Sixth Workshop on African Natural Language Processing (AfricaNLP2025)

Multilingual and Multicultural-aware LLMs

Vienna, Austria
31 July 2025

ISBN: 979-8-3313-2399-8

Printed from e-media with permission by:

Curran Associates, Inc.
57 Morehouse Lane
Red Hook, NY 12571

Some format issues inherent in the e-media version may also appear in this print version.

Association for Computational Linguistics
209 N. Eighth Street
Stroudsburg, Pennsylvania 18360

Phone: 1-570-476-8006
Fax: 1-570-476-0860

acl@aclweb.org

Additional copies of this publication are available from:

Curran Associates, Inc.
57 Morehouse Lane
Red Hook, NY 12571 USA
Phone: 845-758-0400
Fax: 845-758-2633
Email: curran@proceedings.com
Web: www.proceedings.com

AfricaNLP 2025

Sixth Workshop on African Natural Language Processing (AfricaNLP 2025): Multilingual and Multicultural-aware LLMs

Proceedings of the Workshop

July 31, 2025

The AfricaNLP organizers gratefully acknowledge the support from the following sponsors.

Sponsored By

Google DeepMind

Meta

Order copies of this and other ACL proceedings from:

Association for Computational Linguistics (ACL)
317 Sidney Baker St. S
Suite 400 - 134
Kerrville, TX 78028
USA
Tel: +1-855-225-1962
acl@aclweb.org

Introduction

We are pleased to present the proceedings of the Sixth Workshop on African Language Processing (AfricaNLP 2025), held on July 31st, 2025 in Vienna, Austria. The theme for this year's workshop is "Multilingual and Multicultural-aware LLMs," reflecting the need for language technology to be tailored to all users, especially those on the African continent.

These proceedings are the first archival proceedings of the AfricaNLP workshop, and this is the first time the workshop has been held at ACL. We accepted approximately 60% of accepted papers, reflecting our desire to balance inclusion and selectivity. In addition to the 28 archival papers that appear in the proceedings, 7 non-archival papers were also presented at the workshop.

We would like to thank the sponsors of the workshop for their generous support: Google DeepMind, Apple, Distributed AI Research Institute (DAIR), Masakhane, and Meta.

With gratitude,
The AfricaNLP 2025 Organizers

Organizing Committee

General Chair

David Ifeoluwa Adelani, McGill University and Mila

Program and Publication Chair

Constantine Lignos, Brandeis University

Sponsorship Chairs

Henok Ademtew, Vella AI
Shamsuddeen Muhammad, Imperial College London
Clemencia Siro, University of Amsterdam

Mentoring and Communications Chair

Everlyn Asiko Chimoto, University of Cape Town and Lelapa AI

Local and Virtual Chair

Israel Abebe Azime, Saarland University

Organizers

Aremu Anuoluwapo, Lelapa AI
Happy Buzaaba, Princeton University
Rooweither Mabuya, SADiLaR
Andiswa Bukula, SADiLaR
Bonaventure F. P. Dossou, McGill University and Mila
Mmbasibidi Setaka, SADiLaR
Idris Abdulmumin, University of Pretoria

Program Committee

Reviewers

Idris Abdulmumin, David Ifeoluwa Adelani, Henok Biadglign Ademtew, Simbiat Ajao, Emmanuel Akanji, Bunmi Akinremi, Jesujoba Oluwadara Alabi, Felermino D. M. A. Ali, Victor Jotham Ashioya, Busayo Awobade

Edward Bayes, Tadesse Destaw Belay, Happy Buzaaba

Yonas Chanie, Emmanuel Kigen Chesire

Sudhansu Bala Das, Muhammad Umar Diginsa, Emmanuel Dorley, Bonaventure F. P. Dossou

Khalid Elmadani, Naome A Etori

Elodie Gauthier, Gideon George, Agam Goyal, David Guzmán, Tajuddeen Gwadabe

Cari Beth Head

Raphael Iyamu

Sandeep Kumar Jha, Adejumobi Monjolaoluwa Joshua

Sulaiman Kagumire, Börje F. Karlsson, Aditi Khandelwal, Alfred Malengo Kondoro, Sujay S Kumar

Melaku Lake, Sven Lampe, Eric Le Ferrand, En-Shiun Annie Lee, Senyu Li, Weiran Lin

Dunstan Matekenya, Evans Gesura Mecha, Francois Meyer, Anjishnu Mukherjee, Elie Mulamba, Raghavan Muthuregunathan

Abdou Mohamed Naira, Antony Ndolo, Mulubrhan Abebe Nerea, Gebregziabihier Nigusie

Perez Ogayo, Kelechi Ogueji, Odunayo Ogundepo, Jessica Ojo, Ifeoma Okoh, Akintunde Oladipo, Flora Oladipupo, Jeffrey Otoibhi

Chester Palen-Michel, Ted Pedersen, Van-Thuy Phi

Stephen D. Richardson, Nathaniel Romney Robinson

Elizabeth Salesky, Fabian David Schmidt, Tajwaa Scott, Walelign Tewabe Sewunetie, Olamide Shogbamu, Rashidat Damilola Sikiru, Yueqi Song

Jiayi Wang

Seid Muhie Yimam, Hao Yu

Tolúlopé Ògúnrèmí

Invited Talk

Building with Africa: Afrocentric Natural Language Processing

Muhammad Abdul-Mageed
The University of British Columbia

Abstract: Africa's linguistic landscape is one of the richest in the world, with over 2,000 languages and dialects spoken across the continent. This diversity creates a unique environment for innovation in natural language technologies. In this talk, I will describe our collaborative journey to close the technology gap and bring African languages into mainstream NLP research. I will focus on seven key publications—Towards Afrocentric NLP, AfroLID, SERENGETI, Cheetah, Toucan, Sahara, and Voice of a Continent—outlining the goals that drove each project, the obstacles we overcame and the insights we gained along the way. Finally, I will examine the impact that culturally rooted NLP systems can have on African communities, from richer digital communication and the preservation of linguistic heritage to more inclusive and equitable technological innovation.

Bio: Muhammad Abdul-Mageed is the Canada Research Chair in Natural Language Processing and Machine Learning and is an Associate Professor at the University of British Columbia. As director of the UBC Deep Learning & NLP Group, co-director of the SSHRC I Trust Artificial Intelligence partnership and co-lead of the SSHRC Ensuring Full Literacy initiative, his work develops multilingual, multimodal and cross-cultural large-language models that are culturally sensitive, equitable, efficient and socially aware. These models advance applications across speech, language and vision—supporting improved human health, more engaging learning, safer social networking and reduced information overload. His research has been funded by the Gates Foundation (through Clear Global), NSERC, the Canada Foundation for Innovation, with additional support from Google, AMD and Amazon. He has authored over 180 peer-reviewed publications, advised the Government of Canada on generative AI policy, and delivered invited lectures, keynotes and panel presentations in more than 25 countries. His work has been featured in outlets such as MIT Technology Review, The Globe and Mail, Euronews and Libération.

Invited Talk
Mapping Progress in African NLP

Jesujoba Oluwadara Alabi
Saarland University

Abstract: NLP research on African languages is active and growing, even though recent efforts—including work on large language models—have primarily focused on high-resource languages. In the past 5 years, there has been a surge of interest in African NLP, which we recently surveyed. In this talk, I will present key takeaways from that work: where research has been concentrated, and where new efforts are most needed. I will also present our recent efforts to address some of these gaps and future directions: AFRIDOC-MT, a multilingual document-level translation benchmark targeting health and tech domains, and AfriHuBERT, a compact self-supervised speech model designed to help close the speech technology gap for African languages. Overall, these insights and projects showcase the progress made and the path forward to more inclusive and impactful NLP for African languages.

Bio: Jesujoba Oluwadara Alabi is a PhD candidate and researcher at Saarland University, Germany, advised by Prof. Dr. Dietrich Klakow. His research focuses on natural language processing (NLP) for low-resource (African) languages, with interests in machine translation, speech processing, NLP model adaptation, and interpretability of model adaptation methods. He is a member of the Masakhane community and has contributed to several key projects advancing NLP for African languages. Notably, one of his publications received a Best Paper Award (Global Challenges) at COLING 2022 for developing AfroXLMR, a multilingual pre-trained language model for African languages. Other notable awards include an Area Chair Award at IJCNLP-AACL 2023 and Outstanding Paper Award at NAACL 2025.

Invited Talk
Scaling Speech Recognition for African Languages

Joyce Nakatumba-Nabende
Makerere University

Abstract: Automatic speech recognition (ASR) for African languages remains challenging due to limited labeled data and a lack of practical guidance to build effective systems in low-resource settings. Although pretrained models such as Whisper, XLS-R, MMS, and W2v-BERT have improved access, their comparative performance across languages, training scales, and decoding strategies remains understudied. In this talk, I will discuss the evaluation of ASR models on thirteen African languages, fine-tuning each on training subsets. The talk will also cover the assessment of the impact of language model decoding using n-gram models trained on open-source text. Finally, I will delve into a framework and results for evaluation of ASR models beyond WER and CER metrics.

Bio: Dr. Joyce Nakatumba-Nabende is a senior lecturer in the Department of Computer Science at Makerere University and the current director for the Makerere University Center for Artificial Intelligence. She is a research scientist addressing global and African challenges as part of "CoRE-AI" Africa-Europe Clusters of Research Excellence on Innovation and Technology. Dr. Nakatumba-Nabende has worked on research in the development and application of Artificial Intelligence and machine learning models and contributes to sustainable and equitable outcomes in health and agriculture, advancing digital inclusion, and improving African language representation in AI.

Invited Talk

Building Language Technologies for Low-Resourced Languages

Hellina Hailu Nigatu
University of California, Berkeley

Abstract: In recent years, we have seen an increase in the number of languages included in NLP research. Particularly, "low-resource languages" are gaining attention after decades of neglect from mainstream research. While inclusion in NLP research certainly has benefits for speakers of these languages, there are also some risks in how we design and build NLP systems. In this talk, we will first cover background on what low-resourced languages are and what gaps exist in current NLP research when designing language technologies for speakers of these languages. Then, we will take a magnifying lens and look at a pre-processing step performed in Amharic NLP and its impact on monolingual and cross-lingual model performance for Machine Translation. We will end by connecting to literature on technology-facilitated language change and why it is important for us to critically reflect on each stage of the NLP pipeline.

Bio: Hellina Hailu Nigatu is a PhD Candidate at UC Berkeley. She received her BSc from Addis Ababa University in Electrical Engineering and her MSc from UC Berkeley in Computer Science. Her research is at the intersection of HCI, NLP, and AI Ethics, with a specific focus on languages with limited data available online. Hellina studies how current language technology design fails for speakers of these languages and how we can design better, contextual language technologies with users' needs in mind. Hellina holds fellowships from SIGHPC and FAccT. Her research has won several awards, including the Outstanding Paper Award at EMNLP 2024, the Best Paper Award at Black in AI 2024, and the Research of the Year Award from the Wikimedia Foundation.

Invited Talk

Multilingual Modeling and Evaluation in Llama 4 and Beyond

Sebastian Ruder
Meta

Abstract: Multilingual LLMs have become so powerful that they can be used in real-world conversations in a variety of applications. While this presents many opportunities, it also poses challenges associated with the complexity of natural language. In this talk, I will seek to connect academic research to real-world challenges of multilingual conversational AI. I will first provide an overview of multilinguality in Llama 4, highlighting the importance of evaluation. I will then discuss what it takes to bridge the gap between academic and real-world evaluations. Finally, I will discuss how we can develop models that are useful to speakers in their local context, across the globe and for African languages.

Bio: Sebastian Ruder is a research scientist at Meta based in Berlin, Germany where he is working on multilingual LLMs. Previously, he led the Multilingual team at Cohere and worked as a research scientist at Google DeepMind. He completed his PhD in Natural Language Processing Insight Research Centre for Data Analytics, while working as a research scientist at Dublin-based text analytics startup AYLIEN and studied Computational Linguistics at the University of Heidelberg, Germany and at Trinity College, Dublin.

Table of Contents

Yankari: Monolingual Yoruba Dataset

Maro Akpobi
African Center for Language Preservation
maro@acflp.org

Abstract

This paper presents Yankari, a large-scale monolingual dataset for the Yoruba language, aimed at addressing the critical gap in Natural Language Processing (NLP) resources for this important West African language. Despite being spoken by over 30 million people, Yoruba has been severely underrepresented in NLP research and applications. We detail our methodology for creating this dataset, which includes careful source selection, automated quality control, and rigorous data cleaning processes. The Yankari dataset comprises 51,407 documents from 13 diverse sources, totaling over 30 million tokens. Our approach focuses on ethical data collection practices, avoiding problematic sources and addressing issues prevalent in existing datasets. We provide thorough automated evaluations of the dataset, demonstrating its quality compared to existing resources. The Yankari dataset represents a significant advancement in Yoruba language resources, providing a foundation for developing more accurate NLP models, supporting comparative linguistic studies, and contributing to the digital accessibility of the Yoruba language.

1 Introduction

Natural Language Processing (NLP) has made tremendous strides in recent years, yet these advancements have primarily benefited high-resource languages, leaving many African languages, including Yoruba, underrepresented in NLP research and applications. This paper introduces Yankari, a large-scale, high-quality monolingual dataset for Yoruba, a language spoken by over 30 million people in West Africa. Despite its significant speaker population, Yoruba has long suffered from a lack of comprehensive, ethically-sourced language resources suitable for modern NLP tasks.

Yankari addresses this critical gap by providing a carefully curated corpus of 51,407 documents from 13 diverse sources, totaling over 30 million tokens. Our methodology prioritizes ethical data collection, rigorous quality control, and the preservation of linguistic authenticity. By avoiding problematic sources such as religious texts and machine-translated content, Yankari offers a more balanced and representative sample of contemporary Yoruba language use.

This paper details our data collection and processing pipeline, discusses the challenges encountered in creating resources for low-resource languages, and provides a thorough analysis of the dataset's composition and potential biases. We also offer insights into the ethical considerations surrounding the creation and use of such resources. Through Yankari, we aim to facilitate the development of more accurate and culturally appropriate NLP models for Yoruba, contribute to the preservation of linguistic diversity in the digital age, and provide a replicable approach for creating high-quality datasets for other low-resource languages.

To our knowledge, Yankari represents the first large-scale, non-religious domain monolingual resource created specifically for Yoruba. This work not only provides a valuable asset for Yoruba NLP but also offers a replicable approach for developing similar datasets for other low-resource languages.

Proceedings of the Sixth Workshop on African Natural Language Processing (AfricaNLP 2025), pages 1–6
July 31, 2025

Source	Docs	Type	Domain
yo.wikipedia.org	16 809	Encyclopedia	General
alaroye.org	10 535	News	Current Affairs
www.bbc.com	8 252	News	Current Affairs
www.awikonko.com.ng	5 438	Blog	Culture
yoruba.von.gov.ng	2 542	News	Current Affairs
sportsinyoruba.wordpress.com	2 328	Blog	Sports
www.asejere.net	2 079	Blog	Entertainment
asa.ooduarere.com	1 744	Blog	Culture
radionigeriaibadan.gov.ng	824	News	Current Affairs
iroyinowuro.com.ng	603	News	Current Affairs
oroyoruba.blogspot.com	139	Blog	Culture
yo.globalvoices.org	81	News	Current Affairs
edeyorubarewa.com	33	Blog	Fashion
Total	51 407		

Table 1: Data sources for the Yankari dataset.

2 Related Works

This section examines existing resources for Yoruba NLP, highlighting their limitations and the need for a comprehensive, ethically-sourced Yoruba dataset.

2.1 Monolingual Yoruba Datasets

2.1.1 Yorùbá Text C3

Alabi et al. (2020) introduced Yorùbá Text C3, compiled from various web sources including the Bible, JW300 (Agić and Vulić, 2019), books, news articles, and Wikipedia. While broad in scope, this dataset is heavily skewed towards religious content, particularly Christianity. This bias significantly limits its utility for NLG tasks requiring balanced and diverse text. Moreover, the inclusion of JW300 data raises serious ethical and legal concerns. Hutchinson (2024) points out that the Jehovah's Witnesses have explicitly prohibited the use of their data in NLP research, making the continued use of JW300 not just ethically questionable but potentially illegal.

2.1.2 MENYO-20k

Adelani et al. (2021) developed MENYO-20k, a multi-domain English-Yoruba corpus primarily for machine translation tasks. While it offers more diverse content, its relatively small size of 20,100 sentences and focus on translation rather than monolingual text generation limit its applicability for large-scale NLG tasks.

2.2 Multilingual Datasets Including Yoruba

2.2.1 Wura Dataset

The Wura dataset, developed by Oladipo et al. (2023), is a multilingual dataset containing approximately 68,000 Yoruba documents. It integrates content from JW300 and Wikipedia, inheriting similar biases and ethical issues as Yorùbá Text C3. Our manual inspection of the Wura dataset revealed critical quality issues not previously reported, including formatting errors and inappropriate content.

2.2.2 Large-Scale Web-Crawled Corpora

Multilingual datasets such as mC4, OSCAR, and the Afriberta-Corpus also include Yoruba content. However, these datasets often suffer from noise, poor formatting, and limited source diversity. Ogueji et al. (2021) used the Afriberta-Corpus, which primarily sources data from the BBC News and Common Crawl, resulting in a dataset lacking the domain diversity necessary for robust NLG.

Nguyen et al. (2023) introduced CulturaX, covering 167 languages. However, its Yoruba subset showed an alarmingly high duplication rate of 24.48% and contained machine-translated pages, false positives in language detection, and a significant amount of religious text.

2.3 Large-Scale Multilingual Efforts for African Languages

The Cheetah project by Adebara et al. (2024) focuses on natural language generation for 517 African languages, including Yoruba. This ambitious project utilizes existing corpora from various sources, including OSCAR (Ortiz Suárez et al.,

2020), CC-100 (Conneau et al., 2020), Afriberta-Corpus (Ogueji et al., 2021), and mC4 (Xue et al., 2021).

While Cheetah represents a significant step towards improving NLP capabilities for African languages, it faces challenges common to large-scale multilingual efforts. These include potential issues with data quality, bias towards certain domains or text types, and the inclusion of machine-translated content.

2.4 Ethical Considerations in Using Religious Texts

The ethical implications of using religious texts in NLP, particularly for low-resource languages, are profound and often overlooked. Hutchinson (2024) challenges the NLP community's casual approach to sacred texts, arguing that the prevalence of Christian texts in datasets for low-resource languages reflects a legacy of colonialism and missionary work. This creates an ethical dilemma where NLP technologies risk becoming unwitting agents of cultural imperialism and religious proselytism.

3 Motivation for Yankari

Given these severe limitations and ethical concerns in existing resources, there is an urgent need for a high-quality, diverse, and extensive monolingual Yoruba dataset that does not rely on restricted or problematic sources. This is where **Yankari** comes in, directly addressing the gaps and ethical issues left by previous datasets.

Yankari aims to provide a large-scale, ethically sourced corpus that represents a wide range of Yoruba language use. By avoiding the pitfalls of previous datasets, such as over-reliance on religious texts or machine-translated content, Yankari seeks to offer a more balanced and authentic representation of the Yoruba language. This approach aligns with recent calls in the NLP community for more thoughtful and ethical dataset creation, particularly for low-resource languages.

4 Methodology

This section details our approach to creating the Yankari dataset, including data collection, processing, quality assurance steps, and corpus analysis.

4.1 Data Collection

Our data collection process focused on gathering content from diverse, high-quality sources to ensure a representative sample of contemporary Yoruba language use. We carefully selected 13 sources, including news outlets, blogs, educational websites, and Wikipedia. Table 1 provides an overview of these sources and their contributions to the dataset.

4.2 Analysis of Existing Datasets

To inform our data collection and curation process, we conducted a detailed analysis of the Wura dataset (Oladipo et al., 2023). Our investigation revealed several critical issues:

- High repetition: 18.01% of the dataset contains the word 'asteroidi' (asteroid), indicating a significant bias towards astronomical content.
- Duplication: After removing duplicates and cleaning, only 17,103 unique entries remained, representing just 45% of the original dataset.
- Quality issues: We found formatting errors, inappropriate content, and entries in non-Yoruba languages.

These findings highlight the pressing need for more stringent data curation practices in low-resource language datasets. The recent study by Hernandez et al. (2022) on scaling laws and the interpretability of learning from repeated data offers valuable insights that influenced our methodology. Their extensive research reveals that data repetition can severely hinder model performance, particularly by disrupting the balance between memorization and generalization. Additionally, repeated data can obstruct the development of "induction heads," which are vital for in-context learning in large language models. Most importantly, their work underscores the pivotal role that high-quality training data plays in the effectiveness of language models. These insights significantly shaped our careful approach to developing Yankari, underscoring the critical need for rigorous data curation, quality control, and the preservation of diversity in our dataset.

4.3 Data Processing Pipeline

Our data processing pipeline consisted of several key steps:

4.3.1 HTML Parsing and Text Extraction

We implemented a robust HTML parsing system using BeautifulSoup to extract clean text from web pages. This process involved:

- Removing all script and style elements
- Extracting text from relevant HTML tags (e.g., `<p>`, `<h1>`, `<h2>`, etc.)
- Preserving the document structure by maintaining paragraph boundaries

It is important to note that, beyond basic structural parsing, no specific sentence-level filtering based on the presence or absence of terminal punctuation was applied at this stage, as the primary goal was to capture full textual content from the identified relevant HTML elements.

4.3.2 Deduplication

We employed a two-step deduplication process:

1. Exact matching at the document level to remove duplicate web pages
2. Near-duplicate detection at the paragraph level using MinHash and Locality-Sensitive Hashing (LSH) techniques

4.4 Corpus Statistics

Our final Yankari dataset consists of:

- Total number of documents: 51,407
- Total number of tokens: 30,438,702
- Average tokens per document: 592.11

4.5 Domain Analysis

The distribution of web domains in our corpus reflects the diverse sources we targeted. The top 5 domains by number of documents are:

1. yo.wikipedia.org: 32.70%
2. alaroye.org: 20.49%
3. www.bbc.com: 16.05%
4. www.awikonko.com.ng: 10.58%
5. yoruba.von.gov.ng: 4.94%

This distribution ensures a balance between encyclopedic content, news, and cultural discussions, providing a comprehensive representation of written Yoruba across various domains.

4.6 Ethical Considerations and Excluded Content

Throughout our data collection and processing, we prioritized ethical considerations:

- We explicitly removed data from restricted sources, such as those with terms prohibiting use in NLP research.
- We filtered out suspected machine-translated content to maintain linguistic authenticity. This was primarily a manual process conducted by the author, a native Yoruba speaker, during data spot-checking and review. Documents exhibiting unnatural phrasing, common translation artifacts, or content inconsistent with known source characteristics were excluded.
- We removed inappropriate or offensive material to ensure the dataset's suitability for a wide range of applications. This was also a manual review process performed by the author. The guidelines focused on excluding hate speech, explicit adult content, and other materials generally considered unsuitable for a public research dataset.
- We respected copyright and intellectual property rights. Content was sourced primarily from publicly accessible websites. For sources like Wikipedia, explicit open licenses (e.g., CC-BY-SA) were followed. For other public news and blog content without explicit licenses for redistribution, we operated under the principles of fair use for non-commercial research, providing clear attribution via source URLs. Direct contact for explicit redistribution permission was not feasible for every source due to the scale of collection; this is a recognized challenge in web-scale data gathering and is noted as a limitation.

In line with our commitment to transparency, we acknowledge that our content filtering process may have introduced certain biases:

- The removal of very short texts may have disproportionately affected certain types of content.
- Our focus on standard Yoruba may have led to the underrepresentation of regional dialects or colloquial expressions.

- Excluding content with non-Yoruba characters might have removed some culturally relevant content involving code-switching or borrowings.

4.7 Output Format

The final dataset is stored in JSONL format, with each line containing a separate JSON document with the following fields:

- **text**: The main content of the document in Yoruba.
- **url**: The original URL from which the content was sourced.
- **source**: A code indicating the source of the document.

Here is a sample entry:

```
{
  "text": "O ma se o! Ijamba oko
     ofurufu gba emi eeyan marun-
     un...",
  "url": "https://www.awikonko.
     com.ng/2024/03/o-ma-se-o-
     ijamba-oko-ofurufu-gba-emi.
     html",
  "source": "ACFLP"
}
```

4.8 Quality Assurance

To ensure the highest quality of our dataset:

- We involved native Yoruba speakers in the data cleaning and validation process.
- We conducted regular spot checks throughout the data processing pipeline.
- We performed a final manual review of a randomly selected subset of the data to verify its quality and authenticity.

4.9 Limitations and Potential Biases

We acknowledge the following limitations and potential biases in our dataset:

- Internet Bias
- Written Language Bias
- Source Bias
- Temporal Bias
- Standardization Bias

These limitations highlight areas for future work and expansion of the Yankari dataset.

5 Limitations and Ethical Considerations

While the Yankari dataset represents a significant contribution to Yoruba language resources for NLP, it is important to acknowledge its limitations and the ethical considerations that arise from its creation and potential use.

5.1 Representation Bias

- Spoken Language: The dataset does not include samples of spoken Yoruba.
- Informal Variants: Internet sources may favor more formal language use.
- Demographic Skew: Internet access and content creation are not uniformly distributed across all Yoruba-speaking demographics.

5.2 Diacritization Challenges

- Tonal Ambiguity: Incorrect or missing diacritical marks can cause ambiguity.
- Standardization Issues: The lack of a universally adopted standard for Yoruba orthography may result in inconsistencies.

6 Conclusion

The Yankari dataset represents a significant step forward in addressing the resource gap for Yoruba in Natural Language Processing. By providing a large-scale, high-quality, and ethically sourced corpus, we have laid a foundation for advancing NLP research and applications in this important West African language. Our rigorous methodology, which prioritizes data quality, diversity, and ethical considerations, sets a new standard for the development of language resources for low-resource languages.

The creation of Yankari highlights several critical challenges in developing NLP resources for languages like Yoruba, including the scarcity of diverse, high-quality online content, the complexities of automated processing for languages with limited existing NLP tools, and the ethical considerations surrounding data collection and potential misuse. By transparently discussing these challenges and our approaches to addressing them, we hope to contribute to the broader conversation on responsible

AI development for diverse languages and cultures. Future work will focus on rigorously evaluating Yankari's utility in various downstream NLP tasks, such as language modeling, machine translation, and text classification, including comparative performance analyses against other available Yoruba corpora. Such evaluations will further quantify the benefits of Yankari's curated nature and diverse domain coverage.

The dataset is available on Hugging Face: https://huggingface.co/datasets/acflp/YANKARI

Acknowledgments

This work was performed independently. The author received no specific grant from any funding agency in the public, commercial, or not-for-profit sectors for the research described in this manuscript.

References

Ife Adebara, AbdelRahim Elmadany, and Muhammad Abdul-Mageed. 2024. Cheetah: Natural language generation for 517 african languages. *Preprint*, arXiv:2401.01053.

David Adelani et al. 2021. Menyo-20k: A multi-domain english - yoruba corpus for machine translation and domain adaptation. In *Proceedings of the Fourth Workshop on Technologies for MT of Low Resource Languages*.

Željko Agić and Ivan Vulić. 2019. JW300: A wide-coverage parallel corpus for low-resource languages. In *Proceedings of the 57th Annual Meeting of the Association for Computational Linguistics*, pages 3204–3210, Florence, Italy. Association for Computational Linguistics.

Jesujoba Alabi et al. 2020. Massive vs. curated embeddings for low-resourced languages: The case of yorùbá and twi. In *Proceedings of the 12th Language Resources and Evaluation Conference*.

Alexis Conneau, Kartikay Khandelwal, Naman Goyal, Vishrav Chaudhary, Guillaume Wenzek, Francisco Guzmán, Edouard Grave, Myle Ott, Luke Zettlemoyer, and Veselin Stoyanov. 2020. Unsupervised cross-lingual representation learning at scale. In *Proceedings of the 58th Annual Meeting of the Association for Computational Linguistics*, pages 8440–8451.

Danny Hernandez, Tom Brown, Tom Conerly, Nova DasSarma, Dawn Drain, Sheer El-Showk, Nelson Elhage, Zac Hatfield-Dodds, Tom Henighan, Tristan Hume, Scott Johnston, Ben Mann, Chris Olah, Catherine Olsson, Dario Amodei, Nicholas Joseph, Jared Kaplan, and Sam McCandlish. 2022. Scaling laws and interpretability of learning from repeated data. *Preprint*, arXiv:2205.10487.

Ben Hutchinson. 2024. Modeling the sacred: Considerations when using religious texts in natural language processing. *arXiv preprint arXiv:2404.14740*.

Duc Minh Nguyen et al. 2023. Culturax: A cleaned, enormous, and multilingual dataset for large language models in 167 languages. *arXiv preprint arXiv:2309.09400*.

Kelechi Ogueji et al. 2021. Small data? no problem! exploring the viability of pretrained multilingual language models for low-resourced languages. *arXiv preprint arXiv:2011.03823*.

Adewale Oladipo et al. 2023. Wura: A multilingual dataset of african languages. In *Proceedings of the 61st Annual Meeting of the Association for Computational Linguistics*.

Pedro Javier Ortiz Suárez, Laurent Romary, and Benoît Sagot. 2020. A monolingual approach to contextualized word embeddings for mid-resource languages. *Proceedings of the 58th Annual Meeting of the Association for Computational Linguistics*, pages 1703–1714.

Linting Xue, Noah Constant, Adam Roberts, Mihir Kale, Rami Al-Rfou, Aditya Siddhant, Aditya Barua, and Colin Raffel. 2021. mt5: A massively multilingual pre-trained text-to-text transformer. *arXiv preprint arXiv:2010.11934*.

Supervised Machine Learning based Amharic Text Complexity Classification Using Automatic Annotator Tool

Gebregziabihier Nigusie
Mizan-Tepi University
Ethiopia
gerenigusie138@gmail.com

Abstract

Understanding written content can vary significantly based on the linguistic complexity of the text. In the context of Amharic, a morphologically rich and low-resource language, the use of complex vocabulary and less frequent expressions often hinders understanding, particularly among readers with limited literacy skills. Such complexity poses challenges for both human comprehension and NLP applications. Addressing this complexity in Amharic is therefore important for text readability and accessibility. In this study, we developed a text complexity annotation tool using curated list of 1,113 complex Amharic terms. Utilizing this tool, we collected and annotated a dataset comprising 20,084 sentences. Based on the annotated corpus, we developed a text complexity classification model using both traditional and deep learning approaches. For traditional machine learning models, the dataset was vectorized using the Bag-of-Words representation. For deep learning and pre-trained models, we implemented embedding layers based on Word2Vec and BERT, trained on a vocabulary consisting of 24,148 tokens. The experiment is conducted using Support Vector Machine and Random Forest for classical machine learning, and Long Short-Term Memory, Bidirectional LSTM, and BERT for deep learning and pre-trained models. The classification accuracies achieved were 83.5% for SVM, 80.3% for RF, 84.1% for LSTM, 85.0% for BiLSTM, and 89.4% for the BERT-based model. Among these, the BERT-based approaches shows optimal performance for text complexity classifications which have ability to capture long-range dependencies and contextual relationships within the text.

1 Introduction

Natural language processing is recently emerging area in the machine learning research community (Santucci et al., 2020). It is applicable in many areas such as text classification for automatic understanding(Dalal and Zaveri, 2011), Information extraction(Bosco et al., 2018), and sentiment analysis(Seelam et al., 2023). To present language learners and low literacy readers with texts suitable to their level, the morphological, lexical, syntactic, and discursive complexity of a text is to be considered(Nigusie and Tegegne, 2022). NLP became interested in automatically classifying the complexity of a text, typically using lexical features as a key solution for presenting documents appropriate to concerned bodies (Zakaria, 2019).

When organizing documents, utilizing a wide variety of vocabulary, some of those words seem to be unfamiliar to low literacy readers which can cause miss understandability problems and increase document complexity(Nigusie and Tesfa, 2022). This complexity is the degree of difficulty in reading and understanding a text, which can be determined based on a variety of characteristics such as familiarity with words, knowledge demands, and the educational background of readers. The appropriateness of a text for a certain learner group needs to be in line with the proficiency level of the learners (Dina and Banerjee, 2016). The difficulty of vocabulary within a text, caused by unfamiliar or rare words, plays a significant role in content understood. This challenge is highly impacting for second language learners, who often struggle with word recognition and interpretation (Gala and Ziegler, 2016).

Detecting and classifying documents containing such challenging words is an essential step toward text simplification (Shardlow et al., 2020). By categorizing texts according to its difficulty, it is possible to tailor materials to the needs of diverse readers, enhancing accessibility for those with limited literacy, including young learners and non-native speakers (Stefan et al., 2012). Additionally,this classification process helps to improve NLP applications(Sulem et al., 2018).

Proceedings of the Sixth Workshop on African Natural Language Processing (AfricaNLP 2025), pages 7–14
July 31, 2025

1.1 An Overview of the Amharic Language

Amharic is a morphologically rich language belonging to the Semitic language family and is widely spoken in Ethiopia. The language is widely used in Natural Language Processing research (Woldeyohannis and Meshesha, 2022). Amharic texts can contain a wide range of vocabulary, and some lexical items may be unfamiliar to certain readers, particularly second language learners and individuals with low literacy skills, making comprehension challenging (Belete et al., 2015). The Ethiopia Early Grade Reading Assessment studies targeted in grade 2 and grade 3 students for letter/alphabet sound fluency, naming fluency of unfamiliar words, and reading comprehension assessment indicated that Fidel naming fluency in grade 3 scores are significantly higher than those of grade 2 however childrens in all languages have limited skills in reading and understanding unfamiliar words. To overcome such text complexity issues many researches are conducted for different languages such as Text Complexity Classification Based on Linguistic Information for Italian text (Santucci et al., 2020), Efficient Measuring of Readability to Improve Documents Accessibility for Arabic Language (Sulem et al., 2018).

The complexity of text depends on the language script, structure, and morphology which leads to different languages needing to be studied separately for such text complexity problems. So, studying the complexity classification model for the Amharic language helps in solving text complexity for a target population. It can also help to improve the performance of NLP applications, such as parsing, information extraction, and Machine translation. Furthermore, classifying Amharic text complexity is the base for future research on text simplification. Due to this, some works are conducted for such text complexity classification for Amharic text using classical machine learning model (Nigusie and Tegegne, 2022). In previous works, the data collection and annotation process for such Amharic text complexity classification experiments was the big challenge and the work needs to be extended for deep learning models to cover large dataset sizes. So in this study, we attempt to address the problem by developing a new complexity annotation tool and integrating it on the top of the classification models, because text annotation is a critical step toward solving supervised NLP issues. We have developed this new annotation tool for maintaining annotation quality and consistency (Rodolfo et al., 2018). The tool works based on segments large unlabeled Amharic text to sentence level and labels it automatically as complex or non-complex. In this paper, we have compared human annotation with the annotator tool to evaluate its performance, and different supervised machine learning and deep learning algorithms have used for classifying Amharic text complexity using Bag-of-Word(BOW), word2vec and BERT embedding layer as feature extraction techniques.

2 Related work

Assessing the appropriateness of a text for specific readers is particularly important in educational settings, where it helps in selecting content that aligns with learners comprehension levels. It also supports educators in developing textbooks and curricula that are suitable for students abilities (de-la Peña and Luque-Roja, 2021). Additionally, text complexity classification plays a vital role in various NLP applications such as sentiment analysis, text simplification, and machine translation. For non-native readers, ensuring that the complexity of a text matches their language proficiency is essential for effective communication and understanding (Dina and Banerjee, 2016).

A study on reading proficiency for Ethiopia's Achievement Development Monitoring and Evaluation program (Read, 2019) examines key subtasks such as familiar word reading, new word reading, and reading comprehension among early-grade students. The research involved data collected from 459 schools, with assessments conducted on 17,879 students. The findings help evaluate students' ability to understand texts, answer factual questions, and draw inferences from their reading. One of the key conclusions is that using grade level appropriate vocabulary enhances students' reading recognition and comprehension. In another study, supervised machine learning techniques were applied to assess Arabic text complexity (Bessou and Chenni, 2021). The researchers employed Bag-of-Words and TF-IDF feature extraction methods, along with classifiers such as Naïve Bayes, Logistic Regression, Support Vector Machines, and Random Forest. The best performance (87.14%) was achieved using SVM with TF-IDF combined with word based unigrams and bigrams. The study suggests that future work should incorporate syntactic and semantic features for improved classification.

A study by Liu (2017) focused on estimating sentence complexity for Chinese-speaking learners of Japanese, aiming to support their understanding of Japanese functional expressions(Liu, 2017). To address the complexity of Japanese texts for Chinese native speakers, the researchers compiled a dataset of 5,000 sentences and organized them into 2,500 sentence pairs. These were evaluated by 15 native Chinese speakers learning Japanese. The study employed a Support Vector Machine (SVM) model for ranking sentence difficulty, using fivefold cross validation, with each fold training on 4,000 sentences and testing on 1,000. The model achieved an accuracy of 84.4% in ranking sentence difficulty. However, certain features such as the number of verbs, which may influence sentence complexity and the learner's cognitive load were not considered and were suggested for future exploration. With the advancement of deep learning, the focus in text complexity classification has shifted toward neural models(Bosco et al., 2018), the study proposed a Neural Network architecture based on Long Short-Term Memory units, which is capable of automatically learning lexical complexity patterns from data. This model demonstrates the potential to evaluate sentence complexity by distinguishing between complex and simple constructions without relying on hand crafted features.

3 Methodology

For conducting this Amharic text complexity classification work, we have followed an experimental research design for manipulating the effect of different variables such as dataset size, text preprocessing, and feature representation technique on the result of the accuracy of such an Amharic text complexity classification task. The following phases are the main components of our work dataset collection, dataset annotation using both annotator tool and human annotators, preprocessing, word representation, training classical machine learning and deep learning models, and evaluation of the performance of the models.

3.1 Amharic Text Dataset

The dataset used for Amharic text complexity classification is compiled from a diverse range of sources, including academic textbooks (grades 6 through 12) (Alemu et al., 2015) and journal news. These sources were selected due to their inclusion of complex text identified by linguists and book authors. The dataset collection process is a critical component of our research, requiring careful and thorough analysis. In addition to gathering sentences containing complex terms identified by linguists, we conducted a sample survey evaluated by three Amharic linguists. The survey consisted of six pages of Amharic text randomly extracted from student textbooks, news articles, and fiction. Annotators were asked to identify sentences containing unfamiliar words. From this evaluation, 123 sentences were consistently marked as complex by all three annotators.

While collecting data in this manner is time consuming and costly a challenge noted in previous studies (Nigusie and Tegegne, 2022; Nigusie and Tesfa, 2022). We addressed these issues by developing an Amharic text complexity annotation tool. For the classification experiments, we compiled a dataset of 20,084 Amharic sentences. The annotation tool played a crucial role in efficiently collecting this dataset, ensuring an optimal distribution of complex and non-complex sentences.

3.2 Amharic Text Complexity Annotator Tool

Linguistic corpus annotation is a critical step toward solving NLP tasks because these methods are heavily reliant on building machine learning models. The classification model that we have built is based on supervised machine learning and neural network approaches, which employ the analysis of corpus. Annotated data is necessary for building the model that performs complexity classification tasks. Using manually annotated meta data is a time consuming and costly component of many NLP research works, which motivates us to develop a new Amharic text complexity annotator tool that performs sentence annotation from large unlabeled Amharic text. The document is segmented into sentence level then, word tokenization, and root extraction processes are applied to accurately identify the sentence that contains complex terms.

Following analysis, the text proceeds to the annotation phase. Sentences identified as containing complex lexical terms that increase semantic difficulty are tagged as complex, while the sentences do not contain complex elements are tagged as non-complex using the help of the automatic

Amharic text complexity annotator tool.

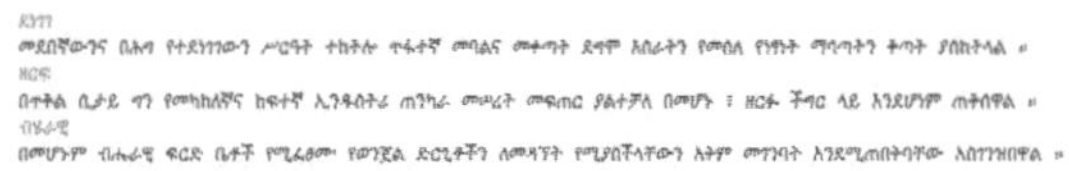

Figure 1: Text complexity annotator tool sample result

To validate the complexity level of the dataset identified by the annotation tool, we have randomly taken 1000 sentences and evaluated them by human annotator. From these total sentences, the human annotator and the tool agreed on 680 sentences.

3.3 Data Preprocessing

This stage is a very common task in NLP applications to have the representative features from the dataset even the way of preprocessing depends on the type of dataset and the language because to develop an optimized model, appropriate data are required, and preprocessing is a vital part of acquiring such data. We have applied different preprocessing stages for our dataset because we have collected the dataset from different sources which contain noise such as special characters and stop words.

3.3.1 Amharic Sentence Segmentation

We have applied sentence segmentation to unlabeled large corpus to detect the sentence boundary and split the document to sentence level (Gillick, 2009). Since the Amharic language has punctuation marks such as ?, ! which occurs at the end of the sentence. This segmentation is a preliminary step for automatic annotation further processing.

3.3.2 Tokenization and Stop-word Removal

In this step, dataset is split into individual tokens. During this process, special characters such as apostrophes, exclamation marks and others are removed, as they contribute little to the models effectiveness and may introduce unnecessary noise during training. Next, stop words which are common words exist frequently in both labels are removed from the dataset. Examples include le (said), wede (to), and ih (this). Eliminating these words reduces the datasets size and complexity, allowing the model to focus on the most relevant features. This step improves both the efficiency and accuracy of the classification model by minimizing irrelevant information (Kaur, 2018; Li et al., 2022).

3.3.3 Normalization

Some Amharic words can be written in a different format for the same representation and function(homophones). To reduce such word variation, we have transformed those words into a single representation (homophone normalization). For example, the phoneme /h/ can be represented by the h, and ha>series of graphemes (Stefano et al., 2022), to reduce such Fidel variation in Amharic words we have applied this normalization.

3.3.4 Morphological analysis

Morphological analysis of highly inflected languages is a non-trivial task and Amharic is one of the most morphologically complex languages (Adam and Maciej, 2014). At this stage, we have reduced morphological variants of Amharic tokens to their representative morpheme by removing affixes. To do this morpheme extraction process, we have used the hybrid technique of our root analyzer algorithm with HornMorpho (Michael, 2011). The reason for a hybrid of such methods is to handle words that are not analyzed by HornMorpho and to enable the analyzer to work on document level analysis.

3.3.5 Sentence Annotation

The purpose of our sentence annotator tool is to automate the labeling of segmented documents based on sentence complexity. During annotation, each segmented and preprocessed sentence is evaluated for the presence of complex terms. Sentences containing complex terms are marked as complex, while those without are designated as non-complex and incorporated into the dataset.

Using the annotator tool instead of a human annotator has a significant advantage in terms of dataset balancing, time saving, and accuracy. The tool helps us to balance complex term distribution in sentences beyond this, it takes an average of 3 minutes to check the sentence that contains complex terms from 10 pages of the document and annotate it automatically, however, when we use a human annotator, it takes an average of 45 - 55 minutes to complete the annotation. In addition to time, human annotators make more mistakes than the annotator tool (Rodolfo et al., 2018). For example, the sentence beseferi yemewedajeti baz inidetetenawetachewi libi nilimi (We do not notice that they are obsessed with being friends in the neighborhood) is annotated as noncomplex by human but when we use the annotator tool identify it as complex sentence due to the existence of the morphologically inflected complex term. Using this Amharic text complexity annotator tool, we have collected a total of 20,084 sentences with 10,084 sentences labeled as complex and 10,000 sentences labeled as noncomplex with a maximum sentence length of 14 and minimal sentence length of 5 tokens after the sentence is preprocessed for train classification models.

3.3.6 Feature extraction

To build a machine learning model for Amharic text complexity classification, it is necessary to apply feature extraction operations on text data, in order to transform it into computer understandable format. We have converted the preprocessed text to numeric format using BOW with bi-gram language modeling to handle the context and order of the tokens for classical machine learning models training. Other Word embedding techniques such as Word2vec is used as feature extraction for LSTM and BiLSTM models which is unsupervised neural network that processes text to create vectors of the word's feature representations. We have selected word2vec because it uses information about the co-occurrence of words in a text corpus (Vahe et al., 2019). For the early emerged pretrained model (BERT) we have used its embedding layer by assigning unique vocabularies of our dataset to the layer this BERT embedding helps to extract features of sentences that contain up to 512 tokens to handle the semantics of long sentences.

4 Supervised Learning Models

Train machine learning models for classifying the document as complex or noncomplex was the next task after the dataset was preprocessed and represented in the form of a numeric vector by computing the linguistic features of text, it is now possible to train the machine learning model. The shift toward using machine learning, rather than relying solely on the annotator tool, is due to its limitation that it can only identify sentences containing terms from a predefined list of complex expressions which will restricts its ability to generalize beyond the terms it was explicitly designed to recognize. For this classification task from classical machine learning, we have conducted experiment on SVM which is a widely used algorithm for binary classification problems, and RF which consists of a combination of tree predictors (Ahmad A. Al et al., 2015).

Beyond those classical algorithms, we have used recently emerging deep neural network models such as LSTM, Bi-LSTM, and transformer-based model BERT. These models have gained more attention because of their ability to model complex features without the necessity of expert involvement and appropriate representations for textual units by considering features that are semantically meaningful and contextual representative (Andrea et al., 2022). These classical machine learning and deep learning models were applied previously for Amharic text complexity classification(Nigusie and Tegegne, 2022; Nigusie and Tesfa, 2022). From such previous studies, the big challenge that we have identified is the dataset collection and annotating process for train these models with large dataset sizes. So to collect a large dataset an automatic means of data collection process is required that motivates us to develop new Amharic text complexity annotation tool and integrate it on the top of the classification models.

4.1 Results of Baseline Machine Learning Models

We have trained SVM by setting hyperparameters, optimization (C=0.9), degree=1, and linear kernel type. The second model we have selected from such classical algorithms is RF using 10 estimators of trees it builds before averaging the predictions, and a random state of 3. The training is conducted using 80/20 data split and the performance of the models is validated using 10-fold cross-validation. The training accuracy of the models was improved from 50% to 85% of SVM and from 50% to 81% of RF using 65 iterations of sampling. At the initial stage, we used 2265 data, and the dataset size was increased by 53 in each iteration. The model's training performance was improved until the dataset size reached 5000. Beyond this, both models cannot show significant improvement. Due to this reason, we have used 6039 sentences to reduce training time and resource usage for these classical machine learning models. The overall experimental result of these two models is summarized in Table 1.

Model	Precision	Recall	F1-score	Accuracy
SVM	84%	84%	84%	83.9%
RF	85%	80%	80%	80.3%

Table 1: Experimental result of classical machine learning models.

4.2 Performance Evaluation of Deep Learning Models

While the classical machine learning models do not scale well to large dataset sizes we have conducted further experiments on recently emerging deep learning and pre-trained transformer-based models to capture the semantics and feature sequence of the data (Andrea et al., 2022). LSTM, BiLSTM, and BERT are used for our experiment from these deep learning models. The pre-trained model BERT has achieved state-of-the-art results in NLP classification tasks and outperforms most of feature based representation methods (Shanshan et al., 2019). To train the BERT pre-trained model we have fine-tuned its base parameters by adding two hidden layers with 64 and 32 neurons respectively and one output layer with two neurons (one for complex and the other is for non-complex class) on the top of the base model. The experiments for these three deep learning models was conducted using 20,084 sentences by applying the 80/10/10 data split rule (16,067 sentences for training, 2,008 sentences for testing, and 2,008 sentences for validation). The BERT model, pre-training on a large corpus and fine-tuning it for specific tasks (Shanshan et al., 2019), has better Amharic text complexity classification with context handling capability. The model scores a validation accuracy of 89.4% and testing accuracy of 89.4%. The model is also preferable for long documents up to 512 tokens in a single sentence (Ahmad A. Al et al., 2015), the training accuracy and loss curve of this pretraind model is depicted in Figure 2.

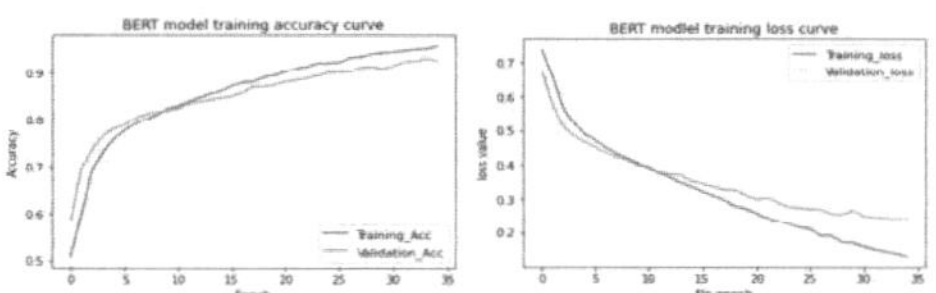

Figure 2: Training accuracy and loss curve of BERT model.

The other two RNN models namely LSTM and BiLSTM models score classification accuracy of 84.1% and 85% respectively. When we compare the BERT model result with these RNN models, BERT has significant accuracy improvement. So we can conclude that the pre-trained model BERT has better Amharic text complexity classification performance. When we compare the result of this BERT model with previous studies on Amharic language text complexity classification(Nigusie and Tesfa, 2022), the newly trained model has more flexibility to handle large features of the dataset that are collected with the help of the newly integrated Amharic text complexity annotator tool, this new annotated tool helps to introduce objectivity for the pre-trained classification model. The experimental evaluation results of these deep learning models are summarized in Table 2.

Model	Precision	Recall	F1-score	Accuracy
BERT	89.4%	89.4%	89.4%	89.4%
BiLSTM	85%	85%	85%	85%
LSTM	85%	84%	84%	84.1%

Table 2: Deep learning models experimental result.

4.3 Error Analysis

Machine learning becoming an important technique to review large volumes of data and discover specific trends and patterns. In some cases, these models are potentially susceptible to bias and some error rates. As we have seen the prediction results of the models using test data they have some error prediction results. The reason for the model miss predictions is because of the existence of the major tokens of some sentences on the opposite side of its actual label or target during training. When we see the sentence betekalayi kekababna ketefetiro gari hibiri yefetere hotlina rzoriti newi maleti yichalali (In general, it can be said that it is a hotel and resort that has created a union/harmony with the environment and nature). Its actual label was complex. However, all three deep learning models predict it as non-complex due to the existence of the words betekalayi (in general), ketefetiro(nature), yefetere (created), and yichalali (possible), in non-complex training dataset more frequent than complex dataset. When we compute the MSE result of the BERT model (which has better classification accuracy), it scores 10.6% error rat

5 Conclusion

In this work, we have designed Amharic text complexity classification model using annotator tool and supervised machine learning. The motivation behind this work is because Amharic language has lexical complexity which is not familiar to low literacy readers and the manual data collection and annotation process for building these complexity classifications models. Beyond this, as we have tested one of the popular machine translation systems called Google translator, the sentences containing these complex terms identified by linguists are translated incorrectly. To address the issue, we have conducted this work for one of morphologically rich languages Amharic. For the experiment, we collected 20,084 sentences using the sentence annotator tool in collaboration with human annotators. The annotation tool filters the document that contains complex terms from unlabeled large Amharic documents by applying different preprocessing stages. Then for the classification problem, we have conducted experiments on both classical (SVM, RF) and deep learning models (LSTM, BiLSTM, and BERT). Based on the experimental results we have got an accuracy of 83.9%(SVM) and 80.3%(RF) using classical machine learning models. However, these traditional machine learning models have limitation of handling sentence context. Due to this reason, we have conducted further experiments on deep learning models (LSTM,Bi-LSTM and BERT). The LSTM scores an accuracy of 84.1%, BiLSTM scores 85%, and BERT scores 89.4% which has better prediction performance than the RNN and classical ML models. Improving dataset collection consistency and annotation quality, classifying Amharic text complexity, and identifying text complexity as one challenging task for ML applications such as machine translations are the main contributions of this study. Syntactic and morphological complexity of the Amharic text are the other types of complexity that need to be studied in the future.

References

Przepiórkowski Adam and Ogrodniczuk Maciej. 2014. Advances in natural language processing. In *Lecture Notes in Computer Science*, pages 1–10.

Sallab Ahmad A. Al, M. Hajj Hazem, Badaro Gilbert, R. Baly, El-Hajj Wassim, and Bashir Shaban Khaled. 2015. Deep learning models for sentiment analysis in arabic. In *ANLP@ACL*, pages 1–24.

D. Alemu, S. Aklilu, and Y. Mengstie. 2015. *Amharic teacher guide grade-9*. FDRE minister of education, Addis Ababa, Ethiopia.

G. Andrea, M. Matteo, Z. Alessandro, and A. Andrea. 2022. A survey on text classification algorithms: From text to predictions. *Information*, 13(83):1–39.

Z. Belete, Z. Mlkt, E. Bezabh, and T. Chekol. 2015. *Amharic teacher guide grade-7*. FDRE minister of education and ABKME Education Bureau, Addis Ababa, Ethiopia.

S. Bessou and G. Chenni. 2021. Efficient measuring of readability to improve documents accessibility for arabic language learners. *ArXiv*, 2109(08648):75–82.

G. Lo Bosco, G. Pilato, and D. Schicchi. 2018. A neural network model for the evaluation of text complexity in italian language: A representation point of view. *Procedia Computer Science*, 145:464–470.

Mita K. Dalal and Mukesh A. Zaveri. 2011. Automatic text classification: A technical review. *International Journal of Computer Applications*, 28:37–40.

C. de-la Peña and María J. Luque-Roja. 2021. Levels of reading comprehension in higher education: Systematic review and meta-analysis. *National Library of Medicine*, 12:1–11.

T. Dina and Banerjee. 2016. *Handbook of Second Language Assessment*. De Gruyter Mouton, Berlin, Boston.

N'uria Gala and Johannes Ziegler. 2016. Reducing lexical complexity as a tool to increase text accessibility for children with dyslexia. In *Proceedings of the Workshop on Computational Linguistics for Linguistic Complexity (CL4LC)*, pages 59–66.

Dan Gillick. 2009. Sentence boundary detection and the problem with the u.s. In *Proceedings of Human Language Technologies: The 2009 Annual Conference of the North American Chapter of the Association for Computational Linguistics, Companion Volume: Short Papers*, pages 241–244.

J. Kaur. 2018. Stopwords removal and its algorithms based on different methods. *International Journal of Advanced Research in Computer Science*, 9(5):81–88.

Xiaofei Li, Daniel Wiechmann, Yu Qiao, and Elma Kerz. 2022. Mantis at tsar-2022 shared task: Improved unsupervised lexical simplification with pretrained encoders. In *Proceedings of the Workshop on Text Simplification, Accessibility, and Readability (TSAR-2022)*, pages 243–250.

J. Liu. 2017. Sentence complexity estimation for chinese-speaking learners of japanese. In *Proceedings of the 31st Pacific Asia Conference on Language, Information and Computation*, pages 296–302, The National University, Philippines.

Gasser Michael. 2011. Hornmorpho: a system for morphological processing of amharic, oromo, and tigrinya. In *COMPUTEL*, pages 2–5.

Gebregziabihier Nigusie and Tesfa Tegegne. 2022. Amharic text complexity classification using supervised machine learning. In *Artificial Intelligence and Digitalization for Sustainable Development (ICAST 2022)*, pages 12–23.

Gebregziabihier Nigusie and Tegegne Tesfa. 2022. Lexical complexity detection and simplification in amharic text using machine learning approach. In *2022 International Conference on Information and Communication Technology for Development for Africa (ICT4DA)*, pages 1–6.

M. Read. 2019. *Reading for Ethiopia S Achievement Developed Monitoring Usaid Reading for Ethiopia S Achievement Developed Monitoring*. Usaid.

Mercado-Gonzales Rodolfo, Pereira-Noriega Jos, S. Cabezudo Marco, and Oncevay Arturo. 2018. Chanot: An intelligent annotation tool for indigenous and highly agglutinative languages in peru. In *International Conference on Language Resources and Evaluation*.

Santucci, V. Santarelli, F. Forti, and L. Spina. 2020. Automatic classification of text complexity. *Applied Sciences*, 10(20):1–19.

Namitha Seelam, Sanjan Pallerla, Reddy Nerella Chaithra, Srikar Yechuri, Shanmugasundaram Hariharan, and Andraju Bhanu Prasad. 2023. Sentiment analysis: Current state and future research perspectives. In *2023 7th International Conference on Intelligent Computing and Control Systems (ICICCS)*, pages 1115–1119.

Y. Shanshan, S. Jindian, and L. Da. 2019. Improving bert-based text classification with auxiliary sentence and domain knowledge. *IEEE Access*, 7:176600–176612.

Matthew Shardlow, Michael Cooper, and Marcos Zampieri. 2020. Complex: A new corpus for lexical complexity prediction from likert scale data. In *Proceedings of the 1st Workshop on Tools and Resources to Empower People with REAding DIfficulties (READI)*, pages 57–62.

Bott Stefan, Rello Luz, Drndarevic Biljana, and Saggion Horacio. 2012. Can spanish be simpler? lexsis: Lexical simplification for spanish. In *International Conference on Computational Linguistics*.

Lusito Stefano, Ferrante Edoardo, and Maillard Jean. 2022. Text normalization for low-resource languages: the case of ligurian. In *COMPUTEL*, pages 1–10.

Elior Sulem, Omri Abend, and Ari Rappoport. 2018. Semantic structural evaluation for text simplification. In *Proceedings of the 2018 Conference of the North American Chapter of the Association for Computational Linguistics: Human Language Technologies, Volume 1 (Long Papers)*, pages 685–696.

T. Vahe, D. John, W. Leigh, D. Alexander, R. Ziqin, K. Olga, P. Kristin A., C. Gerbrand, and J. Anubhav. 2019. Unsupervised word embeddings capture latent knowledge from materials science literature. *Nature*, 571(7763):9598.

Michael M. Woldeyohannis and Million Meshesha. 2022. Usable amharic text corpus for natural language processing applications. *Applied Corpus Linguistics*, 2(3):100033.

M. Zakaria. 2019. Text complexity classification based on linguistic information: Application to intelligent tutoring of esl. *Journal of Data Mining and Digital Humanities*, pages 1–40.

On the Tolerance of Repetition Before Performance Degradation in Kiswahili Automatic Speech Recognition

Kathleen Siminyu[†] **Kathy Reid**[‡] **Rebecca Ryakitimbo**[#]
Britone Mwasaru[⋆] **Chenai Chair**[⋆]
[†]The Distributed AI Research Institute
[‡]School of Cybernetics, Australia National University
[#] Kuza STEAM Generation [⋆] Independent

Abstract

State of the art end-to-end automatic speech recognition (ASR) models require large speech datasets for training. The Mozilla Common Voice project crowd-sources read speech to address this need. However, this approach often results in many audio utterances being recorded for each written sentence.

Using Kiswahili speech data, this paper first explores how much audio repetition in utterances is permissible in a training set before model degradation occurs, then examines the extent to which audio augmentation techniques can be employed to increase the diversity of speech characteristics and improve accuracy.

We find that repetition up to a ratio of 1 sentence to 8 audio recordings improves performance, but performance degrades at a ratio of 1:16. We also find small improvements from frequency mask, time mask and tempo augmentation. Our findings provide guidance on training set construction for ASR practitioners, particularly those working in under-served languages.[1]

1 Introduction

Automatic Speech Recognition(ASR) is the process of converting acoustic speech into text (Washani and Sharma, 2015). This task has gained significance with the increased use of computing systems by humans via voice commands. End-to-end (E2E) speech recognition models have several components that contribute to the development of the overall system. These include an acoustic model which gives the most likely acoustic unit (phone) based on the acoustic properties of the input signal, a language model which can represent the linguistic form of a language, and thus defines the words in this language and how likely they are to occur together and a lexicon which explains the vocabulary at the phone-level (Leino et al., 2015). These models require large volumes of speech data for training.

The accuracy of E2E ASR models is typically evaluated using two metrics - word error rate (WER) and character error rate (CER). WER and CER are defined as the number of word or character insertions, omissions and substitutions in a transcription, divided by the number of matching words or characters respectively (Kamath et al., 2019). WER measures the accuracy of the language model while CER measures the accuracy of the acoustic model. We acknowledge that the suitability of these metrics is contested per Aksënova et al. (2021).

In a bid to reduce error rates, the ASR community continues to call for greater quantities of data to train systems, going from 50 to 500 to 500 hours of speech (Moore, 2003). Speech Recognition datasets are composed of recordings of speech which are accompanied by corresponding texts or transcripts. They can be obtained by taking existing audio recordings, having them transcribed, splitting them into shorter audio segments and aligning the recordings to their transcriptions. This process describes the creation of a spontaneous speech dataset, which is speech produced by a speaker in an informal, dynamic, unrehearsed, casual manner (Tucker and Mukai, 2023). Datasets such as the FAU Aibo Emotion Corpus (Batliner et al., 2008) contain spontaneous speech. In some cases, the script or transcription comes first then audio recordings are created through speakers being prompted to read out the script while recording themselves, resulting in an elicited or read speech dataset. Datasets such as Multilingual LibriSpeech (Pratap et al., 2020) and Mozilla Common Voice (Ardila et al., 2019) are examples of read speech datasets. The Mozilla Common Voice(MCV) dataset is a multilingual speech corpus developed for Auto-

[1]This research was conducted while the authors - Kathleen Siminyu, Rebecca Ryakitimbo, Britone Mwasaru and Chenai Chair - were affiliated to Mozilla Foundation.

Proceedings of the Sixth Workshop on African Natural Language Processing (AfricaNLP 2025), pages 15–23
July 31, 2025

matic Speech Recognition purposes (Ardila et al., 2019). The data collection efforts are entirely crowd-sourced through organising and engaging language communities.

This paper documents work that has focused on the Kiswahili language dataset available on MCV. Kiswahili is a Bantu language originally spoken by the Swahili people of Eastern Africa. It is one of the official languages of the East African Community in addition to being a national language in Tanzania, Kenya, the Democratic Republic of Congo and Uganda. Kiswahili has over 200 million speakers[2]. It is the most widely spoken African language.

The efforts in building the Kiswahili dataset on MCV, are described in greater detail in §3.1. This dataset contains an underlying text corpus of 134,653 Kiswahili sentences and from this, over 700,000 audio clips have been recorded totalling 1,081 hours of audio data. There are over 1,454 individual speakers that have contributed their voices to create the dataset. While these efforts are commendable, the resulting dataset for Kiswahili, MCV 16[3] in some cases has up to 16 corresponding audio recordings to a single sentence. These are instances of different speakers having recorded themselves reading the same sentence out loud.

This work is to help us determine how best to utilise our dataset in training a neural model for speech recognition that is able to generalise well. This set of experiments examines: 1) how much audio repetition, in relation to a sentence, can be included in a training dataset, before this leads to a degradation of performance of the output model, and 2) whether audio augmentation techniques can be employed to reduce repetition and increase diversity (speaking rate, background noise and interference, pitch) within our dataset.

We find that repetition up to a ratio of 1 sentence to 8 audio recordings improves performance, but performance degrades at a ratio of 1:16. Additionally, various augmentation techniques lead to improvements; time mask augmentation led to an improvement of up to 4.2%, tempo augmentation led to an increase of up to 3.36% and frequency mask augmentation led to an increase of up to 2.4%.

2 Prior Work

We infer from speech recognition literature, specifically from the descriptions of the creation of elicited speech datasets, which are comparable to MCV, such as Librispeech (Panayotov et al., 2015) and Multilingual Librispeech (Pratap et al., 2020), that in an ideal data setting we expect a 1:1 ratio of audio to transcript to ensure adequate variety of content in the dataset. In these datasets, the data is derived from read audio books and each book contains only one accompanying audio recording.

While machine learning literature suggests that the more data available to train a model, the better an output system would be (Halevy et al., 2009; Brill, 2003), there is also literature indicating that, particularly in supervised learning scenarios, insufficient samples for learning or repetition within a dataset would lead a model to overfit during training (Ying, 2019). Overfitting is an issue in supervised machine learning where a model is unable to generalize on unseen data, thus performing poorly, despite appearing to generalise on observed data available in the training set (Russell and Norvig, 2010).

Augmentation of data is another strategy that can be used to prevent overfitting. Data augmentation is the generation of synthetic data from already existing data (Ko et al., 2015). Rebai et al. (2017) have shown that data augmentation techniques can be employed to instances where limited data is available with the intent to modify instances of the data so as to increase the amount of training data. These techniques are also used to improve the performance of resulting systems as they serve to introduce variety in training data; frequency and pitch masks can help make the model more robust when faced with background noise and interference in audio recordings, pitch and tempo augmentation can serve to add more 'speakers' to a dataset by adding speakers with the same articulation patterns or creating speakers with new articulation patterns, respectively (Zhang et al., 2023; Zevallos et al., 2022; Ying, 2019).

3 Methodology

3.1 Data Collection

There are several stages in the data collection process on MCV.

3.1.1 Creation and Collection of Sentences

Existing texts can be added onto the platform provided they are in the public domain. This is a requirement because the entirety of the MCV dataset is licensed as CC Zero (CC0). This is a Creative

[2]Swahili gaining popularity globally

[3]Mozilla Common Voice Kiswahili dataset

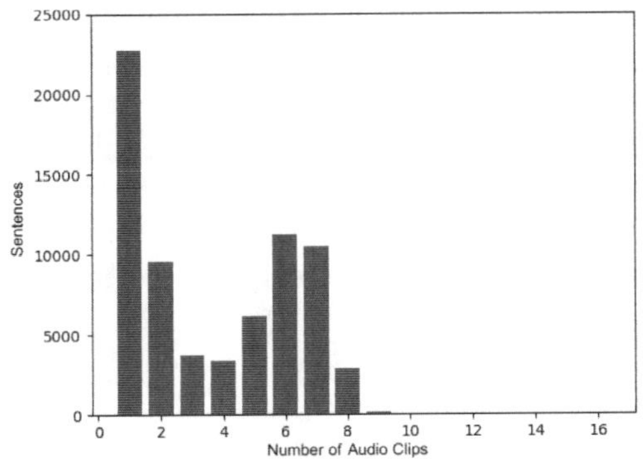

Figure 1: The y-axis shows the number of number of sentences and the x-axis shows the accompanying audios recorded for instances in the validated set.

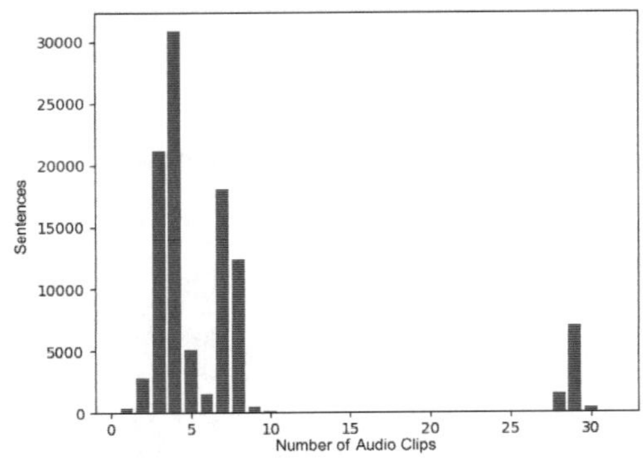

Figure 2: Similar to figure 1, the y-axis shows the number of sentences and the x-axis shows the accompanying audios recorded for sentences. In this case, in addition to the number of clips that have been validated, we include those that have been invalidated and those that are yet to be validated.

Commons License that allows creators to give up their copyright and put their works into the worldwide public domain. CC0 allows re-users to distribute, remix, adapt and build upon the material in any medium or format, with no conditions [4]. Where there is existing text with ownership attributed to an individual or an organisation, and they are willing to waive these rights so that the content is added onto the platform, they need to sign a waiver giving MCV permission [5]. In our work, community initiatives and events have been organised in support of the creation of original Kiswahili texts for addition onto the platform. One example is a partnership with Hekaya Arts Initiative, a writers collective based in Mombasa Kenya, which saw us organise

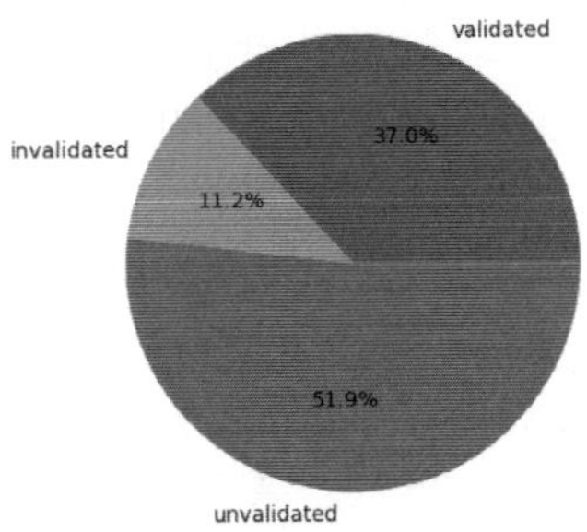

Figure 3: The pie chart shows the percentage of audios that have either been validated, invalidated - has received two or more down-votes - or are yet to be validated (i.e. unvalidated) in version 16 of the MCV Kiswahili dataset.

a series of writing competitions. Submission to the competitions have been added onto the MCV platform and winners in each edition were awarded prizes [6].

3.1.2 Validation of Sentences

These sentences then need to go through a validation process. Each language may have slightly differing requirements for sentence validation. Some general reviewing criteria include ensuring that the spelling and grammar in a sentence are correct, that they are natural and conversational (should be easy to read the sentence), that there is no use of abbreviations or acronyms and that there are no digits in the source text. These should all be written down in full and in text format to avoid ambiguity when reading aloud. Each sentence requires at least 2 up votes to be added onto the MCV platform for voice contributions.

3.1.3 Collection of audio recordings

Contributors can choose the 'Speak' feature on the MCV platform, where a single sentence at a time is displayed and the contributor is prompted to record themselves reading it out loud. New sentences, those that do not yet have an accompanying recording, are prioritised on the platform. Once each sentence has at least one accompanying recording, the sentences then begin being looped over again. Should the voice contributions come in faster than the text contributions, some sentences will have more than one accompanying audio. The platform

[4]Creative Commons Licenses

[5]Common Voice Contribution Agreement for Pre-existing Works

[6]Common Voice, Hekaya Arts Initiative Announce Kiswahili Writing Competition Winners

tracks what sentences an individual contributor has already recorded an audio for, provided they are signed in. They will therefore ideally contribute only one audio recording per sentence. In the event that a 'super' contributor provides an audio for the entire underlying text corpus, they will then start to be presented with sentences for speech elicitation that they have already recorded an audio for. It is therefore possible for a single sentence to have more than one accompanying audio, provided by different speakers. It is also possible, however rare, for there to be duplicates of an individual speaker contributing more than one audio to a single sentence. These features of the platform impact characteristics of the dataset, in terms of creating opportunity for repetition. In our work collecting data for Kiswahili, we experienced significant challenges in accessing text data early on in the project. Our efforts in collecting text were happening concurrently with community efforts to contribute and validate audios. We soon found ourselves with up to 30 audios per sentence for the texts that were seeded onto the platform in the very beginning as evidenced by figure 2, which shows the amount of repetition in all available sentences and their accompanying audios and figure 1, which shows the amount of repetition in the validated subset of the dataset.

3.1.4 Validation of audio recordings

Contributors can choose the 'Listen' feature where they will be prompted to play already recorded audios and to validate them, by giving them a thumbs up, or invalidate them, by giving them a thumbs down, depending on whether or not the audios fit the reviewing criteria provided. This includes listening to ensure that the contents of the audio align with the accompanying text, that the speaker is audible enough and that they do not hesitate or stammer. This validation is important when producing a speech recognition corpus as they will directly impact the quality of models produced. If the transcript and audio recording are not accurate, then the model becomes less likely to be accurate. This validation work is crowd-sourced and takes place in community events[7]. The participants are therefore not trained linguists or language professionals for the most part, they are native speakers of the language. Given the diversity of Kiswahili speakers, and the varying accents available, it is important to curate a diverse group of validators to ensure that this diversity is maintained in the dataset that is curated for Machine Learning. We found that voice validation is not as popular as voice contributions in our community activities. This has resulted in only 48.2% of our dataset having undergone validation (37% validated and 11.2% invalidated), as of the MCV 16 release. This is approximately 400 hours of data that is considered fit for use, i.e. validated, compared to the 1081 hours available. Due to concerns about the quality of unvalidated data, we use only data that is validated and more than half of the data available is left unutilised. Figure 3 shows the validation rate of Kiswahili data in the MCV 16 release.

[7]Common Voice Kiswahili Festival Brings Community Together To Grow Dataset

3.2 Data Pre-processing

The Kiswahili dataset on MCV 16 comes with seven files:

- `validated.tsv` - contains information on the audios that have been validated, i.e. have received at least 2 up-votes
- `reported.tsv` - contains information about sentences that have been reported to have a grammatical or spelling error, having offensive language, having a different language or being difficult to pronounce
- `invalidated.tsv` - contains information of audios that have received at least 2 down-votes, and less than two up-votes
- `other.tsv` - contains information of audios that have neither been validated nor invalidated
- `train.tsv` - contains the list of audios included as part of the training data
- `dev.tsv` - contains the list of audios included as part of the development data used to validate the model's learning during training
- `test.tsv` - contains the list of audios included as part of the test data

In this work, we curate our own experimental splits as opposed to using the train, dev and test splits provided with MCV. We make the decision to use only the instances that have been validated, i.e., those that are listed in the `validated.tsv` file as having been reviewed and verified by Kiswahili speakers. There are approximately 400 hours of validated data in the Kiswahili dataset.

We filter out several subsets that have been created specifically for purposes of evaluation of certain demographic groups. These are data for dialects and variants that are closely related to Kiswahili: Kiunguja, Kibajuni, Kimakunduchi, Kimvita, Kipemba, Kitumbatu and Kiswahili cha Bara ya Tanzania (Kiswahili from Inland Tanzania). These subsets were developed through working with linguists and language experts, work that has been documented (Siminyu et al., 2022).

We investigated the existing CorporaCreator repository[8], a command line tool to create Mozilla Common Voice corpora for use in this work, however it did not provide the flexibility to curate our own evaluation sets, particularly how big they should be. We found that while it is useful to be able to select the number of audio repetitions included in the training set, this changed the composition of the development and test sets in each instance, a behaviour which makes the first set of experiments in this work incomparable. We therefore chose to create our own scripts for data preprocessing.

We split our data into 3 sets, a training set, a development set and a test set, in the ratio 60:20:20.

In constituting our training, development and test sets, we consider several factors:

- That all audios corresponding to a single sentence should only appear in one set
- That all audios contributed by a single speaker should also all be in only one set
- Where a single speaker may have contributed to an individual sentence more than once, we drop duplicate instances

4 Experiments

4.1 Experiment 1: More Data versus Less Repetition Trade-off

In the first set of experiments, we consider a trade-off in constituting the training set. On one hand, an increase in audio repetition, in relation to a single sentence, creates more training data. On the other hand, repetition of audio recordings relative to an individual sentence may decrease the performance of the output model due to overfitting. We increase the text to audio ratio following a geometric progression up to the maximum number of repetitions available, in this case 16, with the intent of drawing a curve that can visualize the results and determine whether there is a point at which more data and more repetition leads to a degradation of performance in the output models. The data is constituted in the following settings;

- 1:1 - each sentence with 1 accompanying audio recording
- 1:2 - each sentence with 2 accompanying audio recordings
- 1:4 - each sentence with 4 accompanying audio recordings
- 1:8 - each sentence with 8 accompanying audio recordings
- 1:16 - each sentence with 16 accompanying audio recordings

We use the Coqui AI Speech-to-Text(STT) toolkit[9] for these experiments. The Coqui STT architecture consists of a recurrent neural network(RNN) with 5 hidden layers, where the first three and the fifth layers are non-recurrent and use a clipped rectified-linear (ReLu) activation function while the fourth layer is a bidirectional recurrent layer. The CTC loss function is used by the network. The system is integrated with an N-gram language model. To identify the ideal hyper-parameter settings, we run several iterations of the experiment with a 1:1 mapping of the data with the following settings:

- `-n_hidden`: 1024, 2048, 5024
- `-reduce_lr_on_plateau`: true
- `-plateau_epochs`: 10
- `-plateau_reduction`: 0.025, 0.05, 0.1
- `-early_stop`: true
- `-es_epochs`: 25
- `-es_min_delta`: 0.01, 0.02, 0.05
- `-dropout_rate`: 0.3
- `-epochs`: 60 (for our hyper-parameter search)

[8]CorporaCreator Github repository

[9]Coqui STT Github repo

Once we have selected the ideal hyperparameters for our experiment, we do training runs with the different sentence to audio ratio settings; 1:1, 1:2, 1:4, 1:8 and 1:16. We then use the best score as a baseline for our second set of experiments.

4.2 Experiment 2: Data Augmentation for More Data

In this set of experiments, we further wish to explore methods that allow us to make maximum use of the data available to us, in spite of the repetition. We explore the use of audio data synthesis methods to augment subsequent repetitions of audio recordings relative to an individual sentence. The following augmentations are applied to the audio recording repetitions:

- Pitch augmentation shifts the pitch of a waveform by scaling it on the frequency axis. By shifting the pitch, we attempt to add to the variety of "speakers" in the dataset, (Bellettini and Mazzini, 2008) particularly as it relates to age given the skew of available data towards younger speakers (Shahnawazuddin et al., 2020)

- Tempo augmentation changes the playback tempo by scaling the waveform along the time axis. This will help our models become robust to speakers with varying speaking rates (Ko et al., 2015)

- Frequency mask augmentation sets frequency-intervals within the augmented samples to zero (silence) at random frequencies. This helps the model to be robust when it encounters background noise and other interferences in audios (Park et al., 2019)

- Time mask augmentation sets time-intervals within the augmented samples to zero (silence) at random positions. This adds variety in a manner similar to the frequency mask, by making models robust to background noises and interferences (Park et al., 2019)

For this experiment, we use the data from the "1:4" (1 sentence with 4 accompanying audio recordings) setting and the results of the first experiment as our baseline, because this setting represents an acceptable amount of repetition before additional data becomes noisy.

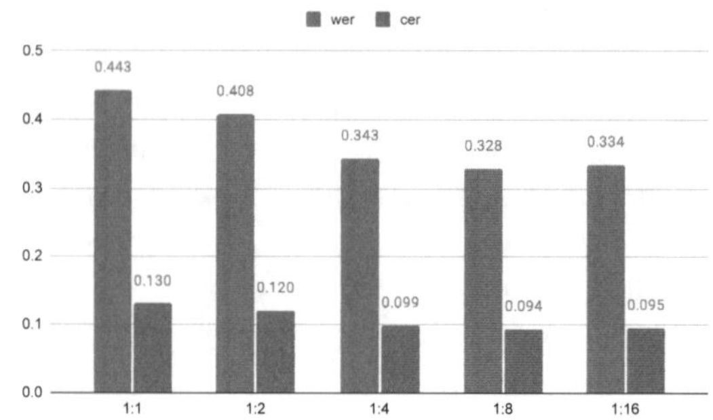

Figure 4: The character error rates and word error rates for the different sentence to audio recordings ratio settings. These steadily decrease with increasing repetition until you reach the 1:8 setting after which there is an increase.

In this experimental setup, given 4 audio recordings relative to one sentence, we vary the ratio of original audio recordings to augmented audio recordings as follows:

- 3:1 - 3 audios in their original form and the final audio recording is augmented. In this case 25% of the data is augmented.

- 2:2 - 2 audios in their original form and 2 of the subsequent repetitions are augmented. In this case 50% of the data is augmented.

- 1:3 - 1 audio is in its original form and 3 of the subsequent repetitions are augmented. In this case, 75% of the data is augmented.

The Coqui AI STT toolkit has implemented a pre-processing pipeline with various augmentation techniques. This feature allows us to set a probability value for each augmentation used. We therefore use the values 0.25 to achieve the "3:1" setting, 0.5 to achieve the "2:2" setting and 0.75 to achieve the "1:3"

We use the ideal hyperparameters selected in experiment 1 to run our experiments.

5 Results

Figure 4 shows results for the first set of experiments in 4.1. It shows WERs and CERs for the different 'sentence to audio ratio' experimental settings, i.e. 1:1, 1:2, 1:4, 1:8 and 1:16. We see a steady decline in both the WERs and CERs, which is consistent with our expectation that with more data, the models' overall performance improves. This is true up to the 1:8 setting, when we get to

Table 1: The CER obtained as well as the percentage change (denoted as Δ) given the baseline when 25%, 50% and 75% of the data is augmented using frequency mask, time mask, tempo and pitch augmentations.

	25% augmentation		50% augmentation		75% augmentation	
	CER	Δ	CER	Δ	CER	Δ
frequency mask	0.097	1.12%	0.096	2.40%	0.096	2.23%
time mask	0.094	4.20%	0.099	-0.44%	0.095	2.65%
tempo	0.100	-2.20%	0.095	3.36%	0.099	-1.20%
pitch	0.319	-224.42%	0.101	-3.39%	0.112	-14.57%

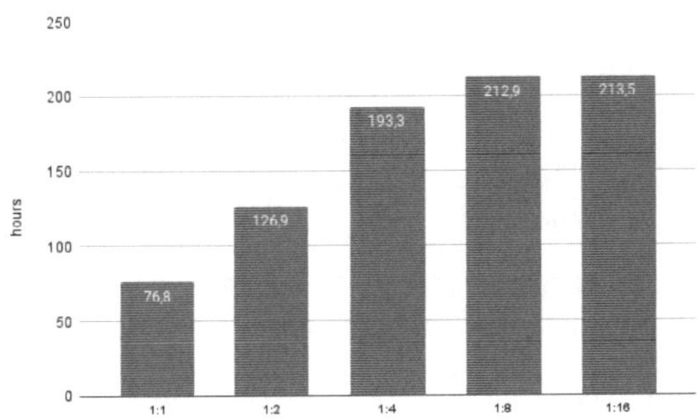

Figure 5: The amount of data, in terms of hours, contained in each of the 'sentence to audio ratio' settings in experiments in 4.1

the 1:16 setting, the performance is seen to deteriorate. This deterioration in performance may be indicative of how much repetition is acceptable, demonstrating that 16 audio instances of the same sentence is too much despite the additional variability introduced by each subsequent audio being read out by a different speaker. Interrogating the amount of data in each setting reveals that the difference between the 1:4 and 1:8 settings is 19 hours while that between the 1:8 and 1:16 settings is 0.6 hours, as shown in figure 5. In investigating duplicate instances, we found evidence of noise. Audios that were included as duplicates beyond the fourth and eighth instance were likely to have received both up-votes and down-votes from the validation process, e.g. 2 up-votes and 1 down-vote, 4 up-votes and 3 down-votes.

We then used the results of the 1:4 experimental setting as our baseline score for comparison in the second set of experiments to exclude these contentious instances.

The results of the second experiment are shown in Table 1. We find that the frequency mask augmentation consistently led to an improvement of up to 2.4% in CER over the baseline score obtained in the first experiment. This is likely due to the great variation of acoustic settings represented in the data, given that this dataset is crowd sourced by communities. It is likely that frequency mask augmentation leads to zero-ing out of noise in audio samples enabling the model to learn more from the speech to be transcribed.

Time mask augmentation led to an improvement in performance when 25% and 75% of the dataset is augmented, up to 4.2%, but a decrease in performance when 50% of the dataset is augmented. Similar to the frequency mask, the time mask leads to zero-ing out of time steps which possibly contain noise.

Tempo augmentation only led to an improvement when 50% of the dataset is augmented and pitch augmentation did not lead to any increase in performance but showed a shocking decrease of -224.42% when 25% of the dataset is augmented. The frequency axis was scaled by a pitch factor of 0.1 to 0.3, which implies a significant lowering of the pitch far below the original which led to audios becoming low-pitched and likely unintelligible. A better approach would have been to alter the pitch progressively by octave, i.e. 0.5 to take it one octave down, 0.25 to take it two octaves down and 2.0 to raise the pitch by one octave.

There are no consistent gains in perfomance across any of the data augmentation settings(25%, 50% or 75%), leading us to conclude once again that selecting the right augmentation type given the data in question is more pertinent. Overall, we have determined that having more data, despite repetition, can be useful and that the choice of an appropriate data augmentation technique can add greater variation in the dataset making it more useful.

6 Future Work

Given the difficulty faced in identifying Kiswahili text data sources, future work could explore data selection methods for speech utterances and/or text data. This could help eliminate redundancies in data and enable better targeted text data collection, and subsequently speech data collection for low-resource languages. Additionally, as there is a lot of data available that we could not use due to lack of validation, we encourage continued community efforts to validate this data. One limitation of this work is that the experiments have been run on a single dataset and a single language, the work would benefit from scaling up to additional languages and datasets as evidence of generalisability to additional contexts. Finally, given some availability of data for dialects and variants closely related to Kiswahili, it would be great to see how the system developed performs when evaluated on speech from these dialects and variants.

7 Conclusions

In this paper, we articulated the data collection method for read speech in MCV and highlighted the constraint of having many recorded audio utterances from a single written sentence when constructing an ASR training set.

To assess how much sentence repetition is permissible, we trained multiple ASR models on Kiswahili data using varying sentence to audio recording ratios, finding that a ratio of 1:8 is optimal, with performance declining at 1:16. Further, we performed multiple forms of audio augmentation, demonstrating some small improvements in CER for time mask augmentation (4.20% improvement) at 25% augmentation and tempo augmentation (3.36% improvement) at 50% augmentation.

The key take-away for ASR practitioners, particularly those working with under-resourced languages having limited speech data, is that it is worthwhile to include repeated sentences in the training set, however the choice of optimal audio augmentation is likely context-dependent.

Acknowledgements

References

Alëna Aksënova, Daan van Esch, James Flynn, and Pavel Golik. 2021. How might we create better benchmarks for speech recognition? In *Proceedings of the 1st Workshop on Benchmarking: Past, Present and Future*, pages 22–34.

Rosana Ardila, Megan Branson, Kelly Davis, Michael Henretty, Michael Kohler, Josh Meyer, Reuben Morais, Lindsay Saunders, Francis M Tyers, and Gregor Weber. 2019. Common voice: A massively-multilingual speech corpus. *arXiv preprint arXiv:1912.06670*.

Anton Batliner, Stefan Steidl, and Elmar Nöth. 2008. Releasing a thoroughly annotated and processed spontaneous emotional database: the fau aibo emotion corpus.

Carlo Bellettini and Gianluca Mazzini. 2008. Reliable automatic recognition for pitch-shifted audio. In *2008 Proceedings of 17th International Conference on Computer Communications and Networks*, pages 1–6. IEEE.

Eric Brill. 2003. Processing natural language without natural language processing. In *International Conference on Intelligent Text Processing and Computational Linguistics*, pages 360–369. Springer.

Alon Halevy, Peter Norvig, and Fernando Pereira. 2009. The unreasonable effectiveness of data. *IEEE intelligent systems*, 24(2):8–12.

Uday Kamath, John Liu, James Whitaker, Uday Kamath, John Liu, and James Whitaker. 2019. Automatic speech recognition. In *Deep Learning for NLP and Speech Recognition*, pages 369–404. Springer.

Tom Ko, Vijayaditya Peddinti, Daniel Povey, and Sanjeev Khudanpur. 2015. Audio augmentation for speech recognition. In *Proc. Interspeech 2015*, pages 3586–3589.

Katri Leino et al. 2015. Maximum a posteriori for acoustic model adaptation in automatic speech recognition. Master's thesis.

Roger K Moore. 2003. A comparison of the data requirements of automatic speech recognition systems and human listeners. In *INTERSPEECH*, pages 2581–2584.

Vassil Panayotov, Guoguo Chen, Daniel Povey, and Sanjeev Khudanpur. 2015. Librispeech: an asr corpus based on public domain audio books. In *2015 IEEE international conference on acoustics, speech and signal processing (ICASSP)*, pages 5206–5210. IEEE.

Daniel S Park, William Chan, Yu Zhang, Chung-Cheng Chiu, Barret Zoph, Ekin D Cubuk, and Quoc V Le. 2019. Specaugment: A simple data augmentation method for automatic speech recognition. *arXiv preprint arXiv:1904.08779*.

Vineel Pratap, Qiantong Xu, Anuroop Sriram, Gabriel Synnaeve, and Ronan Collobert. 2020. Mls: A large-scale multilingual dataset for speech research. *arXiv preprint arXiv:2012.03411*.

Ilyes Rebai, Yessine BenAyed, Walid Mahdi, and Jean-Pierre Lorré. 2017. Improving speech recognition using data augmentation and acoustic model fusion. *Procedia Computer Science*, 112:316–322.

Stuart J Russell and Peter Norvig. 2010. *Artificial intelligence a modern approach*. London.

S Shahnawazuddin, Nagaraj Adiga, Hemant Kumar Kathania, and B Tarun Sai. 2020. Creating speaker independent asr system through prosody modification based data augmentation. *Pattern Recognition Letters*, 131:213–218.

Kathleen Siminyu, Kibibi Mohamed Amran, Abdulrahman Ndegwa Karatu, Mnata Resani, Mwimbi Makobo Junior, Rebecca Ryakitimbo, and Britone Mwasaru. 2022. Corpus development of kiswahili speech recognition test and evaluation sets, preemptively mitigating demographic bias through collaboration with linguists. In *Proceedings of the Fifth Workshop on the Use of Computational Methods in the Study of Endangered Languages*, pages 13–19.

Benjamin V Tucker and Yoichi Mukai. 2023. *Spontaneous Speech*. Cambridge University Press.

Nitin Washani and Sandeep Sharma. 2015. Speech recognition system: A review. *International Journal of Computer Applications*, 115(18).

Xue Ying. 2019. An overview of overfitting and its solutions. In *Journal of physics: Conference series*, volume 1168, page 022022. IOP Publishing.

Rodolfo Zevallos, Nuria Bel, Guillermo Cámbara, Mireia Farrús, and Jordi Luque. 2022. Data augmentation for low-resource quechua asr improvement. *arXiv preprint arXiv:2207.06872*.

Yuanyuan Zhang, Aaricia Herygers, Tanvina Patel, Zhengjun Yue, and Odette Scharenborg. 2023. Exploring data augmentation in bias mitigation against non-native-accented speech. In *2023 IEEE Automatic Speech Recognition and Understanding Workshop (ASRU)*, pages 1–8. IEEE.

Enhancing AI-Driven Farming Advisory in Kenya with Efficient RAG Agents via Quantized Fine-Tuned Language Models

Theophilus Owiti[1], Andrew Kipkebut[1]
[1]Kabarak University, Eldama Ravine Road, Kenya
Correspondence: lowiti@kabarak.ac.ke

Abstract

The integration of Artificial Intelligence (AI) in agriculture has significantly impacted decision-making processes for farmers, particularly in regions such as Kenya, where access to accurate and timely advisory services is crucial. This paper explores the deployment of Retrieval Augmented Generation (RAG) agents powered by fine-tuned quantized language models to enhance AI-driven agricultural advisory services. By optimizing model efficiency through quantization and fine-tuning, our aim is to deliver a specialized language model in agriculture and to ensure real-time, cost-effective and contextually relevant recommendations for smallholder farmers. Our approach takes advantage of localized agricultural datasets and natural language processing techniques to improve the accessibility and accuracy of advisory responses in local Kenyan languages. We show that the proposed model has the potential to improve information delivery and automation of complex and monotonous tasks, making it a viable solution to sustainable agricultural intelligence in Kenya and beyond.

1 Introduction

Despite Open-source and proprietary Pretrained Language Models (PLMs) being trained on large sets of text data, they may lack fundamental principles, in each domain like Agriculture, which govern use of words to predict subsequent words in a sentence. This limitation is demonstrated by the fact that, most LLMs (Large Language Models) today have an exceptionally good global performance but fail in specific task-oriented problems (Josep, 2024). This research focuses on leveraging fine-tuning and quantization techniques for both small and large language models to create specialized models and agents for the agricultural sector in Kenya. While PLMs have demonstrated significant performance on downstream tasks for both high- and low-resourced languages, there is still a large drop in performance for underrepresented African languages during pre-training (Alabi et al., 2022).

Existing efforts, such as AfroLM, majorly focused on a multilingual language model pretrained on 23 African languages using a self-active learning framework. Even though it performs well on various NLP downstream tasks like Named Entity Recognition (NER), text classification, and sentiment analysis (Dossou et al., 2022), these models lack sufficient linguistic and contextual grounding in Kenyan languages and agricultural knowledge.

In the plant health domain, studies have shown that PLMs are useful for text-mining applications but face challenges in low-resource settings due to limited labelled data. For example, research on text mining for plant health hazard detection highlights the need for models

Proceedings of the Sixth Workshop on African Natural Language Processing (AfricaNLP 2025), pages 24–30
July 31, 2025 ©2025 Association for Computational Linguistics

trained on recent, domain-specific agricultural datasets (Jiang et al., 2023). To address these gaps, this research proposes fine-tuning existing PLMs on a corpus of Kenyan agricultural data, enhancing their ability to understand both domain-specific terminology and Kenyan languages. The goal is to develop a compact and efficient quantized language model optimized for agriculture, along with an AI agent capable of both comprehending Kenyan languages and executing task-oriented actions based on natural language inputs.

The absence of specialized agriculture models in Kenyan languages presents a significant gap. Kenyan farmers lack access to adequate and efficient AI-powered solutions that can provide up-to date, localized and contextually relevant agricultural information. Currently, available language models do not incorporate extensive agricultural expertise, nor are they optimized for Kenyan languages, making them ineffective for tasks such as farming guidance, risk assessment, financial literacy, and market insights.

This limitation demonstrates potentially dire consequences in the agricultural sector and Kenya's economy at large. Kenyan farmers struggle to access reliable and actionable farming information, from best planting practices to market trends and financial advice. The available resources are often generic, presented in English or Swahili, and fail to offer localized insights tailored to farmers' specific regions and crops. Sometimes farmers do not have adequate access to extension services. As a result, misinformation and a lack of accessible knowledge contribute to poor farming decisions, lower yields, and financial instability.

While AI-driven agricultural solutions in Kenya primarily focus on weather, soil analysis, crop disease detection, and pest control, they typically follow a three-step approach: detect a problem, offer recommendations, and direct farmers to Agro-vets for solutions. However, these solutions lack a unified access point, personalization and context-aware support that empowers farmers with continuous assistance. LLMs and AI agents have demonstrated their effectiveness in delivering instant, tailored information and executing actions in other domains, yet their potential remains untapped in Kenyan agriculture.

The purpose of the study is to develop a compact and efficient language model that understands Kenyan languages and agricultural terminology while integrating with AI agents to assist farmers. In doing so, our goal is to bridge the knowledge gap in agriculture, improve decision-making, and empower farmers with accessible and language-inclusive AI support.

2 Related Work

Adapting Pre-trained Language Models for African Languages Several efforts to use pretrained models have led to multilingual fine-tuning approaches for African languages. One of the most effective approaches to adapt to a new language is language adaptive fine-tuning (LAFT) — fine-tuning a multilingual PLM on monolingual texts of a language using the pre-training objective. However, adapting to a target language individually takes a large disk space and limits the cross-lingual transfer abilities of the resulting models because they have been specialized for a single language. They performed multilingual adaptive fine-tuning in 17 most resourced African languages and three other high-resource languages widely spoken on the African continent to encourage cross-lingual transfer learning (Alabi et al., 2022). AfroLM a multilingual language model pre-trained from scratch on 23 African languages (the largest effort to date) using our novel self-active learning framework. Pretrained on a dataset significantly (14x) smaller than existing baselines, it outperforms many multilingual pre-trained language models (AfriBERTa, XLMR-base, mBERT) on various NLP downstream tasks like NER and text classification (Dossou et al., 2022).

Tool-calling Other models outperform Text-Davinci-003 and Claude-2, achieve comparable performance to ChatGPT, and is only slightly inferior to GPT4. Besides, models (ToolLLaMA) exhibits robust generalization to previously unseen APIs, requiring only the API documentation to adapt to new APIs effectively. They majorly focus on Supervised fine-tuning to enhance tool calling capabilities with synthesized training data (Qin et al., 2023).

3 Standard and Instruction-based Chain of Thought Annotation

Current LLMs also exceed in areas such as tool calling and reasoning with chain-of-thought (CoT). CoT instruction tuning has drawn attention for its potential to encourage complex, step-by-step reasoning. LLMs can demonstrate CoT abilities with proper prompting and instruction engineering (Liu et al., 2023), but this is something that lacks in most parts of Africa given the state of underrepresented African languages.

Tool-calling is a focus area in this research where we aim to achieve a model that can support tool calling in local Kenyan languages. To achieve this, we focus on adopting Supervised fine-tuning (SFT). It is a method to enhance the tool calling capabilities of LLMs, with the training data often being synthesized. The current data synthesis process generally involves sampling a set of tools, formulating a requirement based on these tools, and generating the call statements (Wang et al., 2024).

Data based on local Agriculture documents have been created with paired translations from vernacular languages to English. We employ an instruction-based format in the dataset, heavily focusing on tuning the training data to employ a Chain of Thought format and focus on tool calling annotation for single-tool calling in Kenyan languages, with standard prompts we focus on enhancing chat completion capabilities based on the corpus that has been translated to specific native Kenyan languages.


```
{
  "api_list": [
    {
      "category_name": "maize",
      "tool_name": "plant_diagnosis",
      "api_name": "CheckPlantHealth",
      "api_description": "Checks for crop health in maize.",
      "required_parameters": ["location", "crop_type"],
      "method": "GET"
    }
  ],
  "query": "Apidho ga oduma, to adak Kisumu, Kenya. Odumba gi nitie gi kumoro ma rateng'. Ango
ma chamo gi?",
  "relevant APIs": [
    [
      "CheckPlantHealth"
    ]
  ],
  "query_id": 1
}
```


Figure 1: Example of the tool calling dataset used with queries in Kenyan languages. This particular training data uses Dholuo.

Construction of the tool-calling dataset for training is split into three stages: collecting existing APIs and creating missing APIs spanning across different categories (such as Agribusiness, Weather, News for Farmers), writing instructions in given languages covering APIs for single-tool scenarios, and the solution path annotation for each instruction (Qin et al., 2023). An example of this is found in Figure 1.

4 Method

To develop a multilingual model specialized in the agricultural domain, we adopted the following steps to achieve the goal of creating a model specialized for a subset of African languages and measuring how well a fine-tuned and quantized PLM can perform in various agricultural tasks in Kenya.

4.1 Data Collection

Data was collected from disparate sources. For instance, the language pair sentences provided by Tech Innovators Network Kenya (THiNK), publicly available websites and documents about agriculture and biblical text extracted using OCR. The THiNK dataset comprised of local-language and swahili pairs[1], therefore, to have a local-language and english pair of each language (Luyha, Luo, Kalenjin, Kidaw'ida-Kiswahili) the dataset comprising of 91,097 sentence pairs was changed to accomodate the manual translation of Swahili words to English. See Table 1 for an example of the Language pair for local-language and swahili sentence pairs.

Language Pair	Train Set Size	Test Set Size	Total Size (bytes)
Kidaw'ida-Kiswahili (dav_swa)	21,329	5,333	1,973,706
Kalenjin-Kiswahili (kln_swa)	28,101	7,026	3,537,847
Dholuo-Kiswahili (luo_swa)	23,446	5,862	4,387,588

Table 1: Total number of language pair sentences provided by THiNK.

4.2 QLoRA for Finetuning

For efficient fine-tuning, we propose using QLoRA (Quantized model weights + Low-Rank Adapters) with the models Llama-2-7B, Llama-3-8B Instruct and Llama-3.1-8B, which reduces memory usage without compromising a model's initial performance as demonstrated in Figure 2. This fine-tuning technique offers several advantages: 4-bit NormalFloat, which outperforms 4-bit Integers and 4-bit Floats in empirical results; Double Quantization, which compresses quantization constants, saving an average of 0.37 bits per parameter; and Paged Optimizers, which mitigate memory spikes caused by gradient checkpointing when processing long-sequence mini-batches (Dettmers et al., 2023).

This approach is informed by the adoption of Quantile Quantization, an optimal data type that estimates the quantile of the input tensor using the empirical cumulative distribution function (Dettmers et al., 2023). While quantization of LLMs has traditionally focused on inference, QLoRA has demonstrated a breakthrough by enabling backpropagation through frozen, quantized weights at large model scales (Belkada et al., 2023).

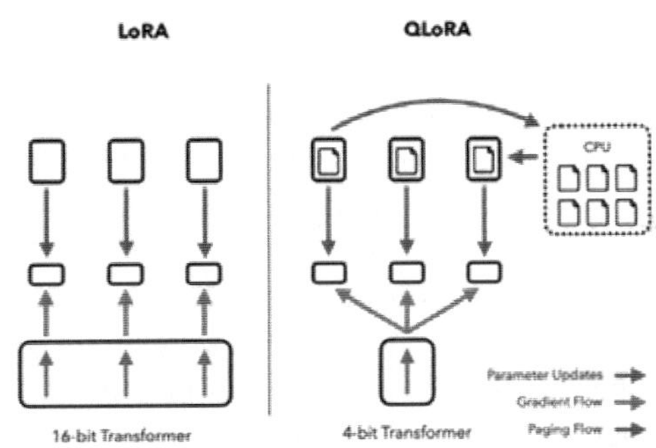

Figure 2: QLORA proves to be efficient than LoRA by quantizing the transformer model to 4-bit precision and using paged optimizers to handle memory spikes. the image is taken from (Dettmers et al., 2023)

4.3 Supervised Fine-tuning

SFT (Supervised Fine-tuning), adapts a pre-trained model to a specific task by taking labelled datasets as input constructed for intended tasks. To be effective, a significant amount of raw data and resources are required to construct and label SFT datasets (Ross et al., 2025).

The research aims to use refined Africa corpora from various languages in Kenya. These data will be further added to standard and chain-of-thought instruction sets with translation pairs from English to local Kenyan languages. During this process of SFT the

[1]https://huggingface.co/datasets/thinkKenya/kenyan-low-resource-language-data

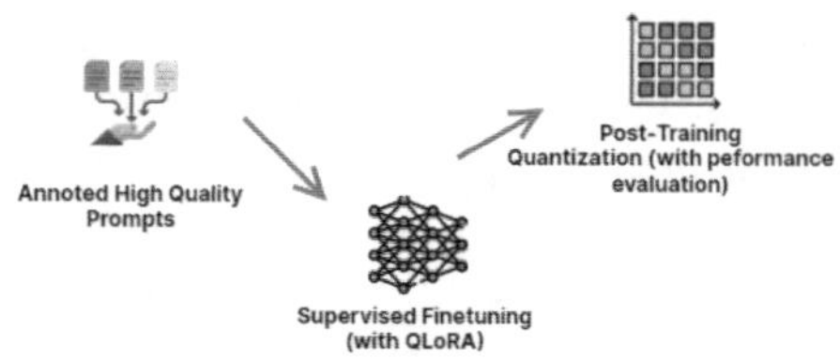

Figure 3: A brief workflow of the training process. This summarizes how the annotated language data is passed over for training to QLoRA and further subjected to testing.

data will then be fed to the training stage where we will use Transformer Reinforcement Learning (TLR)[2] that provides SFTTrainer that makes it straightforward to supervise fine-tune open LLMs, it is a subclass of the Trainer from the transformers library and supports all the same features, including logging, evaluation, and checkpointing, but adds additional quality of life features, including PEFT (parameter-efficient fine-tuning) support including Q-LoRA, or Spectrum (Schmid, 2025) This stage has been indicated on Figure 3.

4.4 Post-Training Quantization

This involves taking our fine-tuned model and quantizing the model parameters during the inference phase. This method does not involve any changes to the training process itself. The dynamic range of parameters is recalculated at runtime, like how we worked with the example matrices (Valenzuela, 2024). This technique allows reducing the size of these increasingly the fine-tuned models with an aim of making it perform better at Agriculture but can also be easily allowed to run on consumer-grade devices with minimal performance depreciation. The quantized model will then be subjected to further testing based on various agricultural areas and the performance will be evaluated and tuned further to achieve optimal results.

[2]https://huggingface.co/docs/trl/index

4.5 RAG Agents and Tool-calling

In this research, we utilize LangGraph to develop an external agent and create Agentic RAG applications that enhance the decision-making process of the deployed model. These applications enable the model to determine whether to retrieve information from the vector store or generate responses directly, as illustrated in Figure 4. Additionally, we extend the agent's capabilities by leveraging LangChain and LangGraph to orchestrate a fine-tuned open-source model deployed on Hugging Face. This allows farmers to interact with the system using natural language to retrieve relevant information and seamlessly access various automated tools for diverse functions.

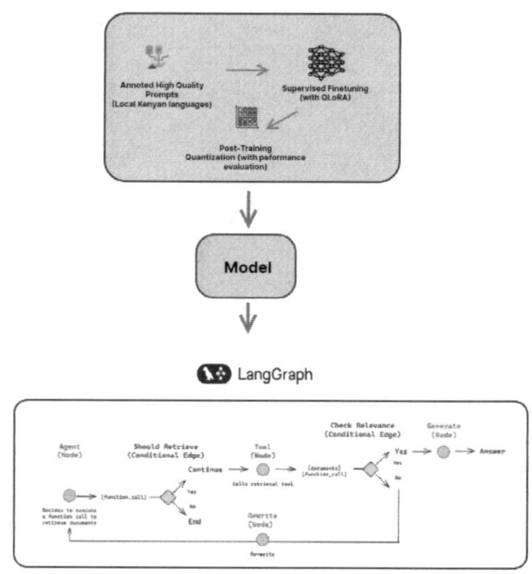

Figure 4: Implementation of the fine-tuned model for AI Agents using LangChain

Beyond this, we will evaluate the in-built too-calling to determine its performance and effectiveness. The capability of tool-calling is achieved by the annotated data set that had CoT format instructions that improves reasoning and also the trained model benefits from the instruction-format based data given during training.

5 Conclusion

This study demonstrates the potential of quantized fine-tuned language models in improving AI-driven farming advisory services through efficient RAG agents. By optimizing model size and computational efficiency, we enable real-time, localized, and cost-effective recommendations tailored to the needs of smallholder farmers in Kenya. Our findings indicate that the proposed approach enhances response accuracy and system performance compared to conventional models, reducing resource constraints while maintaining high-quality advisory outputs. Future work will focus on expanding dataset coverage, integrating multimodal inputs such as satellite imagery, and refining model interpretability to further enhance AI-driven agricultural decision-making in resource-limited environments.

Limitations

Fine-tuning methods utilized in this study have proven to be effective, although, a significant limitation is the scarcity of high-quality, annotated datasets available for fine-tuning models in African languages. The process of creating such datasets is resource-intensive and time-consuming, requiring extensive hours of data preparation. This scarcity of readily available data has created challenges in developing robust and accurate models tailored for the agricultural sector in Kenya and other African contexts.Africa faces a significant shortage of diverse language corpus datasets that authentically capture the nuances of communication in its indigenous languages. To address this, we propose the development of comprehensive, high-quality datasets that reflect the linguistic diversity and cultural contexts of African indigenous languages, enabling more accurate and inclusive natural language processing applications.

Acknowledgments

This research would not have been possible without the exceptional support of our stakeholders. Special thanks to our mentors and colleagues for their valuable insights, feedback, and discussions, which greatly contributed to refining our work. We also recognize the immense support from various open-source communities and developers whose tools, datasets, and frameworks played a crucial role in this study. Furthermore, we appreciate the farmers and agricultural experts in Kenya who shared their experiences, helping us better understand the practical needs of AI-driven farming advisory.

References

O. J. Alabi, I. D. Adelani, M. Mosbach, and D. Klakow. 2022. Adapting pre-trained language models to african languages via multilingual adaptive fine-tuning. In *Proceedings of the 2022 Conference on Computational Linguistics (COLING)*.

Y. Belkada, M. Sun, T. von Köller, S. Mangrulkar, B. Bossan, L. Debut, and S. Liu. 2023. Finetune llms on your own consumer hardware using tools from pytorch and hugging face ecosystem.

T. Dettmers, A. Pagnoni, A. Holtzman, and L. Zettlemoyer. 2023. Qlora: Efficient finetuning of quantized llms. *arXiv preprint arXiv:2305.14314*.

F. P. Dossou, L. A. Tonja, Y. Oreen, S. Osei, A. Oppong, S. Iyanuoluwa, and C. Emezue. 2022. Afrolm: A self-active learning-based multilingual pretrained language model for 23 african languages. In *Proceedings of the Third Workshop on Simple and Efficient Natural Language Processing (SustaiNLP)*, pages 52–64,

Abu Dhabi. Association for Computational Linguistics.

S. Jiang, S. Cormier, A. Rafael, and F. Rousseaux. 2023. Improving text mining in plant health domain with gan and/or pre-trained language model. *Frontiers in Artificial Intelligence*.

F. Josep. 2024. Fine-tuning llms: A guide with examples.

Hanmeng Liu, Zhiyang Teng, Leyang Cui, Chaoli Zhang, Qiji Zhou, and Yue Zhang. 2023. Logicot: Logical chain-of-thought instruction tuning. In *Findings of the Association for Computational Linguistics: EMNLP 2023*, pages 2908–2921.

Yujia Qin, Shihao Liang, Yining Ye, Kunlun Zhu, Lan Yan, Yaxi Lu, Yankai Lin, Xin Cong, Xiangru Tang, Bill Qian, Sihan Zhao, Lauren Hong, Runchu Tian, Ruobing Xie, Jie Zhou, Mark Gerstein, Dahai Li, Zhiyuan Liu, and Maosong Sun. 2023. Toolllm: Facilitating large language models to master 16000+ real-world apis. *arXiv preprint arXiv:2307.16789*.

E. Ross, Y. Kansal, J. Renzella, A. Vassar, and A. Taylor. 2025. Supervised fine-tuning llms to behave as pedagogical agents in programming education. *arXiv preprint arXiv:2502.20527*.

Philipp Schmid. 2025. Fine-tune llms in 2025. Accessed: 2025-03-06.

Andrea Valenzuela. 2024. Quantization for large language models (llms): Reduce ai model sizes efficiently. Accessed: 2025-03-06.

Zezhong Wang, Xingshan Zeng, Weiwen Liu, Liangyou Li, Yasheng Wang, Lifeng Shang, Xin Jiang, and Qun Liu. 2024. Toolflow: Boosting llm tool-calling through natural and coherent dialogue synthesis. *arXiv preprint arXiv:2410.18447*.

Pretraining Strategies using Monolingual and Parallel Data for Low-Resource Machine Translation

Idriss Nguepi Nguefack
AIMS Senegal
inguepi@aimsammi.org

Mara Finkelstein
Google
marafin@google.com

Toadoum Sari Sakayo
AIMS Senegal
tsakayo@aimsammi.org

Abstract

This research article examines the effectiveness of various pretraining strategies for developing machine translation models tailored to low-resource languages. Although this work considers several low-resource languages, including Afrikaans, Swahili, and Zulu, the translation model is specifically developed for Lingala, an under-resourced African language, building upon the pretraining approach introduced by Reid and Artetxe (2021), originally designed for high-resource languages. Through a series of comprehensive experiments, we explore different pretraining methodologies, including the integration of multiple languages and the use of both monolingual and parallel data during the pretraining phase. Our findings indicate that pretraining on multiple languages and leveraging both monolingual and parallel data significantly enhance translation quality. This study offers valuable insights into effective pretraining strategies for low-resource machine translation, helping to bridge the performance gap between high-resource and low-resource languages. The results contribute to the broader goal of developing more inclusive and accurate NLP models for marginalized communities and underrepresented populations. The code and datasets used in this study are publicly available to facilitate further research and ensure reproducibility, with the exception of certain data that may no longer be accessible due to changes in public availability.[1]

1 Introduction

In recent years, pretraining techniques have gained significant popularity and transformed the field of natural language processing (NLP). Pretraining involves training a language model on a large corpus of text data, enabling it to learn general linguistic patterns and representations. The pretrained model can then be fine-tuned for specific downstream tasks, such as sentiment analysis, named entity recognition, or machine translation, leading to substantial performance improvements. While pretraining has shown remarkable success in high-resource languages like English, Spanish, and Chinese, applying these techniques to low-resource languages poses significant challenges. These languages often lack the extensive datasets required for effective pretraining, limiting the performance of NLP models.

Despite these challenges, researchers have actively explored various pretraining techniques tailored to low-resource languages (Costa-Jussà et al., 2022). These approaches include unsupervised and semi-supervised learning, transfer learning, and cross-lingual pretraining (Khoboko et al., 2025). Unsupervised methods leverage large amounts of unlabeled data to learn meaningful representations, while semi-supervised techniques enhance model performance by combining limited labeled data with abundant unlabeled data. Transfer learning involves pretraining a model on a high-resource language and fine-tuning it on a low-resource language, exploiting linguistic similarities (Zheng et al., 2021). Cross-lingual pretraining extends this concept by training models on multiple languages simultaneously, enabling them to learn shared representations.

These techniques hold great promise for advancing NLP in low-resource languages, which are often spoken by marginalized and underrepresented communities. Developing more effective pretraining strategies can help mitigate data scarcity and contribute to more accurate, inclusive, and culturally sensitive NLP models (Adebara et al., 2024). Ensuring that NLP technologies benefit all languages and communities, regardless of available resources, is a crucial step toward linguistic inclusivity (Okolo and Tano, 2024).

In this work, we evaluate the effectiveness of various pretraining techniques for low-resource languages, with a particular focus on Lingala, an

[1] `https://github.com/nguepigit2020/Project1.git`

Proceedings of the Sixth Workshop on African Natural Language Processing (AfricaNLP 2025), pages 31–38
July 31, 2025 ©2025 Association for Computational Linguistics

under-resourced African language. To this end, we combined monolingual and parallel data, hypothesizing that this approach would yield the best results. We pretrained multiple models using methods described in Reid et al. (2021) and Reid and Artetxe (2021), which differ in the types of data used for pretraining. Specifically, we examine the impact of incorporating multiple languages and leveraging both monolingual and parallel data during pretraining. Finally, we evaluated these pretrained models by fine-tuning them on an English-Lingala sequence-to-sequence machine translation task. Our findings offer valuable insights into effective pretraining strategies for low-resource machine translation and contribute to the broader goal of developing more inclusive NLP technologies.

2 Related Work

Most previous studies on multilingual pretraining have primarily relied on monolingual data (Reid et al., 2021; Pires et al., 2019; Song et al., 2019; Liu et al., 2020). While foundational, this approach does not fully exploit the potential of parallel data. Several proposals have attempted to incorporate parallel data into encoder-only models by training two models simultaneously: one encoder-only model trained on the source language and one decoder-only model trained on the target language. During training, the encoder-only model generates hidden representations of the source sentences, which are then used to train the decoder-only model to generate target sentences (Lample and Conneau, 2019; Hu et al., 2020). Some approaches replace words based on a bilingual dictionary, similar to the dictionary denoising objective (Wu et al., 2019), while others use multilingual dictionaries but focus only on high-resource languages (Reid and Artetxe, 2021).

However, these methods often fail to effectively leverage the rich information in parallel data, particularly for low-resource languages. In contrast, sequence-to-sequence models provide a more flexible and natural way to integrate parallel data. Building on the work of Reid and Artetxe (2021), we incorporated parallel corpora into sequence-to-sequence pretraining by feeding concatenated parallel sentences to the encoder and applying different masking strategies. Unlike Reid and Artetxe (2021), our approach specifically targets low-resource languages while maintaining a similar methodology.

Recent advancements in multilingual pretraining have further improved the performance of NLP models for low-resource languages. For example, (Pires et al., 2019) demonstrated that multilingual BERT (mBERT) effectively captures cross-lingual representations, though their study primarily focused on high-resource languages. Similarly, (Song et al., 2019) introduced the MASS framework, which employs a masked sequence-to-sequence pretraining objective to enhance machine translation models. However, these studies did not extensively explore the integration of parallel data for low-resource languages.

Additionally, (Liu et al., 2020) proposed multilingual denoising pretraining for neural machine translation, highlighting the benefits of training on multiple languages. Their work underscored the importance of leveraging both monolingual and parallel data to improve translation quality. Building on these insights, our study extends these pretraining strategies to low-resource languages.

By integrating both monolingual and parallel data during pretraining, we aim to overcome the limitations of existing approaches and develop more effective strategies for low-resource machine translation. Our work contributes to the growing body of research on multilingual pretraining and provides valuable insights into the development of inclusive and accurate NLP models for underrepresented languages.

3 Problem

Despite significant advancements in natural language processing (NLP) and machine translation, the benefits of these technologies are not evenly distributed across all languages. High-resource languages, such as English, Spanish, and Chinese, have seen substantial improvements in translation quality and NLP applications due to the availability of large datasets and extensive research. However, low-resource languages, which are often spoken by marginalized communities and underrepresented populations, continue to lag behind (Costa-Jussà et al., 2022). This disparity poses significant challenges in various domains, including education, healthcare, and digital communication.

In the context of education, the lack of effective machine translation tools for low-resource languages creates a barrier to accessing educational materials and resources. Students and educators in regions where these languages are spoken often rely on materials in high-resource languages, which can hinder comprehension and learning outcomes. Enhancing machine translation for low-resource languages can facilitate the creation and dissemination of educational content in native languages (Steigerwald et al., 2022), thereby improving educational accessibility and effectiveness.

Moreover, in healthcare settings (Al Shamsi et al., 2020), accurate communication is crucial for diagnosing and treating patients. Language barriers can lead to miscommunication, misdiagnosis, and inadequate treatment. Machine translation tools tailored to low-resource languages can help bridge these gaps, ensuring that healthcare providers can effectively communicate with patients who speak these languages.

Additionally, the digital divide is exacerbated by the lack of support for low-resource languages in web-centric applications and technologies (Kreienbrinck et al., 2024). Users who speak these languages often face difficulties in accessing and interacting with digital content, which limits their participation in the global digital economy. By improving machine translation for low-resource languages, we can make digital platforms more inclusive and accessible to a broader range of users (Bella et al., 2023).

This research aims to address these challenges by exploring effective pre-training strategies for machine translation models tailored to low-resource languages. Specifically, we focus on Lingala, an under-resourced African language, and investigate the impact of incorporating multiple languages and both monolingual and parallel data during the pre-training phase. Our goal is to develop more accurate and inclusive NLP models that can enhance communication, education, and digital accessibility for speakers of low-resource languages. By doing so, we hope to contribute to the broader goal of reducing linguistic disparities and promoting equitable access to information and services.

4 Dataset

We utilized various datasets in our pretraining process for different models, including monolingual datasets (English, Lingala, Afrikaans, Swahili, and Zulu), as well as parallel datasets for fine-tuning. To provide a comprehensive summary of the data used for each language, please refer to Table 1 below. It should be noted that we use both monolingual and parallel data for pretraining, while for fine-tuning, only parallel data is used.

4.1 Data Source

We used both parallel and monolingual datasets in our study. Specifically, the parallel datasets were obtained from AfroMT (Reid et al., 2021), a comprehensive benchmark for African language translation. The monolingual datasets Afrikaans, English, Lingala, Swahili, and Zulu were sourced from the open-source CC-100 dataset, which provides a diverse collection of monolingual corpora for various languages. It is worth noting that some of this data may no longer be publicly available. The datasets originate from different sources and vary in size and the number of sentences per language, as detailed in Table 1.

4.2 Data Quality and Preprocessing

To ensure the robustness of our models, we applied several preprocessing steps to clean and augment the data. These steps included tokenization, normalization, and duplicate removal. Additionally, we addressed data imbalance, particularly for low-resource languages like Lingala, by employing techniques such as data augmentation and oversampling. These preprocessing steps were essential for improving the quality and consistency of the datasets used in our experiments.

4.3 Data Split

Based on the number of sentences per language shown in Table 1, we allocated 3,000 sentences each for testing and validation in the parallel data, with the remaining sentences used for training during both pretraining and fine-tuning. For the monolingual data, we designated 10% for testing, 10% for validation, and the remaining 80% for training in each language, but only during the pretraining phase. This data-splitting strategy ensured a balanced and representative dataset for both the pretraining and fine-tuning phases.

5 Models and Methods

This section presents the models and methodologies used in our study, with a focus on the pretraining and fine-tuning processes (see Figure 1). Our goal is to assess the effectiveness of various pretraining techniques and compare their impact on the performance of machine translation models for low-resource languages. Specifically, we pretrain our models on four African languages (Lingala,

Language	Code	Parallel data (En-XX)		Monolingual data	
		Size	Sentences	Size	Sentences
Afrikaans	Af	77MB	749K	1.2G	7979K
Lingala	Ln	45MB	388K	10.3MB	143K
Swahili	Sw	80MB	706K	2G	12000K
Zulu	Zu	75MB	670K	18.6MB	209K
English	En	77MB	-	27.2MB	259K

Table 1: Dataset Description

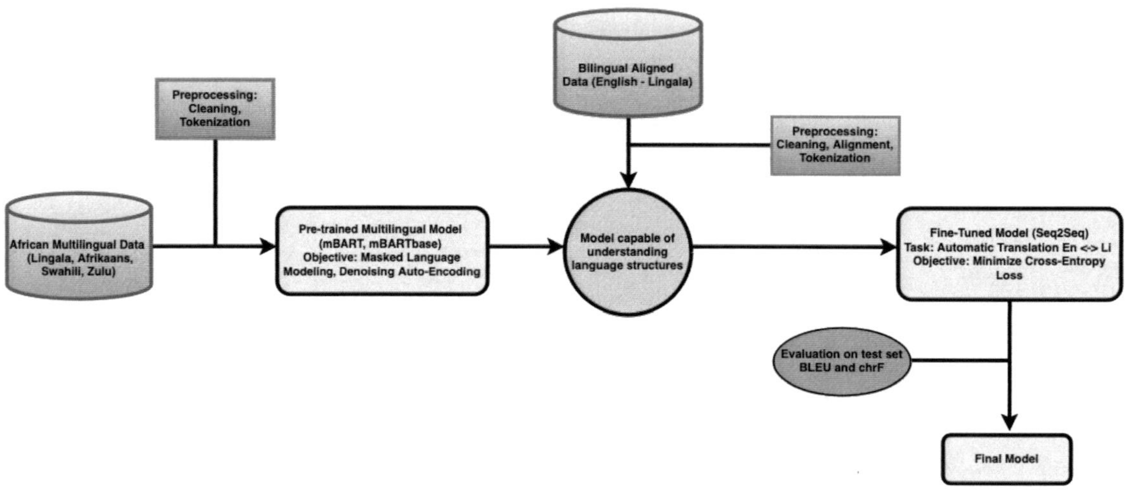

Figure 1: Flowchart from pretraining to finetuning

Afrikaans, Swahili, Zulu) and evaluate them on English-Lingala machine translation tasks.

5.1 Model Architectures

5.1.1 mBART Architecture

The mBART model (Liu et al., 2020) is a sequence-to-sequence denoising autoencoder pretrained on large-scale monolingual corpora spanning 25 languages. It employs a standard Transformer architecture with 12 encoder layers and 12 decoder layers, each featuring a hidden dimension of 1024 and 16 attention heads. The model is trained using a denoising objective, in which the input is corrupted by masking, deleting, or permuting tokens, and the model learns to reconstruct the original sequence. mBART has demonstrated strong performance in multilingual machine translation tasks, particularly in zero-shot and few-shot scenarios.

5.1.2 AfroBART Architecture

The AfroBART model (Reid et al., 2021) is a variant of the BART model specifically designed for African languages. It is pretrained on a combination of monolingual and parallel data from eight African languages, including Lingala. AfroBART employs a Transformer architecture similar to mBART but is adapted to the unique characteristics and data constraints of African languages. The model seeks to address the challenges of low-resource languages by leveraging multilingual pretraining and transfer learning techniques.

6 Hardware and Schedule

We pre-trained our models on a single machine equipped with two NVIDIA T4 GPUs, 32 vCPUs, and 120 GB of RAM, with each pretraining run taking approximately four days. Fine-tuning was conducted on a machine with one NVIDIA T4 GPU, 32 vCPUs, and 60 GB of RAM, requiring about one day to complete.

The computational resources used in this study were sufficient to efficiently handle both pretraining and fine-tuning. The NVIDIA T4 GPUs accelerated the training processes, enabling us to run multiple experiments within a reasonable time frame. Additionally, the ample RAM and vCPUs facilitated smooth execution, allowing us to process large datasets and train complex models without significant bottlenecks.

Pretraining was the most time-intensive phase, requiring up to five days for some experiments, particularly those involving multiple languages and large datasets. In contrast, fine-tuning was relatively faster, taking approximately one day to complete. This efficient use of computational resources and careful time management enabled a thorough evaluation of various pretraining strategies and their impact on machine translation performance for low-resource languages.

6.1 Pretraining

To better understand the impact of different data types on the pretraining strategy, we conducted multiple pretraining sessions, making minor modifications such as altering the type of data or the denoising task used. The details of these pretraining approaches are provided in the following sections.

6.1.1 First Pretraining

For the first experiment, we used only monolingual Lingala data from the AfroMT repository (Reid et al., 2021) (see the dataset description in Table 1). We tokenized all the data using SentencePiece (Kudo and Richardson, 2018), employing a multilingual vocabulary of 80k subwords.

We utilized the mBART implementation and the simple denoising task from the fairseq[2] library (Ott et al., 2019) to train our models. Our setup included a Transformer-base architecture with a hidden dimension of 768, a feed forward size of 3072, and 6 layers for both the encoder and decoder. The maximum sequence length was set to 1024, and we trained our models with a batch size of 1024 for 100k iterations on a single NVIDIA T4 GPU, with 32 vCPUs and 60 GB of RAM. The training process lasted approximately 24 hours.

6.1.2 Second Pretraining

For this experiment, we used both the monolingual data of all languages, except English, for the denoising task and the parallel data of all languages for the translation task. This approach combined two tasks (denoising and translation) on two different types of data. While this method was proposed in (Reid and Artetxe, 2021), it focused primarily on high-resource languages; we applied the same approach but focused on low-resource languages.

Regarding the hyper-parameters, we used SentencePiece (Kudo and Richardson, 2018) to tokenize all the data, employing a multilingual vocabulary of 80K sub-words. We also used the mBART implementation from the fairseq2 (Ott et al., 2019) library to train our model. Our configuration included a Transformer-based architecture with a hidden dimension of 768, a feed forward size of 3072, and 6 layers for both the encoder and decoder. The maximum sequence length was set to 1024, and we trained our model with a batch size of 1024 for 100K iterations. The model contained approximately 162 million parameters and the training lasted 4 days.

6.1.3 Third Pretraining

For this experiment, we used monolingual data from all languages (Afrikaans, English, Lingala, Swahili and Zulu) for the denoising task, as well as parallel data from all languages (English-Lingala, English-Afrikaans, English-Swahili, and English-Zulu) for the translation task. This experiment combined two pretraining tasks (denoising and translation) using two different types of data (monolingual and parallel). It is worth noting that we selected a random sample of 10MB of monolingual data from the English language. By incorporating all languages in this phase, we aimed to achieve a more permanent model.

Regarding the hyper-parameters, we used the same configuration as in the previous experiment. The model had approximately 162 million parameters, and training lasted for 5 days. We later resumed this experiment with the same configuration but increased the English data from 10MB to 112MB.

6.1.4 Fourth Pretraining

We conducted a fourth experiment in which we used only the parallel and monolingual data of two languages, English and Lingala. It should be noted that we used the same tasks and hyperparameters as in the previous experiment. Regarding pre-training time, it took about two days.

6.2 Finetuning

This section summarizes the various fine-tuning experiments we conducted on existing models, including those we pre-trained ourselves. We utilized the parallel data described in Table 1 to fine-tune all pre-trained models, with a primary focus on machine translation between English and Lingala.

As a baseline, we started by fine-tuning the mBART (Liu et al., 2020) model, which is pre-

[2]https://github.com/facebookresearch/fairseq

trained on 25 high-resource languages but does not include Lingala. Next, we fine-tuned the AfroBART (Reid et al., 2021) model, which is pretrained solely on low-resource monolingual data, including Lingala. Finally, we proceeded to fine-tune our own pre-trained models.

We evaluated the system outputs using two automatic evaluation metrics: detokenized BLEU (Papineni et al., 2002) and chrF (Popović, 2015). While BLEU is a standard metric for machine translation, we use chrF to measure performance at the character level, given the morphological richness of the languages in the AfroMT benchmark. Both metrics were calculated using the SacreBLEU library.

7 Results and Discussion

As shown in Table 2, we performed fine-tuning on five pretrained models with highly varied structures. We used the mBART and AfroBART models as starting points to train an automatic translation model from English to Lingala. Evaluation of this model showed that AfroBART outperforms mBART in terms of both BLEU and chrF scores. This can be explained by the fact that the monolingual data used to pretrain AfroBART includes Lingala, the target language of the translation, whereas mBART is pretrained only on high-resource languages.

The BLEU and chrF scores of Experiment 1 are significantly lower than those of mBART and AfroBART. This can be attributed to the fact that the data used to pretrain our experimental model consisted solely of monolingual data from a single language (Lingala), while mBART is pretrained on 25 languages, and AfroBART is trained on 8 African languages, including Lingala. Therefore, we can reasonably conclude that pretraining on multiple languages positively impacts the performance of the resulting translation model.

The scores obtained from the evaluation of the model in Experiment 1 led us to consider another approach that involved using both monolingual and parallel data during the pretraining phase. This approach resulted in a gain of 2 BLEU points and 2 chrF points compared to Experiment 1. Therefore, we can confidently state that the strategy used in this experiment is more beneficial in terms of both BLEU and chrF scores compared to Experiment 1.

We conducted an additional experiment in which we introduced a 10 MB random sample of monolingual English data. This resulted in notably low scores, as shown in Table 2. Subsequently, we increased the size of the English monolingual data to 112 MB, which led to a gain of 4 BLEU points and 3 chrF points.

Finally, we conducted a final experiment using only the parallel and monolingual data of English and Lingala. We observed a significant decrease in both the BLEU and chrF scores, as shown in Table 2. From this, we can affirm that pretraining a model that includes other African languages is more effective than pretraining a model solely on the source and target languages.

8 Conclusion

In conclusion, our study aimed to investigate pretraining strategies for machine translation models using low-resource languages. We conducted a series of experiments, gradually introducing monolingual and parallel data to pretrained models.

We first fine-tuned a pretrained model using only parallel data from the source and target languages. Next, we added monolingual data to the pretraining process, which resulted in a significant improvement in the model's BLEU and chrF scores.

Then, we introduced a random sample of English monolingual data, which led to very low scores. However, when we increased the size of the English monolingual data, we observed a notable improvement in the model's translation performance.

Finally, we conducted an experiment using parallel and monolingual data from both English and Lingala. We observed a decrease in BLEU and chrF scores. However, when we pretrained the model using multiple African languages, including the low-resource language, we saw a positive impact on translation performance. Our study underscores the importance of considering pretraining strategies for low-resource languages in machine translation.

It is worth noting that the pretraining approach we used was introduced by Reid and Artetxe (2021), but it originally focused solely on high-resource languages. Our study demonstrates that this approach can also be beneficial for low-resource languages. Interestingly, mBART, which was not pretrained on any African languages, still outperformed our multilingual pretraining setup in some cases. While the scores were close, mBART performed slightly better, which may be attributed to its larger model size, more extensive pretraining on high-quality data, or architectural advantages. This suggests that pretraining on high-resource lan-

Model	BLEU	chrF	Pretrained Data	Lingala include
mBART	28.5	54.03	Monolingual	✗
AfroBART	29.33	54.67	Monolingual	✓
Experiment 1 6.1.1	25.34	51.26	Monolingual	✓
Experiment 2 6.1.2	27.38	53.24	Monolingual & Parallel	✓
Experiment 3 6.1.3	21.8	48.16	Monolingual & Parallel	✓
Experiment 3^+ 6.1.3	25.18	51.11	Monolingual & Parallel	✓
Experiment 4 6.1.4	21.02	48.92	Monolingual & Parallel	✓

Table 2: **Finetuning on top of English and Lingala**

guages may still offer transferable benefits to low-resource scenarios. Future research in this area can explore different pretraining techniques and incorporate more linguistic knowledge to further improve the performance of machine translation models for low-resource languages.

Limitations

Despite the valuable insights gained from this study, there are several limitations to consider. The availability and quality of data for low-resource languages, such as Lingala, significantly impact the effectiveness of the pretraining strategies. Additionally, the findings may not generalize to all low-resource languages due to linguistic differences. Computational resources required for pretraining and fine-tuning can also be prohibitive, and the reliance on BLEU and chrF scores may not fully capture translation quality, especially for morphologically rich languages. Future work should explore more diverse data sources and evaluation methods, such as human evaluation, to better address these challenges.

9 Acknowledgments

We would like to extend our heartfelt appreciation to the African Institute for Mathematical Sciences (AIMS) and the African Master's of Machine Intelligence (AMMI) program. Their unwavering support and provision of top-notch machine learning training have been instrumental in the success of our project. We are truly grateful for their guidance and assistance throughout this endeavor.

In addition, we would like to express our deep gratitude to Google for generously granting us access to the Google Cloud Platform (GCP). This invaluable resource enabled us to conduct our experiments with utmost efficiency and effectiveness. We recognize the significant contribution that this grant has made to our research.

Furthermore, we would like to extend a special acknowledgment to the dedicated AMMI staff. Their exceptional assistance and unwavering support have been invaluable to us. Their expertise and commitment have played a crucial role in the development and execution of our project.

References

Ife Adebara, AbdelRahim Elmadany, and Muhammad Abdul-Mageed. 2024. Cheetah: Natural language generation for 517 african languages. *arXiv preprint arXiv:2401.01053*.

Hilal Al Shamsi, Abdullah G Almutairi, Sulaiman Al Mashrafi, and Talib Al Kalbani. 2020. Implications of language barriers for healthcare: a systematic review. *Oman medical journal*, 35(2):e122.

Gábor Bella, Paula Helm, Gertraud Koch, and Fausto Giunchiglia. 2023. Towards bridging the digital language divide. *arXiv preprint arXiv:2307.13405*.

Marta R Costa-Jussà, James Cross, Onur Çelebi, Maha Elbayad, Kenneth Heafield, Kevin Heffernan, Elahe Kalbassi, Janice Lam, Daniel Licht, Jean Maillard, et al. 2022. No language left behind: Scaling human-centered machine translation. *arXiv preprint arXiv:2207.04672*.

Junjie Hu, Melvin Johnson, Orhan Firat, Aditya Siddhant, and Graham Neubig. 2020. Explicit alignment objectives for multilingual bidirectional encoders. *arXiv preprint arXiv:2010.07972*.

Pitso Walter Khoboko, Vukosi Marivate, and Joseph Sefara. 2025. Optimizing translation for low-resource languages: Efficient fine-tuning with custom prompt engineering in large language models. *Machine Learning with Applications*, page 100649.

Annika Kreienbrinck, Saskia Hanft-Robert, and Mike Mösko. 2024. Usability of technological tools to overcome language barriers in health care: a scoping review protocol. *BMJ open*, 14(3):e079814.

Taku Kudo and John Richardson. 2018. Sentencepiece: A simple and language independent subword tokenizer and detokenizer for neural text processing. *arXiv preprint arXiv:1808.06226*.

Guillaume Lample and Alexis Conneau. 2019. Cross-lingual language model pretraining. *arXiv preprint arXiv:1901.07291*.

Yinhan Liu, Jiatao Gu, Naman Goyal, Xian Li, Sergey Edunov, Marjan Ghazvininejad, Mike Lewis, and Luke Zettlemoyer. 2020. Multilingual denoising pre-training for neural machine translation. *Transactions of the Association for Computational Linguistics*, 8:726–742.

Chinasa T Okolo and Marie Tano. 2024. Closing the gap: A call for more inclusive language technologies.

Myle Ott, Sergey Edunov, Alexei Baevski, Angela Fan, Sam Gross, Nathan Ng, David Grangier, and Michael Auli. 2019. fairseq: A fast, extensible toolkit for sequence modeling. *arXiv preprint arXiv:1904.01038*.

Kishore Papineni, Salim Roukos, Todd Ward, and Wei-Jing Zhu. 2002. Bleu: a method for automatic evaluation of machine translation. In *Proceedings of the 40th annual meeting of the Association for Computational Linguistics*, pages 311–318.

Telmo Pires, Eva Schlinger, and Dan Garrette. 2019. How multilingual is multilingual bert? *arXiv preprint arXiv:1906.01502*.

Maja Popović. 2015. chrf: character n-gram f-score for automatic mt evaluation. In *Proceedings of the tenth workshop on statistical machine translation*, pages 392–395.

Machel Reid and Mikel Artetxe. 2021. Paradise: Exploiting parallel data for multilingual sequence-to-sequence pretraining. *arXiv preprint arXiv:2108.01887*.

Machel Reid, Junjie Hu, Graham Neubig, and Yutaka Matsuo. 2021. Afromt: Pretraining strategies and reproducible benchmarks for translation of 8 african languages. *arXiv preprint arXiv:2109.04715*.

Kaitao Song, Xu Tan, Tao Qin, Jianfeng Lu, and Tie-Yan Liu. 2019. Mass: Masked sequence to sequence pre-training for language generation. *arXiv preprint arXiv:1905.02450*.

Emma Steigerwald, Valeria Ramírez-Castañeda, Débora YC Brandt, András Báldi, Julie Teresa Shapiro, Lynne Bowker, and Rebecca D Tarvin. 2022. Overcoming language barriers in academia: Machine translation tools and a vision for a multilingual future. *BioScience*, 72(10):988–998.

Shijie Wu, Alexis Conneau, Haoran Li, Luke Zettlemoyer, and Veselin Stoyanov. 2019. Emerging cross-lingual structure in pretrained language models. *arXiv preprint arXiv:1911.01464*.

Francis Zheng, Machel Reid, Edison Marrese-Taylor, and Yutaka Matsuo. 2021. Low-resource machine translation using cross-lingual language model pre-training. In *Proceedings of the First Workshop on Natural Language Processing for Indigenous Languages of the Americas*, pages 234–240.

Designing and Contextualising Probes for African Languages

Wisdom Aduah
African Institute for Mathematical Sciences
South Africa
wizzy@aims.ac.za

Francois Meyer
Department of Computer Science
University of Cape Town
francois.meyer@uct.ac.za

Abstract

Pretrained language models (PLMs) for African languages are continually improving, but the reasons behind these advances remain unclear. This paper presents the first systematic investigation into probing PLMs for linguistic knowledge about African languages. We train layer-wise probes for six typologically diverse African languages to analyse how linguistic features are distributed. We also design control tasks, a way to interpret probe performance, for the MasakhaPOS dataset. We find PLMs adapted for African languages to encode more linguistic information about target languages than massively multilingual PLMs. Our results reaffirm previous findings that token-level syntactic information concentrates in middle-to-last layers, while sentence-level semantic information is distributed across all layers. Through control tasks and probing baselines, we confirm that performance reflects the internal knowledge of PLMs rather than probe memorisation. Our study applies established interpretability techniques to African-language PLMs. In doing so, we highlight the internal mechanisms underlying the success of strategies like active learning and multilingual adaptation.

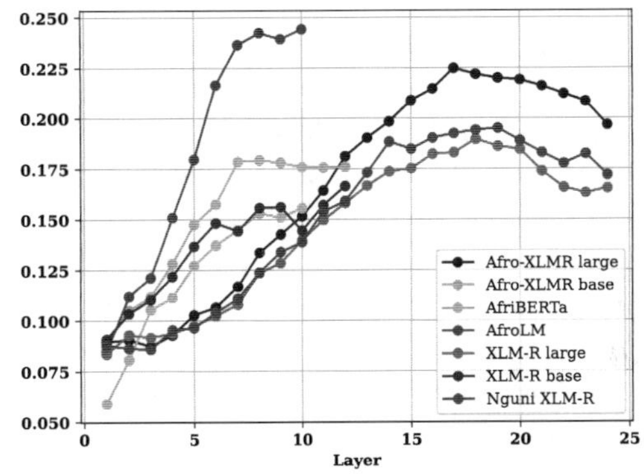

Figure 1: POS probe performance (selectivity), averaged over 6 African languages.

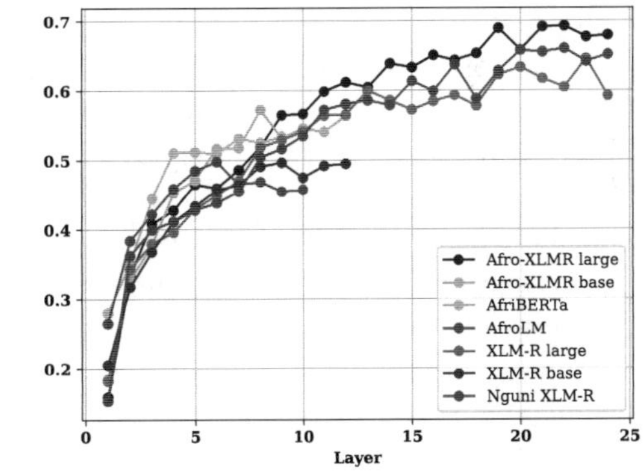

Figure 2: NER probe gains (over random baselines) across layers, averaged over 6 African languages.

1 Introduction

The past few years have seen the proliferation of pretrained language models (PLMs) across various domains including education, healthcare, and finance (Hadi et al., 2024). The blackbox nature of these models, paired with their increasing size and complexity, has prompted the growing subfield of NLP interpretability (Luo and Specia, 2024). These methods aim for insights into the internal mechanisms underlying the success and failures of PLMs. One of the earliest interpretability methods to gain traction in NLP was probing (Alain and Bengio, 2017), which trains a classifier on intermediate PLM representations. Probing measures to what extent specific linguistic features, such as part-of-speech (POS) categories or semantic concepts, are encoded in hidden layers.

Probing provides insights into the internal mechanisms of PLMs by revealing how models acquire, store, and leverage linguistic information in hidden layers. This allows NLP practitioners to better understand the mechanisms by which PLMs succeed in certain tasks, and can also point to the underlying reasons for failing in others. Besides contributing to a greater, linguistically grounded understanding of PLM computations, probing also has the poten-

Proceedings of the Sixth Workshop on African Natural Language Processing (AfricaNLP 2025), pages 39–51
July 31, 2025

Model	Layers	Params	Swahili	Igbo	Hausa	Luganda	isiXhosa	Naija
XLM-R-base (Conneau et al., 2020)	12	270M	★★	☆☆	★★	☆☆	★★	☆☆
XLM-R-large (Conneau et al., 2020)	24	550M	★★	☆☆	★★	☆☆	★★	☆☆
AfroXLMR-base (Alabi et al., 2022)	12	270M	★★	★★	★★	☆☆	★★	★★
AfroXLMR-large (Alabi et al., 2022)	24	550M	★★	★★	★★	☆☆	★★	★★
Nguni-XLMR (Meyer et al., 2024)	24	550M	★☆	★☆	★☆	☆☆	★★	☆☆
AfriBERTa (Ogueji et al., 2021)	10	126M	★★	★★	★★	☆☆	☆☆	★★
AfroLM (Dossou et al., 2022)	10	264M	★★	★★	★★	★★	★★	★★

Table 1: Language coverage of PLMs. ☆☆ indicates no data from the language was included in pretraining or adaptation. ★☆ shows the language was included in the base model but not in the adapted model. ★★ shows the model was either pretrained or adapted for the language.

tial to contribute to performance gains by guiding the finetuning process for downstream tasks. For example, knowing which layers encode specific properties can inform which layers should be targetted for finetuning, optimising both performance and efficiency (Katinskaia and Yangarber, 2024).

Probing is an established tool in NLP interpretability, having been extensively applied and studied across different settings. One area where it has yet to be applied is the growing body of work on PLMs for African languages. Most African languages are under-represented in the pretraining data of multilingual PLMs, which limits their performance. Efforts to address this gap have led to the development of PLMs targeting African languages, such as AfriBERTa (Ogueji et al., 2021), AfroLM (Dossou et al., 2022), and AfroXLMR (Alabi et al., 2022). These models leverage strategies such as cross-lingual transfer (Conneau et al., 2020), active learning (Dossou et al., 2022), and multilingual adaptive fine-tuning (MAFT) (Alabi et al., 2022) to improve performance for low-resource languages.

Despite this progress, there is limited understanding of how these PLMs encode African languages internally, which is where probing holds promise. Most probing research targets higher-resourced languages such as English, French, and Russian (Arps et al., 2024; Katinskaia and Yangarber, 2024; Conneau et al., 2018; Hou et al., 2024). Previous works have explored some low-resource languages, such as Tagalog, Hindi and Tamil (Arora et al., 2023; Li et al., 2024), but to the best of our knowledge, there has been no research targeting African languages.

In this paper, we conduct the first systematic probing study for PLMs focussed on African languages. We design probes for POS tagging, named entity recognition (NER), and news topic classification (NTC), using the MasakhaPOS (Dione et al., 2023), MasakhaNER (Adelani et al., 2022), and MasakhaNEWS (Adelani et al., 2023) datasets respectively. We train probes on seven masked PLMs (listed in Table 1), representing different approaches to developing PLMs for low-resource languages. We evaluate how syntactic and semantic information is encoded for six African languages, which cover different language families and varying levels of data availability, as shown in Table 1.

To interpret probe accuracies, one has to isolate the contribution of model-encoded knowledge, as opposed to the probe itself learning the task. To enable such probe interpretability for African languages, we design a control task (Hewitt and Liang, 2019) for MasakhaPOS. Control tasks are synthetic tasks that measure to what extent probes can learn a task without model-encoded knowledge. Our control task enables researchers to contextualise probing results for MasakhaPOS.

Our main findings can be summarised as follows:

1. Word-level linguistic knowledge (POS, NER) concentrates in middle layers, while sentence-level information (NTC) is spread out.

2. The inclusion of target languages in pretraining or multilingual adaptation improves probe performance across all tasks.

3. Cross-lingual transfer improves probe performance for languages not in pretraining, but less so for low-resource language families.

2 Background

PLMs for African Languages Multilingual modelling has been leveraged in different ways to build PLMs for African languages. The massively multilingual XLM-R (Conneau et al., 2020) is trained on 100 languages, of which only 8 are African languages. AfroXLMR (Alabi et al., 2022) improves performance by adapting XLM-R for 17 African languages, while Nguni-XLMR (Meyer et al., 2024) adapts XLM-R for the four Nguni languages (isiXhosa, isiZulu, isiNdebele, and Siswati). AfriBERTa (Ogueji et al., 2021) is a smaller model pretrained from scratch on 11 African languages on less than 1GB data. AfroLM (Dossou et al., 2022) is also trained from scratch on 23 African languages, using self-active learning (the model learns to identify beneficial training samples).

Contextualising Probe Performance Probes are not direct measures of model-encoded knowledge, since the probe itself can contribute to performance by learning the task. Probing studies use baselines, such as majority class prediction (Belinkov et al., 2017; Conneau et al., 2018) or probes trained on random representations (Zhang and Bowman, 2018; Conneau et al., 2018; Chrupała et al., 2020; Tenney et al., 2019b), to contextualize performance.

However, even random baselines may encode information that a sophisticated classifier could exploit. As an alternative, Hewitt and Liang (2019) propose control tasks: pairing word types with random labels to neutralise the linguistic information required for the original task. They define selectivity as the difference between original task and control task accuracy. Selectivity captures the contribution of linguistic knowledge to probe performance, so it is a more reliable measure of model knowledge than raw probe accuracies. To enable probe contextualisation for African languages, we design a control task for the MasakhaPOS dataset.

3 Probing Framework

3.1 Probe Design

Some works advocate for linear probes (Alain and Bengio, 2017; Hewitt and Liang, 2019), arguing that they are less prone to memorisation, while others argue that some linguistic features might not be linearly separable in the representation space (Conneau et al., 2018; Pimentel et al., 2020).

For our experiments, we select a probe to strike a balance between complexity and simplicity. Our probe classifier is a multilayer perceptron (MLP) with a single hidden layer of 50 neurons, which we formally define as

$$\mathbf{y} = f(\mathbf{W_2}\,\sigma(\mathbf{W_1}\mathbf{x} + \mathbf{b_1}) + \mathbf{b_2}), \quad (1)$$

where $\mathbf{x} \in \mathbb{R}^n$ is the input representation, $\mathbf{W_1} \in \mathbb{R}^{m \times n}$ is the weight matrix for the hidden layer, $\mathbf{W_2} \in \mathbb{R}^{k \times m}$ is the weight matrix for the output layer, $\mathbf{b_1} \in \mathbb{R}^m$ and $\mathbf{b_2} \in \mathbb{R}^k$ are bias vectors, $\sigma(\cdot)$ is the ReLu activation function, and $f(\cdot)$ is a softmax function for label prediction.

For POS tagging and NER, we define a word-level task as a function f that maps an input sequence X to an output sequence Y. That is $f : X \longrightarrow Y$, where X is a sequence of contextualized hidden representations (embeddings) of the input text, and Y is the sequence of output labels corresponding to the words encoded by X. Given that some words are tokenized into multiple subwords, we use the first subword in each word to represent the word in the classifier.

For news topic classification (NTC), we define a sentence-level task similarly. Instead of passing word embeddings to the probe classifier, we pass the embedding of the special token for sequence classification (e.g. <s> for XLM-R). We truncate inputs consisting of more tokens than the maximum sequence length of PLMs.

3.2 MasakhaPOS Control Task

As discussed in section 2, control tasks (Hewitt and Liang, 2019) can be used to contextualise probe results. A probe could achieve a high raw accuracy by learning to map word types to labels, without relying on linguistic knowledge. For example, a probe classifier could learn to map the embedding of "walk" to the POS tag "verb", by learning the mapping between word type and label (instead of the mapping between syntactic role and label). Hewitt and Liang (2019) propose *selectivity* as an alternative to raw accuracy. Selectivity is defined as the difference between linguistic task accuracy and the control accuracy. As a measure, it isolates the contribution of model-encoded linguistic knowledge to probe performance.

A control task is designed in two steps:

1. Define the random control behavior for each word type i.e. assign a label *randomly* to each word in the vocabulary.

2. Deterministically label the original task corpus based on control behaviour i.e. annotate each word with its assigned random label.

To define a control task for MasakhaPOS, we randomly map each unique word in the dataset to a random POS tag. Next, we use this synthetic mapping to re-annotate the train / validation / test set. As per Hewitt and Liang (2019), when creating the random mapping (the control behaviour) we sample POS tags according to their empirical distribution in the original MasakhaPOS dataset. Control tasks are designed to have both structure and randomness. Our MasakhaPOS contains structure in that a word type is always mapped to the same tag, but the assignment is random in that it is independent of the linguistic role of words.

3.3 NTC and NER Probe Baselines

Control tasks define word-level control behaviour, so they are not applicable to sentence-level tasks. To interpret NTC probes, we compare the performance of probes trained on PLMs to those trained on random contextual representations. Following Hewitt and Manning (2019), we use an untrained bi-LSTM, and mean-pooling word-level outputs to produce a single sentence representation. Probes trained on these outputs can leverage contextual information, but no linguistic knowledge.

NER is a word-level task, so controls tasks could plausibly be designed for MasakhaNER. However, the procedure is complicated by the fact that NER is actually a *span-level* task (named entities can span multiple words). It is not obvious how to extend the control behaviour design of Hewitt and Liang (2019) to multi-word spans. To contextualise NER results, we randomly re-initialise the architectures of our seven probed PLMs to serve as random baselines (Zhang and Bowman, 2018; Conneau et al., 2018). We estimate model-encoded knowledge by subtracting the F1 score of a random model from the F1 score of the corresponding PLM. For each layer, we refer to this as the probe *gain* over the random baseline.

4 Experimental Setup

4.1 Data

Both MasakhaPOS (Dione et al., 2023) and MasakhaNER (Adelani et al., 2022) cover 20 African languages. MasakhaNEWS (Adelani et al., 2023) covers 16 African languages and contains news articles annotated with one of seven topic labels (business, entertainment, health, politics, religion, sports, technology).

4.2 Languages

The six language in our study (Swahili, Igbo, Hausa, Luganda, isiXhosa, and Naija Pidgin) are included in all three Masakhane[1] datasets. We chose

Language	Family	Region	mC4 tokens
Swahili	Bantu	East	1B
Igbo	Volta-Niger	West	90m
Hausa	Chadic	West	200m
Luganda	Bantu	East	0
isiXhosa	Bantu	Southern	60m
Naija Pidgin	Creole	West	0

Table 2: The languages used in our study. The number is tokens in the mC4 corpus (Xue et al., 2021) serves to give an indication of broader data availability.

these languages specifically to cover several language families, a broad range of data availability, and varying levels of representation in existing PLMs (as shown in Table 1). As shown in Table 2, the languages cover four language families across East, West, and Southern Africa.

4.3 PLMs

The seven PLMs selected for our study represent established approaches to developing PLMs for African languages. XLM-R-base and XLM-R-large (Conneau et al., 2020) employ massively multilingual pretraining, while AfroXLMR-base, AfroXLMR-large (Alabi et al., 2022), and Nguni-XLMR-large (Meyer et al., 2024) adapt XLM-R to a more limited set of African languages. AfroXLMR takes a broader adaptation approach than Nguni-XLMR, which focusses only on the four Nguni languages, a group of related languages which includes isiXhosa. AfriBERTa (Ogueji et al., 2021) represents memory-efficient pretraining – it is our smallest model both in terms of parameters and training data size. AfroLM (Dossou et al., 2022) represents sample-efficient pretraining, since its self-active learning maximizes available data by identifying beneficial training samples.

5 Results

We plot probing results for POS, NER, and NTC respectively in Figure 3, Figure 4, and Figure 5. We report and compare best-layer results for each language, model, and task in Table 3.

5.1 POS Tagging

We evaluate our POS probes based on selectivity, which is computed using the MasakhaPOS control task described in subsection 3.2. As shown in Figure 3, the PLMs exhibit positive selectivity across all layers for all languages, except in the case of Igbo. This aligns with previously reported PLM results for MasakhaPOS (Dione et al., 2023), where

[1]https://www.masakhane.io/

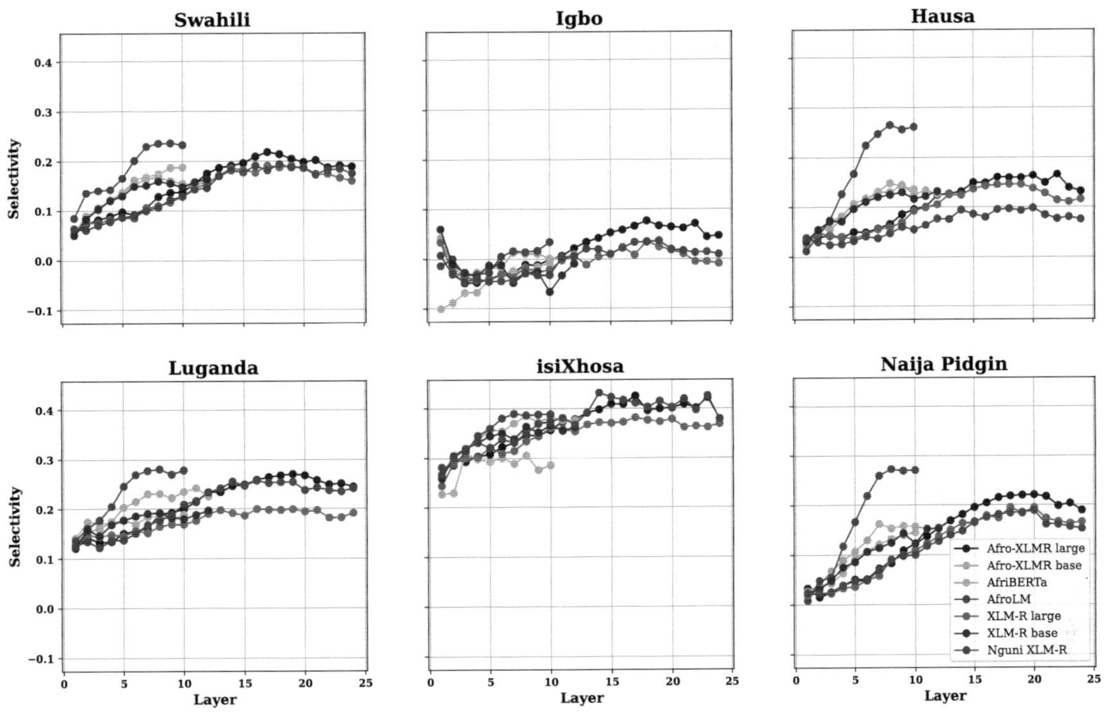

Figure 3: Probe selectivity for POS tagging (the difference between MasakhaPOS accuracy and control task accuracy), across all layers and 6 African languages.

POS tagging accuracies for Igbo were lower than all other languages. Igbo is from the Volta-Niger family, which is under-represented in the datasets of all seven models (as shown in Table 4 in the appendix). This limits the benefit of cross-lingual transfer for Igbo.

For all other languages, POS selectivity is consistently positive, indicating that syntactic roles are reliably being encoded in the hidden representations of the PLMs. A clear pattern emerges in the distribution of POS information across layers. Probe selectivity is low in early layers, increases steadily in middle layers, peaks and plateaus in deeper layers, and finally decreases slightly in final layers. This pattern aligns with existing literature showing that middle-to-last-layers encode syntactic features more effectively (Rogers et al., 2020).

AfroLM stands out as encoding a high amount of POS information, achieving the highest selectivity overall on four of the six languages. While the exact reason for this is unknown, it is possible that self-active learning is used to select training examples that improve the model's syntactic knowledge during pretraining. Among the deeper models, AfroXLMR-large exhibits the greatest internal syntactic knowledge overall, even achieving reasonable selectivity scores for Igbo in deeper layers. The difference in selectivity between AfroXLMR and XLM-R highlights the ability of multilingual adaptation to encode linguistic knowledge about specific languages. Similarly, Nguni-XLMR, exhibits the best probe performance for isiXhosa, one of its four target languages.

We include the raw probe accuracies for POS tagging in Figure 6 in the appendix. The accuracies are quite high, comparing favourably to previously reported PLM performance for MasakhaPOS (Dione et al., 2023).

5.2 NER

To contextualise our NER probes, we compute the per-layer difference between the F1 scores of probes trained on PLMs and their re-initialised counterparts (described in subsection 3.3). As shown in Figure 4, probes trained on PLMs consistently exhibit performance gains over random baselines across all layers and languages. The general trends observed for NER probes are similar to those of POS probes. AfroXLMR achieves the highest probe gains across different languages, while Nguni-XLMR does particularly well for isiXhosa. As in POS tagging, probe performance peaks in

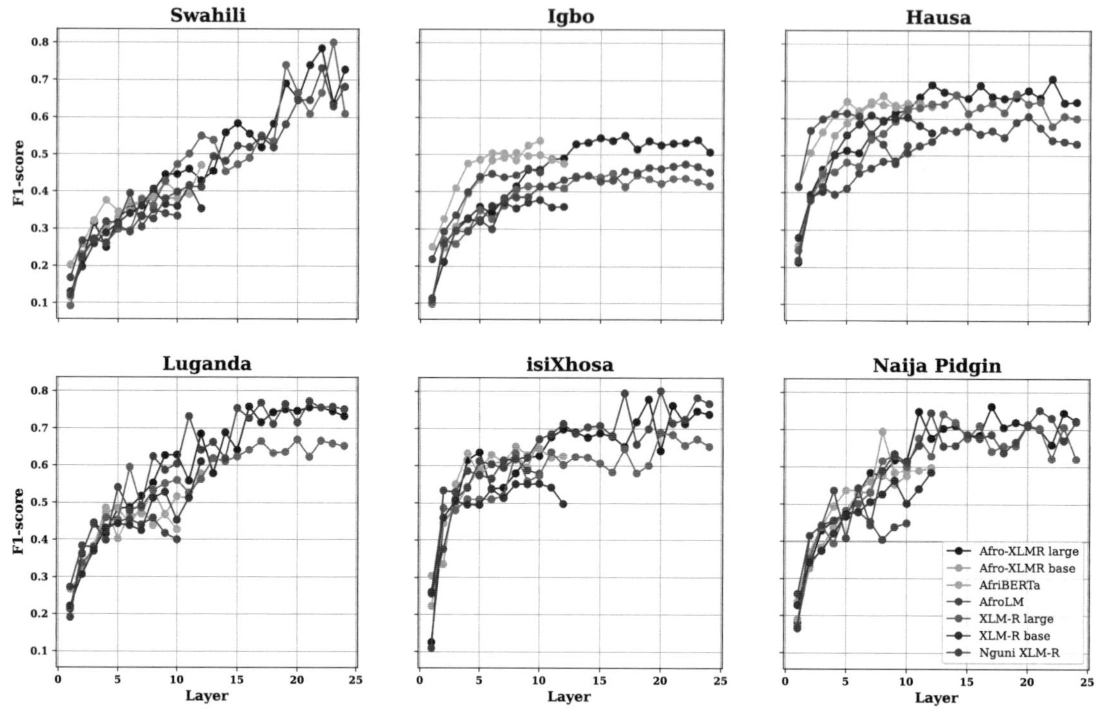

Figure 4: Probe performance gains for NER tagging (F1 improvements over randomly re-initialised PLM architectures), across all layers and 6 African languages.

middle-to-later layers.

We also observe evidence of cross-lingual knowledge representation. Luganda is not included in the pretraining data of either AfroXLMR or NguniXLMR but both exhibit high probe performance gains for Luganda than AfroLM, which is pretrained on Luganda. Luganda is of the Bantu language family, which is better represented than other families in the pretraining data of our PLMs (as shown in Table 4 in the appendix). This shows that the PLMs are encoding linguistic similarities between different languages. This cross-lingual representation learning is the mechanism behind the impressive zero-shot performance of PLMs previously reported on MasakhaNER (Adelani et al., 2022).

5.3 News Topic Classification (NTC)

To contextualise our NTC probes, we compare the classification accuracies of probes trained on PLMs and probes trained on random, contextual baselines (described in subsection 3.3). Figure 5 plots probe accuracies alongside random baseline performance. As for POS and NER, multilingual adaptation enhances sentence-level representations for target languages. Beyond this, NTC probing results diverge from the trends reported for POS and NER.

Probe accuracy remains relatively consistent across layers, which aligns with previous work showing that sentence-level semantic information is spread across layers (Tenney et al., 2019a). The one exception to this is Luganda, which exhibits high variance across layers and is the only language for which some PLM layers fall below random probe performance. We are unable to explain this behaviour. It is possible that the data scarcity of Luganda (see Table 2) is a contributing factor and that, unlike for syntactic knowledge, cross-lingual semantic knowledge does not transfer as effectively.

5.4 Analysing Trends Across Tasks

Table 3 lists results for the top-performing layer for each PLM, across all languages and tasks. For each PLM and language, it also shows to what extent the language is represented by the model: (1) not included at all, (2) included in pretraining but not adaptation, or (3) included in pretraining or adaptation. The table reveals trends that hold across all three tasks.

Multilingual adaptation is known to be a reliable method to improve downstream performance for low-resource languages. Our results show that this

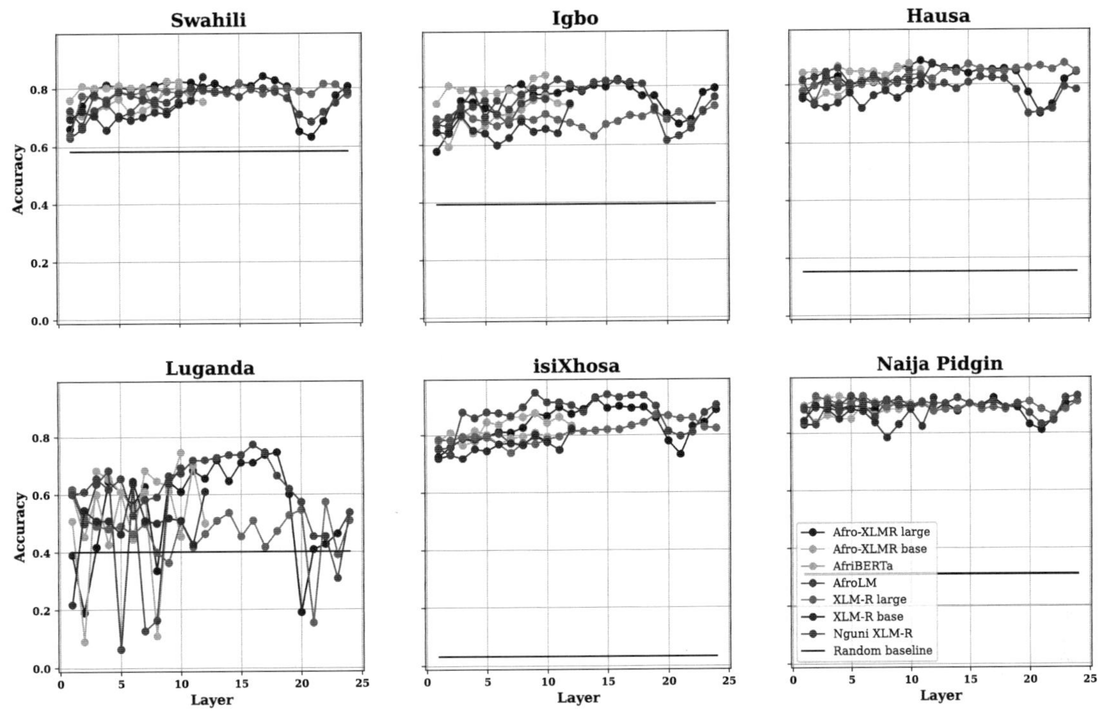

Figure 5: Probe accuracy for news topic classification (visualised in comparison to a random contextual baseline) across all layers and 6 African languages.

is being achieved, in part, by enhancing internal representations of target languages. AfroXLMR-large and Nguni-XLMR-large have the most instances of top-performing layers (six cases each). AfroXLMR-large performs best across Swahili, Igbo, and Hausa, all three of which belong to different language families. The multilingual adaptation of AfroXLMR is highly effective at enhancing linguistic feature encoding across typologically diverse languages. Nguni-XLMR-large performs best for isiXhosa and Luganda (which is also of the Bantu language family). The more focussed, linguistically oriented adaptation of Nguni-XLMR effectively enhances linguistic knowledge for a more limited set of related languages.

A clear pattern in Table 3 is the fact that all top-performing layers (except two) occur in PLMs that represent probed languages in their final pretraining stage (either during adaptation or in pretraining without subsequent adaptation). Best-layer performances (**boldface** in the table) almost always co-occur with maximal language representation (★★). The only exception to this is Luganda, for which Nguni-XLMR-large achieves two best-layer results. While we have previously discussed evidence of zero-shot cross-lingual representation learning, it is clear that including languages in pretraining is essential for encoding language-specific syntactic and semantic knowledge.

6 Conclusion

This paper presents a systematic analysis of the linguistic knowledge encoded in PLMs for African languages. Through extensive probing experiments across seven PLMs and six typologically diverse African languages, we highlight trends in how PLMs represent syntactic and semantic information. To contextualise our results we design a control task for POS tagging and employ randomly initialised baselines to compare against NER and NTC probing results. We show that multilingual adaptation reliably enhances hidden representations for target languages. While token-level linguistic knowledge is primarily encoded in middle and deeper layers, sentence-level semantic information is distributed across layers. We find evidence that cross-lingual learning enhances representations for low-resource languages, such as Luganda, but cannot be relied on to do so for under-represented languages, such as Igbo. We hope this work inspires further research at the intersection of interpretability and NLP for African language.

		Swahili	Igbo	Hausa	Luganda	isiXhosa	Naija
XLM-R-base	Language coverage	★★	☆☆	★★	☆☆	★★	☆☆
	POS selectivity	16.39	5.98	13.15	19.23	36.32	15.39
	NER gain	41.54	37.79	60.84	60.95	55.16	58.46
	NTC accuracy	84.03	74.23	87.38	64.55	82.15	92.11
XLM-R-large	Language coverage	★★	☆☆	★★	☆☆	★★	☆☆
	POS selectivity	19.09	3.29	14.54	19.97	38.15	19.56
	NER gain	**79.98**	45.03	66.63	66.95	68.97	74.20
	NTC accuracy	81.93	73.20	87.38	61.82	86.87	92.76
AfroXLMR-base	Language coverage	★★	★★	★★	☆☆	★★	★★
	POS selectivity	16.73	4.22	14.40	24.18	38.48	16.28
	NER gain	47.07	50.55	66.06	57.7	65.27	69.52
	NTC accuracy	80.46	76.80	86.12	70.00	87.54	90.79
AfroXLMR-large	Language coverage	★★	★★	★★	☆☆	★★	★★
	POS selectivity	21.82	**7.62**	16.56	26.97	42.49	22.03
	NER gain	78.41	**55.20**	**70.63**	75.79	77.96	**76.27**
	NTC accuracy	**84.24**	82.47	**88.33**	74.55	92.93	90.79
Nguni-XLMR-large	Language coverage	★☆	★☆	★☆	☆☆	★★	☆☆
	POS selectivity	19.09	3.6	9.76	25.67	**43.13**	18.92
	NER gain	73.10	47.52	60.57	**77.28**	**80.18**	58.46
	NTC accuracy	80.25	82.47	83.28	**77.27**	**94.61**	**92.76**
AfriBERTa	Language coverage	★★	★★	★★	☆☆	☆☆	★★
	POS selectivity	18.79	-0.82	14.77	18.85	30.87	14.55
	NER gain	42.45	53.78	64.52	48.75	67.36	57.80
	NTC accuracy	82.56	**84.02**	87.38	74.55	81.48	92.76
AfroLM	Language coverage	★★	★★	★★	★★	★★	★★
	POS selectivity	**23.64**	3.37	**26.55**	**27.98**	38.92	**27.28**
	NER gain	39.45	46.33	61.21	45.90	62.07	47.97
	NTC accuracy	76.05	76.29	85.80	69.09	80.47	92.76

Table 3: Best-layer performance for each probing task, with best task performance overall indicated in **boldface**. We show this alongside model language coverage to indicate how language inclusion improves probe performance. ☆☆ indicates no language included in pretraining or adaptation, ★☆ shows the language was included in the base model but not in the adapted model, while ★★ shows the model was either pretrained or adapted for the language.

Limitations

As discussed in Section 2, designing control tasks for NER proved challenging. While control tasks are primarily designed for word-level tasks, NER presents complications because named entities often span multiple words. This makes it difficult to apply the typical control task framework in a meaningful way. Instead, we relied on random baselines, which, although commonly used, are known to have certain limitations (Belinkov, 2022; Hewitt and Liang, 2019).

In this study, we used the first subword as input for the classifier to align tokens with their hidden representations. However, even the choice of subword pooling strategy can make a difference in probing performance (Ács et al., 2021). Other pooling strategies, such as last subword, mean pooling, or attention over subwords, could provide different insights, especially for morphologically rich languages with high subword tokenization rates. Future work should systematically compare the effects of different subword pooling strategies across various syntactic and semantic tasks for African languages.

Acknowledgements

Wisdom Aduah was a Google DeepMind scholar at AIMS South Africa, in the AI for Science Masters program when he conducted this research.

References

Judit Ács, Ákos Kádár, and András Kornai. 2021. Subword pooling makes a difference. In *Proceedings of the 16th Conference of the European Chapter of the Association for Computational Linguistics, EACL 2021*. Association for Computational Linguistics.

David Adelani, Graham Neubig, Sebastian Ruder, Shruti Rijhwani, Michael Beukman, Chester Palen-Michel, Constantine Lignos, Jesujoba Alabi, Shamsuddeen Muhammad, Peter Nabende, Cheikh M. Bamba Dione, Andiswa Bukula, Rooweither Mabuya, Bonaventure F. P. Dossou, Blessing Sibanda,

Happy Buzaaba, Jonathan Mukiibi, Godson Kalipe, Derguene Mbaye, Amelia Taylor, Fatoumata Kabore, Chris Chinenye Emezue, Anuoluwapo Aremu, Perez Ogayo, Catherine Gitau, Edwin Munkoh-Buabeng, Victoire Memdjokam Koagne, Allahsera Auguste Tapo, Tebogo Macucwa, Vukosi Marivate, Mboning Tchiaze Elvis, Tajuddeen Gwadabe, Tosin Adewumi, Orevaoghene Ahia, Joyce Nakatumba-Nabende, Neo Lerato Mokono, Ignatius Ezeani, Chiamaka Chukwuneke, Mofetoluwa Oluwaseun Adeyemi, Gilles Quentin Hacheme, Idris Abdulmumin, Odunayo Ogundepo, Oreen Yousuf, Tatiana Moteu, and Dietrich Klakow. 2022. MasakhaNER 2.0: Africa-centric transfer learning for named entity recognition. In *Proceedings of the 2022 Conference on Empirical Methods in Natural Language Processing*, pages 4488–4508, Abu Dhabi, United Arab Emirates. Association for Computational Linguistics.

David Ifeoluwa Adelani, Marek Masiak, Israel Abebe Azime, Jesujoba Alabi, Atnafu Lambebo Tonja, Christine Mwase, Odunayo Ogundepo, Bonaventure F. P. Dossou, Akintunde Oladipo, Doreen Nixdorf, Chris Chinenye Emezue, Sana Al-azzawi, Blessing Sibanda, Davis David, Lolwethu Ndolela, Jonathan Mukiibi, Tunde Ajayi, Tatiana Moteu, Brian Odhiambo, Abraham Owodunni, Nnaemeka Obiefuna, Muhidin Mohamed, Shamsuddeen Hassan Muhammad, Teshome Mulugeta Ababu, Saheed Abdullahi Salahudeen, Mesay Gemeda Yigezu, Tajuddeen Gwadabe, Idris Abdulmumin, Mahlet Taye, Oluwabusayo Awoyomi, Iyanuoluwa Shode, Tolulope Adelani, Habiba Abdulganiyu, Abdul-Hakeem Omotayo, Adetola Adeeko, Abeeb Afolabi, Anuoluwapo Aremu, Olanrewaju Samuel, Clemencia Siro, Wangari Kimotho, Onyekachi Ogbu, Chinedu Mbonu, Chiamaka Chukwuneke, Samuel Fanijo, Jessica Ojo, Oyinkansola Awosan, Tadesse Kebede, Toadoum Sari Sakayo, Pamela Nyatsine, Freedmore Sidume, Oreen Yousuf, Mardiyyah Oduwole, Kanda Tshinu, Ussen Kimanuka, Thina Diko, Siyanda Nxakama, Sinodos Nigusse, Abdulmejid Johar, Shafie Mohamed, Fuad Mire Hassan, Moges Ahmed Mehamed, Evrard Ngabire, Jules Jules, Ivan Ssenkungu, and Pontus Stenetorp. 2023. MasakhaNEWS: News topic classification for African languages. In *Proceedings of the 13th International Joint Conference on Natural Language Processing and the 3rd Conference of the Asia-Pacific Chapter of the Association for Computational Linguistics (Volume 1: Long Papers)*, pages 144–159, Nusa Dua, Bali. Association for Computational Linguistics.

Jesujoba O. Alabi, David Ifeoluwa Adelani, Marius Mosbach, and Dietrich Klakow. 2022. Adapting pre-trained language models to African languages via multilingual adaptive fine-tuning. In *Proceedings of the 29th International Conference on Computational Linguistics*, pages 4336–4349, Gyeongju, Republic of Korea. International Committee on Computational Linguistics.

Guillaume Alain and Yoshua Bengio. 2017. Understanding intermediate layers using linear classifier probes.

Arnav Arora, Lucie-aimée Kaffee, and Isabelle Augenstein. 2023. Probing pre-trained language models for cross-cultural differences in values. In *Proceedings of the First Workshop on Cross-Cultural Considerations in NLP (C3NLP)*, pages 114–130, Dubrovnik, Croatia. Association for Computational Linguistics.

David Arps, Laura Kallmeyer, Younes Samih, and Hassan Sajjad. 2024. Multilingual nonce dependency treebanks: Understanding how language models represent and process syntactic structure. In *Proceedings of the 2024 Conference of the North American Chapter of the Association for Computational Linguistics: Human Language Technologies (Volume 1: Long Papers)*, pages 7822–7844, Mexico City, Mexico. Association for Computational Linguistics.

Yonatan Belinkov. 2022. Probing Classifiers: Promises, Shortcomings, and Advances. *Computational Linguistics*, 48(1):207–219.

Yonatan Belinkov, Nadir Durrani, Fahim Dalvi, Hassan Sajjad, and James Glass. 2017. What do neural machine translation models learn about morphology? In *Proceedings of the 55th Annual Meeting of the Association for Computational Linguistics (Volume 1: Long Papers)*, pages 861–872, Vancouver, Canada. Association for Computational Linguistics.

Grzegorz Chrupała, Bertrand Higy, and Afra Alishahi. 2020. Analyzing analytical methods: The case of phonology in neural models of spoken language. In *Proceedings of the 58th Annual Meeting of the Association for Computational Linguistics*, pages 4146–4156, Online. Association for Computational Linguistics.

Alexis Conneau, Kartikay Khandelwal, Naman Goyal, Vishrav Chaudhary, Guillaume Wenzek, Francisco Guzmán, Edouard Grave, Myle Ott, Luke Zettlemoyer, and Veselin Stoyanov. 2020. Unsupervised cross-lingual representation learning at scale. In *Proceedings of the 58th Annual Meeting of the Association for Computational Linguistics*, pages 8440–8451, Online. Association for Computational Linguistics.

Alexis Conneau, German Kruszewski, Guillaume Lample, Loïc Barrault, and Marco Baroni. 2018. What you can cram into a single $&!#* vector: Probing sentence embeddings for linguistic properties. In *Proceedings of the 56th Annual Meeting of the Association for Computational Linguistics (Volume 1: Long Papers)*, pages 2126–2136, Melbourne, Australia. Association for Computational Linguistics.

Cheikh M. Bamba Dione, David Ifeoluwa Adelani, Peter Nabende, Jesujoba Alabi, Thapelo Sindane, Happy Buzaaba, Shamsuddeen Hassan Muhammad, Chris Chinenye Emezue, Perez Ogayo, Anuoluwapo Aremu, Catherine Gitau, Derguene Mbaye, Jonathan

Mukiibi, Blessing Sibanda, Bonaventure F. P. Dossou, Andiswa Bukula, Rooweither Mabuya, Allahsera Auguste Tapo, Edwin Munkoh-Buabeng, Victoire Memdjokam Koagne, Fatoumata Ouoba Kabore, Amelia Taylor, Godson Kalipe, Tebogo Macucwa, Vukosi Marivate, Tajuddeen Gwadabe, Mboning Tchiaze Elvis, Ikechukwu Onyenwe, Gratien Atindogbe, Tolulope Adelani, Idris Akinade, Olanrewaju Samuel, Marien Nahimana, Th'eog'ene Musabeyezu, Emile Niyomutabazi, Ester Chimhenga, Kudzai Gotosa, Patrick Mizha, Apelete Agbolo, Seydou Traore, Chinedu Uchechukwu, Aliyu Yusuf, Muhammad Abdullahi, and Dietrich Klakow. 2023. MasakhaPOS: Part-of-speech tagging for typologically diverse African languages. In *Proceedings of the 61st Annual Meeting of the Association for Computational Linguistics (Volume 1: Long Papers)*, pages 10883–10900, Toronto, Canada. Association for Computational Linguistics.

Bonaventure F. P. Dossou, Atnafu Lambebo Tonja, Oreen Yousuf, Salomey Osei, Abigail Oppong, Iyanuoluwa Shode, Oluwabusayo Olufunke Awoyomi, and Chris Emezue. 2022. AfroLM: A self-active learning-based multilingual pretrained language model for 23 African languages. In *Proceedings of The Third Workshop on Simple and Efficient Natural Language Processing (SustaiNLP)*, pages 52–64, Abu Dhabi, United Arab Emirates (Hybrid). Association for Computational Linguistics.

Muhammad Usman Hadi, Qasem Al Tashi, Abbas Shah, Rizwan Qureshi, Amgad Muneer, Muhammad Irfan, Anas Zafar, Muhammad Bilal Shaikh, Naveed Akhtar, Jia Wu, et al. 2024. Large language models: a comprehensive survey of its applications, challenges, limitations, and future prospects. *Authorea Preprints*.

John Hewitt and Percy Liang. 2019. Designing and interpreting probes with control tasks. In *Conference on Empirical Methods in Natural Language Processing*. Association for Computational Linguistics.

John Hewitt and Christopher D. Manning. 2019. A structural probe for finding syntax in word representations. In *Proceedings of the 2019 Conference of the North American Chapter of the Association for Computational Linguistics: Human Language Technologies, Volume 1 (Long and Short Papers)*, pages 4129–4138, Minneapolis, Minnesota. Association for Computational Linguistics.

Jue Hou, Anisia Katinskaia, Lari Kotilainen, Sathianpong Trangcasanchai, Anh-Duc Vu, and Roman Yangarber. 2024. What do transformers know about government? In *Proceedings of the 2024 Joint International Conference on Computational Linguistics, Language Resources and Evaluation (LREC-COLING 2024)*, pages 17459–17472, Torino, Italia. ELRA and ICCL.

Anisia Katinskaia and Roman Yangarber. 2024. Probing the category of verbal aspect in transformer language models. In *Findings of the Association for Computational Linguistics*, pages 3347–3366, United States. The Association for Computational Linguistics. Findings of the Association for Computational Linguistics : NAACL 2024 ; Conference date: 16-06-2024 Through 21-06-2024.

Daoyang Li, Mingyu Jin, Qingcheng Zeng, Haiyan Zhao, and Mengnan Du. 2024. Exploring multilingual probing in large language models: A cross-language analysis. *Preprint*, arXiv:2409.14459.

Haoyan Luo and Lucia Specia. 2024. From understanding to utilization: A survey on explainability for large language models. *Preprint*, arXiv:2401.12874.

Francois Meyer, Haiyue Song, Abhisek Chakrabarty, Jan Buys, Raj Dabre, and Hideki Tanaka. 2024. NGLUEni: Benchmarking and adapting pretrained language models for nguni languages. In *Proceedings of the 2024 Joint International Conference on Computational Linguistics, Language Resources and Evaluation (LREC-COLING 2024)*, pages 12247–12258, Torino, Italia. ELRA and ICCL.

Kelechi Ogueji, Yuxin Zhu, and Jimmy Lin. 2021. Small data? no problem! exploring the viability of pretrained multilingual language models for low-resourced languages. In *Proceedings of the 1st Workshop on Multilingual Representation Learning*, pages 116–126, Punta Cana, Dominican Republic. Association for Computational Linguistics.

Tiago Pimentel, Josef Valvoda, Rowan Hall Maudslay, Ran Zmigrod, Adina Williams, and Ryan Cotterell. 2020. Information-theoretic probing for linguistic structure. In *Proceedings of the 58th Annual Meeting of the Association for Computational Linguistics*, pages 4609–4622, Online. Association for Computational Linguistics.

Anna Rogers, Olga Kovaleva, and Anna Rumshisky. 2020. A primer in BERTology: What we know about how BERT works. *Transactions of the Association for Computational Linguistics*, 8:842–866.

Ian Tenney, Dipanjan Das, and Ellie Pavlick. 2019a. BERT rediscovers the classical NLP pipeline. In *Proceedings of the 57th Annual Meeting of the Association for Computational Linguistics*, pages 4593–4601, Florence, Italy. Association for Computational Linguistics.

Ian Tenney, Patrick Xia, Berlin Chen, Alex Wang, Adam Poliak, R Thomas McCoy, Najoung Kim, Benjamin Van Durme, Sam Bowman, Dipanjan Das, and Ellie Pavlick. 2019b. What do you learn from context? probing for sentence structure in contextualized word representations. In *International Conference on Learning Representations*.

Linting Xue, Noah Constant, Adam Roberts, Mihir Kale, Rami Al-Rfou, Aditya Siddhant, Aditya Barua, and Colin Raffel. 2021. mT5: A massively multilingual pre-trained text-to-text transformer. In *Proceedings of the 2021 Conference of the North American Chapter of the Association for Computational Linguistics: Human Language Technologies*, pages 483–498, Online. Association for Computational Linguistics.

Kelly Zhang and Samuel Bowman. 2018. Language modeling teaches you more than translation does: Lessons learned through auxiliary syntactic task analysis. In *Proceedings of the 2018 EMNLP Workshop BlackboxNLP: Analyzing and Interpreting Neural Networks for NLP*, pages 359–361, Brussels, Belgium. Association for Computational Linguistics.

A Data Information

	Bantu (%)	Volta-Niger (%)	Afro-Asiatic (%)	Others (%)
XLM-R	33.3	0.0	6.3	60.4
AfroXLMR	28.0	5.8	7.4	58.8
AfriBERTa	0.0	7.4	16.0	76.6
AfroLM	32.8	9.7	18.4	39.1

Table 4: Distribution of African datasets by language family

B Figures

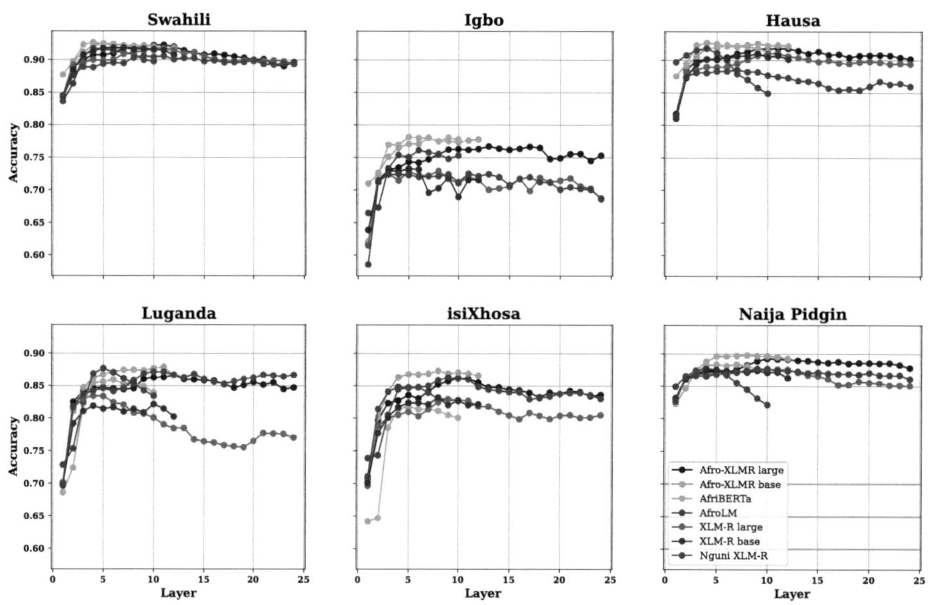

Figure 6: Raw accuracies for POS tagging.

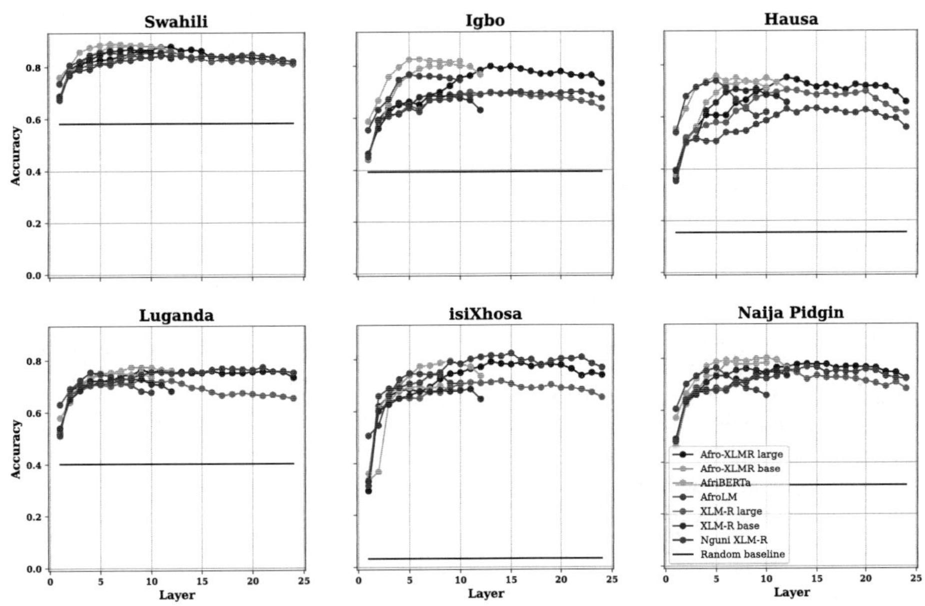

Figure 7: Raw F1-scores for Named Entity Recognition.

Building a Functional Machine Translation Corpus for Kpelle

Kweku Andoh Yamoah[1] **Jackson Weako**[2] **Emmanuel J. Dorley**[1]
[1]University of Florida
[2]Liberia Language Institute
kyamoah@ufl.edu, weakojackson@gmail.com, edorley@ufl.edu

Abstract

In this paper, we introduce the first publicly available English-Kpelle dataset for machine translation, comprising over 2,000 sentence pairs drawn from everyday communication, religious texts, and educational materials. By fine-tuning Meta's No Language Left Behind (NLLB) model on two versions of the dataset, we achieved BLEU scores of up to 30 in the Kpelle-to-English direction, demonstrating the benefits of data augmentation. Our findings align with NLLB-200 benchmarks on other African languages, underscoring Kpelle's potential for competitive performance despite its low-resource status. Beyond machine translation, this dataset enables broader NLP tasks, including speech recognition and language modeling. We conclude with a roadmap for future dataset expansion, emphasizing orthographic consistency, community-driven validation, and interdisciplinary collaboration to advance inclusive language technology development for Kpelle and other low-resourced Mande languages.

1 Introduction

Several notable initiatives have sought to address the challenges of low-resource languages, particularly in Africa. Collaborative projects like Masakhane (Nekoto et al., 2020; Orife et al., 2020) have created and publicly released several machine translation datasets and baseline models for African languages (Nekoto et al., 2020; Orife et al., 2020; Nakatumba-Nabende et al., 2024). The Lacuna Fund has also played a vital role in accelerating the creation of openly accessible text and speech datasets for various African languages (Nakatumba-Nabende et al., 2024; Asamoah Owusu et al., 2022; Vydrin et al., 2022; Asmelash Teka Hadgu et al., 2022; Wanjawa et al., 2024; Adelani et al., 2022). Additionally, there is Meta's "No Language Left Behind" (NLLB) project aimed to develop high-quality machine translation systems for over 200 languages, including many low-resource languages in Africa (Team et al., 2022). Despite these efforts, languages such as the Kpelle language have not been explored, leaving the language marginalized in natural language processing (NLP) research.

Kpelle is a language primarily spoken in Liberia and Guinea, with over one million speakers across these two countries (Vydrin, 2018). It is classified as a macro-language due to distinct variants—Liberian Kpelle and Guinean Kpelle—that, while closely related, constitute separate linguistic entities (Vydrin, 2018). Belonging to the Southwestern subgroup of the broader Mande language family, Kpelle is part of a larger linguistic family that includes approximately 70 languages spoken by at least 25 million native speakers and an additional 30 million second-language speakers throughout West Africa (Konoshenko, 2008; Vydrin, 2018). Within Liberia specifically, Kpelle represents the largest indigenous language, spoken by approximately 20% of the population (Vydrin, 2018).

Although Kpelle boasts a considerable number of speakers, it remains largely absent from digital platforms, including AI tools. Kpelle is a low-resourced language, which means the language lacks sufficient digital resources to support the development of NLP applications. Therefore, by extension, Kpelle faces the same challenges that are unique to low-resourced languages. These challenges include data scarcity (Kusampudi et al., 2021; Maillard et al., 2023; Nakatumba-Nabende et al., 2024; Nguyen et al., 2022), data quality(data limited to specific domains like religious texts) (Nakatumba-Nabende et al., 2024; Maillard et al., 2023; Kusampudi et al., 2021; Team et al., 2022), multilingualism, and dialectical variations(difficulty determining boundaries within dialects) (Konoshenko, 2024).

To address this significant gap, we present the first-ever dataset for Kpelle. This dataset is de-

Proceedings of the Sixth Workshop on African Natural Language Processing (AfricaNLP 2025), pages 52–63
July 31, 2025

signed for machine translation and language learning of Kpelle and English and vice versa. Our work aims to lay the foundations for intensive research for Kpelle and other low resource Liberian languages, enabling the development of NLP applications and solutions that can enhance the way speakers of the language interact with everyday technologies. This paper begins with an introduction highlighting our work's foundations and motivations. The continuing sections present the related work for machine translation for African languages. We then present the history of the Kpelle language, examining its unique linguistic features. Following that, we discuss the dataset creation process and the corpus benchmarking using the NLLB model and the results obtained. Our contributions are as follows:[1] *(a) Created a bilingual English-Kpelle corpus that has 3234 translation pairs. (b) The methodological data collection, cleaning, and alignment approach offers a replicable framework for other researchers working with low-resource languages. (c) Benchmarked the dataset on NLLB achieving a BLEU of ≈ 30 for kpe_Latn → eng_Latn translation and a BLEU of ≈ 24 eng_Latn → kpe_Latn translation.*

2 Related Work

2.1 Review of Efforts in Low-Resource Language Datasets

The development of robust NLP tools for low-resource languages is limited by data scarcity, creating significant challenges for tasks like machine translation. Addressing this challenge has prompted various initiatives to expand language coverage and improve translation quality. Community-led projects like Masakhane have played a pivotal role in building datasets and models for African languages through a collaborative approach involving researchers and native speakers (Nakatumba-Nabende et al., 2024; Akinfaderin, 2020). The Lacuna Fund has further supported these efforts by funding the creation of open-source text and speech resources for African languages (Akinfaderin, 2020; Nakatumba-Nabende et al., 2024; Asamoah Owusu et al., 2022; Vydrin et al., 2022; Asmelash Teka Hadgu et al., 2022; Wanjawa et al., 2024; Adelani et al., 2022). Meta's ambitious "No Language Left Behind" (NLLB) project has made significant progress in building machine translation systems for over 200 languages, including many that are under-resourced (Team et al., 2022). The NLLB Team et al. (2022) used data mining to transform vast monolingual datasets into new training data for low-resource languages and employed new modeling approaches, like the Sparsely Gated Mixture of Experts, to improve translation quality (Team et al., 2022). However, NLLB (Team et al., 2022), like many other initiatives, primarily focuses on languages with established written standards, leaving languages with limited or no written traditions largely unaddressed .

Beyond large-scale projects, creating specialized corpora has proven vital in addressing the data diversity and domain adaptation needs of specific languages and regions (Agyei et al., 2024; Maillard et al., 2023). The Twi-2-ENG corpus from (Agyei et al., 2024) is a recent example, providing a comprehensive resource for the Twi language, encompassing a wide range of genres relevant to Ghanaian Twi-speaking communities. This corpus aims to support NLP applications like machine translation and linguistic research by offering a searchable platform for accurate translations and a deeper understanding of Twi linguistics (Agyei et al., 2024; George et al., 2024; Williams et al., 2018). Another example is the LORELEI program, initiated by DARPA, which targets research and development of language technologies that aim to reduce the dependency on manually transcribed and translated corpora (Nguyen et al., 2022; Agyei et al., 2024; Goyal et al., 2021). This program has facilitated the collection of language samples and data for several African languages, including Hausa, Zulu, Yoruba, Twi, Somali, Swahili, and Wolof, contributing to the growth of language resources for these languages (Agyei et al., 2024; Goyal et al., 2021; Team et al., 2022).

2.2 Prior Work on the Mande Language Family

Existing NLP research on the Mande languages primarily focuses on individual languages, with limited cross-linguistic studies or comprehensive datasets representing the broader family (Vydrin, 2018). A few studies have investigated specific linguistic phenomena, such as the origin of the S-O-V-X word order (Vydrin, 2018), motion events in Bambara (Vydrin, 2018), and the evolution of tonal systems (Konoshenko, 2008; Vydrin, 2018). Efforts in language documentation and corpus creation for Mande languages have also been undertaken (George et al., 2024; Nakatumba-Nabende

[1]Dataset is made available at https://huggingface.co/datasets/IARG-UF/English-Kpelle-Corpus

et al., 2024; Akinfaderin, 2020; Team et al., 2022). For instance, a grammatical sketch of Beng, a Southern Mande language, has been developed (Paperno, 2014). Additionally, research on the Kakabe language, a Western Mande language, has focused on prosody in grammar (Vydrina, 2017). However, these efforts typically focus on individual languages or specific linguistic phenomena, and thus do not provide comprehensive resources or datasets necessary for cross-lingual NLP applications across the broader Mande language family.

2.3 Gap Filled by the Kpelle Dataset

The Kpelle Dataset aims to address a critical gap in the current research by providing the first, publicly available bilingual dataset for the Kpelle language. Despite being one of the most widely spoken languages in Liberia and Guinea, Kpelle remains severely underrepresented in NLP research, lacking any existing publicly available datasets. This absence stems from several factors, including Kpelle's status as a low-resource language with limited digital presence, the complexities arising from its dialectal variations across Guinea and Liberia (Konoshenko, 2008; Vydrin, 2018), and the lack of standardized orthography (Konoshenko, 2024). The dataset from this work will provide a much-needed resource for developing and evaluating NLP tools for Kpelle, enabling advancements in tasks like machine translation, language modeling, and speech recognition. By making this dataset publicly available, the project contributes to the broader goal of promoting language diversity and inclusion for African Languages.

3 Overview of Kpelle

As previously mentioned, Kpelle belongs to the Southwestern Mande branch of the larger Mande language family. Figure 1 illustrates how Kpelle fits within this broader linguistic context, demonstrating its relationship to other languages spoken throughout Liberia.

Kpelle boasts of a rich oral tradition, with storytelling, proverbs, and songs playing a pivotal role in preserving the history and cultural values of the people (Thach, 1981). Oral tradition has been key in maintaining the language across generations, especially since written text is limited (Thach, 1981). Also, Kpelle faces challenges in representation and expansive linguistic research due to its low-resources status.

Further, external influences have impacted the Kpelle language. In the 19th and 20th centuries, interactions with European colonizers and neighboring ethnic groups introduced new vocabulary into the language (Thach, 1981). However, Kpelle has kept its core linguistic structure and continues to thrive as a means of communication and cultural identity for its speakers (Thach, 1981).

3.1 Linguistic Features

In this paper, we focus on **Liberian Kpelle** which exhibits distinct linguistic features that set it apart within the Mande Language family.

3.1.1 Phonetics

Kpelle uses a sound system with a rich array of consonants and vowels (Thach, 1981; Vydrin, 2018; Konoshenko, 2024; Thach et al., 1981). Notably, it includes labiovelar stops such as /gb/ and /kp/, which are said simultaneously at the velar and bilabial places of articulation and represent single consonant sounds (Thach, 1981; Thach et al., 1981; Vydrin, 2018). These sounds are relatively rare in global languages and contribute to Kpelle's unique phonological profile. The vowel system in Kpelle has seven oral vowels and their nasal counterparts, making for a complex vocalic inventory (Vydrin, 2018). Dialectical variations influence pronunciation, particularly with the /s/ sound (Thach, 1981). In some regions, the /s/ can resemble the English /s/; in others, it may sound like /ʃ/ (as in "ship") or /h/ (Thach, 1981). These forms of variations can pose difficulties for language learners.

3.1.2 Syntax

Kpelle follows a Subject-Verb-Object(SVO) sentence structure, which aligns with the syntactic patterns of many languages in the world, including English (Thach, 1981; Vydrin, 2018; Konoshenko, 2008). This syntactic structure facilitates the translation of Kpelle to English to some extent. Kpelle also distinguishes between dependent and independent nouns, akin to the idea of inalienable and alienable possession seen in other languages (Thach, 1981; Vydrin, 2018). For example, body parts and kinship terms are treated differently grammatically compared to other nouns, affecting possessive constructions (Thach, 1981; Vydrin, 2018).

Modifiers in Kpelle usually follow the nouns they describe (Thach, 1981), and the language employs postpositions rather than prepositions (Vydrin, 2018). Verb serialization is also a feature

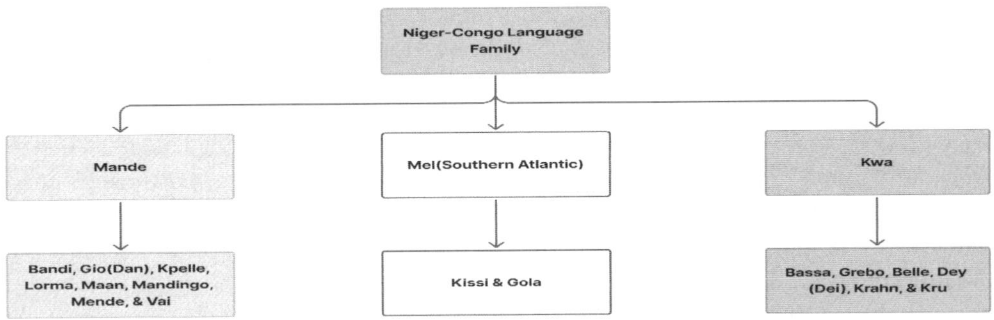

Figure 1: Overview of Liberian language family under the Niger-Congo Branch.

in Kpelle (Heine and Reh, 1984), where multiple verbs are used sequentially to convey complex actions or events without conjunctions.

3.1.3 Grammar

Kpelle grammar has a complex system of pronouns that reflect distinctions in person, number, and sometimes gender (Thach, 1981; Vydrin, 2018). The verb system marks tenses, aspect, and mood through affixes and particles (Thach, 1981; Thach et al., 1981). For example, there are specific markers for past, present, and future tenses and for completed and ongoing actions (Thach et al., 1981).

Noun classes in Kpelle are less prominent than in some other African languages but do exist and can affect agreement within the sentence (Vydrin, 2018). Kpelle employs emphatic particles like *'bé'* to convey emphasis or focus within a sentence (Thach, 1981). Since tone and stress are primarily used to convey lexical and grammatical meaning (Thach, 1981; Thach et al., 1981; Vydrin, 2018)- these particles play an important role in adding nuance and emphasis without altering the tonal structure.

3.1.4 Tonality

Liberian Kpelle is a tonal language, meaning that the pitch at which a syllable is said can change the word's meaning entirely (Thach, 1981; Thach et al., 1981; Vydrin, 2018; Konoshenko, 2024, 2008). Kpelle features three tone levels: high, mid, and low (Thach, 1981; Vydrin, 2018; Konoshenko, 2008). Tones can be level (staying the same throughout the syllable) or contour (changing pitch within the syllable) (Thach, 1981; Thach et al., 1981; Konoshenko, 2008). This tonal system is essential for distinguishing words that are otherwise identical phonetically (Konoshenko, 2008). For example, (Konoshenko, 2008) presents that "simple words in Kpelle form several groupings according to the tonal patterns which are assigned to these words lexically," and the groupings can be binned into categories known as *tonal classes* (Konoshenko, 2008). Also, a single syllable pronounced with a high tone might mean one thing (*lá, meaning mouth*); in a mid-tone, that same syllable communicates (*la, meaning it*), while the same syllable with a low tone means something entirely different (*là, meaning if*) (Thach, 1981).

Tone also plays a grammatical role in Kpelle, affecting verb tenses and aspects (Konoshenko, 2008). Tonal patterns indicate whether an action is completed, ongoing, or habitual. This reliance on tone adds a layer of complexity to Kpelle learning and computational processing since accurate tonal representation is critical, especially for this work. Table 1 presents the tones seen in Kpelle with examples.

Table 1: Tonal Levels in Kpelle adapted from (Thach, 1981; Weako, 2024)

Tonal Level	**Mark**	**Kpelle Example**	**English Version**
High	´	zóo	native doctor
Mid	no mark/¯	tuna	rain
Low	`	nyɔ̀ɔ	be afraid
High-Low	ˆ	sâa	today
Mid-High-Low	ˆ	tisô	sneeze
Low-High	ˇ	kǒ	to plant
Nasal	˜	sã	to dance

3.1.5 Writing System

Historically, Kpelle has been primarily an oral language, but people have worked to develop writing systems that promote literacy and documentation. An example is the Kpelle syllabary created by Chief Gbili in the 1930s, an indigenous script designed to represent the sounds of Kpelle (African 671, 2019). However, few people use this script today (African 671, 2019).

More commonly, Kpelle is written using Latin-based orthography (Vydrin, 2018). This system has been influenced by various scholars and linguists, such as William E. Welmers, who worked on developing practical orthographies for African languages in the mid-20th century (Konoshenko, 2008). The Latin-based orthography often has diacritical marks to show tonal variations (Konoshenko, 2024; Thach, 1981); moreover, the lack of standardization leads to inconsistencies in written materials (Konoshenko, 2024; Thach, 1981).

The Kpelle dictionary by (Leidenfrost and McKay, 2005) incorporates tonal markings and provides valuable resources for language learners and researchers (Thach, 1981; Konoshenko, 2008). Materials from the Kpelle Literacy Center in Totota also use the Latin script to promote written literacy among native speakers of Kpelle (Thach, 1981). The absence of a universally accepted orthography remains challenging, considering the variations between Liberian and Guinean Kpelle (Thach, 1981; Konoshenko, 2008).

4 Dataset Creation

Creating the English-Kpelle dataset involved planning and execution to ensure the data's relevance, accuracy, and cultural appropriateness. Our primary goal was to compile a corpus facilitating effective communication for individuals who may not speak Kpelle, particularly in everyday social interactions and essential services. This section outlines the data collection sources and methods, preprocessing steps, and translation alignment processes used in building the dataset.

4.1 Data Collection

4.1.1 Sources

The sources used in building the dataset covered a combination of practical and culturally relevant scenarios:

Travel and Tourism Phrases. We identified common phrases and questions frequently asked by tourists and travelers when they visit a new location. Usually, due to their unfamiliar disposition to the place, we focused on phrases that covered greetings, inquiries about locations, costs, weather conditions, and other essential interactions. The phrases were sourced from the following respected travel and language teaching website: *Business Insider's Travel Language Phrases*(Abadi, 2018), *EF Education First's Essential Phrases*(B, 2018), *Online Teachers UK's English for Tourism and Travel* (Writer, 2017), *Go Overseas' Language Phrases Before Travelling* (Perez, 2022), *Accessible Travel Phrasebook by Premiki* (Limited, 2018), and *Wikivoyage's Afrikaans Phrasebook* (Wikivoyage, 2005).

Religious Texts. Religious literature, like the Bible, often contains a wealth of translated material that can be valuable for language datasets. We added a few excerpts from publicly available religious texts that have been translated into Kpelle.

Educational Material. Significant portions of the dataset were sourced from the book *A Learner Directed Approach to Kpelle by Sharon V. Thach* (Thach, 1981), *English-Kpelle Dictionary, with a Grammar Sketch and English-Kpelle Finder List* (Leidenfrost and McKay, 2005), *We Have Come To Learn Kpelle* (Ricks, 2009). These resources had bilingual content, including matching English-Kpelle sentence pairs, standalone English paragraphs, and standalone Kpelle paragraphs.

4.1.2 Methods

Data Extraction. We gathered a list of essential phrases and sentences relevant to everyday communication from the travel and tourism websites. These phrases were selected based on their frequency of use and utility in facilitating introductory interaction.

Translation. For English or Kpelle paragraphs that did not have the corresponding translation, we engaged a native Kpelle speaker with linguistic expertise to provide accurate translations.

Segmentation of Paragraphs. In cases where the source material provided paragraphs rather than individual sentences, we segmented the text into sentence pairs. This approach increased the granularity of the dataset, making it suitable for machine translation tasks.

Expert Verification. All translated sentences were reviewed by Kpelle language experts to verify the accuracy of the translations, the correctness of tone and grammar, and the appropriateness of context.

4.2 Data Preprocessing

4.2.1 Cleaning

The raw data collected contained inconsistencies such as typographical errors, informal language, and irrelevant content. We performed a thorough cleaning process to remove these anomalies. This included spell-checking, correcting grammatical errors, and eliminating duplicate entries. Special attention was given to resolving translation inconsistencies, especially where multiple translations existed for a single English phrase. The most accurate and contextually appropriate translation was selected based on expert advice.

4.2.2 Normalization

Given Kpelle's lack of a universally accepted writing system, we adopted the Latin-based orthography commonly used in educational materials and literacy programs. Diacritical marks were standardized to represent tonal variations accurately. All text data was encoded using UTF-8 Unicode to ensure compatibility across different platforms and tools. This was essential for preserving special characters and tonal markers unique to Kpelle. To maintain consistency, all text was converted to a standard case format, except where capitalization was necessary for proper nouns and the beginning of sentences.

4.2.3 Segmentation

The text was segmented into individual sentences using punctuation cues and linguistic rules specific to Kpelle. This process was manually verified due to the potential for misinterpretation by automated tokenizers not tailored to Kpelle. Within sentences, words were tokenized based on whitespace and morphological patterns. This facilitated subsequent processing tasks such as alignment and statistical analysis. Kpelle often uses contractions and compound words. These were carefully identified and treated according to linguistic guidelines to ensure accurate tokenization.

5 Dataset Statistics and Analysis

5.1 Quantitative Overview

The dataset has 3234[2] entries corresponding to unique Kpelle-English translation pairs. Typically, each entry has one Kpelle sentence paired with its English equivalent; however, some entries contain sentences under a single translation unit (e.g., compound or complex sentences kept intact to preserve context). In total, the dataset contains 30,021 words (14,790 in Kpelle and 15,231 in English) and 4,369 sentences (2,202 in Kpelle and 2,167 in English). The longest sentences contain 70 Kpelle words and 49 English words, with the shortest being a single word in either language. Moreover, there are 4,702 unique Kpelle words and 3,579 unique English words, resulting in an overall vocabulary of 8,281 entries. These statistics make this the largest publicly available bilingual English–Kpelle resource to date.

[2]This count refers specifically to Version 2 of our dataset, which extends the initial 1,518 sentence pairs to 2,005 and increases word entries from 1,181 to 1,229.

5.2 Sentence Length

After our distribution analysis, we observed that most of the English sentences ranged from 3 to 15 words, with an average length of around 8 words per sentence. The Kpelle sentences vary more due to certain functional words' presence (or absence) and the possibility of encoding multiple concepts in a single phrase. However, the average Kpelle sentence length approximates 7 words, with most sentences falling between 3 and 12.

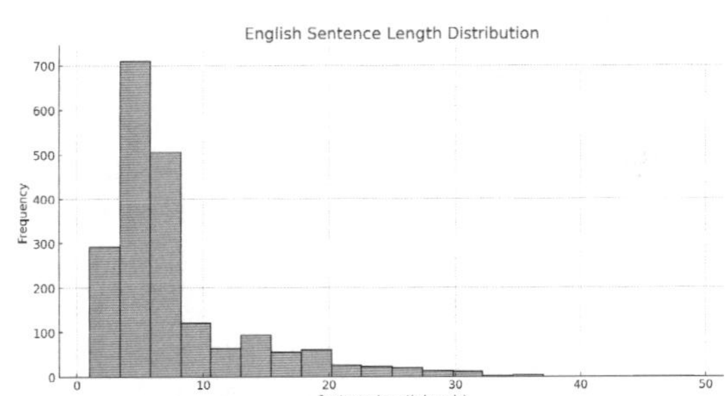

(a) English sentence length distribution

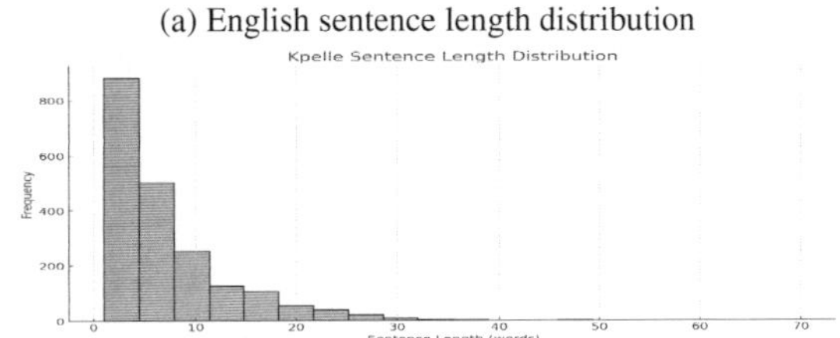

(b) Kpelle sentence length distribution

Figure 2: Sentence length distributions for English (top) and Kpelle (bottom), illustrating the corpus's inherent variability.

The wide range of sentence lengths reflects the dataset's inclusion of both simple and more complex utterances. Short, single-word sentences often correspond to exclamations, greetings, or short prompts, while longer sentences derive from religious or educational materials that contain embedded clauses and descriptive text.

5.3 Vocabulary Frequency

In terms of vocabulary, the top ten most frequent english words were *man (116), good (93), town (93), want (83), go (75), going (65), one (61), house (59), baby (54), went (53)*. Similarly, the top ten most frequent Kpelle words were *su (177), pâi (143), la (123), kaa (123), kɛ̀ (112), mɛ (108)ni, pɔ̂ri (104), li (101), kɛ (99), kɛ̂i (82)*.

Even though we remove common stop words, frequent English words indicate a high presence of articles, pronouns, and commonly used verbs, mirroring everyday conversational usage. On the Kpelle side, repeated use of function words like ***a, da,*** and ***e*** underscores similar syntactic necessities. These observations led to an English Hapax Legomena (words that appear once) of 1732 and a Kpelle Hapax Legomena of 2714.

A high number of hapax legomena suggests a rich and diverse vocabulary, but it also indicates that many words appear in the dataset with minimal frequency. This sparsity could pose challenges for certain NLP models, as low-frequency words often result in less robust embeddings and higher rates of out-of-vocabulary (OOV) tokens.

5.4 Domain Coverage

We conducted a keyword-based classification across common categories to understand the dataset's topical breadth. Table 2 shows that **Daily Conversation (664)** and **Household (214)** predominate, while underrepresented categories were **Religion (27)**, **Health (21)**, and **Education (14)**. It is worth noting that around 30% of the dataset remains unclassified, reflecting idiomatic expressions and content not easily mapped to predefined categories. However, the broad coverage of the dataset, given the number of entries, ensures the dataset can serve a variety of use cases.

5.5 Observations and Challenges

Even though we adopt a standardized Latin-based script, Kpelle orthography's dynamic and evolving nature continues to introduce spelling and tone-marking variations throughout the dataset. These inconsistencies highlight the broader challenges of documenting a language with limited written traditions and underscore the importance of ongoing refinement in orthographic conventions. Additionally, the low representation of domains such as

Domain	**Number of Sentences**
Daily Conversation	664
Household	214
Business & Finance	142
Family	93
Time & Events	91
Nature & Environment	80
General Purpose	59
Religion	27
Health	21
Travel & Tourism	19
Education	14
Unclassified	581

Table 2: Distribution of Sentences by Domain

Religion, Health, and Education highlights future avenues for data collection to achieve more balanced coverage. The distribution of topics also shows that key domains, such as Religion, Health, and Education, remain underrepresented, emphasizing potential areas for future data collection and corpus expansion to achieve more balanced coverage.

6 Experiments and Benchmarking

This section presents our machine translation experiments and benchmarking using the NLLB model by (Team et al., 2022). We describe our baseline models, outline the fine-tuning process, report quantitative results using standard evaluation metrics, and provide an analysis comparing our outcomes with previously reported NLLB-200 performance in other African languages. Figure 3 visually summarize this process.

6.1 Baseline Models and Experimental Setup

Given its strong performance across low-resource African languages, we leveraged Meta's NLLB model as a baseline. Our experiments focus on two Kpelle dataset versions:**Version 1 (V1)** contains 1,667 Kpelle and 1,638 English sentences (3,852 and 2,952 unique words). **Version 2 (V2)** benefits from data augmentation efforts, yielding 2,202 Kpelle and 2,167 English sentences (4,702 and 3,579 unique words). We aimed to assess how expanding the corpus (from 1,518 to 2,005 translation pairs) affects translation quality in both English $\rightarrow$ Kpelle (eng_Latn $\rightarrow$ kpe_Latn) and Kpelle $\rightarrow$ English (kpe_Latn $\rightarrow$ eng_Latn). We split each dataset into two sets, train and test, according to a 9:1 ratio and hold out the test set. Then, these sets were fine-tuned for 10k, 30k, and 60k steps on top of NLLB using Adafactor as the optimizer

(a) Fine-tuning NLLB-200 with Kpelle. (b) Translation example using the fine-tuned model.

Figure 3: NLLB-200 fine-tuning with Kpelle: (a) Model adaptation for bidirectional translation, and (b) a sample translation.

with a batch size of 8, constrained by the memory requirements of the Quadro RTX 6000 GPU, training times ranged between 30 minutes to 6 hours, dependent on the number of steps and the version of the dataset. We trained a Kpelle-specific tokenizer (a SentencePiece model (Kudo and Richardson, 2018)) on data from Penedo et al. (2024) to handle out-of-vocabulary tokens and then enriched the standard NLLB tokenizer with any missing tokens, ensuring compatibility with the model's subword vocabulary. Finally, we used sacreBLEU (Post, 2018) to measure BLEU, 1–4-gram precision, brevity penalty (BP), hypothesis/reference lengths, and chrF2++ to evaluate the fine-tuned model.

6.2 Results

	eng_Latn → kpe_Latn							
	Steps	BLEU	chrF2++	Precision (1-4 grams)				BP
				1-gram	2-gram	3-gram	4-gram	
NLLB	10k	**24.09**	38.24	49.3	28.7	20.5	16.8	0.913
	30k	**24.46**	38.20	50.2	29.1	20.6	16.8	0.918
	60k	**24.00**	38.19	50.1	28.2	19.5	16.1	0.930
NLLB V2	10k	19.80	**38.26**	49.6	25.4	15.5	10.0	0.942
	30k	19.97	**38.42**	49.1	24.6	15.2	10.2	0.961
	60k	20.79	**38.83**	51.5	26.9	16.9	11.4	0.915
	kpe_Latn → eng_Latn							
	Steps	BLEU	chrF2++	Precision (1-4 grams)				BP
				1-gram	2-gram	3-gram	4-gram	
NLLB	10k	23.16	38.29	42.5	24.7	18.6	14.7	1.000
	30k	24.31	39.60	44.1	26.6	19.4	15.3	1.000
	60k	23.65	39.41	43.1	25.2	18.9	15.2	1.000
NLLB V2	10k	**26.39**	**40.22**	50.0	30.6	20.9	15.2	0.999
	30k	**30.03**	**44.00**	52.4	34.0	24.7	18.4	1.000
	60k	**30.28**	**44.28**	53.4	34.5	24.8	18.3	1.000

Table 3: NLLB performance when fine-tuned on two versions of the English-Kpelle dataset (V1 and V2) at 10k, 30k, and 60k steps. Metrics (BLEU, chrF2++, 1–4-gram precision, and BP) are reported for both eng_Latn→kpe_Latn and kpe_Latn→eng_Latn. Bold scores denote the best performance.

Table 3 summarizes the results for NLLB fine-tuned on V1 and V2 of the Kpelle dataset across 10k, 30k, and 60k training steps.

We observe that moving from **V1** (1,518 entries) to **V2** (2,005 entries) improved BLEU scores in some scenarios, particularly for kpe_Latn → eng_Latn translation at higher step counts (e.g., 30k, 60k). This outcome aligns with the broader expectation that additional in-domain data can boost model performance in low-resource settings. Further, we also observe that increasing the fine-tuning steps from 10k to 30k and 60k generally yielded incremental gains for both versions. However, the improvements were again more pronounced when translating from Kpelle to English. In contrast, eng_Latn → kpe_Latn translation showed modest gains, suggesting that further optimization may be necessary to achieve comparable results in translation quality for Kpelle.

6.3 Analysis and Comparison with NLLB-200 Benchmarks

Reports by Team et al. (2022) highlight NLLB-200's performance across multiple African languages (e.g., Hausa, Igbo, Swahili, Yoruba). As shown in Table 4, M2M-100, MMTAfrica, and NLLB-200 yield varying BLEU and chrF2++ scores for these languages. Given the differences in language structure, dataset sizes, and domain coverage, cross-lingual comparisons should be made cautiously. However, **the scores we observe for Kpelle (BLEU in the range of 20–30 depending on the direction and training steps) are generally consistent with NLLB-200's range for other African languages.**.

	eng_Latn–xx			xx–eng_Latn		
	MMTAfrica	M2M-100*	NLLB-200	MMTAfrica	M2M-100*	NLLB-200
hau_Latn	-/-	4.0/-	**33.6/53.5**	-/-	16.3/-	**38.5/57.3**
ibo_Latn	21.4/37.2	19.9/-	**25.8/41.4**	15.4/38.9	12.0/-	**35.5/54.4**
lug_Latn	-/-	7.6/-	**16.8/39.8**	-/-	7.7/-	**27.4/46.7**
luo_Latn	-/-	13.7/-	**18.0/38.5**	-/-	11.8/-	**24.5/43.7**
swh_Latn	40.1/53.1	27.1/-	37.9/**58.6**	28.4/56.1	25.8/-	**48.1/66.1**
wol_Latn	-/-	8.2/-	**11.5/29.7**	-/-	7.5/-	**22.4/41.2**
xho_Latn	27.1/44.9	-/-	**29.5/48.6**	21.7/48.6	-/-	**41.9/59.9**
yor_Latn	12.0/28.3	13.4/-	**13.8/25.5**	9.0/30.6	9.3/-	**26.6/46.3**
zul_Latn	-/-	19.2/-	**36.3/53.3**	-/-	19.2/-	**43.4/61.5**

Table 4: BLEU/chrF2++ performance on selected African languages (eng_Latn ↔ xx) for MMTAfrica, M2M-100*, and NLLB-200 from (Team et al., 2022).

Our kpe_Latn → eng_Latn best BLEU of **30.28** at 60k steps surpasses NLLB-200's lower-bound performances (22.4 BLEU on Wolof), mid-range(24.5 BLEU on Luo, 26.6 BLEU on Youruba, 27.4 BLEU on Luganada) results, though it remains below the model's high performance (48.1 BLEU on Swahili). The eng_Latn → kpe_Latn translation lags slightly behind, reaching approximately **24.46** BLEU with V1 at 30k steps. This result is comparable and higher to NLLB-200's results ($\approx$ 25.8 BLEU in some languages) but lower than its highest observed values (37.9 BLEU in Swahili). Kpelle translations have the potential to reach NLLB-200's highest performance levels with further data augmentation and fine-tuning. However, language-specific nuances, such as Kpelle's orthographic variations, limited standardization, and relatively small corpus size, currently limit model performance.

7 Conclusion

This paper introduced the first publicly available English-Kpelle dataset for machine translation. Our corpus has over 2,000 translation pairs from diverse domains, such as daily conversation, household activities, and religious texts. We demonstrated the dataset's usability by fine-tuning Meta's NLLB model on two corpus versions. Our experiments revealed that data augmentation significantly benefits translation performance, particularly in the Kpelle-to-English direction at higher fine-tuning steps. These findings highlight the importance of domain-specific data expansion in enhancing translation quality for low-resource languages. Moreover, comparative analysis against reported NLLB-200 results highlights the potential for Kpelle NLP systems to achieve competitive performance levels, given continued data curation and iterative fine-tuning.

8 Limitations

1. **Dataset Expansion and Domain Coverage:** While we have made progress in building a representative English-Kpelle dataset, some gaps remain. Future efforts could focus on collecting domain-specific materials from underrepresented categories such as nature, environment, and specialized technical fields to enhance the domain coverage of the dataset further. Adding more varied dialectal data is also essential to capture the linguistic richness of Kpelle more comprehensively.

2. **Broader NLP Applications:** Beyond machine translation, the dataset can be a foundation for other NLP tasks, including speech recognition, language modeling, and sentiment analysis. We intend to explore these avenues, building on the groundwork established here to develop robust and context-aware Kpelle language tools.

3. **Limited Cross Model Evaluation:** Our current evaluation relies exclusively on fine-tuning Meta's NLLB model. While NLLB provides a strong baseline for low-resource translation, this restricts our understanding of how the dataset performs across diverse architectures. As future work, we plan to benchmark an expanded version of the dataset on additional models, including M2M-100 and BLOOMZ, to better assess transferability and generalization. We also intend to incorporate complementary evaluation metrics, such as TER and METEOR, to provide a more comprehensive analysis of model performance.

4. **Lack of Qualitative Error Analysis:** The current scope of this work sought to present the first English-Kpelle dataset and understand Kpelle's potential by benchmarking on a strong baseline like Meta's NLLB model. Given this, we failed to conduct a qualitative error analysis on the translation generated for the held-out test set. In future work, we plan to introduce human evaluation loops where native Kpelle speakers assess translation quality and identify systematic errors. This feedback will guide targeted model improvements and support a more fine-grained understanding of the dataset's linguistic challenges.

8.1 Call to Action

We invite researchers, linguists, and language technology enthusiasts to collaborate in expanding and refining this dataset. By contributing additional Kpelle text resources, validating translations, or developing novel NLP techniques, the research community can help bridge the digital divide faced by low-resource languages. We hope the work presented here will spark renewed interest in Kpelle and other underrepresented Mande languages, ultimately driving innovation and inclusivity in multilingual NLP.

9 Acknowledgments

We acknowledge the contributions of Mr. Aaron D. Y. Pope, Cuttington University, and Mr. Better Jallah, University of Liberia, who served us our Kpelle translation experts, providing Kpelle translation pairs for gathered English sentences and words.

References

Mark Abadi. 2018. I've been to 25 countries and i can tell you there are only 11 phrases you need to get by anywhere.

David Ifeoluwa Adelani, Jesujoba Oluwadara Alabi, Angela Fan, Julia Kreutzer, Xiaoyu Shen, Machel Reid, Dana Ruiter, Dietrich Klakow, Peter Nabende, Ernie Chang, Tajuddeen Gwadabe, Freshia Sackey, Bonaventure F. P. Dossou, Chris Chinenye Emezue, Colin Leong, Michael Beukman, Shamsuddeen Hassan Muhammad, Guyo Dub Jarso, Oreen Yousuf, Andre Niyongabo Rubungo, Gilles Hacheme, Eric Peter Wairagala, Muhammad Umair Nasir, Benjamin Ayoade Ajibade, Tunde Oluwaseyi Ajayi, Yvonne Wambui Gitau, Jade Abbott, Mohamed Ahmed, Millicent Ochieng, Anuoluwapo Aremu, Perez Ogayo, Jonathan Mukiibi, Fatoumata Ouoba Kabore, Godson Koffi Kalipe, Derguene Mbaye, Allahsera Auguste Tapo, Victoire Memdjokam Koagne, Edwin Munkoh-Buabeng, Valencia Wagner, Idris Abdulmumin, Ayodele Awokoya, Happy Buzaaba, Blessing Sibanda, Andiswa Bukula, and Sam Manthalu. 2022. A Few Thousand Translations Go a Long Way! Leveraging Pre-trained Models for African News Translation. *arXiv preprint*. ArXiv:2205.02022.

University of Wisconsin-Madison Students in African 671. 2019. Kpelle- history and brief intro. Lesson on syllabary and alphabet. Publisher: Pressbooks.

Emmanuel Agyei, Xiaoling Zhang, Stephen Bannerman, Ama Bonuah Quaye, Sophyani Banaamwini Yussi, and Victor Kwaku Agbesi. 2024. Low resource twi-english parallel corpus for machine translation in multiple domains (twi-2-eng). *Deleted Journal*, 27.

Adewale Akinfaderin. 2020. HausaMT v1.0: Towards English–Hausa neural machine translation. In *Proceedings of the Fourth Widening Natural Language Processing Workshop*, pages 144–147, Seattle, USA. Association for Computational Linguistics.

D. Asamoah Owusu, A. Korsah, B. Quartey, S. Nwolley Jnr., D. Sampah, D. Adjepon-Yamoah, and L. Omane Boateng. 2022. Github - ashesi-org/financial-inclusion-speech-dataset: A speech dataset to support financial inclusion created by ashesi university and nokwary technologies with funding from lacuna fund. `https://github.com/Ashesi-Org/Financial-Inclusion-Speech-Dataset`. [online] GitHub.

Asmelash Teka Hadgu, Gebrekirstos G. Gebremeskel, and Abel Aregawi. 2022. Machine Translation Benchmark Dataset for Languages in the Horn of Africa. Original-date: 2021-12-05T14:04:38Z.

Sara B. 2018. 13 important phrases to know in your second language.

Gideon George, Olubayo Adekanmbi, and Anthony Soronnadi. 2024. TangaleNLP: Building po tangle to english parallel corpora and machine translation of the tangle (tangale) language. In *5th Workshop on African Natural Language Processing*.

Naman Goyal, Cynthia Gao, Vishrav Chaudhary, Peng-Jen Chen, Guillaume Wenzek, Da Ju, Sanjana Krishnan, Marc'Aurelio Ranzato, Francisco Guzman, and Angela Fan. 2021. The flores-101 evaluation benchmark for low-resource and multilingual machine translation. *Preprint*, arXiv:2106.03193.

B. Heine and M. Reh. 1984. *Grammaticalization and Reanalysis in African Languages*. H. Buske.

Maria Konoshenko. 2024. Quotatives in guinean and liberian kpelle: A study of parallel bible corpora and non-biblical texts. *Acta Linguistica Petropolitana*, 19(3):558–583.

Maria Yu Konoshenko. 2008. Tonal systems in three dialects of the kpelle language. *Mandenkan*.

Taku Kudo and John Richardson. 2018. Sentencepiece: A simple and language independent subword tokenizer and detokenizer for neural text processing. *CoRR*, abs/1808.06226.

Siva Subrahamanyam Varma Kusampudi, Anudeep Chaluvadi, and Radhika Mamidi. 2021. Corpus creation and language identification in low-resource code-mixed Telugu-English text. In *Proceedings of the International Conference on Recent Advances in Natural Language Processing (RANLP 2021)*, pages 744–752, Held Online. INCOMA Ltd.

Theodore E. Leidenfrost and John S. McKay. 2005. *Kpelle-English Dictionary, with a Grammar Sketch and English-Kpelle Finder List*. Language-Literacy-Literature and Bible Translation Center- Lutheran Church in Liberia, Totota.

Lonely Planet Global Limited. 2018. 35 languages covered accessible travel phrasebook.

Jean Maillard, Cynthia Gao, Elahe Kalbassi, Kaushik Ram Sadagopan, Vedanuj Goswami, Philipp Koehn, Angela Fan, and Francisco Guzman. 2023. Small data, big impact: Leveraging minimal data for effective machine translation. In *Proceedings of the 61st Annual Meeting of the Association for Computational Linguistics (Volume 1: Long Papers)*, pages 2740–2756, Toronto, Canada. Association for Computational Linguistics.

Joyce Nakatumba-Nabende, Claire Babirye, Peter Nabende, Jeremy Francis Tusubira, Jonathan Mukiibi, Eric Peter Wairagala, Chodrine Mutebi, Tobius Saul Bateesa, Alvin Nahabwe, Hewitt Tusiime, and Andrew Katumba. 2024. Building text and speech benchmark datasets and models for low-resourced east african languages: Experiences and lessons. *Applied AI Letters*, 5(2):e92.

Wilhelmina Nekoto, Vukosi Marivate, Tshinondiwa Matsila, Timi Fasubaa, Taiwo Fagbohungbe, Solomon Oluwole Akinola, Shamsuddeen Muhammad, Salomon Kabongo Kabenamualu, Salomey Osei, Freshia Sackey, Rubungo Andre Niyongabo, Ricky Macharm, Perez Ogayo, Orevaoghene Ahia, Musie Meressa Berhe, Mofetoluwa Adeyemi, Masabata Mokgesi-Selinga, Lawrence Okegbemi, Laura Martinus, Kolawole Tajudeen, Kevin Degila, Kelechi Ogueji, Kathleen Siminyu, Julia Kreutzer, Jason Webster, Jamiil Toure Ali, Jade Abbott, Iroro Orife, Ignatius Ezeani, Idris Abdulkadir Dangana, Herman Kamper, Hady Elsahar, Goodness Duru, Ghollah Kioko, Murhabazi Espoir, Elan van Biljon, Daniel Whitenack, Christopher Onyefuluchi, Chris Chinenye Emezue, Bonaventure F. P. Dossou, Blessing Sibanda, Blessing Bassey, Ayodele Olabiyi, Arshath Ramkilowan, Alp Öktem, Adewale Akinfaderin, and Abdallah Bashir. 2020. Participatory research for low-resourced machine translation: A case study in African languages. In *Findings of the Association for Computational Linguistics: EMNLP 2020*, pages 2144–2160, Online. Association for Computational Linguistics.

Vinh Van Nguyen, Ha Nguyen, Huong Thanh Le, Thai Phuong Nguyen, Tan Van Bui, Luan Nghia Pham, Anh Tuan Phan, Cong Hoang-Minh Nguyen, Viet Hong Tran, and Anh Huu Tran. 2022. KC4MT: A high-quality corpus for multilingual machine translation. In *Proceedings of the Thirteenth Language Resources and Evaluation Conference*, pages 5494–5502, Marseille, France. European Language Resources Association.

Iroro Orife, Julia Kreutzer, Blessing Sibanda, Daniel Whitenack, Kathleen Siminyu, Laura Martinus, Jamiil Toure Ali, Jade Abbott, Vukosi Marivate, Salomon Kabongo, Musie Meressa, Espoir Murhabazi, Orevaoghene Ahia, Elan van Biljon, Arshath Ramkilowan, Adewale Akinfaderin, Alp Öktem, Wole Akin, Ghollah Kioko, Kevin Degila, Herman Kamper, Bonaventure Dossou, Chris Emezue, Kelechi Ogueji, and Abdallah Bashir. 2020. Masakhane – machine translation for africa. *Preprint*, arXiv:2003.11529.

Denis Paperno. 2014. Sample texts in beng. *Mandenkan*, pages 106–111.

Guilherme Penedo, Hynek Kydlíček, Vinko Sabolčec, Bettina Messmer, Negar Foroutan, Martin Jaggi, Leandro von Werra, and Thomas Wolf. 2024. Fineweb2: A sparkling update with 1000s of languages.

Olivia Christine Perez. 2022. Helpful language phrases to learn before you travel | go overseas.

Matt Post. 2018. A call for clarity in reporting BLEU scores. In *Proceedings of the Third Conference on Machine Translation: Research Papers*, pages 186–191, Belgium, Brussels. Association for Computational Linguistics.

Paul Kanmu Ricks. 2009. *Kwaa Pa Kpelee-Woo Maa Kori(We Have Come to Learn Kpelle)*, first edition. Cuttington University.

NLLB Team, Marta R. Costa-jussà, James Cross, Onur Çelebi, Maha Elbayad, Kenneth Heafield, Kevin Heffernan, Elahe Kalbassi, Janice Lam, Daniel Licht, Jean Maillard, Anna Sun, Skyler Wang, Guillaume Wenzek, Al Youngblood, Bapi Akula, Loic Barrault, Gabriel Mejia Gonzalez, Prangthip Hansanti, John Hoffman, Semarley Jarrett, Kaushik Ram Sadagopan, Dirk Rowe, Shannon Spruit, Chau Tran, Pierre Andrews, Necip Fazil Ayan, Shruti Bhosale, Sergey Edunov, Angela Fan, Cynthia Gao, Vedanuj Goswami, Francisco Guzmán, Philipp Koehn, Alexandre Mourachko, Christophe Ropers, Safiyyah Saleem, Holger Schwenk, and Jeff Wang. 2022. No language left behind: Scaling human-centered machine translation. *Preprint*, arXiv:2207.04672.

Sharon V Thach. 1981. *A Learner Directed Approach to Kpelle. A Handbook on Communication and Culture with Dialogs, Texts, Cultural Notes, Exercises, Drills and Instructions [microform] / Sharon V. Thach and Others*. Distributed by ERIC Clearinghouse. Also contributed by Michigan State Univ., East Lansing. African Studies Center. Accessed: 20 February 2025 via National Library of Australia.

S.V. Thach, D.J. Dwyer, and Michigan State University. African Studies Center. 1981. *Kpelle, a Reference Handbook of Phonetics, Grammar, Lexicon and Learning Procedures*. [Prepared] for the United States Peace Corps at the African Studies Center of Michigan State University.

Valentin Vydrin. 2018. Mande languages.

Valentin Vydrin, Jean-Jacques Meric, Kirill Maslinsky, Andrij Rovenchak, Allashera Auguste Tapo, Sebastien Diarra, Christopher Homan, Marco Zampieri, and Michael Leventhal. 2022. Machine learning dataset development for manding languages. urlhttps://github.com/robotsmali-ai/datasets.

Alexandra Vydrina. 2017. *A corpus-based description of Kakabe, a Western Mande language: prosody in grammar*. Theses, Institut National des Langues et Civilisations Orientales.

Barack Wanjawa, Lilian D. A. Wanzare, Florence Indede, Owen McOnyango, Edward Ombui, and Lawrence Muchemi. 2024. Kencorpus: Kenyan Languages Corpus.

Jackson Weako. 2024. Libtralo kpelle keyboard help. *Keyman.com*.

Contributors Wikivoyage. 2005. West germanic language, spoken in south africa and namibia.

Adina Williams, Nikita Nangia, and Samuel Bowman. 2018. A broad-coverage challenge corpus for sentence understanding through inference. In *Proceedings of the 2018 Conference of the North American Chapter of the Association for Computational Linguistics: Human Language Technologies, Volume 1 (Long Papers)*, pages 1112–1122, New Orleans, Louisiana. Association for Computational Linguistics.

Liam G.-Staff Writer. 2017. English for tourism: Essential uk travel phrases with examples.

Exploring Transliteration-Based Zero-Shot Transfer for Amharic ASR

Hellina Hailu Nigatu
hellina_nigatu@berkeley.edu
UC Berkeley
USA, CA

Hanan Aldarmaki
hanan.aldarmaki@mbzuai.ac.ae
MBZUAI
UAE, Abu Dhabi

Abstract

The performance of Automatic Speech Recognition (ASR) depends on the availability of transcribed speech datasets—often scarce or non-existent for many of the world's languages. This study investigates alternative strategies to bridge the data gap using zero-shot cross-lingual transfer, leveraging transliteration as a method to utilize data from other languages. We experiment with transliteration from various source languages and demonstrate ASR performance in a low-resourced language, Amharic. We find that source data that align with the character distribution of the test data achieve the best performance, regardless of language family. We also experiment with fine-tuning with minimal transcribed data in the target language. Our findings demonstrate that transliteration, particularly when combined with a strategic choice of source languages, is a viable approach for improving ASR in zero-shot and low-resourced settings.

1 Introduction

Automatic Speech Recognition (ASR) is an essential technology used in digital accessibility, video captioning, and virtual assistants. The performance of ASR models depends on the availability of large transcribed speech data for supervised training; yet, such data is lacking for the majority of the world's languages. Attempts to address this data resource gap include data augmentation techniques via self-training and speech synthesis (Bartelds et al., 2023; Kahn et al.), transfer learning by multilingual pre-training alongside high-resourced languages (Radford et al., 2022), or zero-shot transfer (Żelasko et al., 2020; Feng et al., 2021). Zero-shot approaches are particularly appealing in low-resourced settings as they eliminate the requirement of aligned data in the target language.

Languages use different writing scripts; hence, direct zero-shot transfer to the target language writing system may not be possible. Prior works address this challenge by relying on phonetic transcriptions, namely the International Phonetic Alphabet (IPA), as a universal system that can be applied zero-shot to unseen languages (e.g. Feng et al., 2021). While IPA representations are beneficial for building text-free speech recognition systems for unwritten languages, they are not suitable for use cases where users interact directly with the ASR output, such as automatic dictation or video captioning, as most people cannot decode IPA. Another challenge in zero-shot ASR is that languages have different phonetic distributions. In such cross-lingual settings, a deeper investigation of the choice of transfer languages can improve performance (Do et al., 2022; Khare et al., 2021).

We explore how to best utilize transliteration as a mechanism for zero-shot ASR transfer. We focus on a single low-resourced language, Amharic, as a target language, and experiment with Arabic, Xhosa, French, and Spanish as our transfer languages. We selected Arabic and Xhosa based on language family and shared phonetic distribution(§3.1), and French and Spanish as high-resourced but unrelated languages. We automatically transliterate the transcriptions of the transfer languages to our target language script and experiment with zero-shot transfer with wav2vec2 XLS-R and GMM-HMM models (§3.3). While zero-shot speech recognition generally has high error rates (Gao et al., 2021), our approach demonstrates improvements over prior work and gives insights into best practices for cross-lingual transfer.[1]

Contributions Our results demonstrate how transliteration can be used for effective zero-shot transfer even when the source language does not fully cover the phonemes of the target language (§5.2). With only 22 hours of data from transfer

[1]Data, code and models will be aviable at https://github.com/hhnigatu/ASR-via-Translitration

Proceedings of the Sixth Workshop on African Natural Language Processing (AfricaNLP 2025), pages 64–73
July 31, 2025

languages–which is just 4% of the data size used in prior work–zero-shot transfer through transliteration results in performance gains over existing baselines (§5.3). In addition, with 10 minutes up to one hour of target language data, we find that transliteration offers an effective means for data augmentation, resulting in up to ∼30% absolute reduction in CER compared to augmentation with source language scripts (§5.4).

2 Related Work

In this section, we describe prior work on zero-shot ASR, the use of transliteration for ASR transfer, Amharic ASR, and the impact of transfer language selection in cross-lingual ASR.

Zero-Shot ASR: Prior work has explored zero-shot cross-lingual ASR, mainly relying on IPA-based transcriptions and measuring Phoneme Error Rates (PER) (Xu et al., 2022) or Phonetic Token Error Rates (PTER) (Żelasko et al., 2020). Cross-lingual settings involve shared acoustic models trained on single or multiple languages and tested on an unseen language(s). However, performance in this zero-shot setting has high error rates, in the 70-90% range (Gao et al., 2021). Prior work has relied on linguistic knowledge to improve zero-shot ASR under these constraints: Xu et al. (2022) mapped phonemes across transfer and target languages based on edit distance between articulatory features to capture Out-Of-Vocabulary (OOV) phonemes in the target language. Gao et al. (2021) improve zero-shot ASR by adding language embeddings to capture "phylogenetic similarity and phone inventory" of the target language, in addition to masking phonetic tokens that do not exist in the target language. However, IPA-based cross-lingual ASR requires mapping back to the original orthography of the target languages when used in user-facing applications. Additionally, PER and PTER do not reflect the performance at the word level, which is the basic unit for many languages.

Amharic ASR: Prior works have investigated both zero-shot and supervised ASR systems for Amharic. Tachbelie et al. (2014) found that using morphemes in lexical and language modeling led to improved performance gain for Amharic with GMM-HMM models. In multilingual settings, Whisper (Radford et al., 2022) which contains 32 hours of Amharic speech with translated English corpus reports a 140% WER. MMS (Pratap et al., 2023) which contains Amharic speech data achieved 52.9% WER with CTC decoding and 30.1% WER with an external language model for Amharic. Previous work (Feng et al., 2021) included Amharic in a cross-lingual setting and found that, when using a monolingual 3-gram language model for decoding, the PER for Amharic was 74.8% on the Babel (Gales et al., 2014) data. Żelasko et al. (2020) got a similar performance for Amharic in zero-shot cross-lingual transfer with a PTER of 75.2% on the Babel dataset.

Transfer Language Selection: Prior work showed that phonetic similarity of transfer and target languages improves performance (Khare et al., 2021; Tachbelie et al., 2020a). Phonemes that are not shared between transfer and target languages suffer in cross-lingual ASR (Li et al., 2022; Khare et al., 2021). Do et al. (2022) found that languages that had higher Angular Similarity of Phoneme Frequencies (ASPF) scores were better transfer languages for cross-lingual Text-To-Speech (TTS) as compared to selecting a transfer language based on language family. Tachbelie et al. (2020b) used phonetic overlap to select a transfer language for training an acoustic model and test ASR performance on the target language. However, Tachbelie et al. (2020b) used a phonetic dictionary and language model in the target language.

Transliteration: When the transfer language orthography is different from the target language, one potential solution is to use transliteration. By transliterating all transcripts in a multilingual setting to a single writing system, models can benefit from cross-lingual transfer more effectively (Datta et al.). Transliteration has also been used as a data augmentation strategy: Khare et al. (2021) found that further pre-training a model on transliterated English data before finetuning on target language data improved performance for all languages in their experiments except Amharic. To the best of our knowledge, zero-shot transfer with transliteration has not been explored.

3 Transliteration-Based Zero-Shot ASR for Amharic

As described in the previous section, most previous works on zero-shot ASR are based on phonetic transcriptions, which limits the usability of the resulting ASR system. In addition, previous works show relatively poor performance in zero-shot Amharic ASR, even as measured in phoneme error rates, compared to other languages. We utilize transliteration as a means to achieve zero-shot ASR directly in the target language orthography. Additionally, we experiment with four transfer languages, looking at phonetic coverage and approximation through transliteration. We experiment with fine-tuning a XLS-R model for zero-shot ASR. Additionally, we experiment with GMM-HMM models with a Language Model (LM) trained in the target language data. We report performance in terms of Word Error Rate (WER), Character Error Rate (CER), and Phone Token Error Rate (PTER).

3.1 Source & Target Languages

There are several strategies for selecting transfer languages in cross-lingual speech systems, such as using similarity in unigram phonetic distribution for ASR (Khare et al., 2021), or Angular Similarity of Phoneme Frequencies (ASPF) (Do et al., 2022). Mismatch in phonetic inventories between source and target languages presents a challenge for cross-lingual zero-shot ASR, which degrades performance (§2). We experiment with transfer language (1) from the same language family (Arabic) (2) maximum unigram phonetic coverage (Xhosa), and (3) unrelated higher resourced languages (Spanish and French).

Target Language: Amharic is an Afro-Semitic language spoken in Ethiopia. It is written using the Ge'ez script (Adugna, 2023) and has an Abugida[2] writing system, which consists of consonant-vowel sequences written as a unit. Amharic has 38 phonemes (31 consonants and 7 vowels) (Leslau, 2000). It includes glottalized sounds or ejectives[3] that are not found in many higher-resourced languages (Tachbelie et al., 2014).

Source Language: Arabic is an Afro-Semitic language, which is the same language family as Amharic. The Arabic language has only three vowels with long and short versions (ara, 2023) and short vowels are not always marked in writing as they are in the form of diacritics (Contributors to Wikimedia projects, 2023).

Source Language: Xhosa is a Niger-Congo language spoken in Southern Africa. It uses the Latin script and is known for having a heavy load of click sounds[4]. Xhosa has 30 common phonemes with Amharic, the highest coverage from all of our other transfer languages. Specifically, Xhosa covers the 5 ejective phonemes (k', p',t', /t͡s'/,/t͡ʃ'/) in Amharic that are not found in any of the other three transfer languages.

Source Language: Spanish is an Indo-European language that uses the Latin script. It has 5 vowels and fewer than 20 consonants (Hualde, 2005); it only covers 21 out of the 38 phonemes in Amharic. Spanish is considered a high-resourced language based on the availability of data, the number of speakers, and the availability of language technologies.

Source Language: French is an Indo-European language that also uses the Latin script. It is also considered a high-resourced language. French covers 23 of the 38 phonemes of Amharic.

3.2 Transliteration

We transliterate the transfer language transcriptions to the target language script. None of the languages fully cover the phonemes in the target language (see Table 2). There are also phonemes in the source languages that do not exist in Amharic. In both cases, the transliteration process approximates the phonemes to the target language in a way that maximizes coverage; as an example, the Arabic غ /ɣ/ character is transliterated into the Ge'ez 'ግ'/g/. For Xhosa, French, and Spanish we used the `google-transliteration-api`[5] and for Arabic, we built a rule-based transliterator.

Language	Original Word	Lexicon Entry	Pronunciation
Arabic	رَحِمَ /raħima/	ራሒማ rahima	ር ኣ ሕ ኢ ም ኣ r a h i m a
Xhosa	waguqa /waguk!a/	ዋጉቃ /waguk'a/	ው ኣ ግ ኡ ቅ ኣ w a gu k' a
Amharic	ጠቀሜታ t'ək'əmeta	ጠቀሜታ t'ək' əmeta	ጥ ኧ ቅ ኧ ም ኤ ት ኣ t'ək' əmeta

Table 1: **Sample lexicon entries for training (Arabic and Xhosa) and testing (Amharic).** We show both original and IPA transcriptions for readability.

3.3 Models

GMM-HMM are traditional ASR models, in which the distribution of acoustic features at each time step is modeled as Gaussian Mixture Models (GMMs), and the transitions between phones (or sub-phones) are modeled using HMMs. For inference, a word-level grammar transducer G, a pronunciation lexicon L, context dependency graph C, and learned HMM states H are used to create a WFST graph for decoding. To use this architecture

[2]https://www.omniglot.com/writing/ethiopic.htm

[3]`https://wals.info/chapter/7`

[4]https://www.omniglot.com/writing/xhosa.htm

[5]`pypi.org/project/google-transliteration-api`

in zero-shot transfer, we create a training lexicon using the transliterated words from our transfer languages. Each entry in the lexicon consists of a transliterated source language word, along with the sequence of Ge'ez characters which we use in place of phonemes. For the pronunciation lexicon, we split the consonant-vowel sequences of the Ge'ez script so each resulting character represents a single phoneme[6]. Table 1 presents sample lexicon entries. For decoding, we use an Amharic lexicon and language model. Hence, the L and G graphs at test time include words in the target language, which are combined with the H and C graphs trained on the transliterated transfer language data to create our decoding graph. This way, the model is equipped with knowledge of the target language without the need for aligned speech data.

XLS-R-53 is a self-supervised end-to-end neural acoustic model pre-trained on 56k hours of 53 languages (Conneau et al., 2021). The model can be fine-tuned for speech recognition by adding a linear projection layer and optimizing it using the CTC loss (Conneau et al., 2021). For our proposed transliteration-based zero-shot ASR, we use the audio and transliterated transcripts from the source languages to fine-tune the XLS-R model. Hence, the model is trained to directly predict the graphemes of our target language.

4 Experimental Settings

In this section, we describe the datasets we used for our experiments, the training settings for our models and the language combinations we tried.

4.1 Datasets

Table 2 shows the datasets we used for each of our transfer languages. For Arabic, the majority of speech data sets do not contain diacritics (Aldarmaki and Ghannam, 2023), which is a shortcoming that may negatively impact the effectiveness of transliteration[7]. Hence, we used the ClArTTS dataset (Kulkarni et al., 2023), which consists of read speech by a single male speaker in Classical Arabic and is transcribed with complete diacritics. To control for the effect of data size on performance, we downsample all train sets to match the size of the smallest set, which is around 12 hours.

For Amharic, we use two publicly available datasets: FLEURS (Conneau et al., 2022) and ALFFA (Tachbelie et al., 2014). FLEURS is a 102-way parallel read corpus of sentences translated from English Wikipedia with about 12 hours of speech per language. The Amharic test set of FLEURS includes 516 utterances. In all our experiments with the FLEURS test set, we ran both the hypothesis and predictions through Whipser's normalizer[8]. ALFFA contains about 20 hours of Amharic speech from the news domain. The transcriptions for ALFFA have been segmented using Morfessor (Creutz and Lagus, 2005) to obtain morphemes; we manually reconstructed the test set transcriptions, which has 359 utterances, as we are interested in word-level performance. We also used the Babel dataset (Gales et al., 2014), which contains scripted phone conversation data, to compare to prior work. We resampled all data to 16 kHz.

4.2 GMM-HMM Model

Training We trained triphone GMM-HMM models using the Kaldi[9] toolkit on the transliterated Arabic and Xhosa data[10]. As described in §3, we used the transliterated words in the two languages to create the training lexicon. For decoding in Amharic, we created a lexicon using text data in the Amharic language from (Azime and Mohammed, 2021). For experiments using a single source language for training, we used the same training lexicon with transliterated words from both languages to avoid OOV characters in decoding. Hence, phonemes that are not in Arabic but are in Xhosa, for example, would be initialized but not trained.

Monolingual vs Multilingual Transfer For our GMM-HMM experiments, we selected the languages with the highest and lowest phonetic coverage with our target language: Arabic and Xhosa. We trained monolingual models using data from each language and multilingual transfer models with data combined from the two languages.

4.3 wav2vec2 XLS-R

Training As described in §3, we fine-tune XLS-R using transliterated data from our transfer languages. We used the XLS-R 53 model (Conneau

[6]For instance, ራ /ra/ is split into ር /r/ and አ /a/ characters.

[7]We performed preliminary experiments without diacritic marks and obtained poor performance.

[8]`https://pypi.org/project/whisper-normalizer`

[9]`https://kaldi-asr.org`

[10]We experimented with speaker adaptive training (SAT), but found that speaker-independent triphone models perform better. This is in line with prior work (Rouhe et al., 2022) with low-resourced languages using GMM-HMM.

Language	Language Family	No. of Common Phonemes	Source Dataset	Domain	Hours
Arabic	Afro-Semitic	19	ClArTTS (Kulkarni et al., 2023)	Religious	12
French	Indo-European	23	VoxPopuli (Wang et al., 2021)	Parliament	211
Spanish	Indo-European	21	Common Voice 9.0 (Ardila et al., 2020)	Diverse	408*
Xhosa	Niger-Congo	30	NCHLT isiXhosa Speech Corpus (de Vries et al., 2014)	Diverse	56

Table 2: **Comparison of phoneme overlap and datasets used for transfer languages.** Xhosa has the highest number of common phonemes with Amharic, while Spanish has the lowest. The datasets vary by domain and duration, with the Spanish dataset showing the number of validated hours. All datasets were down-sampled to match the size of the Arabic dataset for uniformity.

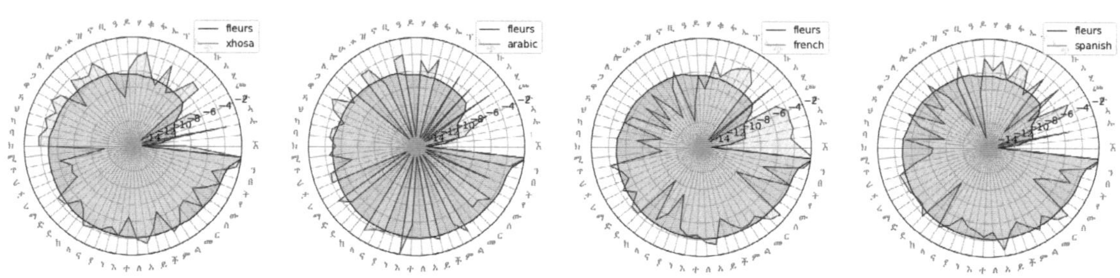

(a) Xhosa (b) Arabic (c) French (d) Spanish

Figure 1: **Log frequency of characters in the train sets (yellow) compared with the FLEURS test set (blue).** Only characters that have a minimum relative frequency of 0.01 in all sets are included in the visualization.

		ALFFA		FLEURS	
		WER	CER	WER	CER
GMM-HMM	Arabic	97.23	84.07	97.93	87.31
	Xhosa	92.94	75.74	93.17	76.24
	Combined	**92.23**	75.12	**93.16**	77.40
XLS-R	Arabic	100.33	86.67	100.10	82.72
	Xhosa	99.91	78.70	99.91	77.88
	Combined	99.85	**73.46**	99.81	**73.72**
XLS-R + LM	Combined	99.14	77.98	99.17	78.57

Table 3: **Zero-shot performance on test sets for Amharic using GMM-HMM and XLS-R models** We report performance on training with Arabic only, Xhosa only, or both (combined) data.

et al., 2021) which has 317M parameters. The model was trained on a total of 56K hours of data from 53 languages, which includes Arabic, French, and Spanish but not Amharic or Xhosa[11]. We experimented with different learning rates [3e-5, 1e-4, 1e-6, 3e-4] and used a linear learning rate scheduler with 500 steps as warmup. We trained for a maximum of 18.5K steps, with early stopping based on the performance on the validation set. All our experiments were conducted on two 24GB Titan RTX GPUs with CUDA Version 11.2.

Monolingual vs Multilingual Transfer We experiment with monolingual transfer where we train on an equal amount of transliterated data from each of the transfer languages separately. This results in four models trained on transliterated transcripts and speech data in each of the transfer languages. Then, we trained on pairs of the four languages resulting in 6 unique pairs for multi-lingual transfer.

Comparison with GMM-HMM Models To compare with the GMM-HMM models, we used data from (Azime and Mohammed, 2021) to train a trigram language model for decoding using the SIRLM[12] toolkit. The shallow fusion with this external LM is used only in comparison with GMM-HMM performance, ensuring our results in other settings are fully zero-shot.

5 Results

In this section, we report the results of the various experimental settings described above.

5.1 Transfer with GMM-HMM

As Table 3 shows, we find that the GMM-HMM models outperform the XLS-R models in zero-shot settings in terms of WER. The XLS-R model, on

[11]The model includes Arabic data from Common Voice. While Xhosa is not included, XLS-R training data include Zulu, a related and mutually intelligible language to Xhosa (Spiegler et al., 2010).

[12]http://www.speech.sri.com/projects/srilm

		ALFFA		FLEURS	
		WER	CER	WER	CER
Monolingual	Arabic	100.33	86.67	100.10	82.72
	Xhosa	**99.91**	78.70	**99.91**	**77.88**
	Spanish	101.67	**75.25**	121.72	81.46
	French	116.95	87.29	140.81	84.09
Multilingual	French-Arabic	98.79	85.57	100.11	87.57
	French-Xhosa	**99.19**	82.10	99.95	87.29
	French-Spanish	99.51	73.14	105.19	74.08
	Spanish-Arabic	99.87	69.70	115.06	72.71
	Spanish- Xhosa	99.63	**69.61**	103.24	**70.39**
	Arabic-Xhosa	99.85	73.46	**99.81**	73.72

Table 4: **Performance of models trained on monolingual and multilingual settings.** Models trained on Spanish and Xhosa data significantly outperform the models trained on Arabic and French. Pairing the least-performing transfer languages with the better-performing ones improves performance.

Training Set	ALFFA	FLEURS
Arabic	7.65%	1.78%
French	11.23%	4.02%
Spanish	2.05%	0.08%
Xhosa	3.12%	0.03%

Table 5: **Percentage of characters that are not found in the test sets but are found in the training set of the transliterated data.** Each percentage quantifies how much percent of the total number of characters in the total training set the unique characters account for.

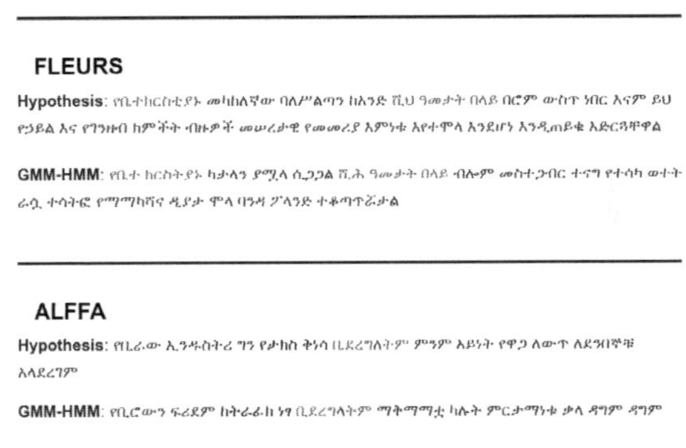

Figure 2: **Samples showing the predictions of the GMM-HMM model trained on Arabic-Xhosa data.** While the full sentences of the predictions do not make sense, highlighted in green are words and characters that the model correctly predicted.

the other hand, achieved similar or slightly better CER, but much higher WER, as the model was unable to predict correct words in the target language. In the GMM-HMM set-up, we enforce the language structure during test time through an Amharic lexicon and an Amharic LM. Adding an external LM for decoding with the XLS-R model improved the WER but only slightly, which shows the advantage of the HMM model where target language structure can be incorporated at decoding time. We see these patterns in examples for both test sets using the Arabic-Xhosa combined model in Figure 2. While the full sentences do not make sense, we see highlighted in green full words that were captured by the GMM-HMM model. In the ALFFA example in Figure 2, we see the first word highlighted in red having a similar sound with the word in the hypothesis but a completely unrelated meaning: the word in the hypothesis says "ye biraw" meaning "The beer" while the word in the prediction says "ye birow" meaning "The bureau." Table 3 also presents results using Arabic-only and Xhosa-only data for training; we find that the Xhosa-only models outperform the Arabic-only models. This is likely due to the higher coverage of Amharic phonemes in Xhosa compared to Arabic. The best performance is achieved when both languages are combined.

5.2 Transfer with XLS-R

Monolingual Transfer We find that the monolingual XLS-R model trained on Xhosa outperforms all the other models for both dataset, except for CER on the ALFFA dataset where the Spanish-trained model outperforms (see Table 4). The French model is the least-performing model in both settings across both metrics. Interestingly, French performs worse than Spanish despite having a higher overlap with Amharic phonemes. We hypothesize the good performance of the Xhosa model can be explained by the coverage of 30 out of 38 of the Amharic phonemes by Xhosa. Additionally, since we did soft approximation through transliteration (§3.2), we hypothesize that even if the phoneme is not present in the language, the transliteration might still approximate the character

Method	LM	No. Languages	Train Data Hours	PER/PTER
Prior Work				
Feng et al. (2021) Cross Mono-tg	3-gram	12	554.40	74.80
Żelasko et al. (2020) Cross	None	12	554.40	75.20
Ours				
Xhosa-Arabic	None	2	22	76.32
Spanish-Xhosa	None	2	22	**73.54**

Table 6: **Comparison of our top two best performing models with prior work reported performance.** With just 4% of training data size and two transfer languages, our best performing model outperforms the reported PTER in zero-shot ASR for Amharic.

representing the phoneme.

To understand the performance gap further, we looked at the distribution of the characters in the test sets and the transliterated training data of each of the languages. Figure 1 shows radar plots of each distribution in terms of log frequencies (the log is used to enable interpretable visualization of the power distribution of characters). Due to the large number of composite characters in the Amharic script, we only show the characters that have a minimum relative normalized frequency of 0.01 in each set. The plots show a clear pattern: both Xhosa and Spanish train sets have better coverage of the frequent characters in the test set. Arabic is missing many of the frequent characters, and French includes a high relative frequency of characters that are infrequent in the test set. As Table 5 shows, both French and Arabic have characters that are not found in the test set that account for a higher percentage of their total number of characters. For example, characters that are in the training set of transliterated French but not in the ALFFA test set account for 11.23% of the total. On the other hand, for both Spanish and Xhosa training sets, the characters that exist in the training set but do not exist in the test set account for less than 4% of the total. This analysis suggests that character distribution plays a larger role than phoneme coverage in zero-shot performance.

Multilingual Transfer In testing with models trained by combining two languages, we find that the combination of Spanish and Xhosa gives the best performance, which is expected since the two languages had the top two best performances in the single-language setting. The combination of the least-performing models resulted in an improvement over performance in either of the languages independently for ALFFA (86.67% with Arabic only and 87.29% in French only to 85.57% in French-Arabic combined) However, for FLEURS, the performance degraded, with a 3% absolute increase of CER from the French-only model and 5% increase in the CER from the Arabic-only model. We also find that pairing the least performing transfer languages with the better performing languages improves performance on the single-language models: pairing Arabic and Xhosa data reduced CER from the Arabic-only model by a 10% absolute drop for both test sets.

5.3 Comparison with Baselines

We compare with two prior works that experiment with Amharic in zero-shot: Feng et al. (2021) trained hybrid DNN-HMM models with training data from 12 phonetically diverse languages and tested cross-lingually on Amharic. Żelasko et al. (2020) trained an end-to-end ASR model with CTC loss on 12 languages and tested on Amharic. Both works train models with IPA transcriptions and report Phone Error Rate (PER) and Phone Token Error Rate (PTER) respectively on the Babel dataset. In Table 6, we show the reported results for our two best models on Babel and compare them to the baselines. Since our models are trained to predict graphemes of the target language, we use LanguageNet grapheme-to-phone (g2p)[13] converter, which is also used in (Żelasko et al., 2020), to covert our model predictions and Babel hypothesis to IPA. We then calculate PTER on the IPA transcriptions. With just 4% of training data size compared to prior work, our best-performing model trained with only two languages outperforms the baselines.

5.4 Few-Shot Fine-Tuning

As noted in Section 2, performance in zero-shot cross-lingual ASR typically has high error rates, even at the phoneme level. Hence, we investigate the performance of further fine-tuning of the ASR models in low-resource settings, where we only use 10 minutes to 1 hour of target language data. In this setting, the transliterated data serve as a

[13]https://github.com/uiuc-sst/g2ps

		WER/CER without LM				WER/CER with LM			
		ALFFA		FLEURS		ALFFA		FLEURS	
10 minutes	Amharic Only	**101.08**	79.77	**101.16**	78.32	99.32	84.74	98.91	81.74
	Source script + Amharic	101.94	78.38	104.06	76.91	99.12	81.32	99.12	78.52
	Transliterated + Amharic	102.87	**71.42**	102.98	**70.72**	**98.80**	**66.99**	**97.72**	**70.21**
20 minutes	Amharic Only	100.52	80.38	101.35	80.37	99.57	83.02	99.44	80.67
	Source script + Amharic	101.61	69.54	100.72	68.17	99.02	71.19	97.47	68.13
	Transliterated + Amharic	**95.32**	**42.22**	**92.41**	**40.34**	**83.41**	**38.10**	**80.24**	**36.42**
30 minutes	Amharic Only	101.29	74.68	100.55	73.96	98.89	79.23	98.64	78.08
	Source script + Amharic	99.54	51.86	98.84	49.37	91.37	50.16	89.09	46.73
	Transliterated + Amharic	**91.46**	**36.75**	**88.25**	**33.88**	**76.00**	**32.04**	**70.01**	**28.46**
1 hour	Amharic Only	83.55	30.34	**74.77**	**26.29**	**64.30**	26.76	**55.95**	23.19
	Source script + Amharic	99.54	51.01	99.41	47.48	77.10	35.31	71.85	30.90
	Transliterated + Amharic	**82.57**	**30.19**	75.51	26.54	66.67	**25.77**	57.91	**21.47**

Table 7: **Performance of XLS-R further fine-tuned with small amounts of Amharic data, from 10 minutes to 1 hour.** We compared direct fine-tuning on Amharic data, vs. fine-tuning first with transfer language data, original script, or transliterated script.

form of data augmentation, where the model is first fine-tuned on the source languages, then further optimized on the target language. For these experiments, we used a linear learning rate scheduler with 100 steps as warmup and we trained models with smaller steps depending on data size to avoid overfitting. For comparison, we (1) directly fine-tune XLS-R on the target Amharic data and (2) fine-tune XLS-R with transfer language data without transliteration then further fine-tune on Amharic data. The results are shown in Table 7.

We note how further fine-tuning with small amounts of supervised data in the target language results in significant performance improvements. With 20 minutes or more, we observe large reductions in error rates. We observe that the model trained on the transliterated data outperforms both the model trained on original source transcripts (up to 30% absolute reduction in CER) as well as the model directly fine-tuned on Amharic data alone. The performance gap between the three setups is most pronounced as the data is smaller, indicating the benefits of using transliteration with carefully selected transfer languages for low-resource ASR. Compared to zero-shot, we observe roughly 40% and 10% absolute reduction in CER and WER, respectively with 30 minutes of Amharic data.

6 Discussion

Our experiments show how to use transliteration for zero-shot transfer in low-resourced settings. With just a fraction of the training data size compared to prior work, our best-performing model outperforms the reported performance on Amharic in a zero-shot setting. Additionally, by training on transliterated data, we predict directly in the target language orthography.

Error rates in zero-shot ASR are generally high for direct use of the systems (Gao et al., 2021). However, zero-shot approaches give us insights to how to best select transfer languages when we have limited data available. In line with prior work, we find that languages that have high unigram phonetic coverage with the target language are better transfer languages. Further, we find that through soft approximation via transliteration, even languages that do not have high phonetic coverage can be good transfer languages. Our analysis reveals that transfer languages with the least post-transliteration rate of Out-Of-Vocabulary (OOV) characters in the target test set perform best as transfer languages, regardless of their language family or degree of inherent phonetic coverage.

In zero-shot settings, GMM-HMM models result in significantly lower WER, which is ascribed to the fact that the models incorporate the target language lexicon in decoding, unlike the end-to-end models that lack such linguistic knowledge without supervised training. However, CER is much lower using the XLS-R model. In low-resource settings, with 10 minutes to 1 hour of training data in the target language, transliteration results in improved performance compared to direct fine-tuning on the target language or using the transfer languages without transliteration.

7 Conclusion

In this study, we explored the use of transliteration for zero-shot and low-resource cross-lingual ASR transfer. We find that, with careful selection of source languages, using ~22 hours of source data, we can build zero-shot ASR systems that can transcribe words directly in the target language orthography. With small amounts of transcribed data in the target language, large reductions in error rates can be achieved through using transliteration for data augmentation.

Limitations

While our results show promising results for zero-shot transfer for Amharic, there are several avenues for improvement. First, the Arabic and French data are domain-limited. The Arabic data is further constrained by having a single speaker. As discussed in Section 4.1, we could not find multi-speaker diverse domain data with diacritic markers for Arabic. While this is a limitation, it is also reflective of the real state of building language technologies for low-resourced languages. Our current work explores how far we can go with data and tools that are currently available to us in a low-resourced setting. For future work, we will explore using automated methods for adding diacritic markers to existing Arabic datasets. Additionally, we were limited to trying multilingual transfers with just two transfer languages due to compute resource constraints. However, our results still demonstrate that our transliteration-based approach outperforms the previously reported performance for zero-shot ASR for Amharic. Future work can explore adding more languages and trying more combinations of languages in the multi-lingual setting. Additionally, our work focused on just one target language; future work could explore our approach on more languages.

References

2023. The Arabic Alphabet: Vowels. [Online; accessed 14. Dec. 2023].

Gabe Adugna. 2023. Research: Language Learning - Amharic: Home. [Online; accessed 14. Dec. 2023].

Hanan Aldarmaki and Ahmad Ghannam. 2023. Diacritic Recognition Performance in Arabic ASR. In *Proc. INTERSPEECH 2023*, pages 361–365.

Rosana Ardila, Megan Branson, Kelly Davis, Michael Kohler, Josh Meyer, Michael Henretty, Reuben Morais, Lindsay Saunders, Francis Tyers, and Gregor Weber. 2020. Common voice: A massively-multilingual speech corpus. In *Proceedings of the Twelfth Language Resources and Evaluation Conference*, pages 4218–4222, Marseille, France. European Language Resources Association.

Israel Abebe Azime and Nebil Mohammed. 2021. An amharic news text classification dataset. In *AfricaNLP*.

Martijn Bartelds, Nay San, Bradley McDonnell, Dan Jurafsky, and Martijn Wieling. 2023. Making More of Little Data: Improving Low-Resource Automatic Speech Recognition Using Data Augmentation. *ACL Anthology*, pages 715–729.

Alexis Conneau, Alexei Baevski, Ronan Collobert, Abdelrahman Mohamed, and Michael Auli. 2021. Unsupervised Cross-Lingual Representation Learning for Speech Recognition.

Alexis Conneau, Min Ma, Simran Khanuja, Yu Zhang, Vera Axelrod, Siddharth Dalmia, Jason Riesa, Clara Rivera, and Ankur Bapna. 2022. FLEURS: Few-shot Learning Evaluation of Universal Representations of Speech. *arXiv*.

Contributors to Wikimedia projects. 2023. Arabic diacritics - Wikipedia. [Online; accessed 14. Dec. 2023].

Mathias Creutz and K. Lagus. 2005. Unsupervised morpheme segmentation and morphology induction from text corpora using morfessor 1.0.

Arindrima Datta, Bhuvana Ramabhadran, Jesse Emond, Anjuli Kannan, and Brian Roark. Language-Agnostic Multilingual Modeling. In *ICASSP 2020 - 2020 IEEE International Conference on Acoustics, Speech and Signal Processing (ICASSP)*, pages 04–08. IEEE.

Nic J. de Vries, Marelie H. Davel, Jaco Badenhorst, Willem D. Basson, Febe de Wet, Etienne Barnard, and Alta de Waal. 2014. A smartphone-based ASR data collection tool for under-resourced languages. *Speech Communication*, 56:119–131.

Phat Do, Matt Coler, Jelske Dijkstra, and Esther Klabbers. 2022. Text-to-Speech for Under-Resourced Languages: Phoneme Mapping and Source Language Selection in Transfer Learning. *ACL Anthology*, pages 16–22.

Siyuan Feng, Piotr ˙Zelasko, Laureano Moro-Vel´azquez, Ali Abavisani, Mark Hasegawa-Johnson, Odette Scharenborg, and Najim Dehak. 2021. How Phonotactics Affect Multilingual and Zero-Shot ASR Performance.

M. Gales, K. Knill, A. Ragni, and S. Rath. 2014. Speech recognition and keyword spotting for low-resource languages: Babel project research at CUED. *Workshop on Spoken Language Technologies for Under-resourced Languages*.

Heting Gao, Junrui Ni, Yang Zhang, Kaizhi Qian, Shiyu Chang, and Mark Hasegawa-Johnson. 2021. Zero-Shot Cross-Lingual Phonetic Recognition with External Language Embedding.

José Ignacio Hualde. 2005. The sounds of spanish.

Jacob Kahn, Ann Lee, and Awni Hannun. Self-Training for End-to-End Speech Recognition. In *ICASSP 2020 - 2020 IEEE International Conference on Acoustics, Speech and Signal Processing (ICASSP)*, pages 04–08. IEEE.

Shreya Khare, Ashish R. Mittal, Anuj Diwan, Sunita Sarawagi, P. Jyothi, and Samarth Bharadwaj. 2021. Low Resource ASR: The Surprising Effectiveness of High Resource Transliteration. *Interspeech*.

Ajinkya Kulkarni, Atharva Kulkarni, Sara Abedalmon'em Mohammad Shatnawi, and Hanan Aldarmaki. 2023. ClArTTS: An Open-Source Classical Arabic Text-to-Speech Corpus. In *Proc. INTERSPEECH 2023*, pages 5511–5515.

Wolf Leslau. 2000. *Introductory grammar of Amharic*, volume 21. Otto Harrassowitz Verlag.

Xinjian Li, Florian Metze, David R. Mortensen, Alan W. Black, and Shinji Watanabe. 2022. ASR2K: Speech Recognition for Around 2000 Languages without Audio.

Vineel Pratap, Andros Tjandra, Bowen Shi, Paden Tomasello, Arun Babu, Sayani Kundu, Ali Elkahky, Zhaoheng Ni, Apoorv Vyas, Maryam Fazel-Zarandi, Alexei Baevski, Yossi Adi, Xiaohui Zhang, Wei-Ning Hsu, Alexis Conneau, and Michael Auli. 2023. Scaling Speech Technology to 1,000+ Languages. *arXiv*.

Alec Radford, Jong Wook Kim, Tao Xu, Greg Brockman, Christine McLeavey, and Ilya Sutskever. 2022. Robust Speech Recognition via Large-Scale Weak Supervision. *arXiv*.

Aku Rouhe, Anja Virkkunen, Juho Leinonen, and Mikko Kurimo. 2022. Low Resource Comparison of Attention-based and Hybrid ASR Exploiting wav2vec 2.0. In *Proc. Interspeech 2022*, pages 3543–3547.

Sebastian Spiegler, Andrew van der Spuy, and Peter A. Flach. 2010. Ukwabelana - An open-source morphological Zulu corpus. *ACL Anthology*, pages 1020–1028.

Martha Yifiru Tachbelie, Solomon Teferra Abate, and Laurent Besacier. 2014. Using different acoustic, lexical and language modeling units for ASR of an under-resourced language – Amharic. *Speech Communication*, 56:181–194.

Martha Yifiru Tachbelie, Solomon Teferra Abate, and Tanja Schultz. 2020a. Analysis of GlobalPhone and Ethiopian languages speech corpora for multilingual ASR. In *Proceedings of the Twelfth Language Resources and Evaluation Conference*, pages 4152–4156, Marseille, France. European Language Resources Association.

Martha Yifiru Tachbelie, Solomon Teferra Abate, and Tanja Schultz. 2020b. DNN-based multilingual automatic speech recognition for Wolaytta using Oromo speech. In *Proceedings of the 1st Joint Workshop on Spoken Language Technologies for Under-resourced languages (SLTU) and Collaboration and Computing for Under-Resourced Languages (CCURL)*, pages 265–270, Marseille, France. European Language Resources association.

Changhan Wang, Morgane Riviere, Ann Lee, Anne Wu, Chaitanya Talnikar, Daniel Haziza, Mary Williamson, Juan Pino, and Emmanuel Dupoux. 2021. VoxPopuli: A large-scale multilingual speech corpus for representation learning, semi-supervised learning and interpretation. In *Proceedings of the 59th Annual Meeting of the Association for Computational Linguistics and the 11th International Joint Conference on Natural Language Processing (Volume 1: Long Papers)*, pages 993–1003, Online. Association for Computational Linguistics.

Qiantong Xu, Alexei Baevski, and Michael Auli. 2022. Simple and Effective Zero-shot Cross-lingual Phoneme Recognition.

Piotr Żelasko, Laureano Moro-Velázquez, Mark Hasegawa-Johnson, Odette Scharenborg, and Najim Dehak. 2020. That Sounds Familiar: An Analysis of Phonetic Representations Transfer Across Languages.

Fine-tuning Whisper Tiny for Swahili ASR: Challenges and Recommendations for Low-Resource Speech Recognition

Avinash Kumar Sharma, Manas R Pandya, Arpit Shukla
{zda23m011, zda23b019, zda23m007}@iitmz.ac.in
Indian Institute of Technology Madras, Zanzibar Campus

Abstract

Automatic Speech Recognition (ASR) technologies have seen significant advancements, yet many widely spoken languages remain underrepresented. This paper explores the fine-tuning of OpenAI's Whisper Tiny model (39M parameters) for Swahili, a lingua franca for over 100 million people across East Africa. Using a dataset of 5,520 Swahili audio samples, we analyze the model's performance, error patterns, and limitations after fine-tuning. Our results demonstrate the potential of fine-tuning for improving transcription accuracy, while also highlighting persistent challenges such as phonetic misinterpretations, named entity recognition failures, and difficulties with morphologically complex words. We provide recommendations for improving Swahili ASR, including scaling to larger model variants, architectural adaptations for agglutinative languages, and data enhancement strategies. This work contributes to the growing body of research on adapting pre-trained multilingual ASR systems to low-resource languages, emphasizing the need for approaches that account for the unique linguistic features of Bantu languages.

1 Introduction

Automatic Speech Recognition (ASR) has revolutionized human-computer interaction, but many widely spoken languages, including Swahili, remain underrepresented in ASR technology. Swahili (Kiswahili) is a lingua franca for over 100 million people across East Africa, yet its presence in modern speech recognition systems is minimal compared to high-resource languages like English, Mandarin, and Spanish.

This study explores the fine-tuning of OpenAI's Whisper Tiny model - a lightweight variant of the Whisper ASR system - for Swahili speech recognition. Whisper, trained on an extensive 680k hour multilingual dataset, shows promise across multiple languages but requires targeted adaptation for low-resource languages like Swahili to perform effectively. We investigate the impact of fine-tuning on model performance, focusing on transcription accuracy, error patterns, and the challenges of adapting compact ASR models for low-resource languages.

To guide this research, we aim to answer the following key questions:
How does fine-tuning the Whisper Tiny model (39M parameters) improve its performance for Swahili speech recognition? What are the main transcription errors observed in the fine-tuned model, and how can they be addressed? What are the challenges of using compact ASR models for low-resource languages, and how can they be mitigated through training strategies and architectural adaptations?

By addressing these questions, this work contributes to the ongoing effort to improve ASR for languages with limited digital resources, paving the way for more inclusive speech technologies. Our findings highlight the importance of fine-tuning for low-resource languages and provide actionable recommendations for future research and development in Swahili ASR.

2 Background and Related Work

2.1 Automatic Speech Recognition for Low-Resource Languages

Developing ASR systems for low-resource languages like Swahili comes with significant challenges, primarily due to the scarcity of transcribed speech data. Most state-of-the-art ASR models rely on large-scale paired audio-text datasets, which are often unavailable for such languages. Recent advances in transfer learning have enabled the adaptation of models pre-trained on high-resource languages, allowing ASR systems to perform well even with limited native-language data (Besacier et al., 2014). Fine-tuning these models is critical

Proceedings of the Sixth Workshop on African Natural Language Processing (AfricaNLP 2025), pages 74–81

to achieving optimal performance, as it allows the system to adapt to the unique phonetic and linguistic characteristics of the target language. Our study explores this process by fine-tuning the Whisper Tiny model for Swahili, evaluating its performance and identifying areas for improvement.

2.2 The Whisper ASR System

OpenAI's Whisper model represents a major step forward in multilingual ASR Radford et al. (2023). Trained on a diverse dataset of 680,000 hours of labeled audio, it offers robust transcription capabilities across multiple languages. The Whisper family consists of models of varying sizes, ranging from Tiny (39M parameters) to Large (1.5B parameters), each balancing computational efficiency and transcription accuracy. Researchers have successfully fine-tuned Whisper for several low-resource languages, such as Amharic (Abdou Mohamed et al., 2024), Yoruba (Ahia et al., 2024), and Nepali (Ghimire et al., 2024). Despite these advancements, comprehensive studies on Whisper's adaptation for Swahili remain limited. Our work addresses this gap by evaluating the impact of fine-tuning on Swahili ASR performance, providing insights into the challenges and opportunities of adapting compact ASR models for low-resource languages.

While ASR for major languages has seen substantial advances, Swahili ASR development remains limited despite its widespread use. Recent efforts include work by Tunde-Onadele and Chao (2022) who developed initial speech recognition models for Swahili using traditional Hidden Markov Model approaches. In the neural era, several pre-trained models have been adapted for Swahili, including wav2vec 2.0 variants (Akash, 2023; SpeechBrain Team, 2022) which leverage self-supervised learning on unlabeled audio. These efforts, however, often lack detailed documentation of the fine-tuning process and error analysis specific to Swahili's linguistic characteristics. Our work complements these efforts by providing a systematic analysis of fine-tuning a compact transformer-based model and documenting language-specific challenges.

3 Methodology

3.1 Dataset Characteristics

This study utilized a comprehensive Swahili speech dataset comprising 5,520 audio samples with corresponding transcriptions.

The dataset was sourced from KenSpeech (Awino et al., 2022), and from an initial pool of approximately 6,300 samples. The audio files were scraped in batches with appropriate processing delays to ensure data integrity. Each audio file was paired with its corresponding transcript, creating a parallel corpus suitable for ASR model training.
We filtered transcripts using automatic language detection via the `langdetect` library. Transcripts predominantly identified as Swahili were retained, while those detected as primarily English were excluded. This filtering process ensured the linguistic purity necessary for training a robust Swahili ASR system.

3.1.1 Length Distributions

The dataset's transcript lengths follow a roughly normal distribution, with a slight negative skew. The majority of samples (69.7%) contain between 21-40 words, indicating a prevalence of medium-length utterances suitable for ASR training. Figure 1 shows the distribution of transcript lengths by category.

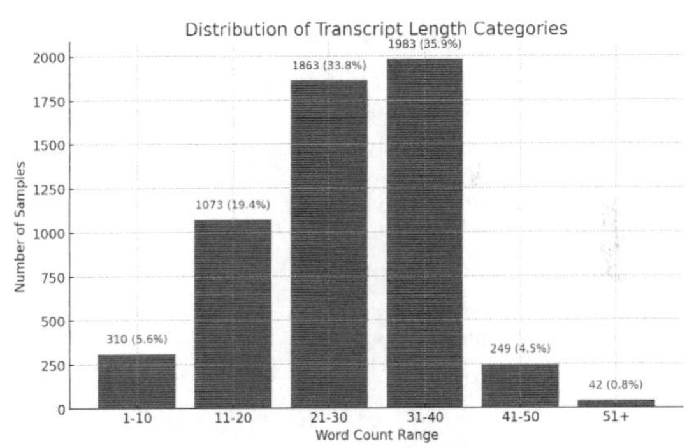

Figure 1: Distribution of Transcript Length Categories showing the number of samples in each word count range. The 21-30 and 31-40 word ranges contain the majority of samples (69.7%).

The detailed frequency distribution of word counts is illustrated in Figure 2, showing the mean and median values.

The tokenized transcripts exhibit a similar distribution pattern but with higher values, as illustrated in Figure 3. This reflects the nature of subword tokenization, where individual words are often split into multiple tokens, particularly in morphologically rich languages like Swahili.

Through the statistical analysis, we find that the Swahili transcriptions averaged 27.23 words and 71.5 tokens, with maximums of 67 words and 170 tokens; medians were slightly higher than means.

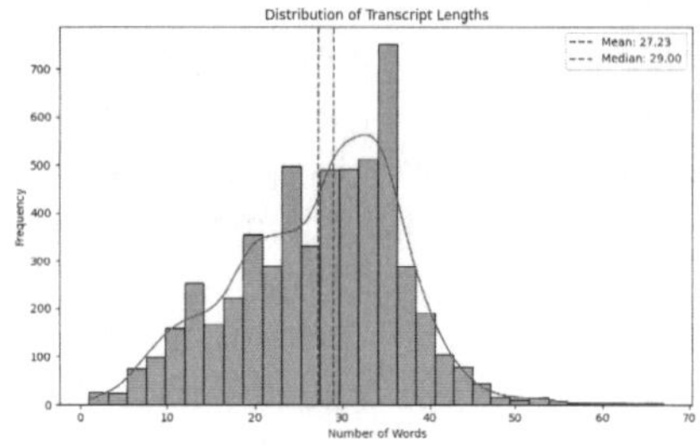

Figure 2: Histogram of Transcript Lengths showing the frequency distribution of word counts. The mean (27.23 words) and median (29.00 words) are indicated by vertical dashed lines.

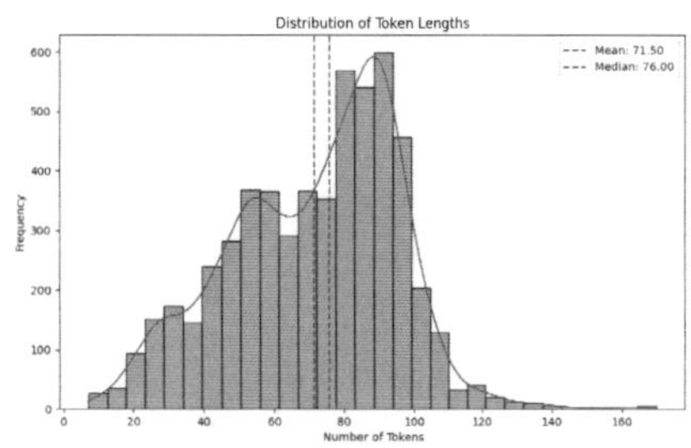

Figure 3: Distribution of Token Lengths across the dataset. The mean (71.50 tokens) and median (76.00 tokens) are indicated by vertical dashed lines, showing the increased granularity when words are tokenized.

3.1.2 Data Partitioning

To facilitate model training and evaluation, the dataset was partitioned using a standard 80/20 split, resulting in a Training set of 4,416 samples (80%), and a Validation set of 1,104 samples (20%).

This partitioning strategy ensures sufficient data for model training while retaining an adequate portion for validation to assess generalization performance. The stratified splitting approach maintained similar transcript length distributions across both sets to prevent evaluation bias.

3.2 Model Architecture[1]

This study employed OpenAI's Whisper Tiny model as the foundation for Swahili ASR development. The Whisper family of models represents a state-of-the-art approach to multilingual speech recognition, with variants ranging from Tiny (39M parameters) to Large (1.5B parameters).

[1]The configuration is in the Appendix A

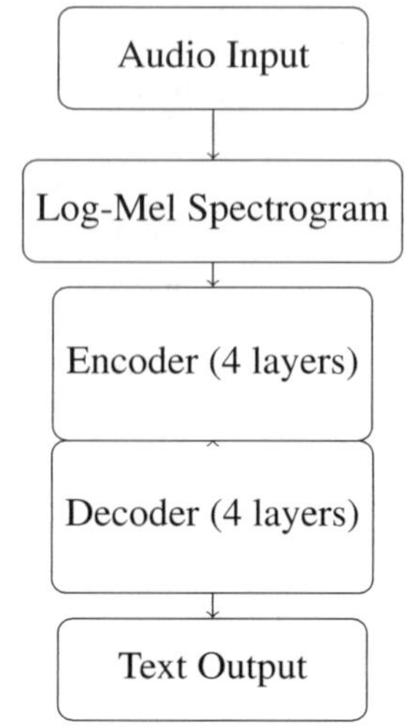

Figure 4: Simplified diagram of the Whisper model architecture, showing the processing pipeline from audio input to text output through the encoder-decoder transformer structure.

3.2.1 Whisper Tiny Specifications

The Whisper Tiny model (OpenAI, 2023), selected for its computational efficiency while maintaining reasonable performance, features the architectural specifications shown in Table 1.

Component	Specification
Model type	Encoder-decoder transformer
Parameter count	39 million
Encoder layers	4
Decoder layers	4
Model dimension	384
Attention heads	6
Audio feature extractor	CNN
Maximum context length	3,000 frames ($\approx$ 30s)

Table 1: Architectural Specifications of Whisper Tiny Model

Compared to larger Whisper variants, the Tiny model offers substantially reduced computational requirements while retaining the core architectural elements that enable effective speech recognition. Figure 4 illustrates the overall architectural design of the Whisper model.

3.2.2 Audio Processing Pipeline

The Whisper architecture processes audio through a multi-stage pipeline designed to efficiently transform raw audio into transcribed text:

Audio Preprocessing: Raw audio is resampled to 16 kHz and converted into 80-channel log-Mel spectrograms with 25ms windows and 10ms stride. **Encoder Processing**: The encoder, consisting of 4 transformer layers with 4 attention heads each, processes these spectrograms to create contextual audio representations. This stage captures the acoustic and phonetic features of the input speech. **Decoder Generation**: The decoder, also comprising 4 transformer layers, generates text tokens autoregressively based on the encoded representations. The decoder incorporates cross-attention mechanisms that attend to the encoder outputs, enabling the model to align speech features with textual elements. **Token Prediction**: At each decoding step, the model predicts the next token from a multilingual vocabulary of approximately 50,000 tokens, which includes subword units for Swahili and other languages.

3.2.3 Adaptation for Swahili

While the base Whisper Tiny model includes some support for Swahili through its multilingual pretraining, specific adaptations were implemented to enhance its performance:

Language-Specific Initialization: The decoder was initialized with Swahili language ID tokens to bias generation toward Swahili output.

Task Configuration: The model was configured specifically for transcription tasks rather than translation, focusing its capabilities on accurate within-language processing.

4 Results

4.1 Training Progress

The model was trained for both 5 and 100 epochs, with evaluation metrics captured at intermediate and final stages. The 5-epoch training proceeded without significant technical issues, though some audio processing challenges were observed. The extended 100-epoch training demonstrated substantial improvements, with validation loss decreasing steadily and WER improving from 82.95% to 30.62%, highlighting the benefits of extended fine-tuning for low-resource languages.

Compared to the small Whisper model trained by Pplantiga on Hugging Face (Plantinga, 2025), which achieved a WER of 27.62%, our tiny model, with a WER of 30.62%, offers a better trade-off by significantly reducing complexity, even though the performance is slightly lower.

4.2 Training and Validation Dynamics

Table 2 summarizes the Training and Validation metrics for both 5-epoch and 100-epoch training regimes.

Metric	5 Epochs	100 Epochs
Training Loss	0.8426	0.0001
Validation Loss	1.2317	1.5977
WER	82.95%	30.62%

Table 2: Metrics for 5-Epoch and 100-Epoch Training

The 100-epoch model achieved a WER of 30.62%, representing a 63.1% improvement over the 5-epoch model. This reduction in WER underscores the importance of extended training for low-resource languages, though challenges remain in achieving practical usability (typically <20% WER).

4.3 Qualitative Error Analysis

A detailed examination of model outputs revealed several recurring error patterns, with notable improvements in the 100-epoch model.

4.3.1 Phonetic Approximations

The model frequently produced phonetically plausible but incorrect transcriptions, as shown in Table 3. While the 100-epoch model reduced errors like double vowel omissions and segmentation issues, challenges persisted.

Reference	5-Epoch Prediction	100-Epoch Prediction
muunganisho wa maarifa asilia na sayansi ya kisasa utaleta jitihada ya ubindamu kuleta amani na mazingira yetu ushauri wangu	m**u**nganisho wa maarifa asilia na sayansi **za** **g**isasa utal**i**ta jiti**a**da ya ubin**a** **damu** kuleta amani na mazin**gi** **rahetu** ushauri wangu	muunganisho wa maarifa asilia na sayansi ya kisasa utaleta jitihada ya ubindamu kuleta amani na mazingira yetu ushauri wangu

Table 3: Example of Phonetic Approximation Errors

4.3.2 Named Entity Recognition

The model exhibited difficulty with proper nouns, as demonstrated in Table 4. The 100-epoch model showed slight improvements but still struggled with non-Swahili names.

Reference	5-Epoch Prediction	100-Epoch Prediction
moto shuleni bweni la shule ya st brigid's kiminini liliteketea jana usiku hakuna mwanafunzi aliyejeruhiwa lakini uchunguzi umeaanza	moto **shule ya ni** bweni la shule ya **sandbridge it kimi mini** ililitaketea jana usiku hakuna mwanafunzi aliye jeruhiwa **na kini** uchunguzi ume**han za**	moto shuleni bweni la shule ya st brigid's kiminini liliteketea jana usiku hakuna mwanafunzi aliyejeruhiwa lakini uchunguzi umeaanza

Table 4: Example of Named Entity Recognition Errors

4.3.3 Repetitive Pattern Generation

In several instances, the model produced repetitive, non-informative output, particularly when encountering challenging audio, as shown in Table 5. The 100-epoch model reduced the frequency of such errors but did not eliminate them entirely.

Reference	5-Epoch Prediction	100-Epoch Prediction
murang'a viongozi wa kidini wazidiwa na hisia hasa wanapohudhuria maombolezo	**mwanamke bomba tunawakata wakati wa kisii kwa kama kama kama kama kama kama kama kama kama...**	murang'a viongozi wa kidini wazidiwa na hisia **hasira waziri waadi wa wadhaingizaa kutangaza**

Table 5: Example of Repetitive Pattern Generation

4.3.4 Sentence Length Correlation

Analysis indicated that transcription accuracy had a moderate negative correlation with sentence length, with longer sentences generally exhibiting higher error rates. This trend persisted in the 100-epoch model, though the magnitude of the correlation was slightly reduced.

5 Discussion

5.1 Model Capacity Limitations

The high Word Error Rate (WER) observed in the 5-epoch model (82.95%) suggests that the Whisper Tiny model's capacity (39M parameters) is insufficient for robust Swahili ASR. The 100-epoch model achieved a WER of 30.62%, demonstrating significant improvement but still falling short of practical usability.

5.2 Linguistic Challenges in Swahili ASR

Several linguistic features of Swahili present particular challenges for ASR systems:

5.2.1 Morphological Complexity

As an agglutinative language, Swahili constructs words by combining multiple morphemes. A single Swahili verb can encode information about subject, object, tense, aspect, and mood through prefixes and suffixes. This complexity increases the vocabulary space and makes word boundary detection challenging, as evidenced by errors like splitting *jitihada* into *jiti ada*. The 100-epoch model showed slight improvements in handling morphologically complex words but still struggled with segmentation.

5.2.2 Tonal Variations

While Standard Swahili is not strictly tonal, variations in intonation can affect meaning, particularly in regional dialects. The model's difficulty with certain phonetic distinctions may be partially attributed to inadequate representation of tonal features. Extended training reduced some phonetic errors but did not fully address this challenge.

5.2.3 Dialectal Diversity

Swahili exhibits significant dialectal variation across East Africa, with notable differences between Tanzanian and Kenyan varieties. The dataset's regional representation may impact the model's ability to generalize across dialectal boundaries. The 100-epoch model showed improved generalization but still struggled with dialect-specific variations.

5.3 Data Considerations

The size of the training dataset (5,520 samples ≈ 19.7 hours) is relatively small compared to datasets used for high-resource language ASR development, which often include tens of thousands of hours of audio. Table 6 provides a comparison with other ASR datasets.

Dataset	Size	Language
Current Study	19.7 hours	Swahili
LibriSpeech	960 hours	English
Common Voice	1,400+ hours	Multiple lang.
High-resource ASR	10,000+ hours	Various

Table 6: Comparison of Dataset Sizes for ASR Development

The limited data diversity may constrain the model's ability to generalize to varied speakers, acoustic environments, and linguistic contexts. Extended training improved performance but did not fully compensate for the dataset's limitations.

6 Future Work

Based on our findings from both 5-epoch and 100-epoch fine-tuning, we propose several recommendations for improving Swahili ASR performance:

6.1 Model Architecture Enhancements

Table 7 summarizes our recommendations for scaling to larger model variants, which could further reduce the WER observed in our experiments.

1. Scale to Larger Model Variants	
The most immediate improvement would likely come from utilizing larger Whisper models:	
Base	74M parameters - Recommended minimum for Swahili ASR, with expected WER improvements of 30-50% over Tiny.
Small	244M parameters - Optimal balance of performance and efficiency, often achieving WERs below 30%.
Medium	769M parameters - For research contexts with sufficient computational resources, offering potential for further improvement.

Table 7: Model Scaling Recommendations

Table 8 presents our recommendations for architectural adaptations to better handle Swahili's linguistic features.

2. Architectural Adaptations	
Consider modifications to the base Whisper architecture to better accommodate Swahili's linguistic features:	
Tokenization	Enhanced subword tokenization specifically designed for agglutinative languages to address segmentation errors.
Attention	Augmented attention mechanisms to better capture long-range dependencies in morphologically complex words.
Audio Features	Additional acoustic feature extraction layers to better represent tonal variations and phonetic nuances.

Table 8: Architectural Adaptation Recommendations

6.2 Training Methodology Improvements

1. **Extended training duration**: Our 100-epoch training demonstrated significant WER improvements, suggesting that longer training durations are beneficial for low-resource languages. Early stopping based on validation performance can prevent overfitting.

2. **Learning rate scheduling**: Implement more sophisticated learning rate schedules, such as cosine annealing with warm restarts, to improve optimization dynamics and convergence.

3. **Hyperparameter optimization**: Conduct systematic grid search or Bayesian optimization of key hyperparameters, including batch size and learning rate, to maximize performance.

4. **Progressive training**: Implement a curriculum learning approach where the model initially trains on shorter, simpler utterances before progressing to more complex examples, as longer sentences remain challenging.

6.3 Data Enhancement Strategies

Table 9 outlines our recommended data enhancement strategies to address the limitations of the current dataset.

7 Conclusion

This study evaluated fine-tuning the Whisper Tiny model for Swahili ASR with 5-epoch and 100-epoch training regimes. The 100-epoch model

Strategy	Approach
Data augmentation	Time stretching, pitch shifting, background noise, room impulse response, speed perturbation (0.9x, 1.0x, 1.1x)
Data quality	Review audio-transcript pairs for misalignments or errors.
Dialectal balancing	Represent major Swahili dialects to improve regional generalization.
Additional sources	Public archives, parliamentary proceedings, educational materials, user recordings.

Table 9: Recommended Data Enhancement Strategies

achieved a WER of 30.62%, significantly better than the 5-epoch model (82.95%). However, performance remains below practical utility, highlighting challenges in adapting compact ASR models for low-resource languages.

Error patterns, such as phonetic approximations and difficulties with named entity recognition and dialectal variations, suggest limitations in capturing Swahili's linguistic complexities. While extended training reduced some errors, issues with morphologically complex words persist.

This research contributes to adapting multilingual ASR systems for low-resource languages and emphasizes the need for approaches tailored to Bantu languages like Swahili. The work should focus on:
Evaluating larger Whisper models for scalability. Developing architectural adaptations for Swahili and Bantu languages. Creating more diverse Swahili speech datasets. Exploring multitask learning approaches. Developing ASR systems for languages like Swahili is a crucial step toward more inclusive speech technology for diverse linguistic communities.

Limitations

This study has several limitations. First, only the Whisper Tiny model was used, which may not represent the performance of larger Whisper variants for Swahili ASR. Second, the dataset, with 5,520 samples, is small, potentially limiting exposure to diverse Swahili speech patterns. Third, we focused on the standard Swahili dialect without accounting for regional variations. Fourth, further hyperparameter optimization could improve results, despite training for 100 epochs. Finally, our evaluation based on Word Error Rate may not fully reflect the semantic accuracy or practical usability of the transcriptions.

References

Noreen Abdou Mohamed, Arbi Allak, Karim Gaanoun, Ibrahim Benelallam, Zineb Erraji, and Ahmed Bahafid. 2024. Multilingual speech recognition initiative for african languages. *International Journal of Data Science and Analytics*, pages 1–16.

Orevaoghene Ahia, Ayeni Aremu, David Abagyan, Hila Gonen, David I. Adelani, David Abolade, Noah A. Smith, and Yulia Tsvetkov. 2024. Voices unheard: Nlp resources and models for yorúbá regional dialects. *arXiv preprint arXiv:2406.19564*.

P. B. Akash. 2023. Xlsr swahili model. `https://huggingface.co/Akashpb13/Swahili_xlsr`.

David Awino, Lawrence Muchemi, Lilian D. A. Wanzare, Evans Ombui, Bernard Wanjawa, Ochieng McOnyango, and Florence Indede. 2022. Kenspeech: Swahili speech transcriptions. `https://doi.org/10.7910/DVN/YHXJSU`.

Laurent Besacier, Etienne Barnard, Alexey Karpov, and Tanja Schultz. 2014. Automatic speech recognition for under-resourced languages: A survey. *Speech Communication*, 56:85–100.

Ram Rijal Ghimire, Prajwal Poudyal, and Bal Krishna Bal. 2024. Improving on the limitations of the asr model in low-resourced environments using parameter-efficient fine-tuning. In *Proceedings of the 21st International Conference on Natural Language Processing (ICON)*, pages 408–415.

OpenAI. 2023. Whisper: A universal speech recognition model. [Accessed: 9-Mar-2025].

Peter Plantinga. 2025. Whisper small model for swahili.

Alec Radford, Jong Wook Kim, Tao Xu, Greg Brockman, Christine McLeavey, and Ilya Sutskever. 2023. Robust speech recognition via large-scale weak supervision. In *International Conference on Machine Learning*, pages 28492–28518. PMLR.

SpeechBrain Team. 2022. Asr wav2vec2 model for swahili. `https://huggingface.co/speechbrain/asr-wav2vec2-dvoice-swahili`.

Olamide Tunde-Onadele and Joseph Chao. 2022. Speech recognition for low-resource languages: Case study on swahili. In *Proceedings of the 3rd Workshop on Computational Methods for Endangered Languages*, pages 148–152.

Appendix

A Fine-Tuning Configuration

The adaptation of the Whisper Tiny model for Swahili ASR was accomplished through a targeted fine-tuning process optimized for efficient learning while preventing overfitting. Table 10 details the hyperparameters selected for this fine-tuning procedure.

Hyperparameter	Value
Batch size	8
Gradient accumulation steps	4
Effective batch size	32 (8 × 4)
Learning rate	5e-5
Learning rate scheduler	Linear with warmup
Warmup ratio	0.1
Number of epochs	5 / 100
Optimizer	AdamW
Weight decay	0.01
Mixed precision	FP16 (enabled)
Gradient checkpointing	Enabled
Language configuration	Forced decoder IDs set to Swahili
Maximum generation length	225 tokens

Table 10: Hyperparameters for Whisper Tiny Fine-tuning

The selection of these hyperparameters was guided by several considerations:

Memory Optimization: The combination of a moderate batch size (8) with gradient accumulation steps (4) yielded an effective batch size of 32, balancing between statistical efficiency and GPU memory constraints.

Learning Dynamics: The learning rate of 5e-5 with a warmup ratio of 0.1 was chosen to allow gradual adaptation of the pre-trained weights while avoiding destructive updates early in training.

Computational Efficiency: Mixed precision training (FP16) and gradient checkpointing were enabled to optimize GPU memory usage and accelerate training without sacrificing model quality.

Language Specificity: Forced decoder IDs ensured that the model generated Swahili text regardless of the detected language in the audio, which was critical for focused adaptation.

A.1 Training Infrastructure

The fine-tuning was conducted on a high-performance computing environment with the specifications shown in Table 11.

Component	Specification
GPU	NVIDIA A100
GPU Memory	16GB VRAM
Training Framework	PyTorch 1.13 HuggingFace Transformers
Training Duration	34 minutes (5 epochs) 11 hours (100 epochs)
Total Training Steps	690 (5 epochs) 13,500 (100 epochs)

Table 11: Training Infrastructure Specifications

Who Wrote This? Identifying Machine vs Human-Generated Text in Hausa

Babangida Sani[1,3], **Aakansha Soy**[1], **Sukairaj Hafiz Imam**[2,3], **Ahmad Mustapha**[1,3], **Lukman Jibril Aliyu**[3], **Idris Abdulmumin**[3,4], **Ibrahim Said Ahmad**[2,3,5], **Shamsuddeen Hassan Muhammad**[2,3,6]

[1]Kalinga University, [2]Bayero University, Kano, [3]HausaNLP

[4]DSFSI, University of Pretoria, [5]Northeastern University, [6]Imperial College London

correspondence: bsani480@gmail.com

Abstract

The advancement of large language models (LLMs) has allowed them to be proficient in various tasks, including content generation. However, their unregulated usage can lead to malicious activities such as plagiarism and generating and spreading fake news, especially for low-resource languages. Most existing machine-generated text detectors are trained on high-resource languages like English, French, etc. In this study, we developed the first large-scale detector that can distinguish between human- and machine-generated content in Hausa. We scraped seven Hausa-language media outlets for the human-generated text and the Gemini-2.0 flash model to automatically generate the corresponding Hausa-language articles based on the human-generated article headlines. We fine-tuned four pre-trained Africentric models (AfriTeVa, AfriBERTa, AfroXLMR, and AfroXLMR-76L) on the resulting dataset and assessed their performance using accuracy and F1-score metrics. AfroXLMR achieved the highest performance with an accuracy of 99.23% and an F1 score of 99.21%, demonstrating its effectiveness for Hausa text detection. Our dataset is made publicly available[1] to enable further research.

Keywords: *Large Language Model (LLM), Natural Language Processing (NLP), Hausa, Transformer, Gemini, Fine-tune*

1 Introduction

Hausa is among the most spoken Chadic languages, belonging to the Afroasiatic phylum. Over 100 million people are estimated to speak the language, with the majority of speakers living in Northern Nigeria and the Republic of Niger, respectively (Inuwa-Dutse, 2021). However, from computational linguistics, it is regarded as a low-resource language, having insufficient resources to support tasks involving Natural Language Processing (NLP; Adam et al. 2023; Muhammad et al. 2023).

Hausa language is written in either the Latin (or ***Boko***) and Arabic (or ***Ajami***) script (Jaggar, 2006). The *Boko* script, existing since the 1930s, was introduced by the British colonial administration, and is used in education, government, and digital communication. The *Ajami* script, an order writing system of the Hausa language that existed in pre-colonial times, is used mostly in religious, cultural, and informal writing. For the purpose of our work, and as Hausa is widely written nowadays, we scraped and generated data based on the Latin-based script.

Large language models (LLMs) are becoming mainstream and easily accessible, ushering in an explosion of machine-generated content over various channels, such as news, social media, question-answering (QA) forums, educational, and even academic contexts (Wang et al., 2023). The human-like quality of texts generated by LLMs models for different languages including Hausa language is always advancing, allowing them to generate diverse content. LLMs, intentionally or unintentionally, have the potential to be used to create and propagate harmful or misleading content, such as fake news or hate speech (Xie et al., 2024), or even fake or artificial scholarship. To ensure the authenticity, accuracy, and trustworthiness of content, there is a need for machine-generated text detectors. Extensive research has been undertaken to differentiate between machine-generated texts (MGTs) and human-generated texts (HGTs), primarily employing model-based approaches (Wang et al., 2023; Alshammari, 2024; Ji et al., 2024).

In existing studies, (i) focus has mainly been on high-resource languages like English; (ii) there are no reliable detectors for detecting human vs. AI-generated text in the Hausa language; (iii) ensuring content authenticity is difficult, especially for low resource languages like Hausa (Ji et al., 2024). We

[1]https://github.com/TheBangis/hausa_corpus

Proceedings of the Sixth Workshop on African Natural Language Processing (AfricaNLP 2025), pages 82–88

aim, therefore, to develop an automatic detector to classify human-generated and machine-generated text in Hausa, focused on the news domain, hence filling this gap. The following are our contributions:

- We are the first to develop a Hausa detector that is capable of differentiating HGT and MGT in Hausa. We believe it would help in ensuring content authenticity in digital communication, academia, and mitigating fake news.
- We curated a dataset that consists of human-generated data by scraping seven Hausa media outlets and machine-generated data using Gemini, addressing the lack of high-quality data in the area.
- By focusing on the Hausa language, we contribute to the expanding NLP capabilities for low-resource languages.
- All our resources will be open-source to encourage future academic research in the Hausa language.

2 Related Work

2.1 Detection of MGTs before ChatGPT

Radford et al. (2019) raised concerns regarding using machine-generated text for malicious purposes such as spam, fake news, plagiarism, and disinformation. The GLTR (Giant Language Model Test Room) tool (Gehrmann et al., 2019), released in June 2019, is an open-source system for detecting GPT-2-generated text using baseline statistical methods. Later that year, OpenAI enhanced the Roberta model (Liu et al., 2019) by introducing a dedicated GPT-2 detector (Radford et al., 2019). Another major advancement was the GROVER model (Zellers et al., 2019), which can both generate and detect fake news. With 5,000 self-generated articles and extensive real news content, GROVER achieved a 92% detection accuracy, surpassing models like the Plug and Play Language Model (PPLM) (Dathathri et al., 2019) and BERT (Devlin et al., 2019). Another study by Ippolito et al. (2019) examines the detection of machine-generated texts (MGTs) from GPT-2 with decoding strategies such as top-k, untruncated random sampling, and nucleus sampling in English. They discovered that optimized BERT was best but had poor cross-strategy generalization, whereas automatic classifiers performed better than humans, who misclassified AI text more than 30% of the time. AraGPT-2 (Antoun et al., 2020) introduced the first advanced Arabic language model that aides in distinguishing human-written and machine-generated Arabic text.

2.2 Detection of MGTs after ChatGPT

The launch of ChatGPT in late 2022 and later sequential models like GPT-4, Gemini, Claude, Llama, DeepSeek, etc., have posed new challenges as machine-generated texts (MGTs) mimic human writing styles more effectively than ever before. This raises concerns and the need for detection models to discern between HGTs and MGTs in different fields, such as academia, to mitigate plagiarism. In 2024, a study by Jawaid et al. (2024) presents a systemic approach for discerning between HWTs and MGTs using a combination of deep learning models, textual feature-based models, and machine learning models. Similarly, Xie et al. (2024) used eight traditional machine learning models and integrate statistical analysis, linguistic patterns, sentiment analysis and fact-checking as factors to differentiate between human-generated and machine-generated content across the three different datasets. In another study, Mitrović et al. (2023) examines ChatGPT-generated short text detection using DistilBERT and a perplexity-based classifier on online reviews, creating three datasets: human-written, ChatGPT-generated, and ChatGPT-rephrased. DistilBERT achieved 98% accuracy on original AI-generated text but only 79% on rephrased text, indicating the challenge of detecting AI-rewritten text.

3 Methodology

3.1 Datasets

We used both human-generated text (HGTs) and machine-generated text (MTGTs) for the Hausa language in the news domain. We collected 2,586 HGTs from seven different local and international news outlets and generated equal amounts of texts for the MGTs by leveraging the Gemini-2.0-flash closed-source model. We merged the datasets into a single file and created a source column to label whether a text is a HGT or MGT and then shuffled the data for effective training and evaluation. Table 1 displays selected samples from our HGT and MGT dataset used in the experiments and Table 2 provides information on the composition of our

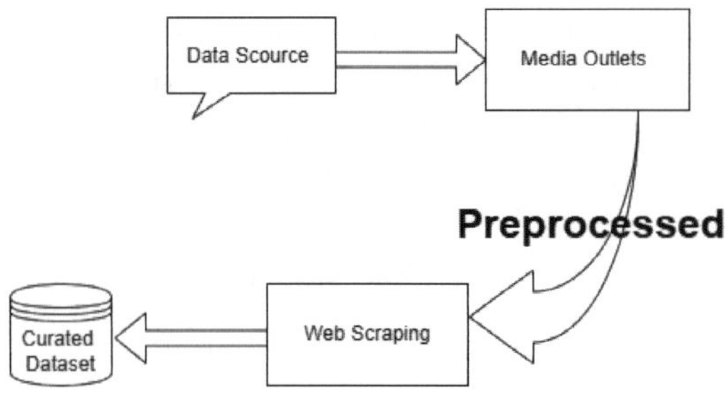

Figure 1: Overview of the pipeline's data collection for human-generated texts.

dataset in terms of the number of sentences, words, and unique words.

Human-Generated Data The human-generated data was extracted from seven different local and international online news outlet websites written in the Hausa language through web scraping, structured into headlines and content. Initially, we extracted 3,700 news articles; and after automatically filtering out unwanted texts, we preprocessed the dataset to remove rows with empty content, reducing the news articles to exactly 2,586. Figure 1 shows an overview of the pipeline's data collection process for human-generated data.

Machine-Generated Data For the machine-generated text, we used the Gemini-2.0 flash model, through Google AI Studio, to automatically generate corresponding Hausa news articles based on each of the article headlines in the human-generated text. The dataset consists of headlines, content, and a word count for every article so that the text length of the generated article is near or equal to the actual article. To produce the machine-generated articles, we processed the dataset in batches of 10 and checked whether machine-generated text existed and initiated missing values where required. For every batch, the model generated full articles from the headlines, and after every batch, progress was saved so as not to lose data, and a 10-second delay was added between batches to avoid exceeding API limits. This iterative process continued until machine-generated articles were created for all headlines.

Data Processing

The data collected, particularly the human-generated data, was noisy, containing many duplicates, English content, and other markup language symbols. Furthermore, some rows in the generated data produced an error message, while others included headlines that required cleaning. We identified and removed all unwanted content, including URLs, in both datasets before merging them into a single file to ensure effective training of our detection model.

Subdomain Analysis In order to get a clearer view of our dataset, we carried out an analysis of how articles are distributed in different news subdomains. The aim was to see how the content is distributed in terms of categories like politics, health, sports, business, entertainment, religion, and technology. Table 3 shows the distribution of news articles in different subdomains of the dataset.

The dataset is dominated by political content, which makes up more than half, 53.5% of the total articles. Categories such as health, 10.4% and sports, 9.7% have moderate representation, whereas business, 8.8%, entertainment, 7.9%, religion, 5.2%, and technology, 4.5% are less represented in the dataset.

Data Splits and Contamination Avoidance To ensure robust evaluation, we split the dataset into training (80%), validation (10%), and test (10%) sets, with no overlap of headlines across splits. Each headline (and its associated human and machine-generated articles) was grouped and assigned to a single split to avoid contamination. This ensures that the model does not encounter semantically similar content across training and evaluation phases. The dataset consists of 5172 samples (2586 human-generated and 2586 machine-generated), corresponding to 2586 unique headlines. These were divided into 2068 headlines (4136 samples) for training, 258 headlines (516 samples) for validation, and 260 headlines (520 samples) for testing.

4 Experiments setup

For our experiments, we utilized four Afri-centric transformer pre-trained language models: three multilingual and one monolingual. These models were selected due to their prior optimization for African languages, including Hausa. The models are AfriTeVa (Jude Ogundepo et al., 2022), AfroXLMR-76L (Adelani et al., 2023), AfroXLMR (Alabi et al., 2022), and AfriBERTa (Ogueji et al., 2021), respectively. Each pre-trained language model was fine-tuned on our constructed dataset by training it up 3 epochs. The models were optimized with AdamW, with a learning rate

Headline	Human-Generated Text	Machine-Generated Text
Man City ta kusan kammala aukar mai tsaron baya Reis	Manchester City ta kusan kammala cinikin matashin an wasan Palmeiras mai tsaron baya, Vitor Reis. City ta auki matakai tana zawarcin an wallon tawagar Brazil, yanzu dai ta kai ga cewa sauran iris ungiyar Etihad ta kammala sayen mai shekara 19. Tun farko Palmeiras ta so rie mai tsaron bayan har zuwa gasar cin kofin duniya, domin a lokacin zai kara tsada...	Manchester City na gab da kammala sayen an wasan baya mai suna Reis daga ungiyar Benfica. Rahotanni sun bayyana cewa, tattaunawa ta yi nisa sosai kuma ana sa ran za a cimma yarjejeniya a cikin 'yan kwanaki masu zuwa. Reis, wanda ya taka rawar gani a gasar Portugal, ya burge koci Pep Guardiola wanda ke neman arfafa layin tsaron ungiyarsa...
Matar Havertz ta samu saonnin cin zarafi a kafar sada zumunta	Matar Kai Havertz ta sanar da samun saonnin cin mutunci da zarafi a kafar sada zumunta, bayan tashi wasan da Manchester United ta fitar da Arsenal a FA Cup ranar Lahadi. Ta kuma ce cikin saonnin da ta samu har da na barazana da aka yi musu da an cikin da ko haifarsa ba a yi ba. Havertz mai shekara 25, ya barar da damar makin da ya kamata ya ci wallayen da zai kai Arsenal zagayen gaba a FA Cup, amma ya yi ta barar da wallaye. Bayan da suka tashi 1-1 har da arin lokacin, sai aka je bugun fenariti, inda mai tsare ragar United, Altay Bayindir ya tare wadda Havertz ya buga...	Matar an wasan wallon afa na asar Jamus, Kai Havertz, wato Sophia Weber ta fuskanci zazzafan cin zarafi a shafukan sada zumunta bayan wasan da ungiyar wallon afa ta Arsenal ta buga da Bayern Munich a gasar zakarun Turai. Masu amfani da shafukan sada zumunta sun yi wa Sophia ruwan zagi da maganganu masu ata rai, inda suka danganta rashin nasarar ungiyar Arsenal da arancin arfin mijinta a filin wasa. Wasu daga cikin saonnin sun yi nuni da cewa Sophia ce sanadiyyar rashin taka rawar gani na Havertz, yayin da wasu suka yi amfani da kalmomi masu zafi da cin mutunci...
Yadda wani farar fata ya kashe mata biyu ya bai wa alade gawarsu a Afirka ta Kudu	Labarin matan nan guda biyu da ake zargin wani farar fata da kashe su a gonarsa sannan ya mia wa alade gawarsu ya cinye na ci gaba da tayar da hankali a asar Afirka ta Kudu. Matan guda biyu da suka haa da Maria Makgato mai shekaru 45 da Lucia Ndlovu mai shekaru 34 dai an yi zargin cewa farar fatar ya harbe su ne a lokacin da suka shiga gonarsa domin neman abinci a kusa da Polokwane da ke arewacin lardin Limpopo na Afirka ta Kudun. An zargi farar fatar da jefa wa alade gawar matan a wani mataki na oarin oye shaidar abin da ya faru....	A wani lamari mai ban tsoro da takaici, wani farar fata ya aikata wani mugun aiki a kasar Afirka ta Kudu, inda ya kashe wasu mata biyu sannan ya bai wa alade gawarsu. Wannan lamari ya girgiza al'ummar kasar, ya kuma haifar da fushin jama'a, musamman a tsakanin bakaken fata. Rahotanni sun bayyana cewa, wanda ake zargin, wanda ba a bayyana sunansa ba tukuna, ya yi amfani da wani makami ne wajen kashe matan biyu a wani gida da ke wani yanki na kasar. Bayan ya aikata wannan aika-aika, sai ya dauki gawarwakin matan ya kai su wani gona da ake kiwon alade, inda ya jefa su a cikin kejin aladun...
Yadda fasinjojin Algeria suka makale a Paris	Yan Algeria 26 da za su koma gida daga Birtaniya sun makale a filin jirgin saman Charles de Gaulle da ke birnin Paris makonni uku da suka gabata. Fasinjojin wadanda suka hada da yara mata biyu da wata tsohuwa mai shekara 75 sun shigo Faransa ne a ranar 26 ga watan Fabareru daga filin jirgin sama na Heathrow...	A ranar Laraba, daruruwan fasinjojin jirgin sama 'yan kasar Aljeriya sun shiga halin kaka-nika-yi a filin jirgin sama na Charles de Gaulle da ke birnin Paris. Fasinjojin, wadanda suka yi niyyar komawa gida bayan ziyara ko tafiye-tafiye daban-daban, sun makale ne sakamakon soke jirage da kamfanonin jiragen sama suka yi ba zato ba tsammani...
Yan wasa 10 da hankali zai karkata kansu a AFCON	Nan da sa'o'i kaan ne, nahiyar Afrika za ta au harama ta ko'ina inda za a ria jin sowar magoya baya sakamakon Gasar cin Kofin nahiyar ta 2023, da za a fara karo na 34 a asar Cote d'Ivoire. Fitattun 'yan wasan nahiyar Afrika da suka yi fice a duniya za su baje-koli, daga ranar 13 ga watan Janairu zuwa 11 ga watan Fabrairu...	Gasar cin kofin nahiyar Afirka ta 2023 (AFCON) na gabatowa, kuma a wannan shekara ma, kamar yadda aka saba, akwai 'yan wasan da za su ja hankalin masoya kwallon kafa a fadin nahiyar da ma duniya baki daya. Daga cikin dubban 'yan wasan da za su fafata a wannan gasa, akwai wasu da ake ganin za su yi fice fiye da sauran saboda irin bajintar da suke nunawa a kungiyoyinsu da kuma kasashensu...
Babu gaskiya a zargin da shugaban sojin Nijar ya yi wa Najeriya - Ribadu	NUHU RIBADU Mai bai wa shugaban Najeriya shawara kan harkokin tsaro Malam Nuhu Ribau, ya nuna takaicinsa kan wasu zarge-zarge da shugaban mulkin sojin Nijar, Janar Abdulrahman Tchiani, ya yi yayin hirarsa da kafar talabijin in asar ranar Laraba. Shi dai Janar Tchiani ya zargi Najeriya da ba asar Faransa hadin kai wajen ba 'yan bindiga mafaka da kuma oarin kafa sansani a arewacin Najeriya, don shirya yadda za su far wa asarsa...	Mai ba shugaban kasa shawara kan harkokin tsaro, Nuhu Ribadu, ya yi watsi da zargin da shugaban sojin Nijar ya yi wa Najeriya, yana mai cewa babu gaskiya a cikin zargin. Ribadu ya bayyana haka ne a wata tattaunawa da manema labarai a Abuja, inda ya yi karin haske kan batun da ya jawo cece-kuce a 'yan kwanakin nan...

Table 1: Sample entries from our Human and Machine-Generated Hausa dataset

Statistic	Count
Total Sentences	6,737
Total Words	3,376,976
Unique Words	49,883

Table 2: Statistics of the dataset used in Hausa Machine-generated text detection.

Subdomain	Proportion (%)
Politics	53.50
Health	10.38
Sports	9.72
Business	8.79
Entertainment	7.94
Religion	5.19
Technology	4.49

Table 3: Distribution of the news articles across different subdomains.

of 1e-5, a batch size of 8, and a maximum sequence length of 512, with evaluation performed after each epoch. Table Table 4 shows the combinations of hyperparameters used to train the four models. The experiments were performed using PyTorch and Hugging Face Transformers. Upon completion, each fine-tuned model and tokenizer was saved and pushed to the Hugging Face Hub.

5 Results and Discussion

5.1 Results

Table 5 shows the performance of the fine-tuned models. The models' good performances indicate

Hyperparameter	Value
optimizer	AdamW
epochs	3
batch size	8
learning rate	1e-5

Table 4: Hyperparameters used for training the pre-trained language models.

their capabilities to distinguish between machine- and human-generated news texts written in Hausa language. Consistent in many downstream tasks, AfroXLMR performed the best, with an accuracy of 0.9923 and an F1 score of 0.9921. This is followed by AfriTeVa and AfriBERTa with an accuracy of 0.9884 and 0.9807 and an F1 score of 0.9881 and 0.9805, respectively, while AfroXLMR-76L had the lowest performance with an accuracy of 0.9672 and an F1 score of 0.9674. However, the overall performance indicates that all the developed models are very capable of detecting texts that are automatically generated from human-written news articles.

5.2 Discussion

The results of our experiments reveal the efficacy of pre-trained language models in detecting between human-generated text (HGTs) and machine-generated text (MGTs) in the Hausa language. AfroXLMR, was the best-performing model, achieved an accuracy of 99.23% on the test set and an F1 score of 99.21%, indicating its efficacy in identifying text origins with minimal misclassification. This suggests that multilingual pre-trained language models optimized for African languages can be fine-tuned effectively for low-resource language tasks such as MGT detection. Relative to the other three models, AfriTeVa, AfriBERTa, and AfroXLMR-76L showed different levels of performance. AfriTeVa achieved an accuracy of 98.84% on the test set, followed by AfriBERTa with 98.07% accuracy on the test set and lastly the AfroXLMR-76L achieved the lowest accuracy of 96.72% on the test set. This difference can be due to model architecture, pretraining data, and optimization methods.

6 Conclusion and Future Work

In this paper, we introduced the first large-scale effort to develop a detector capable of distinguishing between human-generated text (HGT) and machine-generated text (MGT) in the Hausa language. The study consists of two main parts. Firstly, we created a dataset consisting of both human-generated and machine-generated. Next, we developed and evaluated the detectors by fine-tuning four Afri-centric pre-trained language models on the dataset. The models are AfriTeVa, AfriBERTa, AfroXLMR, and AfroXLMR-76L. We trained the models multiple times to optimize hyperparameters and enhance performance. The experimental results revealed the efficacy of the proposed models, with AfroXLMR outperforming the other models, achieving an accuracy of 99.23% and an F1 score of 99.21%.

Model	Accuracy	F1 Score
AfriTeVa	0.9884	0.9881
AfriBERTa	0.9807	0.9805
AfroXLMR	**0.9923**	**0.9921**
AfroXLMR-76L	0.9672	0.9674

Table 5: Results and performance of the fine-tuned models. The best-performing model is highlighted in bold.

This study not only advances the detection of human-generated text and machine-generated text in a low-resource language such as Hausa but also shows that multilingual models optimized for African languages can be effectively adapted for detecting machine-generated text in low-resource languages. Support for low-resource languages is continuously improving across various large language models (LLMs). As a result, effective detection is important to prevent the spread of misinformation and disinformation, which are often facilitated by these models. We anticipate that this study will offer a comprehensive assessment of detection capabilities and enhance the ongoing academic discourse on identifying content generated by language models especially in underserved languages.

For future research, we aim to extend the dataset to cover diverse domains beyond news articles such as social media posts, academic writing, and books, as well as increasing the dataset size for better model generalization. Secondly, we aim to create real-time detection frameworks for use on digital platforms to help mitigate the propagation of AI-driven misinformation. Thirdly, exploring the use of the GPTs and other large language models in identifying machine-generated Hausa text. Using these models, with their high-level knowledge of language and context, detection accuracy could be enhanced. Lastly, to expand detection capabilities to other low-resource African languages, future research might explore cross-language transfer learning.

7 Limitations

Our study also has some limitations. First, we focused only on one domain when creating our dataset, which is news articles. The training was limited to three epochs, and a small batch size of 8 across all the models, which may impact the models' performance. Another limitation is that machine-generated texts were created using only the Gemini-2.0-flash model. While this model is high-performing, relying solely on a single source may limit the stylistic diversity of generated texts.

Acknowledgments

We thank HausaNLP Community for generously providing access to the Google Colab GPU Premium Version, greatly enhancing our model's training efficiency and supporting this research.

References

Fatima Muhammad Adam, Abubakar Yakubu Zandam, and Isa Inuwa-Dutse. 2023. Detection of offensive and threatening online content in a low resource language. *arXiv preprint arXiv:2311.10541*.

David Ifeoluwa Adelani, Hannah Liu, Xiaoyu Shen, Nikita Vassilyev, Jesujoba O Alabi, Yanke Mao, Haonan Gao, and Annie En-Shiun Lee. 2023. Sib-200: A simple, inclusive, and big evaluation dataset for topic classification in 200+ languages and dialects. *arXiv preprint arXiv:2309.07445*.

Jesujoba O. Alabi, David Ifeoluwa Adelani, Marius Mosbach, and Dietrich Klakow. 2022. Adapting pre-trained language models to African languages via multilingual adaptive fine-tuning. In *Proceedings of the 29th International Conference on Computational Linguistics*, pages 4336–4349, Gyeongju, Republic of Korea. International Committee on Computational Linguistics.

Hamed Alshammari. 2024. *AI-Generated Text Detector for Arabic Language*. Ph.D. thesis, University of Bridgeport.

Wissam Antoun, Fady Baly, and Hazem Hajj. 2020. Aragpt2: Pre-trained transformer for arabic language generation. *arXiv preprint arXiv:2012.15520*.

Sumanth Dathathri, Andrea Madotto, Janice Lan, Jane Hung, Eric Frank, Piero Molino, Jason Yosinski, and Rosanne Liu. 2019. Plug and play language models: A simple approach to controlled text generation. *arXiv preprint arXiv:1912.02164*.

Jacob Devlin, Ming-Wei Chang, Kenton Lee, and Kristina Toutanova. 2019. Bert: Pre-training of deep bidirectional transformers for language understanding. In *Proceedings of the 2019 conference of the North American chapter of the association for computational linguistics: human language technologies, volume 1 (long and short papers)*, pages 4171–4186.

Sebastian Gehrmann, Hendrik Strobelt, and Alexander M Rush. 2019. Gltr: Statistical detection and visualization of generated text. *arXiv preprint arXiv:1906.04043*.

Isa Inuwa-Dutse. 2021. The first large scale collection of diverse hausa language datasets. *arXiv preprint arXiv:2102.06991*.

Daphne Ippolito, Daniel Duckworth, Chris Callison-Burch, and Douglas Eck. 2019. Automatic detection of generated text is easiest when humans are fooled. *arXiv preprint arXiv:1911.00650*.

P J Jaggar. 2006. Hausa. *Elsevier Ltd*, pages 222–225.

Urwah Jawaid, Rudra Roy, Pritam Pal, Srijani Debnath, Dipankar Das, and Sivaji Bandyopadhyay. 2024. Human vs machine: An automated machine-generated text detection approach. In *Proceedings of the 21st International Conference on Natural Language Processing (ICON)*, pages 215–223.

Jiazhou Ji, Ruizhe Li, Shujun Li, Jie Guo, Weidong Qiu, Zheng Huang, Chiyu Chen, Xiaoyu Jiang, and Xinru Lu. 2024. Detecting machine-generated texts: Not just" ai vs humans" and explainability is complicated. *arXiv preprint arXiv:2406.18259*.

Odunayo Jude Ogundepo, Akintunde Oladipo, Mofetoluwa Adeyemi, Kelechi Ogueji, and Jimmy Lin. 2022. AfriTeVA: Extending ?small data? pretraining approaches to sequence-to-sequence models. In *Proceedings of the Third Workshop on Deep Learning for Low-Resource Natural Language Processing*, pages 126–135, Hybrid. Association for Computational Linguistics.

Yinhan Liu, Myle Ott, Naman Goyal, Jingfei Du, Mandar Joshi, Danqi Chen, Omer Levy, Mike Lewis, Luke Zettlemoyer, and Veselin Stoyanov. 2019. Roberta: A robustly optimized bert pretraining approach. *arXiv preprint arXiv:1907.11692*.

Sandra Mitrović, Davide Andreoletti, and Omran Ayoub. 2023. Chatgpt or human? detect and explain. explaining decisions of machine learning model for detecting short chatgpt-generated text. *arXiv preprint arXiv:2301.13852*.

Shamsuddeen Hassan Muhammad, Idris Abdulmumin, Abinew Ali Ayele, Nedjma Ousidhoum, David Ifeoluwa Adelani, Seid Muhie Yimam, Ibrahim Sa'id

Ahmad, Meriem Beloucif, Saif M. Mohammad, Sebastian Ruder, Oumaima Hourrane, Pavel Brazdil, Alipio Jorge, Felermino Dário Mário António Ali, Davis David, Salomey Osei, Bello Shehu Bello, Falalu Ibrahim, Tajuddeen Gwadabe, Samuel Rutunda, Tadesse Belay, Wendimu Baye Messelle, Hailu Beshada Balcha, Sisay Adugna Chala, Hagos Tesfahun Gebremichael, Bernard Opoku, and Stephen Arthur. 2023. AfriSenti: A Twitter sentiment analysis benchmark for African languages. In *Proceedings of the 2023 Conference on Empirical Methods in Natural Language Processing*, pages 13968–13981, Singapore. Association for Computational Linguistics.

Kelechi Ogueji, Yuxin Zhu, and Jimmy Lin. 2021. Small data? no problem! exploring the viability of pretrained multilingual language models for low-resourced languages. In *Proceedings of the 1st Workshop on Multilingual Representation Learning*, pages 116–126, Punta Cana, Dominican Republic. Association for Computational Linguistics.

Alec Radford, Jeffrey Wu, Rewon Child, David Luan, Dario Amodei, Ilya Sutskever, et al. 2019. Language models are unsupervised multitask learners. *OpenAI blog*, 1(8):9.

Yuxia Wang, Jonibek Mansurov, Petar Ivanov, Jinyan Su, Artem Shelmanov, Akim Tsvigun, Chenxi Whitehouse, Osama Mohammed Afzal, Tarek Mahmoud, Toru Sasaki, et al. 2023. M4: Multi-generator, multi-domain, and multi-lingual black-box machine-generated text detection. *arXiv preprint arXiv:2305.14902*.

Yaqi Xie, Anjali Rawal, Yujing Cen, Dixuan Zhao, Sunil K Narang, and Shanu Sushmita. 2024. Mugc: Machine generated versus user generated content detection. *arXiv preprint arXiv:2403.19725*.

Rowan Zellers, Ari Holtzman, Hannah Rashkin, Yonatan Bisk, Ali Farhadi, Franziska Roesner, and Yejin Choi. 2019. Defending against neural fake news. *Advances in neural information processing systems*, 32.

Automatic Speech Recognition for African Low-Resource Languages: Challenges and Future Directions

Sukairaj Hafiz Imam[1,10], **Babangida Sani**[2,10], **Dawit Ketema Gete**[3], **Bedru Yimam Ahamed**[4], **Ibrahim Said Ahmad**[1,5,10], **Idris Abdulmumin**[6,10], **Seid Muhie Yimam**[7,9], **Muhammad Yahuza Bello**[1], **Shamsuddeen Hassan Muhammad**[1,8,10]

[1]Bayero University, Kano, [2]Kalinga University, [3]Debre Birhan University, [4]Wollo University, [5]Northeastern University, [6]University of Pretoria, [7]University of Hamburg, [8]Imperial College London, [9]EthioNLP, [10]HausaNLP

Abstract

Automatic Speech Recognition (ASR) technologies have transformed human-computer interaction; however, low-resource languages in Africa remain significantly underrepresented in both research and practical applications. This study investigates the major challenges hindering the development of ASR systems for these languages, which include data scarcity, linguistic complexity, limited computational resources, acoustic variability, and ethical concerns surrounding bias and privacy. The primary goal is to critically analyze these barriers and identify practical, inclusive strategies to advance ASR technologies within the African context. Recent advances and case studies emphasize promising strategies such as community-driven data collection, self-supervised and multilingual learning, lightweight model architectures, and techniques that prioritize privacy. Evidence from pilot projects involving various African languages showcases the feasibility and impact of customized solutions, which encompass morpheme-based modeling and domain-specific ASR applications in sectors like healthcare and education. The findings highlight the importance of interdisciplinary collaboration and sustained investment to tackle the distinct linguistic and infrastructural challenges faced by the continent. This study offers a progressive roadmap for creating ethical, efficient, and inclusive ASR systems that not only safeguard linguistic diversity but also improve digital accessibility and promote socioeconomic participation for speakers of African languages.

1 Introduction

ASR has emerged as an innovative technology, enabling natural interactions between humans and computers in various applications, including virtual assistants, transcription services, language learning, and accessibility tools. However, the development of ASR systems has primarily concentrated on high-resource languages like English and Mandarin, thereby sidelining African languages, which are spoken by hundreds of millions across the continent. This digital exclusion not only restricts access to vital technologies but also put at risk the preservation of linguistic and cultural heritage. (Abate et al., 2020a; Alabi et al., 2024).

African languages are complex, described by rich morphology, tonal variation, and substantial dialectal diversity. These features, combined with a severe lack of annotated speech data, limited computational infrastructure, and underdeveloped linguistic tools, constitute significant challenges for ASR development. In addition, ethical concerns, such as algorithmic bias, under-representation of certain dialects, and insufficient privacy protections, further disrupt the progress. The underdevelopment of ASR for African languages represents both a technological gap and a socio-linguistic bias that must be addressed with urgency and care (Nzeyimana, 2023; Tachbelie and Abate, 2023; Martin and Wright, 2023; Jacobs et al., 2023; Gutkin et al., 2020; Sirora and Mutandavari, 2024).

The aim of this paper is to critically examine the primary challenges which hinder the advancement of ASR for African low-resource languages while also identifying emerging strategies that provide viable paths forward. The specific objectives include (i) analyzing the linguistic, technical, and ethical barriers to ASR development, (ii) exploring current solutions including self-supervised learning, community-driven data initiatives, and lightweight modeling, and (iii) proposing future directions that promote the creation of inclusive, efficient, and context-aware ASR systems suitable for deployment across diverse African low-resource languages.

The remainder of this paper is structured as follows: Section 2 provides background information and reviews the relevant literature. Section 3 explores the significant challenges facing the devel-

Proceedings of the Sixth Workshop on African Natural Language Processing (AfricaNLP 2025), pages 89–94

opment of automatic speech recognition (ASR) for African languages, while Section 4 highlights promising future directions. The paper concludes in Section 5 with final reflections and considerations regarding the broader implications of inclusive ASR development.

2 Background and Literature Analysis

Automatic Speech Recognition technologies have experienced significant advances in recent years. The field has progressed from traditional techniques, such as Hidden Markov Models (HMMs), to more innovative methodologies that employ deep learning and transformer-based architectures. This transformation marks a pivotal shift in the landscape of speech recognition. Although HMMs established the fundamental principles by using statistical methods to interpret spoken language, they are insufficient to address the complexities inherent in contemporary speech patterns (El Ouahabi et al., 2023; Badji et al., 2020).

African languages exhibit remarkable diversity, characterized by intricate morphological structures, sophisticated tonal variations, and a wide variety of dialects. For example, Yoruba and Wolaitta are two prominent tonal languages that employ variations in pitch; even a slight alteration in tone can entirely change the meaning of a phrase (Caubrière and Gauthier, 2024; Abdou Mohamed et al., 2024). Amharic and Tigrinya exemplify the rich cultural heritage of their speakers, characterized by their morphological complexity. These languages feature intricate systems of conjugation and inflection, which contribute to their vibrancy and expressiveness (Koffi, 2020; Tachbelie et al., 2020; Ibrahim et al., 2022).

In order to improve the performance of ASR systems for African languages, recent research has explored modern techniques such as self-supervised learning (SSL), multilingual training, and dynamic data enhancement (Ejigu and Asfaw, 2024; Caubrière and Gauthier, 2024). Despite the substantial advancements in this field, progress is frequently limited by the scarcity of high-quality datasets and the limited availability of computational resources. These factors present significant challenges for research in this area of study (Shamore et al., 2023; Nzeyimana, 2023).

On another hand, there are numerous ethical concerns towards the current ASR research. For example, speakers of underrepresented dialects often encounter bias against their languages, which compromises the reliability and accuracy of these systems. Furthermore, concerns regarding privacy invasion remain a problem, particularly when ASR technology is utilized for sensitive applications, such as in legal or medical environments (Martin and Wright, 2023; Jimerson et al., 2023).

3 Challenges in ASR for African low-resource Languages

Despite the increasing interest in ASR for African low-resource languages, several ongoing challenges disrupt the development of effective and inclusive systems. These disruptions are both technical and socio-linguistic contexts and must be systematically addressed to ensure equitable access to speech technologies throughout the continent.

3.1 Data Scarcity

A significant challenge in developing ASR systems for African languages is the scarcity of high-quality, annotated speech datasets. While initiatives like Mozilla Common Voice offer valuable resources, the variability in recording conditions, speaker representation, and audio quality can undermine the usability and overall representativeness of the data. Moreover, the absence of domain-specific and balanced datasets limits the ability of models to effectively generalize across various speech contexts and user demographics. (Abubakar et al., 2024; Azunre and Ibrahim, 2023).

3.2 Linguistic Complexity

African languages possess a rich linguistic diversity, characterized by complex morphological structures and tonal features that causes significant challenges for ASR systems. In tonal languages such as Yoruba and Wolaitta, even small variations in pitch can completely change the meaning of a word and this will cause complication in accuracy. Similarly, languages like Amharic and Tigrinya display extensive inflection and derivation, resulting in high rates of out-of-vocabulary (OOV) words and making it challenging for ASR systems to process word forms that were not encountered during training.(Koffi, 2020; Abate et al., 2020b).

3.3 Limited Computational Resources

Most of the African research institutions and developers encounter infrastructural challenges, particularly when it comes to accessing high-performance computing resources. Training and fine-tuning modern ASR models, especially those utilizing large transformer architectures, often demand powerful GPUs and sufficient memory. In areas with limited technological infrastructure, this causes a considerable obstacle to local innovation and experimentation with State-of-the-art methods. (Abubakar et al., 2024; Zellou and Lahrouchi, 2024; Kivaisi et al., 2023).

3.4 Environmental Noise and Dialectal Variation

Real-world deployment of ASR systems in African low-resource languages commonly involves highly variable acoustic conditions. Background noise, overlapping speech, and informal speaking styles, mostly in public spaces such as markets, schools, and clinics, can significantly reduce recognition accuracy. Furthermore, the wide range of dialects, accents, and speech patterns across regions adds another layer of complexity. Many existing ASR systems struggle to adapt to this diversity due to limited training data that captures intra-language variation (Ramanantsoa, 2023; Babatunde et al., 2023).

3.5 Ethical and Social Considerations

ASR technologies continuously reflect biases contained in the datasets they are trained on. For African low-resource languages, this can result in unbalanced performance across dialects, social groups, and gender identities which may lead to systematic exclusion or misrepresentation of certain users. Moreover, when deployed in sensitive fields like healthcare, ASR systems raise significant privacy concerns, especially in situations where data protection policies are either weak or not enforced. If we don't pay careful attention to ethics, inclusivity, and user trust, these technologies may end up reinforcing existing inequalities instead of helping to resolve them. (Martin and Wright, 2023; Afonja et al., 2024).

In summary, the advancement of ASR systems for African low-resource languages faces several challenges, including data scarcity, linguistic complexity, computational constraints, acoustic variability, and ethical considerations. Addressing these issues demands innovative, context-sensitive approaches that extend beyond traditional ASR design. The following section delves into emerging research directions and practical strategies aimed at overcoming these barriers and promoting the development of inclusive, efficient, and ethical ASR systems, specifically in the diverse linguistic landscape of Africa.

4 Future Direction

To address the challenges in developing ASR systems for African low-resource languages, researchers must adopt innovative and inclusive strategies. The following directions outline key areas for future work:

4.1 Expanding and Diversifying Datasets

Enhancing speech datasets through community engagement is a fundamental initial step towards improved ASR systems. Local contributors have effectively collected diverse voice data that represents a variety of accents, dialects, and environments on platforms such as Mozilla Common Voice. (Abubakar et al., 2024; Alabi et al., 2024; Ogunremi et al., 2023). Furthermore, techniques for generating synthetic data, including noise injection, speed variation, and voice cloning, can significantly enhance both the quality of the dataset and the model's ability to generalize effectively. (Ejigu and Asfaw, 2024).

4.2 Addressing Linguistic Complexity

The morphological complexity and tonal diversity in most African languages present considerable obstacles in the model generalization, therefore, Future models should adopt subword-level representations, such as morpheme-based modelling, to effectively handle vast inflection and derivation patterns. Additionally, advancements in grapheme-to-phoneme (G2P) conversion techniques are crucial for precisely correlating written representations with their respective pronunciations, especially in tonal languages. (Emiru et al., 2021; Abubakar et al., 2024; Ogunremi et al., 2023).

4.3 Improving Computational Efficiency

Resource constraints in various regions of Africa necessitate the design of lightweight ASR models. By optimizing model architecture and reducing the number of parameters, it is possible to preserve performance while lowering computational demands. Additionally, techniques like transfer learning and fine-tuning of pre-trained models can further decrease training time and energy consumption, making ASR development feasible even in low-resource environments (Olatunji et al., 2023; Afonja et al., 2024; Nzeyimana, 2023).

4.4 Ethical and Inclusive ASR Systems

To promote fairness, future automatic speech recognition (ASR) systems should be trained on diverse and representative datasets. This inclusivity is crucial for mitigating biases, particularly for speakers of dialects and accents that have traditionally been under-represented. Furthermore, incorporating privacy-preserving techniques, such as federated learning, enables models to learn from decentralized data while safeguarding user confidentiality. These strategies are particularly significant in sensitive areas like healthcare. (Martin and Wright, 2023; Afonja et al., 2024)

4.5 Applications in Real-World Contexts

Improving noise robustness is a crucial requirement for the successful implementation of ASR systems in real-world, acoustically diverse environments. By using advanced signal processing techniques and noise-cancellation algorithms, ASR models can sustain high performance even in challenging settings such as crowded healthcare facilities and dynamic educational spaces (El Ouahabi et al., 2023). Empirical evidence affirms this potential; for instance, in rural Ghana, a Twi-based ASR system used in clinical settings achieved 85% clinician satisfaction, despite a modest reduction in accuracy in high-noise wards. Similarly, a Shona-based educational application in Zimbabwe led to a 30% reduction in mispronunciation rates and doubled student engagement. These results highlight the tangible effectiveness and contextual relevance of domain-specific, noise-resilient ASR technologies in meeting the unique needs of African communities. (Doumbouya et al., 2021; El Ouahabi et al., 2023; Sirora and Mutandavari, 2024).

4.6 Field Trials and Performance Metrics

Community-driven data initiatives have shown great potential in enhancing ASR for African languages. A project for Yorùbá using Mozilla Common Voice collected over 120 hours of speech data from a diverse group of 250 speakers. A two-stage quality control process achieved a 92% clip-acceptance rate. Fine-tuning a Wav2Vec2 model on this data reduced the word error rate significantly, from 28% to 17%, underlining the effectiveness of foundational data collection for tonal languages.

A highly efficient ASR model for edge devices was developed by (Nzeyimana, 2023), which utilized quantization and pruning on a transformer-based architecture to reduce its size from 300 MB to 50 MB. This optimization allowed real-time inference on a Raspberry Pi 4 with a real-time factor of 0.8×, introducing a slight increase in WER from 22% to 25%, while still maintaining acceptable latency and CPU usage. The results demonstrate the potential for deploying advanced ASR systems in resource-constrained environments.

(Olatunji et al., 2023) emphasizes the importance of diversity by collecting speech (Pan-Africa dataset) from 200 speakers in both clinical and general domains. A self-supervised Wav2Vec2 model was fine-tuned, leading to over a 10% relative reduction in word error rate (WER) for clinical transcription tasks, showcasing how application-specific datasets can improve ASR robustness.

The "Iroyinspeech" corpus, developed by (Ogunremi et al., 2023), includes a vast number of Yorùbá utterances from both urban and rural dialects. When used in a multilingual fine-tuning framework, this expanded dataset decreased word error rates (WER) on rural-accented speech by about 15%, highlighting the significance of dialectal diversity and community involvement in ASR development.

(Ramanantsoa, 2023) highlights the potential of using existing audio archives to improve transcription accuracy. Researchers achieved over 80% accuracy in transcribing real-world radio broadcasts through targeted harvesting and dynamic noise augmentation. This demonstrates that even under-resourced languages can benefit from strategic use of publicly available audio to develop effective ASR models.

Table 1 presents a summary of the challenges that disrupt the development of ASR and outlines potential future directions.

5 Conclusion

ASR technologies gave significant promise for improving digital accessibility, preserving linguistic heritage, and promoting socio-economic inclusion for low-resource languages in Africa. However, challenges such as limited annotated datasets, complex linguistic structures, and ethical considerations disrupt advancement. To improve ASR performance, solutions like self-supervised learning, multilingual modeling, and synthetic data generation have been suggested. Future research should emphasise the development of high-quality datasets through community-driven initiatives and

Challenges	Future Directions	Authors
Data Scarcity: Lack of annotated datasets for training ASR models.	Expanding Datasets: Leveraging community-driven platforms like Mozilla Common Voice.	(Abubakar et al., 2024; Azunre and Ibrahim, 2023; Alabi et al., 2024; ?)
Linguistic Complexity: Tonal variations and morphological richness.	Advanced Modeling: Using self-supervised learning (SSL) and multilingual training.	(Koffi, 2020; Caubrière and Gauthier, 2024)
Computational Constraints: Limited access to computational resources.	Lightweight Architectures: Developing efficient models for low-resource settings.	(Abubakar et al., 2024; Nzeyimana, 2023)
Noise and Variability: Background noise and dialectal diversity.	Robustness to Noise: Enhancing ASR systems to handle noisy environments.	(Ramanantsoa, 2023; El Ouahabi et al., 2023)
Ethical and Social Issues: Bias against underrepresented dialects.	Reducing Bias: Training on diverse datasets to improve inclusivity.	(Martin and Wright, 2023; Afonja et al., 2024)
Privacy Concerns: Use of ASR in sensitive applications like healthcare.	Privacy Protection: Implementing federated learning to protect user data.	(Martin and Wright, 2023; Afonja et al., 2024)
Lack of Standardized Linguistic Tools: Absence of pronunciation dictionaries.	Grapheme-to-Phoneme (G2P) Conversion: Improving G2P for tonal languages.	(Abate et al., 2020b; Emiru et al., 2021)
High Out-of-Vocabulary (OOV) Rates: Due to morphological richness.	Morpheme-Based Models: Focusing on subword units for better recognition.	(Tachbelie and Abate, 2023; Abate et al., 2020a)
Difficulty in Data Collection: Limited availability of native speakers.	Synthetic Data Generation: Using data augmentation techniques like speed perturbation.	(Fantaye et al., 2020; Ejigu and Asfaw, 2024)
Dialectal Diversity: Variability in accents and speaking styles.	Domain-Specific ASR: Tailoring systems for specific domains like healthcare, education, etc.	(Babatunde et al., 2023; Doumbouya et al., 2021)

Table 1: Challenges and Future Directions in ASR Research

the development of models capable of addressing tonal variations and morphological complexities in African languages. It is very important to use privacy-preserving methods for ethical deployment, especially in sensitive contexts. Lightweight ASR architectures will facilitate use in resource-constrained environments. Achieving meaningful progress necessitates collaboration among linguists, technologists, policymakers, and local communities to ensure that African languages are supported and preserved in the digital age.

References

Solomon Teferra Abate, Martha Yifiru Tachbelie, and Tanja Schultz. 2020a. Deep neural networks based automatic speech recognition for four ethiopian languages. In *ICASSP 2020-2020 IEEE International Conference on Acoustics, Speech and Signal Processing (ICASSP)*, pages 8274–8278. IEEE.

Solomon Teferra Abate, Martha Yifiru Tachbelie, and Tanja Schultz. 2020b. Multilingual acoustic and language modeling for ethio-semitic languages. In *Interspeech*, pages 1047–1051.

Naira Abdou Mohamed, Anass Allak, Kamel Gaanoun, Imade Benelallam, Zakarya Erraji, and Abdessalam Bahafid. 2024. Multilingual speech recognition initiative for african languages. *International Journal of Data Science and Analytics*, pages 1–16.

Abdulqahar Mukhtar Abubakar, Deepa Gupta, and Susmitha Vekkot. 2024. Development of a diacritic-aware large vocabulary automatic speech recognition for hausa language. *International Journal of Speech Technology*, 27(3):687–700.

Tejumade Afonja, Tobi Olatunji, Sewade Ogun, Naome A Etori, Abraham Owodunni, and Moshood Yekini. 2024. Performant asr models for medical entities in accented speech. *arXiv preprint arXiv:2406.12387*.

Jesujoba O Alabi, Xuechen Liu, Dietrich Klakow, and Junichi Yamagishi. 2024. Afrihubert: A self-supervised speech representation model for african languages. *arXiv preprint arXiv:2409.20201*.

Paul Azunre and Naafi Dasana Ibrahim. 2023. Breaking the low-resource barrier for dagbani asr: From data collection to modeling. In *4th Workshop on African Natural Language Processing*.

Oreoluwa Boluwatife Babatunde, Emmanuel Akeweje, Sharon Ibejih, Victor Tolulope Olufemi, and Sakinat Oluwabukonla Folorunso. 2023. Automatic speech recognition for nigerian-accented english. In *Deep Learning Indaba 2023*.

Aliou Badji, Youssou Dieng, Ibrahima Diop, Papa Alioune Cisse, and Boubacar Diouf. 2020. Automatic speaker recognition (asr) application in the monitoring of plhiv in the cross-border area between the gambia, guinea-bissau and senegal. In *Proceedings of the 10th International Conference on Information Systems and Technologies*, pages 1–9.

Antoine Caubrière and Elodie Gauthier. 2024. Africa-centric self-supervised pre-training for multilingual speech representation in a sub-saharan context. *arXiv preprint arXiv:2404.02000*.

Moussa Doumbouya, Lisa Einstein, and Chris Piech. 2021. Using radio archives for low-resource speech recognition: towards an intelligent virtual assistant for illiterate users. In *Proceedings of the AAAI Conference on Artificial Intelligence*, volume 35, pages 14757–14765.

Yohannes Ayana Ejigu and Tesfa Tegegne Asfaw. 2024. Large scale speech recognition for low resource language amharic, an end-to-end approach.

Safâa El Ouahabi, Sara El Ouahabi, and Mohamed Atounti. 2023. Comparative study of amazigh speech recognition systems based on different toolkits and approaches. In *E3S Web of Conferences*, volume 412, page 01064. EDP Sciences.

Eshete Derb Emiru, Shengwu Xiong, Yaxing Li, Awet Fesseha, and Moussa Diallo. 2021. Improving amharic speech recognition system using connectionist temporal classification with attention model and phoneme-based byte-pair-encodings. *Information*, 12(2):62.

Tessfu Geteye Fantaye, Junqing Yu, and Tulu Tilahun Hailu. 2020. Investigation of automatic speech recognition systems via the multilingual deep neural network modeling methods for a very low-resource language, chaha. *Journal of Signal and Information Processing*, 11(1):1–21.

A. Gutkin, I. Demirsahin, O. Kjartansson, C. Rivera, and K. Túbòsún. 2020. Developing an open-source corpus of Yoruba speech. In *Proceedings of the Annual Conference of the International Speech Communication Association, INTERSPEECH*, volume 2020-Octob, pages 404–408.

U. A. Ibrahim, M. M. Boukar, and M. A. Suleiman. 2022. Development of Hausa acoustic model for speech recognition. *International Journal of Advanced Computer Science and Applications*, 13(5):503–508.

C. Jacobs, N. C. Rakotonirina, E. A. Chimoto, B. A. Bassett, and H. Kamper. 2023. Towards hate speech detection in low-resource languages: Comparing ASR to acoustic word embeddings on Wolof and Swahili. In *Proceedings of the Annual Conference of the International Speech Communication Association, INTERSPEECH*, volume 2023-Augus, pages 436–440.

R. Jimerson, Z. Liu, and E. Prud'hommeaux. 2023. An (unhelpful) guide to selecting the right ASR architecture for your under-resourced language. In *Proceedings of the Annual Meeting of the Association for Computational Linguistics*, volume 2, pages 1008–1016.

Alexander R Kivaisi, Qingjie Zhao, and Jimmy T Mbelwa. 2023. Swahili speech dataset development and improved pre-training method for spoken digit recognition. *ACM Transactions on Asian and Low-Resource Language Information Processing*, 22(7):1–24.

Ettien Koffi. 2020. A tutorial on acoustic phonetic feature extraction for automatic speech recognition (asr) and text-to-speech (tts) applications in african languages. *Linguistic Portfolios*, 9(1):11.

Joshua L Martin and Kelly Elizabeth Wright. 2023. Bias in automatic speech recognition: The case of african american language. *Applied Linguistics*, 44(4):613–630.

Antoine Nzeyimana. 2023. Kinspeak: Improving speech recognition for kinyarwanda via semi-supervised learning methods. *arXiv preprint arXiv:2308.11863*.

Tolulope Ogunremi, Kola Tubosun, Anuoluwapo Aremu, Iroro Orife, and David Ifeoluwa Adelani. 2023. \{I} r\{o} y\{i} nspeech: A multi-purpose yor\{u} b\'{a} speech corpus. *arXiv preprint arXiv:2307.16071*.

Tobi Olatunji, Tejumade Afonja, Aditya Yadavalli, Chris Chinenye Emezue, Sahib Singh, Bonaventure FP Dossou, Joanne Osuchukwu, Salomey Osei, Atnafu Lambebo Tonja, Naome Etori, et al. 2023. Afrispeech-200: Pan-african accented speech dataset for clinical and general domain asr. *Transactions of the Association for Computational Linguistics*, 11:1669–1685.

Falia Ramanantsoa. 2023. Voxmg: An automatic speech recognition dataset for malagasy. In *4th Workshop on African Natural Language Processing*.

Selamu Shamore, Amin Tuni Gure, and Mohammed Abebe Yimer. 2023. Hadiyyissa automatic speech recognition using deep learning approach. In *2023 International Conference on Information and Communication Technology for Development for Africa (ICT4DA)*, pages 144–149. IEEE.

L. W. Sirora and M. Mutandavari. 2024. A deep learning automatic speech recognition model for shona language. *International Journal of Innovative Research in Computer and Communication Engineering*, 12(9).

Martha Yifiru Tachbelie and Solomon Teferra Abate. 2023. Lexical modeling for the development of amharic automatic speech recognition systems. *Language Resources and Evaluation*, 57(3):963–984.

Martha Yifiru Tachbelie, Solomon Teferra Abate, and Tanja Schultz. 2020. Dnn-based multilingual automatic speech recognition for wolaytta using oromo speech. In *Proceedings of the 1st Joint Workshop on Spoken Language Technologies for Under-resourced languages (SLTU) and Collaboration and Computing for Under-Resourced Languages (CCURL)*, pages 265–270.

Georgia Zellou and Mohamed Lahrouchi. 2024. Linguistic disparities in cross-language automatic speech recognition transfer from arabic to tashlhiyt. *Scientific Reports*, 14(1):313.

SabiYarn: Advancing Low Resource Languages with Multitask NLP Pretraining

Jeffrey Otoibhi
drjeffreypaul@gmail.com

Oduguwa Damilola
University of Lagos
oduguwadamilola40@gmail.com

Okpare David
dave@datached.com

Abstract

The rapid advancement of large language models (LLMs) has revolutionized natural language processing, yet a significant challenge persists: the under representation of low-resource languages. This paper introduces SABIYARN, a novel 125M parameter decoder-only language model specifically designed to address this gap for Nigerian languages. Our research demonstrates that a relatively small language model can achieve remarkable performance across multiple languages even in a low-resource setting when trained on carefully curated task-specific datasets. We introduce a multitask learning framework designed for computational efficiency, leveraging techniques such as sequence packing to maximize token throughput per batch. This allows SABIYARN to make the most of a limited compute budget while achieving strong performance across multiple NLP tasks.

This paper not only highlights the effectiveness of our approach but also challenges the notion that only massive models can achieve high performance in diverse linguistic contexts, outperforming models over 100 times its parameter size on specific tasks such as translation (in both directions), Named Entity Recognition, Text Diacritization, and Sentiment Analysis in the low-resource languages it was trained on. SabiYarn-125M represents a significant step towards democratizing NLP technologies for low-resource languages, offering a blueprint for developing efficient, high-performing models tailored to specific linguistic regions. Our work paves the way for more inclusive and culturally sensitive AI systems, potentially transforming how language technologies are developed and deployed in linguistically diverse areas like Nigeria and beyond.

1 Introduction

The field of natural language processing (NLP) has witnessed remarkable advancements in recent years, driven by the development of large-scale, pre-trained language models. These powerful models have demonstrated impressive capabilities in handling a variety of language-related tasks, from text generation to language understanding, and emergent reasoning abilities as they scale to ever-increasing model sizes (Wei et al., 2022). Despite the remarkable progress in NLP, the performance of large language models (LLM) in African languages remains suboptimal. Recent studies, such as the analysis by (Ojo et al., 2023), highlight the significant performance gap between African languages and high-resource languages such as English in the state-of-the-art large language models, including LLaMa 2 (Touvron et al., 2023), and GPT-4 (Achiam et al., 2023). Their findings reveal that while GPT-4 achieves average or impressive results on classification tasks, it performs poorly on generative tasks like machine translation, while LLaMa 2 recorded the worst performance due to its English-centric pretraining and limited multilingual capabilities. These results underscore the urgent need to address the under representation of African languages in LLMs, ensuring they are not left behind as these technologies continue to evolve.

To address this gap, we present SABIYARN-125M, a decoder-only foundational (pre-trained) language model specifically designed to support the major languages spoken in Nigeria. Our model tackles two main challenges in developing NLP solutions for Nigerian languages: limited computational resources and a scarcity of high-quality data sources. Using a diverse training dataset and a multitask learning approach, this model aims to provide versatile and inclusive language technology that can empower Nigerian communities and contribute to the global NLP landscape. Our model is pre-trained on a diverse dataset covering nine Nigerian languages: Yoruba, Igbo, Hausa, Pidgin English, Fulani, Fulah, Fulfulde, Uhrobo, and Efik. Previ-

Proceedings of the Sixth Workshop on African Natural Language Processing (AfricaNLP 2025), pages 95–107
July 31, 2025

ous models have predominantly focused on the four major Nigerian Languages, Yoruba, Igbo, Pidgin, and Hausa. Our work builds on this foundation by extending further language coverage beyond the four major Nigerian Languages, to include several underrepresented languages, increasing language diversity and enabling our model SABIYARN to perform various NLP tasks while preserving cultural and linguistic nuances.

We adopt a mixture of training strategies, including a technique called Sequence Packing (Krell et al., 2022)) for the efficient processing of sequences to speed up pretraining and minimize wasted attention computation, task-conditioning prompts inspired by (Raffel et al., 2020), a multi-task learning objective (Zhang and Yang, 2021) and a custom loss computation strategy that leverages sequence packing, ensuring the model learns precisely from the task-relevant information. This hybrid approach allows us to maximize the potential of each parameter given the limited resources, achieving impressive results across a range of NLP tasks, including Named Entity Recognition, Topic classification, Translation, Diacritization, and Sentiment Analysis, even in zero-shot settings.

In the following sections, we detail our methodology, present our results, and discuss the implications of our findings for the future of NLP in Nigeria and potentially other linguistically diverse regions. Our work contributes to the democratization of NLP technologies but also paves the way for more inclusive AI solutions that respect and preserve linguistic diversity.

2 Related Work

The rapid advancement of large language models (LLMs) has revolutionized natural language processing (NLP), with models like GPT (Radford and Narasimhan, 2018) demonstrating the power of scaling decoder-only architectures. These models, pre-trained with multi-task instructions, have achieved human-level performance in zero-shot and few-shot settings (Brown et al., 2020), setting a new standard for NLP. However, a critical limitation persists: the underrepresentation of low-resource languages, particularly African languages, in these advancements. This gap has motivated research into developing specialized models that address the unique challenges of low-resource linguistic contexts.

Early efforts to address this gap, such as AFRIBERTA (Ogueji et al., 2021), marked a significant step forward. AfriBERTa, a 126M-parameter encoder-only model, was pre-trained on 11 African languages and outperformed larger multilingual models like XLM-R (Conneau et al., 2020) and MBert (Devlin et al., 2019) on African language benchmarks. This success highlighted the potential of smaller, high-quality models tailored to low-resource languages, challenging the assumption that larger models are always superior. However, AfriBERTa's encoder-only architecture limited its applicability to generative tasks, leaving a gap for decoder-based models that could better handle tasks like text generation and diacritization.

Further advancements by (Hedderich et al., 2020) and (Alabi et al., 2022) explored fine-tuning and adaptation techniques for African languages. While (Hedderich et al., 2020) focused on single-language adaptation, (Alabi et al., 2022) introduced Multi-Language Adaptation Fine-Tuning (MAFT), which extended adaptation to multiple languages. Their work resulted in Afro-XLM-R[1], a model that outperformed AfriBERTa by leveraging techniques like non-African language token removal. Despite these improvements, these models remained encoder-based and relied on large-scale multilingual pretraining, which often dilutes the representation of low-resource languages. Recent successes in Large Language Models (LLMs) have highlighted the superiority of decoder-only architectures in various NLP tasks, necessitating re-evaluating approaches to modeling Nigerian languages. Efforts such as (Buzaaba* et al., 2024) and (Mwongela et al., 2024) have explored the decoder-only architectures for low-resourced African languages. However these models were fine-tuned or adapted from pretrained base models. Our approach considers pretraining the model entirely from scratch.

We argue that decoder-only models offer unique advantages, such as multi-task learning and emergent abilities that arise with scaling, (Wei et al., 2022). These capabilities are reflected in our model, SABIYARN, which excels at tasks it was not necessarily pre-trained on, such as inter-language translation between Nigerian languages. This underscores the potential of decoder-only architectures to better capture the linguistic intricacies and practical utility of these languages. The trend of scaling LLMs

[1]https://huggingface.co/Davlan/afro-xlmr-large

to larger parameter sizes has dominated NLP research, with larger models demonstrating improved reasoning and zero-shot capabilities. However, (Hoffmann et al., 2022) revealed that many models are under-trained relative to their compute budgets, emphasizing the need for efficient training strategies. This finding is particularly relevant for low-resource languages, where data scarcity and computational constraints make large-scale training impractical. Recent work has also shown that smaller models, when trained on carefully curated datasets, can achieve competitive performance (Abdin et al., 2024), challenging the necessity of massive models for low-resource settings. Notable data collection efforts like WURA (Oladipo et al., 2023), a publicly available high-quality dataset for African languages, that builds on mC4[2] and amounts to 19GB of African texts on various tasks, aim to tackle the problem of high-quality African data.

Despite these advancements, Nigerian languages remain severely underrepresented in NLP research. Existing models often fail to capture the linguistic and cultural nuances of these languages, limiting their practical applicability. This gap underscores the need for a targeted, resource-efficient approach that prioritizes high-quality data curation and efficient parameter utilization. Our work, SABIYARN, addresses this need by introducing a 125M-parameter decoder-only model specifically trained for Nigerian languages. By leveraging a multi-task learning framework (Zhang and Yang, 2021) and adhering to Chinchilla scaling laws, SABIYARN demonstrates that smaller, meticulously trained models can achieve remarkable performance in low-resource settings, offering a viable alternative to the prevailing trend of massive, indiscriminate scaling.

3 Methodology

This section details the development of SABIYARN-125M, including the dataset collation, processing, model architecture, and training.

3.1 Dataset Curation and Cleaning

The preparation of our datasets involved a meticulous process of collation, deduplication, task-specific tagging, and tokenization. This section outlines our methodology for ensuring the datasets were optimally structured for our multi-task learning approach.

[2]urlhttps://paperswithcode.com/dataset/mc4

The training dataset for SabiYarn was curated through a comprehensive effort that involved manually aggregating relevant data sets from sources such as Hugging face and the BBC Africa news website. The resulting dataset comprised approximately 114.7 million samples, representing 10.1 billion tokens (see Table 7 and Table 8 for data distribution), encompassing a diverse range of text data in various Nigerian languages, including the bible, news articles, social media posts, literary works, and educational resources for different NLP tasks. These tasks include: text generation, translation, sentiment and topic classification, text summarization, headline generation, text diacritization, text cleaning, instruction following and reasoning.

The text diacritization and cleaning datasets were generated by introducing random noise into a portion of the already collated data. For each character in the original data, there was a 15% probability of applying a random modification. This modification involved either inserting a random character or deleting the original character.

To ensure dataset quality and relevance, a rigorous cleaning and filtering process was applied to all collected datasets. This involved the following techniques:

- **Manual Scrutiny**: Duplicates, unwanted samples, and unreadable characters were manually identified and removed.
- **Normalization**: Text formats were standardized for consistency, including the conversion of Unicode characters to their language equivalents.
- **Quality Refinement**: Data integrity issues were addressed. This included removing data exhibiting social, gender, and sexual biases (identified during manual selection), filtering out repeated nonsensical characters using regular expressions, and excluding poor-quality samples. All sentence lengths and single-word translations were considered, while empty strings were discarded. This was a time-intensive but crucial step.

The resulting dataset is a rich and diverse corpus that captures linguistic nuances and incorporates cultural contexts specific to the target (9) Nigerian languages including English. However, the complete dataset has not yet been made publicly available.

3.2 Dataset Task Assignment

For each dataset described in the previous section, we undertook a manual review process to determine its suitability for specific NLP tasks. This critical step ensured that each dataset was appropriately matched to tasks such as translation, sentiment classification, named entity recognition, topic classification, instruction-following and so on.

3.2.1 Task-Specific Tagging

Upon establishing the task relevance of each dataset, we implemented a unique tagging system. This system involves the use of task-specific tag pairs, designed to clearly demarcate the input and output segments of each data sample. The tagging process follows this structure:

- A unique start tag is prepended to the input text segment.
- A corresponding end tag is appended after the input text, followed by the output text.

For instance, in a sentiment classification task:

```
<classify>I love rice!<sentiment> positive
```

Here, `<classify>` and `<sentiment>` are the task-specific tags, "I love rice!" is the input text, and "positive" is the output text. Other tags can be seen in Table 9

3.2.2 Rationale for Tagging

This tagging approach serves several crucial purposes.

1. **Task Identification**: It allows the model to identify the specific NLP task associated with each input during training and inference.
2. **Input-Output Demarcation**: It clearly separates the input text from the expected output, facilitating more effective learning of the input-output relationship through focused loss computation.
3. **Multi-Task Learning**: Using consistent tagging for different tasks, we enable the model to learn multiple tasks within a unified framework.

3.3 Tokenization

SabiYarn-125M utilizes the Bloom tokenizer, a BPE tokenizer pretrained on a curated dataset to effectively handle the linguistic nuances and diacritics of 9 Nigerian languages. Informed by the vocabulary sizes of GPT-2 and Mistral v3 tokenizers, and considering the training corpus's linguistic diversity, we established a vocabulary size of 52,050 tokens. A vocabulary size of 52k was chosen to achieve a compromise between adequate coverage across 9 languages and practical compute/memory limitations. This decision is supported by the findings of (Dagan et al., 2024), who suggest that increasing vocabulary size, and consequently decreasing sequence length, may lead to diminished performance as a result of reduced FLOPS efficiency during training. Task-specific tags were incorporated as special tokens during tokenizer training.

The trained tokenizer was subsequently used to tokenize the cleaned training data into a stream of token ID sequences, which were stored in a binary file in `uint8` format. During this process, a validation set comprising approximately 6 million tokens was generated by random sampling and stored in a separate binary file.

3.4 Model Architecture

SabiYarn-125M is a 125-million-parameter language model based on the Generative Pre-trained Transformer J (GPT-J) architecture. To enhance generalization, particularly in low-resource settings, we extend the attention module's output vectors with additional information via a feedforward network in each transformer block following the design used in GPT-J[3] (see comparison in Fig 1). However, we employed a trainable positional embedding layer unlike the rotary embedding layer seen in GPT-J's architecture. This choice was motivated by the hypothesis that trainable embeddings could offer greater flexibility in learning positional relationships within a smaller parameter space, potentially leading to faster convergence and improved performance compared to fixed rotary embeddings at this scale. We believe that this design enables the model to handle a wide range of NLP tasks with limited data. See Table 1 for specific details.

The model features 12 layers, 12 attention heads, an embedding size of 768, and a context length of 1024, and employs learned positional embeddings, optimizing its learning capacity. These specifications align with the GPT-2 medium model.

[3] `https://www.eleuther.ai/artifacts/gpt-j`

Model Name	n_{params}	n_{layers}	d_{model}	n_{heads}	d_{head}	Context Length	Learning Rate
SabiYarn-125M	125M	12	768	12	64	1024	6.0×10^{-5}

Table 1: SabiYarn Model Specifications

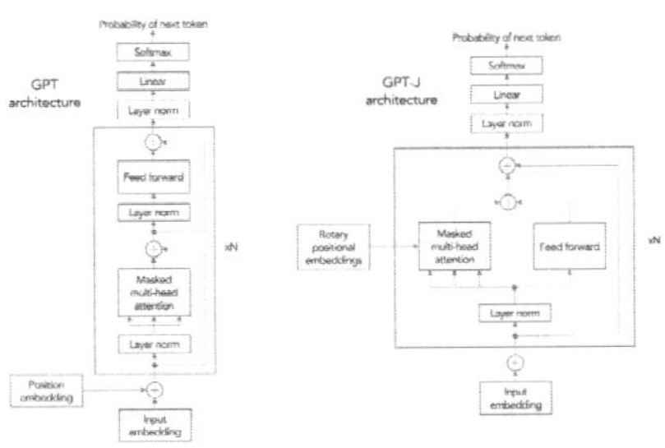

Figure 1: GPT-J architecture

3.5 Pretraining

SabiYarn-125M was pre-trained using causal language modeling with a multitask objective on a diverse, multilingual Nigerian corpus. This joint training enriches shared linguistic representations, improving next-word prediction and generalizing across tasks and languages. By increasing effective training data size and diversity (crucial for underrepresented languages), the model develops stronger token representations, enhancing language understanding and prediction. This multitask framework yields transferable and effective representations for various NLP applications, boosting performance and versatility. Table 8 presents the token distribution per language and task.

During model pretraining, we implemented a comprehensive masking strategy to prevent information leakage and ensure robust learning. Our approach consisted of two key components:

1. **Task dependent, token-level masking:** During training, when processing packed token sequences, a custom mask is applied for next-token prediction. If a sequence includes task-specific tags (e.g., for translation or NER, detailed in table 9), all tokens between these paired tags (representing the typical input) are masked out when calculating the cross-entropy loss on the shifted target sequence. This strategy trains the model to predict not only subsequent tokens generally but also to generate the correct output sequence conditioned on the presence of a downstream task and its corresponding input. This masking mechanism is illustrated in Fig 2).

2. **Sequence Packing:** We isolated attention calculations to prevent information leakage between different data samples in a batch, ensuring that each sample's processing remained independent.

As visualized in Figure 2, this dual masking approach created a more challenging learning environment that encourages the model to develop a genuine understanding of linguistic patterns rather than relying on shortcuts or memorization. Using this technique, we significantly improved the model's ability to learn task-specific features and generalize to unseen data.

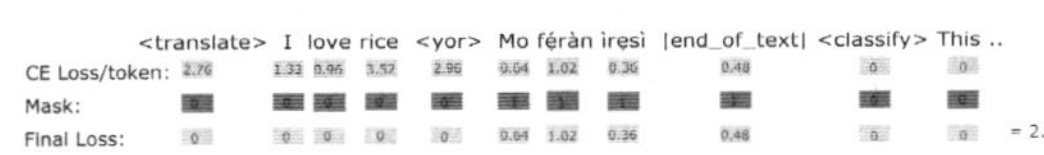

Figure 2: Masking during loss computation

The model was trained on a single 24GB GPU, token ID sequences of length 1,024 (block size) were randomly sampled from the binary file to form batches of size 12. A gradient accumulation step of 40 was used, resulting in an effective token batch size of 406000 tokens, in conjunction with a cosine learning rate scheduler with a maximum learning rate of 6×10^{-4} and a minimum learning rate of 6×10^{-5}. Training was carried out with precision bfloat16 to optimize memory usage and accelerate training without compromising quality.

4 Evaluation and Results

4.1 Evaluation Methodology

The performance of SabiYarn-125M was evaluated across a spectrum of NLP tasks relevant to the Nigerian linguistic landscape. To ensure a comprehensive and reproducible assessment, we adopted the benchmark datasets and tasks used by (Ojo et al., 2023), including Translation, News Classification, Named Entity Recognition (NER), Sentiment Analysis, Text Diacritization, and Text Cleaning. These datasets, MASAKHANEWS (Adelani et al., 2023) for news classification, AFRISENTI (Muhammad et al., 2023) for sentiment analysis, and MASAKHANER(Adelani et al., 2021) for named entity recognition, provide a robust framework for assessing the model's capabilities across diverse African languages. By adhering to these established benchmarks, we facilitate a fair and meaningful comparison between SabiYarn-125M and existing state-of-the-art language models.

4.2 Fine-tuning

In addition to evaluating the base pre-trained model, we fine-tuned SabiYarn-125M on the training sets of the benchmark datasets mentioned above. This process yielded several specialized models, each designed to excel in specific NLP tasks:

- **SabiYarn-finetune**: Fine-tuned on the aggregated training sets of all benchmark datasets, encompassing all four Nigerian languages (Yoruba, Igbo, Hausa, and Pidgin) and including back-translation data.
- **SabiYarn-translate**: Optimized for translation tasks, fine-tuned on the benchmark translation dataset and its corresponding back-translations across all languages.
- **SabiYarn-topic**: Optimized for topic classification, fine-tuned on the combined multilingual topic classification dataset.
- **SabiYarn-sentiment**: Optimized for sentiment analysis, fine-tuned on the aggregated sentiment classification dataset across all languages.
- **SabiYarn-NER**: Optimized for Named Entity Recognition, fine-tuned on the combined NER dataset spanning all languages.
- **SabiYarn-diacritics-cleaner**: Optimized for text diacritization and cleaning across all languages.

It should be noted that our approach diverges from that of M2M-100, which employed separate fine-tuning processes for each language and translation direction. We adopted a unified fine-tuning strategy across languages, a method employed in various multilingual models. To create the dataset for text diacritization and cleaning fine tuning tasks, we utilized pre-existing datasets and applied custom transformations. For diacritization, we selectively removed diacritical marks with a 50% - 100% probability, creating pairs of original and diacritic-free text. For text cleaning, we introduced controlled noise to the text, simulating common errors and inconsistencies found in real-world data. The resulting datasets were split into train, validation, and test sets, with 15,000, 1,000, and 5,000 samples respectively for each language and task.

5 Results and Discussion

The subsequent sections provide a detailed analysis of the performance of SabiYarn-125M across the evaluated tasks. We present comparative results against existing models and discuss the implications of our findings for low-resource language processing in the African context.

5.1 Task-specific Performance

Translation: SabiYarn, despite its significantly smaller size (125M parameters), demonstrates competitive performance in machine translation tasks, particularly excelling in forward translation for Igbo and pidgin and backward translation for Yoruba. While larger models like mT0-MT (13B) and M2M-100 (418M) achieve higher scores in several categories, SabiYarn's performance is remarkable considering its parameter efficiency. The model's strong performance in Nigerian Pidgin (Pcm) translation, outperforming many larger models, highlights its effectiveness in handling this unique linguistic context. However, the reliability of the evaluation is somewhat constrained by the benchmark dataset's use of only a single reference translation per source sentence. This is particularly limiting for Nigerian languages such as Yoruba, where multiple valid translations are often possible, potentially underestimating the models' true capabilities. Additionally, SabiYarn's tendency to avoid verbosity and its occasional struggle with coherence during translation present areas for future improvement, suggesting that refining the model's ability to balance conciseness with contextual understanding could further enhance its performance.

Sentiment Analysis: SabiYarn, with only 125M parameters, demonstrates impressive performance in sentiment analysis across Nigerian languages, achieving average accuracies of 66.0% (SabiYarn-Sentiment) and 65.3% (SabiYarn-Finetune). While AfroXLMR-Large (550M parameters) leads in most categories as seen in Table 4, SabiYarn consistently outperforms larger models like GPT4 and

Task	avg	Yor	Hau	Ibo	Pcm
Text Diacritization	96.9	**100.0**	-	93.7	-
Text Cleaning	71.3	77.83	54.67	**81.54**	71.17

Table 2: **Text Diacritization and Cleaning Results**. We show the **BLEU** score of **SabiYarn-diacritics-cleaner**.

Model Name	Size	avg	Yor	Hau	Ibo	Pcm
xx-en						
SabiYarn-Translate	125M	40.9	31.2	32.3	46.4	54.9
SabiYarn-Finetune	125M	41.1	29.1	34.4	46.0	54.9
M2M-100	418M	38.3	35.1	35.1	46.1	36.7
mT0	13B	36.0	35.7	32.0	31.2	44.9
mT0-MT	13B	**45.7**	**40.8**	**38.1**	**46.8**	56.9
GPT4	-	27.2	13.6	14.7	21.8	**58.8**
Llama2	13B	29.0	20.8	17.4	23.1	54.8
en-xx						
SabiYarn-Translate	125M	41.3	34.8	31.6	43.3	55.4
SabiYarn-Finetune	125M	41.4	34.4	30.72	42.3	58.0
M2M-100	418M	**48.3**	**35.9**	**43.3**	**50.0**	**64.0**
mT0	13B	19.9	6.3	15.4	23.5	34.2
mT0-MT	13B	31.3	15.2	23.11	38.5	48.3
GPT4	-	35.8	18.1	36.1	35.7	53.4
Llama2	13B	15.7	10.4	14.7	16.3	21.4

Table 3: **Machine Translation Results**: Comparison of ChrF score of SABIYARN and results obtained from Jessica et al. (2023)

Llama2 (13B parameters) across all languages. Notably, SabiYarn-Finetune surpasses AfroXLMR-Large in Nigerian Pidgin (Pcm), highlighting its effectiveness in low-resource languages. The consistent performance of the model in various Nigerian languages (63.6% to 66.8%) emphasizes its robustness and efficiency in handling multilingual sentiment analysis tasks with significantly fewer parameters.

News Classification: In news classification (Table 5), SabiYarn-Topic showcases remarkable performance with an average F1 score of 87. 03%. This is particularly impressive when compared to much larger models like mT0 (41.6%) and GPT4 (55.45%). SabiYarn even outperforms the larger AfroXLMR-Large model in Nigerian Pidgin (pcm) with a score of 96.3%. This demonstrates SabiYarn's strong capability in understanding and categorizing news content in Nigerian languages, despite its smaller size.

Named Entity Recognition: SabiYarn-Finetune achieves the highest F1 score of 93.4, outperforming all other models, including the larger AfroXLMR-Large (550M) and prompting-based LLMs like GPT-4 and Llama2 (Table 6). In contrast, larger models like mT0 and mT0-MT fail to perform well in this task, scoring 0.0, while GPT-4 and Llama2 achieve modest results of 55.6 and 17.8, respectively. This may underscore the limitations of prompting-based methods for NER tasks compared to specialized fine-tuned models such as SabiYarn.

Text Diacritization: The results for text diacritization, as shown in Table 2, demonstrate the model's strong performance in this task. SabiYarn-diacritics-cleaner model achieved a perfect BLEU score of 100.0 for Yoruba and a high score of 93.7 for Igbo. These results indicate the model's exceptional ability to accurately restore diacritical marks, particularly in Yoruba text, and its strong performance in Igbo, suggesting its potential for improving text processing in these languages.

Text Cleaning: As seen in Table 2, The model achieves the highest BLEU score of 77.83 for Yoruba, indicating strong performance in this language. However, performance varies significantly between languages, with Hausa scoring the lowest at 54.67, probably due to the lack of diacritics in this language, suggesting room for improvement in handling linguistic diversity and complexity.

6 Conclusion

Although originally trained in Nigerian languages, SabiYarn-125M represents a significant advancement in the field of natural language processing (NLP) for languages with limited data. By encompassing a diverse range of languages and offering a comprehensive suite of NLP functionalities, this model establishes a robust foundation for the potential transformation of language technology not only in Nigeria but across the African continent, thus making a substantial contribution to the global NLP community.

The development of SabiYarn-125M is driven by several key objectives:

1. **Empowering Researchers:** This model serves as a versatile foundation for future research and development, facilitating the creation of more culturally relevant and impactful language technologies.

2. **Addressing Linguistic Diversity:** By supporting multiple Nigerian languages, SabiYarn-125M tackles the unique challenges posed by Africa's rich linguistic landscape.

Model Name	Size	avg	Yor	Hau	Ibo	Pcm
SabiYarn-Sentiment	125M	66.0	65.0	66.1	66.0	66.0
SabiYarn-Finetune	125M	65.3	64.8	66.0	63.6	**66.8**
AfroXLMR-Large	550M	**75.0**	**74.1**	**80.7**	**79.5**	**68.7**
Prompting of LLMs						
mT0	13B	41.6	35.6	40.5	26.7	63.6
mT0-MT	13B	34.4	23.7	36.1	27.2	50.7
GPT4	-	55.0	55.6	41.8	66.7	57.7
Llama2	13B	27.8	24.0	25.5	35.1	24.3

Table 4: **Sentiment Analysis Results**: Comparison of Accuracy score of SABIYARN and results obtained from (Ojo et al., 2023)

Model Name	Size	avg	Yor	Hau	Ibo	Pcm
SabiYarn-Topic	125M	90.9	89.0	**90.2**	87.7	96.7
SabiYarn-Finetune	125M	87.03	84.4	82.1	85.3	67.8
AfroXLMR-Large	550M	**92.95**	**94.0**	92.2	**93.4**	92.1
AfriTeVa-V2	428M	91.2	92.3	89.4	86.1	**96.8**
Prompting of LLMs						
mT0	13B	41.6	35.6	40.5	26.7	63.6
mT0-MT	13B	34.4	23.7	36.1	27.2	50.7
GPT4	-	55.45	55.6	41.8	66.7	57.7
Llama2	13B	27.22	24.0	25.5	35.1	24.3

Table 5: **News Classification Results** We compare the F1-score of **SabiYarn** with that of the current **SOTA** models.

Model Name	Size	avg
SabiYarn-NER	125M	93.2
SabiYarn-Finetune	125M	**93.4**
AfroXLMR-Large	550M	84.6
Prompting of LLMs		
mT0	13B	0.0
mT0-MT	13B	0.0
GPT4	-	55.6
Llama2	13B	17.8

Table 6: **Named Entity Recognition Results**: We compare the F1 score of SABIYARN with results obtained from (Ojo et al., 2023).

3. **Enhancing NLP Capabilities:** The model's wide array of functionalities paves the way for advanced applications in machine translation, sentiment analysis, named entity recognition, and beyond.

Looking ahead, SabiYarn-125M opens up numerous avenues for future research:

- **Expansion to Additional Languages:** Future iterations could incorporate more African languages, further enhancing the model's versatility and impact.
- **Domain-Specific Adaptations:** Researchers could fine-tune newer versions of the model for specific domains such as healthcare, education, or legal applications, tailoring it to address sector-specific challenges.
- **Cross-Lingual Transfer Learning:** Investigating the model's capacity for cross-language fine-tuning across related African languages could yield valuable insights for low-resource language processing.

In conclusion, SabiYarn-125M represents a significant step towards bridging the gap in NLP research and technology for underrepresented languages. By showcasing the model's capabilities and potential applications, we hope to inspire and encourage further advancements in this field, ultimately contributing to the preservation and empowerment of Africa's rich linguistic heritage in this digital age and a more inclusive and equitable global language technology ecosystem.

Limitations

The scope of our evaluation was necessarily limited to the aforementioned Nigerian languages due to two critical constraints: the acute scarcity of high-quality, diverse datasets for African languages, and the limited availability of substantial computational resources. These limitations not only underscore the challenges inherent in low-resource language research but also highlight a systemic issue in the field of artificial intelligence as it pertains to linguistically diverse regions. The paucity of comprehensive datasets and the computational divide present significant barriers to advancing NLP capabilities across the African continent. This situation urgently calls for a multi-faceted approach: increased investment in data collection and curation for African languages, enhanced allocation of computational resources for research in these areas, and a concerted effort to build local AI research capacity. Addressing these challenges is crucial not only for advancing NLP technologies in the region but also for ensuring that the benefits of AI are equitably distributed across diverse linguistic communities. Future research must prioritize these areas to foster a more inclusive and representative landscape in global NLP development.

Acknowledgments

We extend our sincere gratitude to all who contributed to this research. First, we thank our academic advisors for their invaluable guidance and feedback, and the Nigerian/African language experts for their expertise in curating and validating the benchmark datasets. We also acknowledge the open-source community, particularly the developers of tools like PyTorch and Accelerate, which were instrumental to our work. Additionally, we are grateful to our colleagues in Natural Language Processing and African language research for laying the groundwork that inspired this study.

Finally, we express profound appreciation to our families, friends, and loved ones for their unwavering support and encouragement throughout this journey. While many have contributed to this work, any errors or oversights remain our responsibility.

References

Marah Abdin, Jyoti Aneja, Hany Awadalla, Ahmed Awadallah, Ammar Ahmad Awan, Nguyen Bach, Amit Bahree, Arash Bakhtiari, Jianmin Bao, Harkirat Behl, et al. 2024. Phi-3 technical report: A highly capable language model locally on your phone. *arXiv preprint arXiv:2404.14219*.

OpenAI Josh Achiam, Steven Adler, Sandhini Agarwal, Lama Ahmad, Ilge Akkaya, Florencia Leoni Aleman, Diogo Almeida, Janko Altenschmidt, Sam Altman, Shyamal Anadkat, Red Avila, Igor Babuschkin, Suchir Balaji, Valerie Balcom, Paul Baltescu, Haim ing Bao, Mo Bavarian, Jeff Belgum, Irwan Bello, Jake Berdine, Gabriel Bernadett-Shapiro, Christopher Berner, Lenny Bogdonoff, Oleg Boiko, Made laine Boyd, Anna-Luisa Brakman, Greg Brockman, Tim Brooks, Miles Brundage, Kevin Button, Trevor Cai, Rosie Campbell, Andrew Cann, Brittany Carey, Chelsea Carlson, Rory Carmichael, Brooke Chan, Che Chang, Fotis Chantzis, Derek Chen, Sully Chen, Ruby Chen, Jason Chen, Mark Chen, Benjamin Chess, Chester Cho, Casey Chu, Hyung Won Chung, Dave Cummings, Jeremiah Currier, Yunxing Dai, Cory Decareaux, Thomas Degry, Noah Deutsch, Damien Deville, Arka Dhar, David Dohan, Steve Dowling, Sheila Dunning, Adrien Ecoffet, Atty Eleti, Tyna Eloundou, David Farhi, Liam Fedus, Niko Felix, Sim'on Posada Fishman, Juston Forte, Is abella Fulford, Leo Gao, Elie Georges, Christian Gibson, Vik Goel, Tarun Gogineni, Gabriel Goh, Raphael Gontijo-Lopes, Jonathan Gordon, Morgan Grafstein, Scott Gray, Ryan Greene, Joshua Gross, Shixiang Shane Gu, Yufei Guo, Chris Hallacy, Jesse Han, Jeff Harris, Yuchen He, Mike Heaton, Jo hannes Heidecke, Chris Hesse, Alan Hickey, Wade Hickey, Peter Hoeschele, Brandon Houghton, Kenny Hsu, Shengli Hu, Xin Hu, Joost Huizinga, Shantanu Jain, Shawn Jain, Joanne Jang, Angela Jiang, Roger Jiang, Haozhun Jin, Denny Jin, Shino Jomoto, Billie Jonn, Heewoo Jun, Tomer Kaftan, Lukasz Kaiser, Ali Kamali, Ingmar Kanitscheider, Nitish Shirish Keskar, Tabarak Khan, Logan Kilpatrick, Jong Wook Kim, Christina Kim, Yongjik Kim, Hendrik Kirchner, Jamie Ryan Kiros, Matthew Knight, Daniel Kokotajlo, Lukasz Kondraciuk, Andrew Kondrich, Aris Konstantinidis, Kyle Kosic, Gretchen Krueger, Vishal Kuo, Michael Lampe, Ikai Lan, Teddy Lee, Jan Leike, Jade Leung, Daniel Levy, Chak Li, Rachel Lim, Molly Lin, Stephanie Lin, Ma teusz Litwin, Theresa Lopez, Ryan Lowe, Patricia Lue, Anna Makanju, Kim Malfacini, Sam Manning, Todor Markov, Yaniv Markovski, Bianca Martin, Katie Mayer, Andrew Mayne, Bob McGrew, Scott Mayer McKinney, Christine McLeavey, Paul McMillan, Jake McNeil, David Medina, Aalok Mehta, Jacob Menick, Luke Metz, Andrey Mishchenko, Pamela Mishkin, Vinnie Monaco, Evan Morikawa, Daniel P. Mossing, Tong Mu, Mira Murati, Oleg Murk, David M'ely, Ashvin Nair, Reiichiro Nakano, Rajeev Nayak, Arvind Neelakantan, Richard Ngo, Hyeonwoo Noh, Ouyang Long, Cullen O'Keefe, Jakub W. Pachocki, Alex Paino, Joe Palermo, Ashley Pantuliano, Giambattista Parascandolo, Joel Parish, Emy Parparita, Alexandre Passos, Mikhail Pavlov, Andrew Peng, Adam Perelman, Filipe de Avila Belbute Peres, Michael Petrov, Henrique Pondé de Oliveira Pinto, Michael Pokorny, Michelle Pokrass, Vitchyr H. Pong, Tolly Powell, Alethea Power, Boris Power, Elizabeth Proehl, Raul Puri, Alec Radford, Jack W. Rae, Aditya Ramesh, Cameron Raymond, Francis Real, Kendra Rimbach, Carl Ross, Bob Rotsted, Henri Roussez, Nick Ryder, Mario D. Saltarelli, Ted Sanders, Shibani Santurkar, Girish Sastry, Heather Schmidt, David Schnurr, John Schulman, Daniel Selsam, Kyla Sheppard, Toki Sherbakov, Jessica Shieh, Sarah Shoker, Pranav Shyam, Szymon Sidor, Eric Sigler, Maddie Simens, Jordan Sitkin, Katarina Slama, Ian Sohl, Benjamin Sokolowsky, Yang Song, Natalie Staudacher, Felipe Petroski Such, Natalie Summers, Ilya Sutskever, Jie Tang, Nikolas A. Tezak, Madeleine Thompson, Phil Tillet, Amin Tootoonchian, Elizabeth Tseng, Preston Tuggle, Nick Turley, Jerry Tworek, Juan

Felipe Cer'on Uribe, Andrea Vallone, Arun Vijayvergiya, Chelsea Voss, Carroll L. Wainwright, Justin Jay Wang, Alvin Wang, Ben Wang, Jonathan Ward, Jason Wei, CJ Weinmann, Akila Welihinda, Peter Welinder, Jiayi Weng, Lilian Weng, Matt Wiethoff, Dave Willner, Clemens Winter, Samuel Wolrich, Hannah Wong, Lauren Workman, Sherwin Wu, Jeff Wu, Michael Wu, Kai Xiao, Tao Xu, Sarah Yoo, Kevin Yu, Qim ing Yuan, Wojciech Zaremba, Rowan Zellers, Chong Zhang, Marvin Zhang, Shengjia Zhao, Tianhao Zheng, Juntang Zhuang, William Zhuk, and Barret Zoph. 2023. Gpt-4 technical report.

David Ifeoluwa Adelani, Jade Abbott, Graham Neubig, Daniel D'souza, Julia Kreutzer, Constantine Lignos, Chester Palen-Michel, Happy Buzaaba, Shruti Rijhwani, Sebastian Ruder, Stephen Mayhew, Israel Abebe Azime, Shamsuddeen Muhammad, Chris Chinenye Emezue, Joyce Nakatumba-Nabende, Perez Ogayo, Anuoluwapo Aremu, Catherine Gitau, Derguene Mbaye, Jesujoba Alabi, Seid Muhie Yimam, Tajuddeen Gwadabe, Ignatius Ezeani, Rubungo Andre Niyongabo, Jonathan Mukiibi, Verrah Otiende, Iroro Orife, Davis David, Samba Ngom, Tosin Adewumi, Paul Rayson, Mofetoluwa Adeyemi, Gerald Muriuki, Emmanuel Anebi, Chiamaka Chukwuneke, Nkiruka Odu, Eric Peter Wairagala, Samuel Oyerinde, Clemencia Siro, Tobius Saul Bateesa, Temilola Oloyede, Yvonne Wambui, Victor Akinode, Deborah Nabagereka, Maurice Katusiime, Ayodele Awokoya, Mouhamadane MBOUP, Dibora Gebreyohannes, Henok Tilaye, Kelechi Nwaike, Degaga Wolde, Abdoulaye Faye, Blessing Sibanda, Orevaoghene Ahia, Bonaventure F. P. Dossou, Kelechi Ogueji, Thierno Ibrahima DIOP, Abdoulaye Diallo, Adewale Akinfaderin, Tendai Marengereke, and Salomey Osei. 2021. Masakhaner: Named entity recognition for african languages. *Preprint*, arXiv:2103.11811.

David Ifeoluwa Adelani, Marek Masiak, Israel Abebe Azime, Jesujoba Alabi, Atnafu Lambebo Tonja, Christine Mwase, Odunayo Ogundepo, Bonaventure F. P. Dossou, Akintunde Oladipo, Doreen Nixdorf, Chris Chinenye Emezue, sana al azzawi, Blessing Sibanda, Davis David, Lolwethu Ndolela, Jonathan Mukiibi, Tunde Ajayi, Tatiana Moteu, Brian Odhiambo, Abraham Owodunni, Nnaemeka Obiefuna, Muhidin Mohamed, Shamsuddeen Hassan Muhammad, Teshome Mulugeta Ababu, Saheed Abdullahi Salahudeen, Mesay Gemeda Yigezu, Tajuddeen Gwadabe, Idris Abdulmumin, Mahlet Taye, Oluwabusayo Awoyomi, Iyanuoluwa Shode, Tolulope Adelani, Habiba Abdulganiyu, Abdul-Hakeem Omotayo, Adetola Adeeko, Abeeb Afolabi, Anuoluwapo Aremu, Olanrewaju Samuel, Clemencia Siro, Wangari Kimotho, Onyekachi Ogbu, Chinedu Mbonu, Chiamaka Chukwuneke, Samuel Fanijo, Jessica Ojo, Oyinkansola Awosan, Tadesse Kebede, Toadoum Sari Sakayo, Pamela Nyatsine, Freedmore Sidume, Oreen Yousuf, Mardiyyah Oduwole, Tshinu Tshinu, Ussen Kimanuka, Thina Diko, Siyanda Nxakama, Sinodos Nigusse, Abdulmejid Johar, Shafie Mohamed, Fuad Mire Hassan, Moges Ahmed Mehamed, Evrard Ngabire, Jules Jules, Ivan Ssenkungu, and Pontus Stenetorp. 2023. Masakhanews: News topic classification for african languages. *Preprint*, arXiv:2304.09972.

Jesujoba O. Alabi, David Ifeoluwa Adelani, Marius Mosbach, and Dietrich Klakow. 2022. Adapting pre-trained language models to African languages via multilingual adaptive fine-tuning. In *Proceedings of the 29th International Conference on Computational Linguistics*, pages 4336–4349, Gyeongju, Republic of Korea. International Committee on Computational Linguistics.

Tom Brown, Benjamin Mann, Nick Ryder, Melanie Subbiah, Jared D Kaplan, Prafulla Dhariwal, Arvind Neelakantan, Pranav Shyam, Girish Sastry, Amanda Askell, et al. 2020. Language models are few-shot learners. *Advances in neural information processing systems*, 33:1877–1901.

Happy Buzaaba*, Alexander Wettig*, David Ifeoluwa Adelani, and Christiane Fellbaum. 2024. Model card for afrollama. `https://huggingface.co/Masakhane/afro-llama`. Accessed: 2025-03-06.

Alexis Conneau, Kartikay Khandelwal, Naman Goyal, Vishrav Chaudhary, Guillaume Wenzek, Francisco Guzmán, Edouard Grave, Myle Ott, Luke Zettlemoyer, and Veselin Stoyanov. 2020. Unsupervised cross-lingual representation learning at scale. *Preprint*, arXiv:1911.02116.

Gautier Dagan, Gabriel Synnaeve, and Baptiste Rozière. 2024. Getting the most out of your tokenizer for pre-training and domain adaptation. *Preprint*, arXiv:2402.01035.

Jacob Devlin, Ming-Wei Chang, Kenton Lee, and Kristina Toutanova. 2019. Bert: Pre-training of deep bidirectional transformers for language understanding. *Preprint*, arXiv:1810.04805.

Michael A. Hedderich, David Adelani, Dawei Zhu, Jesujoba Alabi, Udia Markus, and Dietrich Klakow. 2020. Transfer learning and distant supervision for multilingual transformer models: A study on african languages. *Preprint*, arXiv:2010.03179.

Jordan Hoffmann, Sebastian Borgeaud, Arthur Mensch, Elena Buchatskaya, Trevor Cai, Eliza Rutherford, Diego de Las Casas, Lisa Anne Hendricks, Johannes Welbl, Aidan Clark, et al. 2022. Training compute-optimal large language models. *arXiv preprint arXiv:2203.15556*.

Mario Michael Krell, Matej Kosec, Sergio P. Perez, Mrinal Iyer, and Andrew W Fitzgibbon. 2022. Efficient sequence packing without cross-contamination: Accelerating large language models without impacting performance.

Shamsuddeen Hassan Muhammad, Idris Abdulmumin, Abinew Ali Ayele, Nedjma Ousidhoum, David Ifeoluwa Adelani, Seid Muhie Yimam, Ibrahim Sa'id

Ahmad, Meriem Beloucif, Saif M. Mohammad, Sebastian Ruder, Oumaima Hourrane, Pavel Brazdil, Felermino Dário Mário António Ali, Davis David, Salomey Osei, Bello Shehu Bello, Falalu Ibrahim, Tajuddeen Gwadabe, Samuel Rutunda, Tadesse Belay, Wendimu Baye Messelle, Hailu Beshada Balcha, Sisay Adugna Chala, Hagos Tesfahun Gebremichael, Bernard Opoku, and Steven Arthur. 2023. Afrisenti: A twitter sentiment analysis benchmark for african languages. *Preprint*, arXiv:2302.08956.

Stanslaus Mwongela, Jay Patel, Sathy Rajasekharan, Lyvia Lusiji, Francesco Piccino, Mfoniso Ukwak, and Ellen Sebastian. 2024. Afrollama 3. Accessed: 2025-03-06.

Kelechi Ogueji, Yuxin Zhu, and Jimmy Lin. 2021. Small data? no problem! exploring the viability of pretrained multilingual language models for low-resourced languages. In *Proceedings of the 1st Workshop on Multilingual Representation Learning*, pages 116–126, Punta Cana, Dominican Republic. Association for Computational Linguistics.

Jessica Ojo, Kelechi Ogueji, Pontus Stenetorp, and David Ifeoluwa Adelani. 2023. How good are large language models on african languages? *arXiv preprint arXiv:2311.07978*.

Akintunde Oladipo, Mofetoluwa Adeyemi, Orevaoghene Ahia, Abraham Toluwalase Owodunni, Odunayo Ogundepo, David Ifeoluwa Adelani, and Jimmy Lin. 2023. Better quality pre-training data and t5 models for African languages. In *Proceedings of the 2023 Conference on Empirical Methods in Natural Language Processing*, pages 158–168, Singapore. Association for Computational Linguistics.

Alec Radford and Karthik Narasimhan. 2018. Improving language understanding by generative pre-training.

Colin Raffel, Noam Shazeer, Adam Roberts, Katherine Lee, Sharan Narang, Michael Matena, Yanqi Zhou, Wei Li, and Peter J Liu. 2020. Exploring the limits of transfer learning with a unified text-to-text transformer. *Journal of machine learning research*, 21(140):1–67.

Hugo Touvron, Louis Martin, Kevin Stone, Peter Albert, Amjad Almahairi, Yasmine Babaei, Nikolay Bashlykov, Soumya Batra, Prajjwal Bhargava, Shruti Bhosale, Dan Bikel, Lukas Blecher, Cristian Canton Ferrer, Moya Chen, Guillem Cucurull, David Esiobu, Jude Fernandes, Jeremy Fu, Wenyin Fu, Brian Fuller, Cynthia Gao, Vedanuj Goswami, Naman Goyal, Anthony Hartshorn, Saghar Hosseini, Rui Hou, Hakan Inan, Marcin Kardas, Viktor Kerkez, Madian Khabsa, Isabel Kloumann, Artem Korenev, Punit Singh Koura, Marie-Anne Lachaux, Thibaut Lavril, Jenya Lee, Diana Liskovich, Yinghai Lu, Yuning Mao, Xavier Martinet, Todor Mihaylov, Pushkar Mishra, Igor Molybog, Yixin Nie, Andrew Poulton, Jeremy Reizenstein, Rashi Rungta, Kalyan Saladi, Alan Schelten, Ruan Silva, Eric Michael Smith, Ranjan Subramanian, Xiaoqing Ellen Tan, Binh Tang, Ross Taylor, Adina Williams, Jian Xiang Kuan, Puxin Xu, Zheng Yan, Iliyan Zarov, Yuchen Zhang, Angela Fan, Melanie Kambadur, Sharan Narang, Aurelien Rodriguez, Robert Stojnic, Sergey Edunov, and Thomas Scialom. 2023. Llama 2: Open foundation and fine-tuned chat models. *Preprint*, arXiv:2307.09288.

Jason Wei, Yi Tay, Rishi Bommasani, Colin Raffel, Barret Zoph, Sebastian Borgeaud, Dani Yogatama, Maarten Bosma, Denny Zhou, Donald Metzler, Ed H. Chi, Tatsunori Hashimoto, Oriol Vinyals, Percy Liang, Jeff Dean, and William Fedus. 2022. Emergent abilities of large language models. *Transactions on Machine Learning Research*. Survey Certification.

Yu Zhang and Qiang Yang. 2021. A survey on multi-task learning. *IEEE transactions on knowledge and data engineering*, 34(12):5586–5609.

A Appendix

A.1 HuggingFace Datasets Used (Non-exhaustive)

- ayymen/Pontoon-Translations
- igbo_ner
- chymaks/Igbo_ner
- yoruba_wordsim353
- yoruba_gv_ner
- yoruba_bbc_topics
- HausaNLP/HausaVG
- hausa_voa_ner
- Arnold/hausa_common_voice
- moro23/hausa_ng
- vpetukhov/bible_tts_hausa
- mangaphd/hausaBERTdatatrain
- masakhane/masakhaner2
- masakhane/afriqa
- sbmaruf/forai_ml_masakhane_mafand
- masakhane/afriqa-gold-passages
- HausaNLP/HausaVQA
- masakhane/mafand
- mozilla-foundation/common_voice_12_0

Table 7: Detailed breakdown of number of samples per language per task

Language	Trans	Class	Sum	Headline	Instruct	Monolingual	Diac	Clean	Total
English	0	32,536	0	53	2,243,235	11,097,016	0	6,869,858	20,242,698
Yoruba	729,878	21,572	15,572	56,564	5,016,319	11,673,886	3,602,690	381,418	21,497,899
Hausa	2,619,081	29,171	17,721	320,945	3,435,696	11,797,952	0	2,579,220	20,799,786
Igbo	6,377,666	30,265	41,303	162,148	4,967,183	14,376,298	3,393,839	4,056,681	33,405,383
Pidgin	8,988,159	12,087	145,815	289,865	512,816	4,564,139	0	3,650,887	18,163,768
Urhobo	129,668	0	162,970	0	198	32,711	0	0	325,547
Fulfulde	0	0	0	0	0	126,000	0	0	126,000
Fulah	4,018	0	751	0	2,526	134,968	0	0	142,263
Efik	0	0	0	0	0	9,567	0	0	9,567
Total	18,848,470	125,631	384,132	829,575	16,177,973	53,812,537	6,996,529	17,538,064	114,712,911

Table 8: Detailed breakdown of number of tokens per language per task

Language	Trans	Class	Sum	Headline	Instruct	Monolingual	Diac	Clean	Total
English	-	295,542	-	100,612	290,387,169	493,068,409	-	650,222,243	1,434,073,975
Yoruba	115,188,816	603,945	9,030,269	14,666,102	646,467,834	834,162,538	242,229,137	135,178, 107	1,997,526,748
Hausa	250,989,822	617,583	8,761,900	63,429,798	386,761,152	1,186,571,221	-	483,250,638	2,380,382,114
Igbo	609,811,051	530,117	18,338,768	24,977,727	646,811,000	751,549,672	161,485,201	533,371,421	2,746,874,957
Pidgin	298,282,535	276,284	95,768,701	52,113,111	112,421,167	308,031,286	-	580,618,346	1,447,511,430
Urhobo	6,451,518	-	97,198,864	-	56,358	893,162	-	-	104,599,902
Fulfulde	-	-	-	-	-	3,677,103	-	-	3,677,103
Fulah	286,795	-	436,133	-	1,069,200	9,953,441	-	-	11,745,569
Efik	-	-	-	-	-	139,740	-	-	139,740
Total	1,281,010,537	2,323,471	229,534,635	155,287,350	2,083,973,880	3,588,046,572	403,714,338	2,382,640,755	10,126,531,538

- mc4
- cyanic-selkie/wikianc
- HausaNLP/afrisenti-lid-data
- HausaNLP/NaijaSenti-Twitter
- HausaNLP/Naija-Lex
- wikimedia/wikipedia
- gsarti/flores_101
- opus100
- castorini/africlirmatrix
- severo/flores_101
- graelo/wikipedia
- igbo_english_machine_translation
- iamwille/igbo-translation
- castorini/wura
- csebuetnlp/xlsum
- cis-lmu/GlotStoryBook
- wili_2018
- cis-lmu/Glot500
- google/fleurs
- google/xtreme_s
- masakhane/masakhanews
- masakhane/afriqa_wiki_en_fr_100
- bigscience/xP3all
- CohereForAI/aya_collection_language_split
- udhr
- mtek2000/yoruba_newsclass_topic
- mxronga/cultura-x-deduped-yoruba
- mxronga/yoruba-proverbs-parallel-corpora
- ayymen/Weblate-Translations

article booktabs caption

B Previous Section

Some text before the tables. This is to demonstrate the spacing.

Table 9: Task-specific tags used for multi-task training

Task	Start Tag	End Tag
Translation	<translate>	<lang>:
Sentiment Classification	<classify>	<sentiment>:
Topic Classification	<classify>	<topic>:
Instruction Following	<prompt>	<response>:
Headline Generation	<title>	<headline>:
Text Diacritization	<diacritize>	<lang>:
Question Generation	<prompt>	<response>:
Question-Answering	<prompt>	<response>:
Text Summarization	<summarize>	<summary>:
Text Cleaning	<clean>	<lang>:

Table 10: Language tags used for multi-lingual training

Language	Tag
Yoruba	<yor>
Hausa	<hau>
Igbo	<ibo>
English	<eng>
Urhobo	<urh>
Fulah	<ful>
Efik	<efi>
Nigerian Pidgin	<pcm>

Retrieval-Augmented Generation Meets Local Languages for Improved Drug Information Access and Comprehension.

Ahmad Ibrahim Ismail, Bashirudeen Ibrahim Opeyemi,
Olubayo Adekanmbi, Ife Adebara
Data Science Nigeria (DSN), Lagos, Nigeria
{ahmad, olubayo, ife}@datasciencenigeria.ai,
bashirudeenopeyemi772@gmail.com

Abstract

Medication errors are among the leading causes of avoidable harm in healthcare systems across the world. A large portion of these errors stem from inefficient information retrieval processes and lack of comprehension of drug information. In low-resource settings, these issues are exacerbated by limited access to updated and reliable sources, technological constraints, and linguistic barriers. Innovations to improve the retrieval and comprehension of drug-related information are therefore poised to reduce medication errors and improve patient outcomes. This research employed open-source Retrieval-Augmented Generation (RAG) integrated with multilingual translation and Text-to-Speech (TTS) systems. Using open-source tools, a corpus was created from prominent sources of medical information in Nigeria and stored as high-level text embeddings in a Chroma database. Upon user query, relevant drug information is retrieved and synthesized using a large language model. This can be translated into Yoruba, Igbo, and Hausa languages, and converted into speech through the TTS system, addressing the linguistic accessibility gap. Evaluation of the system by domain experts indicated impressive overall performance in translation, achieving an average accuracy of 73%, and the best performance observed in Hausa and Yoruba. TTS results were moderately effective (mean = 57%), with Igbo scoring highest in speech clarity (68%). However, tonal complexity, especially in Yoruba, posed challenges for accurate pronunciation, highlighting the need for language-specific model fine-tuning. Addressing these linguistic nuances is essential to optimize comprehension and practical utility in diverse healthcare settings .The results demonstrates system's the potential to improve access to drug information, enhance comprehension, and reduce linguistic barriers. These technologies could substantially mitigate medication errors and improve patient safety. This study offers valuable insights and practical guidelines for future implementations aimed at strengthening global medication safety practices.

1 Introduction

The traditional medication information retrieval and communication has always been plagued with a myriad of issues broadly and rightly categorised as "medication errors". Medication errors are the leading cause of avoidable harm in healthcare systems around the world, together with unsafe medication practices. A medication error is defined by the United States National Coordinating Council for Medication Error Reporting and Prevention as any avoidable incident that could result in the improper use of medication or harm to a patient while the medication is in the hands of a healthcare professional, patient, or consumer (National Coordinating Council for Medication Error Reporting and Prevention).

The World Health Organization recognises that medication error occurs in prescribing, transcribing, dispensing, and administering (World Health Organization, 2023). Therefore, medical information retrieval and communication must be optimised for efficiency, effectiveness and precision.

Drug information is usually retrieved manually from multiple sources, especially in low-resource settings. A study by (Ogbonna and Okoye, 2021) found that Nigeria's most common sources of drug information are the Nigerian Essential Medicines Index (EMDEX), the British National Formulary, Pharmacopoeias and product information leaflets (PILs) included in drug packages by manufacturers.

While all this information is usually readily available for healthcare professionals, studies suggest professionals in developed climes more frequently access the best-quality information, with the only barrier reported being time (Seidel et al., 2023). However, available drug information sources in low-resource settings are usually of lower quality

Proceedings of the Sixth Workshop on African Natural Language Processing (AfricaNLP 2025), pages 108–114
July 31, 2025

and mostly outdated. The retrieval process is also slow and ineffective due to factors like drug availability, slow internet access, and a large population of patients (Abdel-Latif et al., 2022).

Patients, caregivers and consumers of medications are also involved in creating medication errors. Many information sources are accessible to consumers, caregivers and patients, including physicians and pharmacists, digital platforms and resources, printed materials like PILs and Drug information centers (DICs). While people worldwide have access to these various drug information sources, the quality, availability, and effectiveness of these sources differ widely, similar to the aforementioned trend among healthcare providers. Studies show that people from around the world read PILs, less than half understand the intended information while some even reported anxiety and confusion after consulting drug information sources (Rašković et al., 2024; Al Jeraisy et al., 2023; Owusu et al., 2020).

The most prominent recommendation from all the studies cited above is to explore ways to improve communication in the different drug information sources and optimise the information retrieval process. This aligns with (Okoye and Ogbonna, 2022)'s stress of the need to include and prioritise local languages in health service delivery.

Retrieval-Augmented Generation (RAG) is an advanced technique in natural language processing that enhances the capabilities of large language models (LLMs) by integrating them with external information retrieval systems, allowing them to access and incorporate up-to-date, domain-specific knowledge during the generation process, thereby improving the accuracy and reliability of their responses. This technique has attained wide adoption as it solves the most pervasive problem of LLM hallucination. (Lewis et al.).

This research leverages RAG to allow LLMs and translation models access and work with correct and up-to-date medical information from structured and unstructured formats to produce an application that aims to improve the retrieval and enhance the comprehension of drug information by healthcare providers, patients and caregivers to reduce medication errors. This research leverages open-source models and libraries to allow interested parties to freely tweak, modify and use the source code available on the GitHub repository to progress the aim of this research.

2 Literature Review

2.1 Retrieval-Augmented Generation in Healthcare

Large Language Models (LLMs) have demonstrated remarkable capabilities in medical language tasks, even answering medical exam questions with high accuracy in the United States (Sohn et al., 2024). However, their adoption in healthcare has been limited due to their potentials to hallucinate (generate confident but incorrect outputs) and limited access to up-to-date knowledge . In the medical field, precision is essential; an incorrect fact or dosage can carry serious risks. To mitigate these issues, RAG has emerged as a key strategy. RAG systems integrate external knowledge retrieval into the LLM's generation process, providing relevant context from trusted data sources to enhance accuracy (Miao et al., 2024).

The integration of RAG with medical NLP has shown clear benefits in improving the factual accuracy of AI outputs. A 2025 systematic review and meta-analysis of RAG in biomedicine found that augmenting LLMs with retrieval significantly improved performance, yielding a pooled 1.35× increase in accuracy over base LLMs (95% CI 1.19–1.53, p = 0.001). The review which analyzed 20 studies from 2023–2024 and identified common trends in how RAG is implemented (e.g. types of knowledge sources and evaluation methods), found that many of these studies demonstrate that RAG can markedly reduce LLM hallucinations and bias, making the outputs more trustworthy for medical use. The study ultimately proposing guidelines for safe clinical deployment of RAG-powered applications (Liu et al., 2025).

A team of researchers developed Almanac, a retrieval-augmented LLM for clinical decision support, which was evaluated on 130 realistic clinical scenarios. The RAG-augmented model showed an 18% improvement in factual accuracy of its recommendations (evaluated by physicians) compared to the base model, along with gains in completeness and safety (Zakka et al., 2023). Similarly, another team introduced the Rationale-Guided RAG (RAG2), achieving up to 6.1% higher accuracy by refining retrieval queries through model-generated rationales, further reducing the risk of misinformation in medical contexts (Sohn et al., 2024). MEDIC, an LLM-driven system augmented with domain-specific guidelines was developed with the aim of substantially reducing medication errors in online pharmacies. It was able to effectively standardize prescription directions and translate complex medical jargon into clear, patient-understandable instructions. This system achieved 33% reduction in medication errors as a direct result of improved patient comprehension of drug-related communications, and medication adherence (Pais et al., 2024).

In a low-resource context, a study showcased the potential of RAG to improve drug insight generation from local medical databases by creating a chatbot called "Drug Insights". This chatbot, tailored to the needs of frontline healthcare workers in Nigeria was able to effectively bridge the gap in drug information access (Owoyemi et al., 2025). RAG serves as an "open-book" exam mode for LLMs, ensuring their answers are supported by real sources rather than just the model's internal training data.

2.2 Cross-Lingual Applications in Healthcare

Most advanced medical NLP solutions, including RAG-augmented systems, have been developed in a handful of high-resource languages, primarily English. This poses a barrier in multilingual societies and low-resource settings, where patients and health workers often speak and read in local languages. Bridging the language gap is crucial for equitable healthcare information access.

Recent efforts in multilingual and cross-lingual NLP aim to enable medical AI systems that can operate across diverse languages, either by building multilingual models or by coupling translation modules with information retrieval. One early demonstration of such an approach developed a multilingual question-answering system for rural healthcare information access. Their prototype was a full NLP pipeline that incorporated named entity recognition (NER) on user queries, translated the queries into English (the language of the medical knowledge base), retrieved relevant information, and then generated answers which could be translated back into the user's local language (Vinod et al., 2021). Their model was designed to be low-resource and language-agnostic, targeting "indigenous languages" spoken in rural areas of developing countries. It enabled users to ask health questions in their native language and receive answers based on global medical knowledge. Their results demonstrated that such systems could be employed in healthcare systems to provide advice on common health issues and even produce preliminary summaries of patient health records for clinician review.

Subsequent projects have continued this line of work. The AwezaMed initiative in South Africa created a speech-to-speech translator for maternal healthcare during COVID-19 pandemic, enabling communication between English-speaking doctors and patients speaking indigenous languages to disseminate timely knowledge about prevention and treatment (Hu et al., 2025).

2.3 Applications in Low- and Middle-Income Countries

The confluence of RAG and multilingual NLP opens up especially exciting opportunities for low- and middle-income countries. Many LMICs face severe shortages of healthcare professionals, and those in practice often serve multilingual populations with limited resources. AI systems that provide decision support and information in local languages could help bridge gaps in healthcare delivery (Okoye and Ogbonna, 2022).

Open access RAG tools are particularly valuable in LMICs, where cost and proprietary systems are barriers, an open framework allows local innovation and continuous improvement by the community. The inclusion of regional experts in building these tools ensures that the solutions are culturally and linguistically appropriate.

3 Methodology

3.1 Data Collection and Extraction

This research utilises data from Nigeria's most prominent medical information sources. This information was extracted into text format using Python libraries[1] like PyMuPDF for PDF files, requests and beautifulsoup for data sourced from the web. These libraries are standard in NLP and offer the best to extract data while maintaining inherent semantic relationships. They also allowed us to store and access the metadata of the source documents to create a large corpus, an important process for our pipeline during the synthesis stage, as it allows the LLM in our work to make the best decisions.

[1] PyMuPDF is a lightweight PDF and XPS parsing library `https://pymupdf.readthedocs.io/`, Requests is a simple and elegant HTTP library`https://docs.python-requests.org/`, and BeautifulSoup is a Python library for parsing and scraping HTML and XML `https://beautiful-soup-4.readthedocs.io/`.

3.2 Data Preprocessing

The handy regex library was used in this research to clean data. This process involved removing excessive blank lines, fixing hyphenated words at line breaks (e.g., "exam- nple" to "example"), normalising spacing around punctuations, removing extra spaces before new lines, matching and removing unnecessary patterns like those seen in indexes and appendixes, and reconstructing broken paragraphs. The RecursiveCharacterTextSplitter class from the LangChain framework[2] was used to divide the clean text into manageable chunks. It works by splitting texts using a predefined sequence of characters, proceeding recursively through the list until the resulting segment meets the desired length criteria (chunk_size=1024). Setting the parameter 'chunk_overlap=100' allows characters to overlap between consecutive chunks, ensuring context continuity across segments. This also enables the definition and access of a structured data schema, where essential drug information, e.g., name, class, indication, interactions, contraindication, etc., defined in the source materials are maintained.

3.3 Vectorization and Vector Storage

multilingual-e5-large[3], an open-source, state-of-the-art, high-performance, multilingual text embedding model developed by Microsoft and available on Huggingface[4] was used to convert the text chunks into vector embeddings. These embeddings were then stored in Chroma[5], an open-source vector database designed to store and retrieve vector embeddings efficiently. Integrating the Chroma vector store with metadata support enables efficient management and retrieval of embeddings, facilitating accurate nearest-neighbor searches based on the default Euclidean distance metric.

3.4 Drug Information Generation

With the knowledge base in the Chroma database, the system employs a retrieval-augmented generation (RAG) approach to synthesising and generating drug-related information. When a query is submitted, a similarity search is performed within the database to retrieve the most relevant drug-related information from the indexed knowledge sources. The retrieved texts containing structured pharmaceutical details are then passed as contextual input to a large language model (OpenAI's GPT 3.5 turbo[6]), which analyses the retrieved context, extracts essential details, and synthesises a concise, coherent, and medically relevant response.

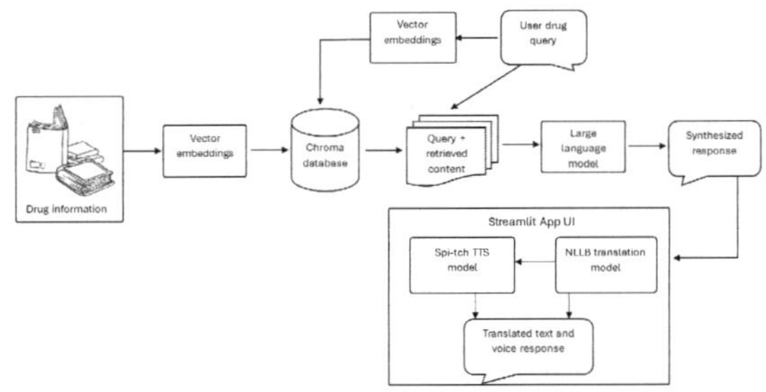

Figure 1: System flowchart

3.5 Translation

To achieve the aim of this research, the output synthesised by the LLM must be available to the end user in local languages. To facilitate this, the research employed Meta's NLLB[7], a multilingual machine translation model capable of translating between 200 languages, including many low-resource languages.

3.6 Text to Speech (TTS)

Spi-tch[8] Text-to-Speech (TTS) system was utilized to convert textual drug information into spoken output across the Yoruba, Igbo, and Hausa languages. Along with support for these languages, Spi-tch offers a selection of eight unique voices, each with distinct attributes, to enhance specific features of the synthesised speech. To ensure accurate pronunciation, especially in tonal languages like Yoruba, we applied Spitch's tone-marking feature before speech generation, allowing the model to pronounce words properly during synthesis. The audio outputs generated were in 'wav' format, facilitating seamless integration into our application.

4 Result

The output of this research is a RAG-powered chat application (built on streamlit) that leverages a cor-

[2]https://www.langchain.com/

[3]https://huggingface.co/intfloat/multilingual-e5-large

[4]Hugging Face is an AI platform that hosts open-source platform that machine learning models, datasets, and tools. http://https://huggingface.co/

[5]https://docs.trychroma.com/docs/overview/introduction

[6]https://openai.com

[7]https://huggingface.co/docs/transformers/model_doc/nllb

[8]https://docs.spi-tch.com/getting-started/welcome

pus of leading drug information data in the region. The system is built on various open-source tools to facilitate reproducibility and wrapped around a user friendly UI (see Appendix 6) using Streamlit.

The notebooks and codes used are available on GitHub

4.1 Evaluation Strategy

The system was evaluated by three independent groups of licensed pharmacists, who assessed the text and voice translation components based on a structured evaluation framework. Each group was given 20 prompts, with Group 2 generating additional domain-specific questions based on their clinical expertise. The evaluation criteria focused on three key aspects:
1. Drug Information Accuracy – The accuracy and completeness of drug-related information retained in the translated output.
2. Language Output Accuracy – The correctness of translations in the target languages (Yoruba, Igbo, and Hausa).
3. Structure of Output/Completion – The final output's coherence, grammatical structure, and completeness.

4.2 Drug Information in Local Languages

For text translation, results were recorded separately for each of the three languages (Yoruba, Igbo, and Hausa) and aggregated across the three evaluators. The overall average score for text translation was (73%), indicating high accuracy and completeness in the system's ability to translate drug-related information.
Yoruba Language had the highest scores (80%), showing strong accuracy in language fluency and drug information retention. Hausa followed closely, while Igbo had slightly lower performance, particularly in Drug Information Accuracy, where it recorded the lowest score of 60% in one evaluation.

Criteria	Yoruba	Igbo	Hausa
Language Output	8	7	7
Drug Information	7	6	9
Output Structure	7	6	9
Total Score (%)	**23 (77)**	**20 (67)**	**24 (80)**
Average Score (%)	**22 (73)**	**20.3 (68)**	**22.3 (74)**

Table 1: Evaluation Summary for language translation output.

4.3 Drug Information Voice Output (TTS)

For speech generation, the average score across all languages was 57%, indicating a moderate level of accuracy and output structure compared to text translation. Igbo (70%) was the highest-performing language, showing strong audio output accuracy. Yoruba performed the lowest, with one evaluator scoring it 40% due to pronunciation clarity and structure issues.

Evaluation Criteria	Yoruba	Igbo	Hausa
Language Output	4	7	7
Drug Information	5	6	5
Output Structure	5	6	5
Total Score (%)	**11 (36)**	**21 (70)**	**19 ()**
Average Score (%)	**14.3 (48)**	**20.3 (68)**	**18.0 (60)**

Table 2: Evaluation Summary for TTS output.

5 Discussions

This study aimed to address the critical issue of medication error from different barriers from the healthcare practitioners, patients, and caregivers by emphasising the importance of accurate, accessible and comprehensible drug information, particularly in low resource settings. It leveraged a Retrieval-Augmented Generation (RAG) system integrated with open-source language, translation and voice models. It demonstrated significant potential to enhance drug information retrieval and comprehension, thus contributing to reduced medication errors. The system can serve as an intelligent assistant for healthcare professionals, enabling them to counsel patients who speak only their local language and thereby strengthen understanding, compliance, and adherence to prescribed medications. The findings showed the robust performance of the retrieval process and the text translation component. The highest accuracy was achieved for the Yoruba language, with a better average recorded for the Hausa language, indicating effective linguistic adaptability of the multilingual model. The moderate performance of Igbo text translations, particularly in Drug Information Accuracy, underscores the need for further training or fine-tuning of the language model on domain-specific data. Conversely, the Text-to-Speech (TTS) component exhibited more varied performance. The Igbo language audio translations showed the highest accuracy, indicating effective phonetic adaptation and clarity. In contrast, Yoruba audio outputs exhibited lower performance, primarily due to pronunciation issues inherent in the tonal complexities of the language. This highlights the critical need for improving TTS models, especially for tonal languages, to enhance user comprehension and ensure accurate drug information delivery.

6 Conclusion

This research shows that implementing RAG into multilingual translation and TTS systems could enhance drug information knowledge availability, accessibility and comprehension, especially in low resource settings. This encouraging result in the accuracy of the text translation, findings from domain experts still show the need for improvement in the TTS system. However, this research has proven that an RAG-powered system is a viable tool for future efforts to improve medication information comprehension and reduce medication error.

References

Mohamed Mahmoud Abdel-Latif, Hosny Ahmed Elewa, and Amal Abd El.Moneim Soliman El-Kholy. 2022. Perceptions and attitudes of hospital' prescribers towards drug information sources and prescribing practices. *Brazilian Journal of Pharmaceutical Sciences*, 58:e20498. Accessed: 2025-03-09.

Majed Al Jeraisy, Heba Alshammari, Mashael Albassam, Kholoud Al Aamer, and Mostafa A. Abolfotouh. 2023. Utility of patient information leaflet and perceived impact of its use on medication adherence. *BMC Public Health*, 23(488). Accessed: 2025-03-09.

S. Hu and 1 others. 2025. Natural language processing technologies for public health in africa: Scoping review. *Journal of Medical Internet Research*, 27:e68720.

Patrick Lewis, Ethan Perez, Aleksandra Piktus, Fabio Petroni, Vladimir Karpukhin, Naman Goyal, Heinrich Küttler, Mike Lewis, Wen-tau Yih, Tim Rocktäschel, Sebastian Riedel, and Douwe Kiela. Retrieval-augmented generation for knowledge-intensive nlp tasks. *arXiv preprint arXiv:200 ::contentReference[oaicite:0]index=0.*

S. Liu and 1 others. 2025. Improving large language model applications in biomedicine with retrieval-augmented generation: a systematic review, meta-analysis, and clinical development guidelines. *Journal of the American Medical Informatics Association (JAMIA)*. Ahead of print.

C. Miao and 1 others. 2024. Integration of retrieval-augmented generation (rag) in clinical practice: Enhancing clinical decision support and information retrieval in nephrology. *Medicina*, 60(3):445.

National Coordinating Council for Medication Error Reporting and Prevention. About medication errors. Accessed: 2025-03-09.

Brian O. Ogbonna and Ijeoma Mary-Ann Okoye. 2021. Utilization of drug information services in selected tertiary hospitals in enugu state, nigeria. *Journal of Current Biomedical Research*, 1(1):15–22. Accessed: 2025-03-09.

Ijeoma Okoye and Brian O. Ogbonna. 2022. Drug information services utilization in nigeria from 1980-2020: A narrative review of related studies. *Journal of Current Biomedical Research*, 2(4):380–390. Accessed: 2025-03-09.

J. Owoyemi and 1 others. 2025. "drug insights" – an open-source rag chatbot for medication lookup in africa. *medRxiv preprint*.

Frederick W. A. Owusu, Genevieve Naana Yeboah, Rahel Adutwiwah Aboagye, Cedric Dzidzor K. Amengor, and Philomena Entsie. 2020. The role of the patient information leaflet in patients' medication therapy: A case study within the kumasi metropolis of ghana. *The Scientific World Journal*, 2020:2489137. Accessed: 2025-03-09.

C. Pais and 1 others. 2024. Large language models for preventing medication direction errors in online pharmacies. *Nature Medicine*, 30(6):1574–1582.

Aleksandar Rašković, Maja Steinbach, Snežana Mugoša, Jovan Baljak, Dušan Prodanović, Stanislav Sabo, Dragica Bukumirić, Boris Milijašević, and Milica Paut Kusturica. 2024. Patient information leaflets: How do patients comprehend and understand drug information? *Archives of Pharmacy Practice*, 15(1):7–11. Accessed: 2025-03-09.

Pia Seidel, Bo Rolander, Anna L. Eriksson, Ulf Lindahl, Susanna M. Wallerstedt, Staffan Hägg, and Anders Kling. 2023. Drug information sources in professional work—a questionnaire study on physicians' usage and preferences (the drug information study). *European Journal of Clinical Pharmacology*, 79:767–774.

J. Sohn and 1 others. 2024. Rationale-guided rag for medical question answering. *arXiv preprint arXiv:2411.00300*.

V. Vinod and 1 others. 2021. Multilingual medical qa and information retrieval for rural health. In *ICLR AI4PH Workshop*.

World Health Organization. 2023. Global burden of preventable medication-related harm in health care: a systematic review. Technical report. Accessed: 2025-03-09.

C. Zakka and 1 others. 2023. Almanac — retrieval-augmented language models for clinical medicine. *NEJM AI*, 2(3).

Appendix

Appendix A: Streamlit Screenshot

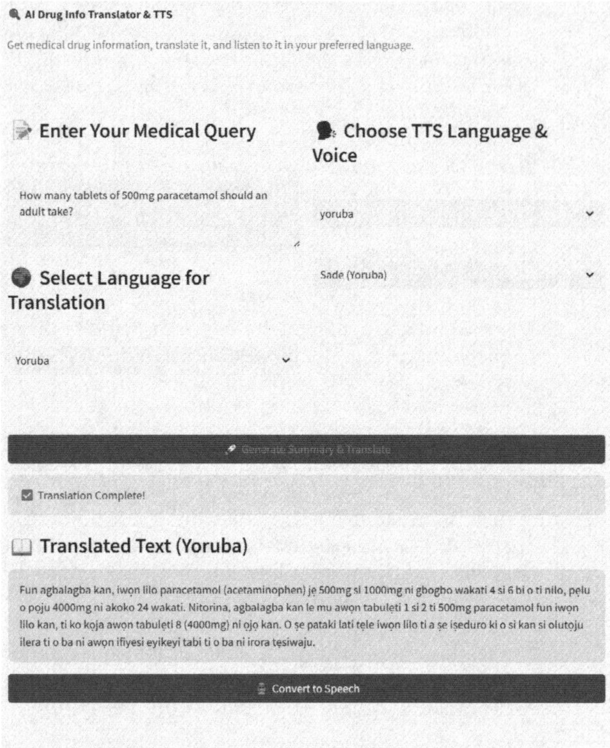

Figure 2: An image of the system running on Streamlit with sample query and output.

Appendix B: GitHub Repository

The full source code for this project is available at: `https://bit.ly/RAGDRUGINFOLANGUAGE`

Story Generation with Large Language Models for African Languages

Catherine Nana Nyaah Essuman
African Institute for Mathematical Sciences
University of Cape Town
catherine@aims.ac.za

Jan Buys
University of Cape Town
jan.buys@uct.ac.za

Abstract

The development of Large Language Models (LLMs) for African languages has been hindered by the lack of large-scale textual data. Previous research has shown that relatively small language models, when trained on synthetic data generated by larger models, can produce fluent, short English stories, providing a data-efficient alternative to large-scale pretraining. In this paper, we apply a similar approach to develop and evaluate small language models for generating children's stories in isiZulu and Yoruba, using synthetic datasets created through translation and multilingual prompting. We train six language-specific models varying in dataset size and source, and based on the GPT-2 architecture. Our results show that models trained on synthetic low-resource data are capable of producing coherent and fluent short stories in isiZulu and Yoruba. Models trained on larger synthetic datasets generally perform better in terms of coherence and grammar, and also tend to generalize better, as seen by their lower evaluation perplexities. Models trained on datasets generated through prompting instead of translation generate similar or more coherent stories and display more creativity, but perform worse in terms of generalization to unseen data. In addition to the potential educational applications of the automated story generation, our approach has the potential to be used as the foundation for more data-efficient low-resource language models.

1 Introduction

In recent years, pretrained transformer language models have been used as the foundation of NLP systems for text generation, understanding and summarizing, and information extraction (Razumovskaia et al., 2024). However, most of the advancements have been concentrated on high-resource languages (HRLs) such as English and French, leaving low-resource languages (LRLs) and African languages in particular underrepresented in advancements in Language Models (LMs). Some of these languages, despite having millions of speakers, lack sufficient data online to train robust LMs or develop and deploy systems that can cater for their speakers. While many efforts have been made to create LMs, the lack of suitable datasets remains a significant challenge. In response, recent research has focused on creating datasets for African languages, either through manual annotations or through synthetic data generation (Adelani et al., 2023; Tonja et al., 2024; Adelani et al., 2025).

The use of synthetic data has proven to be essential for training LMs in low-resource settings. Liu et al. (2024) argues that synthetic data addresses data scarcity, allowing models to generalize better while high-quality synthetic data helps to avoid biases. Gunasekar et al. (2023) also demonstrates that synthetic generated datasets with high quality can enhance model learning. Our work is motivated by TinyStories (Eldan and Li, 2023) which uses curated synthetic data consisting of short stories using simple language to train small language models. That work shows that high-quality synthetic data can enable small models to match the performance of larger models by focusing on coherent and diverse content.

The aim of this paper is to investigate whether a similar approach can be applied to generate high-quality synthetic stories in low-resource languages, which can then be used to train small but capable language models. We train six models based on the GPT-2 architecture from scratch for isiZulu and Yoruba, using synthetic datasets of different sizes and approaches to generate children's stories. We evaluate the performance of these models using both qualitative and quantitative analysis in order to investigate whether LMs trained on synthetic LRL data can produce coherent and fluent stories. We compare the performance of models trained on

Proceedings of the Sixth Workshop on African Natural Language Processing (AfricaNLP 2025), pages 115–125
July 31, 2025 ©2025 Association for Computational Linguistics

the translated stories to that of models trained on stories generated by prompting from a multilingual model.

2 Related Work

Generating stories with LLMs has proven to be a promising approach to generating texts that are coherent and appealing. TinyStories (Eldan and Li, 2023) showed that even small-scale models can generate fluent short stories, offering a promising approach to train effective story generation models with less computational resources. This result offers a promising path to develop models for low-resource languages (LRLs) in settings that also frequently lack the infrastructure required for large-scale pretraining.

Razumovskaia et al. (2024) investigated cross-lingual story generation by generating stories in multiple languages from a single plan in English. This work complements the findings of Eldan and Li (2023), drawing attention to the versatility of LLMs across languages, which is critical for African languages lacking considerable data. The two studies stress the importance of building LLMs that are capable of generating coherent stories in resource constrained environments, which is a major challenge for African languages. In a different approach, the GROVE framework (Wen et al., 2023) uses Retrieval-Augmented Generation (RAGs) to enhance the coherence and complexity of stories. This approach further underscores the importance of extra information (whether through cross-lingual plans or the retrieval of evidence) to improve the quality of stories. Both methods show that making use of external information can improve the capability of LLMs generations.

In our research, we build upon these ideas by using two methods for synthetic data generation: translation of existing stories into isiZulu and Yoruba using a multilingual translation model, and directly prompting a multilingual model to generate stories in both target languages, in order to create LMs which can generate stories in isiZulu and Yoruba.

3 Methodology

3.1 Dataset Generation

We follow two approaches to generate synthetic datasets: machine translation of English stories to the target languages, and prompting a multilingual language model to generate stories in the target languages.

We use the `TinyStories`[1] (Eldan and Li, 2023) dataset as the source of English stories to be translated. This dataset consists of stories generated by prompting GPT-3.5 and GPT-4. The prompts selected random keywords from a set of 3,000 nouns, verbs, and adjectives to generate stories aimed at children aged 3 to 5 years. The dataset contains approximately 2 million unique stories, but for the purpose of this study, an eighth (250,000), of these stories were used. The stories were translated from English into both isiZulu and Yoruba using the state-of-the-art Seamless Massively Multilingual and Multimodal Machine Translation (Seamless M4T-V2) model version 2 (Communication et al., 2023).

For the second data generation approach we utilized **`AfroLlama`**[2], a multilingual text generation model developed by Jacaranda Health, which was fine-tuned from Meta AI's Llama 3, to generate synthetic stories directly in the isiZulu and Yoruba. To generate the stories, we created prompts varying in content but with a consistent structure in the target languages aimed at guiding the model to produce children stories. Example prompts are shown in Table 1. We generated 10,000 unique short stories about different characters, with a clear beginning, middle and end.

All together we created six synthetic datasets:

- **isiZulu and Yoruba Large: 250,000** stories from the TinyStories dataset, translated into isiZulu and Yoruba.
- **isiZulu and Yoruba Mini: 10,000** stories sampled from the initial set of 250,000 TinyStories, translated into isiZulu and Yoruba.
- **isiZulu and Yoruba Prompt: 10,000** stories generated by prompting Afro Llama to generate stories in isiZulu and Yoruba.

We split each of the datasets into training (70%), validation (20%) and evaluation (10%) sets.

3.2 Model Initialization & Pretraining

For the models trained in this study, we initialized the weights randomly, meaning that no pretrained model weights were used during the training process. We trained the models entirely on the synthetic datasets generated from our corpus, with no

[1]https://huggingface.co/datasets/roneneldan/TinyStories
[2]https://huggingface.co/Jacaranda/AfroLlama_V1

	Prompt
1	Ko̱ itan awo̱n o̱mo̱de ni Yoruba nipa Lily ati Max ti o gba e̱bun airote̱le̱, o ni ipari ti o dara.
2	So̱ itan awo̱n o̱mo̱de ni Yoruba nibiti Emma nilo lati gafara fun o̱re̱ re̱ Thabo, o ni opin irora.
3	Bhala indaba emfushane yezingane ngesiZulu lapho uZandile no-Oliver behlangana nesilwane esikhulumayo, inesiphetho esihle kakhulu.
4	Xoxa izindaba zezingane ngesiZulu ngoNomsa owafunda izifundo ezibalulekile ngokuhlanganyela.

Table 1: Prompts for story generation in Yobura (1 & 2) and Zulu (3 & 4)

use of external corpora or multilingual pretraining. While this approach allows for an investigation of model performance based purely on the synthetic data, the lack of real-world language exposure may limit the models' ability to generalize effectively to unseen data. Training from scratch on synthetic data could result in biases that differ from those seen in models pre-trained on real-world data. Our motivation was to isolate the effects of our synthetic dataset and avoid potential transfer effects from external corpora.

3.3 Pre-processing & Model Training

We trained six language-specific models, one for each of the generated synthetic datasets. The text was tokenized with Byte-Level Byte-Pair Encoding (BPE) (Wang et al., 2020) for isiZulu and SentencePiece BPE (Kudo and Richardson, 2018) for Yoruba. Table 2 shows the number of tokens in each of the datasets.

We train story generation models using the GPT-2 (Generative Pre-trained Transformer 2) architecture, which is a transformer-based autoregressive language model (Radford et al., 2019). At its core lies the transformer decoder block introduced by (Vaswani et al., 2017), which uses self-attention mechanisms to process sequential data. Our implementation is based on Andrej Kaparthy's nanoGPT model [3]. Our models are smaller than the "small" variant of GPT-2, with the specifications given in Table 3. The model size is 30.59M parameters for the isiZulu models and 29.20M parameters for the Yoruba models. The model sizes were chosen in proportion to the size of the available training data, while allowing for computational feasibility in a low-resource setting. The aim is to show that with an even smaller model, fluent, coherent stories can still be generated in a low-resource language.

[3]https://github.com/karpathy/nanoGPT

3.4 Generating Stories from the Trained Models

We use the models trained on our isiZulu and Yoruba datasets to generate new stories. We evaluate the models by evaluating the quality of the generated stories. Some evaluations also use the held-out evaluation datasets from the original datasets generated by translation or prompting. We generate 1,000 stories from each of the models to ensure there is enough data to evaluate the performance of the models based on the chosen evaluation metrics. To generate a story we prompt the model with the start token and sample stories using the hyperparameter values given in Table 4. We set these hyperparameters to ensure a balance between diversity and coherence in the generated stories. The maximum number of tokens of 512 is equal to the model context length during training. A temperature of 0.7 is used to ensure diversity in the model generations, while top-k sampling with k=50 limits the number of possible next words from which the model can sample to maintain coherence.

3.5 Evaluation Metrics

In order to assess the quality of our generated sample stories and the performance of our models, we employ a number of evaluation metrics:

1. **Perplexity** is a normalized measure of the probability of text scored by the model:

$$\text{PPL} = e^{-\frac{1}{N}\Sigma_{n=1}^{N} logP(w_n|w_1,w_2,\cdots,w_{n-1})}, \quad (1)$$

which exponentiates the average Negative Log Likelihood, where N is the number of tokens in the evaluation set and $w_1, w_2, \cdots, w_N$ are the tokens.

2. **Diversity** We consider two metrics. Lexical Diversity, also known as Type-Token Ratio (TTR), measures the variety of vocabulary

Dataset	ZuluLarge	YorubaLarge	ZuluMini	YorubaMini	ZuluPrompt	YorubaPrompt
Train	28,809,839	41,056,131	1,193,167	1,694,424	1,035,290	1,208,521
Validation	7,200,689	10,264,075	297,977	424,016	259,003	302,424
Evaluation	3,928,142	5,658,137	161,736	235,508	141,535	164,736

Table 2: Dataset sizes (number of tokens) for the generated synthetic datasets

Hyperparameter	Value
Layers	6
Attention Heads	6
Embedding Dimension	384
Dropout Rate	0.2

Table 3: Transformer architecture hyperparameters

Hyperparameter	Value
Maximum new Tokens	512
Temperature	0.7
Top-k Sampling	50

Table 4: Story Generation Hyperparameters

used in the generated stories:

$$\text{TTR} = \frac{\text{Number of Unique Words}}{\text{Total Number of Words}} \tag{2}$$

Semantic Similarity measures how different the generated stories are from each other in terms of meaning, which helps us to understand if our model is creative in generating unique stories:

$$\text{Cosine Similarity} = \frac{\mathbf{A} \cdot \mathbf{B}}{||\mathbf{A}|| \times ||\mathbf{B}||} \tag{3}$$

where $\mathbf{A}$ and $\mathbf{B}$ are the sentence embeddings of two different stories, and $||\mathbf{A}||$ and $||\mathbf{B}||$ are their respective magnitudes. We compute the semantic similarity score by performing pairwise comparisons between all stories within each generated set and evaluation set, averaging the cosine similarity scores.

3. **Quality evaluation using Gemini** We follow the methodology of Eldan and Li (2023), which prompted GPT-4 to score the generated stories. We prompt Gemini 1.5 Pro, an LLM developed by Google, to score the generated and reference evaluation set stories from each of the six models based on Grammar, Coherence, Plot, and Creativity. Each of the categories are scored out of 10 and an overall score is also given. The prompt used for this evaluation is shown in Table 5.

Prompt
Grade these isiZulu and Yoruba stories out of 40 based on: 1. Grammar (10) 2. Coherence (10) 3. Plot (10) 4. Creativity (10) Provide short comments (1-2 sentences) for each category in the format: - Grammar: [score], [comment] - Coherence: [score], [comment] - Plot: [score], [comment] - Creativity: [score], [comment] Overall Score: [score]

Table 5: Prompt for Story Evaluation

Model	Train Loss	Val Loss
isiZuluPlus	2.566	2.687
YorubaPlus	1.906	1.948
isiZuluLite	0.442	5.424
YorubaLite	1.094	2.547
isiZuluGuide	0.417	4.035
YorubaGuide	0.758	2.660

Table 6: Train and Validation Losses for the Models

4 Results and Discussion

We refer to the six trained models as follows:

- **isiZulu and Yoruba Plus Models:** This refers to the models trained on the isiZulu Large and Yoruba Large datasets.
- **isiZulu and Yoruba Lite Models:** This refers to the models trained on the isiZulu Mini and Yoruba Mini datasets.
- **isiZulu and Yoruba Guide Models:** This refers to the models trained on the isiZulu Prompt and Yoruba Prompt datasets.

Table 6 shows the training and validation losses for each of the six models after training for 20 epochs.

4.1 Model Evaluation

The results for the model evaluation, using Perplexity and the Diversity Scores (Token-Type Ratio and

Model	Perplexity of ↓ Generated Stories	Perplexity of ↓ Evaluation Sets	TTR for ↑ Generated Stories	TTR for ↑ Evaluation Sets	Semantic Similarity of ↑ Generated Stories	Semantic Similarity of ↑ Evaluation Sets
isiZuluPlus	34.37	15.82	0.0653	0.1210	0.6549	**0.7603**
YorubaPlus	**5.92**	7.47	0.0158	0.0284	0.7505	0.7474
isiZuluLite	40.83	14.33	**0.0743**	0.1202	0.7044	0.7657
YorubaLite	7.43	**7.13**	0.0181	0.0273	**0.7567**	0.7479
isiZuluGuide	15.98	154.05	0.0545	**0.0816**	0.7453	0.7530
YorubaGuide	14.42	275.62	0.0208	0.0316	0.7451	0.7449

Table 7: Perplexity, Type-Token Ratio, and Semantic Similarity for Generated Stories & Evaluation Datasets

Semantic Similarity) are given in Table 7.

We calculate the **perplexity** of each set of generated stories with the model used to generate the respective set of stories. The comparison reveals several key insights. YorubaPlus has the lowest perplexity of 5.92 for generating stories, indicating that it is more confident and accurate in generating coherent stories compared to the other models. This is in contrast to isiZuluPlus, which has a higher perplexity of 34.37, suggesting isiZuluPlus struggles more to generate coherent, accurate stories.

Additionally we calculate the perplexity of the Large evaluation sets for each language across each of the models. This allows comparing these perplexity results across models; lower perplexity indicates better generalization. On the evaluation sets, YorubaPlus still performs well with a perplexity of 7.47, whereas isiZuluPlus has a perplexity of 15.82, which is better but still higher than YorubaPlus, showing that the Yoruba model generalizes more effectively.

Similarly, isiZuluLite has a higher perplexity of 40.83 for generating stories, indicating that it is less confident in generating coherent text compared to YorubaLite, which has a perplexity of 7.43. YorubaLite performs significantly better in both generation and evaluation, with perplexities of 7.43 and 7.13, respectively, suggesting better generalization and more accurate generation.

When analyzing models trained with datasets generated through prompting, isiZuluGuide has a perplexity of 15.98 for generating stories, which is lower than that of isiZuluLite but still relatively high. However, isiZuluGuide displays a much higher perplexity of 154.05 on the evaluation sets, indicating that although it generates relatively good stories consistent with the training data, it struggles to generalize to unseen data. Note that this mismatch is due to the different training data source (which the Lite and Plus models have the same training data source, just using different data sizes).

For YorubaGuide, the perplexity for generating stories is 14.42, which is higher than YorubaLite (7.43) but lower than isiZuluGuide. However, the evaluation perplexity for YorubaGuide is 275.62, which is much higher than YorubaLite's 7.13, suggesting that YorubaGuide has significant challenges in generalization.

This **TTR (Type-Token Ratio)** is in the range of zero and one, where a higher TTR value indicates more diverse vocabulary usage. The comparison of TTR scores highlights several trends based on training data size and dataset type. isiZuluLite has a higher TTR of 0.0743 compared to isiZuluPlus' 0.0653, suggesting that models trained on smaller datasets may exhibit more lexical diversity, with this effect being more noticeable in isiZulu than in Yoruba.

When comparing models trained on prompted versus translated datasets, isiZuluGuide shows a lower TTR of 0.0545, indicating less vocabulary diversity than isiZuluLite (0.0743) and isiZuluPlus (0.0653). Conversely, models trained on Yoruba datasets generated through prompting (YorubaGuide: 0.0208) show more lexical diversity than the models trained on translated datasets (YorubaLite: 0.0181, YorubaPlus: 0.0158). Furthermore, evaluation sets consistently exhibit higher TTR scores than generated stories, indicating that evaluation datasets have richer vocabulary. For example, the TTR of the isiZuluLite evaluation set is 0.1202 compared to the generated stories' TTR of 0.0743. This suggests that while the models capture some token variety, the generated stories still lack the vocabulary richness seen in the evaluation sets, highlighting limitations in vocabulary diversity during story generation.

The **semantic similarity** scores are in the range of zero to one, with a score close to zero indicating no similarity between stories, and a score close to one indicating high similarity. The comparison of semantic similarity scores highlights the impact of training data size and dataset type. Models trained on larger datasets (250,000 stories) tend to have lower semantic similarity scores compared to those trained on smaller datasets (10,000 stories) for generated stories. For example, isiZuluPlus scores 0.6549, while isiZuluLite scores 0.7044, suggesting that larger datasets lead to slightly less similar stories in isiZulu. However, this trend is not as pronounced in Yoruba models, where YorubaLite scores 0.7567 and YorubaPlus 0.7505, indicating that dataset size has less impact on generated story similarity for Yoruba.

Models trained on prompt-generated datasets (isiZuluGuide: 0.7453, YorubaGuide: 0.7451) show more consistent semantic similarity scores compared to those trained on translated datasets, like isiZuluLite (0.7044), suggesting that models trained on datasets generated through prompting leads to more stable story generation. When comparing the generated stories to the evaluation sets, the evaluation datasets consistently show higher similarity scores. For example, isiZuluPlus' generated stories score 0.6549, while the evaluation set score 0.7603. This pattern is seen across all models, with the isiZulu models showing larger gaps between generated stories and the evaluation set, indicating more diversity in the generated stories compared to the evaluation dataset. Note that here we use the evaluation sets corresponding to each of the models, which explains why the Plus and Lite model results are very close to each other, with the Guide results diverging.

For the **Quality Evaluation**, we score a subset of 200 stories generated from each of the models and 200 stories from our evaluation datasets (which were generated through translation or prompting). Gemini 1.5 Pro is prompted to give a score of out 10 for each of the following categories: Grammar, Coherence, Plot and Creativity. Table 8 presents the average scores for each of the categories.

When comparing models trained on 250,000 stories (isiZuluPlus and YorubaPlus) to those trained on 10,000 stories (isiZuluLite and YorubaLite), the impact of dataset size is evident. Larger datasets result in better performance in grammar and coherence, as seen with YorubaPlus scoring 7.196 in grammar compared to YorubaLite's 6.865, and isiZuluPlus scoring 5.120 in coherence compared to isiZuluLite's 3.475. However, no significant differences are observed in creativity and plot scores, suggesting that these aspects depend more on the nature of the story than the dataset size. Models trained on datasets generated through prompting, such as isiZuluGuide and YorubaGuide, outperform their translation-based counterparts (isiZuluLite and YorubaLite) in grammar and creativity, with isiZuluGuide scoring 6.830 in grammar and 5.490 in creativity compared to isiZuluLite's 4.615 and 3.955. Similarly, YorubaGuide improves creativity with a score of 5.890 compared to 4.910 for YorubaLite, indicating that prompting can enhance diversity in training data. When comparing the generated stories to the evaluation datasets, the evaluation sets consistently score higher across all categories, demonstrating that while the models capture certain quality aspects, they fall short in fully replicating the complexities of the original stories generated through translation and prompting. For example, the isiZuluPlus evaluation set scores 8.650 in grammar, higher than the generated story score of 6.440, and YorubaLite's evaluation set scores 5.775 for creativity compared to 3.955 for the generated stories.

4.2 Example Generations

Figure 1 shows two examples of generated stories, one from the YorubaPlus model and one from the isiZuluGuide model, along with their English translations.

4.3 Discussion

Overall, across the six models, we see differences in model performance between the isiZulu and Yoruba models, as well as between models trained on datasets generated through prompting versus translation.

YorubaPlus consistently shows the lowest perplexity scores, indicating better coherence and generalization, both for generating stories and for the evaluation sets. In contrast, isiZuluPlus and models trained with prompting (isiZuluGuide, YorubaGuide) show higher perplexities, especially during evaluation, indicating they struggle with generalization to unseen data. This demonstrates that while datasets generated through prompting may help with generating more coherent stories during training, it does not necessarily improve the model's ability to generalize across unseen data. However, the smaller size of the prompt-generated training sets is a possible confounding factor here. Models trained on larger datasets (YorubaPlus and isiZuluPlus), tend to generalize better, as seen by their lower evaluation perplexities.

Models trained on smaller datasets tend to have a higher lexical diversity than those trained on larger

Generated Story - YorubaPlus

Ìgbà kan wà tí e̱ye̱ kékeré kan wà tí orúko̱ rè̱ ń jé̱ Tweety. Tweety fé̱ràn láti máa fò lo̱ sókè lójú ò̱run, kó sì máa bá àwo̱n ò̱ré̱ ré̱ ṣeré. Ló̱jó̱ kan, nígbà tí Tweety ń fò lo̱, ó rí adágún omi kan tó lé̱wà ní òdìkejì adágún náà. Ó fé̱ sún mó̱ o̱n, àmó̱ ó ga jù fún un. Tweety so̱ pé: "Mo lè ràn é̱ló̱wó̱". Tweety àti Tweety jo̱ gbé e̱ye̱ kékeré náà kúrò nínú adágún náà. Lé̱yìn tí e̱ye̱ kékeré náà ti fò lo̱, Tweety so̱ pé: "O ṣeun fún ìrànló̱wó̱ re̱, Tweety kékeré. Inú mi dùn pé o ràn mí ló̱wó̱". Láti o̱jó̱ ye̱n ni Tweety àti Tweety ti di ò̱ré̱ tímó̱tímó̱, tí wó̱n sì máa ń jo̱ máa ṣeré lójoojúmó̱.

English Translation - YorubaPlus

There was a little bird that was called Tweety. Tweety liked to fly in the sky, and one day when he was flying, he found a beautiful pond on the other side of the lake. He wanted to get closer, but it was too high for him. Tweety said, "I can help you." Tweety and the little bird together helped the little bird out of the pond. After the little bird flew away, Tweety said, "Thank you for your help, little Tweety. I'm happy you helped me." From that day on, Tweety and the little bird became close friends and played together every day.

Generated Story - isiZuluGuide

Kwesinye isikhathi, kwakukhona umfana ogama lakhe lingu Liam owayehlala edolobhaneni elincane. Wayenobungani obukhulu nomndeni wakhe nabangane bakhe, kodwa wayezizwa eyedwa kancane. Ngelinye ilanga, uLiam wahlangana nentombazane egama layo lingu Zinhle. Njengoba bengazi omunye nomunye, baqala ukuba ngabangane bokuphila okujabulisayo ndawonye. Bahamba baya ohambweni ndawonye, babelana ngamabali nezindaba, futhi benza izinkumbulo eziningi ezimnandi. Ekugcineni, ubungani babo babuthuthukiswa ngaphezu kokuba ngabangani, futhi bobabili babazi ukuthi bazohlale bekhona komunye nomunye.

English Translation - isiZuluGuide

Once upon a time, there was a boy named Liam who lived in a small town. He had a great friendship with his family and friends, but he felt a little lonely. One day, Liam met a girl named Zinhle. As they got to know each other, they began to be friends and share exciting adventures together. They went on journeys, shared stories, and created many wonderful memories. Eventually, their friendship grew beyond just being friends, and they both knew they would always be there for each other.

Figure 1: Example generated stories and their English translations from YorubaPlus and isiZuluGuide

Model	Grammar		Coherence		Plot		Creativity	
	Gen	Eval	Gen	Eval	Gen	Eval	Gen	Eval
isiZuluPlus	6.440	8.650	5.120	8.650	3.860	5.725	4.475	5.735
YorubaPlus	7.196	8.205	5.412	8.8805	4.185	5.675	5.155	5.620
isiZuluLite	4.615	8.635	3.475	8.885	2.495	5.815	3.955	5.775
YorubaLite	6.865	8.340	5.195	8.655	4.070	5.675	4.910	5.545
isiZuluGuide	6.830	8.545	4.925	8.295	4.020	5.365	5.490	5.780
YorubaGuide	7.475	8.270	5.340	8.065	4.170	5.160	5.890	5.535

Table 8: Average Scores for isiZulu and Yoruba Models and Evaluation Datasets

datasets, as is shown by the high TTR and semantic similarity scores. Models trained on small datasets may produce stories with more varied vocabulary, but will lead to generated stories with high similarity among them. We see this more in the isiZulu models as compared to that of the Yoruba models, which suggests that the size of the dataset has an impact on features across these languages.

Models trained on datasets generated through prompting tend to produce semantic similarity and TTR scores that are comparable to those trained on datasets generated through translations. The isiZulu models produce stable outputs from the prompting-based datasets as compared to the translation-based datasets.

In terms of quality evaluation, the results suggest that models trained on datasets generated through prompting generally perform better in creativity compared to the models trained on translated datasets. This reinforces the idea that models which are trained on stories generated through prompting may be better at capturing imaginative elements in the story generation procedure.

Models trained on large datasets tend to perform better in terms of grammar and coherence of the generated stories. This implies models may need to be trained on larger datasets to be able to capture the linguistic features of African languages. However, scores in the creativity and plot categories are not highly sensitive to the data size, indicating that training on a large synthetic dataset may not be enough to enhance creativity and plot of the generation process. The Gemini quality evaluation confirms that while our models can generate stories that perform well grammatically and with coherence, they struggle in producing creative stories with a consistent plot.

Histograms of the distribution of the Gemini scores per category over each of the model's generated stories and the evaluation dataset stories are given in Appendix A.

5 Conclusion

This paper investigated the feasibility of training models for story generation in low-resource African languages using synthetic data. The results show that it is possible to train models that can generate grammatical and coherent stories, which is promising in particular considering the relatively small training data sizes. Models trained on stories generated through prompting an existing large multilingual model showed particular strength in terms of the quality of the generated outputs, but displayed less generalization than models trained on translated stories, which exhibit more diversity. Overall, in addition to providing new datasets of children stories in isiZulu and Yoruba, which might be of practical usage, e.g. in reading tutoring applications, our results suggest that pretraining on controlled synthetic datasets might be a promising avenue for future investigation of pretraining general-purpose low-resource language models.

Limitations

Our approach relies on the availability of sufficiently high-quality translation models or multilingual LLMs for the target languages, which are not always available for low-resource African languages. However, translation models generally require less training data than general-purpose multilingual language modeling training. Adding generation constraints or quality filters could help to improve synthetic data quality in lower-resource settings. Larger synthetic training datasets would likely have led to higher-quality models, however the study was performed within limited available computational resources. Pretraining models on a combination of real and synthetic data is likely to lead to better models. Fine-tuning and evaluating the models on instruction tuning datasets will enable better evaluation of the potential of this approach to scale beyond story generation.

Acknowledgements

Catherine Essuman was financially supported by Google DeepMind African Institute for Mathematical Sciences (AIMS) AI for Science Master's program. This work is based on the research supported in part by the National Research Foundation of South Africa (Grant Number 151601).

References

David Ifeoluwa Adelani, Marek Masiak, Israel Abebe Azime, Jesujoba Alabi, Atnafu Lambebo Tonja, Christine Mwase, Odunayo Ogundepo, Bonaventure F. P. Dossou, Akintunde Oladipo, Doreen Nixdorf, Chris Chinenye Emezue, Sana Al-azzawi, Blessing Sibanda, Davis David, Lolwethu Ndolela, Jonathan Mukiibi, Tunde Ajayi, Tatiana Moteu, Brian Odhiambo, and 46 others. 2023. MasakhaNEWS: News topic classification for African languages. In *Proceedings of the 13th International Joint Conference on Natural Language Processing and the 3rd Conference of the Asia-Pacific Chapter of the Association for Computational Linguistics (Volume 1: Long Papers)*, pages 144–159, Nusa Dua, Bali. Association for Computational Linguistics.

David Ifeoluwa Adelani, Jessica Ojo, Israel Abebe Azime, Jian Yun Zhuang, Jesujoba Oluwadara Alabi, Xuanli He, Millicent Ochieng, Sara Hooker, Andiswa Bukula, En-Shiun Annie Lee, Chiamaka Ijeoma Chukwuneke, Happy Buzaaba, Blessing Kudzaishe Sibanda, Godson Koffi Kalipe, Jonathan Mukiibi, Salomon Kabongo Kabenamualu, Foutse Yuehgoh, Mmasibidi Setaka, Lolwethu Ndolela, and 8 others. 2025. IrokoBench: A new benchmark for African languages in the age of large language models. In *Proceedings of the 2025 Conference of the Nations of the Americas Chapter of the Association for Computational Linguistics: Human Language Technologies (Volume 1: Long Papers)*, pages 2732–2757, Albuquerque, New Mexico. Association for Computational Linguistics.

Seamless Communication, Loïc Barrault, Yu-An Chung, Mariano Cora Meglioli, David Dale, Ning Dong, Paul-Ambroise Duquenne, Hady Elsahar, Hongyu Gong, Kevin Heffernan, John Hoffman, Christopher Klaiber, Pengwei Li, Daniel Licht, Jean Maillard, Alice Rakotoarison, Kaushik Ram Sadagopan, Guillaume Wenzek, Ethan Ye, and 49 others. 2023. Seamlessm4t: Massively multilingual & multimodal machine translation. *Preprint*, arXiv:2308.11596.

Ronen Eldan and Yuanzhi Li. 2023. Tinystories: How small can language models be and still speak coherent english? *Preprint*, arXiv:2305.07759.

Suriya Gunasekar, Yi Zhang, Jyoti Aneja, Caio César Teodoro Mendes, Allie Del Giorno, Sivakanth Gopi, Mojan Javaheripi, Piero Kauffmann, Gustavo de Rosa, Olli Saarikivi, Adil Salim, Shital Shah, Harkirat Singh Behl, Xin Wang, Sébastien Bubeck, Ronen Eldan, Adam Tauman Kalai, Yin Tat Lee, and Yuanzhi Li. 2023. Textbooks are all you need. *Preprint*, arXiv:2306.11644.

Taku Kudo and John Richardson. 2018. SentencePiece: A simple and language independent subword tokenizer and detokenizer for neural text processing. In *Proceedings of the 2018 Conference on Empirical Methods in Natural Language Processing: System Demonstrations*, pages 66–71, Brussels, Belgium. Association for Computational Linguistics.

Ruibo Liu, Jerry Wei, Fangyu Liu, Chenglei Si, Yanzhe Zhang, Jinmeng Rao, Steven Zheng, Daiyi Peng, Diyi Yang, Denny Zhou, and Andrew M. Dai. 2024. Best practices and lessons learned on synthetic data. In *First Conference on Language Modeling*.

Alec Radford, Jeff Wu, Rewon Child, David Luan, Dario Amodei, and Ilya Sutskever. 2019. Language models are unsupervised multitask learners.

Evgeniia Razumovskaia, Joshua Maynez, Annie Louis, Mirella Lapata, and Shashi Narayan. 2024. Little red riding hood goes around the globe: Crosslingual story planning and generation with large language models. In *Proceedings of the 2024 Joint International Conference on Computational Linguistics, Language Resources and Evaluation (LREC-COLING 2024)*, pages 10616–10631, Torino, Italia. ELRA and ICCL.

Atnafu Lambebo Tonja, Bonaventure F. P. Dossou, Jessica Ojo, Jenalea Rajab, Fadel Thior, Eric Peter Wairagala, Anuoluwapo Aremu, Pelonomi Moiloa, Jade Abbott, Vukosi Marivate, and Benjamin Rosman. 2024. Inkubalm: A small language model for low-resource african languages. *Preprint*, arXiv:2408.17024.

Ashish Vaswani, Noam Shazeer, Niki Parmar, Jakob Uszkoreit, Llion Jones, Aidan N. Gomez, Łukasz Kaiser, and Illia Polosukhin. 2017. Attention is all you need. In *Proceedings of the 31st International Conference on Neural Information Processing Systems*, page 6000–6010.

Changhan Wang, Kyunghyun Cho, and Jiatao Gu. 2020. Neural machine translation with byte-level subwords. *Proceedings of the AAAI Conference on Artificial Intelligence*, 34(05):9154–9160.

Zhihua Wen, Zhiliang Tian, Wei Wu, Yuxin Yang, Yanqi Shi, Zhen Huang, and Dongsheng Li. 2023. GROVE: A retrieval-augmented complex story generation framework with a forest of evidence. In *Findings of the Association for Computational Linguistics: EMNLP 2023*, pages 3980–3998, Singapore. Association for Computational Linguistics.

A Appendix

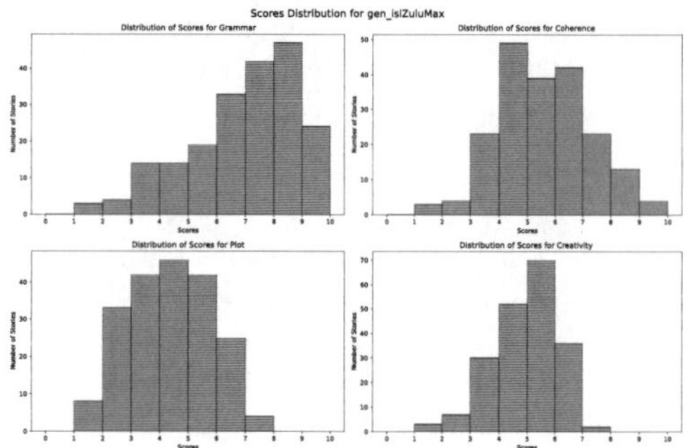

Figure 2: Gemini Score Distribution for isiZulu-Plus Model Generations

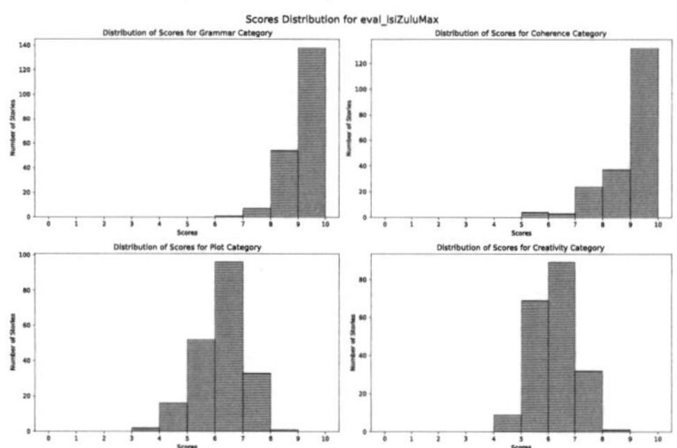

Figure 3: Gemini Score Distribution for isiZulu-Plus Evaluation Set

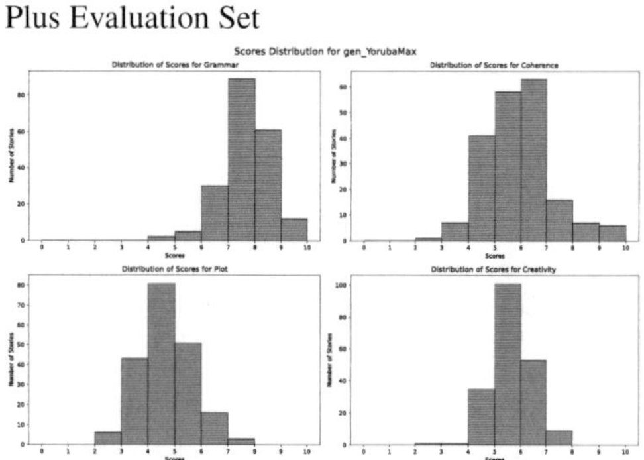

Figure 4: Gemini Score Distribution for YorubaPlus Model Generations

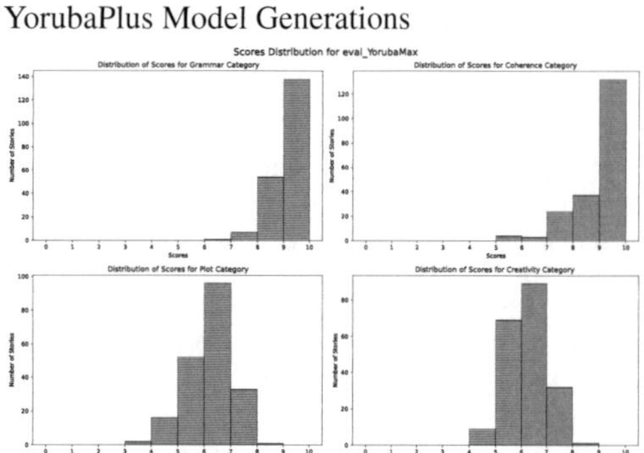

Figure 5: Gemini Score Distribution for YorubaPlus Evaluation Set

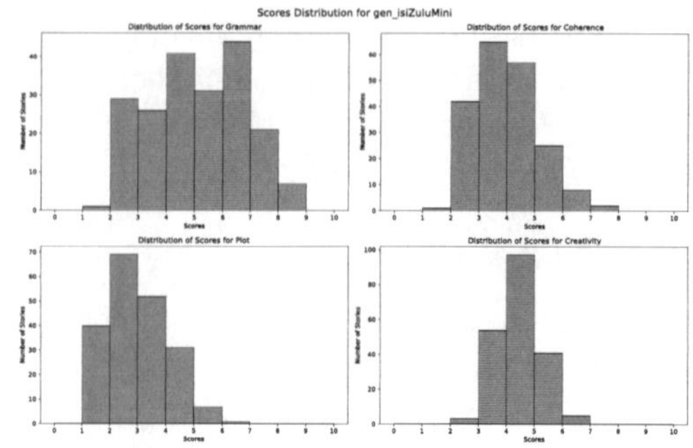

Figure 6: Gemini Score Distribution for isiZul-uLite Model Generations

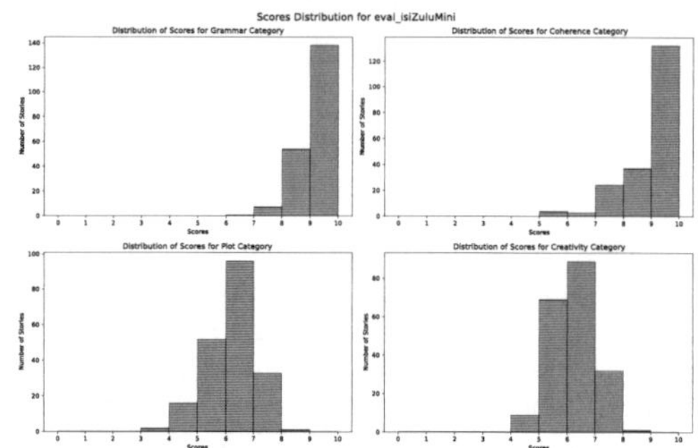

Figure 7: Gemini Score Distribution for isiZul-uLite Evaluation Set

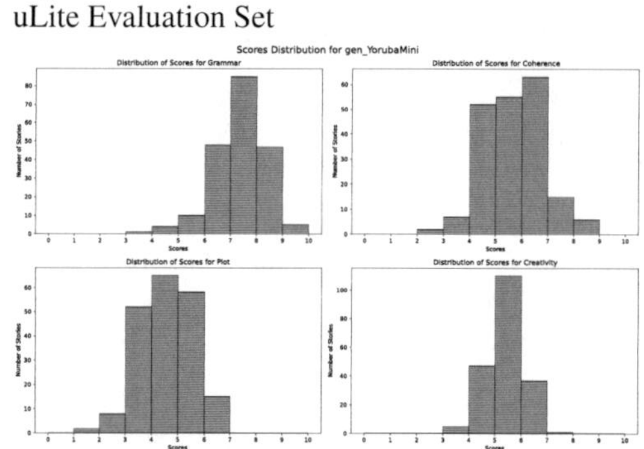

Figure 8: Gemini Score Distribution for YorubaLite Model Generations

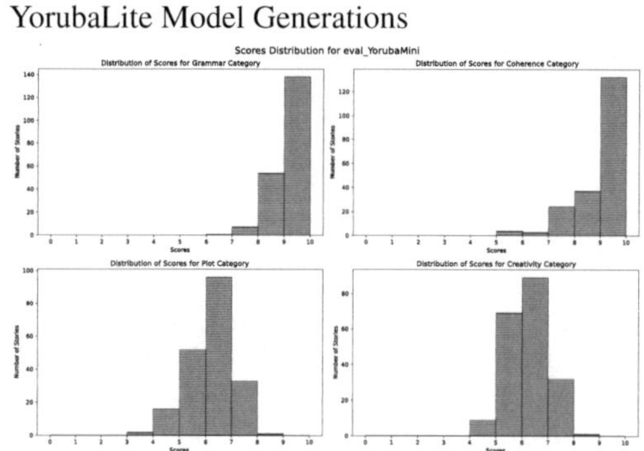

Figure 9: Gemini Score Distribution for YorubaLite Evaluation Set

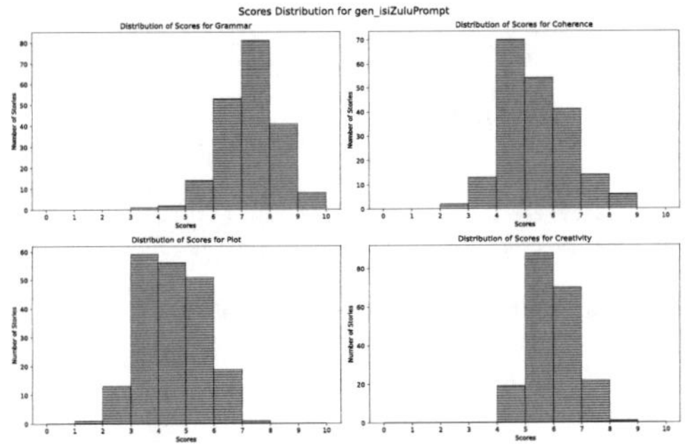

Figure 10: Gemini Score Distribution for isiZuluGuide Model Generations

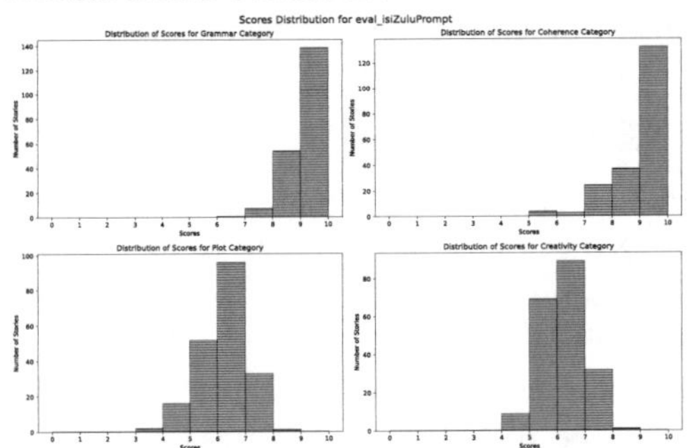

Figure 11: Gemini Score Distribution for isiZuluGuide Evaluation Set

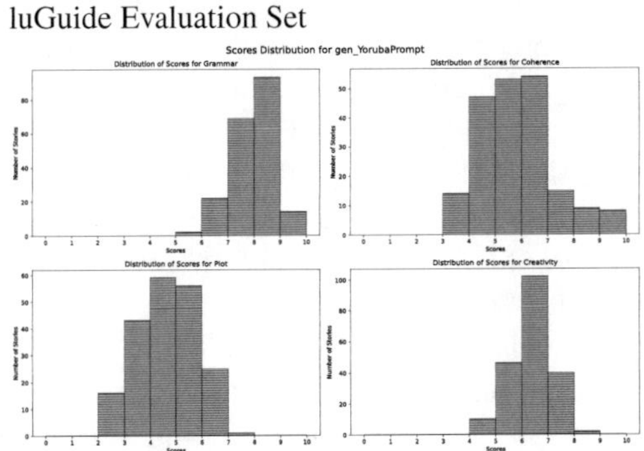

Figure 12: Gemini Score Distribution for YorubaGuide Model Generations

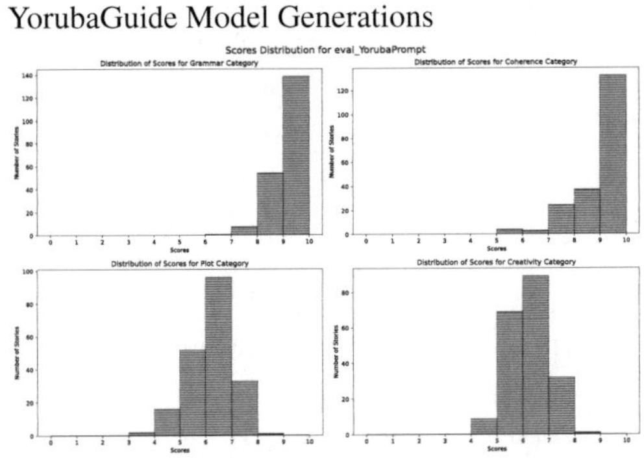

Figure 13: Gemini Score Distribution for YorubaGuide Evaluation Set

Command R7B Arabic: A Small, Enterprise Focused, Multilingual, and Culturally Aware Arabic LLM

Yazeed Alnumay*, **Alexandre Barbet***, **Anna Bialas***, **William Darling***,
Shaan Desai*, **Joan Devassy***, **Kyle Duffy***, **Stephanie Howe***,
Olivia Lasche*, **Justin Lee***, **Anirudh Shrinivason***, **Jennifer Tracey***

Cohere

Abstract

Building high-quality large language models (LLMs) for enterprise Arabic applications remains challenging due to the limited availability of digitized Arabic data. In this work, we present a data synthesis and refinement strategy to help address this problem, namely, by leveraging synthetic data generation and human-in-the-loop annotation to expand our Arabic training corpus. We further present our iterative post training recipe that is essential to achieving state-of-the-art performance in aligning the model with human preferences, a critical aspect to enterprise use cases. The culmination of this effort is the release of a small, 7B, open-weight model that outperforms similarly sized peers in head-to-head comparisons and on Arabic-focused benchmarks covering cultural knowledge, instruction following, RAG, and contextual faithfulness.

1 Introduction

Multilingual language models are evolving rapidly (Huang et al., 2024b), yet specific languages and capabilities remain underdeveloped, particularly in enterprise applications. While state-of-the-art models continue to improve, they often struggle to adapt to linguistic and professional needs in languages like Arabic (Gabriel Nicholas, 2023), the most spoken language in Africa (Zucchet, 2024). This challenge becomes even more pronounced when additional constraints are introduced: the need to keep the model small to ensure accessibility even with limited resources, overcoming data scarcity, and accounting for linguistic nuances that do not translate well from English, all the while prioritizing rapid iteration to stay aligned with the fast-moving market. To address these issues, we developed a post-training approach that efficiently tailors cutting-edge models to specialized capabilities. This report outlines our methodology and findings, offering insights into adapting LLMs for language-specific and professional domains.

2 Related Work

With the recent rapid development in LLMs (Zhao et al., 2024), some focus was placed on improving model multilingualism through second language acquisition techniques (Huang et al., 2024b). These techniques aim to circumvent data scarcity in languages other than English by adding other language capabilities to English models, which is more data efficient. For instance, the Llama 3 family of models adds a final pretraining stage by adding multilingual pretraining data mixed with English (Grattafiori et al., 2024). These techniques have been applied to Arabic-centric models, such as ALLaM (Bari et al., 2025), Jais (Sengupta et al., 2023; Inception, 2024), AceGPT (Huang et al., 2024a; Zhu et al., 2024; Liang et al., 2024), and Fanar (Fanar Team et al., 2025). These projects primarily focused on pretraining data mixture, staging, and tokenizer innovations, including vocabulary expansion (ALLaM), iterative vocabulary expansion (AceGPT), and morphology-based tokenization (Fanar). While they contribute strong foundational models for the community, they do not offer computationally efficient post-training methods.

Post-training has become essential for building robust models (Wei et al., 2022; Kumar et al., 2025; Ouyang et al., 2022). Many research labs have contributed to the open-source community by documenting modern post-training techniques. Notable examples include Tülu 3 (Lambert et al., 2025), which provides a comprehensive overview of general post-training methods, and Aya Expanse (Dang et al., 2024), which focuses on multilingual adaptation.

Our work builds on these efforts by developing a systematic, iterative, and comprehensive approach to efficiently adapt LLMs for languages. Specifi-

*Equal contribution. Authors appear in alphabetical order by second name.

Proceedings of the Sixth Workshop on African Natural Language Processing (AfricaNLP 2025), pages 126–135
July 31, 2025

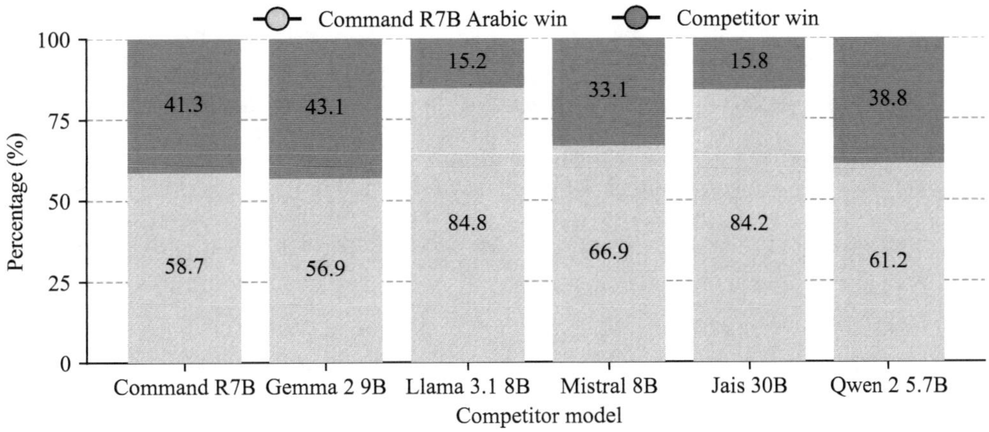

Figure 1: Evaluations on enterprise usability factors (mArenaHard, described in Section 4). Auto win-rates on Arabic version of LMSYS Arena "Hard" human preference tasks (Dang et al., 2024). Command R7B Arabic outperforms all listed similarly-sized models.

cally, we leverage iterative tuning (Grattafiori et al., 2024) methods that rely on best-of-N sampling to generate instruction and preference data via automated reward models or human preference (Yuan et al., 2024). We also further reduce compute requirements by incorporating model merging techniques (Goddard et al., 2024; Yang et al., 2024).

3 Methods

Our training procedure is illustrated in Figure 2. We start by selecting a strong starting model (Section 3.1), on which we perform three distinct training phases: *(i)* supervised fine-tuning (SFT) (Wei et al., 2022), for which we employ iterative dataset refinement techniques (Sections 3.2 and 3.3), *(ii)* off-policy (offline) preference tuning, and *(iii)* iterative preference tuning. The latter two are described in Section 3.4. After each training phase, we merge expert models into a single general model (Section 3.5).

3.1 Base Model Selection

As a starting checkpoint, we chose Command R7B (Cohere, 2024; Cohere et al., 2025) - a strong, general purpose, and open-weight model already trained on a large corpus of multilingual data, including Arabic, and specialized to enterprise use-cases. Additionally, Robinson et al. (2025) showed that Cohere models excel in dialectal Arabic compared to other open-weight models. Our primary objective was to reach state-of-the-art performance in Arabic enterprise use cases while preserving the model's performance on other core capabilities. Starting from an already polished checkpoint meant we could spend more effort on our data and training efforts that refined Arabic-specific tasks.

3.2 Multilingual Arbitrage for Capability Enhancement

Previous work by Aya (Odumakinde et al., 2024) has demonstrated that synthetic data generation is crucial for achieving state-of-the-art performance, and this is especially true for domains with limited data availability such as Arabic. However, a key challenge when training Arabic LLMs is the distinctive difference between Arabic and English. Not only do these languages differ in syntax and morphology, but there are also variations in cultural and contextual nuances that make literal translation challenging. For example, lexical control tasks such as length adherence and structured generation are awkward or nonsensical when translated to Arabic.

To address this, we implemented a human-in-the-loop approach:

- We collaborated with expert annotators to translate IFEval (Zhou et al., 2023) instructions into Arabic. Additionally, we augmented the set with two instructions specific to the Arabic language: “add N diacritics to the response” and “use a specific grammatical verb to start sentences”. This ensured better alignment with Arabic linguistic and cultural nuances.

- These instructions were used as seeds to

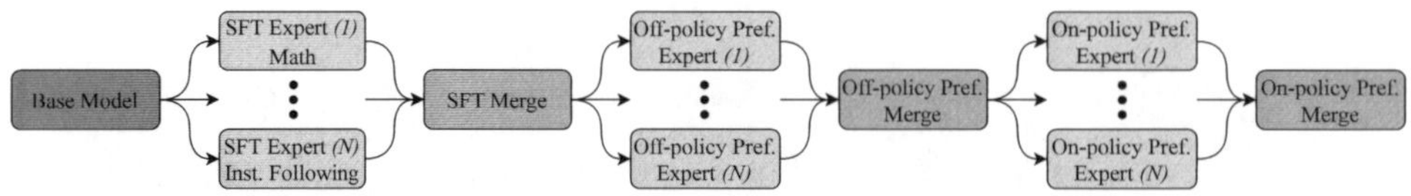

Figure 2: Outline of Command R7B Arabic's training processes with three training stages, each training multiple experts that are merged into a single general model. For instance, in the SFT stage, multiple SFT expert models are trained to excel in specific domains, such as mathematics or instruction following. These experts are subsequently merged to create a generalist SFT model via parameter-wise linear interpolation of the experts' weights.

synthetically generate instruction following prompts in Arabic and subsequently the corresponding completions.

- In accordance with the work done in Aya's Multilingual Arbitrage (Odumakinde et al., 2024), we scored and filtered completions using a reward model, a panel of LLM judges for Arabic natural language quality, and max reward difference for preference pair dataset creation.

This targeted approach ensured that the model learned to follow instructions naturally in Arabic, which is apparent in arena style win-rates where our model is consistently favored over other competitor models, as shown in Figure 1.

3.3 Dataset Curation and Iterative Supervised Refinement

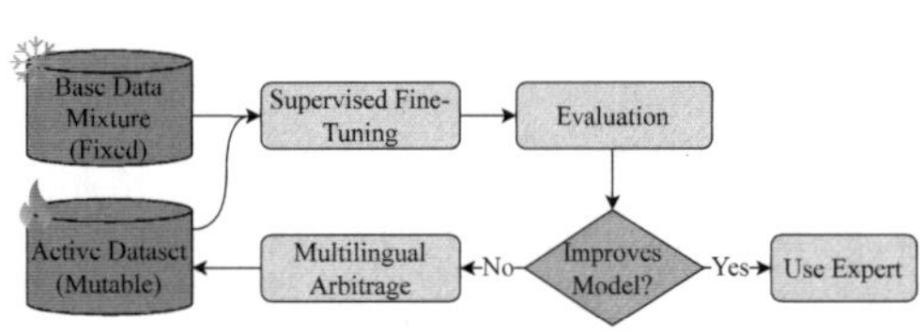

Figure 3: Flowchart for our iterative supervised refinement approach. It ensures that all datasets used improve targeted model performance by mixing a base data mixture with a targeted dataset that is iteratively improved via multilingual arbitrage.

The availability of high-quality Arabic datasets is a well-documented challenge (Gabriel Nicholas, 2023). We aimed to incorporate both publicly available datasets, including ArMATH (Alghamdi et al., 2022), ArabicaQA (Abdallah et al., 2024), and synthetically generated datasets, while enforcing a high-quality data standard. With this in mind, we defined the Iterative Supervised Refinement during Supervised Fine-Tuning (SFT) training phase as a process to optimize our dataset composition. The steps are illustrated in Figure 3 and are as follows:

1. Define a base data mix consisting of high-quality instruction-tuning data.

2. For each new dataset in consideration, add it to the base data mixture and fine-tune the model.

3. Evaluate the resulting model using a benchmark evaluation harness to measure the impact of the new dataset.

4. If the dataset improves performance in any critical capability, retain it for the next iteration.

5. If no improvement was observed, apply Multilingual Arbitrage, refining the prompts before re-running the process.

This approach enabled us to design an optimal dataset mixture that maximized the model's instruction-following capabilities while maintaining a high standard for data quality.

3.4 Preference Tuning for Final Model Optimization

Since we initialized from a strong Command R7B model, it was essential to ensure that enhancements in Arabic did not degrade performance on other benchmarks. Similar to the methodology described by Aya (Üstün et al., 2024), we used two stages of preference tuning as final polishing steps to improve model performance and align it with human preferences. In the first phase, we performed offline preference training on general preference datasets to refine the model's conversational fluency. In the second phase, we ran iterative preference training, incorporating an Arabic-translated reasoning and math-focused dataset (Alghamdi et al., 2022), which proved particularly beneficial for maintaining high performance across diverse enterprise use cases. Both preference tuning stages utilize the direct preference optimization (DPO) (Rafailov et al., 2024) algorithm.

Benchmark	R7B Arabic	R7B (Cohere et al., 2025)	Gemma 9B (Gemma Team et al., 2024)	Llama 3.1 8B (Grattafiori et al., 2024)	Qwen 2.5 7B (Yang et al., 2025)	Ministral 8B (Mistral, 2024)
AlGhafa-Native	**82.2**	81.5	81.3	80.1	80.2	76.6
ArabicMMLU	60.9	59.7	**62.4**	56.6	61.2	53.6
IFEval AR	**69.0**	57.8	67.8	48.4	62.4	49.3
TyDIQA-GoldP Arabic	**83.0**	79.9	76.4	65.9	60.9	57.7
FaithEval Arabic	**51.6**	49.9	47.0	40.9	49.9	25.5
Average	**69.3**	65.8	67.0	58.4	62.9	52.5

Table 1: Full performance comparison against competitor models on Arabic-specific benchmarks. The highest score in each row is in **bold**. Command R7B Arabic is best-in-class compared to similarly sized models on all Arabic benchmarks, with the exception of ArabicMMLU.

3.5 Expert Model Merging

After completing the iterative supervised refinement procedure described in Section 3.3 to create multiple expert models from various datasets, one path forward is to retrain a new generalist model by combining appropriate datasets based on the insights obtained from these experiments. However, we can eliminate computational redundancy by merging various expert models. This is a common practice with mature frameworks (Goddard et al., 2024). The literature lacks conclusive theoretical foundations for the effectiveness of model merging, but extensive experimentation has shown it is a successful strategy in practice (Yang et al., 2024).

To reduce the expert merge search space, we only considered linear merges (Utans, 1996) of the expert models. We tested several weighting schemes based on the importance of each capability and the size of each expert's training data. In the end, our best model was obtained by assigning equal weight to each expert.

In practice, model merging reduces computational cost. However, it complicates replication and adds an additional source of potential errors.

4 Experiments and Results

4.1 Arabic Language

To measure the performance of various models in general Arabic language generation and understanding, as well as enterprise use-cases, such as grounding model generation with enterprise-specific data via RAG and precise instruction following, we utilized the following evaluation suite:

- **IFEval AR**: An internal Arabic translation of the original English dataset (Zhou et al., 2023) with 541 test samples. It measures a model's precise instruction following ability, with instructions such as "use at least 300 words" or "do not use commas."

- **AlGhafa-Native**: The subset[1] of AlGhafa (Almazrouei et al., 2023) tasks which were curated by native Arabic speakers, which encapsulates the following:
  - MCQ Exams AR (562 samples) (Hardalov et al., 2020).
  - Belebele AR Dialects (5,400 samples) and Belebele AR MSA (900 samples) (Bandarkar et al., 2024).
  - AraFacts balanced (80 samples) (Sheikh Ali et al., 2021).
  - SOQAL (155 samples) (Mozannar et al., 2019).
  - XGLUE (155 samples) (Liang et al., 2020).
  - Rating sentiment no neutral (8,000 samples) and rating sentiment (6,000 samples) from the HARD-Arabic-Dataset (Elnagar et al., 2018).
  - Sentiment (1,725 samples) (Abu Farha et al., 2021).

  We report the unweighted average percentage performance across all tasks.

- **TyDiQA-GoldP Arabic**: The 921 samples in Arabic from the original TyDiQA (Clark et al., 2020) golden passage (GoldP) secondary task, in which models are provided with a question and a single passage that contains the question's answer. Models are prompted to determine the substring in the passage that answers the question.

[1] https://huggingface.co/datasets/OALL/AlGhafa-Arabic-LLM-Benchmark-Native

Benchmark	R7B Arabic	R7B (Cohere et al., 2025)	Gemma 9B (Gemma Team et al., 2024)	Llama 3.1 8B (Grattafiori et al., 2024)	Qwen 2.5 7B (Yang et al., 2025)	Ministral 8B (Mistral, 2024)
BBH (Suzgun et al., 2022)	36.2	36.0	**42.1**	29.9	34.9	25.8
MuSR (Sprague et al., 2024)	**11.9**	10.2	9.7	8.4	8.5	8.4
GPQA (Rein et al., 2023)	7.9	7.8	**14.8**	2.4	5.5	4.5
MMLU Pro (Wang et al., 2024)	29.4	28.6	32.0	30.7	**36.5**	30.7
IfEval (Zhou et al., 2023)	**83.3**	77.1	74.4	78.6	75.9	59.0
MATH* (Hendrycks et al., 2021b)	19.6	29.9	19.1	19.3	50.0	19.6
Average	31.4	31.6	32.1	28.2	**35.2**	22.0

* The MATH benchmark used in this leaderboard changed in early January due to a DMCA takedown notice for the original benchmark.

Table 2: Performance comparison of R7B Arabic against similarly sized models on multiple benchmarks. The highest score in each row is in **bold**. Command R7B Arabic retains most of the general and English capabilities of its base model, Command R7B, as indicated by the similar average scores.

- **ArabicMMLU** (Koto et al., 2024): Inspired by the original MMLU (Hendrycks et al., 2021a) in English, ArabicMMLU is a collection of 14,575 native Arabic multiple choice questions focusing on knowledge and reasoning. It covers 40 tasks at various education levels (elementary to college) and regions (North Africa, Levant, and Gulf).

- **FaithEval Arabic**: An internal Arabic translation of a 500 sample subset of the original English dataset (Ming et al., 2024). It measures the model's RAG performance when provided with unanswerable, inconsistent, or counterfactual contexts.

- **Multilingual ArenaHard** (Dang et al., 2024): A machine translation of 500 questions from the original English LMArena (formerly LMSYS) Arena-Hard-Auto (Li et al., 2024) prompts into various other languages. We limit our evaluation to the Arabic subset. The evaluation uses GPT-4o as a judge to compare completions from two different models.

Table 1 shows results compared to other models in the same size category. The Command R7B Arabic model outperforms all baselines across key Arabic benchmarks, achieving an average score of 69.3, surpassing Command R7B (65.8) and Gemma 9B (67.0). It performs at the top of its size class in the following benchmarks: Cultural Knowledge (AlGhafa-Native), Instruction Following (IFEval AR) validating our human-in-the-loop data strategy, RAG Question Answering (TyDiQA-GoldP Arabic), and RAG Faithfulness (FaithEval Arabic). In General Knowledge (ArabicMMLU), Command R7B Arabic scores third, while staying competitive with Gemma 9B and Qwen 2.7.

4.2 General Capabilities

Retaining general capabilities is essential for the model to be helpful in enterprise settings. We thoroughly measured our model's performance and present the results of the standardized Hugging Face Open LLM Leaderboard benchmarks (Fourrier et al., 2024; Gao et al., 2021). Table 2 shows that our model excels in IfEval and MuSR, achieving the highest scores among similarly sized models. Notably, it outperforms the initial checkpoint on all benchmarks except for MATH, possibly due to the change in methodology.

These benchmark results (Table 1 and Table 2), coupled with auto win-rate data (Figure 1), validate that our approach effectively enhances Arabic language capabilities while maintaining robust performance in enterprise applications.

5 Conclusion

In this work, we rapidly iterated to develop Command R7B Arabic, a small, yet competent Arabic LLM optimized for enterprise applications. By leveraging synthetic data generation, multilingual arbitrage, and human-in-the-loop interventions, we significantly improved instruction following, retrieval-augmented generation (RAG), and question answering capabilities in Arabic. However, transferring knowledge from English-centric datasets to Arabic remains an open challenge. Future work should explore more effective adaptation strategies, ensuring higher linguistic and factual alignment across languages.

Limitations

Our work focuses on Modern Standard Arabic (MSA), which is widely used in formal and professional settings but differs significantly from spoken dialects across the Arabic-speaking world. While

MSA provides a strong foundation for enterprise applications, real world use cases often involve dialectal Arabic, which varies by region and context. Future work should explore dialect adaptation strategies to improve robustness across diverse Arabic varieties.

We adapted Faithfulness (FaithEval Arabic), Question Answering (TyDi QA Arabic), and Instruction Following (IFEval AR) to measure enterprise-relevant capabilities. Still, these benchmarks remain proxies rather than direct tests of real-world deployment challenges. The effectiveness of our model in enterprise workflows can only be fully validated through real-world deployment and user feedback.

Acknowledgments

This work was a collaboration between many teams in Cohere. We would like to particularly acknowledge the following people who supported the project through advice and maintenance of our core infrastructure:

Modeling Team: Théo Dehaze, Jesse Willman, Lewis Stott, Florian Strub, Jay Alammar, Matthias Gallé, Samuel Cahyawijaya, Alexandre Bérard, Wei-Yin Ko, Kocmi Tom, Dennis Aumiller, Nathan Grinsztajn, Phil Blunsom, Jon Ander Campos, Yi Chern Tan, Sander Land, Nithya Govindarajan, Nick Jakobi, Adrien Morisot, Olivia Markham;

C4AI: Sungjin Hong, Alejandro Salamanca, Marzieh Fadaee, Ahmet Üstün, Sara Hooker;

Infrastructure: Cécile Robert-Michon, Jessica Xie, Adi Bongale, Ace Eldeib, Sudip Roy, Manoj Govindassamy, Maxime Brunet, Jeremy Pekmez, Terrence Zhao, Renjie Huang;

Applied ML Team: Neeral Beladia, Gokce Keskin, Utsav Garg, Jason Jung, Hemangani Nagarajan, Sanal Shivaprasad, Sam Passaglia, Edmond Wen, Trushant Kalyanpur, Vivek Muppalla, Evren Tumer, Harri Bell-Thomas;

Annotators: Arwa Alaya, Noha Shehata , Eyas Shanaah , Abdullah Omran, Nermeen Isaac, Izzat Homsi, Mahmoud Mansour, Mayar Soliman, Israr Wahid, Vanessa Choueiry, Mona Knobloch, Fatima Zahra Zyad;

Annotator Operations: Claire Cheng, Trisha Starostina, Brenda Malacara Lopez;

Leadership: Aidan Gomez, Martin Kon, Saurabh Baji, Phil Blunsom;

External partners: Neha Sengupta, Ali El Filali.

References

Abdelrahman Abdallah, Mahmoud Kasem, Mahmoud Abdalla, Mohamed Mahmoud, Mohamed Elkasaby, Yasser Elbendary, and Adam Jatowt. 2024. Arabicaqa: A comprehensive dataset for arabic question answering. *Preprint*, arXiv:2403.17848.

Ibrahim Abu Farha, Wajdi Zaghouani, and Walid Magdy. 2021. Overview of the WANLP 2021 shared task on sarcasm and sentiment detection in Arabic. In *Proceedings of the Sixth Arabic Natural Language Processing Workshop*, pages 296–305, Kyiv, Ukraine (Virtual). Association for Computational Linguistics.

Reem Alghamdi, Zhenwen Liang, and Xiangliang Zhang. 2022. ArMATH: a dataset for solving Arabic math word problems. In *Proceedings of the Thirteenth Language Resources and Evaluation Conference*, pages 351–362, Marseille, France. European Language Resources Association.

Ebtesam Almazrouei, Ruxandra Cojocaru, Michele Baldo, Quentin Malartic, Hamza Alobeidli, Daniele Mazzotta, Guilherme Penedo, Giulia Campesan, Mugariya Farooq, Maitha Alhammadi, Julien Launay, and Badreddine Noune. 2023. AlGhafa evaluation benchmark for Arabic language models. In *Proceedings of ArabicNLP 2023*, pages 244–275, Singapore (Hybrid). Association for Computational Linguistics.

Lucas Bandarkar, Davis Liang, Benjamin Muller, Mikel Artetxe, Satya Narayan Shukla, Donald Husa, Naman Goyal, Abhinandan Krishnan, Luke Zettlemoyer, and Madian Khabsa. 2024. The belebele benchmark: a parallel reading comprehension dataset in 122 language variants. In *Proceedings of the 62nd Annual Meeting of the Association for Computational Linguistics (Volume 1: Long Papers)*, page 749–775. Association for Computational Linguistics.

M Saiful Bari, Yazeed Alnumay, Norah A. Alzahrani, Nouf M. Alotaibi, Hisham Abdullah Alyahya, Sultan AlRashed, Faisal Abdulrahman Mirza, Shaykhah Z. Alsubaie, Hassan A. Alahmed, Ghadah Alabduljabbar, Raghad Alkhathran, Yousef Almushayqih, Raneem Alnajim, Salman Alsubaihi, Maryam Al Mansour, Saad Amin Hassan, Dr. Majed Alrubaian, Ali Alammari, Zaki Alawami, Abdulmohsen Al-Thubaity, Ahmed Abdelali, Jeril Kuriakose, Abdalghani Abujabal, Nora Al-Twairesh, Areeb Alowisheq, and Haidar Khan. 2025. ALLam: Large language models for arabic and english. In *The Thirteenth International Conference on Learning Representations*.

Jonathan H. Clark, Eunsol Choi, Michael Collins, Dan Garrette, Tom Kwiatkowski, Vitaly Nikolaev, and Jennimaria Palomaki. 2020. Tydi qa: A benchmark for information-seeking question answering in typologically diverse languages. *Preprint*, arXiv:2003.05002.

Cohere. 2024. Introducing command r7b: Fast and efficient generative ai.

Team Cohere, :, Aakanksha, Arash Ahmadian, Marwan Ahmed, Jay Alammar, Milad Alizadeh, Yazeed Alnumay, Sophia Althammer, Arkady Arkhangorodsky, Viraat Aryabumi, Dennis Aumiller, Raphaël Avalos, Zahara Aviv, Sammie Bae, Saurabh Baji, Alexandre Barbet, Max Bartolo, Björn Bebensee, Neeral Beladia, Walter Beller-Morales, Alexandre Bérard, Andrew Berneshawi, Anna Bialas, Phil Blunsom, Matt Bobkin, Adi Bongale, Sam Braun, Maxime Brunet, Samuel Cahyawijaya, David Cairuz, Jon Ander Campos, Cassie Cao, Kris Cao, Roman Castagné, Julián Cendrero, Leila Chan Currie, Yash Chandak, Diane Chang, Giannis Chatziveroglou, Hongyu Chen, Claire Cheng, Alexis Chevalier, Justin T. Chiu, Eugene Cho, Eugene Choi, Eujeong Choi, Tim Chung, Volkan Cirik, Ana Cismaru, Pierre Clavier, Henry Conklin, Lucas Crawhall-Stein, Devon Crouse, Andres Felipe Cruz-Salinas, Ben Cyrus, Daniel D'souza, Hugo Dalla-Torre, John Dang, William Darling, Omar Darwiche Domingues, Saurabh Dash, Antoine Debugne, Théo Dehaze, Shaan Desai, Joan Devassy, Rishit Dholakia, Kyle Duffy, Ali Edalati, Ace Eldeib, Abdullah Elkady, Sarah Elsharkawy, Irem Ergün, Beyza Ermis, Marzieh Fadaee, Boyu Fan, Lucas Fayoux, Yannis Flet-Berliac, Nick Frosst, Matthias Gallé, Wojciech Galuba, Utsav Garg, Matthieu Geist, Mohammad Gheshlaghi Azar, Ellen Gilsenan-McMahon, Seraphina Goldfarb-Tarrant, Tomas Goldsack, Aidan Gomez, Victor Machado Gonzaga, Nithya Govindarajan, Manoj Govindassamy, Nathan Grinsztajn, Nikolas Gritsch, Patrick Gu, Shangmin Guo, Kilian Haefeli, Rod Hajjar, Tim Hawes, Jingyi He, Sebastian Hofstätter, Sungjin Hong, Sara Hooker, Tom Hosking, Stephanie Howe, Eric Hu, Renjie Huang, Hemant Jain, Ritika Jain, Nick Jakobi, Madeline Jenkins, JJ Jordan, Dhruti Joshi, Jason Jung, Trushant Kalyanpur, Siddhartha Rao Kamalakara, Julia Kedrzycki, Gokce Keskin, Edward Kim, Joon Kim, Wei-Yin Ko, Tom Kocmi, Michael Kozakov, Wojciech Kryściński, Arnav Kumar Jain, Komal Kumar Teru, Sander Land, Michael Lasby, Olivia Lasche, Justin Lee, Patrick Lewis, Jeffrey Li, Jonathan Li, Hangyu Lin, Acyr Locatelli, Kevin Luong, Raymond Ma, Lukáš Mach, Marina Machado, Joanne Magbitang, Brenda Malacara Lopez, Aryan Mann, Kelly Marchisio, Olivia Markham, Alexandre Matton, Alex McKinney, Dominic McLoughlin, Jozef Mokry, Adrien Morisot, Autumn Moulder, Harry Moynehan, Maximilian Mozes, Vivek Muppalla, Lidiya Murakhovska, Hemangani Nagarajan, Alekhya Nandula, Hisham Nasir, Shauna Nehra, Josh Netto-Rosen, Daniel Ohashi, James Owers-Bardsley, Jason Ozuzu, Dennis Padilla, Gloria Park, Sam Passaglia, Jeremy Pekmez, Laura Penstone, Aleksandra Piktus, Case Ploeg, Andrew Poulton, Youran Qi, Shubha Raghvendra, Miguel Ramos, Ekagra Ranjan, Pierre Richemond, Cécile Robert-Michon, Aurélien Rodriguez, Sudip Roy, Sebastian Ruder, Laura Ruis, Louise Rust, Anubhav Sachan, Alejandro Salamanca, Kailash Karthik Saravanakumar, Isha Satyakam, Alice Schoenauer Sebag, Priyanka Sen, Sholeh Sepehri, Preethi Seshadri, Ye Shen, Tom Sherborne, Sylvie Shang Shi, Sanal Shivaprasad, Vladyslav Shmyhlo, Anirudh Shrinivason, Inna Shteinbuk, Amir Shukayev, Mathieu Simard, Ella Snyder, Ava Spataru, Victoria Spooner, Trisha Starostina, Florian Strub, Yixuan Su, Jimin Sun, Dwarak Talupuru, Eugene Tarassov, Elena Tommasone, Jennifer Tracey, Billy Trend, Evren Tumer, Ahmet Üstün, Bharat Venkitesh, David Venuto, Pat Verga, Maxime Voisin, Alex Wang, Donglu Wang, Shijian Wang, Edmond Wen, Naomi White, Jesse Willman, Marysia Winkels, Chen Xia, Jessica Xie, Minjie Xu, Bowen Yang, Tan Yi-Chern, Ivan Zhang, Zhenyu Zhao, and Zhoujie Zhao. 2025. Command a: An enterprise-ready large language model. *Preprint*, arXiv:2504.00698.

John Dang, Shivalika Singh, Daniel D'souza, Arash Ahmadian, Alejandro Salamanca, Madeline Smith, Aidan Peppin, Sungjin Hong, Manoj Govindassamy, Terrence Zhao, Sandra Kublik, Meor Amer, Viraat Aryabumi, Jon Ander Campos, Yi-Chern Tan, Tom Kocmi, Florian Strub, Nathan Grinsztajn, Yannis Flet-Berliac, Acyr Locatelli, Hangyu Lin, Dwarak Talupuru, Bharat Venkitesh, David Cairuz, Bowen Yang, Tim Chung, Wei-Yin Ko, Sylvie Shang Shi, Amir Shukayev, Sammie Bae, Aleksandra Piktus, Roman Castagné, Felipe Cruz-Salinas, Eddie Kim, Lucas Crawhall-Stein, Adrien Morisot, Sudip Roy, Phil Blunsom, Ivan Zhang, Aidan Gomez, Nick Frosst, Marzieh Fadaee, Beyza Ermis, Ahmet Üstün, and Sara Hooker. 2024. Aya expanse: Combining research breakthroughs for a new multilingual frontier. *Preprint*, arXiv:2412.04261.

Ashraf Elnagar, Yasmin S Khalifa, and Anas Einea. 2018. Hotel arabic-reviews dataset construction for sentiment analysis applications. *Intelligent natural language processing: Trends and applications*, pages 35–52.

Fanar Team, Ummar Abbas, Mohammad Shahmeer Ahmad, Firoj Alam, Enes Altinisik, Ehsannedin Asgari, Yazan Boshmaf, Sabri Boughorbel, Sanjay Chawla, Shammur Chowdhury, Fahim Dalvi, Kareem Darwish, Nadir Durrani, Mohamed Elfeky, Ahmed Elmagarmid, Mohamed Eltabakh, Masoomali Fatehkia, Anastasios Fragkopoulos, Maram Hasanain, Majd Hawasly, Mus'ab Husaini, Soon-Gyo Jung, Ji Kim Lucas, Walid Magdy, Safa Messaoud, Abubakr Mohamed, Tasnim Mohiuddin, Basel Mousi, Hamdy Mubarak, Ahmad Musleh, Zan Naeem, Mourad Ouzzani, Dorde Popovic, Amin Sadeghi, Husrev Taha Sencar, Mohammed Shinoy, Omar Sinan, Yifan Zhang, Ahmed Ali, Yassine El Kheir, Xiaosong Ma, and Chaoyi Ruan. 2025. Fanar: An arabic-centric multimodal generative ai platform. *Preprint*, arXiv:2501.13944.

Clémentine Fourrier, Nathan Habib, Alina Lozovskaya, Konrad Szafer, and Thomas Wolf. 2024. Open llm leaderboard v2. `https://huggingface.co/spaces/open-llm-leaderboard/open_llm_leaderboard`.

Aliya Bhatia Gabriel Nicholas. 2023. Lost in translation: Large language models in non-english content analysis. *Center for Democracy & Technology*.

Leo Gao, Jonathan Tow, Stella Biderman, Sid Black, Anthony DiPofi, Charles Foster, Laurence Golding, Jeffrey Hsu, Kyle McDonell, Niklas Muennighoff, Jason Phang, Laria Reynolds, Eric Tang, Anish Thite, Ben Wang, Kevin Wang, and Andy Zou. 2021. A framework for few-shot language model evaluation.

Gemma Team, Morgane Riviere, Shreya Pathak, Pier Giuseppe Sessa, Cassidy Hardin, Surya Bhupatiraju, Léonard Hussenot, Thomas Mesnard, Bobak Shahriari, Alexandre Ramé, Johan Ferret, Peter Liu, Pouya Tafti, Abe Friesen, Michelle Casbon, Sabela Ramos, Ravin Kumar, Charline Le Lan, Sammy Jerome, Anton Tsitsulin, Nino Vieillard, Piotr Stanczyk, Sertan Girgin, Nikola Momchev, Matt Hoffman, Shantanu Thakoor, Jean-Bastien Grill, Behnam Neyshabur, Olivier Bachem, Alanna Walton, Aliaksei Severyn, Alicia Parrish, Aliya Ahmad, Allen Hutchison, Alvin Abdagic, Amanda Carl, Amy Shen, Andy Brock, Andy Coenen, Anthony Laforge, Antonia Paterson, Ben Bastian, Bilal Piot, Bo Wu, Brandon Royal, Charlie Chen, Chintu Kumar, Chris Perry, Chris Welty, Christopher A. Choquette-Choo, Danila Sinopalnikov, David Weinberger, Dimple Vijaykumar, Dominika Rogozińska, Dustin Herbison, Elisa Bandy, Emma Wang, Eric Noland, Erica Moreira, Evan Senter, Evgenii Eltyshev, Francesco Visin, Gabriel Rasskin, Gary Wei, Glenn Cameron, Gus Martins, Hadi Hashemi, Hanna Klimczak-Plucińska, Harleen Batra, Harsh Dhand, Ivan Nardini, Jacinda Mein, Jack Zhou, James Svensson, Jeff Stanway, Jetha Chan, Jin Peng Zhou, Joana Carrasqueira, Joana Iljazi, Jocelyn Becker, Joe Fernandez, Joost van Amersfoort, Josh Gordon, Josh Lipschultz, Josh Newlan, Ju yeong Ji, Kareem Mohamed, Kartikeya Badola, Kat Black, Katie Millican, Keelin McDonell, Kelvin Nguyen, Kiranbir Sodhia, Kish Greene, Lars Lowe Sjoesund, Lauren Usui, Laurent Sifre, Lena Heuermann, Leticia Lago, Lilly McNealus, Livio Baldini Soares, Logan Kilpatrick, Lucas Dixon, Luciano Martins, Machel Reid, Manvinder Singh, Mark Iverson, Martin Görner, Mat Velloso, Mateo Wirth, Matt Davidow, Matt Miller, Matthew Rahtz, Matthew Watson, Meg Risdal, Mehran Kazemi, Michael Moynihan, Ming Zhang, Minsuk Kahng, Minwoo Park, Mofi Rahman, Mohit Khatwani, Natalie Dao, Nenshad Bardoliwalla, Nesh Devanathan, Neta Dumai, Nilay Chauhan, Oscar Wahltinez, Pankil Botarda, Parker Barnes, Paul Barham, Paul Michel, Pengchong Jin, Petko Georgiev, Phil Culliton, Pradeep Kuppala, Ramona Comanescu, Ramona Merhej, Reena Jana, Reza Ardeshir Rokni, Rishabh Agarwal, Ryan Mullins, Samaneh Saadat, Sara Mc Carthy, Sarah Cogan, Sarah Perrin, Sébastien M. R. Arnold, Sebastian Krause, Shengyang Dai, Shruti Garg, Shruti Sheth, Sue Ronstrom, Susan Chan, Timothy Jordan, Ting Yu, Tom Eccles, Tom Hennigan, Tomas Kocisky, Tulsee Doshi, Vihan Jain, Vikas Yadav, Vilobh Meshram, Vishal Dharmadhikari, Warren Barkley, Wei Wei, Wenming Ye, Woohyun Han, Woosuk Kwon, Xiang Xu, Zhe Shen, Zhitao Gong, Zichuan Wei, Victor Cotruta, Phoebe Kirk, Anand Rao, Minh Giang, Ludovic Peran, Tris Warkentin, Eli Collins, Joelle Barral, Zoubin Ghahramani, Raia Hadsell, D. Sculley, Jeanine Banks, Anca Dragan, Slav Petrov, Oriol Vinyals, Jeff Dean, Demis Hassabis, Koray Kavukcuoglu, Clement Farabet, Elena Buchatskaya, Sebastian Borgeaud, Noah Fiedel, Armand Joulin, Kathleen Kenealy, Robert Dadashi, and Alek Andreev. 2024. Gemma 2: Improving open language models at a practical size. *Preprint*, arXiv:2408.00118.

Charles Goddard, Shamane Siriwardhana, Malikeh Ehghaghi, Luke Meyers, Vladimir Karpukhin, Brian Benedict, Mark McQuade, and Jacob Solawetz. 2024. Arcee's mergekit: A toolkit for merging large language models. In *Proceedings of the 2024 Conference on Empirical Methods in Natural Language Processing: Industry Track*, pages 477–485.

Aaron Grattafiori, Abhimanyu Dubey, Abhinav Jauhri, Abhinav Pandey, Abhishek Kadian, Ahmad Al-Dahle, Aiesha Letman, Akhil Mathur, Alan Schelten, Alex Vaughan, et al. 2024. The llama 3 herd of models. *arXiv preprint arXiv:2407.21783*.

Momchil Hardalov, Todor Mihaylov, Dimitrina Zlatkova, Yoan Dinkov, Ivan Koychev, and Preslav Nakov. 2020. Exams: A multi-subject high school examinations dataset for cross-lingual and multilingual question answering. *arXiv preprint arXiv:2011.03080*.

Dan Hendrycks, Collin Burns, Steven Basart, Andy Zou, Mantas Mazeika, Dawn Song, and Jacob Steinhardt. 2021a. Measuring massive multitask language understanding. *Preprint*, arXiv:2009.03300.

Dan Hendrycks, Collin Burns, Saurav Kadavath, Akul Arora, Steven Basart, Eric Tang, Dawn Song, and Jacob Steinhardt. 2021b. Measuring mathematical problem solving with the math dataset. *Preprint*, arXiv:2103.03874.

Huang Huang, Fei Yu, Jianqing Zhu, Xuening Sun, Hao Cheng, Dingjie Song, Zhihong Chen, Abdulmohsen Alharthi, Bang An, Juncai He, Ziche Liu, Zhiyi Zhang, Junying Chen, Jianquan Li, Benyou Wang, Lian Zhang, Ruoyu Sun, Xiang Wan, Haizhou Li, and Jinchao Xu. 2024a. Acegpt, localizing large language models in arabic. *Preprint*, arXiv:2309.12053.

Kaiyu Huang, Fengran Mo, Xinyu Zhang, Hongliang Li, You Li, Yuanchi Zhang, Weijian Yi, Yulong Mao, Jinchen Liu, Yuzhuang Xu, et al. 2024b. A survey on large language models with multilingualism: Recent advances and new frontiers. *arXiv preprint arXiv:2405.10936*.

Inception. 2024. Jais family model card. *Hugging Face*.

Fajri Koto, Haonan Li, Sara Shatanawi, Jad Doughman, Abdelrahman Boda Sadallah, Aisha Alraeesi, Khalid Almubarak, Zaid Alyafeai, Neha Sengupta, Shady Shehata, Nizar Habash, Preslav Nakov, and Timothy Baldwin. 2024. ArabicMMLU: Assessing massive multitask language understanding in arabic. In *Findings of the Association for Computational Linguistics: ACL 2024*.

Komal Kumar, Tajamul Ashraf, Omkar Thawakar, Rao Muhammad Anwer, Hisham Cholakkal, Mubarak Shah, Ming-Hsuan Yang, Phillip H. S. Torr, Salman Khan, and Fahad Shahbaz Khan. 2025. Llm post-training: A deep dive into reasoning large language models. *Preprint*, arXiv:2502.21321.

Nathan Lambert, Jacob Morrison, Valentina Pyatkin, Shengyi Huang, Hamish Ivison, Faeze Brahman, Lester James V. Miranda, Alisa Liu, Nouha Dziri, Shane Lyu, Yuling Gu, Saumya Malik, Victoria Graf, Jena D. Hwang, Jiangjiang Yang, Ronan Le Bras, Oyvind Tafjord, Chris Wilhelm, Luca Soldaini, Noah A. Smith, Yizhong Wang, Pradeep Dasigi, and Hannaneh Hajishirzi. 2025. Tulu 3: Pushing frontiers in open language model post-training. *Preprint*, arXiv:2411.15124.

Tianle Li, Wei-Lin Chiang, Evan Frick, Lisa Dunlap, Tianhao Wu, Banghua Zhu, Joseph E. Gonzalez, and Ion Stoica. 2024. From crowdsourced data to high-quality benchmarks: Arena-hard and benchbuilder pipeline. *Preprint*, arXiv:2406.11939.

Juhao Liang, Zhenyang Cai, Jianqing Zhu, Huang Huang, Kewei Zong, Bang An, Mosen Alharthi, Juncai He, Lian Zhang, Haizhou Li, Benyou Wang, and Jinchao Xu. 2024. Alignment at pre-training! towards native alignment for arabic LLMs. In *The Thirty-eighth Annual Conference on Neural Information Processing Systems*.

Yaobo Liang, Nan Duan, Yeyun Gong, Ning Wu, Fenfei Guo, Weizhen Qi, Ming Gong, Linjun Shou, Daxin Jiang, Guihong Cao, Xiaodong Fan, Ruofei Zhang, Rahul Agrawal, Edward Cui, Sining Wei, Taroon Bharti, Ying Qiao, Jiun-Hung Chen, Winnie Wu, Shuguang Liu, Fan Yang, Daniel Campos, Rangan Majumder, and Ming Zhou. 2020. XGLUE: A new benchmark dataset for cross-lingual pre-training, understanding and generation. In *Proceedings of the 2020 Conference on Empirical Methods in Natural Language Processing (EMNLP)*, pages 6008–6018, Online. Association for Computational Linguistics.

Yifei Ming, Senthil Purushwalkam, Shrey Pandit, Zixuan Ke, Xuan-Phi Nguyen, Caiming Xiong, and Shafiq Joty. 2024. Faitheval: Can your language model stay faithful to context, even if "the moon is made of marshmallows". *Preprint*, arXiv:2410.03727.

Mistral. 2024. Ministral 8b instruct model card. *Hugging Face*.

Hussein Mozannar, Karl El Hajal, Elie Maamary, and Hazem Hajj. 2019. Neural arabic question answering. *Preprint*, arXiv:1906.05394.

Ayomide Odumakinde, Daniel D'souza, Pat Verga, Beyza Ermis, and Sara Hooker. 2024. Multilingual arbitrage: Optimizing data pools to accelerate multilingual progress. *Preprint*, arXiv:2408.14960.

Long Ouyang, Jeff Wu, Xu Jiang, Diogo Almeida, Carroll L. Wainwright, Pamela Mishkin, Chong Zhang, Sandhini Agarwal, Katarina Slama, Alex Ray, John Schulman, Jacob Hilton, Fraser Kelton, Luke Miller, Maddie Simens, Amanda Askell, Peter Welinder, Paul Christiano, Jan Leike, and Ryan Lowe. 2022. Training language models to follow instructions with human feedback. *Preprint*, arXiv:2203.02155.

Rafael Rafailov, Archit Sharma, Eric Mitchell, Stefano Ermon, Christopher D. Manning, and Chelsea Finn. 2024. Direct preference optimization: Your language model is secretly a reward model. *Preprint*, arXiv:2305.18290.

David Rein, Betty Li Hou, Asa Cooper Stickland, Jackson Petty, Richard Yuanzhe Pang, Julien Dirani, Julian Michael, and Samuel R. Bowman. 2023. Gpqa: A graduate-level google-proof q&a benchmark. *Preprint*, arXiv:2311.12022.

Nathaniel R. Robinson, Shahd Abdelmoneim, Kelly Marchisio, and Sebastian Ruder. 2025. Al-qasida: Analyzing llm quality and accuracy systematically in dialectal arabic. *Preprint*, arXiv:2412.04193.

Neha Sengupta, Sunil Kumar Sahu, Bokang Jia, Satheesh Katipomu, Haonan Li, Fajri Koto, William Marshall, Gurpreet Gosal, Cynthia Liu, Zhiming Chen, Osama Mohammed Afzal, Samta Kamboj, Onkar Pandit, Rahul Pal, Lalit Pradhan, Zain Muhammad Mujahid, Massa Baali, Xudong Han, Sondos Mahmoud Bsharat, Alham Fikri Aji, Zhiqiang Shen, Zhengzhong Liu, Natalia Vassilieva, Joel Hestness, Andy Hock, Andrew Feldman, Jonathan Lee, Andrew Jackson, Hector Xuguang Ren, Preslav Nakov, Timothy Baldwin, and Eric Xing. 2023. Jais and jais-chat: Arabic-centric foundation and instruction-tuned open generative large language models. *Preprint*, arXiv:2308.16149.

Zien Sheikh Ali, Watheq Mansour, Tamer Elsayed, and Abdulaziz Al-Ali. 2021. AraFacts: The first large Arabic dataset of naturally occurring claims. In *Proceedings of the Sixth Arabic Natural Language Processing Workshop*, pages 231–236, Kyiv, Ukraine (Virtual). Association for Computational Linguistics.

Zayne Sprague, Xi Ye, Kaj Bostrom, Swarat Chaudhuri, and Greg Durrett. 2024. Musr: Testing the limits of chain-of-thought with multistep soft reasoning. *Preprint*, arXiv:2310.16049.

Mirac Suzgun, Nathan Scales, Nathanael Schärli, Sebastian Gehrmann, Yi Tay, Hyung Won Chung, Aakanksha Chowdhery, Quoc V. Le, Ed H. Chi, Denny Zhou, and Jason Wei. 2022. Challenging big-bench tasks and whether chain-of-thought can solve them. *Preprint*, arXiv:2210.09261.

Ahmet Üstün, Viraat Aryabumi, Zheng Yong, Wei-Yin Ko, Daniel D'souza, Gbemileke Onilude, Neel Bhandari, Shivalika Singh, Hui-Lee Ooi, Amr Kayid, Freddie Vargus, Phil Blunsom, Shayne Longpre, Niklas Muennighoff, Marzieh Fadaee, Julia Kreutzer, and Sara Hooker. 2024. Aya model: An instruction finetuned open-access multilingual language model. In

Proceedings of the 62nd Annual Meeting of the Association for Computational Linguistics (Volume 1: Long Papers), pages 15894–15939, Bangkok, Thailand. Association for Computational Linguistics.

Joachim Utans. 1996. Weight averaging for neural networks and local resampling schemes. In *Proc. AAAI-96 Workshop on Integrating Multiple Learned Models. AAAI Press*, pages 133–138. Citeseer.

Yubo Wang, Xueguang Ma, Ge Zhang, Yuansheng Ni, Abhranil Chandra, Shiguang Guo, Weiming Ren, Aaran Arulraj, Xuan He, Ziyan Jiang, Tianle Li, Max Ku, Kai Wang, Alex Zhuang, Rongqi Fan, Xiang Yue, and Wenhu Chen. 2024. Mmlu-pro: A more robust and challenging multi-task language understanding benchmark. *Preprint*, arXiv:2406.01574.

Jason Wei, Maarten Bosma, Vincent Y. Zhao, Kelvin Guu, Adams Wei Yu, Brian Lester, Nan Du, Andrew M. Dai, and Quoc V. Le. 2022. Finetuned language models are zero-shot learners. *Preprint*, arXiv:2109.01652.

An Yang, Baosong Yang, Beichen Zhang, Binyuan Hui, Bo Zheng, Bowen Yu, Chengyuan Li, Dayiheng Liu, Fei Huang, Haoran Wei, Huan Lin, Jian Yang, Jianhong Tu, Jianwei Zhang, Jianxin Yang, Jiaxi Yang, Jingren Zhou, Junyang Lin, Kai Dang, Keming Lu, Keqin Bao, Kexin Yang, Le Yu, Mei Li, Mingfeng Xue, Pei Zhang, Qin Zhu, Rui Men, Runji Lin, Tianhao Li, Tianyi Tang, Tingyu Xia, Xingzhang Ren, Xuancheng Ren, Yang Fan, Yang Su, Yichang Zhang, Yu Wan, Yuqiong Liu, Zeyu Cui, Zhenru Zhang, and Zihan Qiu. 2025. Qwen2.5 technical report. *Preprint*, arXiv:2412.15115.

Enneng Yang, Li Shen, Guibing Guo, Xingwei Wang, Xiaochun Cao, Jie Zhang, and Dacheng Tao. 2024. Model merging in llms, mllms, and beyond: Methods, theories, applications and opportunities. *Preprint*, arXiv:2408.07666.

Weizhe Yuan, Richard Yuanzhe Pang, Kyunghyun Cho, Xian Li, Sainbayar Sukhbaatar, Jing Xu, and Jason Weston. 2024. Self-rewarding language models. *Preprint*, arXiv:2401.10020.

Wayne Xin Zhao, Kun Zhou, Junyi Li, Tianyi Tang, Xiaolei Wang, Yupeng Hou, Yingqian Min, Beichen Zhang, Junjie Zhang, Zican Dong, Yifan Du, Chen Yang, Yushuo Chen, Zhipeng Chen, Jinhao Jiang, Ruiyang Ren, Yifan Li, Xinyu Tang, Zikang Liu, Peiyu Liu, Jian-Yun Nie, and Ji-Rong Wen. 2024. A survey of large language models. *Preprint*, arXiv:2303.18223.

Jeffrey Zhou, Tianjian Lu, Swaroop Mishra, Siddhartha Brahma, Sujoy Basu, Yi Luan, Denny Zhou, and Le Hou. 2023. Instruction-following evaluation for large language models. *Preprint*, arXiv:2311.07911.

Jianqing Zhu, Huang Huang, Zhihang Lin, Juhao Liang, Zhengyang Tang, Khalid Almubarak, Abdulmohsen Alharthik, Bang An, Juncai He, Xiangbo Wu, Fei Yu, Junying Chen, Zhuoheng Ma, Yuhao Du, He Zhang, Emad A. Alghamdi, Lian Zhang, Ruoyu Sun, Haizhou Li, Benyou Wang, and Jinchao Xu. 2024. Second language (arabic) acquisition of llms via progressive vocabulary expansion. *Preprint*, arXiv:2412.12310.

Elinor Zucchet. 2024. African languages: The top 70 most spoken languages in Africa — berlitz.com. `https://www.berlitz.com/blog/what-are-most-spoken-languages-africa`. [Accessed 27-04-2025].

Challenges and Limitations in Gathering Resources for Low-Resource Languages: The Case of Medumba

Tatiana Moteu Ngoli[1], MBUH Christabel[1], NJEUNGA YOPA[1]
[1]Metchoup
contact@metchoup.org

Abstract

Low-resource languages face significant challenges in natural language processing due to the scarcity of annotated data, linguistic resources, and the lack of language standardization, which leads to variations in grammar, vocabulary, and writing systems. This issue is particularly observed in many African languages, which significantly reduces their usability. To bridge this barrier, this paper investigates the challenges and limitations of collecting datasets for the Medumba language, a Grassfields Bantu language spoken in Cameroon, in the context of extremely low-resource natural language processing. We mainly focus on the specificity of this language, including its grammatical and lexical structure. Our findings highlight key barriers, including (1) the challenges in typing and encoding Latin scripts, (2) the absence of standardized translations for technical and scientific terms, and (3) the challenge of limited digital resources and financial constraints, highlighting the need to improve data strategies and collaboration to advance computational research on African languages. We hope that our study informs the development of better tools and policies to make knowledge platforms more accessible to extremely low-resource language speakers. We further discuss the representation of the language, data collection, parallel corpus development.

1 Introduction

The field of natural language processing (NLP) has made tremendous progress in improving low-resource languages in recent years. However, many languages remain underrepresented in computational linguistics. This is the case of Medumba, a Cameroonian language spoken by approximately 200.000 people in the western part of the country. Studies have been conducted on this particular language but these studies date back to the 90s, and focus primarily on its grammatical, structural, and phonological aspects(Nganmou, 1991, Tchiegang, 1978, Kachin, 1990) . In addition, NLP researchers have developed benchmark datasets and parallel corpus covering specific language families, such as MasakhaNER (Adelani et al., 2021) the Sawa corpus (De Pauw et al., 2009), MasakhaNEWS (Adelani et al., 2023), WebCrawl African (Vegi et al., 2022) but, without including some extremely low-resource languages such as Medumba.

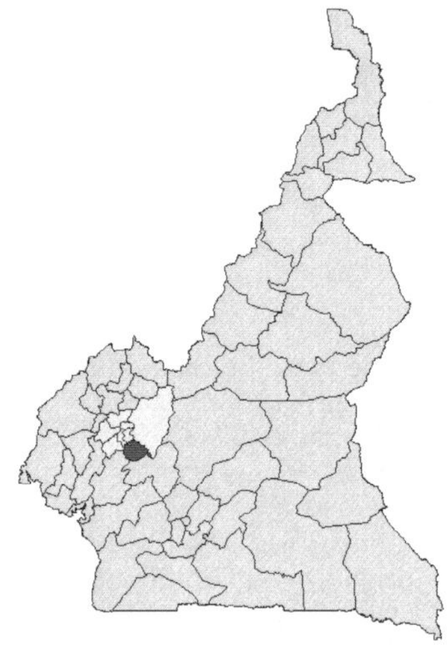

Figure 1: Representation of Medumba language

A language is considered as low-resource language by its limited linguistic resources and data, posing challenges in NLP in learning robust language patterns (Magueresse et al., 2020). On the other hand, Joshi et al. (2021) categorizes languages in six classes based on the availability of labeled and unlabeled data: *(The Left-Behinds (0), (The Scraping-Bys (1), The Hopefuls (2), The Rising Stars (3), The Underdogs (4)*, and *The Winners (5)*. In a simplified form, class 0 languages have neither labeled nor unlabeled data; class 1-4 languages have unlabeled data, but their labeled data quantity varies from virtually non-existent to high and, class 5 languages have both high volumes of labeled and

Proceedings of the Sixth Workshop on African Natural Language Processing (AfricaNLP 2025), pages 136–142
July 31, 2025 ©2025 Association for Computational Linguistics

unlabeled data. However, the Medumba language might belong to either class 0 or 1 as it is very hard to find available resources, thus highlighting the need of more investigations into this particular language.

This study explores methods for building NLP resources for the Medumba language, contributing to the broader goal of enhancing language technology for African languages. We designed our analysis to mainly answer the research question: *What are the challenges and limitations of gathering and annotating an extremely low-resource language?*. To answer this question, we created a parallel French-Medumba corpus consisting of 2050 sentences translated by a professional linguist.

"Our study reveals a significant gap in categorization between the source language (French) and the target language (Medumba), making it difficult to find adequate equivalents due to the language's complexity. We summarize the main contributions of this paper as follows:

- We collected French sentences from open-source repositories related to African contexts from the web and asked a professional linguist to translate them
- We present the language background and the methodologies used to translate the sentences
- We present some baseline model results and discuss their performance
- We highlight the challenges and limitations encountered during data collection and propose solutions to overcome them

2 Related works

In this section, we provide an overview of related studies on extremely low-resource languages, specifically Medumba.

Research on Cameroonian languages has recently seen an evolution in the field of NLP. Echu (2004) investigate into the multilingualism and language policy since the colonial period of Cameroon while Olson and Meynadier (2015) assess the articulation and phonology of bilabial trills and vowels in Medumba. Moreover, a syntax of A-dependencies in Bamileke Medumba have been study (Keupdjio, 2020), and more recently, Zimmermann and Kouankem (2024) discuss the structural realization of contrastive focus in the Grassfields Bantu language Bamileke Medumba, and

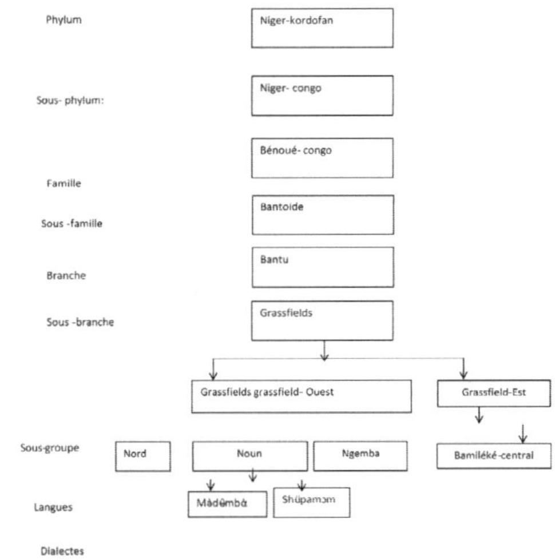

Figure 2: Family tree of the Medumba language.

Kouankem (2022) analyses the interaction between the syntactic structure and the semantic outcome of serial verb constructions in Medumba. Althought these studies investigates the Medumba language, the are more focused on the structural syntax and semantical aspect of the language, without highlighting the challenges of translating text into Medumba. In this study, we investigate the challenges of gathering resources in the medumba by highlighting the methodology, the challenges and some techniques used to translate sentences from a source language to the Medumba language.

3 Medumba language

3.1 Background

The Medumba (mèdum̂bà) language is a Bamileke language primarily spoken in Cameroon in the Ndé department, West region, with the main settlements being *Bangangté, Bangoulap, Bakong, Bahouoc, Bagnoun, Bawouok, Tonga, Bamaha, Bagnoun*. It is also spoken in the North-West by the *Bahouoc* in the Bali district (futher details can be found in Figure 2). According to the Ethnology [1], this language belongs to Niger-Congo language family, the Eastern Grassfields group, and the Central Bamileke subgroup with over 210.000 speakers (htt, 2018). Medumba belongs to zone 9 of the Southern Grassfield languages, with Alcam code [997] (BIKOI, 2018). The Medumba language has a dialectal variant called nsî ntuñ spoken in *Tonga, Bandounga, Bassamba* and in part of *Bazou*. The standard reference variant is known as *bangangte*.

[1]https://www.ethnologue.com/language/byv/

Medumba language is governed by a set of rules. In terms of morphology, Medumba is monosyllabic, i.e the morphemes of this language are initially formed of one syllable. We can have examples like t´α/father, m´α/mother, nkʉǹ/the news, f´α/work, nvəǹ/the chief, etc. We also find disyllable and trisyllable words such as: ngəláη/paternal uncles or aunts, mɛǹntʉǹ/someone, ngàzìfə/the learner, etc. The morphemes of the Medumba language always begin with consonants and the tones are essentially marked on the vowels and on the consonant η. Vowels, on the other hand, always occupy the medial and final position in a word. The grammatical classes of this language are nouns, prepositions, adverbs, adjectives, conjunctions, verbs and pronouns. There are 5 noun classes, including 3 singular classes (classes 1, 3 and 5) and two plural classes (classes 4 and 6). The formation of the plural is done according to the noun class concerned. In general, the word (ba) is used as a plural marker. Compound nouns are written as a single word.
Syntactically, the sentence in Medumba generally follows the SVO (Subject-Verb-Object) structure. A set of orthographic principles governs this language. The following principles serve as examples:

- Do not write the same consonant twice in a word. This would simply mean that if at the time of pronunciation, we perceive a sound twice, we replace the first one with a sound that is close to the first, unless the first sound is separated from the second by the glottal stop. Example: bɛ̀ttə will be written bɛ̀dtə , sà´

- The vowel /ɔ/ is never placed before /g/ and /η/ even if it is heard when pronouncing a word. Example: lɔη will be written loη in this word; the grapheme o is not read /ou/ as its alphabet requires, but it is read as /ɔ/

The phonology of Medumba is made up of 32 letters including ten 10 vowels, 22 consonants and five (5 tones. The different vowels of the Medumba language are / a, e, ∂, ϵ, i, u, 0, α, o, O /. Depending on the points of articulation, Table 1 and Table 2 summarize the classification of its different vowels.

The vowels of the Medumba language can be closed, half-closed, half-open or open. Among these vowels, we have two pairs of vowels that are represented differently in spelling, but are read the same way. These are (i/e and u and o). The concept of aspiration is crucial in distinguishing writing from reading. The consonants are b, d, c, k, f, s, g, j, h, sh, gh, l, m, n, v, z, y, η, ny, ‘, w and ts. Moreover, Kouankem (2012) summarizes these letters according to their place of articulation as follows, the punctual tones found in the Medumba language are the high tone, the low tone and the mid tone. The modulated tones are: the falling tone and the rising tone. In the writing of this language, the high tone and the low tone are not marked.

	Anterior	**Central**	**Posterior**
Closed	i	ʉ	u
Half-closed	e	-	o
Half-open	ϵ	∂	ɔ
Open	-	α	a

Table 1: Medumba vowels

3.2 Data collection

We mainly worked on the translation of 2050 sentences from French to Medumba collected on the web. The sentences come from various categories and are based on African contexts (e.g. *Un seul projet est réalisé au Cameroun ou dans le cadre de la CEMAC un vaste programme de production d'engrais à la mesure des besoins de notre agriculture*); More examples can be found in Figure 3. This study made it possible to identify the specific obstacles linked to the absence of lexical equivalents and the differences in linguistic categorization between French and Medumba. To overcome these challenges, we adopted a methodical approach including:

- Consulting native speakers and existing documents on the Medumba lexicon
- Using translation techniques such as explanation and adaptation
- Lexical creation or neologism while respecting the grammatical principles of the target language
- Validation of translations with the Medumba language development committee

4 Methodology

We conducted a qualitative study based on the analysis of discussions from online forums and African content creators. We applied analysis to identify recurring problems and concerns encountered by

	Bilabial	Labio-dental	Alveolaire dental	Palatal	Velaire	Glottal
Plosives	b	-	t d	-	k	-
Nasals	m	-	n	-	η	-
Fricatives	-	f v	s sh z ts	-	gh	h
Glides	-	-	-	y	w	-
Laterals	-	-	l	-	-	-

Table 2: Medumba consonants

French	Medumba
Un seul réalisée au Cameroun ou dans le cadre de la CEMAC un vaste programme de production d'engrais à la mesure des besoins de notre agriculture.	Tà' nsâg nkăzìn nənàb mĩcá' bò ghʉ̂ Kàmərún kə ntʉ̂m CEMAC mbɑ́ à kû'nì nũm nzĩ zəbə ngɑ́mnà lɑ́
D'autres suivront avec l'aménagement du cours de la Sanaga.	Tsəmò' à' sə̂' bô nənàb ntsə̆ Sanaga
Notre pays ne fait pas exception en Afrique.	Zəbə lá' kə̂' tàg Àflìkà
La lutte contre le VIH/SIDA est une préoccupation importante pour les Synergies Africaines.	Zwə̆' VIH/SIDA bə ɑ̃ tà' nù tânjòŋ á cwɛ̆d ngʉ̀dni tàmtə ghăfà' Aflìkà
M Samuel MVONDO AYOLO Directeur du Cabinet Civil de la Présidence de la République avec rang et prérogatives de Ministre.	Tɑ̌ Samuel MVONDO AYOLO, ngàcàgtə Cabinet Civil ndɑ́ngɔ̀ bô bin nkâmngɔ̀
Pour d'autres il n'est pas toujours aisé de réunir toutes les pièces que l'administration exige.	À bə̂ ntâ tsəmô' bənntʉ̀n nə kʉ́mtə njôŋ fə̆ ŋwà'nì ngàcàgtə cwɛ̆d mbɛ̂dtə lɑ́
Le jeune garçon est le fils d'une cousine à elle et n'avait alors que 10 ans à cette époque.	Mɛ̆n mɑ́ndûm lĩ bə nshûm bə̌mɑ́ ĩ. À ná' ngʉ̂ ɑ̃ ngʉ̀' ghám ngəláŋ bò ná' ndô' ĩ lɑ́
Des campagnes de sensibilisation sont aussi organisées sur les dangers de la drogue.	Bó cwɛ̆d nɑ̀b nkăzìn nətúm nzĩ'tə bəntʉ̀n nũm cɔ̀kəbwɔ̀ fùkəbwɔ̀
Absente du domicile conjugal depuis vendredi dernier, la veuve du défunt n'est revenue que ce mardi dans la soirée.	Mbɑ́ mfôg mɛ̆nnzwĩ lĩ ná' tùm ndɑ̃ ndú ĩ mfɛ̆nntɑ̂nndʉ́b, ntʉ̂' bɛ̆nnjàm ɑ̂ mvə̆dnjʉ́ mfɛ̆nntɑ̂nnkā'ə̄
Je crois que ce monument est une belle réalisation.	Mə kwâ mbə sə̂n lôŋlá' lĩ bə ɑ́ bwɔ̂ fà'

Figure 3: Samples translated sentences.

contributors. To improve the translation, we inquired whenever we were faced with a complex term whose translation was not immediately apparent. We thus verified the non-existence of the term itself before moving on to adopting a specific translation technique. For some terms, we drew inspiration from their explanations in French to translate them. In addition, we drew inspiration from the principle of forming the grammatical category to be translated in the target language to create a new word designating the term in the source language.

4.1 Medumba Dataset

The Medumba dataset is a translated version of French sentences collected from open-source repositories such as GitHub [2], covering multiple topics. After preprocessing, we use 31,679 tokens to train our baseline models. The dataset statistics are shown in Table 3. Furthermore, we split the dataset into train and test to train our baselines models as showed in 4.

4.2 Baselines Performance

To conduct our experiments, we chose to fine-tune custom pre-trained machine translation models, as our parallel corpus includes Medumba, a language not supported by most existing models. This approach enables the model to learn translation patterns specific to Medumba. For instance, we fine-tuned models such as opus-mt-fr-en[3], mbart50[4], and t5-small[5]. The results are reported in Table 5.

As metrics, we use:

- **BLEU** (Bilingual Evaluation Understudy): A metric that calculates n-gram precision for various n-gram lengths (typically 1 to 4) and combines these scores using a geometric mean. It also incorporates a brevity penalty to address the issue of overly short translations.

- **COMET** (Cross-lingual Optimized Metric for Evaluation of Translation): A metric that employs machine learning models to evaluate translations. Unlike traditional metrics, it does not rely solely on surface-level text comparisons. It assesses translations based on fluency, adequacy, and the preservation of meaning.

- **TER** (Translation Edit Rate): A metric that calculates the minimum number of edits required to transform a machine translation into one of the reference translations. The score is normalized by the total number of words in the reference translation.

The results reveal that only the T5-small model achieves a high BLEU score, while the other two models exhibit higher COMET scores. Since COMET is effective in scenarios requiring a deeper

[2] https://github.com/

[3] https://huggingface.co/Helsinki-NLP/opus-mt-fr-en

[4] https://huggingface.co/sarubi/mbart-50

[5] https://huggingface.co/google/flan-t5-small

	Tokens	Nbr documents	Vocab size
fr	33304	2052	6786
byv	31679	2052	4542

Table 3: Datasets tokens count

Train	Test
1846	206

Table 4: Datasets split

understanding of translation quality, it is particularly useful for evaluating translations where contextual and semantic accuracy are more important than literal word-for-word correspondence—an evaluation criterion well aligned with the characteristics of our Medumba dataset. The other results were expected, given the limited size of our dataset.

5 Challenges and Limitations

The translation of the 2.050 sentences from French to Medumba was mainly hampered by the lack of adequate equivalent terms in the target language and differences in categorization between the two languages.

5.1 Challenges related to platform interfaces and language support

The Medumba language uses the Latin alphabet, which requires complex diacritical characters, making typing cumbersome. Platform updates sometimes disrupt existing input methods, causing frustration among contributors. In addition, we have faced some challenges in translating scientific and technological terms due to lack of consensus on local language equivalents. For example, terms like *spammer robots* or *word processing* had to be translated using periphrases in Medumba, while others, such as *JavaScript* and *thermal power station* remain untranslatable due to a lack of corresponding concepts. It was also impossible to translate scientific concepts from physics, such as *thermal power station* and *hydroelectric dam*, because there are no equivalents or realities that could provide inspiration for a satisfactory adaptation of these words. Some legal terms or expressions, such as *decree*, *democracy*, *order*, *Commander of the National Order of Value* and *State of the General Staff*, etc., have no equivalents in the Medumba language and have been maintained as borrowings in the target language. All in all, the absence of direct equivalents in the Medumba language has led to the use of periphrases and borrowings. On the other hand, the lack of spelling uniformity complicates access to information. Medumba has a great deal of variability in the writing of words and many homophones, which hinders the performance of search engines and automatic correctors. Furthermore, the difference in categorization between the Medumba language and the French language has also hampered the translation of certain specific concepts such as *ambassador* and *charge of mission* in two very different contexts, but the Medumba language classifies both under the generic term *ngàntùm/envoye*.

Models	BLEU	COMET	TER
opus-mt-fr-en	15.82	**0.80**	82.51
mbart50	20.36	**0.80**	77.15
T5-small	**83.20**	0.42	94.97

Table 5: Baselines results. Values in bold represent high scores.

5.2 Financial and material barriers

The lack of access to reliable internet, digital libraries and reference materials has greatly hampered work and generated significant costs. Furthermore, there is a shortage of online media, there are many African platforms [6] [7] [8] created, but very few promote Medumba. The Medumba language has a radio called Radio Medumba, however it is only accessible in the Ndé department. This media serves as a channel for broadcasting Medumba language learning programs through games, stories and the popularization of new words created by the Medumba language development committee mainly in the Medumba area. This implies that accessibility to this radio is limited. Given this reality, we therefore rely heavily on our own internal research work.

6 Conclusion

In this study, we investigate the challenges and limitations of gathering resources for an extremely low-resource language: Medumba. We present the language's background, the methodology used to translate sentences from French to Medumba, and particularly highlight the challenges encountered

[6] https://www.languagesafrica.com

[7] https://github.com/masakhane-io/lafand-mt

[8] https://github.com/masakhane-io/masakhane-mt

during the translation process. Our findings reveal that discrepancies in categorization between the source and target languages contribute to translation complexity. To address these limitations and advance the state of the art in low-resource languages, future research should explore additional techniques for resource gathering and enhance translation capabilities for extremely low-resource languages.

References

2018. Issue information. *IPPR Progressive Review*, 25(2):107–107.

David Ifeoluwa Adelani, Jade Abbott, Graham Neubig, Daniel D'souza, Julia Kreutzer, Constantine Lignos, Chester Palen-Michel, Happy Buzaaba, Shruti Rijhwani, Sebastian Ruder, Stephen Mayhew, Israel Abebe Azime, Shamsuddeen Muhammad, Chris Chinenye Emezue, Joyce Nakatumba-Nabende, Perez Ogayo, Anuoluwapo Aremu, Catherine Gitau, Derguene Mbaye, Jesujoba Alabi, Seid Muhie Yimam, Tajuddeen Gwadabe, Ignatius Ezeani, Rubungo Andre Niyongabo, Jonathan Mukiibi, Verrah Otiende, Iroro Orife, Davis David, Samba Ngom, Tosin Adewumi, Paul Rayson, Mofetoluwa Adeyemi, Gerald Muriuki, Emmanuel Anebi, Chiamaka Chukwuneke, Nkiruka Odu, Eric Peter Wairagala, Samuel Oyerinde, Clemencia Siro, Tobius Saul Bateesa, Temilola Oloyede, Yvonne Wambui, Victor Akinode, Deborah Nabagereka, Maurice Katusiime, Ayodele Awokoya, Mouhamadane MBOUP, Dibora Gebreyohannes, Henok Tilaye, Kelechi Nwaike, Degaga Wolde, Abdoulaye Faye, Blessing Sibanda, Orevaoghene Ahia, Bonaventure F. P. Dossou, Kelechi Ogueji, Thierno Ibrahima DIOP, Abdoulaye Diallo, Adewale Akinfaderin, Tendai Marengereke, and Salomey Osei. 2021. Masakhaner: Named entity recognition for african languages. *Preprint*, arXiv:2103.11811.

David Ifeoluwa Adelani, Marek Masiak, Israel Abebe Azime, Jesujoba Alabi, Atnafu Lambebo Tonja, Christine Mwase, Odunayo Ogundepo, Bonaventure F. P. Dossou, Akintunde Oladipo, Doreen Nixdorf, Chris Chinenye Emezue, sana al azzawi, Blessing Sibanda, Davis David, Lolwethu Ndolela, Jonathan Mukiibi, Tunde Ajayi, Tatiana Moteu, Brian Odhiambo, Abraham Owodunni, Nnaemeka Obiefuna, Muhidin Mohamed, Shamsuddeen Hassan Muhammad, Teshome Mulugeta Ababu, Saheed Abdullahi Salahudeen, Mesay Gemeda Yigezu, Tajuddeen Gwadabe, Idris Abdulmumin, Mahlet Taye, Oluwabusayo Awoyomi, Iyanuoluwa Shode, Tolulope Adelani, Habiba Abdulganiyu, Abdul-Hakeem Omotayo, Adetola Adeeko, Abeeb Afolabi, Anuoluwapo Aremu, Olanrewaju Samuel, Clemencia Siro, Wangari Kimotho, Onyekachi Ogbu, Chinedu Mbonu, Chiamaka Chukwuneke, Samuel Fanijo, Jessica Ojo, Oyinkansola Awosan, Tadesse Kebede, Toadoum Sari Sakayo, Pamela Nyatsine, Freedmore Sidume, Oreen Yousuf, Mardiyyah Oduwole, Tshinu Tshinu, Ussen Kimanuka, Thina Diko, Siyanda Nxakama, Sinodos Nigusse, Abdulmejid Johar, Shafie Mohamed, Fuad Mire Hassan, Moges Ahmed Mehamed, Evrard Ngabire, Jules Jules, Ivan Ssenkungu, and Pontus Stenetorp. 2023. Masakhanews: News topic classification for african languages. *Preprint*, arXiv:2304.09972.

Charles BIKOI. 2018. *BINAM BIKOI Ch.- (dir.)- Atlas linguistique du Cameroun, 2012, Yaoundé, éd. Cerdotola, 399 p.*

Guy De Pauw, Peter Waiganjo Wagacha, and Gilles-Maurice de Schryver. 2009. The SAWA corpus: A parallel corpus English - Swahili. In *Proceedings of the First Workshop on Language Technologies for African Languages*, pages 9–16, Athens, Greece. Association for Computational Linguistics.

George Echu. 2004. The language question in cameroon. *Linguistik online*, 18.

Pratik Joshi, Sebastin Santy, Amar Budhiraja, Kalika Bali, and Monojit Choudhury. 2021. The state and fate of linguistic diversity and inclusion in the nlp world. *Preprint*, arXiv:2004.09095.

Brigitte Kachin. 1990. *The phonological adaptation of English loan words in Medumba.*

Hermann Sidoine Keupdjio. 2020. *The syntax of A'-dependencies in Bamileke Medumba.* Ph.D. thesis, Universitu of British Columbia.

Constantine Kouankem. 2012. The syntax of the medumba determiner phrase. *Yaounde: University of Yaounde I dissertation.*

Constantine Kouankem. 2022. Issues on serial verb constructions in medumba. *Language in Africa.*

Alexandre Magueresse, Vincent Carles, and Evan Heetderks. 2020. Low-resource languages: A review of past work and future challenges. *Preprint*, arXiv:2006.07264.

Alise Nganmou. 1991. *Modalités verbales: Temps, Aspect et Mode en Mdūmba.* Ph.D. thesis, Université de Yaoundé I.

Kenneth Olson and Yohann Meynadier. 2015. On medumba bilabial trills and vowels.

Luc Tchiegang. 1978. Bangangté-deutsch-konversationsbuch. Thesis, Saarbrücken: Universität des Saarlandes.

Pavanpankaj Vegi, Sivabhavani J, Biswajit Paul, Abhinav Mishra, Prashant Banjare, Prasanna K R, and Chitra Viswanathan. 2022. WebCrawl African : A multilingual parallel corpora for African languages. In *Proceedings of the Seventh Conference on Machine Translation (WMT)*, pages 1076–1089, Abu Dhabi, United Arab Emirates (Hybrid). Association for Computational Linguistics.

Malte Zimmermann and Constantine Kouankem. 2024. Focus fronting in a language with in situ marking: The case of mdmbà. *Languages*, 9(4).

YodiV3: NLP for Togolese Languages with Eyaa-Tom Dataset and the Lom Metric

Justin E. Bakoubolo[1], **Catherine Nana Nyaah Essuman**[1], **Messan Agbobli, PhD**[1,2], Ahoefa Kansiwer, PhD[1,2], Kpona Sekpane Kpatika[1], Notou Your Timibe, PhD[1,3], Agossou, PhD[1,4], Guedela Bakouya, PhD[1,2], Bruno Koukoudjoe, PhD[1,2], Samuel Kossi Mawouena Afola[1] et al.[1]

[1]Umbaji

[2]University of Lomé

[3]University of Kara

[4]UCAO-UUT

Abstract

Most of the 40+ languages spoken in Togo are severely under-represented in Natural Language Processing (NLP) resources. We present **YodiV3**, a comprehensive approach to developing NLP for ten Togolese languages (plus two major lingua francas) covering machine translation, speech recognition, text-to-speech, and language identification. We introduce **Eyaa-Tom**, a new multi-domain parallel corpus (religious, healthcare, financial, etc.) for these languages. We also propose the **Lom metric**, a scoring framework to quantify the AI-readiness of each language in terms of available resources. Our experiments demonstrate that leveraging large pretrained models (e.g.NLLB for translation, MMS for speech) along with YodiV3 leads to significant improvements in low-resource translation and speech tasks. This work highlights the impact of integrating diverse data sources and pretrained models to bootstrap NLP for underserved languages, and outlines future steps for expanding coverage and capability.

1 Introduction

Togo is home to dozens of languages, including *Ewè*, *Kabyè*, *Tem* (Kotokoli), and many others spoken by millions collectively. However, most of these languages lack the data and tools needed for modern NLP applications. The scarcity of machine translation (MT) systems, speech technologies, and even basic linguistic resources (e.g.digital dictionaries) hinders information access and technology inclusion for the related communities. Recent advances in multilingual NLP have started to include a few Togolese languages—for instance, Facebook AI's *No Language Left Behind* (NLLB) project released MT models for Ewè and Kabyè [Team et al., 2022], and their *Massively Multilingual Speech* (MMS) initiative produced speech recognition and synthesis models covering those languages [Pratap et al., 2023]. Yet, these models often struggle on domain-specific content and other local languages not covered in training.

In this work, we address the above gaps by developing an end-to-end NLP pipeline for 10 key Togolese languages. First, we assembled a new dataset called **Eyaa-tom**[1] comprising parallel text (and audio) in multiple domains such as religious texts, healthcare, financial operations. Using this data, we train **YodiV3**, a multilingual model which supports translation, as well as speech recognition (ASR) and text-to-speech (TTS) components for selected languages.

Additionally, we introduce the **Lom metric** ("lom" meaning "score" in Nawdm) to quantify the state of language technology readiness for each language. The Lom metric aggregates the availability of core resources like a Bible or liturgical text, a dictionary, MT, ASR, TTS, language identification, and OCR models. This provides a quick overview of which languages are more digitally equipped and which need more attention.

We report experiments showing that YodiV3 improves translation quality and speech in low-resource settings by leveraging domain-specific data and as well as large fine-tunned models. We also present the Lom scores for the ten languages, revealing significant disparities: e.g., Ewè and Kabyè lead with much higher scores, whereas languages like Mina need more resources. Our results underscore the importance of targeted data collection and the integration of existing models to support "the last mile" languages. We conclude with our plans to incorporate more datasets and extend coverage to additional Togolese languages, further bridging the NLP divide.

- We present the first multi-domain NLP dataset for 10 Togolese languages, including

[1]*Eyaa-tom* means "People words'" in Kabyè.

Proceedings of the Sixth Workshop on African Natural Language Processing (AfricaNLP 2025), pages 143–149
July 31, 2025 ©2025 Association for Computational Linguistics

20k+ parallel audio-text segments and additional annotated resources.

- We develop and evaluate baseline models for ASR, TTS, NMT, and language identification (LID) on these languages, demonstrating the feasibility of NLP with minimal resources.
- We introduce the *Lom* metric, which consolidates various resource indicators into a single score for each language, revealing disparities and guiding future work.

2 Related Work

Research on NLP for low-resource languages has gained momentum in recent years. Projects like Masakhane have leveraged participatory approaches to create translation datasets and models for numerous African languages [Nekoto et al., 2020]. For speech, the Mozilla Common Voice project released crowdsourced speech corpora for languages such as Swahili, Luganda, and Kabyle [Ardila et al., 2020], providing a foundation for ASR in some African languages. However, many languages of West Africa remain underrepresented in these initiatives.

Closer to our focus, Tonja et al. surveyed NLP for Ethiopian languages, highlighting the challenges of limited data and orthographic complexities. Our work is similar in spirit, but targets languages of Togo, which have distinct linguistic characteristics (many are Niger-Congo languages with tonal systems) and even fewer existing resources. To our knowledge, no comprehensive NLP dataset or benchmarks existed for the Togolese languages prior to this work. Also, a comprehensive examination of the current state of Natural Language Processing (NLP) in Kenya is presented in the paper titled "State of NLP in Kenya: A Survey" by Cynthia Jayne Amol et al. This survey delves into ongoing efforts in dataset creation, machine translation, sentiment analysis, and speech recognition for Kenyan languages such as Kiswahili, Dholuo, Kikuyu, and Luhya. Despite these advancements, the authors highlight that the development of NLP in Kenya remains constrained by limited resources and tools, leading to the under-representation of most Kenyan languages in digital spaces. The paper critically evaluates available datasets and existing NLP models, emphasizing the need for large-scale language models and better digital representation of Kenyan languages. Additionally, it analyzes key NLP applications tailored to local linguistic needs and explores the governance, policies, and regulations shaping the future of AI and NLP in Kenya, proposing a strategic roadmap to guide future research and development efforts.

In the speech domain, recent advances in self-supervised learning have shown promise for low-resource ASR; for example, wav2vec 2.0 pretraining [Baevski et al., 2020] can drastically reduce the data needed to train speech recognizers. We capitalize on such advances in our ASR models. For TTS, while classic autoregressive architectures like Tacotron 2 [Shen et al., 2018] produce high-quality speech, they can be impractical with limited data and compute. Non-autoregressive models such as Glow-TTS [Kim et al., 2020] offer faster and more data-efficient synthesis, which we explore in our setting. Our work ties these threads together by building a full pipeline (ASR $\rightarrow$ NMT $\rightarrow$ TTS, with LID) for multiple truly low-resource languages.

African Language Identification and Models. One foundational effort for African NLP is language identification (LID). Adebara et al. introduced **AfroLID**, a neural LID toolkit covering 517 African languages, which significantly outperforms previous LID tools on many African languages. Building on such resources, [Adebara et al., 2023] developed **SERENGETI**, a massively multilingual language model for 517 African languages. These works, led by the UBC NLP group, demonstrate the feasibility of broad-coverage models for African languages, including those of Togo. However, LID and language models alone do not directly provide translation or speech technology, which are our focus.

Masakhane and African NLP Initiatives. The Masakhane research community has spearheaded collaborative NLP projects for African languages. For example, the **Masakhane MT** project mobilized researchers to create machine translation datasets and baselines for numerous African languages [Orife et al., 2020]. Similarly, **MasakhaNER** provided high-quality named entity recognition data for ten African languages [Adelani et al., 2021] including Ewè. Our work is inspired by these community-driven efforts, and we extend the spirit of Masakhane to Togo by focusing on local languages and tasks (MT, ASR, TTS) that have immediate real-world application (e.g. healthcare information delivery).

Multilingual Translation and Speech by Big Tech. NLLB (*No Language Left Behind*) by Meta AI released MT models for 200+ languages, including Ewè and Kabyè, achieving unprecedented coverage [Team et al., 2022]. This demonstrated that low-resource languages can be handled within a single massive model given sufficient training data and compute. Meanwhile, Meta's **MMS** project (*Massively Multilingual Speech*) scaled speech technology (ASR, TTS, and spoken LID) to over 1,000 languages [Pratap et al., 2023] including the majority of the languages mentioned in this work. MMS included ASR/TTS models for Ewè and Kabyè, which we leverage as starting points. Our work differs in that, we build a new architecture based on the transformer architecture and incorporate some new neural quantization layers (to reduce costs) and adapt these large models on our curated Togolese datasets, focusing on specific domains (like religious or financial speech) where out-of-the-box NLLB/MMS performance may be suboptimal. We also address languages not covered by NLLB/MMS (e.g. Adja), using a combination of data augmentation and smaller neural models.

3 Dataset Creation: Eyaa-Tom

To enable training and evaluation of NLP models for Togolese languages, we built the **Eyaa-Tom** dataset. Eyaa-Tom consists of parallel text (and audio) in 10 local languages of Togo, with translations to French and English. The languages covered are: Ewè, Kabyè, Adja,Tem (Kotokoli), Moba, Lamba(Togo), Konkomba, Mina (Gen), Bassar, Nawdm. While some of them seem to be related, some dialects have evolved and tend to be now considered as languages, (i.e. Mina has its own alphabet and syntax despite the strong relationships with Ewè). The dataset present a clear separation between the dialects and languages with the intent of improving quality of service and further achieve research.

An overview of the dataset contents for each language can be seen in Table 1.

As shown in Table 1, each language has at least 2,000 parallel language pair sentences from religious texts with another language. These were obtained from publicly available translations. Many of these languages also had audio recordings collected (via the community contributions platform for specific and service phrases).We manually aligned a portion of this audio with the text to use for ASR, Speech translation, and TTS training namely. In addition to the religious domain, we collected parallel corpora in other domains for a subset of languages. For example, we are working with the community to translate financial and healthcare services sentences. Furthermore, we constructed a named entity list of over 1,500 Togolese personal names and locations, across several languages to support NER tasks.

The dataset was created through a combination of methods:

Community Contributions : A significant portion of the data was gathered via the *Umbaji Community Contribution Platform*—an online platform developed by the Umbaji community specifically to collect datasets for African languages. This platform enabled volunteers and native speakers to contribute text and audio in their local languages, ensuring a wide and authentic representation of linguistic data.

Field Research : Another major component of the dataset is collecting through fieldwork conducted by our linguists. They visit rural areas and work closely with local communities, including traditional chieftaincies, to gather texts, oral histories, poems, and other culturally significant materials in local languages. This approach ensures the inclusion of diverse linguistic features and contexts that might not be available in written form.

Collaboration with Mozilla Common Voice : We collaborated with Mozilla Common Voice, contributing over 2,000 validated voice samples for at least four of the languages in our dataset. This collaboration helped in expanding the spoken data component and aligning it with global standards for open-source language datasets.[Mozilla, 2025a][Mozilla, 2025d][Mozilla, 2025b][Mozilla, 2025c]

In this process, community contributors were actively engaged, with informed consent obtained prior to participation, and incentives provided to encourage contributions. Additionally, linguists were fairly compensated for their expertise, ensuring high-quality linguistic data. To foster inclusivity, we prioritized gender representation by intentionally recruiting a significant number of women, reinforcing our commitment to equitable data collection practices.

Overall, Eyaa-Tom provides a unique blend of

Language	Min. Religious (sentences or utterances)	Min. Other (utterances)	Min Total (utterances)
Ewè	2,000	2,961	4,961
Kabyè	2,000	2,316	4,316
Tem	2,000	2,316	4,316
Moba	2,000	2,483	2,483
Lamba(Togo)	2,000	2,316	4,316
Adja	2,000	2,316	4,316
Mina (Gen)	2,000	2,316	4,316
Bassar	2,000	2,316	4,316
Nawdm	2,000	3,410	5410
Konkomba	2,000	2,316	4,316

Table 1: Eyaa-Tom dataset statistics: number of parallel sentence pairs by domain for each Togolese language. "Religious" denotes primarily scripture and liturgical texts (often with corresponding audio). "Other" includes secular domains (healthcare, finance, public service) and additional named-entity lists.

domain-specific data tailored to real-world use cases in Togo. While modest in size compared to high-resource benchmarks, it is the first to offer such comprehensive parallel and spoken data across numerous Togolese languages. Data quality is ensured through community review and consistent orthography.

Integration with Hugging Face : Portions of the dataset are also hosted on Hugging Face, making it easily accessible to the broader machine learning and NLP research community.[Umbaji, 2025]

4 Model: YodiV3

We developed **YodiV3**, a multi-faceted model architecture that addresses both text and speech tasks for the ten languages. YodiV3 consists of several components:

Machine Translation (MT). YodiV3 includes an encoder-decoder neural translation model that can translate between each Togolese language and French/English.

Automatic Speech Recognition (ASR). We explore two approaches: (1) a standard *auto-regressive* Transformer model that generates translations one token at a time, and (2) a *non-auto-regressive* (NAR) model aimed at faster inference and which is less compute intensive. YodiV3's ASR component is currently capable of recognizing speech in at least the two main languages (Ewè, Kabyè) with reasonable accuracy (as shown in Section 6), and provides baseline models for the others that can be improved with more data.

Text-to-Speech (TTS). Similarly we built a TTS system namely for Ewè (since Ewè has more data for training). Additionally, we developed a voice cloning approach for "Togolese-accented" French and English: essentially, we fine-tuned an English/French TTS model on a small set of recordings from Togolese speakers, so that the synthesized French/English maintains the accent characteristics. This is useful for public service announcements where code-switching occurs. YodiV3's TTS module can thus speak in Ewè, Kabyè, and Togolese accented French/English. Extending TTS to the other languages is future work, likely requiring significantly more recording efforts.

Deployment The TTS and ASR models are constantly deployed and maintained through the community's Whatsapp AI chatbot and community contributions interface.

5 The Lom Metric

To quantify the state of NLP support for each language, we propose the **Lom metric**. This metric aggregates the presence of various foundational resources and technologies for a given language. We consider eight factors: (1) availability of a major **WOG** corpus (*Word of God*, i.e., a significant religious text such as the Bible), (2) a digital **Dictionary**/lexicon, (3) an **NMT** system (Neural Machine Translation), (4) an **ASR** system, (5) a **TTS** system, (6) a **Speech LID** model (SLID), (7) a **Text LID** model (TLID), and (8) an **OCR** system for printed text. For each language, we assign 1 point if the resource is available (even in prototype form), or 0 if not. The Lom score (0–8) is the sum of points. Table 2 presents the status for the ten languages in our study.

From Table 2, we can see Ewè and Kabyè have the maximum Lom score (7/8), reflecting that they have a Bible, a published dictionary, and we have developed or leveraged MT, ASR, TTS, and LID, for it.

The Lom metric is a purely qualitative metric useful for guiding resource allocation: languages with very low scores need basic resource creation (data collection, orthography standardization), while those with mid-level scores might benefit from targeted projects (e.g., developing a TTS for Mina, or an ASR for Adja). It also provides an easy way to communicate to stakeholders or funders on how a language is positioned in terms of digital readiness.

6 Experiments and Preliminary Results

We conducted experiments to evaluate the performance of YodiV3 on translation and speech tasks, using the Eyaa-Tom data. Rather than exhaustively tuning the models, we focus on highlighting key results that demonstrate the effectiveness of our approach.

Machine Translation Quality. Improved performance on tasks such as NER for Togolese names as compared to all the models tested.

Speech-to-Text & Text-to-Speech Evaluation. Auto-regressive model show increased accuracy on many more tokens inputs, but overall, models incorporating neural non-auto-regressive quantization needs less compute but tend to be less precise for the initial tests.

Finally, our experiments reaffirm insights from prior work: multi-domain data is vital for performance. For instance, when evaluating Ewè→French translation specifically on health-related sentences, the model trained with our health subset achieved 30+ BLEU score, whereas a model trained only on religious text fell below 15 BLEU score on the same health test, demonstrating the importance of in-domain data. This aligns with observations by Team et al. [2022] that low-resource MT models benefit greatly from any domain-specific data available. Similarly, our use of pretrained models mirrors the success of Pratap et al. [2023] in showing that massive multilingual pretraining can jump-start speech technology for languages that lack sufficient data.

7 Conclusion and Future Work

We presented YodiV3 and the Eyaa-Tom dataset as steps toward inclusive NLP for Togo's languages. Our experiments show that combining carefully curated data with large pretrained models can yield workable translation and speech systems even for extremely low-resource languages. We also introduced the Lom metric, which revealed how unevenly resources are distributed across languages, providing a road-map for future resource development.

In the future, we plan to integrate additional existing datasets and models to further improve and expand YodiV3. This includes incorporating new releases from projects like Masakhane (e.g., any Togo-specific NLP datasets) or updates from the NLLB/MMS teams. We aim to extend the Eyaa-Tom corpus to more languages of Togo (such as Akebu, Ikposso, and others) to eventually cover all major language groups in the country.

Additionally, we will explore semi-supervised and active learning techniques to make the most of limited data, and continue to refine the Lom metric (possibly weighting the categories by importance or difficulty).

The AR model is based on a Transformers architecture similar to mBART. The NAR model uses a conditional masked language model (e.g., Levenshtein Transformer) which we train from scratch on our data. Both models are trained on the Eyaa-Tom parallel text. We found that fine-tuning the pretrained NLLB model greatly stabilizes training for the low-resource languages and yields higher translation quality.

These would allow us to publish our final work and compare it to exiting models and work.

Another important future direction is deployment: we intend to provide an API to work with local organizations to deploy YodiV3's translation and TTS capabilities in real-world settings (e.g., rural clinics or community radio). Such deployment will provide feedback to guide further research (for instance, identifying which errors are most critical to fix). We also foresee expanding our evaluation to include human evaluation with native speakers for translation quality and user acceptance of TTS and ASR. Future work would

Lang	WOG	Dict.	NMT	ASR	TTS	SLID	TLID	OCR	Lom
Ewè	Y	Y	Y	Y	Y	Y	Y	N	7
Kabyè	Y	Y	Y	Y	Y	Y	Y	N	7
Tem	Y	Y	Y	Y	Y	Y	Y	N	7
Adja	Y	Y	N	N	N	N	Y	N	3
Moba	Y	Y	Y	Y	Y	Y	Y	N	7
Lamba(Togo)	Y	-	N	N	N	N	Y	N	-
Konkomba	Y	Y	Y	Y	Y	Y	Y	N	7
Mina	Y	Y	N	N	N	N	Y	N	3
Bassar	Y	Y	Y	Y	Y	Y	Y	N	7
Nawdm	Y	Y	Y	Y	Y	Y	Y	N	7
Ifè	Y	Y	Y	Y	Y	Y	Y	N	7

Table 2: Lom metric evaluation for Togolese languages as of 2024. "Y" indicates the resource/technology is available (at least in experimental form), "N" indicates not yet available. WOG = presence of a significant religious text corpus; Dict. = digital dictionary or word list; NMT = machine translation; ASR = speech recognition; TTS = speech synthesis; SLID = spoken language identification; TLID = text language identification; OCR = optical character recognition. The final Lom score is out of 1.

Model	Translation		SNR/Classification		Speech Synthesis	
	Ewè	Kabyè	Ewè	Kabyè	Ewè	Kabyè
V1,zindi	—	—	0.97	—	—	—
V2, B^2	—	—	0.1	0.33	—	—
V3, T	0.90	0.88	—	—	—	—
V3,ASR	—	—	0.50	0.5		—
V3,TTS	—	—	—	—	0.88	0.87

Table 3: Performance of multiple models across tasks and languages on the Eyaa-Tom dataset. This table is the history of Yodi and its performance. For each task it features accuracy. Translation is measured from and to french. It also features improvements done since the last publication. SNER stands for Spoken Name Entity Recognition. YodiV1,zindi is the final V1 version, not train on Eyaa-Tom however, developed owing to a competition on zindi and presents the best performances

also include a scientific comparison between cognate languages in Togo and similarities between them. By iteratively improving data, models, and evaluation metrics, we hope to steadily raise the Lom scores for all Togolese languages, ensuring none are left behind in the NLP revolution.

References

Ife Adebara, AbdelRahim Elmadany, Muhammad Abdul-Mageed, and Alcides Alcoba Inciarte. 2022. Afrolid: A neural language identification tool for african languages. In *Proceedings of LREC 2022*, pages 2540–2547, Marseille, France.

Ife Adebara, AbdelRahim Elmadany, Muhammad Abdul-Mageed, and Alcides Alcoba Inciarte. 2023. Serengeti: Massively multilingual language models for africa. *arXiv preprint*.

D. I. Adelani, J. Abbott, G. Neubig, D. D'souza, J. Kreutzer, C. Lignos, C. Palen-Michel, H. Buzaaba, S. Rijhwani, S. Ruder, S. Mayhew, I. A. Azime, S. H. Muhammad, C. C. Emezue, J. Nakatumba-Nabende, P. Ogayo, A. Diallo, A. Akinfaderin, T. Marengereke, and 2 others. 2021. Masakhaner: Named entity recognition for african languages. *Transactions of the Association for Computational Linguistics*, 9:1116–1131.

R. Ardila, M. Branson, and K. Davis et al. 2020. Common voice: A massively-multilingual speech corpus. In *Proceedings of LREC 2020.*

A. Baevski, Y. Zhou, A. Mohamed, and M. Auli. 2020. wav2vec 2.0: A framework for self-supervised learning of speech representations. In *NeurIPS 2020.*

J. Kim, S. Kim, J. Kong, and S. Yoon. 2020. Glow-tts: A generative flow for text-to-speech via monotonic alignment search. In *NeurIPS 2020.*

Mozilla. 2025a. Common voice dataset for ajg.

Mozilla. 2025b. Common voice dataset for gej.

Mozilla. 2025c. Common voice dataset for kdh.

Mozilla. 2025d. Common voice dataset for nmz.

Wilhelmina Nekoto, Vukosi Marivate, Tshinondiwa Matsila, Timi Fasubaa, Taiwo Fagbohungbe, Solomon Oluwole Akinola, Shamsuddeen Muhammad, Salomon Kabongo Kabenamualu, Salomey Osei, Freshia Sackey, Rubungo Andre Niyongabo, Ricky Macharm, Perez Ogayo, Orevaoghene Ahia, Musie Meressa Berhe, Mofetoluwa Adeyemi, Masabata Mokgesi-Selinga, Lawrence Okegbemi, Laura Martinus, and 28 others. 2020. Participatory research for low-resourced machine translation: A case study in African languages. In *Findings of the Association for Computational Linguistics: EMNLP 2020*, pages 2144–2160, Online. Association for Computational Linguistics.

I. Orife, D. I. Adelani, J. O. Alabi, K. Amponsah-Kaakyire, I. A. Azime, T. S. Bateesa, H. Buzaaba, C. Chukwuneke, A. Diallo, B. F. P. Dossou, R. Eiselen, C. C. Emezue, A. Faye, D. Gebreyohannes, T. R. Gwadabe, M. A. Hedderich, . O. Ishola, M. Katusiime, D. Klakow, and 13 others. 2020. Masakhane – machine translation for africa. *arXiv preprint*.

V. Pratap, E. Adjaye, T. D. Nguyen, A. Babu, T. Likhomanenko, P. Andrews, C. Fuegen, and R. Collobert. 2023. Mms: Scaling speech technology to 1,000+ languages. In *Proceedings of EMNLP 2023*.

J. Shen, R. Pang, and R. Weiss et al. 2018. Natural tts synthesis by conditioning wavenet on mel spectrogram predictions. In *Proceedings of ICASSP 2018*.

NLLB Team, Marta R. Costa-jussà, James Cross, Onur Çelebi, Maha Elbayad, Kenneth Heafield, Kevin Heffernan, Elahe Kalbassi, Janice Lam, Daniel Licht, Jean Maillard, Anna Sun, Skyler Wang, Guillaume Wenzek, Al Youngblood, Bapi Akula, Loic Barrault, Gabriel Mejia Gonzalez, Prangthip Hansanti, and 20 others. 2022. No language left behind: Scaling human-centered machine translation. *Preprint*, arXiv:2207.04672.

A. L. Tonja, T. D. Belay, and I. A. Azime et al. 2023. Natural language processing in ethiopian languages: Current state, challenges, and opportunities. In *Proceedings of RAIL 2023*.

Umbaji. 2025. Eyaa-tom dataset.

Challenging Multimodal LLMs with African Standardized Exams: A Document VQA Evaluation

Victor Olufemi **Oreoluwa Babatunde** **Kausar Moshood** **Emmanuel Bolarinwa**
LyngualLabs
{victor, oreoluwa, kausar, emmanuel}@lyngualabs.org

Abstract

Despite rapid advancements in multimodal large language models (MLLMs), their ability to process low-resource African languages in document-based visual question answering (VQA) tasks remains limited. This paper evaluates three state-of-the-art MLLMs—GPT-4o, Claude-3.5 Haiku, and Gemini-1.5 Pro—on WAEC/NECO standardized exam questions in Yoruba, Igbo, and Hausa. We curate a dataset of multiple-choice questions from exam images and compare model accuracies across two prompting strategies: (1) using English prompts for African language questions, and (2) using native-language prompts. While GPT-4o achieves over 90% accuracy for English, performance drops below 40% for African languages, highlighting severe data imbalance in model training. Notably, native-language prompting improves accuracy for most models, yet no system approaches human-level performance, which reaches over 50% in Yoruba, Igbo, and Hausa. These findings emphasize the need for diverse training data, fine-tuning, and dedicated benchmarks that address the linguistic intricacies of African languages in multimodal tasks, paving the way for more equitable and effective AI systems in education.

1 Introduction

The rapid advancements in artificial intelligence (AI) have led to the emergence of multimodal large language models (MLLMs) capable of processing and understanding both textual and visual information (Peng et al., 2023; Ahuja et al., 2024). Notable examples include OpenAI's GPT, Anthropic's Claude and Google's Gemini. These models exhibit impressive capabilities in interpreting combined visual-textual inputs, allowing them to extract text from images and answer questions about that content. However, their ability to accurately process text from images in low-resource languages remains an open question (Adelani et al., 2025). Despite the progress in multilingual NLP, most state-of-the-art models are primarily trained on high-resource languages, resulting in suboptimal performance for many African languages. Low-resource languages are severely underrepresented in the datasets used to train and evaluate MLLMs (Joshi et al., 2020; Adelani et al., 2025), and African languages such as Yoruba, Igbo, and Hausa present unique linguistic and orthographic challenges that differ significantly from dominant languages on which these models are typically trained. (Orife et al., 2020). The scarcity of high-quality training data for these languages exacerbates the performance disparity between high- and low-resource languages (Nayak et al., 2024). Recent benchmarks confirm that multimodal models perform very well on English but struggle on many African languages due to data limitations (Ahuja et al., 2024)

1.1 WAEC and NECO: Importance in West African Education

The West African Examinations Council (WAEC) and the National Examinations Council (NECO) play a crucial role in standardized education across West Africa. These organizations administer high-stakes secondary school examinations that assess students' proficiency in core subjects, including language proficiency in English as well as indigenous languages like Yoruba, Igbo, and Hausa. WAEC and NECO exams serve as key determinants of academic progression, influencing university admissions and career opportunities. Standardized exams such as WAEC and NECO provide an objective measure of students' knowledge, making them an appealing testbed for evaluating AI models' natural language understanding abilities in structured educational contexts. By leveraging real-world examination content, this study assesses whether state-of-the-art MLLMs can process structured educational material effectively in African languages.

Proceedings of the Sixth Workshop on African Natural Language Processing (AfricaNLP 2025), pages 150–157
July 31, 2025

1.2 Research Objectives

This study aims to systematically evaluate the performance of GPT-4o, Claude-3.5 Haiku and Gemini-1.5 Pro in natural language comprehension for African languages by addressing the following objectives:

- **Objective 1:** Assess the ability of multimodal LLMs to accurately extract and process text from WAEC/NECO examination images.
- **Objective 2:** Compare performance under different prompt languages, analyzing whether using English vs. native-language prompts affects answer accuracy.

2 Related Works

2.1 Multimodal Large Language Models and Their Capabilities

Multimodal large language models integrate multiple data modalities, such as text and images, to enhance comprehension and reasoning (Peng et al., 2023; Ahuja et al., 2024). These models build on advances in vision-language pre-training that combine visual encoders with language models (Radford et al., 2021; Li et al., 2023). State-of-the-art MLLMs have achieved impressive performance on many text-based visual tasks, including image captioning, document understanding, and visual question answering. In general, these models perform well on tasks in high-resource languages. However, studies have shown that their effectiveness diminishes significantly in low-resource languages such as Yoruba, Igbo, and Hausa (Adelani et al., 2025; Schneider and Sitaram, 2024)). For instance, the IrokoBench evaluation found a substantial drop in GPT-4o's performance on African language understanding compared to English. Similarly, a culturally diverse VQA benchmark (Romero et al., 2024) demonstrated that even powerful vision-language models fail to generalize across linguistically diverse or culturally unfamiliar inputs. (Zhang et al., 2023) introduced M3Exam, a multilingual, multimodal exam benchmark, and reported major performance discrepancies between high-resource and low-resource languages. While current MLLMs can process Latin-script inputs with high accuracy, they struggle with the complex morphology and orthographic variations present in many African languages (Liu et al., 2023). This gap underscores that simply scaling to multimodal inputs is not sufficient for broad multilingual competency.

2.2 Challenges in Multilingual NLP for Low-Resource African Languages

The lack of training data remains a fundamental challenge in multilingual NLP research, particularly for African languages (Adelani et al., 2025). Unlike English or other widely spoken languages, Yoruba, Igbo, and Hausa have relatively limited corpora and annotated datasets available for training or fine-tuning large models. This data scarcity negatively impacts model performance on both text-only and multimodal tasks (Schneider and Sitaram, 2024)). Even large multilingual language models like XLM-R (Conneau et al., 2020) or BLOOM struggle on African languages that were underrepresented in their training data. In addition, many African languages have unique linguistic properties – for example, tonal phonology and extensive use of diacritics in Yoruba, or complex noun classes in some Bantu languages – which prove difficult for pre-trained LLMs to handle. These orthographic and grammatical nuances are often lost or misinterpreted by models not specifically adapted to them (Orife et al., 2020). Recent studies such as (Nayak et al., 2024) highlight that vision-language models exhibit poor understanding of culturally or linguistically specific content, reinforcing the importance of developing benchmarks that reflect real-world linguistic diversity. There have been efforts to bolster NLP for African languages – for example, the Masakhane project's participatory approach to machine translation (Nekoto et al., 2020) and the creation of language-specific models like AfriBERTa (Ogueji et al., 2021), but these are text-only initiatives. Until similar resources and benchmarks are created on the multimodal front, AI models will continue to exhibit biases favoring high-resource languages over under-represented ones (Ahuja et al., 2024; Lu et al., 2024). Our work addresses this gap by providing a focused evaluation on Yoruba, Igbo, and Hausa, thereby pushing towards more inclusive multimodal model development.

2.3 Optical Character Recognition and Text Processing in Multimodal AI

Optical Character Recognition (OCR) plays a crucial role in multimodal AI by enabling models to extract text from images. However, existing OCR-focused evaluations – for example, the comprehensive OCRBench suite (Li et al., 2023) – indicate that current MLLMs often struggle with non-Latin scripts, accented characters, and handwritten text. Even models like GPT-4 and Claude that are adept at English OCR can falter when faced with, say, a scanned Hausa document or Yoruba text with tone marks. Kosmos-2, a recent grounded multimodal model (Peng et al., 2023), introduced new capabilities for aligning text with visual regions, but its effectiveness on low-resource African languages remains unclear, as it was primarily evaluated on mainstream languages and object-centric tasks. In our study, we do not explicitly re-evaluate OCR accuracy at the character level; instead, we assess how well multimodal LLMs handle the output of OCR in a downstream task – specifically, answering multiple-choice questions based on exam images. By leveraging real WAEC/NECO exam questions, our evaluation extends prior research and provides new insights into OCR performance within an African educational context. In particular, our results can reveal whether state-of-the-art models accurately interpret the extracted text (including any diacritics or uncommon characters) and use it correctly to select answers. This complements existing OCR benchmarks by focusing on end-to-end comprehension: from image to extracted text to answer selection.

2.4 Standardized Exam Benchmarks in AI Research

Standardized exams have become a widely adopted benchmark for evaluating AI models. The structured format of exam questions—where each item follows a consistent style and has a known correct answer offers a controlled environment for assessing an AI's reading comprehension, reasoning, and problem-solving abilities. Several recent studies have used exam-based benchmarks to evaluate large language models. For example, M3Exam (Zhang et al., 2023) compiles real multilingual exam questions and shows that GPT-4o and similar models perform well on high-resource languages but struggle on under-represented languages. Similarly, the MEGAVERSE benchmark (Ahuja et al., 2024) evaluated LLMs across 83 languages and highlighted substantial performance gaps in low-resource linguistic settings. Our study follows a similar methodology of exam-driven evaluation but narrows the focus specifically to structured educational content in popular Nigerian languages. By concentrating on WAEC/NECO multiple-choice questions in Yoruba, Igbo, and Hausa, we provide an in-depth look at model capabilities in a context that had not been examined in prior multilingual benchmarks. This approach also complements efforts like Hendrycks et al.(2021)'s MMLU, which included a broad range of subjects and some languages: we add the dimension of image-based text understanding in an educational assessment scenario.

3 Methodology

3.1 Dataset Curation

The dataset for this study was curated from past WAEC and NECO examination questions in Yoruba, Igbo, Hausa, and English. We targeted multiple-choice questions (MCQs) from recent years to ensure a representative sample of modern usage. The curation process involved several steps:

3.1.1 Data Collection

We obtained past examination papers from students and bookshops that sell educational materials. However, acquiring exam questions for language subjects (Hausa, Igbo, Yoruba) online proved extremely challenging, if not nearly impossible, due to their limited availability compared to more widely documented subjects. To ensure a sizable dataset in each target language, we focused on examination papers from the years 2008–2024.

3.1.2 Question Segmentation

Each question' was manually cropped from scanned examination sheets to isolate it as an individual image. This ensured that each image contained exactly one question for the model to answer, standardizing the input format. Only multiple-choice questions were included to maintain a uniform evaluation style.

3.1.3 Answer Key Verification

Many exams came with official answer keys, which we treated as gold-standard answers. For questions lacking official keys (or in cases where only the exam paper was available), we consulted linguistic and subject matter experts fluent in Yoruba, Igbo, or Hausa to determine the correct answer. These expert-verified answers were cross-checked to ensure accuracy.

3.1.4 Categorization

Each question was labeled by language (Yoruba, Igbo, Hausa, or English) and by exam year. This allows us to perform year-wise or language-wise analysis of the results. We ensured a roughly balanced number of questions per language where possible, though English had a naturally larger pool. This dataset of exam questions forms the basis for our evaluation. By using real educational content, we ensure that the evaluation is grounded in tasks that have practical importance and linguistic richness. Table 1 below summarizes the provisional composition of the dataset:

Year	English	Yoruba	Igbo	Hausa
2008	0	20	0	0
2009	0	16	0	0
2010	0	19	0	0
2011	0	20	0	0
2012	0	17	0	0
2013	0	20	0	0
2014	0	20	0	0
2015	0	19	0	0
2016	0	20	0	0
2017	0	0	0	0
2018	29	19	0	0
2019	30	19	0	0
2020	30	19	0	0
2021	60	38	24	0
2022	60	40	45	20
2023	60	36	45	20
2024	0	36	0	36
Total	**269**	**378**	**114**	**76**

Table 1: Dataset composition by year and language. WAEC and NECO Combined

3.2 Model Selection and Evaluation Criteria

We selected three state-of-the-art multimodal LLMs for benchmarking: GPT-4o (OpenAI), Claude-3.5 Haiku (Anthropic), and Gemini-1.5 pro (Google DeepMind). These models although uneven in sizes were chosen due to their cutting-edge performance and diverse origins (industry leaders in AI). We accessed GPT-4o, Claude-3.5 Haiku, and Gemini-1.5 Pro via their official API endpoints, While other emerging models (such as Mistral) could be considered, we limited our testing to these three due to time and resource constraints. Our evaluation was based on two primary criteria:

- **Answer Accuracy:** The percentage of questions for which the model's answer matched the expert-verified correct answer. This is a direct measure of performance on the multiple-choice questions.
- **Language-wise Performance:** We compare accuracy across the four languages (English, Yoruba, Igbo, Hausa) to identify any performance disparities.

3.3 Experimental Setup

We designed a uniform evaluation pipeline and prompting strategy to ensure a fair comparison between models. Key aspects of the experimental setup are outlined below:

3.3.1 Prompting Strategy

We employed two query strategies for each question image:

1. An English-prompted query.
2. A native-language-prompted query.

In the English prompt condition, the model was instructed in English (e.g., "Analyze the image and answer the question") while being given an image containing a Yoruba/Igbo/Hausa question. In the native prompt condition, we translated the instruction into the question's language (Yoruba, Igbo, or Hausa) so that the model received the prompt in the same language as the question. This allows us to test whether prompting in the local language improves understanding or not. Each model thus answers every question twice: once with an English prompt and once with a native-language prompt.

3.3.2 Temperature Setting

While most API parameters were left at their defaults, we explicitly set the temperature to 0.1 to ensure minimal randomness and greater response consistency across model runs. This controlled setting ensures that each model selects the most probable answer rather than generating diverse outputs.

3.3.3 Multiple-Choice Answering Format

To reduce variability in how models produce answers and to minimize open-ended generation issues (e.g., hallucinations), we prompted the models to choose one of the options A, B, C, D, E for each question. We adopted a best-practice format inspired by prior VQA benchmarks (e.g., CVQA): the model is instructed to assign a probability score to each option and then select the option with the highest probability. In practice, we implemented this by instructing the model to output a JSON object with scores, which forces the model to make a single choice.

3.3.4 Human Evaluation via Independent NLP Community

A crucial component of our methodology involved human evaluation using participants from an independent NLP community. They have a network of linguistics enthusiasts, including students with a keen interest in language processing. We engaged a subset of students from this community to answer the same multiple-choice exam questions that were presented to the AI models. The students were selected based on their fluency in Yoruba, Igbo, or Hausa, but they were not necessarily language experts. Their responses provide a useful baseline to compare human vs. model performance on these questions. (This human study was conducted with appropriate consent and is intended for qualitative comparison, not as a rigorous benchmark.)

3.3.5 Prompt Template

We crafted a consistent system message for all models, emphasizing the task and format. Below is a simplified example of the prompt content used (shown here in English for brevity):

System Prompt:

> "You are a knowledgeable assistant for answering exam questions. Carefully read the question in the image and evaluate each of the four choices. Provide the answer by indicating the option (A, B, C, D, or E) with the highest probability of being correct, along with probability scores for each option in JSON format."

User Prompt:

> "Analyze the following question image and determine the correct answer (A, B, C, D, or E). Respond in JSON with your probabilities for each option."

For native-language trials, the prompts were translated appropriately (e.g., to Yoruba). All models were thus given a very similar cue and format requirement, to the extent their API allowed system instructions.

3.4 Evaluation Metric

We used a strict accuracy metric for each model's responses. A model receives a score of 1 for a question if its highest-probability choice matches the correct answer, and 0 otherwise. We then compute overall accuracy as well as per-language accuracy.

The above methodology enables a controlled and fair evaluation of each model's ability to interpret exam images and answer questions in multiple languages. All model outputs and metadata are logged for analysis.

4 Results

The evaluation results provide insights into the performance of GPT-4o, Gemini-1.5 Pro, and Claude-3.5 Haiku on multiple-choice exam questions in Yoruba, Hausa, Igbo, and English. We analyze accuracy under two prompting conditions:

1. Prompting in English.
2. Prompting in the respective African language.

We also compare the models' performance to human baseline scores.

4.1 Model Performance Across Languages

The Table 2 below presents the accuracy scores for each model across different languages and prompt conditions:

Prompt	GPT-4o Accuracy	Gemini-1.5 Pro Accuracy	Claude-3.5 Haiku Accuracy
Yoruba Exam Questions			
Yoruba Prompt	32.80% (124/378)	29.63% (112/378)	26.72% (101/378)
English Prompt	31.74% (121/378)	33.86% (128/378)	25.92% (98/378)
Hausa Exam Questions			
English Prompt	39.47% (30/76)	36.84% (28/76)	28.95% (22/76)
Hausa Prompt	43.42% (33/76)	44.74% (34/76)	23.68% (18/76)
English Exam Questions			
English Prompt	90.33% (243/269)	73.61% (198/269)	55.39% (149/269)
Yoruba Prompt	79.55% (214/269)	72.49% (195/269)	39.03% (105/269)
Hausa Prompt	80.30% (216/269)	72.86% (196/269)	40.89% (110/269)
Igbo Prompt	81.04% (218/269)	72.12% (194/269)	36.43% (98/269)
Igbo Exam Questions			
English Prompt	27.19% (31/114)	31.58% (36/114)	18.42% (21/114)
Igbo Prompt	28.95% (33/114)	35.96% (41/114)	23.68% (27/114)

Table 2: Accuracy scores for GPT-4o, Gemini, and Claude across different languages and prompt conditions.

4.2 Key Observations

- **Higher Accuracy in English:** As expected, models performed significantly better on English-only questions, with GPT-4o achieving the highest accuracy (90.33%), followed by Gemini-1.5 Pro (73.61%) and Claude -3.5 Haiku (55.39%). This confirms that the models handle high-resource languages much better than low-resource ones.
- **Effect of Prompting English Questions in African Languages:** Interestingly, when English questions were prompted in Yoruba,

Hausa, and Igbo, accuracy dropped compared to using English prompts. GPT-4o's accuracy dropped from 90.33% (English prompt) to 79.55% (Yoruba prompt), 80.30% (Hausa prompt), and 81.04% (Igbo prompt). Gemini-1.5 Pro and Claude-3.5 Haiku showed similar trends, highlighting how translation and linguistic context impact comprehension.

- **Native Language Prompts Improve Accuracy:** For Yoruba, Hausa, and Igbo, prompting the model in the native language generally resulted in higher accuracy than when the prompt was in English. The effect was particularly noticeable in Hausa (e.g., GPT-4o: 43.42% Hausa-prompted vs. 39.47% English-prompted).

4.3 Comparison with Human Performance

We also compared model results with human performance, where participants from an independent NLP community answered the same exam questions. The results are presented in Table 3 below:

Language	Human Accuracy
Hausa	68.0%
Igbo	52.3%
Yoruba	56.0%

Table 3: Comparison of human accuracy on multiple-choice exam questions across three African languages.

Human accuracy was significantly higher than all model performances across the three African languages, reinforcing that even non-expert humans outperform state-of-the-art AI models on structured educational tasks in Yoruba, Igbo, and Hausa.

These results provide strong evidence of the performance gap between AI models and human linguistic abilities, particularly in low-resource African languages.

5 Discussion

The results indicate several key trends regarding multimodal LLMs' performance in African languages. Below, we discuss the implications of these findings and analyze potential causes and areas for improvement.

5.1 Performance Disparities Across Languages

Our findings confirm that AI models struggle significantly with low-resource languages, particularly in the context of document VQA for standardized exams. The sharp decline in accuracy from 90.33% in English (GPT-4o) to below 40% for Yoruba, Hausa, and Igbo underscores the severe data imbalance in model training. Despite advancements in multilingual AI, African languages remain underrepresented in training datasets, leading to weaker comprehension and reasoning abilities when processing structured educational assessments. This highlights the critical need for more inclusive AI models capable of handling the complexities of standardized exam content in low-resource languages.

5.2 Effect of Native vs. English Prompting

A critical takeaway from the study is that models perform better when prompted in the same language as the question. This trend was particularly consistent for GPT-4o and partially observed in Gemini and Claude. The improvement suggests that prompting in the target language helps models better interpret syntactic and semantic nuances, likely because it reduces the additional complexity of cross-language interpretation.

However, this trend was not uniform across all languages and models. For example, Gemini performed slightly better when prompted in English for Yoruba questions, suggesting that some models may rely on English as an anchor for reasoning. This discrepancy warrants further investigation into the internal translation and tokenization processes of multimodal LLMs.

5.3 Human vs. AI Performance Gap

Human participants vastly outperformed all models, with an average accuracy of 56.0% (Yoruba), 52.3% (Igbo), and 68% (Hausa). This performance gap is expected, but its magnitude is striking, especially considering that the human evaluators were not expert linguists, but student enthusiasts from an independent NLP community. The disparity suggests that AI models lack fundamental linguistic and contextual understanding needed for structured educational tasks in African languages.

This reinforces the need for more diverse and representative training datasets to improve multimodal AI comprehension of African languages. It also suggests the potential for fine-tuning or adaptation strategies to boost model performance in these languages.

6 Conclusion

This study evaluated the performance of state-of-the-art multimodal large language models—GPT-4o, Gemini, and Claude—on structured educational tasks in Yoruba, Igbo, and Hausa. Our findings reveal several key takeaways:

- **Performance disparities exist across languages,** with models performing significantly better in English than in African languages for VQA in standardized exams.

- **Prompting in native languages improves model accuracy,** particularly for GPT-4o, suggesting a need for further multilingual optimization.

- **AI models still lag behind human performance,** with human participants from an independent NLP community achieving much higher accuracy than all models.

These results highlight the challenges of multimodal NLP for African languages and emphasize the need for greater linguistic inclusivity in AI training data and model design.

7 Future Work

Future research can build upon this study by expanding and improving multimodal datasets for African languages, ensuring high-quality resources that help bridge performance gaps. Fine-tuning large language models (LLMs) with domain-specific data could further enhance their comprehension and reasoning capabilities in these languages. Additionally, the development of standardized evaluation benchmarks for African multimodal NLP would enable systematic model comparisons. Investigating OCR accuracy for African scripts is another crucial area, as many languages have unique orthographic systems that present distinct challenges. Finally, broadening the scope beyond Yoruba, Igbo, and Hausa to include a wider range of African languages would provide a more comprehensive understanding of NLP challenges on the continent.

References

David Ifeoluwa Adelani, Jessica Ojo, Israel Abebe Azime, Jian Yun Zhuang, Jesujoba O. Alabi, Xuanli He, Millicent Ochieng, Sara Hooker, Andiswa Bukula, En-Shiun Annie Lee, Chiamaka Chukwuneke, Happy Buzaaba, Blessing Sibanda, Godson Kalipe, Jonathan Mukiibi, Salomon Kabongo, Foutse Yuehgoh, Mmasibidi Setaka, Lolwethu Ndolela, Nkiruka Odu, Rooweither Mabuya, Shamsuddeen Hassan Muhammad, Salomey Osei, Sokhar Samb, Tadesse Kebede Guge, Tombekai Vangoni Sherman, and Pontus Stenetorp. 2025. Irokobench: A new benchmark for african languages in the age of large language models. *Preprint*, arXiv:2406.03368.

Sanchit Ahuja, Divyanshu Aggarwal, Varun Gumma, Ishaan Watts, Ashutosh Sathe, Millicent Ochieng, Rishav Hada, Prachi Jain, Mohamed Ahmed, Kalika Bali, and Sunayana Sitaram. 2024. MEGAVERSE: Benchmarking large language models across languages, modalities, models and tasks. In *Proceedings of the 2024 Conference of the North American Chapter of the Association for Computational Linguistics: Human Language Technologies (Volume 1: Long Papers)*, pages 2598–2637, Mexico City, Mexico. Association for Computational Linguistics.

Alexis Conneau, Kartikay Khandelwal, Naman Goyal, Vishrav Chaudhary, Guillaume Wenzek, Francisco Guzmán, Edouard Grave, Myle Ott, Luke Zettlemoyer, and Veselin Stoyanov. 2020. Unsupervised cross-lingual representation learning at scale. In *Proceedings of the 58th Annual Meeting of the Association for Computational Linguistics*, pages 8440–8451, Online. Association for Computational Linguistics.

Dan Hendrycks, Collin Burns, Steven Basart, Andy Zou, Mantas Mazeika, Dawn Song, and Jacob Steinhardt. 2021. Measuring massive multitask language understanding. *Preprint*, arXiv:2009.03300.

Pratik Joshi, Sebastin Santy, Amar Budhiraja, Kalika Bali, and Monojit Choudhury. 2020. The state and fate of linguistic diversity and inclusion in the NLP world. In *Proceedings of the 58th Annual Meeting of the Association for Computational Linguistics*, pages 6282–6293, Online. Association for Computational Linguistics.

Junnan Li, Dongxu Li, Silvio Savarese, and Steven Hoi. 2023. Blip-2: Bootstrapping language-image pre-training with frozen image encoders and large language models. *Preprint*, arXiv:2301.12597.

Haotian Liu, Chunyuan Li, Qingyang Wu, and Yong Jae Lee. 2023. Visual instruction tuning. *Preprint*, arXiv:2304.08485.

Yujie Lu, Dongfu Jiang, Wenhu Chen, William Yang Wang, Yejin Choi, and Bill Yuchen Lin. 2024. Wildvision: Evaluating vision-language models in the wild with human preferences. *Preprint*, arXiv:2406.11069.

Shravan Nayak, Kanishk Jain, Rabiul Awal, Siva Reddy, Sjoerd Van Steenkiste, Lisa Anne Hendricks, Karolina Stanczak, and Aishwarya Agrawal. 2024. Benchmarking vision language models for cultural understanding. In *Proceedings of the 2024 Conference on Empirical Methods in Natural Language Processing*, pages 5769–5790, Miami, Florida, USA. Association for Computational Linguistics.

Wilhelmina Nekoto, Vukosi Marivate, Tshinondiwa Matsila, Timi Fasubaa, Taiwo Fagbohungbe, Solomon Oluwole Akinola, Shamsuddeen Muhammad, Salomon Kabongo Kabenamualu, Salomey Osei, Freshia Sackey, Rubungo Andre Niyongabo, Ricky Macharm, Perez Ogayo, Orevaoghene Ahia, Musie Meressa Berhe, Mofetoluwa Adeyemi, Masabata Mokgesi-Selinga, Lawrence Okegbemi, Laura Martinus, Kolawole Tajudeen, Kevin Degila, Kelechi Ogueji, Kathleen Siminyu, Julia Kreutzer, Jason Webster, Jamiil Toure Ali, Jade Abbott, Iroro Orife, Ignatius Ezeani, Idris Abdulkadir Dangana, Herman Kamper, Hady Elsahar, Goodness Duru, Ghollah Kioko, Murhabazi Espoir, Elan van Biljon, Daniel Whitenack, Christopher Onyefuluchi, Chris Chinenye Emezue, Bonaventure F. P. Dossou, Blessing Sibanda, Blessing Bassey, Ayodele Olabiyi, Arshath Ramkilowan, Alp Öktem, Adewale Akinfaderin, and Abdallah Bashir. 2020. Participatory research for low-resourced machine translation: A case study in African languages. In *Findings of the Association for Computational Linguistics: EMNLP 2020*, pages 2144–2160, Online. Association for Computational Linguistics.

Kelechi Ogueji, Yuxin Zhu, and Jimmy Lin. 2021. Small data? no problem! exploring the viability of pretrained multilingual language models for low-resourced languages. In *Proceedings of the 1st Workshop on Multilingual Representation Learning*, pages 116–126, Punta Cana, Dominican Republic. Association for Computational Linguistics.

Iroro Orife, David I. Adelani, Timi Fasubaa, Victor Williamson, Wuraola Fisayo Oyewusi, Olamilekan Wahab, and Kola Tubosun. 2020. Improving yorùbá diacritic restoration. *Preprint*, arXiv:2003.10564.

Zhiliang Peng, Wenhui Wang, Li Dong, Yaru Hao, Shaohan Huang, Shuming Ma, and Furu Wei. 2023. Kosmos-2: Grounding multimodal large language models to the world. *Preprint*, arXiv:2306.14824.

Alec Radford, Jong Wook Kim, Chris Hallacy, Aditya Ramesh, Gabriel Goh, Sandhini Agarwal, Girish Sastry, Amanda Askell, Pamela Mishkin, Jack Clark, Gretchen Krueger, and Ilya Sutskever. 2021. Learning transferable visual models from natural language supervision. *Preprint*, arXiv:2103.00020.

David Romero, Chenyang Lyu, Haryo Akbarianto Wibowo, Teresa Lynn, Injy Hamed, Aditya Nanda Kishore, Aishik Mandal, Alina Dragonetti, Artem Abzaliev, Atnafu Lambebo Tonja, Bontu Fufa Balcha, Chenxi Whitehouse, Christian Salamea, Dan John Velasco, David Ifeoluwa Adelani, David Le Meur, Emilio Villa-Cueva, Fajri Koto, Fauzan Farooqui, Frederico Belcavello, Ganzorig Batnasan, Gisela Vallejo, Grainne Caulfield, Guido Ivetta, Haiyue Song, Henok Biadglign Ademtew, Hernán Maina, Holy Lovenia, Israel Abebe Azime, Jan Christian Blaise Cruz, Jay Gala, Jiahui Geng, Jesus-German Ortiz-Barajas, Jinheon Baek, Jocelyn Dunstan, Laura Alonso Alemany, Kumaranage Ravindu Yasas Nagasinghe, Luciana Benotti, Luis Fernando D'Haro, Marcelo Viridiano, Marcos Estecha-Garitagoitia, Maria Camila Buitrago Cabrera, Mario Rodríguez-Cantelar, Mélanie Jouitteau, Mihail Mihaylov, Mohamed Fazli Mohamed Imam, Muhammad Farid Adilazuarda, Munkhjargal Gochoo, Munkh-Erdene Otgonbold, Naome Etori, Olivier Niyomugisha, Paula Mónica Silva, Pranjal Chitale, Raj Dabre, Rendi Chevi, Ruochen Zhang, Ryandito Diandaru, Samuel Cahyawijaya, Santiago Góngora, Soyeong Jeong, Sukannya Purkayastha, Tatsuki Kuribayashi, Teresa Clifford, Thanmay Jayakumar, Tiago Timponi Torrent, Toqeer Ehsan, Vladimir Araujo, Yova Kementchedjhieva, Zara Burzo, Zheng Wei Lim, Zheng Xin Yong, Oana Ignat, Joan Nwatu, Rada Mihalcea, Thamar Solorio, and Alham Fikri Aji. 2024. Cvqa: Culturally-diverse multilingual visual question answering benchmark. *Preprint*, arXiv:2406.05967.

Florian Schneider and Sunayana Sitaram. 2024. M5 – a diverse benchmark to assess the performance of large multimodal models across multilingual and multicultural vision-language tasks. *Preprint*, arXiv:2407.03791.

Wenxuan Zhang, Sharifah Mahani Aljunied, Chang Gao, Yew Ken Chia, and Lidong Bing. 2023. M3exam: A multilingual, multimodal, multilevel benchmark for examining large language models. *Preprint*, arXiv:2306.05179.

MOZ-Smishing: A Benchmark Dataset for Detecting Mobile Money Frauds

Felermino D. M. A. Ali[1,2,3], **Saide M. Saide**[3], **Rui Sousa-Silva**[2], **Henrique Lopes Cardoso**[1]

[1]LIACC, Faculdade de Engenharia, Universidade do Porto, Rua Dr. Roberto Frias, 4200-465, Porto, Portugal

[2]CLUP, Faculdade de Letras da Universidade do Porto, Via Panorâmica, 4150-564, Porto, Portugal

[3]DEI, Faculdade de Engenharia da Universidade Lúrio, Pemba, 3203, Cabo-Delgado, Mozambique

{up202100778, hlc}@fe.up.pt, saide.saide@unilurio.ac.mz, rssilva@letras.up.pt

Abstract

Despite the increasing prevalence of smishing attacks targeting Mobile Money Transfer systems, there is a notable lack of publicly available SMS phishing datasets in this domain. This study seeks to address this gap by creating a specialized dataset designed to detect smishing attacks aimed at Mobile Money Transfer users. The data set consists of crowd-sourced text messages from Mozambican mobile users, meticulously annotated into two categories: legitimate messages and smishing attempts. The messages are written in Portuguese, often incorporating microtext styles and linguistic nuances unique to the Mozambican context. We also investigate the effectiveness of LLMs in detecting smishing. Using in-context learning approaches, we evaluate the models' ability to identify smishing attempts without requiring extensive task-specific training. The data set is released under an open license at the following link: https://huggingface.co/datasets/MOZNLP/MOZ-Smishing

1 Introduction

Mobile Money Transfer (MMT) systems have emerged as a transformative financial technology, particularly in developing countries where traditional banking infrastructure is often inadequate or inaccessible. These systems have revolutionized financial inclusion by providing essential services to underserved populations, enabling users to deposit, withdraw, transfer money, pay for goods and services, and access credit and savings—all through the convenience of a mobile device. In regions such as Sub-Saharan Africa, where traditional banking adoption remains low, MMT systems have become a cornerstone of economic activity and financial empowerment.

According to GSMA (2024b), the global adoption of MMT systems has reached unprecedented levels, with over 1.75 billion registered accounts worldwide as of 2024. These systems process an estimated \$1.4 trillion annually, equivalent to approximately \$2.7 million per minute. Sub-Saharan Africa has emerged as the most active region for MMT adoption, driven by the widespread use of platforms such as M-Pesa, Airtel Money, and MTN Mobile Money. However, this rapid growth has also attracted the attention of cybercriminals, making MMT users increasingly vulnerable to fraud (INTERPOL, 2020).

Mobile money fraud has become a significant concern across Africa, with the number of victims rising sharply in recent years. This alarming trend underscores the urgent need for fraud detection and mitigation strategies. Therefore, various solutions have been proposed to address this challenge (GSMA, 2024a), with a growing emphasis on leveraging advanced technologies such as Artificial Intelligence and Machine Learning to detect and prevent fraudulent activities (Delvia Arifin et al., 2016; Balim and Gunal, 2019; Ghourabi et al., 2020; Ghourabi, 2021; Jain and Gupta, 2018, 2019; Jain et al., 2020; Mishra and Soni, 2020, 2021; Roy et al., 2020; Sonowal and Kuppusamy, 2018). However, the scarcity of high-quality, domain-specific datasets hinders the development of effective AI-based fraud detection systems. These solutions are inherently data-hungry, requiring a large amount of labeled data to train deployable models. Unfortunately, few publicly available datasets exist for smishing identification and other types of mobile money fraud, limiting the progress of research in this critical area.

In this study, we aim to bridge this gap by contributing a benchmark dataset specifically designed for smishing identification in the context of MMT. This dataset is constructed to reflect real-world scenarios and includes a set of smishing attempts targeting real mobile money users. Additionally, we evaluate the performance of existing LLMs using in-context learning techniques to assess their effectiveness in detecting smishing attempts. Our

Proceedings of the Sixth Workshop on African Natural Language Processing (AfricaNLP 2025), pages 158–166
July 31, 2025

findings provide valuable insights into the potential of LLMs for fraud detection and highlight areas for future research and development.

2 Literature Review

One of the most widely used datasets for smishing detection is the one proposed by Almeida et al. (2013). This dataset contains 5,574 text messages, divided into 4,827 legitimate messages and 747 fraudulent messages. While this dataset has been influential in advancing research in smishing detection, it has notable limitations. First, the dataset contains a relatively small number of smishing examples, which may limit the generalizability of models trained on it. Second, the dataset is exclusively composed of English-language text messages, which restricts its applicability to non-English-speaking regions where smishing fraud is also prevalent.

Other publicly available datasets, such as those proposed by Timko and Rahman (2024) and Chen and Kan (2012), also focus primarily on English-language content and general smishing or spam messages, rather than targeting the specific context of mobile money fraud. While these datasets have contributed to the development of spam and fraud detection systems, they do not adequately address the unique linguistic and contextual nuances of MMT-related fraud, particularly in regions where English is not the primary language.

To address the language gap, some researchers have proposed datasets that include other non-English languages. For example, Yadav et al. (2011), Ghourabi (2021) and Mambina et al. (2022), have developed datasets that besides English also included Hindi, Arabic and Swahili respectively.

In general, all existing data sets often lack a specific focus on mobile money fraud, instead addressing more general forms of SMS spam or smishing. Our work seeks to address these gaps by introducing a novel dataset focused on Portuguese-language text messages, with a particular emphasis on smishing attempts targeting MMT users. Similar to Mambina et al. (2022); Timko and Rahman (2024), this data set was constructed using community-based approaches, where we crowd-sourced both smishing and legitimate messages.

3 Dataset Collection

We gathered data from users of MMT services in Mozambique, a country currently experiencing a wave in the adoption of such services. The MMT landscape in Mozambique is dominated by several prominent platforms, including M-PESA, E-Mola, and mKesh, which are operated by the country's major telecom providers: Vodacom, Movitel, and Tmcel, respectively. However, the rapid growth of these services has also led to an increase in fraudulent activities targeting users. For instance, Vodacom, the operator of M-Pesa, reported that approximately 80 people fall victim to fraudulent mobile money transactions daily in Mozambique. This alarming trend underscored the necessity to study and understand these scams. To address this, we crowd-sourced fraudulent messages from users, including those who had already been victimized by such schemes.

The data collection methodology comprised the following steps:

Crowdsourcing Smishing Messages: We launched a campaign inviting people to join a dedicated WhatsApp group. Participants were encouraged to share suspicious or fraudulent text messages they had received, particularly those from unknown sources that appeared to target their mobile money accounts. Clear instructions were provided to guide participants in identifying these messages, emphasizing the importance of sharing only those texts that they believed were attempts to defraud them or cause financial loss. Participants could share these messages either by submitting screenshots or forwarding the text directly to the group.

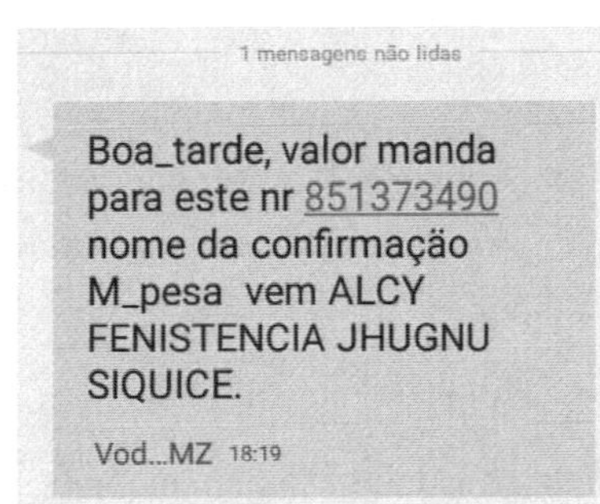

Figure 1: A Sample of a smishing text message.

Crowdsourcing Legitimate Messaging: Similarly, we invited participants to share messages that they considered legitimate. We encouraged them to submit messages related to MMT topics, as well as other non-fraudulent messages. This helped us build a balanced data set for comparative analysis.

Data Preprocessing: We preprocessed the collected data by performing the following steps. First, all message screenshots were transcribed in plain text format. Next, we identified and removed duplicate messages. Finally, all personal identifiers within the legitimate messages were anonymized to ensure user privacy.

The final dataset contains 552 instances of smishing messages and 2,009 legitimate text messages. Figure 2 illustrates the embedding space of both categories using UMAP (Uniform Manifold Approximation and Projection for Dimension Reduction) clustering (McInnes et al., 2020), highlighting their distribution. Furthermore, Table 1 presents a sample of 8 data points, which showcases examples of legitimate and smishing messages from our dataset.

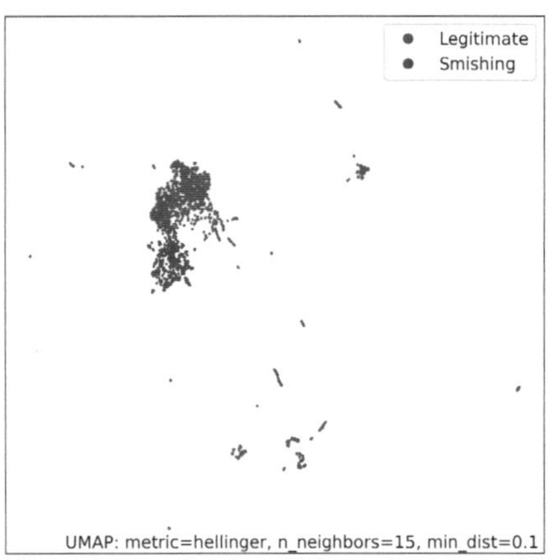

Figure 2: UMAP clustering, where blue points represent legitimate messages, whereas red points are smishing messages

4 Exploratory Data Analysis

4.1 Smishing Tactics

To further our analysis of the tactics used by scammers, we conducted a content analysis on the collected smishing messages. Our analysis identified several recurring patterns and social engineering tactics used by scammers. These tactics primarily aim to deceive users into transferring monetary funds directly or inadvertently, ultimately resulting in financial loss. We identified the following tactics:

Bulk SMS: We collected a total of 692 text messages from our dataset. After preprocessing, we identified that 140 messages were duplicates. Interestingly, the persistence of duplicate messages provided valuable information on the operational strategies of scammers. Since identical messages appear to be disseminated to a large number of recipients via multiple phone numbers, it suggests that scammers target various random recipients simultaneously, thereby increasing the chances that at least some victims will fall into their trap. Furthermore, we observed that scammers frequently used different accounts or contact numbers in various messages. This deliberate strategy presumably serves as a mechanism to avoid detection and tracking.

Pretending an Existing Transaction was Previously Arranged: Scammers create a psychological trap that a transaction was previously agreed upon by vaguely referencing prior interactions or conversations, as exemplified by ambiguous phrases like:

- *"aquele valor"* ("that amount of money").

Creating Urgency and Pressure: Scammers attempt to induce panic or urgency, prompting immediate action from their victims. Typical tactics used by scammers manipulate victims into quick, and often irrational, include using the following phases:

- *"manda agora"* ("send now");
- *"tem problema a minha conta M-pesa"* ("my M-pesa account has a problem");
- *"meu telefone caiu em água"* ("my phone fell into water");
- *"já podes mandar"* ("you can send it now").

Impersonation of Trusted Parties or Familiar Contacts: Scammers use impersonation techniques that involve pretending to be trusted persons such as family members or friends. They frequently use informal language and familiar salutations such as *"amigo/a"* ("friend"), *"man"*, or typical greetings such as:

- *"oi," "boa tarde," "bom dia"* (informal salutations).

Text Message	Target Label
Bom dia pai sou eu sua filha estou a espera desse valor quero pagar matricula	Legitimate
Bom dia bro, podes mandar aquele valor para o meu número aguardo teu sinal	Legitimate
Bom dia Rosinha peço para me mandar 500 Mts no M-Pesa pago no final do mês	Legitimate
Kmk brow, tudo bem? Peço que me envies aquele valor para minha conta m-pesa, estou a precisar.	Legitimate
Manda o valor neste número,858773567.M-pesa vem em nome de Manuel Vasco R.Ok	Smishing
bom dia, este valor enviame nesta conta: 857491433 vem em nome de ROSA MILIONE FERRO	Smishing
Esta bem.O valor podes mandar para este Nr 841898297 vem em nome e Castro Jos Fabio!	Smishing
Man Esse Valor Manda Neste Numero 857170842 M,pesa Vem Abel Vasco	Smishing

Table 1: Sample messages from the dataset. Phone numbers used to receive fraudulent payments are shown in blue, the MMT platforms exploited by scammers are marked in red, and the names under which fraudsters registered their MMT accounts are highlighted in green.

Impersonating Common Names: Scammers increase the authenticity and credibility of scam messages by carefully selecting common local names. The names identified in the messages include:

- Top 5 frequent **First Names:** *"Maria", "Luisa", "Alberto", "Ana".*
- Top 5 frequent **Surnames:** *"João", "José", "Mário", "Joaquim", "Manuel"*
- **Mozambican family names:** *"Siquice", "Chacuanda", "Nhampossa", "Páisse", "Mustafa", "Mapisse", "Nhalungo", "Cuamba", "Mutucua", "Machava", "Malangisse", etc.*

Fake Technical or Emergency Problems: Many messages exploit scenarios involving fictitious technical difficulties or emergencies to justify the use of an unfamiliar phone number. Frequent examples found in messages are:

- *"minha conta tem problema"* ("my account has an issue"),
- *"meu número não tá receber dinheiro"* ("my number can't receive money anymore"),
- *"telefone desligado," "telefone caiu na água"* ("phone is off," "phone fell in water").

Politeness and False Courtesy: Scammers strategically incorporate polite and courteous expressions into their messages, lowering the victims' guard and diminishing suspicion. Instances include phrases such as:

- *"desculpe pelo incómodo"* ("sorry for the inconvenience"),
- *"por favor"* ("please"),
- *"bom dia," "boa tarde"* ("good morning," "good afternoon").

Small Mistakes, Microtext, and Typographical Errors: Finally, deliberate typographical errors or microtext were frequently observed in smishing messages, making them resemble authentic informal texts. We noticed many intentionally casual errors or informal grammar, thus giving messages a natural, rushed appearance. Scammers may also use these errors to avoid automated filtering or spam detection systems. Examples include abbreviations, improper capitalization, simplified spelling, or grammatically inconsistent phrases, making the messages appear realistic and spontaneous, and reducing skepticism.

4.2 Mobile Money Platforms used by Scammers

Our analysis revealed that scammers frequently exploit various MMT platforms to receive illicit funds. Among the most commonly used platforms are M-Pesa, E-mola, and Ponto-24. We observed a strong preference for the use of M-Pesa. This preference may be attributed to M-Pesa's status as one of the oldest and largest MMT platforms in the market, with a widespread user base and high transaction volumes. However, this trend also highlights a critical vulnerability within these platforms, as they appear to be susceptible to exploitation by criminals for this type of illicit activity. The lack of robust mechanisms to track and flag suspicious transactions on these platforms further exacerbates the problem.

Furthermore, our analysis revealed that the phone numbers used to receive fraudulent funds are typically unique and not reused in different smishing messages (see Figure 3). This suggests that scammers use a "one-time use" strategy for these numbers, likely to avoid detection and complicate efforts to trace the transactions. Interestingly, we identified a recurring pattern in the phone numbers used by these criminals. Specifically, the numbers often featured consecutive prefixes (see Figure 4), indicating that attackers may have access to a sequence of SIM cards purchased in bulk. This pattern implies a level of organization and resourcefulness among the scammers, as they appear to systematically acquire and deploy multiple SIM cards to facilitate their schemes.

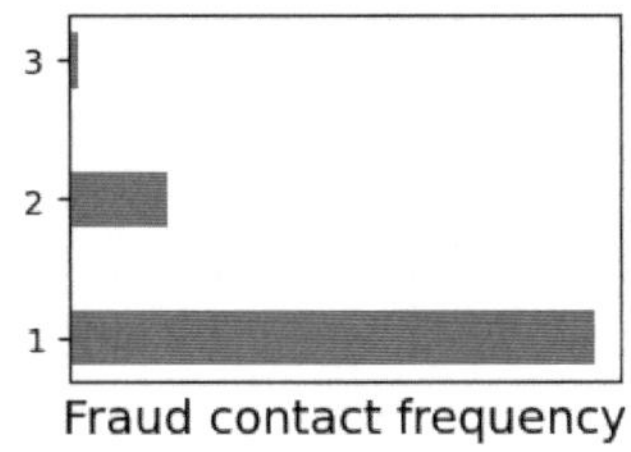

Figure 3: Phone number frequency on smishing messages

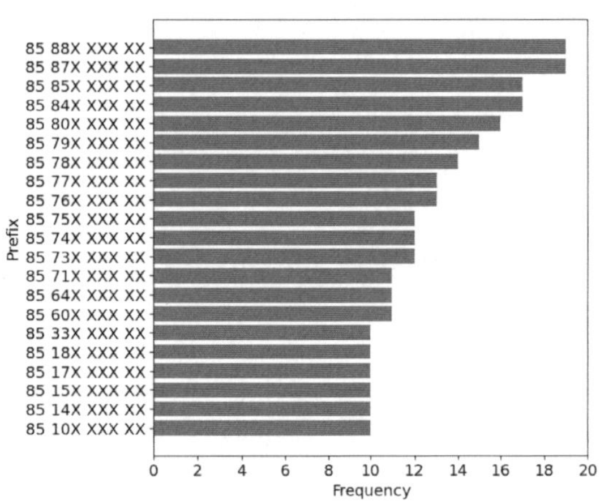

Figure 4: Top frequent four digits prefix

5 Experiments and Results

This section describes our experimental setup, presents the results from benchmarking various LLMs for smishing detection, and discusses the implications of these results in the context of mobile money transfer fraud detection. Specifically, we explore in-context learning capabilities across multiple LLMs using various few-shot prompting scenarios.

5.1 Experimental Setup

Using our newly constructed dataset, we conducted experiments to evaluate the effectiveness of state-of-the-art LLMs in detecting smishing messages. The selected models for our evaluation included *Dolly-v2-12B* (Conover et al., 2023), an open-source conversational model developed by Databricks; *Mistral-Small-24B* (Jiang et al., 2024), developed by Mistral AI; *Qwen2.5-14B*, a multilingual language model introduced by Alibaba (Yang et al., 2024); and *EuroLLM-9B*, an LLM specially optimized for multilingual European language tasks (Martins et al., 2025).

Each model was assessed using an in-context learning approach, in which carefully designed prompts incorporated balanced examples of legitimate and smishing messages. Furthermore, model performance was evaluated under multiple learning scenarios, including 0-shot and few-shot settings. To ensure consistency and reproducibility, all models received a standardized prompt (see Figure 5 and Figure 7), outlining the task and providing examples labeled as "*Legitimate*" or "*Smishing*".

Prompt Template

Below are examples of messages classified as Positive (indicating intent of smishing or phishing) or Negative (indicating no intent of smishing or phishing):

Input: "*Bom dia, o valor melhor mandar para este nr 858798603 Mpesa nome Israel Robate Charimba, o meu atingiu limite.*"
Output: Positive

Input: "*Irmã peço pra me mandar mil mt.*"
Output: Negative

...

Input: "*Ok Aquele Valor Manda Para Este Nr D M-pesa 846861650 E Nome D Essinate Jofres*"
Output:

Figure 5: Example of the few-shot prompt template

We measured the performance of each model using commonly adopted evaluation metrics in binary classification tasks, including the F1-score for each class (Smishing and Legitimate), and the Macro-F1 average across the classes to account for potential imbalances in class distribution.

All experiments were executed on 4 NVIDIA A10 GPU cards.

5.2 Experimental Results

The results of our experiments are presented in Table 2. Qwen2.5-14B notably achieved the highest overall performance among the evaluated mod-

#shot	F1	EuroLLM-9B pt	EuroLLM-9B en	dolly-v2-12b pt	dolly-v2-12b en	Qwen2.5-14B pt	Qwen2.5-14B en	Mistral-Small-24B pt	Mistral-Small-24B en
0-shot	Legitimate	0.69	0.59	0.45	0.48	**0.69**	**0.63**	0.51	0.51
	Smishing	0.43	0.41	0.3	0.28	**0.49**	**0.48**	0.45	0.45
	Macro	0.56	0.5	0.38	0.38	**0.59**	**0.55**	0.48	0.48
1-shot	Legitimate	0.0	0.54	0.2	0.51	**0.63**	0.56	0.54	**0.63**
	Smishing	0.33	0.42	0.33	0.32	**0.5**	0.47	0.46	**0.5**
	Macro	0.17	0.48	0.26	0.41	**0.56**	0.51	0.5	**0.56**
2-shot	Legitimate	0.4	0.34	0.15	0.59	**0.62**	0.6	0.58	**0.65**
	Smishing	0.4	0.41	0.37	0.39	**0.5**	0.49	0.48	**0.52**
	Macro	0.4	0.38	0.26	0.49	**0.56**	0.55	0.53	**0.58**
4-shot	Legitimate	0.22	0.52	0.08	0.65	**0.7**	**0.72**	0.62	0.69
	Smishing	0.36	0.46	0.36	0.42	**0.54**	**0.56**	0.5	0.54
	Macro	0.29	0.49	0.22	0.53	**0.62**	**0.64**	0.56	0.62
6-shot	Legitimate	0.32	0.56	0.05	0.64	**0.75**	**0.77**	0.68	0.74
	Smishing	0.38	0.47	0.36	0.42	**0.58**	**0.6**	0.53	0.57
	Macro	0.35	0.51	0.21	0.53	**0.67**	**0.68**	0.61	0.65
8-shot	Legitimate	0.32	0.62	0.03	0.71	**0.79**	**0.8**	0.72	0.78
	Smishing	0.38	0.5	0.36	0.46	**0.61**	**0.62**	0.55	0.6
	Macro	0.35	0.56	0.19	0.59	**0.7**	**0.71**	0.63	0.69
16-shot	Legitimate	0.67	0.8	0.08	0.87	**0.87**	**0.86**	0.78	0.83
	Smishing	0.5	0.62	0.36	0.53	**0.71**	**0.69**	0.6	0.65
	Macro	0.58	0.71	0.22	0.7	**0.79**	**0.78**	0.69	0.74

Table 2: Performance of the models different few-shot settings with Portuguese and English prompts, with the highest values shown in bold.

els, with F1-scores consistently higher in most scenarios, reaching a Macro F1-score of 0.79 in the 16-shot learning setting. Mistral-Small-24B and EuroLLM-9B also demonstrated improvements as the number of few-shot examples increased, though their absolute performance remained somewhat lower than Qwen2.5-14B across the scenarios tested.

The experimental results consistently show that adding task-specific examples boosts the model's detection performance. As the number of few-shot examples increased from 0-shot to 16-shot, most models improved their classification performance (see Figure 6), highlighting the crucial role that appropriate in-context learning can fill when applying general-purpose LLMs to specialized tasks.

Nevertheless, it was observed that models attained higher performance in classifying legitimate messages compared to smishing messages. This difference highlights an ongoing difficulty in using general-purpose LLMs to detect smishing. The models' weaker performance on smishing messages indicates they may have trouble picking up on the subtle hints, microtexts, or spelling that often characterize smishing messages. This finding opens the door to further exploration and refinement, possibly through focused fine-tuning and collection of more examples.

English versus Portuguese prompting As shown in Table 6, LLMs generally performed better when prompted in English, which is expected given their predominantly English training data. Nonetheless, some models, such as Qwen2.5 and Mistral, achieved results in Portuguese whose quality competes with those in English, reflecting the increasing multilingual capabilities of modern LLMs. English prompts also resulted in more stable and consistent improvements as the number of shots increased. In contrast, Portuguese prompts led to a decline in performance for models like Dolly, which exhibited notable fluctuations as the number of Portuguese shots increased. This contrast highlights Dolly's stronger alignment with English inputs.

6 Conclusion

In our study, we address an existing research gap in combating smishing attacks aimed at users of mobile money transfer platforms, specifically in a non-English context. To this end, we introduced a public, domain-specific, crowdsourced Portuguese language dataset designed explicitly for the task of detecting, and understanding smishing messages targeting mobile money users. Our exploratory data

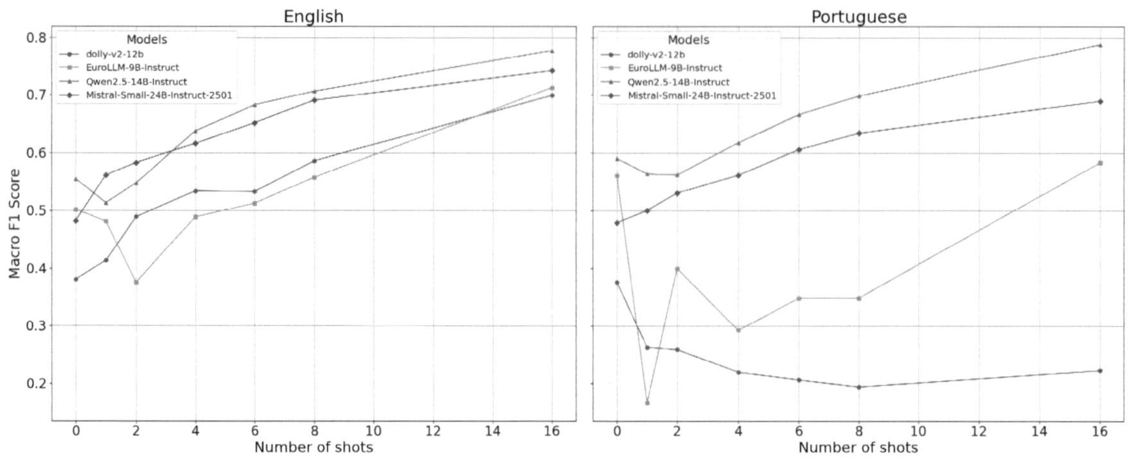

Figure 6: Macro F1 Scores for different models across few-Shot Settings

analysis revealed critical tactics and strategies employed by attackers, offering valuable insights that could facilitate the enhancement of user awareness campaigns and security tools.

Finally, our comprehensive experiments provided essential benchmarks evaluating how large language models perform through an in-context learning approach on this specific domain task. Our findings showed that models such as the multilingual Qwen2.5-14B demonstrated strong performance, particularly as more contextual examples were provided in the prompt scenarios.

Our research clearly underscores the potential of large language models to detect mobile money transfer fraud using careful task-oriented prompting strategies. However, the continued vulnerability of these platforms emphasizes a critical need for further training, fine-tuning domain-specific models, and improving general language AI capabilities to achieve greater sensitivity to linguistic nuances of text related to smudges.

Limitations

Despite the promising findings of this study, several critical limitations and constraints must be recognized:

Limited Computational Resources: The most significant limitation was the constrained computational capacity available through our hardware (4 NVIDIA A10 GPUs), which prevented us from experimenting with larger, state-of-the-art LLMs such as Llama-3.3-70B, Deepseek-R1-70B or Falcon. The inclusion of larger models may yield higher performances, but verifying this premise would require substantially larger computing resources than the ones at our disposal.

Lack of Temporal Dimension: Our dataset represents smishing messages collected within a specific time period and in the context of Mozambique. Thus, only static snapshot features of scams, which continually evolve, are captured. Further studies should capture longitudinal samples to track evolving fraud approaches and maintain effective detection.

Acknowledgments

This work was financially supported by UID/00027 - Artificial Intelligence and Computer Science Laboratory (LIACC), funded by Fundação para a Ciência e a Tecnologia (FCT), I.P./MCTES through national funds. Felermino Ali is supported by a PhD grant (with reference SFRH/BD/151435/2021), funded by FCT, as well as supported by the Base (UIDB/00022/2020) and Programmatic (UIDP/00022/2020) projects of the Centre for Linguistics of the University of Porto.

The authors thank everyone who contributed to the construction of the data set. Special thanks to Ekoko Clesh, Ednilson Sarmento, Clinton Uachave, Noémia Viegas, and all our colleagues and students at Lurio University, who have been actively conducting the data collection.

References

Tiago Almeida, José María Hidalgo, and Tiago Silva. 2013. Towards SMS spam filtering: Results under a new dataset.

Caner Balim and Efnan Sora Gunal. 2019. Automatic detection of smishing attacks by machine learning methods. In *2019 1st International Informatics and Software Engineering Conference (UBMYK)*, pages 1–3.

Tao Chen and Min-Yen Kan. 2012. Creating a live, public short message service corpus: the nus sms corpus. *Language Resources and Evaluation*.

Mike Conover, Matt Hayes, Ankit Mathur, Jianwei Xie, Jun Wan, Sam Shah, Ali Ghodsi, Patrick Wendell, Matei Zaharia, and Reynold Xin. 2023. Free dolly: Introducing the world's first truly open instruction-tuned llm.

Dea Delvia Arifin, Shaufiah, and Moch. Arif Bijaksana. 2016. Enhancing spam detection on mobile phone short message service (sms) performance using fp-growth and naive bayes classifier. In *2016 IEEE Asia Pacific Conference on Wireless and Mobile (APWiMob)*, pages 80–84.

Abdallah Ghourabi. 2021. Sm-detector: A security model based on bert to detect smishing messages in mobile environments. *Concurrency and Computation: Practice and Experience*, 33(24):e6452.

Abdallah Ghourabi, Mahmood A. Mahmood, and Qusay M. Alzubi. 2020. A hybrid cnn-lstm model for sms spam detection in arabic and english messages. *Future Internet*, 12(9).

GSMA. 2024a. Mobile money fraud typologies and mitigation strategies. Technical report, GSMA.

GSMA. 2024b. The state of the industry report on mobile money 2024. Technical report, GSMA.

INTERPOL. 2020. Mobile money and organized crime in africa. Technical report, INTERPOL.

Ankit Kumar Jain and B. B. Gupta. 2019. Feature based approach for detection of smishing messages in the mobile environment. *J. Inf. Technol. Res.*, 12(2):17–35.

Ankit Kumar Jain and B.B. Gupta. 2018. Rule-based framework for detection of smishing messages in mobile environment. *Procedia Computer Science*, 125:617–623. The 6th International Conference on Smart Computing and Communications.

Ankit Kumar Jain, Sumit Kumar Yadav, and Neelam Choudhary. 2020. A novel approach to detect spam and smishing sms using machine learning techniques. *Int. J. E-Services Mob. Appl.*, 12(1):21–38.

Albert Q Jiang, Alexandre Sablayrolles, Antoine Roux, Arthur Mensch, Blanche Savary, Chris Bamford, Devendra Singh Chaplot, Diego de las Casas, Emma Bou Hanna, Florian Bressand, et al. 2024. Mixtral of experts. *arXiv preprint arXiv:2401.04088*.

Iddi S. Mambina, Jema D. Ndibwile, and Kisangiri F. Michael. 2022. Classifying swahili smishing attacks for mobile money users: A machine-learning approach. *IEEE Access*, 10:83061–83074.

Pedro Henrique Martins, Patrick Fernandes, João Alves, Nuno M. Guerreiro, Ricardo Rei, Duarte M. Alves, José Pombal, Amin Farajian, Manuel Faysse, Mateusz Klimaszewski, Pierre Colombo, Barry Haddow, José G.C. de Souza, Alexandra Birch, and André F.T. Martins. 2025. Eurollm: Multilingual language models for europe. *Procedia Computer Science*, 255:53–62. Proceedings of the Second EuroHPC user day.

Leland McInnes, John Healy, and James Melville. 2020. Umap: Uniform manifold approximation and projection for dimension reduction. *Preprint*, arXiv:1802.03426.

Sandhya Mishra and Devpriya Soni. 2020. Smishing detector: A security model to detect smishing through sms content analysis and url behavior analysis. *Future Gener. Comput. Syst.*, 108:803–815.

Sandhya Mishra and Devpriya Soni. 2021. Dsmishsms-a system to detect smishing sms. *Neural computing & applications*, 108:1–18.

Pradeep Kumar Roy, Jyoti Prakash Singh, and Snehasish Banerjee. 2020. Deep learning to filter sms spam. *Future Generation Computer Systems*, 102:524–533.

Gunikhan Sonowal and K S Kuppusamy. 2018. SmiDCA: An Anti-Smishing Model with Machine Learning Approach. *The Computer Journal*, 61(8):1143–1157.

Daniel Timko and Muhammad Lutfor Rahman. 2024. Smishing dataset i: Phishing sms dataset from smishtank.com. In *Proceedings of the Fourteenth ACM Conference on Data and Application Security and Privacy*, CODASPY '24, page 289–294, New York, NY, USA. Association for Computing Machinery.

Kuldeep Yadav, Ponnurangam Kumaraguru, Atul Goyal, Ashish Gupta, and Vinayak Naik. 2011. Smsassassin: Crowdsourcing driven mobile-based system for sms spam filtering. In *Proceedings of the 12th Workshop on Mobile Computing Systems and Applications*, HotMobile '11, page 1–6, New York, NY, USA. Association for Computing Machinery.

An Yang, Baosong Yang, Beichen Zhang, Binyuan Hui, Bo Zheng, Bowen Yu, Chengyuan Li, Dayiheng Liu, Fei Huang, Haoran Wei, et al. 2024. Qwen2. 5 technical report. *arXiv preprint arXiv:2412.15115*.

A Portuguese Prompt

Portuguese Prompt

A seguir estão exemplos de mensagens classificadas como Positivas (indicando intenção de smishing ou phishing) ou Negativas (indicando ausência de intenção de smishing ou phishing):

Input: "Bom dia, o valor melhor mandar para este nr 858798603 Mpesa nome Israel Robate Charimba, o meu atingiu limite."
Output: Positiva

Input: "Irmã peço pra me mandar mil mt."
Output: Negativa

...
Input: "Ok Aquele Valor Manda Para Este Nr D M-pesa 846861650 E Nome D Essinate Jofres"
Output:

Figure 7: Portuguese prompt template

In-Domain African Languages Translation Using LLMs and Multi-armed Bandits

Pratik Rakesh Singh, Kritarth Prasad, Mohammadi Zaki and Pankaj Wasnik
Media Analysis Group, Sony Research India
{pratik.singh, kritarth.prasad, mohammadi.zaki, pankaj.wasnik}@sony.com

Abstract

Neural Machine Translation (NMT) systems face significant challenges when working with low-resource languages, particularly in domain adaptation tasks. These difficulties arise due to limited training data and suboptimal model generalization, As a result, selecting an optimal model for translation is crucial for achieving strong performance on in-domain data, particularly in scenarios where fine-tuning is not feasible or practical. In this paper, we investigate strategies for selecting the most suitable NMT model for a given domain using bandit-based algorithms, including Upper Confidence Bound, Linear UCB, Neural Linear Bandit, and Thompson Sampling. Our method effectively addresses the resource constraints by facilitating optimal model selection with high confidence. We evaluate the approach across three African languages and domains, demonstrating its robustness and effectiveness in both scenarios where target data is available and where it is absent.

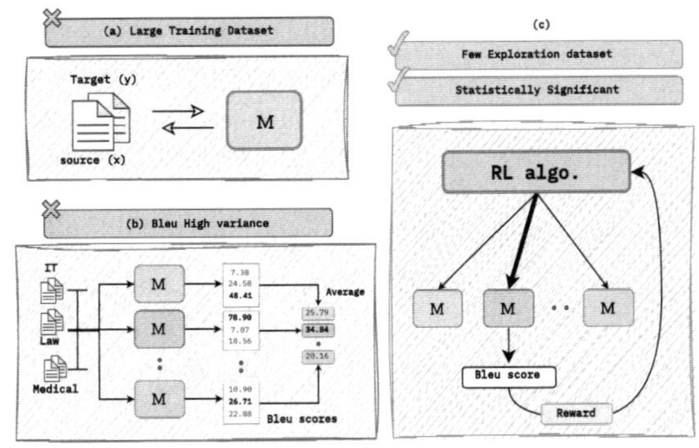

Figure 1: Motivation for Reinforcement Learning for model selection in machine translation: (a) Using a large dataset for training may be inefficient or impractical for low-resource settings, (b) BLEU scores vary significantly across domains, making model selection unreliable, (c) Reinforcement learning enables efficient model selection with fewer data and statistical significance.

1 Introduction

Advancements in multilingual machine translation models have significantly expanded language coverage, enabling translations even for low-resource languages. These models have also demonstrated strong performance in general domains, such as News, Movies, and more (Barrault et al., 2020) (Saunders, 2022a). Additionally, with the rise of large language models, methods like few-shot learning and in-context learning have shown notable improvements in domain adaptation tasks (Garcia et al., 2023) (Aycock and Bawden, 2024). Despite these advancements, the performance of these models remains highly dependent on the quality and scope of pre-training data as well as the model size, particularly for low-resource languages. It is common for a model to perform well in one domain but struggle in another, which presents a significant challenge in the selection of the most suitable NMT system for a given task.

A commonly used approach for domain adaptation in Neural Machine Translation (NMT) tasks is fine-tuning NMT models on in-domain data using various strategies (Chu and Wang, 2018). As shown in Figure 1 (a), this approach faces significant challenges, particularly in low-resource settings where in-domain data is scarce. Moreover, fine-tuning often leads to a degradation in performance on general-domain data due to the issue of catastrophic forgetting (Thompson et al., 2019), further complicating the task of maintaining robust model performance across different domains.

Selection-based approaches have gained significant attention in recent Neural Machine Translation (NMT) systems, where the task is to identify the best possible model from a given set. A widely adopted method for this is the use of a Selection Block (SB) (Salazar et al., 2020) (Liu and Liu, 2021), which reranks models based on the spe-

Proceedings of the Sixth Workshop on African Natural Language Processing (AfricaNLP 2025), pages 167–175
July 31, 2025 ©2025 Association for Computational Linguistics

cific task at hand. In recent years, reinforcement learning (RL)-based approaches have emerged as promising techniques for optimizing the selection of these models (Prasad et al., 2025). However, a limitation of many of these approaches is their reliance on large amounts of data to demonstrate performance gains over individual NMT systems.

One potential approach is to select the best model, which is trained on a general-domain dataset, and assume it will perform well on the in-domain dataset without the need for fine-tuning. Typically, one would evaluate models on the test dataset using common machine translation metrics, such as BLEU, to determine the best-performing model. However, in resource-constrained settings, these metrics can exhibit high variance, and there is often limited control over the statistical significance of the observed differences. This issue is illustrated in Figure 1 (b), where the mean of these metrics might provide a misleading impression of the best NMT system. In such cases, a few outlier examples could skew the BLEU score, leading to the wrong selection of the model. Moreover, a single evaluation does not capture the full variability in system performance, particularly when working with a small validation set. This underscores the need for model selection methods that not only choose the best NMT systems but also provide a statistical basis for the selection process, thereby mitigating the risks of misleading conclusions based on limited data.

To address the above challenges of model selection for Domain adaptation in resource-constrained settings, one possible approach could be to estimate the most optimal NMT system using fewer data samples, thereby reducing the reliance on large datasets. This can be achieved through the use of bandit-based algorithms (Zhou, 2016) (Bouneffouf et al., 2020), which allow for efficient exploration and exploitation of model performance, facilitating the identification of the best-performing system for the given domain with minimal data. As shown in Figure 1 (c), by leveraging these techniques, it is possible to make more informed decisions about model selection, even when In-domain data availability is limited, ensuring effective performance in low-resource scenarios. Our key contributions are summarized as follows:

- We propose a bandit-based approach to estimate optimal systems for a domain in a resource-constraint setting.
- We evaluate our approach on English to multiple African languages in multiple domains and report the performance of the popular bandit algorithms when applied to domain-specific model selection task.

2 Related works and Motivation

Domain Adaptation in Neural Machine Translation (NMT) refers to methods aimed at adjusting translation models trained on general-domain data to perform effectively in specific target domains with distinctive characteristics (Saunders, 2022b). Effective domain adaptation typically addresses data scarcity and domain mismatch (Pang et al., 2024) issues through data-centric and model-centric approaches. Data-centric strategies include back-translation using monolingual target data (Poncelas et al., 2019; Jin et al., 2020), forward-translation and self-learning (Chinea-Ríos et al., 2017), and synthetic data generation via noise introduction or lexicon-based methods (Vaibhav et al., 2019; Hu et al., 2019; Peng et al., 2020; Zhang et al., 2022). Model-centric approaches introduce domain-specific parameters or modules like domain tagging, embedding manipulation, adapter-based methods, and pointer-generators leveraging dictionaries (Kobus et al., 2017; Stergiadis et al., 2021; Pham et al., 2019; Bapna and Firat, 2019; Chen et al., 2021).

In low-resource scenarios, approaches such as data augmentation through bilingual lexicon-based replacements, transfer learning, and pretrained multilingual models have been employed (Nag et al., 2020; Liu et al., 2021). However, despite significant progress in both DA and low-resource NMT, domain adaptation techniques remain underexplored and challenging specifically for low-resource languages, where often the only available parallel data are very limited (Siddhant et al., 2022; Ranathunga et al., 2023).

Selection-Based Approach Recently, various selection methods have been introduced prior to the fusion step in multi-agent candidate selection. Significant research has focused on summarization tasks, including training reranking models based on evaluation metrics (Ravaut et al., 2023), employing contrastive learning for effective candidate ranking (Liu and Liu, 2021), and utilizing pairwise ranking methods to directly compare candidate summaries (Jiang et al., 2023). In the field of

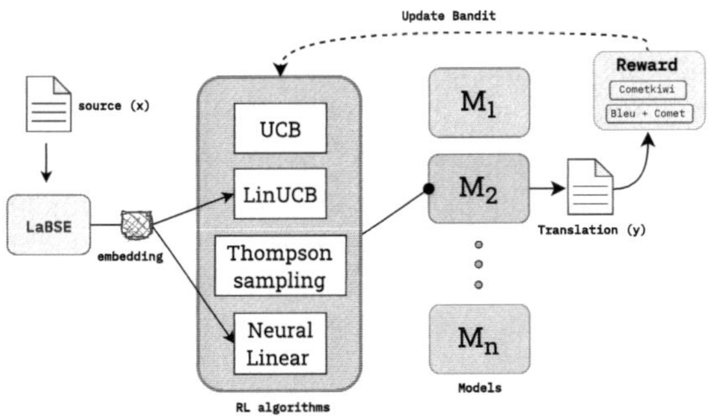

Figure 2: Block diagram of the proposed bandit-based model selection strategy.

neural machine translation (NMT), recent studies by (Prasad et al., 2025) have explored model selection strategies using a DQN-based approach. However, all these selection methods require substantial amounts of parallel data for effective training. Notably, limited research has investigated contextual bandit (Lu et al., 2010) approaches, which require significantly less data, to generalize agent selection based on provided context in low-resource machine translation scenarios.

Motivation for Bandit based approach A major challenge in Low-Resource Machine Translation (LRMT) is the scarcity of high-quality training datasets. This issue is further compounded in domain-specific translation, where the data becomes even more limited. While general-domain NMT systems exhibit reasonable performance across a broad range of tasks, their efficacy significantly fluctuates across different domains and languages. To mitigate this variability and identify the most effective NMT model for a given task with limited data, an optimal selection strategy is essential. This strategy must not only consider the available training data but also provide statistically-backed confidence in the model's selection.

Bandit-based approaches have been widely explored in recommendation systems, where recommendations are generated based on past interactions with users (Silva et al., 2022). This methodology is well-suited for selecting optimal NMT systems in scenarios where only a small in-domain dataset is available, utilizing an appropriate reward function for NMT performance (Boursier and Perchet, 2024) (Nguyen et al., 2017). Furthermore, reference-less reward mechanisms offer a promising avenue for applying these bandit-based methods in target-free domain-specific machine translation tasks, as demonstrated by recent works (Obuchowski et al., 2024).

3 Methodology

As previously discussed, selecting the best model from a pool by evaluating a subset of data and then applying it to the entire test set is both computationally expensive and unreliable. Determining the necessary sample size to ensure the optimality of the chosen model becomes extremely important in such cases. Hence we take a more principled way to dynamically choose the machine translation model on-the-fly by treating the model selection process as a multi-armed bandit problem. We explore popular bandit algorithms designed for regret minimization, which, under mild theoretical assumptions, are proven to achieve (near-)optimal cumulative rewards over time. Below, we provide a brief overview of our methodology, as illustrated in Figure 2.

Each source sentence x is passed through a Language-agnostic BERT Sentence Encoder (LaBSE) to obtain a feature vector which we denote by overloading $x \in \mathbb{R}^d$. This vector x acts as the context vector in the contextual bandit algorithms considered in this work. The MT system pool act as the arms $\{M_1, M_2, \ldots, M_n\}$ in our multi-armed bandit setup. Once the arm is chosen by the MAB algorithm, the corresponding MT system is chosen to translate the source sentence x to obtain y in the target language. Next, a reward is generated depending on x, y and whether a reference gold translation is available (see the next section for detail on 'reward') to obtain a scalar r.

Next, we provide a brief explanation of the arm selection strategy and update rules for each of the bandit algorithms we explore.

Upper Confidence Bound (UCB): UCB (Auer et al., 2002) relies on the principle of Optimism in the Face of Uncertainty (OFU). It selects the arm that maximizes an 'upper confidence bound' of its estimated reward.

Select arm:

$$a_t := \underset{a \in \{M_1, M_2, \ldots, M_n\}}{\arg\max} \left(\hat{\mu}_a(t) + \alpha \sqrt{\frac{\log t}{N_a(t)}} \right)$$

Update empirical means of all arms.

where $\hat{\mu}_a(t)$ is the empirical reward obtained from pulling arm a till round t, $N_a(t)$ is the number of times arm a is pulled till round t, and α is a confidence parameter.

Thompson Sampling (TS): Thompson Sampling (Thompson, 1933) is a Bayesian approach where we maintain a posterior distribution over each arm's expected reward and sample from it. In particular, in our case we maintain a Beta distribution over each arm's reward which has two parameters α, β which are initially set to 0. The arm selection and parameter update rules are as follows:

Select arm:

$$a_t := \arg\max_{a \in \{M_1, M_2, \ldots, M_n\}} \quad \theta_a \sim P(\cdot|\alpha_a, \beta_a)$$

Update:

$$\alpha_a \leftarrow \alpha_a + r, \beta_a \leftarrow \beta_a + 1 - r$$

Linear UCB (LinUCB): LinUCB (Li et al., 2010; Abbasi-yadkori et al., 2011) extends UCB to contextual bandits, assuming that rewards follow a linear function of the context/feature vector $x_t \in \mathbb{R}^d$ as explained before . In particular, we make the following assumption on the reward function that $\forall t \geq 1$, $r := x^T\theta_a + noise$ for all arms a.

Select arm:

$$a_t := \arg\max_{a \in \{M_1, M_2, \ldots, M_n\}} \left(x_t^T \hat{\theta}_a + \alpha\sqrt{x_t^T A_a^{-1} x_t} \right)$$

where, $A_a := \sum_{s=1}^{t} \mathbb{1}\{a_s == a\} x_s x_s^T$, $b_a := \sum_{s=1}^{t} \mathbb{1}\{a_s == a\} r_s x_s$ and $\hat{\theta}_a := A_a^{-1} b_a$ is the Least Squares estimate of the true parameter θ_a of arm a.

Neural LinUCB (NL): Neural LinUCB (Xu et al., 2020) is a deep-learning extension of LinUCB, replacing the linear model with a neural network that maps features to a latent representation before applying LinUCB. In particular we replace the context vector x by a neural network $f(x : w)$ parameterized by w. The arm selection strategy and the update rule remain the same as in LinUCB with x replaced with $f(x; w)$.

Rewards: The rewards serve as the primary signal in bandit-based settings, guiding both the learning process and decision-making of the algorithms. The main objective in a Multi-Armed Bandit (MAB) problem is to maximize rewards by balancing exploration and exploitation.

In Neural Machine Translation (NMT), model performance is typically evaluated using standard metrics such as BLEU and COMET. These metrics are particularly crucial for assessing how well a model translates within a specific domain. BLEU measures how accurately the model translates domain-specific vocabulary, while COMET evaluates the semantic similarity of the model's output to the reference translation within the given domain. Using these metrics, we consider two types of reward signals as follows:

- **When parallel data is present:** When we have source along with the reference (gold) translation, we consider a combination of BLEU (Post, 2018) and a reference-based comet as shown below. Note that both the BLEU and comet scores have been normalized to lie between [0,1].

  $$\text{Reward} = \lambda \cdot \text{BLEU} + (1 - \lambda) \cdot \text{COMET}.$$

  Here λ is a hyperparameter in [0,1]. In our experiments, we find that $\lambda = 0.4$ achieves the best results in our case.

- **Target-free scenario:** When only the source sentence is present, and the target is absent, which is typically the case in low-resource languages, especially in domain translation task, we use a reference-less MT metric like CometKiwi (Rei, 2022) (normalized between [0,1]), as the reward signal.

The λ is a controllability parameter that enables us to control the influence of metrics on reward, and reward_norm is the normalization value to normalize the metrics.

4 Experimental Setup

Datasets and Evaluation metrics: For our experiments, we utilize parallel datasets for English-to-African language translation, focusing on three African languages: English-to-Yoruba (en-yo), English-to-Swahili (en-sw) and English-to-Igbo (en-ig). We sample 1,000 parallel samples for validation (seed data for model convergence) and testing each. The datasets span three domains: News, Movies, and Religious texts.

- News Domain: We use the Lafand-MT dataset (Adelani *et al.*, 2022), which contains parallel data for English-to-16 African languages, gathered from various news corpora.

Datasets	News Igbo	News Yoruba	News Swahili	Movies Igbo	Movies Yoruba	Movies Swahili	Religious Igbo	Religious Yoruba	Religious Swahili
Aya101	12.98	5.20	23.53	7.48	3.847	23.98	19.03	11.53	5.04
Gemma2 9B	8.17	3.55	24.24	5.21	1.97	25.07	9.48	2.12	3.9
Llama 3.1 8B	4.59	3.28	17.24	2.85	1.09	10.90	6.79	3.43	2.25
Madlad	6.91	1.11	8.92	7.087	1.19	24.47	3.19	1.36	32.36
NLLB	19.73	9.67	27.57	9.60	12.90	**30.78**	34.72	14.96	28.01
UCB	**19.83**	9.539	**28.275**	9.6	12.90	**30.78**	34.72	14.96	32.36
TS	19.48	**9.74**	26.95	9.36	12.88	27.29	34.34	14.34	**32.54**
LinUCB	19.73	9.54	27.80	**9.80**	12.90	29.9	**34.8**	13.7	32.45
NL	19.74	9.67	27.57	9.24	**13.12**	24.37	34.72	**15.67**	32.39

Table 1: Performance on BLEU metrics when Parallel data is present.

Datasets	News Igbo	News Yoruba	News Swahili	Movies Igbo	Movies Yoruba	Movies Swahili	Religious Igbo	Religious Yoruba	Religious Swahili
Aya101	12.98	5.20	23.53	7.48	3.847	23.98	19.03	11.53	5.04
Gemma2 9B	8.17	3.55	24.24	5.21	1.97	25.07	9.48	2.12	3.9
Llama 3.1 8B	4.59	3.28	17.24	2.85	1.09	10.90	6.79	3.43	2.25
Madlad	6.91	1.11	8.92	7.087	1.19	24.47	3.19	1.36	32.36
NLLB	19.73	9.67	27.57	**9.60**	**12.90**	**30.78**	**34.72**	**14.96**	28.01
UCB	**19.83**	9.53	**28.27**	7.48	**12.90**	**30.78**	**34.72**	**14.96**	28.01
TS	19.48	**9.74**	26.95	9.33	12.89	27.95	34.34	14.34	32.54
LinUCB	18.5	9.67	27.5	8.9	**12.90**	29.7	34.54	11.51	**32.67**
NL	19.73	9.67	27.57	7.48	**12.90**	23.98	**34.72**	11.53	32.36

Table 2: Performance on BLEU metrics in Target-Free scenario

- Movies Domain: We leverage the OpenSubtitles dataset (Lison and Tiedemann, 2016), which includes parallel translations of dialogues from various movies and TV shows. This domain is essential for capturing informal language usage and conversational nuances in translations.
- Religious Texts Domain: We compile a dataset from various sources, including CCAligned (El-Kishky et al., 2020) and Tanzil (available at `https://tanzil.net/`), which contains Quran translations in multiple languages. This domain is particularly valuable for translating formal, religious content.

To assess the performance of the models, we rely on BLEU (Papineni et al., 2002), a widely accepted metric in machine translation. BLEU effectively measures the degree of overlap between the model-generated translations and reference translations, capturing the adequacy of domain-specific vocabulary translation, which is specifically effective for In-Domain Translations

Models: We test the effectiveness of our approach by using baselines, which also act as arms for bandits. The models used are a Mixture of LLMs and Foundational models like Aya101 (Üstün et al., 2024), NLLB200 3.3B (NLLB) (Team, 2022), Madlad400 10B (Madlad) (Kudugunta et al., 2023), Gemma2 9B (*et al.*, 2024b) and Llama3.1 8B (*et al.*, 2024a) all the model used for experiments are in its based or pre-trained state.

Choice of Hyper-parameters: For evaluation of our proposed bandit-based strategies, we use four popular arm-selection bandit algorithms that are UCB, LinUCB, Neural Bandit, Thompson Sampling as discussed in detail in Sec. 3. The values of the hyper-parameters specific to each bandit strategy are given in Table 3. The selection of Hyper-parameters was done based on hit and trail method, where initial few sentences of validations were used for convergence of algorithm and the algorithm was tested on rest of the remaining sentences.

Algorithm	Parameter	Value
UCB	λ	[0.4-0.6]
Thompson Sampling	Prior Distribution	Beta(0,0)
LinUCB	α λ	1.5 0.4
Neural LinUCB	Arm model network	2 layer MLP with 50 neurons each

Table 3: Values of hyper-parameters used in our experiments.

5 Results

When parallel data is present: The hyper-parameters are tuned on the validation set and freezed for all the algorithms. The Bandit-based models explored the reward that is a weighted summation of BLEU and reference-based Comet on the exploration set (Section 3 Rewards), the performance is evaluated using 1000 test samples per domain and language. As shown in Table 1, most of the Bandit-based approaches, when selecting the optimal arm, either perform on par with or surpass the best possible NMT model, demonstrating the effectiveness of our proposed method. On average, UCB (Upper Confidence

Bound) achieves superior performance across all languages and domains, outperforming the best model, NLLB, by an average improvement of 2.68% in BLEU score. Additionally, in specific cases—such as Neural Linear Bandit (NL) in the Movies domain for Yoruba, UCB in the News domain for Igbo and Swahili, and Thompson Sampling (TS) in the News domain for Yoruba, Religious, and Swahili the Bandit-based algorithms surpass the performance of the best possible NMT model. This suggests that these algorithms can occasionally select alternative NMT systems, resulting in slight but notable improvements in translation quality. In summary, the results indicate that Bandit-based approaches can effectively identify the best-performing NMT models, even with very small training sets, highlighting the robustness and utility of our proposed training strategy.

Results on Target-free Scenario: In this experiment, we explore the scenario where target translations for the in-domain dataset are unavailable, a common challenge in low-resource language settings. Such cases can be addressed using reference-less rewards (Section 3 Rewards), specifically leveraging CometKiwi-based metrics for NMT evaluation. The exploration of the Bandit-based models follows the same setup as discussed previously, with testing performed on 1000 samples. As shown in Table 2, the Bandit-based approaches successfully identify the best arms for translations even in the absence of target translations for reward generation. Among the various Bandit algorithms, UCB performs the best, followed by LinUCB and NL. Notably, in some instances, the Bandit-based selection slightly outperforms the individual best models, underscoring the flexibility of our approach. This demonstrates that our method can effectively be applied to model selection in target-free domain translation task where reference translations are not available.

6 Conclusion

In this paper, we presented a bandit-based approach for selecting the most suitable NMT model for domain adaptation, particularly in low-resource settings. Our method effectively balances exploration and exploitation by leveraging strategies such as Upper Confidence Bound, Linear UCB, Neural Linear Bandit, and Thompson Sampling, enabling optimal model selection with high confidence. Experimental results across multiple African languages and domains confirm the robustness of our approach, demonstrating its effectiveness both in the presence and absence of target domain data. Our findings highlight the potential of bandit-based methods to improve NMT performance in resource-constrained environments, paving the way for a more efficient and adaptive model selection process.

References

Yasin Abbasi-yadkori, Dávid Pál, and Csaba Szepesvári. 2011. Improved algorithms for linear stochastic bandits. In *Advances in Neural Information Processing Systems*, volume 24. Curran Associates, Inc.

David Adelani *et al.* 2022. A few thousand translations go a long way! leveraging pre-trained models for African news translation. In *Proceedings of the 2022 Conference of the North American Chapter of the Association for Computational Linguistics: Human Language Technologies*, pages 3053–3070, Seattle, United States. Association for Computational Linguistics.

Peter Auer, Nicolò Cesa-Bianchi, and Paul Fischer. 2002. Finite-time analysis of the multiarmed bandit problem. *Machine Learning*, 47(2):235–256.

Seth Aycock and Rachel Bawden. 2024. Topic-guided example selection for domain adaptation in LLM-based machine translation. In *Proceedings of the 18th Conference of the European Chapter of the Association for Computational Linguistics: Student Research Workshop*, pages 175–195, St. Julian's, Malta. Association for Computational Linguistics.

Ankur Bapna and Orhan Firat. 2019. Simple, scalable adaptation for neural machine translation. In *Proceedings of the 2019 Conference on Empirical Methods in Natural Language Processing and the 9th International Joint Conference on Natural Language Processing (EMNLP-IJCNLP)*, pages 1538–1548, Hong Kong, China. Association for Computational Linguistics.

Loïc Barrault, Magdalena Biesialska, Marta R. Costa-jussà, Fethi Bougares, and Olivier Galibert. 2020. Findings of the first shared task on lifelong learning machine translation. In *Proceedings of the Fifth Conference on Machine Translation*, pages 56–64, Online. Association for Computational Linguistics.

Djallel Bouneffouf, Irina Rish, and Charu Aggarwal. 2020. Survey on applications of multi-armed and contextual bandits. In *2020 IEEE Congress on Evolutionary Computation (CEC)*, pages 1–8.

Etienne Boursier and Vianney Perchet. 2024. A survey on multi-player bandits. *Preprint*, arXiv:2211.16275.

Guanhua Chen, Yun Chen, Yong Wang, and Victor O. K. Li. 2021. Lexical-constraint-aware neural machine translation via data augmentation. In *Proceedings of the Twenty-Ninth International Joint Conference on Artificial Intelligence*, IJCAI'20.

Mara Chinea-Ríos, Álvaro Peris, and Francisco Casacuberta. 2017. Adapting neural machine translation with parallel synthetic data. In *Proceedings of the Second Conference on Machine Translation*, pages 138–147, Copenhagen, Denmark. Association for Computational Linguistics.

Chenhui Chu and Rui Wang. 2018. A survey of domain adaptation for neural machine translation. In *Proceedings of the 27th International Conference on Computational Linguistics*, pages 1304–1319, Santa Fe, New Mexico, USA. Association for Computational Linguistics.

Ahmed El-Kishky, Vishrav Chaudhary, Francisco Guzman, and Philipp Koehn. 2020. Ccaligned: A massive collection of cross-lingual web-document pairs. *Preprint*, arXiv:1911.06154.

Xavier Garcia, Yamini Bansal, Colin Cherry, George Foster, Maxim Krikun, Fangxiaoyu Feng, Melvin Johnson, and Orhan Firat. 2023. The unreasonable effectiveness of few-shot learning for machine translation. *Preprint*, arXiv:2302.01398.

Junjie Hu, Mengzhou Xia, Graham Neubig, and Jaime Carbonell. 2019. Domain adaptation of neural machine translation by lexicon induction. In *Proceedings of the 57th Annual Meeting of the Association for Computational Linguistics*, pages 2989–3001, Florence, Italy. Association for Computational Linguistics.

Dongfu Jiang, Xiang Ren, and Bill Yuchen Lin. 2023. LLM-blender: Ensembling large language models with pairwise ranking and generative fusion. In *Proceedings of the 61st Annual Meeting of the Association for Computational Linguistics (Volume 1: Long Papers)*, pages 14165–14178, Toronto, Canada. Association for Computational Linguistics.

Di Jin, Zhijing Jin, Joey Tianyi Zhou, and Peter Szolovits. 2020. A simple baseline to semi-supervised domain adaptation for machine translation. *Preprint*, arXiv:2001.08140.

Catherine Kobus, Josep Crego, and Jean Senellart. 2017. Domain control for neural machine translation. *Preprint*, arXiv:1612.06140.

Sneha Kudugunta, Isaac Caswell, Biao Zhang, Xavier Garcia, Christopher A. Choquette-Choo, Katherine Lee, Derrick Xin, Aditya Kusupati, Romi Stella, Ankur Bapna, and Orhan Firat. 2023. Madlad-400: A multilingual and document-level large audited dataset. *Preprint*, arXiv:2309.04662.

Lihong Li, Wei Chu, John Langford, and Robert E. Schapire. 2010. A contextual-bandit approach to personalized news article recommendation. In *Proceedings of the 19th International Conference on World Wide Web*, WWW '10, page 661–670, New York, NY, USA. Association for Computing Machinery.

Pierre Lison and Jörg Tiedemann. 2016. OpenSubtitles2016: Extracting large parallel corpora from movie and TV subtitles. In *Proceedings of the Tenth International Conference on Language Resources and Evaluation (LREC'16)*, pages 923–929, Portorož, Slovenia. European Language Resources Association (ELRA).

Yixin Liu and Pengfei Liu. 2021. SimCLS: A simple framework for contrastive learning of abstractive summarization. In *Proceedings of the 59th Annual Meeting of the Association for Computational Linguistics and the 11th International Joint Conference on Natural Language Processing (Volume 2: Short Papers)*, pages 1065–1072, Online. Association for Computational Linguistics.

Zihan Liu, Genta Indra Winata, and Pascale Fung. 2021. Continual mixed-language pre-training for extremely low-resource neural machine translation. In *Findings of the Association for Computational Linguistics: ACL-IJCNLP 2021*, pages 2706–2718, Online. Association for Computational Linguistics.

Tyler Lu, David Pal, and Martin Pal. 2010. Contextual multi-armed bandits. In *Proceedings of the Thirteenth International Conference on Artificial Intelligence and Statistics*, volume 9 of *Proceedings of Machine Learning Research*, pages 485–492, Chia Laguna Resort, Sardinia, Italy. PMLR.

Sreyashi Nag, Mihir Kale, Varun Lakshminarasimhan, and Swapnil Singhavi. 2020. Incorporating bilingual dictionaries for low resource semi-supervised neural machine translation. *Preprint*, arXiv:2004.02071.

Khanh Nguyen, Hal Daumé III, and Jordan Boyd-Graber. 2017. Reinforcement learning for bandit neural machine translation with simulated human feedback. *Preprint*, arXiv:1707.07402.

Aleksander Obuchowski, Barbara Klaudel, Piotr Frąckowski, Sebastian Krajna, Wasyl Badyra, Michał Czubenko, and Zdzisław Kowalczuk. 2024. Target-free domain adaptation through cross-adaptation (student abstract). *Proceedings of the AAAI Conference on Artificial Intelligence*, 38(21):23602–23603.

Jianhui Pang, Fanghua Ye, Longyue Wang, Dian Yu, Derek F. Wong, Shuming Shi, and Zhaopeng Tu. 2024. Salute the classic: Revisiting challenges of machine translation in the age of large language models. *Preprint*, arXiv:2401.08350.

Kishore Papineni, Salim Roukos, Todd Ward, and Wei-Jing Zhu. 2002. Bleu: a method for automatic evaluation of machine translation. In *Proceedings of the 40th Annual Meeting on Association for Computational Linguistics*, ACL '02, page 311–318, USA. Association for Computational Linguistics.

Wei Peng, Chongxuan Huang, Tianhao Li, Yun Chen, and Qun Liu. 2020. Dictionary-based data augmentation for cross-domain neural machine translation. *Preprint*, arXiv:2004.02577.

MinhQuang Pham, Josep Crego, François Yvon, and Jean Senellart. 2019. Generic and specialized word embeddings for multi-domain machine translation. In *Proceedings of the 16th International Conference on Spoken Language Translation*, Hong Kong. Association for Computational Linguistics.

Alberto Poncelas, Gideon Maillette de Buy Wenniger, and Andy Way. 2019. Adaptation of machine translation models with back-translated data using transductive data selection methods. *Preprint*, arXiv:1906.07808.

Matt Post. 2018. A call for clarity in reporting BLEU scores. In *Proceedings of the Third Conference on Machine Translation: Research Papers*, pages 186–191, Brussels, Belgium. Association for Computational Linguistics.

Kritarth Prasad, Mohammadi Zaki, Pratik Singh, and Pankaj Wasnik. 2025. Faster machine translation ensembling with reinforcement learning and competitive correction. *Preprint*, arXiv:2501.15219.

Surangika Ranathunga, En-Shiun Annie Lee, Marjana Prifti Skenduli, Ravi Shekhar, Mehreen Alam, and Rishemjit Kaur. 2023. Neural machine translation for low-resource languages: A survey. *ACM Comput. Surv.*, 55(11).

Mathieu Ravaut, Shafiq Joty, and Nancy F. Chen. 2023. Summareranker: A multi-task mixture-of-experts re-ranking framework for abstractive summarization. *Preprint*, arXiv:2203.06569.

Ricardo *et al.* Rei. 2022. CometKiwi: IST-unbabel 2022 submission for the quality estimation shared task. In *Proceedings of the Seventh Conference on Machine Translation (WMT)*, pages 634–645, Abu Dhabi, United Arab Emirates (Hybrid). Association for Computational Linguistics.

Julian Salazar, Davis Liang, Toan Q. Nguyen, and Katrin Kirchhoff. 2020. Masked language model scoring. In *Proceedings of the 58th Annual Meeting of the Association for Computational Linguistics*, pages 2699–2712, Online. Association for Computational Linguistics.

Danielle Saunders. 2022a. Domain adaptation and multi-domain adaptation for neural machine translation: A survey. *Preprint*, arXiv:2104.06951.

Danielle Saunders. 2022b. Domain adaptation and multi-domain adaptation for neural machine translation: A survey. *Preprint*, arXiv:2104.06951.

Aditya Siddhant, Ankur Bapna, Orhan Firat, Yuan Cao, Mia Xu Chen, Isaac Caswell, and Xavier Garcia. 2022. Towards the next 1000 languages in multilingual machine translation: Exploring the synergy between supervised and self-supervised learning. *Preprint*, arXiv:2201.03110.

Nícollas Silva, Heitor Werneck, Thiago Silva, Adriano C.M. Pereira, and Leonardo Rocha. 2022. Multi-armed bandits in recommendation systems: A survey of the state-of-the-art and future directions. *Expert Systems with Applications*, 197:116669.

Emmanouil Stergiadis, Satendra Kumar, Fedor Kovalev, and Pavel Levin. 2021. Multi-domain adaptation in neural machine translation through multidimensional tagging. In *Proceedings of Machine Translation Summit XVIII: Users and Providers Track*, pages 396–420, Virtual. Association for Machine Translation in the Americas.

NLLB Team. 2022. No language left behind: Scaling human-centered machine translation. *Preprint*, arXiv:2207.04672.

Aaron Grattafiori *et al.* 2024a. The llama 3 herd of models. *Preprint*, arXiv:2407.21783.

Gemma Team *et al.* 2024b. Gemma 2: Improving open language models at a practical size. *Preprint*, arXiv:2408.00118.

Brian Thompson, Jeremy Gwinnup, Huda Khayrallah, Kevin Duh, and Philipp Koehn. 2019. Overcoming catastrophic forgetting during domain adaptation of neural machine translation. In *Proceedings of the 2019 Conference of the North American Chapter of the Association for Computational Linguistics: Human Language Technologies, Volume 1 (Long and Short Papers)*, pages 2062–2068, Minneapolis, Minnesota. Association for Computational Linguistics.

William R Thompson. 1933. On the likelihood that one unknown probability exceeds another in view of the evidence of two samples. *Biometrika*, 25(3-4):285–294.

Vaibhav Vaibhav, Sumeet Singh, Craig Stewart, and Graham Neubig. 2019. Improving robustness of machine translation with synthetic noise. In *Proceedings of the 2019 Conference of the North American Chapter of the Association for Computational Linguistics: Human Language Technologies, Volume 1 (Long and Short Papers)*, pages 1916–1920, Minneapolis, Minnesota. Association for Computational Linguistics.

Pan Xu, Zheng Wen, Handong Zhao, and Quanquan Gu. 2020. Neural contextual bandits with deep representation and shallow exploration. *CoRR*, abs/2012.01780.

Hongxiao Zhang, Hui Huang, Jiale Gao, Yufeng Chen, Jinan Xu, and Jian Liu. 2022. Iterative constrained back-translation for unsupervised domain adaptation of machine translation. In *Proceedings of the 29th International Conference on Computational Linguistics*, pages 5054–5065, Gyeongju, Republic of Korea. International Committee on Computational Linguistics.

Li Zhou. 2016. A survey on contextual multi-armed bandits. *Preprint*, arXiv:1508.03326.

Ahmet Üstün, Viraat Aryabumi, Zheng-Xin Yong, Wei-Yin Ko, Daniel D'souza, Gbemileke Onilude, Neel Bhandari, Shivalika Singh, Hui-Lee Ooi, Amr Kayid, Freddie Vargus, Phil Blunsom, Shayne Longpre, Niklas Muennighoff, Marzieh Fadaee, Julia Kreutzer, and Sara Hooker. 2024. Aya model: An instruction finetuned open-access multilingual language model. *Preprint*, arXiv:2402.07827.

HausaNLP: Current Status, Challenges and Future Directions for Hausa Natural Language Processing

Shamsuddeen Hassan Muhammad[1,5,6], **Ibrahim Said Ahmad**[2,5,6], **Idris Abdulmumin**[3,5], **Falalu Ibrahim Lawan**[4,5], **Sukairaj Hafiz Imam**[5,6], **Yusuf Aliyu**[7], **Sani Abdullahi Sani**[8], **Ali Usman Umar**[9], **Tajuddeen Gwadabe**[5], **Kenneth Church**[2], **Vukosi Marivate**[3]

[1]Imperial College London, [2]Northeastern University, [3]Data Science for Social Impact, University of Pretoria, [4]Kaduna State University, [5]HausaNLP, [6]Bayero University, Kano, [7]Universiti Teknologi PETRONAS, [8]University of the Witwatersrand, Johannesburg, [9]Federal University of Lafia

correspondence: s.muhammad@imperial.ac.uk

Abstract

Hausa Natural Language Processing (NLP) has gained increasing attention in recent years, yet remains understudied as a low-resource language despite having over 120 million first-language (L1) and 80 million second-language (L2) speakers worldwide. While significant advances have been made in high-resource languages, Hausa NLP faces persistent challenges including limited open-source datasets and inadequate model representation. This paper presents an overview of the current state of Hausa NLP, systematically examining existing resources, research contributions, and gaps across fundamental NLP tasks: text classification, machine translation, named entity recognition, speech recognition, and question answering. We introduce HAUSANLP[1], a curated catalog that aggregates datasets, tools, and research works to enhance accessibility and drive further development. Furthermore, we discuss challenges in integrating Hausa into large language models (LLMs), addressing issues of suboptimal tokenization, and dialectal variation. Finally, we propose strategic research directions emphasizing dataset expansion, improved language modeling approaches, and strengthened community collaboration to advance Hausa NLP. Our work provides both a foundation for accelerating Hausa NLP progress and valuable insights for broader multilingual NLP research.

1 Introduction

The limits of my language mean the limits of my world. – (Wittgenstein, 1994)

Natural Language Processing (NLP) has made significant progress and revolutionized the way language technology is used in our daily lives. From voice assistants and chatbots to machine translations, text classification, information extraction, and question-answering, NLP enables us to interact with machines in a more natural way (Cambria and White, 2014). One of the recent advances in NLP is emergence of large language models (LLMs) such as ChatGPT, which demonstrated impressive performance in various NLP tasks, such as dialogue generation and arithmetic reasoning (Qin et al., 2023). However, much of this progress has been concentrated on a limited set of high-resource languages (e.g., English and Chinese), where large-scale pre-training corpora are readily available (van Esch et al., 2022). As a result, many languages remain underrepresented in NLP research, including Hausa.

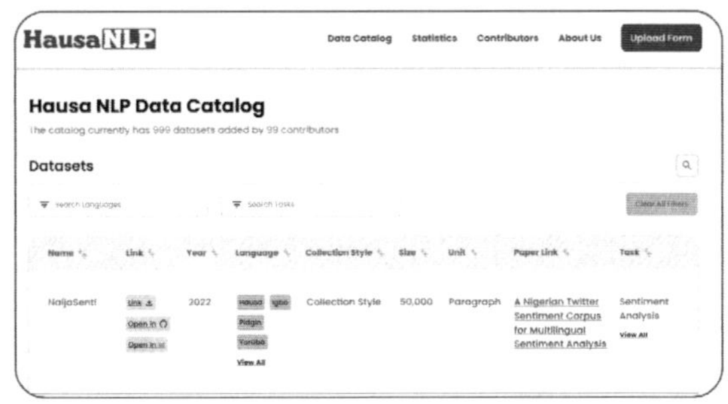

Figure 1: **HausaNLP Catalogue:** A repository of datasets, tools, and research papers on Hausa NLP, developed to improve access to and discovery of Hausa language resources

Hausa is a major Chadic language with rich linguistic and cultural significance within the Afroasiatic family. Originally written in Arabic script (Ajami) during the pre-colonial era, the language has been romanized and now uses the Latin script as its primary writing system. Yet, Arabic influence remains evident in Hausa through loanwords from Arabic (El-Shazly, 1987; Newman, 2022). Most Hausa speakers are found in northern Nigeria and southern Niger. However, its influence has expanded through trade and migration, reaching countries such as Cameroon, Ghana, Benin, Togo, Chad, and Sudan (Inuwa-Dutse, 2023). Hausa has a global presence and is broadcast by several interna-

[1]https://catalog.hausanlp.org

Proceedings of the Sixth Workshop on African Natural Language Processing (AfricaNLP 2025), pages 176–191
July 31, 2025

tional media outlets such as BBC, Deutsche Welle, Voice of America, Voice of Russia, China Radio International, and Radio France Internationale in Hausa —*the most predominant language broadcast internationally in West Africa*.

Despite its importance, diversity, and cultural heritage, Hausa has received relatively little attention in NLP research (Zakari et al., 2021; Muhammad et al., 2025c; Parida et al., 2023). This slows progress in language technology research and development in Hausa and further widens the gap. Recent work on HausaNLP is mostly community-driven efforts such as machine translation (Adelani et al., 2022a; Abdulmumin et al., 2022b), sentiment analysis (Muhammad et al., 2022, 2023), emotion detection (Muhammad et al., 2025c), hate speech detection (Muhammad et al., 2025a), and named entity recognition (Adelani et al., 2022c). However, numerous NLP tasks for Hausa remain understudied, primarily due to the lack of available corpora.

Open-source corpora are key drivers of advancements in NLP. However, Hausa, a well-documented language, lacks open-source corpora that can be used for many NLP tasks. Further, the few available Hausa corpora are dispersed and difficult to access. Therefore, creating and aggregating open-source corpora for Hausa is crucial for the progress of HausaNLP. To address these challenges, this paper makes the following contributions:

- **HausaNLP Catalogue**: We introduce HausaNLP Catalogue, a centralized repository of datasets, tools, and research papers designed to improve accessibility and accelerate progress in Hausa NLP research.

- **Comprehensive Review**: We present a review of Hausa NLP research, analyzing current progress and identifying key challenges in the field.

- **Future Directions**: We explore promising research opportunities and outline recommendations to advance Hausa NLP technologies.

We release the HausaNLP Catalogue as an open, community-driven platform to centralize and accelerate Hausa NLP research. The catalogue serves as a living resource for discovering and sharing datasets, tools, and papers, with ongoing contributions from researchers and practitioners worldwide.

2 Hausa Language

Hausa is the language of the Hausa people (*Hausawa*), primarily spoken in West Africa's sub-Saharan region, with the largest populations in northern Nigeria and southern Niger. Significant Hausa-speaking communities exist across Northern Ghana, Togo, Cameroon, and parts of Sudan, Chad, Mali, Ivory Coast, Libya, Saudi Arabia, and the Central African Republic (Bello, 2015). With approximately 120 million first-language (L1) and 80 million second-language (L2) speakers, Hausa ranks among Africa's most widely spoken languages, second only to Swahili in total speaker count (Hegazy et al.).

While some argue that Hausa may surpass Swahili in total speakers (Newman, 2022), Swahili maintains broader institutional recognition as an official language in four East African nations: Tanzania, Kenya, Uganda, and Rwanda. In contrast, Hausa had limited official recognition until recently, when Niger declared it an official language (El-Shazly, 1987).

Linguistically, Hausa belongs to the Chadic branch of the Afroasiatic language family and is spoken by over 200 million people either as a first language or as a second language, making it a prominent lingua franca in the region (Yakasai, 2025). Hausa has several dialect variations, which are broadly categorized into two major groups: western and eastern dialects. Furthermore, Hausa has regional variations influenced by contact with non-Hausa languages, leading to phonological, morphological, syntactic, and lexical differences (Bello, 2015).

Phonologically, Hausa is a tonal language with three pitch contrasts that distinguish word meanings and grammatical categories. It has 48 phonemes and 36 standard alphabets (Caron, 2012). Morphologically, Hausa uses root-and-pattern templates and affixation to support complex morphological processes including inflection, derivation, modification, reduplication, clipping, blending, and compounding. It also has numerous loanwords from contact language such as Arabic (Ahmed and B., 1970). Syntactically, Hausa follows a subject-verb-object (SVO) word order and uses diverse typological constructions. The language has developed two writing systems: Ajami (Arabic-based script) and Boko (Latin-based script), both actively used in print, broadcasting, and digital media.

Despite its linguistic richness, Hausa remains a

low-resource language in NLP due to limited annotated corpora and tools, hindering the development of language technologies.

3 Current State of Hausa NLP

Several existing works have explored various NLP tasks in Hausa, including text classification, machine translation, named entity recognition, and automatic speech recognition, as shown in Figure 2. This section reviews prior work on Hausa NLP, discusses available datasets, and identifies future research directions.

3.1 Text Classification

Text classification is a method for automatically categorizing texts into distinct, predetermined classes. It is a supervised learning approach, as the classes must be known beforehand to train the model. Text classification can take various forms; however, in the context of Hausa texts, prior studies have primarily focused on sentiment analysis, toxicity detection, or topic classification

Sentiment Analysis Sentiment analysis is a text classification method of categorizing based on the sentiment contained in the text. The method is usually a binary classification, into positive and negative classes, or three classes, into positive, negative, and neutral classes.

Several studies have explored sentiment analysis in Hausa. Abubakar et al. (2021) introduced a sentiment analysis model for Hausa texts, leveraging a corpus of political tweets. Their approach incorporated Hausa lexical features and sentiment intensifiers, achieving an accuracy of 0.71 when employing the SVM classifier. Nevertheless, the dataset size of merely around 200 tweets in the study is grossly inadequate for training supervised learning models.

Muhammad et al. (2022) proposed the first large-scale sentiment dataset for the Hausa language among other Nigerian languages. The paper collected and annotated around 30,000 tweets in the Hausa language. The authors proposed novel methods for tweet collection, filtering, processing, and labeling methods. Additionally, contrary to the other study, they leverage fine-tuning LLMs, attaining a weighted F1-score of 0.81.

Further, Sani et al. (2022) combined machine learning and lexicon-based approaches, achieving 86% accuracy with TF-IDF but struggling with syntactic and semantic nuances. Shehu et al. (2024)

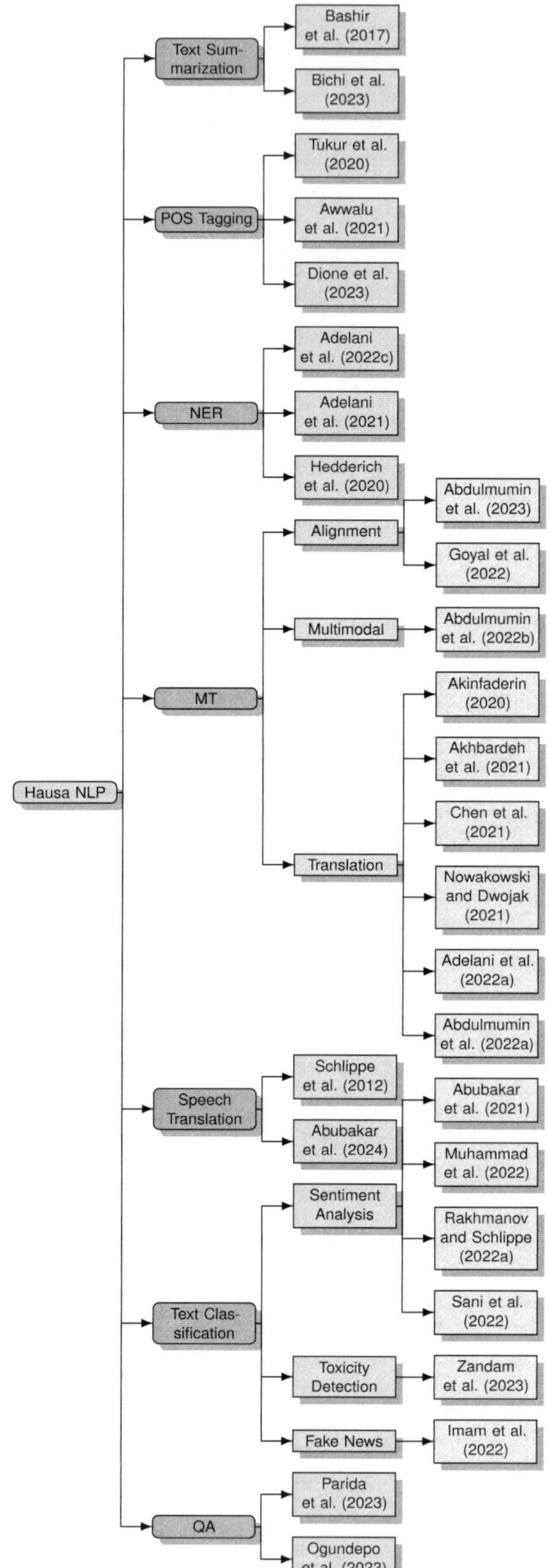

Figure 2: Taxonomy of Hausa NLP Research Progress: Tasks and Associated Publications

integrated CNN, RNN, and HAN with a lexicon dictionary, but the approach yielded a lower accuracy of 68.48%, highlighting the limitations of the bag-of-words model. Mohammed and Prasad (2024) introduced a manually annotated lexicon dataset for social media and product reviews, useful for lexicon-based models but unsuitable for data-driven approaches. To address language-specific challenges, Abdullahi et al. (2024) implemented a normalization process for handling Hausa abbreviations and acronyms, improving the performance of MNB and Logistic Regression. Meanwhile, Ibrahim et al. (2024) proposed a Deep CNN model for aspect and polarity classification in Hausa movie reviews, achieving 92% accuracy but struggling with multi-aspect classification. These studies highlight progress in Hausa sentiment analysis while emphasizing the need for better feature representation, richer datasets, and advanced techniques to handle linguistic complexities.

Future research in Hausa sentiment analysis should focus on high-quality annotated datasets to improve benchmarking (Liu et al., 2024), and domain adaptation to enhance model generalization across different contexts (Hays et al., 2023; Singhal et al., 2023), Cross-lingual sentiment classification offers potential for transferring knowledge from high-resource languages while addressing cultural nuances (Chan et al., 2023; Rakhmanov and Schlippe, 2022b; Yusuf et al., 2024). Further, aspect-based sentiment analysis (ABSA) is crucial for entity-level sentiment detection (Ibrahim et al., 2024; Obiedat et al., 2021), while multimodal approaches integrating text, audio, and visuals remain underexplored (Zhu et al., 2023; Gandhi et al., 2023; Parida et al., 2023). Sentiment analysis using code-mixed remains underexplored in HausaNLP (Shakith and Arockiam, 2024; Yusuf et al., 2023). Finally, explainable sentiment analysis should be explored to improve model transparency (Diwali et al., 2023). Advancing these areas will significantly strengthen Hausa NLP research and applications.

Emotion analysis in text Unlike sentiment analysis, which aims to interpret text and assign polarities (positive, negative, or neutral), emotion analysis focuses on extracting and analyzing fine-grained emotions, known as affects (e.g., happiness, sadness, fear, anger, surprise, and disgust). Muhammad et al. (2025b) is the first work on emotion detection in Hausa. The authors developed a text-based emotion dataset in 29 languages, including Hausa. The dataset is annotated into six emotion classes (anger, fear, joy, sadness, surprise, and disgust) and further categorized into intensity levels: 0 (indicating no emotion), 1 (low emotion), 2 (medium emotion), and 3 (high emotion). This dataset was used in the SemEval shared task (Muhammad et al., 2025b).

Toxicity detection Toxicity detection is a text classification task of detecting toxicity in text. The toxicity could be in the form of hate speech, harassment, and threats. The only work on toxicity detection in Hausa texts is by (Zandam et al., 2023). In the work, the authors developed an online threat detection dataset using both Facebook and Twitter posts. The developed dataset is quite limited with around 801 instances. The Hausa threat detection models are based on machine learning algorithms, achieving the best performance of 0.85 with a random forest algorithm.

Fake news detection The advancement of the internet and social media has accelerated news dissemination, offering both benefits and drawbacks. While crucial information reaches the public swiftly, the downside includes the widespread circulation of fake news. It is increasingly become difficult to distinguish actual news and fake news in the cyberspace. As a result, fake news detection has become an important area of research.

The work of Imam et al. (2022) focused on the creation of fake news detection corpus for Hausa news articles. They developed a corpus of 2600 news articles comprising of real and fake news selected from key topics like: Business, health, entertainment, sports, politics and religion.

Topic Classification News topic classification is a text classification task in NLP that involves categorizing news articles into different categories like sports, business, entertainment, and politics. For Hausa news articles, Adelani et al. (2023) focused on topic classification for African langauges' news articles including Hausa articles. They used both classical machine learning algorithms, and pre-trained LLMs. The best performing model is AfroXLMR-large attaining a weighted F1-score of 0.92.

3.2 Machine Translation

3.2.1 Text Translation

Adelani et al. (2022a) leveraged pre-trained models for African news translation, focusing on 16 under-represented African languages including the Hausa language. For the Hausa language, The Hausa Khamenei [2] corpus contained 5,898 sentences, was used. The study demonstrated the effectiveness of fine-tuning pre-trained models on a few thousand high-quality bitext for adding new languages like Hausa to the models.

Nowakowski and Dwojak (2021) and Chen et al. (2021) participated in the WMT 2021 News Translation Task (Akhbardeh et al., 2021). This involves building a machine translation system for English and Hausa language pairs. The Nowakowski and Dwojak (2021) focused on thorough data cleaning, transfer learning, iterative training, and back-translation. The work experimented with NMT and PB-SMT, using the base Transformer architecture for the NMT models. On the other hand, (Chen et al., 2021) used an iterative back-translation approach on top of pre-trained English-German models and investigated vocabulary embedding mapping.

Akinfaderin (2020) explored English-Hausa machine translation by training LSTM and transformer-based model using the JW300 (Agić and Vulić, 2019) corpus. Abdulmumin et al. (2022a) participated in WMT 2022 Large-Scale Machine Translation Evaluation for the African Languages Shared Task (Adelani et al., 2022b). The work made an attempt to improve Hausa-English (along with other language pairs) machine translation using data filtering techniques. The idea relies on filtering out the noisy or invalid parts of a large corpus, keeping only a high-quality subset thereof. The results show that the performance of the models improved with increased data filtering, indicating the removal of noisy sentences enhanced translation quality.

3.2.2 Multi-Modal Machine Translation

Multimodal machine translation (MMT) focuses on translating languages using multiple modalities of information, not just text. This typically involves combining text with other data sources, such as images, speech, and video. MMT aims to enhance translation quality by incorporating information from other modalities. The goal is to leverage these additional modalities to improve the overall translation process.

Abdulmumin et al. (2022b) presents the ***Hausa Visual Genome (HaVG)***, a multi-modal dataset that contains the description of an image or a section within the image in Hausa and its equivalent in English. HaVG was formed by translating the English description of the images in the Hindi Visual Genome (HVG) into Hausa automatically. Afterward, the synthetic Hausa data was carefully post-edited considering the respective images. The dataset comprises 32,923 images and their descriptions.

3.2.3 Sentence Alignment

Automatic sentence alignment is the process of identifying which sentences in a source text correspond to which sentences in a target text. This task is crucial for creating parallel corpora, where each sentence in one language is aligned with its equivalent translation in another language. Various approaches, including length-based, lexicon-based, and translation-based methods, are employed for sentence alignment. Evaluating alignment quality involves assessing accuracy and effectiveness, considering factors like language pairs and genre.

Abdulmumin et al. (2023) addresses the challenge of limited qualitative datasets for English-Hausa machine translation by automatic sentence alignment. The work presented a qualitative parallel sentence aligner that leverages the closed-access Cohere multilingual embedding [3]. For evaluation, the work used the MAFAND-MT (Adelani et al., 2022a), FLORES (Goyal et al., 2022), a new corpus of 1000 Hausa and English news articles each. The proposed method showed promising results.

3.3 POS

Part-of-speech tagging (POS) is one of the first steps in NLP that involves the tagging (or labeling) of each word in a sentence with the correct part of speech to indicate their grammatical behaviours for computational tasks (Martinez, 2012). POS tagging is very crucial in many NLP tasks like sentiment analysis and information extraction.

While considerable amount of work has been done on POS tagging, only a couple of studies are on Hausa POS tagging. Tukur et al. (2020) proposed a technique for POS tagging of Hausa

[2] https://www.statmt.org/wmt21/translation-task.html

[3] https://docs.cohere.com/docs/multilingual-language-models

sentences using the Hidden Markov Model. They evaluated the model using a manually collected and annotated Hausa corpus sourced from from radio stations. While the study is worthwhile, both the dataset and model are not publicly available.

Awwalu et al. (2021) presents a study on Corpus Based Transformation-Based Learning for Hausa language POS tagging. The research involves corpus development for Hausa language POS tagset. Various models and techniques such as Transformation-Based Learning (TBL), Hidden Markov Model (HMM), and N-Gram models are employed for POS tagging. The main findings indicate that the TBL tagger outperforms HMM and N-Gram taggers in terms of accuracy levels, showcasing the effectiveness of hybrid generative and discriminative taggers.

Dione et al. (2023) created MasakhaPOS, a large POS dataset for 20 diverse African languages. They address the challenges of using universal dependencies (UD) guidelines for these languages, and compare different POS taggers based Conditional Random Field (CRF) and several multilingual Pretrained Language Models (PLMs). For the Hausa part of the project, the data was sourced from *Kano Focus* and *Freedom Radio* to a total of 1504 sentences (train: 753, test:150, and dev: 601).

3.4 Text Summarization

Text summarization is the process of automatically generating a concise and coherent summary of a longer text while retaining its key information and main points (El-Kassas et al., 2021).

Text summarization plays a crucial role in various applications such as information retrieval, document summarization, news aggregation, and content recommendation systems, helping users quickly grasp the main points of lengthy documents or articles.

(Bashir et al., 2017) perhaps conducted one the the earliest works on text summarization for Hausa langauge. The work focused on text summarization based on feature extraction using Naive Bayes model. However, the validity of the work is limited by the small data size of 10 documents from news articles, with each document containing over 600 words. The work of (Bichi et al., 2023) focus on graph-based extractive text summarization method for Hausa text. The study focus on graph-based extractive single-document summarization method for Hausa text by modifying the PageRank algorithm using the normalized common bigrams count between adjacent sentences as the initial vertex score. They evaluated the proposed approach using a manually annotated dataset that comprises of 113 Hausa news articles on various genres. Each news article had two manually generated gold standard summaries, with the length of summaries being 20% of the original article length.

3.5 Question and Answering

Question and Answering (QA) is a branch of natural language processing (NLP) that deals with building systems that can automatically answer questions posed by humans in natural language. QA systems can be useful for various applications, such as virtual assistants, customer support, search engines, and education (Rogers et al., 2023).

Parida et al. (2023) developed a Hausa Visual Question Answering (VQA) dataset called ***HaVQA***. The dataset is a multi-modal dataset for visual question-answering (VQA) tasks in the Hausa language. The dataset was created by manually translating 6,022 English question-answer pairs, which are associated with 1,555 unique images from the Visual Genome dataset. The paper employed state-of-the-art language and vision models for Visual Question Answering and achieved the best performance with the Data-Efficient Image Transformers model proposed by Facebook with a WuPalmer score of 30.85.

(Ogundepo et al., 2023) developed ***AfriQA***, a dataset for cross-lingual open-retrieval question answering for 10 African languages, including the Hausa language. The dataset was developed from Wikipedia articles and manually elicited questions. For Hausa language, the final corpus consist of 1171 instances split into 435 training, 436 development and 300 test sets. The findings of the experiments proves how challenging multilingual retrieval is even for state-of-the-art QA models.

3.6 Named Entity Recognition

Named entity recognition (NER) is a technique of NLP that identifies and classifies named entities in a text, such as person names, organizations, locations, and dates. NER can be useful for various tasks, such as information extraction, search engines, chatbots, and machine translation. There are different methods and tools for NER, such as dictionary-based, rule-based, machine learning-based, and hybrid systems (Li et al., 2022).

Adelani et al. (2021) and Adelani et al. (2022c) created the largest NER corpus for African languages titled ***MasakhaNER 1.0*** and ***MasakhaNER 2.0***. MasakhaNER 1.0 covers 10 African languages, while MasakhaNER 2.0 expanded the corpus to include 10 South African languages, making a total of 20 languages. MasakhaNER 1.0 consists of 2,720 sources from VOA news while MasakhaNER 2.0 consists of 8,165 sourced from Kano Focus and Freedom Radio news channels. Both studies explored various experiments using pretrained language models and other techniques like transfer learning and zero-shot learning.

The work of Hedderich et al. (2020) investigates transfer learning and distant supervision with multilingual transformer models on NER and topic classification in Hausa, isiXhosa and Yoruba languages. The study show that transfer learning from a high-resource language and distant supervision are effective techniques for improving performance in low-resource settings for African languages.

3.7 Automatic Speech Recognition (ASR)

Automatic speech recognition (ASR) is a technology that allows computers to convert spoken language into text. ASR can be used for various purposes, such as voice control, transcription, translation, and accessibility (Yu and Deng, 2016).

Schlippe et al. (2012) focused on developing a Hausa Large Vocabulary Continuous Speech Recognition (LVCSR) system by collecting a corpus of Hausa speech data from native speakers in Cameroon and text data from prominent Hausa websites. The data collected for the study included approximately 8 hours and 44 minutes of speech data from 102 native speakers of Hausa in Cameroon. Additionally, the text corpus consists of roughly 8 million words. The study found that modeling tones and vowel lengths significantly improved recognition performance, leading to a reduction in word error rates.

(Abubakar et al., 2024) focuses on developing a diacritic-aware automatic speech recognition model for the Hausa language. The model uses a large corpus of speech data from the Mozilla Common Voice dataset, which includes a variety of diacritical words and sentences. The Whisper-large model outperforms existing models, achieving a word error rate of 4.23% and a diacritic coverage of 92%. It also has a precision of 98.87%, with a 2.1% diacritic error rate, demonstrating its effectiveness in accurately transcribing Hausa speech. However, Due to the absence of prior ASR systems specifically focused on diacritization in the Hausa language, the authors were unable to make direct comparisons with their results. This lack of benchmarks may limit the ability to fully assess the effectiveness of their proposed model against existing technologies

Future efforts should prioritize developing real-time ASR systems for continuous Hausa speech recognition, enhancing usability across everyday communication and diverse industries. Optimizing computational resources and designing efficient algorithms will enable high-performance ASR systems with reduced power requirements. Further, exploring ASR techniques less reliant on diacritics can broaden usability for varied contexts and users. Finally, integrating ASR with NLP and machine translation can pave the way for comprehensive tools to better serve Hausa-speaking communities.

4 Hausa Representation in Large Language Models (LLMs)

Large language models (LLMs) have made significant strides in supporting multilingual tasks, including those involving low-resource languages like Hausa. Multilingual models such as AfrIBERTa (Ogueji et al., 2021) mBERT (Devlin et al., 2019), InkubaLM (Tonja et al., 2024) XLM-R (Conneau et al., 2020), and BLOOM (Workshop et al., 2023) have incorporated Hausa into their training data, albeit to varying degrees. These models leverage cross-lingual transfer learning to improve performance on languages with limited resources. However, the extent of Hausa representation in these models is often constrained by the scarcity of high-quality, diverse datasets.

The availability and quality of training data are critical factors influencing the performance of large language models (LLMs) on Hausa language tasks. Like many low-resource languages, Hausa faces challenges such as data scarcity, representational bias, and inadequate dataset construction. Existing datasets are often limited in scale and diversity, particularly in capturing dialectal variations and informal text (e.g., social media content). Sani et al. (2025b) highlight these challenges, emphasizing the impact of dialectal variation and tokenization on Hausa sentiment analysis. Their findings underscore the need for more diverse and high-quality datasets to enhance model performance. Without sufficient data, LLMs struggle to achieve robust performance in handling Hausa text, as highlighted by Zhao et al. (2024) and Acikgoz et al. (2024).

In addition to data scarcity, Hausa's linguistic features pose significant challenges for tokenization and language modeling. The language's rich morphology, tonal variations, and complex noun pluralization systems complicate the process of accurately representing it in LLMs. Diacritics and tonal markers, which are critical for meaning, often lead to suboptimal tokenization, resulting in poor representations of the language (Abubakar et al., 2024; Jaggar, 2006). Furthermore, the dialectal diversity within Hausa adds another layer of complexity. Models trained on formal Hausa text frequently struggle to process informal or dialectal variations, as noted by Sani et al. (2025b). This limits their applicability in real-world scenarios where such variations are common.

Another critical issue is bias and representation in existing LLMs. Studies comparing LLM outputs with native speaker responses have revealed discrepancies in how cultural nuances and emotional tones are captured (Ahmad et al., 2024). These biases can lead to outputs that are misaligned with the cultural and linguistic expectations of Hausa speakers, further reducing the utility of LLMs for this language. Addressing these challenges requires innovative approaches, including improved tokenization strategies, dialectal adaptation techniques, and data augmentation methods. By tackling these issues, researchers can develop more robust and inclusive models that better serve Hausa speakers and other low-resource language communities

A promising direction is the development of specialized, lightweight models tailored specifically to Hausa. These custom models could provide more accurate and efficient solutions for Hausa-specific applications (Yang et al., 2024). Additionally, federated prompt tuning offers a pathway to enhance data efficiency and facilitate mutual improvements across languages, benefiting low-resource languages like Hausa (Zhao et al., 2024). Synthetic data generation also presents a valuable opportunity to address data scarcity. By creating high-quality synthetic datasets, researchers can overcome the limitations of limited real-world data and improve the performance of the model (Mahgoub et al., 2024). Together, these approaches, ranging from architectural innovations and specialized models to federated learning and synthetic data, have the potential to significantly advance Hausa representation in LLMs, making them more robust, efficient, and culturally relevant for Hausa speakers.

5 Conclusion

Advancing Hausa NLP requires a multifaceted approach that addresses both technical and community-driven challenges. Below, we outline key areas for future research and development.

Future research should investigate the interplay between tokenization strategies and model initialization to optimize the learning efficiency of Hausa LLMs. Techniques inspired by the BabyLM Challenge (Hu et al., 2024) could be adapted to Hausa, focusing on sample-efficient pretraining and developmentally plausible corpora. Such approaches could mitigate data scarcity while improving model performance, particularly in low-resource settings.

Innovative architectures that support dynamic re-tokenization based on context could significantly enhance the representation of Hausa's linguistic features. These models would adapt tokenization to better capture dialectal variations and morphological complexity, improving generalization across diverse Hausa texts. This is especially important given the language's rich morphology and tonal variations, which are often underrepresented in current models.

Building on the work of Wolf et al. (2023), future studies could explore encoding prosodic features into embeddings to improve the contextual understanding of Hausa. Although prosody carries information beyond text, its integration could enhance model performance, particularly in low-resource settings. This approach could also facilitate better handling of tonal variations in Hausa, which are critical for accurate language representation.

Creating richer and more diverse datasets for Hausa is essential for advancing NLP applications. Future efforts should focus on curating datasets that capture both formal and informal text, as well as dialectal variations. Techniques such as data augmentation, synthetic data generation, and crowdsourcing could help address data scarcity and improve model robustness. Expanding digital resources through initiatives like web crawling and community contributions (Schlippe et al., 2012; Ibrahim et al., 2022) will also play a crucial role.

Engaging the Hausa-speaking community in dataset creation and model evaluation is vital for ensuring that LLMs reflect the linguistic and cultural nuances of Hausa. Collaborative efforts between researchers, linguists, and native speakers could lead to more representative and inclusive models. Community-driven approaches can also help address biases and improve the cultural and emotional representation of Hausa in NLP systems (Ahmad et al., 2024).

Multilingual and cross-lingual transfer learning offers promising opportunities to leverage resources from related languages to enhance Hausa NLP. For instance, the work of Erasmo Ndomba et al. (2025) demonstrates that language-specific tokenizers outperform multilingual tokenizers in tasks like sentiment and news classification for African languages. Interestingly, their findings reveal that a tokenizer trained on Swahili outperformed one trained on Hausa for Hausa-specific tasks, highlighting strong cross-linguistic connections between these languages. This suggests that shared linguistic structures and features among African languages can be harnessed to improve model performance. Future research should explore these cross-linguistic bonds further, leveraging multilingual capabilities and federated learning techniques to enhance Hausa NLP (Zhao et al., 2024).

Adapting and fine-tuning existing LLMs to better handle the unique linguistic features of Hausa is another critical area for future work (Acikgoz et al., 2024; Abubakar et al., 2024). Additionally, addressing biases and ensuring culturally aware models will be essential for creating systems that accurately represent the emotions and nuances of the Hausa language (Ahmad et al., 2024).

References

Habeeba Ibraheem Abdullahi, Muhammad Aminu Ahmad, and Khalid Haruna. 2024. Twitter sentiment analysis for hausa abbreviations and acronyms. *Science World Journal*, 19(1):101–104.

Idris Abdulmumin, Michael Beukman, Jesujoba Alabi, Chris Chinenye Emezue, Everlyn Chimoto, Tosin Adewumi, Shamsuddeen Muhammad, Mofetoluwa Adeyemi, Oreen Yousuf, Sahib Singh, and Tajuddeen Gwadabe. 2022a. Separating grains from the chaff: Using data filtering to improve multilingual translation for low-resourced African languages. In *Proceedings of the Seventh Conference on Machine Translation (WMT)*, pages 1001–1014, Abu Dhabi, United Arab Emirates (Hybrid). Association for Computational Linguistics.

Idris Abdulmumin, Satya Ranjan Dash, Musa Abdullahi Dawud, Shantipriya Parida, Shamsuddeen Muhammad, Ibrahim Sa'id Ahmad, Subhadarshi Panda, Ondřej Bojar, Bashir Shehu Galadanci, and Bello Shehu Bello. 2022b. Hausa visual genome: A dataset for multi-modal English to Hausa machine translation. In *Proceedings of the Thirteenth Language Resources and Evaluation Conference*, pages 6471–6479, Marseille, France. European Language Resources Association.

Idris Abdulmumin, Auwal Abubakar Khalid, Shamsuddeen Hassan Muhammad, Ibrahim Said Ahmad, Lukman Jibril Aliyu, Babangida Sani, Bala Mairiga Abduljalil, and Sani Ahmad Hassan. 2023. Leveraging closed-access multilingual embedding for automatic sentence alignment in low resource languages.

Abdulqahar Mukhtar Abubakar, Deepa Gupta, and Susmitha Vekkot. 2024. Development of a diacritic-aware large vocabulary automatic speech recognition for hausa language. *International Journal of Speech Technology*, 27(3):687–700.

Amina Imam Abubakar, Abubakar Roko, Aminu Muhammad Bui, and Ibrahim Saidu. 2021. An enhanced feature acquisition for sentiment analysis of english and hausa tweets. *International Journal of Advanced Computer Science and Applications*, 12(9).

Emre Can Acikgoz, Mete Erdogan, and Deniz Yuret. 2024. Bridging the bosphorus: Advancing turkish large language models through strategies for low-resource language adaptation and benchmarking. page 242 – 268.

David Adelani, Jesujoba Alabi, Angela Fan, Julia Kreutzer, Xiaoyu Shen, Machel Reid, Dana Ruiter, Dietrich Klakow, Peter Nabende, Ernie Chang, Tajuddeen Gwadabe, Freshia Sackey, Bonaventure F. P. Dossou, Chris Emezue, Colin Leong, Michael Beukman, Shamsuddeen Muhammad, Guyo Jarso, Oreen Yousuf, Andre Niyongabo Rubungo, Gilles Hacheme, Eric Peter Wairagala, Muhammad Umair Nasir, Benjamin Ajibade, Tunde Ajayi, Yvonne Gitau, Jade Abbott, Mohamed Ahmed, Millicent Ochieng, Anuoluwapo Aremu, Perez Ogayo, Jonathan Mukiibi, Fatoumata Ouoba Kabore, Godson Kalipe, Derguene Mbaye, Allahsera Auguste Tapo, Victoire Memdjokam Koagne, Edwin Munkoh-Buabeng, Valencia Wagner, Idris Abdulmumin, Ayodele Awokoya, Happy Buzaaba, Blessing Sibanda, Andiswa Bukula, and Sam Manthalu. 2022a. A few thousand translations go a long way! leveraging pre-trained models for African news translation. In *Proceedings of the 2022 Conference of the North American Chapter of the Association for Computational Linguistics: Human Language Technologies*, pages 3053–3070, Seattle, United States. Association for Computational Linguistics.

David Adelani, Md Mahfuz Ibn Alam, Antonios Anastasopoulos, Akshita Bhagia, Marta R. Costa-jussà, Jesse Dodge, Fahim Faisal, Christian Federmann, Natalia Fedorova, Francisco Guzmán, Sergey Koshelev, Jean Maillard, Vukosi Marivate, Jonathan Mbuya, Alexandre Mourachko, Safiyyah Saleem, Holger Schwenk, and Guillaume Wenzek. 2022b. Findings of the WMT'22 shared task on large-scale machine translation evaluation for African languages. In *Proceedings of the Seventh Conference on Machine Translation (WMT)*, pages 773–800, Abu Dhabi, United Arab Emirates (Hybrid). Association for Computational Linguistics.

David Adelani, Graham Neubig, Sebastian Ruder, Shruti Rijhwani, Michael Beukman, Chester Palen-Michel, Constantine Lignos, Jesujoba Alabi, Shamsuddeen Muhammad, Peter Nabende, Cheikh M. Bamba Dione, Andiswa Bukula, Rooweither Mabuya, Bonaventure F. P. Dossou, Blessing Sibanda, Happy Buzaaba, Jonathan Mukiibi, Godson Kalipe, Derguene Mbaye, Amelia Taylor, Fatoumata Kabore, Chris Chinenye Emezue, Anuoluwapo Aremu, Perez Ogayo, Catherine Gitau, Edwin Munkoh-Buabeng, Victoire Memdjokam Koagne, Allahsera Auguste Tapo, Tebogo Macucwa, Vukosi Marivate, Mboning Tchiaze Elvis, Tajuddeen Gwadabe, Tosin Adewumi, Orevaoghene Ahia, Joyce Nakatumba-Nabende, Neo Lerato Mokono, Ignatius Ezeani, Chiamaka Chukwuneke, Mofetoluwa Oluwaseun Adeyemi, Gilles Quentin Hacheme, Idris Abdulmumin, Odunayo Ogundepo, Oreen Yousuf, Tatiana Moteu, and Dietrich Klakow. 2022c. MasakhaNER 2.0: Africa-centric transfer learning for named entity recognition. In *Proceedings of the 2022 Conference on Empirical Methods in Natural Language Processing*, pages 4488–4508, Abu Dhabi, United Arab Emirates. Association for Computational Linguistics.

David Ifeoluwa Adelani, Jade Abbott, Graham Neubig, Daniel D'souza, Julia Kreutzer, Constantine Lignos, Chester Palen-Michel, Happy Buzaaba, Shruti Rijhwani, Sebastian Ruder, Stephen Mayhew, Israel Abebe Azime, Shamsuddeen H. Muhammad, Chris Chinenye Emezue, Joyce Nakatumba-Nabende, Perez Ogayo, Aremu Anuoluwapo, Catherine Gitau, Derguene Mbaye, Jesujoba Alabi, Seid Muhie Yimam, Tajuddeen Rabiu Gwadabe, Ignatius Ezeani, Rubungo Andre Niyongabo, Jonathan Mukiibi, Verrah Otiende, Iroro Orife, Davis David, Samba Ngom, Tosin Adewumi, Paul Rayson, Mofetoluwa Adeyemi, Gerald Muriuki, Emmanuel Anebi, Chiamaka Chukwuneke, Nkiruka Odu, Eric Peter Wairagala, Samuel Oyerinde, Clemencia Siro, Tobius Saul Bateesa, Temilola Oloyede, Yvonne Wambui, Victor Akinode, Deborah Nabagereka, Maurice Katusiime, Ayodele Awokoya, Mouhamadane MBOUP, Dibora Gebreyohannes, Henok Tilaye, Kelechi Nwaike, Degaga Wolde, Abdoulaye Faye, Blessing Sibanda, Orevaoghene Ahia, Bonaventure F. P. Dossou, Kelechi Ogueji, Thierno Ibrahima DIOP, Abdoulaye Diallo, Adewale Akinfaderin, Tendai Marengereke, and Salomey Osei. 2021. MasakhaNER: Named entity recognition for African languages. *Transactions of the Association for Computational Linguistics*, 9:1116–1131.

David Ifeoluwa Adelani, Marek Masiak, Israel Abebe Azime, Jesujoba Alabi, Atnafu Lambebo Tonja, Christine Mwase, Odunayo Ogundepo, Bonaventure F. P. Dossou, Akintunde Oladipo, Doreen Nixdorf, Chris Chinenye Emezue, sana al azzawi, Blessing Sibanda, Davis David, Lolwethu Ndolela, Jonathan Mukiibi, Tunde Ajayi, Tatiana Moteu, Brian Odhiambo, Abraham Owodunni, Nnaemeka Obiefuna, Muhidin Mohamed, Shamsuddeen Hassan Muhammad, Teshome Mulugeta Ababu, Saheed Abdullahi Salahudeen, Mesay Gemeda Yigezu, Tajuddeen Gwadabe, Idris Abdulmumin, Mahlet Taye, Oluwabusayo Awoyomi, Iyanuoluwa Shode, Tolulope Adelani, Habiba Abdulganiyu, Abdul-Hakeem Omotayo, Adetola Adeeko, Abeeb Afolabi, Anuoluwapo Aremu, Olanrewaju Samuel, Clemencia Siro, Wangari Kimotho, Onyekachi Ogbu, Chinedu Mbonu, Chiamaka Chukwuneke, Samuel Fanijo, Jessica Ojo, Oyinkansola Awosan, Tadesse Kebede, Toadoum Sari Sakayo, Pamela Nyatsine, Freedmore Sidume, Oreen Yousuf, Mardiyyah Oduwole, Tshinu Tshinu, Ussen Kimanuka, Thina Diko, Siyanda Nxakama, Sinodos Nigusse, Abdulmejid Johar, Shafie Mohamed, Fuad Mire Hassan, Moges Ahmed Mehamed, Evrard Ngabire, Jules Jules, Ivan Ssenkungu, and Pontus Stenetorp. 2023. Masakhanews: News topic classification for african languages.

Željko Agić and Ivan Vulić. 2019. JW300: A wide-coverage parallel corpus for low-resource languages. In *Proceedings of the 57th Annual Meeting of the Association for Computational Linguistics*, pages 3204–3210, Florence, Italy. Association for Computational Linguistics.

Ibrahim Said Ahmad, Shiran Dudy, Resmi Ramachandranpillai, and Kenneth Church. 2024. Are generative language models multicultural? a study on hausa culture and emotions using chatgpt. page 98 – 106.

U. Ahmed and Dauda B. 1970. An introduction to classical hausa and major dialects. *Norther Nigeria Publishing Company*.

Farhad Akhbardeh, Arkady Arkhangorodsky, Magdalena Biesialska, Ondřej Bojar, Rajen Chatterjee, Vishrav Chaudhary, Marta R. Costa-jussa, Cristina España-Bonet, Angela Fan, Christian Federmann, Markus Freitag, Yvette Graham, Roman Grundkiewicz, Barry Haddow, Leonie Harter, Kenneth Heafield, Christopher Homan, Matthias Huck, Kwabena Amponsah-Kaakyire, Jungo Kasai, Daniel Khashabi, Kevin Knight, Tom Kocmi, Philipp Koehn, Nicholas Lourie, Christof Monz, Makoto Morishita, Masaaki Nagata, Ajay Nagesh, Toshiaki Nakazawa, Matteo Negri, Santanu Pal, Allahsera Auguste Tapo, Marco Turchi, Valentin Vydrin, and Marcos Zampieri. 2021. Findings of the 2021 conference on machine translation (WMT21). In *Proceedings of the Sixth Conference on Machine Translation*, pages

1–88, Online. Association for Computational Linguistics.

Adewale Akinfaderin. 2020. Hausamt v1. 0: Towards english–hausa neural machine translation. In *Proceedings of the The Fourth Widening Natural Language Processing Workshop*, pages 144–147.

Saminu Mohammad Aliyu, Gregory Maksha Wajiga, Muhammad Murtala, Shamsuddeen Hassan Muhammad, Idris Abdulmumin, and Ibrahim Said Ahmad. 2022. Herdphobia: A dataset for hate speech against fulani in nigeria. In *Seventh Widening Natural Language Processing Workshop (WiNLP)*.

Jamilu Awwalu, Saleh Elyakub Abdullahi, and Abraham Eseoghene Evwiekpaefe. 2021. A corpus based transformation-based learning for hausa text parts of speech tagging. *International Journal of Computing and Digital Systems*, 10:473–490.

Muazzam Bashir, Azilawati Rozaimee, and Wan Malini Wan Isa. 2017. Automatic hausa languagetext summarization based on feature extraction using naïve bayes model. *World Applied Science Journal*, 35(9):2074–2080.

A. Bello. 2015. The dialects of hausa. *Ahmadu Bello University Press.*

Abdulkadir Abubakar Bichi, Ruhaidah Samsudin, Rohayanti Hassan, Layla Rasheed Abdallah Hasan, and Abubakar Ado Rogo. 2023. Graph-based extractive text summarization method for hausa text. *Plos one*, 18(5):e0285376.

Erik Cambria and Bebo White. 2014. Jumping nlp curves: A review of natural language processing research. *IEEE Computational intelligence magazine*, 9(2):48–57.

Bernard Caron. 2012. Hausa grammatical sketch.

Jireh Yi-Le Chan, Khean Thye Bea, Steven Mun Hong Leow, Seuk Wai Phoong, and Wai Khuen Cheng. 2023. State of the art: a review of sentiment analysis based on sequential transfer learning. *Artificial Intelligence Review*, 56(1):749–780.

Pinzhen Chen, Jindřich Helcl, Ulrich Germann, Laurie Burchell, Nikolay Bogoychev, Antonio Valerio Miceli Barone, Jonas Waldendorf, Alexandra Birch, and Kenneth Heafield. 2021. The University of Edinburgh's English-German and English-Hausa submissions to the WMT21 news translation task. In *Proceedings of the Sixth Conference on Machine Translation*, pages 104–109, Online. Association for Computational Linguistics.

Alexis Conneau, Kartikay Khandelwal, Naman Goyal, Vishrav Chaudhary, Guillaume Wenzek, Francisco Guzmán, Edouard Grave, Myle Ott, Luke Zettlemoyer, and Veselin Stoyanov. 2020. Unsupervised cross-lingual representation learning at scale. In *Proceedings of the 58th Annual Meeting of the Association for Computational Linguistics*, pages 8440–8451, Online. Association for Computational Linguistics.

Jacob Devlin, Ming-Wei Chang, Kenton Lee, and Kristina Toutanova. 2019. Bert: Pre-training of deep bidirectional transformers for language understanding.

Cheikh M. Bamba Dione, David Ifeoluwa Adelani, Peter Nabende, Jesujoba Alabi, Thapelo Sindane, Happy Buzaaba, Shamsuddeen Hassan Muhammad, Chris Chinenye Emezue, Perez Ogayo, Anuoluwapo Aremu, Catherine Gitau, Derguene Mbaye, Jonathan Mukiibi, Blessing Sibanda, Bonaventure F. P. Dossou, Andiswa Bukula, Rooweither Mabuya, Allahsera Auguste Tapo, Edwin Munkoh-Buabeng, Victoire Memdjokam Koagne, Fatoumata Ouoba Kabore, Amelia Taylor, Godson Kalipe, Tebogo Macucwa, Vukosi Marivate, Tajuddeen Gwadabe, Mboning Tchiaze Elvis, Ikechukwu Onyenwe, Gratien Atindogbe, Tolulope Adelani, Idris Akinade, Olanrewaju Samuel, Marien Nahimana, Théogène Musabeyezu, Emile Niyomutabazi, Ester Chimhenga, Kudzai Gotosa, Patrick Mizha, Apelete Agbolo, Seydou Traore, Chinedu Uchechukwu, Aliyu Yusuf, Muhammad Abdullahi, and Dietrich Klakow. 2023. MasakhaPOS: Part-of-speech tagging for typologically diverse African languages. In *Proceedings of the 61st Annual Meeting of the Association for Computational Linguistics (Volume 1: Long Papers)*, pages 10883–10900, Toronto, Canada. Association for Computational Linguistics.

Arwa Diwali, Kawther Saeedi, Kia Dashtipour, Mandar Gogate, Erik Cambria, and Amir Hussain. 2023. Sentiment analysis meets explainable artificial intelligence: A survey on explainable sentiment analysis. *IEEE Transactions on Affective Computing*.

Wafaa S. El-Kassas, Cherif R. Salama, Ahmed A. Rafea, and Hoda K. Mohamed. 2021. Automatic text summarization: A comprehensive survey. *Expert Systems with Applications*, 165:113679.

Mohamed Helal Ahmed Sheref El-Shazly. 1987. *The provenance of Arabic loan-words in Hausa: a phonological and semantic study*. University of London, School of Oriental and African Studies (United Kingdom).

Goodwill Erasmo Ndomba, Medard Edmund Mswahili, and Young-Seob Jeong. 2025. Tokenizers for african languages. *IEEE Access*, 13:1046–1054.

Ankita Gandhi, Kinjal Adhvaryu, Soujanya Poria, Erik Cambria, and Amir Hussain. 2023. Multimodal sentiment analysis: A systematic review of history, datasets, multimodal fusion methods, applications, challenges and future directions. *Information Fusion*, 91:424–444.

Naman Goyal, Cynthia Gao, Vishrav Chaudhary, Peng-Jen Chen, Guillaume Wenzek, Da Ju, Sanjana Krishnan, Marc'Aurelio Ranzato, Francisco Guzmán, and Angela Fan. 2022. The Flores-101 evaluation benchmark for low-resource and multilingual machine translation. *Transactions of the Association for Computational Linguistics*, 10:522–538.

Chris Hays, Zachary Schutzman, Manish Raghavan, Erin Walk, and Philipp Zimmer. 2023. Simplistic collection and labeling practices limit the utility of benchmark datasets for twitter bot detection. In *Proceedings of the ACM web conference 2023*, pages 3660–3669.

Michael A. Hedderich, David Adelani, Dawei Zhu, Jesujoba Alabi, Udia Markus, and Dietrich Klakow. 2020. Transfer learning and distant supervision for multilingual transformer models: A study on African languages. In *Proceedings of the 2020 Conference on Empirical Methods in Natural Language Processing (EMNLP)*, pages 2580–2591, Online. Association for Computational Linguistics.

Mahmoud Fahmi Hegazy, Mohammad Ali Nofal, and MA Mahmoud Sayed. A lexical semantic error analysis of arabic-speaking hausa language learners.

Michael Y. Hu, Aaron Mueller, Candace Ross, Adina Williams, Tal Linzen, Chengxu Zhuang, Ryan Cotterell, Leshem Choshen, Alex Warstadt, and Ethan Gotlieb Wilcox. 2024. Findings of the second BabyLM challenge: Sample-efficient pretraining on developmentally plausible corpora. In *The 2nd BabyLM Challenge at the 28th Conference on Computational Natural Language Learning*, pages 1–21, Miami, FL, USA. Association for Computational Linguistics.

Umar Ibrahim, Abubakar Yakubu Zandam, Fatima Muhammad Adam, and Aminu Musa. 2024. A deep convolutional neural network-based model for aspect and polarity classification in hausa movie reviews. *arXiv preprint arXiv:2405.19575*.

Umar Adam Ibrahim, Moussa Boukar Mahatma, and Muhammed Aliyu Suleiman. 2022. Framework for hausa speech recognition.

Sukairaj Hafiz Imam, Abubakar Ahmad Musa, and Ankur Choudhary. 2022. The first corpus for detecting fake news in hausa language. In *Emerging Technologies for Computing, Communication and Smart Cities*, pages 563–576, Singapore. Springer Nature Singapore.

Isa Inuwa-Dutse. 2023. The first large scale collection of diverse hausa language datasets. In *4th Workshop on African Natural Language Processing*.

P.J. Jaggar. 2006. *Hausa*.

Jing Li, Aixin Sun, Jianglei Han, and Chenliang Li. 2022. A survey on deep learning for named entity recognition. *IEEE Transactions on Knowledge and Data Engineering*, 34(1):50–70.

Jiabei Liu, Keqin Li, Armando Zhu, Bo Hong, Peng Zhao, Shuying Dai, Changsong Wei, Wenqian Huang, and Honghua Su. 2024. Application of deep learning-based natural language processing in multilingual sentiment analysis. *Mediterranean Journal of Basic and Applied Sciences (MJBAS)*, 8(2):243–260.

Abeer Mahgoub, Ghada Khoriba, and Elhassan Anas Elsabry. 2024. Mathematical problem solving in arabic: Assessing large language models. volume 244, page 86 – 95.

Angel R. Martinez. 2012. Part-of-speech tagging. *WIREs Computational Statistics*, 4(1):107–113.

Idi Mohammed and Rajesh Prasad. 2024. Lexicon dataset for the hausa language. *Data in Brief*, 53:110124.

Shamsuddeen Muhammad, Idris Abdulmumin, Abinew Ayele, Nedjma Ousidhoum, David Adelani, Seid Yimam, Ibrahim Ahmad, Meriem Beloucif, Saif Mohammad, Sebastian Ruder, Oumaima Hourrane, Alipio Jorge, Pavel Brazdil, Felermino Ali, Davis David, Salomey Osei, Bello Shehu-Bello, Falalu Lawan, Tajuddeen Gwadabe, Samuel Rutunda, Tadesse Belay, Wendimu Messelle, Hailu Balcha, Sisay Chala, Hagos Gebremichael, Bernard Opoku, and Stephen Arthur. 2023. AfriSenti: A Twitter sentiment analysis benchmark for African languages. In *Proceedings of the 2023 Conference on Empirical Methods in Natural Language Processing*, pages 13968–13981, Singapore. Association for Computational Linguistics.

Shamsuddeen Hassan Muhammad, Idris Abdulmumin, Abinew Ali Ayele, David Ifeoluwa Adelani, Ibrahim Said Ahmad, Saminu Mohammad Aliyu, Nelson Odhiambo Onyango, Lilian D. A. Wanzare, Samuel Rutunda, Lukman Jibril Aliyu, Esubalew Alemneh, Oumaima Hourrane, Hagos Tesfahun Gebremichael, Elyas Abdi Ismail, Meriem Beloucif, Ebrahim Chekol Jibril, Andiswa Bukula, Rooweither Mabuya, Salomey Osei, Abigail Oppong, Tadesse Destaw Belay, Tadesse Kebede Guge, Tesfa Tegegne Asfaw, Chiamaka Ijeoma Chukwuneke, Paul Rottger, Seid Muhie Yimam, and Nedjma Djouhra Ousidhoum. 2025a. Afrihate: A multilingual collection of hate speech and abusive language datasets for african languages. *ArXiv*, abs/2501.08284.

Shamsuddeen Hassan Muhammad, David Ifeoluwa Adelani, Sebastian Ruder, Ibrahim Sa'id Ahmad, Idris Abdulmumin, Bello Shehu Bello, Monojit Choudhury, Chris Chinenye Emezue, Saheed Salahudeen Abdullahi, Anuoluwapo Aremu, Alípio Jorge, and Pavel Brazdil. 2022. NaijaSenti: A nigerian Twitter sentiment corpus for multilingual sentiment analysis. In *Proceedings of the Thirteenth Language Resources and Evaluation Conference*, pages 590–602, Marseille, France. European Language Resources Association.

Shamsuddeen Hassan Muhammad, Nedjma Ousidhoum, Idris Abdulmumin, Jan Philip Wahle, Terry Ruas, Meriem Beloucif, Christine de Kock, Nirmal Surange, Daniela Teodorescu, Ibrahim Said Ahmad, David Ifeoluwa Adelani, Alham Fikri Aji, Felermino D. M. A. Ali, Ilseyar Alimova, Vladimir Araujo, Nikolay Babakov, Naomi Baes, Ana-Maria Bucur, Andiswa Bukula, Guanqun Cao, Rodrigo Tufino Cardenas, Rendi Chevi, Chiamaka Ijeoma Chukwuneke, Alexandra Ciobotaru, Daryna Dementieva, Murja Sani Gadanya, Robert Geislinger, Bela Gipp, Oumaima Hourrane, Oana Ignat, Falalu Ibrahim Lawan, Rooweither Mabuya, Rahmad Mahendra, Vukosi Marivate, Andrew Piper, Alexander Panchenko, Charles Henrique Porto Ferreira, Vitaly Protasov, Samuel Rutunda, Manish Shrivastava, Aura Cristina Udrea, Lilian Diana Awuor Wanzare, Sophie Wu, Florian Valentin Wunderlich, Hanif Muhammad Zhafran, Tianhui Zhang, Yi Zhou, and Saif M. Mohammad. 2025b. Brighter: Bridging the gap in human-annotated textual emotion recognition datasets for 28 languages.

Shamsuddeen Hassan Muhammad, Nedjma Ousidhoum, Idris Abdulmumin, Jan Philip Wahle, Terry Ruas, Meriem Beloucif, Christine de Kock, Nirmal Surange, Daniela Teodorescu, Ibrahim Said Ahmad, et al. 2025c. Brighter: Bridging the gap in human-annotated textual emotion recognition datasets for 28 languages. *arXiv preprint arXiv:2502.11926*.

Paul Newman. 2022. *Loanwords*, page 205–211. Cambridge University Press.

Artur Nowakowski and Tomasz Dwojak. 2021. Adam Mickiewicz University's English-Hausa submissions to the WMT 2021 news translation task. In *Proceedings of the Sixth Conference on Machine Translation*, pages 167–171, Online. Association for Computational Linguistics.

Ruba Obiedat, Duha Al-Darras, Esra Alzaghoul, and Osama Harfoushi. 2021. Arabic aspect-based sentiment analysis: A systematic literature review. *IEEE Access*, 9:152628–152645.

Kelechi Ogueji, Yuxin Zhu, and Jimmy Lin. 2021. Small data? no problem! exploring the viability of pretrained multilingual language models for low-resourced languages. In *Proceedings of the 1st Workshop on Multilingual Representation Learning*, pages 116–126, Punta Cana, Dominican Republic. Association for Computational Linguistics.

Odunayo Ogundepo, Tajuddeen Gwadabe, Clara Rivera, Jonathan Clark, Sebastian Ruder, David Adelani, Bonaventure Dossou, Abdou Diop, Claytone Sikasote, Gilles Hacheme, Happy Buzaaba, Ignatius Ezeani, Rooweither Mabuya, Salomey Osei, Chris Emezue, Albert Kahira, Shamsuddeen Muhammad, Akintunde Oladipo, Abraham Owodunni, Atnafu Tonja, Iyanuoluwa Shode, Akari Asai, Anuoluwapo Aremu, Ayodele Awokoya, Bernard Opoku, Chiamaka Chukwuneke, Christine Mwase, Clemencia Siro, Stephen Arthur, Tunde Ajayi, Verrah Otiende, Andre Rubungo, Boyd Sinkala, Daniel Ajisafe, Emeka Onwuegbuzia, Falalu Lawan, Ibrahim Ahmad, Jesujoba Alabi, Chinedu Mbonu, Mofetoluwa Adeyemi, Mofya Phiri, Orevaoghene Ahia, Ruqayya Iro, and Sonia Adhiambo. 2023. Cross-lingual open-retrieval question answering for African languages. In *Findings of the Association for Computational Linguistics: EMNLP 2023*, pages 14957–14972, Singapore. Association for Computational Linguistics.

Shantipriya Parida, Idris Abdulmumin, Shamsuddeen Hassan Muhammad, Aneesh Bose, Guneet Singh Kohli, Ibrahim Said Ahmad, Ketan Kotwal, Sayan Deb Sarkar, Ondřej Bojar, and Habeebah Kakudi. 2023. HaVQA: A dataset for visual question answering and multimodal research in Hausa language. In *Findings of the Association for Computational Linguistics: ACL 2023*, pages 10162–10183, Toronto, Canada. Association for Computational Linguistics.

Chengwei Qin, Aston Zhang, Zhuosheng Zhang, Jiaao Chen, Michihiro Yasunaga, and Diyi Yang. 2023. Is chatgpt a general-purpose natural language processing task solver? *arXiv preprint arXiv:2302.06476*.

Ochilbek Rakhmanov and Tim Schlippe. 2022a. Sentiment analysis for Hausa: Classifying students' comments. In *Proceedings of the 1st Annual Meeting of the ELRA/ISCA Special Interest Group on Under-Resourced Languages*, pages 98–105, Marseille, France. European Language Resources Association.

Ochilbek Rakhmanov and Tim Schlippe. 2022b. Sentiment analysis for hausa: Classifying students' comments. In *Proceedings of the 1st Annual Meeting of the ELRA/ISCA Special Interest Group on Under-Resourced Languages*, pages 98–105.

Anna Rogers, Matt Gardner, and Isabelle Augenstein. 2023. Qa dataset explosion: A taxonomy of nlp resources for question answering and reading comprehension. *ACM Comput. Surv.*, 55(10).

Babangida Sani, Aakansha Soy, Sukairaj Hafiz Imam, Ahmad Mustapha, Lukman Jibril Aliyu, Idris Abdulmumin, Ibrahim Said Ahmad, and Shamsuddeen Hassan Muhammad. 2025a. Who wrote this? identifying machine vs human-generated text in hausa. *arXiv preprint arXiv:2503.13101*.

Muhammad Sani, Abubakar Ahmad, and Hadiza S Abdulazeez. 2022. Sentiment analysis of hausa language tweet using machine learning approach. *Journal of Research in Applied Mathematics*, 8(9):07–16.

Sani Abdullahi Sani, Shamsuddeen Hassan Muhammad, and Devon Jarvis. 2025b. Investigating the impact of language-adaptive fine-tuning on sentiment analysis in Hausa language using AfriBERTa. In *Proceedings of the First Workshop on Language Models for Low-Resource Languages*, pages 101–111, Abu Dhabi, United Arab Emirates. Association for Computational Linguistics.

Tim Schlippe, Edy Guevara Komgang Djomgang, Ngoc Thang Vu, Sebastian Ochs, and Tanja Schultz. 2012. Hausa large vocabulary continuous speech recognition. In *Spoken Language Technologies for Under-Resourced Languages*.

Ayesha Shakith and L Arockiam. 2024. Enhancing classification accuracy on code-mixed and imbalanced data using an adaptive deep autoencoder and xgboost. *The Scientific Temper*, 15(03):2598–2608.

Harisu Abdullahi Shehu, Kaloma Usman Majikumna, Aminu Bashir Suleiman, Stephen Luka, Md Haidar Sharif, Rabie A Ramadan, and Huseyin Kusetogullari. 2024. Unveiling sentiments: A deep dive into sentiment analysis for low-resource languages–a case study on hausa texts. *IEEE Access*.

Peeyush Singhal, Rahee Walambe, Sheela Ramanna, and Ketan Kotecha. 2023. Domain adaptation: challenges, methods, datasets, and applications. *IEEE access*, 11:6973–7020.

Atnafu Lambebo Tonja, Bonaventure F. P. Dossou, Jessica Ojo, Jenalea Rajab, Fadel Thior, Eric Peter Wairagala, Anuoluwapo Aremu, Pelonomi Moiloa, Jade Abbott, Vukosi Marivate, and Benjamin Rosman. 2024. Inkubalm: A small language model for low-resource african languages.

Aminu Tukur, Kabir Umar, and Anas Sa'idu Muhammad. 2020. Parts-of-speech tagging of hausa-based texts using hidden markov model. *Dutse Journal of Pure and Applied Sciences (DUJOPAS)*, 6:303–313.

Pavanpankaj Vegi, Sivabhavani J, Biswajit Paul, Abhinav Mishra, Prashant Banjare, Prasanna K R, and Chitra Viswanathan. 2022. WebCrawl African : A multilingual parallel corpora for African languages. In *Proceedings of the Seventh Conference on Machine Translation (WMT)*, pages 1076–1089, Abu Dhabi, United Arab Emirates (Hybrid). Association for Computational Linguistics.

Ludwig Wittgenstein. 1994. *Tractatus logico-philosophicus*. Edusp.

Lukas Wolf, Tiago Pimentel, Evelina Fedorenko, Ryan Cotterell, Alex Warstadt, Ethan Wilcox, and Tamar Regev. 2023. Quantifying the redundancy between prosody and text. In *Proceedings of the 2023 Conference on Empirical Methods in Natural Language Processing*, pages 9765–9784, Singapore. Association for Computational Linguistics.

BigScience Workshop, :, Teven Le Scao, Angela Fan, Christopher Akiki, Ellie Pavlick, Suzana Ilić, Daniel Hesslow, Roman Castagné, Alexandra Sasha Luccioni, François Yvon, Matthias Gallé, Jonathan Tow, Alexander M. Rush, Stella Biderman, Albert Webson, Pawan Sasanka Ammanamanchi, Thomas Wang, Benoît Sagot, Niklas Muennighoff, Albert Villanova del Moral, Olatunji Ruwase, Rachel Bawden, Stas Bekman, Angelina McMillan-Major, Iz Beltagy, Huu Nguyen, Lucile Saulnier, Samson Tan, Pedro Ortiz Suarez, Victor Sanh, Hugo Laurençon, Yacine Jernite, Julien Launay, Margaret Mitchell, Colin Raffel, Aaron Gokaslan, Adi Simhi, Aitor Soroa, Alham Fikri Aji, Amit Alfassy, Anna Rogers, Ariel Kreisberg Nitzav, Canwen Xu, Chenghao Mou, Chris Emezue, Christopher Klamm, Colin Leong, Daniel van Strien, David Ifeoluwa Adelani, Dragomir Radev, Eduardo González Ponferrada, Efrat Levkovizh, Ethan Kim, Eyal Bar Natan, Francesco De Toni, Gérard Dupont, Germán Kruszewski, Giada Pistilli, Hady Elsahar, Hamza Benyamina, Hieu Tran, Ian Yu, Idris Abdulmumin, Isaac Johnson, Itziar Gonzalez-Dios, Javier de la Rosa, Jenny Chim, Jesse Dodge, Jian Zhu, Jonathan Chang, Jörg Frohberg, Joseph Tobing, Joydeep Bhattacharjee, Khalid Almubarak, Kimbo Chen, Kyle Lo, Leandro Von Werra, Leon Weber, Long Phan, Loubna Ben allal, Ludovic Tanguy, Manan Dey, Manuel Romero Muñoz, Maraim Masoud, María Grandury, Mario Šaško, Max Huang, Maximin Coavoux, Mayank Singh, Mike Tian-Jian Jiang, Minh Chien Vu, Mohammad A. Jauhar, Mustafa Ghaleb, Nishant Subramani, Nora Kassner, Nurulaqilla Khamis, Olivier Nguyen, Omar Espejel, Ona de Gibert, Paulo Villegas, Peter Henderson, Pierre Colombo, Priscilla Amuok, Quentin Lhoest, Rheza Harliman, Rishi Bommasani, Roberto Luis López, Rui Ribeiro, Salomey Osei, Sampo Pyysalo, Sebastian Nagel, Shamik Bose, Shamsuddeen Hassan Muhammad, Shanya Sharma, Shayne Longpre, Somaieh Nikpoor, Stanislav Silberberg, Suhas Pai, Sydney Zink, Tiago Timponi Torrent, Timo Schick, Tristan Thrush, Valentin Danchev, Vassilina Nikoulina, Veronika Laippala, Violette Lepercq, Vrinda Prabhu, Zaid Alyafeai, Zeerak Talat, Arun Raja, Benjamin Heinzerling, Chenglei Si, Davut Emre Taşar, Elizabeth Salesky, Sabrina J. Mielke, Wilson Y. Lee, Abheesht Sharma, Andrea Santilli, Antoine Chaffin, Arnaud Stiegler, Debajyoti Datta, Eliza Szczechla, Gunjan Chhablani, Han Wang, Harshit Pandey, Hendrik Strobelt, Jason Alan Fries, Jos Rozen, Leo Gao, Lintang Sutawika, M Saiful Bari, Maged S. Al-shaibani, Matteo Manica, Nihal Nayak, Ryan Teehan, Samuel Albanie, Sheng Shen, Srulik Ben-David, Stephen H. Bach, Taewoon Kim, Tali Bers, Thibault Fevry, Trishala Neeraj, Urmish Thakker, Vikas Raunak, Xiangru Tang, Zheng-Xin Yong, Zhiqing Sun, Shaked Brody, Yallow Uri, Hadar Tojarieh, Adam Roberts, Hyung Won Chung, Jaesung Tae, Jason Phang, Ofir Press, Conglong Li, Deepak Narayanan, Hatim Bourfoune, Jared Casper, Jeff Rasley, Max Ryabinin, Mayank Mishra, Minjia Zhang, Mohammad Shoeybi, Myriam Peyrounette, Nicolas Patry, Nouamane Tazi, Omar Sanseviero, Patrick von Platen, Pierre Cornette, Pierre François Lavallée, Rémi Lacroix, Samyam Rajbhandari, Sanchit Gandhi, Shaden Smith, Stéphane Requena, Suraj Patil, Tim Dettmers, Ahmed Baruwa, Amanpreet Singh, Anastasia Cheveleva, Anne-Laure Ligozat, Arjun Subramonian, Aurélie Névéol, Charles Lovering, Dan Garrette, Deepak Tunuguntla, Ehud Reiter, Ekaterina Taktasheva, Ekaterina Voloshina, Eli Bogdanov, Genta Indra Winata, Hailey Schoelkopf, Jan-Christoph Kalo, Jekaterina Novikova, Jessica Zosa Forde, Jordan Clive, Jungo Kasai, Ken Kawamura,

Liam Hazan, Marine Carpuat, Miruna Clinciu, Najoung Kim, Newton Cheng, Oleg Serikov, Omer Antverg, Oskar van der Wal, Rui Zhang, Ruochen Zhang, Sebastian Gehrmann, Shachar Mirkin, Shani Pais, Tatiana Shavrina, Thomas Scialom, Tian Yun, Tomasz Limisiewicz, Verena Rieser, Vitaly Protasov, Vladislav Mikhailov, Yada Pruksachatkun, Yonatan Belinkov, Zachary Bamberger, Zdeněk Kasner, Alice Rueda, Amanda Pestana, Amir Feizpour, Ammar Khan, Amy Faranak, Ana Santos, Anthony Hevia, Antigona Unldreaj, Arash Aghagol, Arezoo Abdollahi, Aycha Tammour, Azadeh HajiHosseini, Bahareh Behroozi, Benjamin Ajibade, Bharat Saxena, Carlos Muñoz Ferrandis, Daniel McDuff, Danish Contractor, David Lansky, Davis David, Douwe Kiela, Duong A. Nguyen, Edward Tan, Emi Baylor, Ezinwanne Ozoani, Fatima Mirza, Frankline Ononiwu, Habib Rezanejad, Hessie Jones, Indrani Bhattacharya, Irene Solaiman, Irina Sedenko, Isar Nejadgholi, Jesse Passmore, Josh Seltzer, Julio Bonis Sanz, Livia Dutra, Mairon Samagaio, Maraim Elbadri, Margot Mieskes, Marissa Gerchick, Martha Akinlolu, Michael McKenna, Mike Qiu, Muhammed Ghauri, Mykola Burynok, Nafis Abrar, Nazneen Rajani, Nour Elkott, Nour Fahmy, Olanrewaju Samuel, Ran An, Rasmus Kromann, Ryan Hao, Samira Alizadeh, Sarmad Shubber, Silas Wang, Sourav Roy, Sylvain Viguier, Thanh Le, Tobi Oyebade, Trieu Le, Yoyo Yang, Zach Nguyen, Abhinav Ramesh Kashyap, Alfredo Palasciano, Alison Callahan, Anima Shukla, Antonio Miranda-Escalada, Ayush Singh, Benjamin Beilharz, Bo Wang, Caio Brito, Chenxi Zhou, Chirag Jain, Chuxin Xu, Clémentine Fourrier, Daniel León Periñán, Daniel Molano, Dian Yu, Enrique Manjavacas, Fabio Barth, Florian Fuhrimann, Gabriel Altay, Giyaseddin Bayrak, Gully Burns, Helena U. Vrabec, Imane Bello, Ishani Dash, Jihyun Kang, John Giorgi, Jonas Golde, Jose David Posada, Karthik Rangasai Sivaraman, Lokesh Bulchandani, Lu Liu, Luisa Shinzato, Madeleine Hahn de Bykhovetz, Maiko Takeuchi, Marc Pàmies, Maria A Castillo, Marianna Nezhurina, Mario Sänger, Matthias Samwald, Michael Cullan, Michael Weinberg, Michiel De Wolf, Mina Mihaljcic, Minna Liu, Moritz Freidank, Myungsun Kang, Natasha Seelam, Nathan Dahlberg, Nicholas Michio Broad, Nikolaus Muellner, Pascale Fung, Patrick Haller, Ramya Chandrasekhar, Renata Eisenberg, Robert Martin, Rodrigo Canalli, Rosaline Su, Ruisi Su, Samuel Cahyawijaya, Samuele Garda, Shlok S Deshmukh, Shubhanshu Mishra, Sid Kiblawi, Simon Ott, Sinee Sang-aroonsiri, Srishti Kumar, Stefan Schweter, Sushil Bharati, Tanmay Laud, Théo Gigant, Tomoya Kainuma, Wojciech Kusa, Yanis Labrak, Yash Shailesh Bajaj, Yash Venkatraman, Yifan Xu, Yingxin Xu, Yu Xu, Zhe Tan, Zhongli Xie, Zifan Ye, Mathilde Bras, Younes Belkada, and Thomas Wolf. 2023. Bloom: A 176b-parameter open-access multilingual language model.

S.A. Yakasai. 2025. Tauraruwa harshen hausa jiya da yau: Kalubale da madosa. *Tauraruwa Journal of Hausa Studies*, 1(1):1–9.

Yizhe Yang, Huashan Sun, Jiawei Li, Runheng Liu, Yinghao Li, Yuhang Liu, Yang Gao, and Heyan Huang. 2024. Mindllm: Lightweight large language model pre-training, evaluation and domain application. *AI Open*, 5:1 – 26.

Dong Yu and Lin Deng. 2016. *Automatic speech recognition*, volume 1. Springer.

Aliyu Yusuf, Aliza Sarlan, Kamaluddeen Usman Danyaro, and Abdullahi Sani BA Rahman. 2023. Fine-tuning multilingual transformers for hausa-english sentiment analysis. In *2023 13th International Conference on Information Technology in Asia (CITA)*, pages 13–18. IEEE.

Aliyu Yusuf, Aliza Sarlan, Kamaluddeen Usman Danyaro, Abdullahi Sani BA Rahman, and Mujaheed Abdullahi. 2024. Sentiment analysis in low-resource settings: A comprehensive review of approaches, languages, and data sources. *IEEE Access*.

Rufai Yusuf Zakari, Zaharaddeen Karami Lawal, and Idris Abdulmumin. 2021. A systematic literature review of hausa natural language processing. *International Journal of Computer and Information Technology (2279-0764)*, 10(4).

Abubakar Yakubu Zandam, Fatima Adam Muhammad, and Isa Inuwa-Dutse. 2023. Online threats detection in hausa language. In *4th Workshop on African Natural Language Processing*.

Wanru Zhao, Yihong Chen, Royson Lee, Xinchi Qiu, Yan Gao, Hongxiang Fan, and Nicholas D. Lane. 2024. Breaking physical and linguistic borders: Multilingual federated prompt tuning for low-resource languages.

Linan Zhu, Zhechao Zhu, Chenwei Zhang, Yifei Xu, and Xiangjie Kong. 2023. Multimodal sentiment analysis based on fusion methods: A survey. *Information Fusion*, 95:306–325.

6 Appendex

Table 1: Publicly available Hausa datasets

SN	Source	Domain	Task	Size	Repository
1	(Muhammad et al., 2022)	Tweets	Sentiment Analysis	30k	https://github.com/hausanlp/NaijaSenti/blob/main/README.md
2	Rakhmanov and Schlippe (2022a)	Teachers' evaluation	Sentiment Analysis	40k	https://github.com/MrLachin/HESAC
3	(Aliyu et al., 2022)	Tweets	Hate speech detection	6k	https://github.com/hausanlp/HERDPhobia
3	Adelani et al. (2023)	News	Topic classification	3k	https://github.com/masakhane-io/masakhane-news
4	(Inuwa-Dutse, 2023)	Tweets/News	Machine translation, raw texts		https://github.com/ijdutse/hausa-corpus/tree/master
5	(Dione et al., 2023)	News	POS tagging	1,504 sents.	https://github.com/masakhane-io/masakhane-pos/tree/main/data/hau
6	(Bichi et al., 2023)	News	Summarization	113 articles	https://journals.plos.org/plosone/article/file?type=supplementary&id=10.1371/journal.pone.0285376.s001
7	(Ogundepo et al., 2023)	Wikipedia	Question Answering	1171	https://github.com/masakhane-io/afriqa
8	(Adelani et al., 2021, 2022c)	NER	News	2,720 & 8,165	https://github.com/masakhane-io/masakhane-ner/
9	Adelani et al. (2022a)	Machine Translation	News		https://github.com/masakhane-io/lafand-mt/tree/main
10	(Akhbardeh et al., 2021)	Machine Translation	News & Religious	Numerous	https://data.statmt.org/wmt21/translation-task/
11	(Goyal et al., 2022)	Machine Translation	Wikimedia	$\sim$2000	https://github.com/openlanguagedata/flores
12	(Vegi et al., 2022)	Machine Translation	Web Crawl		https://github.com/pavanpankaj/Web-Crawl-African?tab=readme-ov-file
13	(Sani et al., 2025a)	News	Text Classification	5172	https://github.com/TheBangis/hausa_corpus

Beyond Generalization: Evaluating Multilingual LLMs for Yorùbá Animal Health Translation

Godwin Adegbehingbe, Anthony Soronnadi, Ife Adebara ,Olubayo Adekanmbi
Research & Innovation Department
Data Science Nigeria
Lagos, Nigeria
{Godwin,Anthony,Ife,Olubayo}@datasciencenigeria.ai

Abstract

Machine translation (MT) has advanced significantly for high-resource languages, yet specialized domain translation remains a challenge for low-resource languages. This study evaluates the ability of state-of-the-art multilingual models to translate animal health reports from English to Yorùbá, a crucial task for veterinary communication in underserved regions.We curated a dataset of 1,468 parallel sentences and compared multiple MT models in zero shot and fine-tuned settings. Our findings indicate substantial limitations in their ability to generalize to domain-specific translation, with common errors arising from vocabulary mismatch, training data scarcity, and morphological complexity. Fine-tuning improves performance, particularly for the NLLB 3.3B model, but challenges remain in preserving technical accuracy. These results underscore the need for more targeted approaches to multilingual and culturally aware LLMs for African languages.

1 Introduction

Machine translation (MT) has the potential to improve communication in African languages, but most state-of-the-art models underperform in specialized domains. Yorùbá-speaking communities rely on accurate veterinary translations for disease surveillance and livestock health. However, generic MT models struggle with technical terms and tonal complexities. This study evaluates MT models for domain-specific translation, highlighting challenges and improvements through fine-tuning.

2 Related Work

Recent advances in machine translation (MT) have significantly improved low-resource language translation through transfer learning and unsupervised MT techniques. For African languages, particularly Yorùbá, pre-trained multilingual models like mT5 and mBART (Lee et al., 2022)have shown promising results when fine-tuned on Yorùbá data (Adelani et al., 2022). However, challenges persist in domain-specific applications, especially in specialized fields such as animal health, where standardized terminologies are often absent or underdeveloped (Abenet). Existing MT systems such as NLLB and Google Translate frequently produce erroneous translations of technical terms, highlighting the need for domain-specific fine-tuning (Adebara and Abdul-Mageed, 2022).To address data scarcity in low-resource MT systems, researchers have explored various augmentation techniques. Back-translation has shown promise by creating synthetic parallel data from monolingual target-language content(Jauregi Unanue and Piccardi, 2020), though its effectiveness in preserving technical accuracy remains uncertain for domain-specific translations(Baruah and Singh, 2022).Synthetic data generation techniques have been investigated for neural MT (Tonja et al., 2023), while human-in-the-loop strategies incorporating domain experts (Nunes Vieira, 2019) have emerged as crucial approaches for improving translation quality, particularly in specialized domains (Yang et al., 2023). Evaluation of MT systems in specialized domains requires comprehensive assessment approaches that go beyond traditional metrics. While metrics such as BLEU, AfriComet and chrF provide insights into different aspects of translation quality, (Zappatore and Ruggieri, 2023) argue that specialized domains like biomedical MT require tailored evaluation strategies emphasizing terminology accuracy and practical usability. For Yorùbá animal health translation, these metrics collectively offer a multi-faceted assessment framework: BLEU measures n-gram overlap, AfriComet accounts for semantic accuracy in African languages, and chrF captures character-level precision, particularly valuable for morphologically rich languages like Yorùbá.

Proceedings of the Sixth Workshop on African Natural Language Processing (AfricaNLP 2025), pages 192–194

3 Dataset and Methodology

We introduce VetYorùbá, a curated corpus of 1,468 English-Yorùbá parallel sentences, sourced from veterinary health reports. Data preprocessing included normalization to handle Yorùbá's tonal orthography. We evaluated multiple MT models, including NLLB 3.3B (Team et al., 2022), AfriTeVa (Jude Ogundepo et al., 2022), and mT0, under zero-shot and fine-tuned conditions. Metrics such as BLEU, chrF, and AfriComet were used to assess translation quality.We collected our data from three primary sources: the World Organisation for Animal Health (WOAH) reports focusing on seven epidemiologically significant diseases in the region: Rabies, Avian Influenza, Newcastle Disease, Foot-and-Mouth Disease (FMD), African Swine Fever (ASF), Bovine Tuberculosis, and Peste des Petits Ruminants (PPR). Food and Agriculture Organization (FAO) documentation covering animal health practices, preventive measures, and outbreak management protocols, selected to enhance the corpus's terminological breadth. Real-time epidemiological data extracted using PADI-Web (Valentin et al., 2020), an event-based surveillance tool that aggregates information from both structured (official reports) and unstructured sources (news articles, social media)(Oladipo et al., 2023). We focused on maintaining a balanced representation across different disease contexts and livestock categories.Veterinarians facilitated data curation, while native speakers of Yorùbá translated the sentences. The translations were then validated by veterinarians fluent in Yorùbá.

Split	Size	TTR (English)	TTR (Yoruba)
Train	1172	0.2243	0.1672
Dev	147	0.4706	0.3629
Test	147	0.4592	0.3485

Table 1: Dataset split and Type-Token Ratio(TTR) for English and Yoruba sentences

4 Results and Discussion

Zero-shot translation yielded poor results in all models, with NLLB 3.3B achieving a BLEU score of 2.9. Fine-tuning improved performance significantly, raising BLEU to 45.89 for NLLB 3.3B and enhancing chrF and AfriComet scores. However, translation errors persisted, particularly in complex veterinary terms and tonal variations. These findings highlight the limitations of general-purpose LLMs in handling domain-specific, low-resource languages.

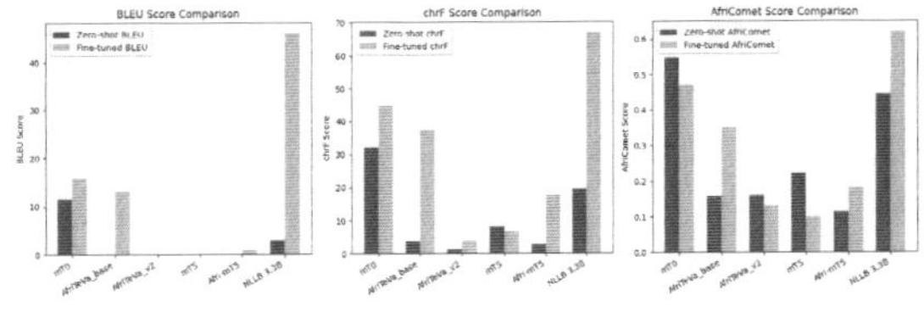

Figure 1: MT Model performance on Yoruba Animal Health Translation

The performance of the machine translation models evaluated was quantified using BLEU (Papineni et al., 2002), chrF (Popović, 2015), and AfriComet (Wang et al., 2024) metrics under both zero-shot and fine-tuned conditions. Overall, fine-tuning on our domain-specific dataset of 1,468 English–Yorùbá sentence pairs resulted in marked improvements across all metrics. In the zero-shot setting, the models generally exhibited low performance, with many struggling to produce coherent translations in the specialized domain of animal health. mT0 achieved a BLEU score of 11.57, while other models such as Afri-mT5 and AfriTeVa_v2 recorded near-zero BLEU scores (0.0003 and 0.005, respectively).Fine-tuning of the models on the curated veterinary dataset significantly improved translation quality. The BLEU score of the mT0 model improved to 15.9, while NLLB 3.3B exhibited the most dramatic gain, rising from 2.9 to 45.89. This improvement was consistently reflected in the chrF scores, with NLLB 3.3B increasing from 19.47 to 66.85. The AfriComet metric further supported these improvements, particularly for the NLLB 3.3B and the AfriTeVa base, whose fine-tuned scores of 62 and 35, respectively, signified better semantic alignment and contextual accuracy in translations.The substantial improvements observed in key models, particularly NLLB 3.3B, confirm that fine-tuning can mitigate the limitations of zero-shot translation (Alabi et al., 2022) and lead to more accurate and reliable translations of technical content in Yorùbá.

5 Conclusion and Future Work

This study underscores the challenges of applying multilingual LLMs to specialized translation tasks in African languages. Although fine-tuning improves performance, key limitations remain, emphasizing the need for tailored approaches integrating linguistic features such as tone and morphology.

Future research would focus on expanding domain-specific corpora and developing African-centric models for technical translation tasks in animal health.

References

T. A. Abenet. Bridging the gap: Legal and medical translation in African indigenous languages. In *Proceedings of ...*

I. Adebara and M. Abdul-Mageed. 2022. Towards afrocentric nlp for african languages: Where we are and where we can go. In *Proceedings of the 60th Annual Meeting of the Association for Computational Linguistics (Volume 1: Long Papers)*, pages 3814–3841, Dublin, Ireland. Association for Computational Linguistics.

D. I. Adelani, J. O. Alabi, A. Fan, J. Kreutzer, X. Shen, M. Reid, D. Ruiter, D. Klakow, P. Nabende, E. Chang, et al. 2022. A few thousand translations go a long way! Leveraging pre-trained models for African news translation. In *Proceedings of the North American Chapter of the Association for Computational Linguistics*.

Jesujoba O. Alabi, David Ifeoluwa Adelani, Marius Mosbach, and Dietrich Klakow. 2022. Adapting pre-trained language models to African languages via multilingual adaptive fine-tuning. In *Proceedings of the 29th International Conference on Computational Linguistics*, pages 4336–4349, Gyeongju, Republic of Korea. International Committee on Computational Linguistics.

Rupjyoti Baruah and Anil Kumar Singh. 2022. *A Clinical Practice by Machine Translation on Low Resource Languages*. CRC Press eBooks.

I. Jauregi Unanue and M. Piccardi. 2020. Pretrained language models and backtranslation for English-Basque biomedical neural machine translation. In *Proceedings of the Fifth Conference on Machine Translation*, pages 826–832, Online. Association for Computational Linguistics.

Odunayo Jude Ogundepo, Akintunde Oladipo, Mofetoluwa Adeyemi, Kelechi Ogueji, and Jimmy Lin. 2022. AfriTeVA: Extending ?small data? pretraining approaches to sequence-to-sequence models. In *Proceedings of the Third Workshop on Deep Learning for Low-Resource Natural Language Processing*, pages 126–135, Hybrid. Association for Computational Linguistics.

En-Shiun Annie Lee, Sarubi Thillainathan, Shravan Nayak, Surangika Ranathunga, David Ifeoluwa Adelani, Ruisi Su, and Arya D. McCarthy. 2022. Pre-trained multilingual sequence-to-sequence models: A hope for low-resource language translation? In *Findings of the Association for Computational Linguistics: ACL 2022*, pages 58–67, Dublin, Ireland. Association for Computational Linguistics.

Lucas Nunes Vieira. 2019. *Post-Editing of Machine Translation*, pages 319–335.

Akintunde Oladipo, Mofetoluwa Adeyemi, Orevaoghene Ahia, Abraham Owodunni, Odunayo Ogundepo, David Adelani, and Jimmy Lin. 2023. Better quality pre-training data and t5 models for African languages. In *Proceedings of the 2023 Conference on Empirical Methods in Natural Language Processing*, pages 158–168, Singapore. Association for Computational Linguistics.

K. Papineni, S. Roukos, T. Ward, and W.-J. Zhu. 2002. BLEU: A method for automatic evaluation of machine translation. In *Proceedings of the 40th Annual Meeting of the Association for Computational Linguistics*, pages 311–318. Association for Computational Linguistics.

Maja Popović. 2015. chrF: character n-gram F-score for automatic MT evaluation. In *Proceedings of the Tenth Workshop on Statistical Machine Translation*, pages 392–395, Lisbon, Portugal. Association for Computational Linguistics.

NLLB Team, Marta R. Costa-jussà, James Cross, Onur Çelebi, Maha Elbayad, Kenneth Heafield, Kevin Heffernan, Elahe Kalbassi, Janice Lam, Daniel Licht, Jean Maillard, Anna Sun, Skyler Wang, Guillaume Wenzek, Al Youngblood, Bapi Akula, Loic Barrault, Gabriel Mejia Gonzalez, Prangthip Hansanti, John Hoffman, Semarley Jarrett, Kaushik Ram Sadagopan, Dirk Rowe, Shannon Spruit, Chau Tran, Pierre Andrews, Necip Fazil Ayan, Shruti Bhosale, Sergey Edunov, and Angela Fan. 2022. No language left behind: Scaling human-centered machine translation. *Preprint*, arXiv:2207.04672.

A. L. Tonja, O. Kolesnikova, A. Gelbukh, and G. Sidorov. 2023. Low-resource neural machine translation improvement using source-side monolingual data. *Applied Sciences*, 13(1201).

Sarah Valentin, Elena Arsevska, Sylvain Falala, Jocelyn de Goër, Renaud Lancelot, Alizé Mercier, Julien Rabatel, and Mathieu Roche. 2020. Padi-web: A multilingual event-based surveillance system for monitoring animal infectious diseases. *Computers and Electronics in Agriculture*, 169:105163.

Jiayi Wang, David Ifeoluwa Adelani, and Agrawal. 2024. Afrimte and africomet: Enhancing comet to embrace under-resourced african languages. *Preprint*, arXiv:2311.09828.

Xinyi Yang, Runzhe Zhan, Derek F. Wong, Junchao Wu, and Lidia S. Chao. 2023. Human-in-the-loop machine translation with large language model. In *Proceedings of Machine Translation Summit XIX, Vol. 2: Users Track*, pages 88–98, Macau SAR, China. Asia-Pacific Association for Machine Translation.

M. Zappatore and G. Ruggieri. 2023. Adopting machine translation in the healthcare sector: A methodological multi-criteria review. *Computer Speech & Language*, page 101582.

Evaluating Robustness of LLMs to Typographical Noise in Yorùbá QA

Paul Okewunmi[1,2*] **Favour James**[1,2] **Oluwadunsin Fajemila**[1,2]
[1]ML Collective
[2]Obafemi Awolowo University
{ptokewunmi, fujames, oefajemila}@student.oauife.edu.ng

Abstract

Generative AI models are primarily accessed through chat interfaces, where user queries often contain typographical errors. While these models perform well in English, their robustness to noisy inputs in low-resource languages like Yorùbá remains underexplored. This work investigates a Yorùbá question-answering (QA) task by introducing synthetic typographical noise into clean inputs. We design a probabilistic noise injection strategy that simulates realistic human typos. In our experiments, each character in a clean sentence is independently altered, with noise levels ranging from 10% to 40%. We evaluate performance across three strong multilingual models using two complementary metrics: (1) a multilingual BERTScore to assess semantic similarity between outputs on clean and noisy inputs, and (2) an LLM-as-judge approach, where the best Yorùbá-capable model rates fluency, comprehension, and accuracy on a 1–5 scale. Results show that while English QA performance degrades gradually, Yorùbá QA suffers a sharper decline. At 40% noise, GPT-4o experiences over a 50% drop in comprehension ability, with similar declines for Gemini 2.0 Flash and Claude 3.7 Sonnet. We conclude with recommendations for noise-aware training and dedicated noisy Yorùbá benchmarks to enhance LLM robustness in low-resource settings.

Figure 1: The top conversation represents a correct response, while the bottom conversation illustrates errors due to typographical noise. The question in the bottom example contains multiple error types, which includes replacement and transposition. As a result, the model fails to understand the query and responds with confusion.

1 Introduction

Large Language Models (LLMs) have transformed the landscape of Natural Language Processing (NLP), enabling advanced reasoning and question-answering (QA) capabilities. These models perform exceptionally well in high-resource languages like English, where extensive training data and noise-handling mechanisms enhance robustness. However, their effectiveness in low-resource languages like Yorùbá remains underexplored (Inuwa-Dutse, 2025).

A key challenge affecting LLM robustness is sensitivity to input variations. Minor typographical errors, such as omitted letters or misplaced diacritics, can significantly degrade model performance. Prior research (Moradi and Samwald, 2021; Vaibhav et al., 2019) has analyzed this phenomenon in English QA tasks, revealing how slight distortions mislead models. However, little is known about its effects in Yorùbá, a tonal language heavily reliant

*Corresponding author.

Proceedings of the Sixth Workshop on African Natural Language Processing (AfricaNLP 2025), pages 195–202
July 31, 2025 ©2025 Association for Computational Linguistics

on diacritics to convey meaning. Misplaced or omitted diacritics can alter words entirely—e.g., "Ògún" (a deity) vs. "ogun" (war) vs. "ogún" (twenty), presenting an even greater risk of misinterpretation (Jimoh et al., 2025).

Despite the linguistic importance of diacritics, Yorùbá text is often written without them in electronic media, most often due to keyboard limitations or user habits, resulting in significant information loss (Jimoh et al., 2025). As illustrated in Figure 1, typographical distortions can lead to misinterpretations that affect model performance in QA tasks. LLMs trained predominantly on high-resource languages may struggle with these nuances, raising a critical question: **How well do LLMs handle typographical errors in Yorùbá question answering?**

Handling noisy text is crucial for real-world applications, particularly in multilingual settings. While typographical perturbations and adversarial attacks have been studied extensively in English, systematic evaluations for Yorùbá are lacking—despite the language being spoken by over 40 million people. Understanding how well LLMs handle noisy Yorùbá input is essential for improving their reliability across diverse linguistic contexts.

To address this gap, we construct a controlled Yorùbá QA dataset with synthetic typographical noise using a probabilistic noise modeling approach. Characters in clean sentences are independently altered at noise levels ranging from 10% to 40%, introducing errors such as insertions, replacements, and transpositions (swapping) based on keyboard adjacency. We also explore a variant where error types are randomly selected, incorporating leet replacements (e.g., 'e' → '3', 'o' → '0', 's' → '$')(Zhang et al., 2022). Model responses to noisy inputs are evaluated against clean text using semantic similarity metrics such as BERTScore (Zhang et al., 2020) and an LLM-as-judge evaluation framework (Zheng et al., 2023).

Our contributions are as follows:

1. We propose a probabilistic noise generation method that simulates human typographical errors in Yorùbá.

2. We systematically evaluate the impact of typographical noise on Yorùbá QA performance using GPT-4o, Gemini 2.0 Flash and Claude 3.7 Sonnet.

3. We provide insights to inform noise-aware training, develop evaluation datasets, and establish benchmarks for assessing typographical robustness in Yorùbá NLP.

2 Related Work

Given the increasing prevalence of chat-based language models facilitating text-based interaction between users and language models, several studies have explored how user-generated typographical errors influence model performance. Previous research has utilized artificially generated noisy datasets created through various simulation methodologies (Kumar et al., 2020; Cai et al., 2022). Specifically, these studies introduced noise by randomly altering a percentage of characters based on proximity within the QWERTY keyboard layout, effectively simulating typical typing errors encountered in real-world interactions.

However, much of this research has primarily concentrated on monolingual settings, predominantly English, neglecting the assessment of multilingual language models with diverse multilingual test scenarios (Moradi and Samwald, 2021; Wang et al., 2023). Consequently, investigations into textual noise have largely been restricted to English-language contexts. Despite impressive performances by large multilingual models across various tasks and languages, their effectiveness tends to diminish significantly when applied to languages other than English, particularly low-resource languages (Etxaniz et al., 2023).

Additionally, existing literature has mainly evaluated transformer-based models such as BERT, suggesting a research gap regarding larger, recently popularized language models (Cooper Stickland et al., 2023). Previous studies demonstrated the robustness of models like BERT, XLM-Roberta, and XLNet against textual noise, noting their commendable performance despite their relatively modest sizes, typically under 0.3 billion parameters. This highlights a clear distinction from contemporary LLMs, which frequently possess parameter counts in the billions, underscoring the necessity for further investigations into their resilience to noisy inputs.

This study addresses the gap between contemporary chat-based LLMs and authentic typographical errors observed in practical usage. It examines the robustness of large language models with multilingual capabilities, specifically using noisy, real-

Error	Example Sentence
None	Kí ló mu ki ẹ̀rọ kọmpútà fi ṣe pàtàkì púpọ ní ayé òde òní?
Replacement	lí ló mu ji ẹ̀fọ kọmpútà fi ṣe pàtàkì púpọ ní ayé òde ònk?
Insertion	Kí ló mu kiu ẹ̀ẹ̀rọ kọmpútà fi ṣe pàtàqkì púpọ ní ayé òde òoní?
Transposition	Kí ló mu ki ẹ̀ọr kmọpútà fi ṣe pàtàkì púpọ ní ayé òde òin?
Random	Kí l0 mu k1 ẹ̀rọ ọkmpútà fi $e pàtàkì púpọ ní ayé pde 0ní

Table 1: Yorùbá text with different error types.

world Yorùbá datasets.

3 Methodology

3.1 Typographical Error Types

To effectively replicate real-world user interactions, we focus on modifying words in ways that reflect common typing errors made during chatbot conversations with LLMs. To assess their impact, we introduce four primary categories of typographical errors using a probabilistic modeling approach:

- **Insertion Errors:** An extra character, either the same as the intended one (double typing) or an adjacent key from a QWERTY keyboard, is inserted immediately after the original character. This simulates accidental keystrokes common in rapid typing.
- **Replacement Errors:** The intended character is replaced with a neighboring key based on the QWERTY layout, mimicking mistyped characters.
- **Transposition (Swap) Errors**: Two adjacent characters swap positions, replicating common finger-slips where typists accidentally invert the order of two neighboring characters.
- **Random Errors:** A combination of insertion, replacement, transposition, and character-to-symbol substitutions (leetspeak errors, e.g., replacing 'e' with '3', 'o' with '0') is applied. This mixed-error category closely reflects real-world, unstructured typing mistakes.

These error types collectively represent realistic erros that can substantially affect the performance of language models, especially in a linguistically sensitive context such as Yorùbá question and answering tasks. Table 1 shows examples of these errors in a sentence.

3.2 Noise Injection Strategy

To precisely evaluate the impact of typographical errors, we employ a probabilistic noise injection approach. Given a clean text sequence of length N, we introduce errors at a predefined rate p, modifying a fraction of characters to simulate real-world typing mistakes.

The number of modified characters, N_e, is determined as:

$$N_e = \lfloor p \times N \rfloor$$

where p is the error rate (e.g., 10%, 20%, 40%).

For each selected character position, one of the previously described error types is applied. The error type is either predetermined (for controlled experiments) or chosen randomly for greater variability.

The noise injection process follows these steps:

1. **Text Tokenization**: The input text is split into individual characters while preserving spaces.
2. **Error Injection**: A random subset of characters, determined by N_e, is selected, and an error type is applied.
3. **Text Reconstruction**: The modified sequence is reconstructed, ensuring that spacing and word boundaries remain intact.

Since the selection of characters to be modified is performed uniformly at random, each character in the text has an equal probability of being selected for modification. The probability that a specific character x_i is selected for modification is:

$$P(x_i \text{ is modified}) = \frac{N_e}{N} = p$$

This implies that every character has an independent probability p of being altered, regardless of its position in the sequence. The overall process is further illustrated in **Algorithm 1**.

Algorithm 1 Probabilistic Typo Injection

Require: Clean text sequence $X = \{x_1, x_2, ..., x_n\}$, error rate p, predefined error mapping T, noise function $\mathcal{N}$

Ensure: Noisy text sequence $X' = \{x'_1, x'_2, ..., x'_n\}$

Compute number of typo errors:

$$N_e = \lfloor p \times n \rfloor$$

Randomly select N_e character positions:

$$P = \text{RandomSample}(\{1, 2, ..., n\}, N_e)$$

```
for i ∈ P do
    Retrieve predefined error type T_i from mapping T
    Apply noise function N based on T_i:
    if T_i = Insertion then
        Insert an adjacent or duplicate character
    else if T_i = Replacement then
        Replace character with a neighboring key
    else if T_i = Transposition then
        Swap adjacent characters
    else if T_i = Random then
        Apply a mix of predefined transformations
    end if
end for
Construct noisy text X' by modifying selected positions in X
return X'
```

4 Experimentation

4.1 Dataset

The dataset used in this study consists of 50 curated Yorùbá QA pairs, carefully selected to ensure a balance between culturally specific questions and general knowledge inquiries. The culturally peculiar questions focus on topics rooted in Yorùbá traditions, language, and history, while the general knowledge questions cover widely known facts that are not restricted to any specific cultural context. The average question length is about 15 words.

Each question in the dataset is structured to encourage detailed responses rather than one-word answers. This design choice ensures that evaluation is not based on exact matches but rather on the LLM's ability to understand the question and generate an accurate and contextually appropriate response.

4.2 Generating Noisy Variants from Dataset

To evaluate the impact of typographical noise on Yorùbá QA, we introduce controlled noise to create variations of the clean questions in the dataset. For each question, we introduce typographical errors at predefined rates. Every question undergoes modifications corresponding to the four error types, with error rates varying from 10% to 40% in increments of 10%. This range ensures that we capture a spectrum of real-world errors, from minor typos to more severe distortions. Increasing noise beyond this threshold could result in unnatural sentences, making evaluation less meaningful.

To account for variability, we generate three distinct variations for each error type at each noise level, ensuring that different subsets of characters are affected. This results in a total of:

$$4 \text{ (error types)} \times 4 \text{ (error rates)} \\ \times 3 \text{ (variations per rate)} = 48$$

noisy versions per sentence. Since we have 50 sentences in our dataset, we end up with a total of:

$$50 \times 48 = 2,400$$

sentences, allowing for a diverse evaluation of model robustness.

Having multiple variations per sentence enhances evaluation depth and reliability. First, it provides a comprehensive assessment of how different types and levels of noise impact model performance. Additionally, by generating multiple variations at the same noise level, we ensure that evaluation results are not biased by a specific character selection, reducing variance and improving statistical significance. Finally, this approach closely reflects real-world typing errors, as users rarely make the same mistake in a fixed pattern.

4.3 Models

Each noisy variation of the dataset is input into the models using the same system prompt to ensure consistency across evaluations. The prompt explicitly instructs the models to limit responses to a maximum of 25 words, balancing computational efficiency with response relevance.

To enforce deterministic outputs, we set the temperature to 0, ensuring a fixed response pattern for each input. The generated responses are logged for further evaluation, enabling direct comparisons between clean and noisy input variations.

4.4 Evaluation Process

We pass the clean questions to the models, using their returned output as a gold standard for comparison. Next, we introduce typographical noise and compare the models' responses to their clean-input counterparts to measure performance degradation.

Model	Error Rate	LLM as Judge			Refusal	BertScore		
		Fluency	Comp.	Acc.	Rate (%)	P	R	F1
Google Gemini	10	4.9	4.9	4.8	0.7	82.4	82.2	82.3
	20	4.8	4.3	4.3	8.4	79.2	79.0	79.1
	30	4.7	3.2	3.1	29.4	76.0	75.3	75.6
	40	4.7	2.3	2.2	59.1	73.4	72.7	73.0
Claude sonnet 3.7	10	4.8	4.9	4.8	1.0	83.0	80.0	84.0
	20	4.7	4.5	4.5	8.0	80.0	78.0	80.0
	30	4.5	3.4	3.3	19.7	77.0	77.0	76.0
	40	4.0	2.1	2.0	35.0	71.0	72.0	73.0
GPT-4 Omni	10	4.9	4.8	4.7	0.4	85.9	85.8	85.9
	20	4.5	4.2	4.1	2.5	81.2	80.9	81.1
	30	4.1	3.1	3.0	13.4	77.1	76.7	76.9
	40	4.2	2.2	1.9	38.1	73.8	73.1	73.4

Table 2: Model Performance Across Error Rates: Fluency, Comprehension, Accuracy, Refusal Rate, and BERTScore

4.4.1 Metrics for Measuring Robustness

BERTScore for Semantic Similarity: To assess how typographical noise affects responses, we compute BERTScore between the model's outputs for clean and noisy inputs. Unlike BLEU (Papineni et al., 2002), which relies on n-grams, BERTScore leverages contextual embeddings from pre-trained models to measure semantic similarity.

However, BERTScore's effectiveness for Yorùbá is limited by the poor quality of its language embeddings in multilingual models, as low-resource languages often lack sufficient training data for robust representations. As a result, while it can measure similarity, it sometimes fails to reflect how dissimilar two Yorùbá sentences truly are, necessitating additional evaluation methods.

LLM-as-a-Judge Evaluation: Given BERTScore's limitations, we use an LLM-as-a-Judge approach, leveraging Google's Gemini 2.0 Flash for human-like evaluation. This method assesses whether the models maintain meaningful understanding despite noise. The system prompt provided to the LLM acting as judge is show in Appendix B.

The evaluation process follows these steps:

1. The clean question and the noisy-response pair are fed to the model.

2. The model scores the response, based on the following:

    - **Fluency**: Grammatical correctness and naturalness.
    - **Comprehension**: Understanding of the question.
    - **Accuracy**: Correctness of the response.

3. The model also classifies responses as either:

    - A valid attempt at answering the question.
    - A refusal or failure to understand, including responses like: *"Mo nílò àlàyé síwájú sí"* ("I need more clarification.") or *"Èmi kò lè dáhùn ìbéèrè yìí."* ("I can't provide an answer.").

This helps us to calculate the refusal rate:

$$\text{Refusal Rate(RR)} = \frac{\text{Number of refusals}}{\text{Total questions asked}}$$

By combining BERTScore with LLM-based evaluation, we obtain a more comprehensive assessment of model performance, capturing both semantic similarity and human-like judgment across varying levels of typographical noise.

5 Results and Findings

Table 2 presents the main results on the effect of varying levels of typographical noise in Yorùbá sentences on LLM, using different evaluation metrics across the three models.

5.1 Overall Performance Trend

The findings reveal that typographical noise severely affects comprehension and accuracy once

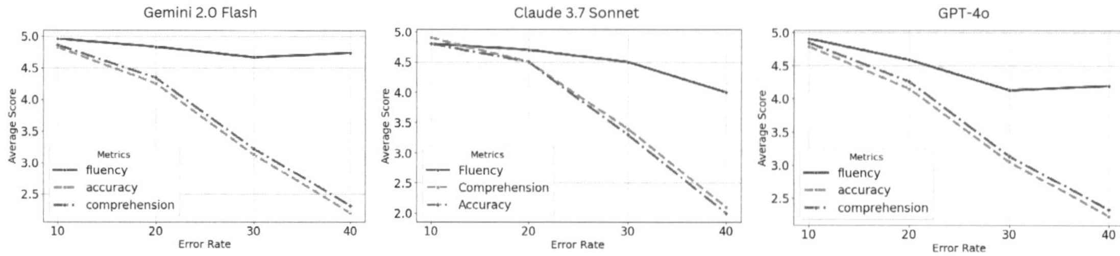

Figure 2: LLM-as-Judge Evaluation of Fluency, Comprehension, and Accuracy Across Error Rates

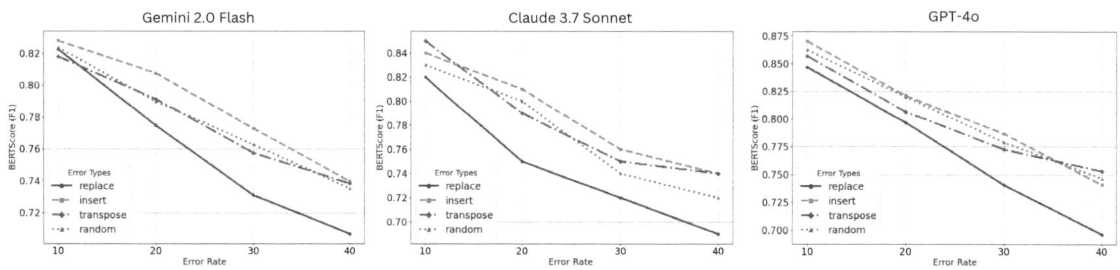

Figure 3: BERTScore (F1) Evaluation Across Error Rates and Error Types

it exceeds 20% - all models show comparable difficulty in extracting meaning from increasingly distorted inputs. Fluency remains relatively stable across all models, indicating that while the models can still generate well-formed sentences, they often misinterpret noisy inputs or in other cases simply say they cannot answer or need more information in a well-written sentence. Similarly, the refusal rate increases significantly after the 20% noise level, indicating that the models refuse to respond as the noise increases. This suggests that, past a certain threshold, models prioritize avoiding incorrect responses over attempting a response based on uncertain input.

5.2 Which type of error has the most significant effect on performance?

Different error types impact performance in different ways, as seen in Figure 3. From the graph, we note that insertion errors introduce minor noise, but do not significantly degrade comprehension. In contrast, replacement errors cause the most substantial drop, as they alter the core word structures. Random and swap errors produced mixed results, but followed a general downward trend.

5.3 Which of the models is more robust?

No one model stands out to be more robust, instead each exhibits some unique trends. For example, in Table 2, we note that at higher noise levels (30-40%) GPT-4o tends to attempt answering the question even when comprehension is very low, but Gemini tries to play it safe by declining to give an answer. From Figure 2, we can see that claude performs slightly better in comprehension than GPT-4o at lower noise levels (10-20%) but deteriorates faster at higher noise rates. Gemini maintains the highest stability in fluency, but its accuracy and comprehension decline significantly at 30% noise and beyond.

5.4 What kind of performance do we see for English

A similar evaluation was conducted on the English translations of the Yorùbá sentences using the same error injection strategy, revealing a stark contrast in model robustness. While Yorùbá comprehension drops rapidly with increasing noise levels, As expected, English maintains high accuarcy and comprehension scores, this is shown in Appendix A. This further illustrates the fact that LLMs are significantly more resilient to typographical noise in English due to greater training data exposure and familiarity with noisy text variations in high-resource languages.

6 Conclusion

This study highlights the critical challenge of maintaining robustness in LLMs under typographical noise within low-resource languages, specifically focusing on Yorùbá, a tonal language highly sensitive to orthographic nuances such as diacritics. Our experimental results underscore the vulnerability of state-of-the-art models (GPT-4 Omni, Gemini 2.0 Flash, and Claude 3.7 Sonnet) to typographical errors in Yorùbá QA tasks. These findings highlight the urgent need for noise-aware training, emphasizing typographical robustness, particularly for low-resource languages like Yorùbá. We recommend for the creation of dedicated, noisy Yorùbá QA benchmarks and noise-aware training strategies to improve real-world robustness of multilingual LLMs.

Limitations

Our research has several limitations that future studies could address. Firstly, the use of synthetic typographical errors may not fully capture the complexity and variability of real-world user-generated typing errors. Collecting genuine noisy Yorùbá data would enhance ecological validity and applicability of findings. Additionally, although the dataset scales up to 2400 samples from an initial set of 50 QA pairs, incorporating more QA pairs would likely enhance generalizability and robustness assessments. Additionally, better semantic similarity metrics tailored specifically to Yorùbá should be developed, given the limitations of multilingual BERTScore. Lastly, periodic re-evaluation using updated LLMs is necessary to reflect continuous advancements in model robustness.

Acknowledgments

We would like to thank Abraham Owodunni, whose initial idea sparked the curiosity that led to this research. His guidance in refining the research question and validating key ideas was invaluable. I also appreciate the support of the MLC Nigeria community of independent researchers, whose encouragement and insights were instrumental throughout the research process.

References

Shanqing Cai, Subhashini Venugopalan, Katrin Tomanek, Ajit Narayanan, Meredith Morris, and Michael Brenner. 2022. Context-aware abbreviation expansion using large language models. In *Proceedings of the 2022 Conference of the North American Chapter of the Association for Computational Linguistics: Human Language Technologies*, pages 1261–1275, Seattle, United States. Association for Computational Linguistics.

Asa Cooper Stickland, Sailik Sengupta, Jason Krone, Saab Mansour, and He He. 2023. Robustification of multilingual language models to real-world noise in crosslingual zero-shot settings with robust contrastive pretraining. In *Proceedings of the 17th Conference of the European Chapter of the Association for Computational Linguistics*, pages 1375–1391, Dubrovnik, Croatia. Association for Computational Linguistics.

Julen Etxaniz, Gorka Azkune, Aitor Soroa, Oier Lopez de Lacalle, and Mikel Artetxe. 2023. Do multilingual language models think better in english? *Preprint*, arXiv:2308.01223.

Isa Inuwa-Dutse. 2025. Naijanlp: A survey of nigerian low-resource languages. *Preprint*, arXiv:2502.19784.

Toheeb A. Jimoh, Tabea De Wille, and Nikola S. Nikolov. 2025. Bridging gaps in natural language processing for yorùbá: A systematic review of a decade of progress and prospects. *Preprint*, arXiv:2502.17364.

Ankit Kumar, Piyush Makhija, and Anuj Gupta. 2020. Noisy text data: Achilles' heel of bert. *Preprint*, arXiv:2003.12932.

Milad Moradi and Matthias Samwald. 2021. Evaluating the robustness of neural language models to input perturbations. In *Proceedings of the 2021 Conference on Empirical Methods in Natural Language Processing*, pages 1558–1570, Online and Punta Cana, Dominican Republic. Association for Computational Linguistics.

Kishore Papineni, Salim Roukos, Todd Ward, and Wei-Jing Zhu. 2002. Bleu: a method for automatic evaluation of machine translation. In *Proceedings of the 40th Annual Meeting of the Association for Computational Linguistics*, pages 311–318, Philadelphia, Pennsylvania, USA. Association for Computational Linguistics.

Vaibhav Vaibhav, Sumeet Singh, Craig Stewart, and Graham Neubig. 2019. Improving robustness of machine translation with synthetic noise. In *Proceedings of the 2019 Conference of the North American Chapter of the Association for Computational Linguistics: Human Language Technologies, Volume 1 (Long and Short Papers)*, pages 1916–1920, Minneapolis, Minnesota. Association for Computational Linguistics.

Haoyu Wang, Guozheng Ma, Cong Yu, Ning Gui, Linrui Zhang, Zhiqi Huang, Suwei Ma, Yongzhe Chang, Sen Zhang, Li Shen, Xueqian Wang, Peilin Zhao, and Dacheng Tao. 2023. Are large language models really robust to word-level perturbations? *Preprint*, arXiv:2309.11166.

Tianyi Zhang, Varsha Kishore, Felix Wu, Kilian Q. Weinberger, and Yoav Artzi. 2020. Bertscore: Evaluating text generation with bert. *Preprint*, arXiv:1904.09675.

Yunxiang Zhang, Liangming Pan, Samson Tan, and Min-Yen Kan. 2022. Interpreting the robustness of neural NLP models to textual perturbations. In *Findings of the Association for Computational Linguistics: ACL 2022*, pages 3993–4007, Dublin, Ireland. Association for Computational Linguistics.

Lianmin Zheng, Wei-Lin Chiang, Ying Sheng, Siyuan Zhuang, Zhanghao Wu, Yonghao Zhuang, Zi Lin, Zhuohan Li, Dacheng Li, Eric Xing, Hao Zhang, Joseph E Gonzalez, and Ion Stoica. 2023. Judging llm-as-a-judge with mt-bench and chatbot arena. In *Advances in Neural Information Processing Systems*, volume 36, pages 46595–46623. Curran Associates, Inc.

A Model Performance on Translated English Questions

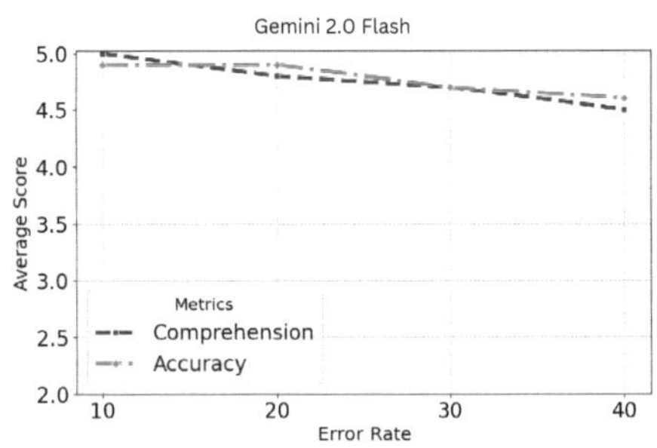

Figure 4: Gemini 2.0 Evaluation of Comprehension and Accuracy Across Error Rates

B System Prompt for LLM-as-Judge Evaluation

LLM-as-Judge System Prompt

You are an expert evaluator of Yoruba language responses. You will be shown a question in Yoruba and the response provided by an AI system. Your task is to rigorously assess the quality of the response.
Important Considerations:

- **Yoruba Language Expertise:** Assume the role of a native Yoruba speaker with deep linguistic knowledge.
- **25-Word Limit:** The AI's response is constrained to a maximum of 25 words.

1. Response Status (Choose One):

- **A. Direct Answer:** The AI provides an answer, even if incorrect.
- **B. Explicit Refusal/Uncertainty:** The AI explicitly refuses to answer or asks for clarification.

Evaluation Criteria (Score 1-5):

- **Fluency:** Is the response grammatically correct and natural?
- **Accuracy:** Does the response correctly address the question?
- **Comprehension:** Does the response demonstrate an understanding of the question?

Swahili News Classification: Performance, Challenges, and Explainability Across ML, DL, and Transformers

Manas Pandya, Avinash Kumar Sharma, Arpit Shukla
{zda23b019, zda23m011, zda23m007}@iitmz.ac.in
Indian Institute of Technology Madras, Zanzibar Campus

Abstract

In this paper, we propose a comprehensive framework for the classification of Swahili news articles using a combination of classical machine learning techniques, deep neural networks, and transformer-based models. By balancing two diverse datasets sourced from Harvard Dataverse and Kaggle, our approach addresses the inherent challenges of imbalanced data in low-resource languages. Our experiments demonstrate the effectiveness of the proposed methodology and set the stage for further advances in Swahili natural language processing.

1 Introduction

The rapid growth of digital news platforms has intensified the need for automated text classification systems. Although substantial progress has been made in natural language processing (NLP) for high-resource languages, low-resource languages such as Swahili remain significantly underrepresented. Swahili, spoken by millions across East Africa, is essential for disseminating information; however, the scarcity of balanced and annotated datasets poses a major challenge for developing robust NLP models.

This study addresses these challenges by leveraging two prominent Swahili news datasets - one from Harvard Dataverse and another from Kaggle. By applying advanced data balancing techniques, we mitigate class imbalances and enhance the reliability of our models. Furthermore, we explore a diverse set of classification methodologies, ranging from traditional machine learning algorithms to deep neural networks and transformer-based architectures. To promote transparency and trust in automated decisions, explainability tools such as LIME and SHAP are suggested as promising avenues for future work, to shed light on the inner workings of these classifiers.

2 Related Work

Text classification has long been a core task in Natural Language Processing (NLP), with early work relying on classical machine learning techniques such as Support Vector Machines (SVM), Naïve Bayes, and Random Forests (Joachims, 1998; McCallum and Nigam, 1998). These methods, despite their simplicity, have shown considerable success in various domains. With the advent of deep learning, models such as Convolutional Neural Networks (CNN) and Long Short-Term Memory (LSTM) networks have been increasingly applied to capture complex sequential dependencies in text data (Kim, 2014; Hochreiter and Schmidhuber, 1997).

In recent years, transformer-based models have revolutionized NLP by leveraging self-attention mechanisms to learn contextual representations at scale (Vaswani et al., 2017; Devlin et al., 2019). These models have not only improved overall performance on benchmark tasks but have also enabled more effective handling of nuanced language phenomena. However, while substantial progress has been made for high-resource languages, low-resource languages like Swahili continue to receive limited attention.

Prior research on Swahili text processing has predominantly utilized traditional machine learning techniques for tasks such as sentiment analysis and named entity recognition (Nyoni et al., 2020). Only recently have deep learning and transformer-based approaches been explored for Swahili. The introduction of models such as AfriBERTa (Ogueji et al., 2021a) and SwahBERTa (Martin et al., 2022) marks a significant step forward, as these pretrained models provide richer contextual embeddings tailored for African languages. Despite these advancements, the application of state-of-the-art transformers to Swahili news classification remains underexplored.

Our work builds upon this diverse body of re-

Proceedings of the Sixth Workshop on African Natural Language Processing (AfricaNLP 2025), pages 203–209
July 31, 2025

search by integrating classical machine learning, deep learning, and transformer-based models for Swahili news classification. By leveraging multiple model architectures and employing advanced explainability techniques, we aim to bridge the gap in low-resource NLP and provide a comprehensive evaluation framework that not only improves classification performance but also enhances model transparency.

3 Data

We use two datasets for Swahili news classification:

Swahili News Classification Dataset The Swahili News Classification Dataset was obtained from Kaggle (Antudre, 2020). It contains Swahili news articles categorized into five classes: *kitaifa* (national), *michezo* (sports), *burudani* (entertainment), *uchumi* (economy), and *kimataifa* (international). Initially, the dataset consists of 22,409 samples across three features. To mitigate class imbalance, undersampling was applied by taking 1,906 samples from each remaining category, resulting in a balanced dataset of 9,530 samples. The data was then split into 7,624 training samples and 1,906 testing samples.

Harvard Swahili News Dataset The Harvard Swahili News Dataset was obtained from Harvard Dataverse (Harvard Dataverse, 2020). This dataset comprises news articles from various Swahili media sources and includes six categories: *kitaifa* (national), *michezo* (sports), *kimataifa* (international), *burudani* (entertainment), *afya* (health), and *biashara* (business). The original dataset contains 31,044 samples across two features. To address class imbalance, undersampling was performed by taking 2,611 samples from each category, yielding a balanced dataset of 15,666 samples. This dataset was partitioned into 12,532 training samples and 3,134 testing samples.

Preprocessing

Prior to model training, both datasets underwent the following preprocessing steps: removal of special characters; conversion of text to lowercase to ensure uniformity; tokenization and stopword removal using Swahili-specific NLP libraries; splitting the data into 80% training and 20% testing sets; and balancing the datasets using undersampling to ensure equal distribution across categories. Tables 1 and 2 summarize the balanced datasets.

Attribute	Swahili News Classification Dataset
Total Samples	9,530
Training Samples	7,624
Testing Samples	1,906
Categories	*kitaifa, michezo, burudani, uchumi, kimataifa*

Table 1: Summary of Swahili News Classification Dataset statistics after preprocessing and balancing.

Attribute	Harvard Swahili News Dataset
Total Samples	15,666
Training Samples	12,532
Testing Samples	3,134
Categories	*kitaifa, michezo, kimataifa, burudani, afya, biashara*

Table 2: Summary of Harvard Swahili News Dataset statistics after preprocessing and balancing.

4 Methodology

4.1 Data Characteristics

Although our primary focus is on the classification of Swahili news, we first analyze important properties of the data that may influence model performance. In particular, we observe the distribution of text length across the different categories in both datasets. Figure 1 present the box-and-whisker plots, illustrating the minimum, first quartile, median, third quartile, and maximum text lengths for each category.

From these plots, a few notable patterns emerge:

Certain categories (e.g., *burudani*) tend to have lower median text lengths, potentially impacting the richness of vocabulary captured and affecting classification performance.

Outliers reaching beyond 20,000 characters in categories such as *kitaifa* may contain in-depth or repeated text, possibly influencing classifier decisions if not handled properly.

Categories with fewer words or shorter articles on average (e.g., *afya* in the Harvard dataset) tend to exhibit slightly lower performance, likely due to less contextual information per sample.

In the subsequent sections, we detail the modeling approaches used to address these challenges.

4.2 Machine Learning Approach[1]

We begin our methodology with classical machine learning algorithms, leveraging `scikit-learn` pipelines. The process involves:

[1]Kindly look at the appendix 'A' for more details about exact implementation of our models

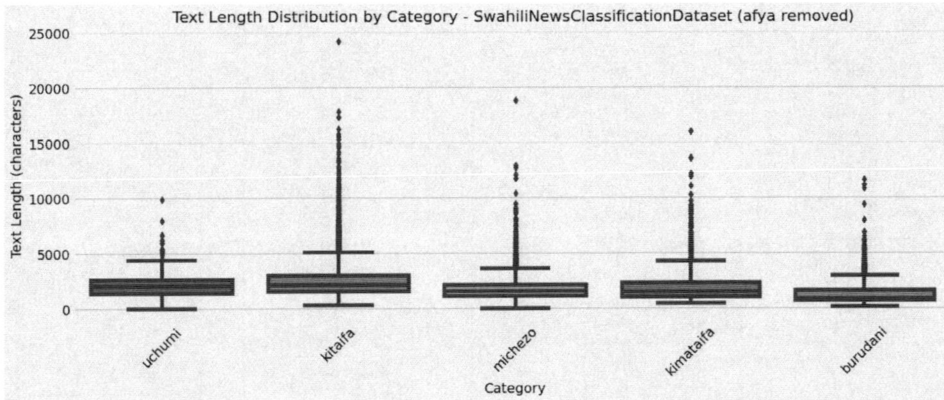

Figure 1: Text Length Distribution by Category — SwahiliNewsClassificationDataset (afya removed).

Text Representation: We apply a `TfidfVectorizer` to convert text into numerical feature vectors, setting `max_features=5000` to limit dimensionality.

Model Training: We train **four models: SVM, Logistic Regression, Random Forest, and XGBoost.** Each model is embedded in a `Pipeline` to ensure reproducible and streamlined experimentation.

Evaluation: We track metrics like accuracy, F1-score, precision, recall, training time, and inference time. Additionally, we save each trained pipeline for later analysis and potential use in explainability methods.

This approach provides initial baselines to compare against the more complex deep learning architectures.

4.3 Deep Learning Approach

To capture rich semantic and syntactic features, we develop PyTorch-based models that utilize embedding layers and sequence-processing components. Specifically, we examine:

BiLSTM: A bidirectional LSTM that can process text from left to right and right to left, capturing long-term dependencies.

CNN: A text-based convolutional neural network that extracts local features via sliding filters.

BiLSTM+CNN: A hybrid model that first uses BiLSTM to glean temporal context, followed by a 1D convolution to capture local n-gram features.

4.3.1 Model Architecture Visualization

Figure 2 illustrates two of our core deep learning architectures side by side. We train all deep models for a fixed number of epochs (e.g., 5), track training and validation losses, and then evaluate on held-out test data to assess generalization.

4.4 Transformer-Based Approach[2]

Transformers leverage self-attention to learn contextual embeddings and have shown state-of-the-art performance in various NLP tasks. We finetune the following models: AfriBERTa (Ogueji et al., 2021b) , XLM-RoBERTa (Conneau et al., 2019), and RoBERTa Swahili (Minixhofer et al., 2022) on our datasets, enabling them to adapt to domain-specific Swahili news content.

4.4.1 Transformer Architecture Visualization

Figure 2 shows a schematic of two representative transformer models used in our experiments. We tokenize the input text using each model's recommended tokenizer and then feed it through the pretrained layers. Finally, a simple classification head produces the output probabilities. We finetune for a small number of epochs (e.g., 3) on our training sets with an early stopping criterion to avoid overfitting.

Implementation Details. We employ the Hugging Face Transformers library for loading and fine-tuning models. Training arguments (`TrainingArguments`) are set with a small batch size (e.g., 4), a learning rate of $2e{-}5$, and a maximum sequence length of 256. F

5 Experimental Results and Discussion

Table 3 summarizes the experimental results across three modeling paradigms: classical machine learning (ML) models, deep learning (DL) models, and transformer-based models. For each dataset, the

[2]See appendix 'A' for more details about exact implementation of our models

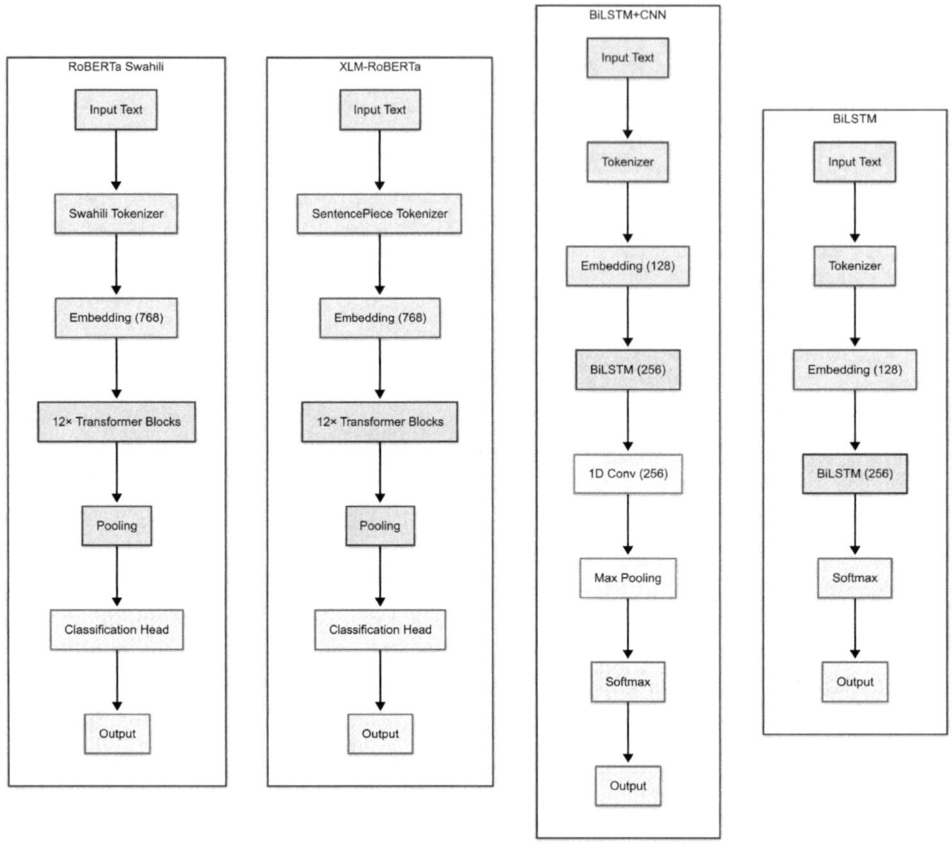

Figure 2: Transformer based and Deep Learning based model Architecture Examples

best performing metric values are highlighted in bold.

Our experimental evaluation reveals several noteworthy insights:

Classical Machine Learning Models: For the SwahiliNews dataset, the SVM model achieved the highest accuracy, F1-score, precision, and recall, indicating robustness in handling the textual features extracted via TF-IDF. Logistic Regression offered faster training and inference times, which may be advantageous in real-time or resource-constrained scenarios. On the Harvard Dataset, SVM again outperformed other ML models in terms of classification metrics, while Logistic Regression maintained computational efficiency.

Deep Learning Models: Among DL models, the CNN architecture outperformed both the BiLSTM and the hybrid BiLSTM+CNN model on the SwahiliNews dataset. In the Harvard Dataset, BiLSTM+CNN and CNN models showed similar effectiveness. CNNs were especially valuable in distinguishing closely related news categories by capturing local features.

Transformer-Based Models: Transformer models, leveraging self-attention, consistently yielded the highest performance across both datasets. Notably, the RoBERTa Base Wechsel Swahili model achieved the best accuracy, F1-score, precision, and recall. While transformers incur longer training and inference times, their ability to capture contextual nuances in Swahili news articles leads to significant performance gains.

Additional Interpretations: Shorter text lengths in some categories, such as entertainment and health, correlated with slightly reduced performance. ML models provide computational efficiency but are generally outperformed by DL and transformer-based models, which offer better predictive robustness. Variations in dataset size and composition emphasize the importance of tailored preprocessing and model fine-tuning; transformer models in particular demonstrated strong adaptability.

Comparison with Prior Work: Compared to the results reported by (Murindanyi et al., 2023), where the best SVM achieved 83% and their CNN-

Dataset	Model	Accuracy	F1-Score	Precision	Recall	Train Time (s)	Inference Time (s)
ML Models							
SwahiliNews	SVM	**0.8898**	**0.8897**	**0.8897**	**0.8898**	142.0781	7.6992
SwahiliNews	Logistic Regression	0.8814	0.8816	0.8820	0.8814	**3.0558**	**0.4052**
SwahiliNews	Random Forest	0.8683	0.8691	0.8718	0.8683	26.3243	0.6207
SwahiliNews	XGBoost	0.8788	0.8791	0.8799	0.8788	80.3573	0.4206
Harvard Dataset	SVM	**0.8535**	**0.8532**	**0.8536**	**0.8535**	299.9927	17.3810
Harvard Dataset	Logistic Regression	0.8462	0.8461	0.8465	0.8462	**4.5977**	**0.5304**
Harvard Dataset	Random Forest	0.8287	0.8285	0.8303	0.8287	47.8084	0.8566
Harvard Dataset	XGBoost	0.8481	0.8480	0.8491	0.8481	127.2364	0.5829
DL Models							
SwahiliNews	BiLSTM	0.5315	0.5007	0.5767	0.5315	44.7930	0.7452
SwahiliNews	CNN	**0.8620**	**0.8630**	**0.8662**	**0.8620**	**3.7755**	**0.0899**
SwahiliNews	BiLSTM_CNN	0.8421	0.8422	0.8515	0.8421	48.2156	0.8496
Harvard Dataset	BiLSTM	0.7128	0.7152	0.7306	0.7128	67.9060	1.2125
Harvard Dataset	CNN	0.8293	0.8292	**0.8330**	0.8293	**5.3939**	**0.1006**
Harvard Dataset	BiLSTM_CNN	**0.8325**	**0.8304**	0.8316	**0.8325**	79.5473	1.3700
Transformer Models							
SwahiliNews	AfriBERTa	0.9355	0.9354	0.9355	0.9355	**709.0182**	**18.5460**
SwahiliNews	XLM-RoBERTa	0.9344	0.9342	0.9344	0.9344	876.8414	22.4779
SwahiliNews	RoBERTa Wechsel sw	**0.9391**	**0.9391**	**0.9393**	**0.9391**	779.2871	20.8529
Harvard Dataset	AfriBERTa	0.9148	0.9141	0.9142	0.9148	**1142.9654**	**29.2730**
Harvard Dataset	XLM-RoBERTa	0.9065	0.9060	0.9064	0.9065	1393.1364	35.0627
Harvard Dataset	RoBERTa Weschel sw	**0.9167**	**0.9165**	**0.9166**	**0.9167**	1248.5649	33.3698

Table 3: Experimental Results. In the table, **Bold** values indicate the best performance per metric per dataset/model and Highlights indicate best overall.

BiLSTM+Attention model achieved 84% test accuracy (with Bagging ensemble at 90%), our SVM, CNN-based, and hybrid models meet or exceed these metrics. Most notably, our transformer-based models set a new state-of-the-art, achieving over 93% test accuracy and demonstrating significant advances in Swahili news classification.

Generalizability: While our experiments are focused on Swahili, many Bantu languages share similar linguistic structures, morphological patterns, and semantic features. As a result, the methodologies and insights presented here may extend to related languages, providing cross-transfer learning and adaptation.

Overall, our experiments show that while ML and DL models offer great baselines and efficiency, transformer-based architectures, especially those fine-tuned, achieve superior classification performance.

6 Challenges

This study has demonstrated that careful model selection and preprocessing can yield robust classification results for Swahili news articles across classical machine learning, deep learning, and transformer-based approaches. Notably, transformer models, particularly the RoBERTa Base Wechsel Swahili model, have shown superior performance in capturing the nuances of Swahili language data, despite increased computational cost. However, several challenges remain that must be addressed to further improve Swahili NLP applications.

A primary challenge is the limited availability of high-quality annotated data for Swahili, which constrains both model training and generalization. The high computational demand of transformer models presents an additional barrier to efficient deployment, particularly in low-resource environments.

Models trained specifically on news data may not transfer well to other domains, such as medical or legal text, making domain adaptation an important area for future research. The complex decision-making processes of transformer models also highlight the ongoing trade-off between predictive performance and interpretability.

Furthermore, Swahili's rich morphology and regional variations continue to complicate tokenization, embedding, and model generalization, necessitating more sophisticated preprocessing strategies.

7 Future Work

In terms of future scope, enriching available datasets through new data sources and advanced data augmentation methods remains essential to mitigate class imbalances and improve representation for underrepresented categories.

A key area for future work is the systematic application and evaluation of advanced interpretability techniques, such as Local Interpretable Model-Agnostic Explanations (LIME) (Ribeiro et al., 2016) and SHAP (Lundberg and Lee, 2017), to provide transparency and insight into model predictions. Additional explorations might include attention-based interpretability in transformers, as well as resource optimization through model compression strategies like knowledge distillation and quantization to facilitate real-time deployment. Extending these models to cross-lingual or multilingual contexts could further enhance their applicability across other low-resource languages.

In future work, we plan to expand the scope of our dataset by collecting and integrating Swahili language data from a wider variety of sources, including additional news outlets, social media platforms, and blogs. By incorporating content from these diverse domains, we aim to construct a more comprehensive and representative corpus that captures the linguistic richness, topical diversity, and informal language use prevalent in real-world Swahili communication.

Such an expanded dataset would not only improve the generalizability and robustness of our models but also enable more nuanced investigations into dialectal variations, code-switching, and emerging trends within the Swahili-speaking digital ecosystem. This approach is expected to facilitate the development of more effective and inclusive NLP systems for Swahili and other low-resource languages., integration into real-world systems, such as live news aggregation platforms requiring real-time inference and continuous learning, remains a critical direction for future practical impact.

8 Conclusion:

In summary, our findings highlight the strengths and trade-offs of different NLP models for Swahili news classification. While classical machine learning models provide interpretable baselines and deep learning models offer balanced performance and efficiency, transformer-based models achieve state-of-the-art results through contextual understanding. Addressing challenges related to data availability, computational efficiency, and especially model interpretability is essential for broader adoption. By tackling these challenges and pursuing the outlined future directions, this research contributes towards advancing NLP for Swahili and other low-resource languages, promoting more inclusive and effective AI applications.

References

Waalbanny Antudre. 2020. Swahili news classification dataset. Available at: `https://www.kaggle.com/datasets/waalbannyantudre/swahili-news-classification-dataset`.

Alexis Conneau, Kartikay Khandelwal, Naman Goyal, Vishrav Chaudhary, Guillaume Wenzek, Francisco Guzmán, Edouard Grave, Myle Ott, Luke Zettlemoyer, and Veselin Stoyanov. 2019. Unsupervised cross-lingual representation learning at scale. *CoRR*, abs/1911.02116.

J. Devlin, M.-W. Chang, K. Lee, and K. Toutanova. 2019. Bert: Pre-training of deep bidirectional transformers for language understanding. In *Proc. NAACL-HLT*.

Harvard Dataverse. 2020. Swahili news dataset. Available at: `https://dataverse.harvard.edu/dataset.xhtml?persistentId=doi:10.7910/DVN/UZHZ3I`.

S. Hochreiter and J. Schmidhuber. 1997. Long short-term memory. *Neural Computation*, 9(8):1735–1780.

T. Joachims. 1998. Text categorization with support vector machines: Learning with many relevant features. In *Proc. European Conference on Machine Learning*.

Y. Kim. 2014. Convolutional neural networks for sentence classification. In *Proc. EMNLP*.

S. M. Lundberg and S.-I. Lee. 2017. A unified approach to interpreting model predictions. In *Advances in Neural Information Processing Systems*.

M. Martin et al. 2022. Swahbert: Enhancing swahili nlp with pretrained transformers. In *Proc. EACL*.

A. McCallum and K. Nigam. 1998. A comparison of event models for naïve bayes text classification. In *Proc. AAAI-98 Workshop on Learning for Text Categorization*.

Benjamin Minixhofer, Fabian Paischer, and Navid Rekabsaz. 2022. WECHSEL: Effective initialization of subword embeddings for cross-lingual transfer of monolingual language models. pages 3992–4006, Seattle, United States. Association for Computational Linguistics.

Sudi Murindanyi, Yiiki Afedra Brian, Andrew Katumba, and Joyce Nakatumba-Nabende. 2023. Explainable machine learning models for swahili news classification. In *7th International Conference on Natural Language Processing and Information Retrieval (NLPIR)*.

P. Nyoni et al. 2020. Comparative analysis of swahili text classification techniques. *Journal of African Language Technology*, 3:45–62.

A. Ogueji et al. 2021a. Afriberta: A pretrained language model for african languages. In *Proc. ACL*.

Kelechi Ogueji, Yuxin Zhu, and Jimmy Lin. 2021b. Small data? no problem! exploring the viability of pretrained multilingual language models for low-resourced languages. In *Proceedings of the 1st Workshop on Multilingual Representation Learning*, pages 116–126, Punta Cana, Dominican Republic. Association for Computational Linguistics.

M. T. Ribeiro, S. Singh, and C. Guestrin. 2016. Why should i trust you? explaining the predictions of any classifier. In *Proc. KDD*.

A. Vaswani et al. 2017. Attention is all you need. In *Advances in Neural Information Processing Systems*.

Appendix

A Implementation Details

This section outlines the implementation details, including model training and hyperparameter tuning for each category of models considered in our study.

A.1 Machine Learning Models

Classical ML models were trained using TF-IDF features with a vocabulary size capped at 5000 terms. For **SVM**, a linear kernel was employed with probability estimation enabled, and the regularization parameter C was selected from $\{0.01, 0.1, 1, 10\}$ using grid search with five-fold cross-validation. **Logistic Regression** was set with a maximum of 1000 iterations for convergence, and C was similarly tuned. **Random Forest** utilized 200 estimators, with maximum depth tuned between 10, 20, and None, and the random state fixed at 42 for reproducibility. **XGBoost** used the multi-log loss evaluation metric and had its number of estimators and learning rate tuned via grid search. All classical models were implemented using the `scikit-learn` pipeline, and optimal hyperparameters were chosen based on F1-score performance on the validation set.

A.2 Deep Learning Models

Deep learning models were implemented with PyTorch and TensorFlow. For the **BiLSTM** model, we used an embedding size of 128, 256 hidden units, and a bidirectional architecture, trained for five epochs. The **CNN** model for text used the same embedding size, a single 1D convolutional layer with 256 filters, and also trained for five epochs. The **BiLSTM+CNN** hybrid model first extracted features using BiLSTM and then applied CNN layers, again training for five epochs. The dataset was tokenized with a vocabulary size of 10,000 and a sequence length of 300. All models used a batch size of 32 and the Adam optimizer with a learning rate of 0.001. Hyperparameters were determined through pilot experiments and validation set performance, with early stopping applied if the validation loss did not improve for two consecutive epochs.

A.3 Transformer-Based Models

Three transformer-based models were fine-tuned using the `transformers` library. **AfriBERTa** and **XLM-RoBERTa** were trained for three epochs with a batch size of 4, a learning rate of 2×10^{-5}, and weight decay of 0.01. The **RoBERTa Base Wechsel Swahili** model was also trained for three epochs, batch size 4, and fine-tuned using gradient accumulation steps of 4. The AdamW optimizer was used for all models, and input text was tokenized to a maximum sequence length of 256 tokens. Hyperparameters were selected through small grid searches on the validation set, with early stopping based on the F1-score.

A.4 Computational Resources

All models were trained on a GPU-enabled environment. **Machine learning models** were executed on CPU, while **deep learning and transformer models** were trained using an NVIDIA Tesla V100 GPU. Training duration varied, with transformer models requiring the most time—averaging between 700 to 1400 seconds per model.

Neural Morphological Tagging for Nguni Languages

Cael Marquard* **Simbarashe Mawere*** **Francois Meyer**
Department of Computer Science
University of Cape Town
{mrqcae001, mwrsim003}@myuct.ac.za, francois.meyer@uct.ac.za

Abstract

Morphological parsing is the task of decomposing words into morphemes, the smallest units of meaning in a language, and labelling their grammatical roles. It is a particularly challenging task for agglutinative languages, such as the Nguni languages of South Africa, which construct words by concatenating multiple morphemes. A morphological parsing system can be framed as a pipeline with two separate components, a segmenter followed by a tagger. This paper investigates the use of neural methods to build morphological taggers for the four Nguni languages. We compare two classes of approaches: training neural sequence labellers (LSTMs and neural CRFs) from scratch and finetuning pretrained language models. We compare performance across these two categories, as well as to a traditional rule-based morphological parser. Neural taggers comfortably outperform the rule-based baseline and models trained from scratch tend to outperform pretrained models. We also compare parsing results across different upstream segmenters and with varying linguistic input features. Our findings confirm the viability of employing neural taggers based on pre-existing morphological segmenters for the Nguni languages.

1 Introduction

The smallest unit of linguistic meaning that a word can be split into is known as a *morpheme* (Matthews, 1991). Morphological parsing is the task of identifying the grammatical role of each morpheme within a word (Puttkammer and Du Toit, 2021). For example, "izinhlobo" (meaning "types" in isiZulu) is split into the morphemes "i-zin-hlobo", which is parsed as "i[NPrePre10] - zin[BPre10] - hlobo[NStem]" (Gaustad and Puttkammer, 2022) (see Figure 1). Each bracketed tag labels the preceding morpheme with its grammatical function and noun class (if applicable).

*Equal contribution.

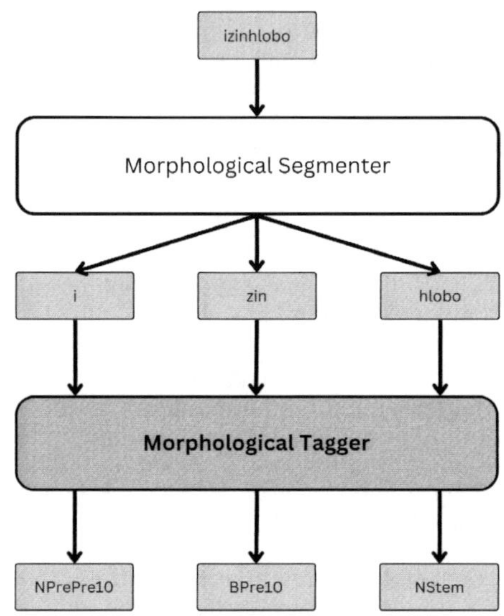

Figure 1: Morphological parsing as a two-step pipeline. We focus on tagging, training our taggers on the outputs of pre-existing morphological segmenters.

Morphological information is especially important for the Nguni languages, a group of related languages (isiNdebele, isiXhosa, isiZulu, and Siswati) spoken across South Africa by more than 23m home language speakers (Eberhard et al., 2019). The Nguni languages are agglutinative, meaning that many words are created by aggregating multiple morphemes (Taljard and Bosch, 2006). They are also written conjunctively—morphemes are concatenated into a single orthographic (space-delimited) word (Taljard and Bosch, 2006). This can produce long, complex word forms consisting of several morphemes, such as the isiXhosa word "andikambuzi", which means "I have not yet asked them", composed of the morphemes "a", "ndi", "ka", "m", "buza", and "i".

As a result of this morphological complexity, morphological parsing is a challenging but important task for the Nguni languages. Despite this, few morphological parsers exist for the Nguni lan-

Proceedings of the Sixth Workshop on African Natural Language Processing (AfricaNLP 2025), pages 210–220

guages. Moreover, no existing parsers use neural methods, despite their established performance gains for linguistic annotation tasks (Min et al., 2023). In this paper we explore the viability of neural morphological parsers for the Nguni languages.

Morphological parsing can be framed as a two-step pipeline (Tsarfaty et al., 2013; Puttkammer and Du Toit, 2021), in which raw text is first segmented into morphemes, which are subsequently tagged with morphological labels. The first part of this pipeline is known as *morphological segmentation*, while the second part is known as *morphological tagging*. We visualise this pipeline for the isiZulu word "izinhlobo" in Figure 1. In this work we focus on the second subtask, morphological tagging. Instead of training models for the entire task, we make use of pre-existing morphological segmenters for the Nguni languages (Moeng et al., 2021) and train neural taggers on top of their output.

We train two classes of neural taggers – neural sequence labellers trained from scratch and finetuned pretrained language models (PLMs). Our models trained from scratch are bi-LSTMs (Hochreiter and Schmidhuber, 1997) and conditional random fields (CRFs) (Lafferty et al., 2001) with bi-LSTM features, using either morpheme or character-level input features. For PLMs, we finetune XLM-R-large (Conneau et al., 2020), Afro-XLMR-large (Alabi et al., 2022), and Nguni-XLMR-large (Meyer et al., 2024), which respectively represent different levels of Nguni-language coverage.

We develop neural taggers based on two types of morphological segmentations: canonical and surface segmentations (Cotterell et al., 2016). Canonical segmentation decomposes a word into its constituent morphemes, in their standardised (precomposed) form. For example, the isiXhosa word "zobomi" is canonically segmented into "za-u-(bu)-bomi", where some of the morphemes undergo spelling changes in word composition (Gaustad and Puttkammer, 2022). Surface segmentation decomposes a word into its constituent *morphs*, which are the surface forms of morphemes as they appear in the composed word. For example, "zobomi" is surface-segmented into "zo-bomi". As demonstrated by this example, the canonical and surface-level segmentation of a word can differ.

We evaluate all our models in two settings. In the first, we test our taggers on the morphological segmentations available in our task dataset (Gaustad and Puttkammer, 2022). This provides an idealised setting in which we evaluate our models on gold-annotated segmentations, which we know to be correct, isolating tagging performance from segmentation mistakes. In the second setting, we test our taggers on the segmentations produced by the neural segmenters of Moeng et al. (2021). These are model-predicted segmentations, so some segmentations will not align with morphological boundaries. This can lead to error propagation, in which segmentation errors degrade tagging performance. However, it also provides us with an estimate of how our taggers fare in a real-world setting in which the entire morphological parsing pipeline is predicted by neural models.

Overall, we evaluate four variants of each model configuration – trained on canonical/surface segmentations, and respectively tested on gold-annotated/model-predicted segmentations. Our study is an extensive investigation into the potential of neural parsers for all four Nguni languages. Our main findings can be summarised as follows:

- Neural parsing comfortably outperforms our rule-based baseline, confirming the benefit of data-driven segmentation and tagging.
- Neural sequence labellers trained from scratch outperform finetuned PLMs on the morphological tagging subtask.
- With no access to gold-annotated morphological segmentations, canonical segmentations consistently leads to better parsing performance than surface segmentations.

We are the first to use neural models to train morphological taggers for the Nguni languages. To the best of our knowledge, our morphological parsing results represent state-of-the-art performance. Our models can be used to incorporate morphological information into downstream NLP models, which holds the potential to improve performance for the morphologically complex Nguni languages.

2 Related Work

Morphological parsing has been extensively studied in NLP (Tsarfaty et al., 2013; Klemen et al., 2023). Traditionally, it is performed by incorporating grammatical and morphological rules from the language into a finite-state transducer. This is a time-consuming process in which linguists construct hand-crafted rules (Chapin and Norton, 1968). As in other tasks of linguistic annotation

(Min et al., 2023), neural models provide an effective, data-driven solution approach to morphological parsing.

Several works have trained a single model for morphological parsing, jointly modelling morphological segmentation and tagging (Seker and Tsarfaty, 2020a; Aleçakır, 2020; Abudouwaili et al., 2023; Yshaayahu Levi and Tsarfaty, 2024). Alternatively, Tsarfaty et al. (2013) propose a two-step architecture for parsing morphologically rich languages by first segmenting them into their morphemes and then tagging the morphemes with labels. Because morphological segmenters for Nguni languages already exist (Moeng et al., 2021), we choose to adopt this two-step pipeline approach, visualised in Figure 1. Despite the drawbacks of error propagation, training neural taggers alone is simpler than training joint segmentation-tagging models. The approach is also more modular, allowing for better segmenters to be substituted in as and when they are developed.

A number of works have developed morphological segmenters, taggers, and parsers for the Nguni languages. ZulMorph (Bosch et al., 2008) is a rule-based canonical segmenter and tagger for isiZulu based on finite-state transducers. Puttkammer and Du Toit (2021) develop data-driven (non-neural) canonical segmenters and taggers for all four Nguni languages. They apply TiMBL (Daelemans et al.), a memory-based learning package, to the segmentation step, and MarMoT (Björkelund et al., 2013; Mueller et al., 2013), a trainable CRF pipeline, to the tagging step. Moeng et al. (2021) were the first to apply neural methods to segmentation, using CRFs (Lafferty et al., 2001), LSTMs (Hochreiter and Schmidhuber, 1997), and Transformers (Vaswani et al., 2023) to train canonical and surface-level segmenters for all four Nguni languages. They found that non-neural CRFs were best for surface segmentation, while Transformers outperformed the other methods in canonical segmentation. Despite recent developments in neural models, such as sequence-to-sequence (Akyürek et al., 2019) and sequence labeling models (Ma and Hovy, 2016), no neural morphological taggers currently exist for the Nguni languages.

3 Tagging Models

We now introduce our neural morphological taggers. Our models are trained on sequences of pre-segmented morphemes as input, and are tasked with assigning a morphological label to each morpheme. By focusing on the morphological tagging component of the morphological parsing pipeline (Figure 1), we can use established approaches to neural sequence tagging.

3.1 Neural sequence labellers

We train two types of neural models from scratch: bidirectional long short-term memory (bi-LSTM) networks (Hochreiter and Schmidhuber, 1997) and conditional random fields (CRFs) (Lafferty et al., 2001) with bi-LSTM features. Bi-LSTMs have previously been successfully applied to POS tagging (Pannach et al., 2022) and morphological segmentation (Moeng et al., 2021) for the Nguni languages.

CRFs are probabilistic models for sequence labelling. A CRF estimates the probability of a given output (label) sequence by modelling the interdependence of labels with each other, as well as their dependence on the input sequence. We use linear-chain CRFs because of their lower computational complexity (compared to higher-order CRFs). Traditionally, CRFs use a set of hand-crafted features to assign probabilities (Moeng et al., 2021). However, instead of designing these features by hand, a neural network can be used to automatically learn the features from the data (Moeng et al., 2021; Lample et al., 2016; Ma and Hovy, 2016). We choose a bi-LSTM to generate these features, as this has previously proved successful in POS tagging (Pannach et al., 2022) and morphological segmentation (Moeng et al., 2021) for the Nguni languages.

We experimented with several design choices for our neural models trained from scratch, varying the following factors:

- **Feature level.** Models were trained on either morpheme-level or character-level input features, represented by learned embeddings in both cases. For morpheme-level features, we replaced rare morphemes (<2 examples in the training data) with a special unknown token to help the model generalise to unseen data. For character-level features, we summed character embeddings to produce morpheme-level input embeddings. Surface models also have lowercase variants of these features.

- **Context level.** Models were trained on single words in isolation, or on entire sentences. Our goal was to investigate whether the additional context available to sentence-level sequence models would improve performance.

Word	Morphological analysis
aliqela	a[RelConc6]-li[BPre5]-qela[NStem]
kwibhunga	ku[LocPre]-i[NPrePre5]-(li)[BPre5]-bhunga[NStem]
izincomo	i[NPrePre10]-zin[BPre10]-como[NStem]

Table 1: Three examples from the isiXhosa part of the dataset used in our experiments (Gaustad and Puttkammer, 2022). Only the relevant aspects are included.

3.2 Pretrained language models

We finetune the following three PLMs on our task:

1. XLM-R-large (Conneau et al., 2020): a massively multilingual PLM trained on more than 100 languages, including isiXhosa.

2. Afro-XLMR-large (Alabi et al., 2022): XLM-R further pretrained on 20 African languages, including isiXhosa and isiZulu.

3. Nguni-XLMR-large (Meyer et al., 2024): XLM-R adapted for the four Nguni languages.

The models were selected to represent increasing levels of Nguni language pretraining coverage: XLM-R includes minimal Nguni data (only isiXhosa), Afro-XLMR adds isiZulu, while Nguni-XLMR specifically targets all four Nguni languages. We examine the degree to which these different levels of Nguni language inclusion influence downstream performance.

4 Experimental Setup

4.1 Dataset

We use the morphologically annotated dataset developed by Gaustad and Puttkammer (2022). It contains sentences from South African government publications, wherein each word is annotated with its morphological parse (segmentation and tags, as shown in Table 1), lemma, and part-of-speech. It contains 1,431 parallel paragraphs with roughly 50k words per language. The data is pre-split 90%/10% into train/test sets. The dataset contains only gold-standard canonical segmentations, so gold-standard surface segmentations were obtained through a script provided by Moeng et al. (2021). Predicted segmentations for both canonical and surface forms were created by applying Moeng et al.'s (Moeng et al., 2021) to the raw text column of the dataset.

4.2 Model Configurations

All our models are monolingually trained and evaluated on isiNdebele, isiXhosa, isiZulu, or Siswati. We evaluate four versions of each neural model, varying morphological input in the following ways.

Segmentation types We train models for both types of morphological segmentation, allowing us to evaluate their respective difficulty.

- Canonical segmentation: decompose words into standardised morphemes (e.g., "zobomi" $\rightarrow$ "za-u-(bu)-bomi").

- Surface segmentation: decompose words into morphs as they appear in composed forms (e.g., "zobomi" $\rightarrow$ "zo-bomi").

Upstream segmentation During testing, we assess performance across both idealised and practical scenarios.

- Gold-annotated segmentations: apply taggers directly to the linguistically annotated, gold-standard morphological segmentations from the task dataset (Gaustad and Puttkammer, 2022). This provides an idealised setting in which morphological segmentations are known to be correct, isolating tagging performance from segmentation errors.

- Model-predicted segmentations: apply taggers to segmentations generated by neural segmenters (Moeng et al., 2021). We retrain their feature-based CRFs and Transformers on our training set to match our data setup. This simulates a real-world pipeline where segmentation is predicted, allowing for error propagation from segmentation to tagging.

4.3 Evaluation

We use F_1 score to evaluate our models. We only evaluate morphological tagging performance, as opposed to full morphological parsing (segmentation + tagging). However, tagging inherently depends on segmentation in our setup, since models are trained on the pre-segmented morpheme sequences.

In our model-predicted segmentation setting, errors in predicted morphological segmentations can result in fewer or more predicted morphemes than morphological tags. As a result, in some instances we have to compute an F_1 score for predicted and target tag sequences of different lengths. We make use of the aligned multiset F_1 score proposed by Seker and Tsarfaty (2020b). This is an adaptation of the aligned segment F_1 score used in CoNLL18

Hyperparameter	Search space
Neural sequence labellers	
Learning rate	$[10^{-6}, 10^{-1}]$
Weight decay	$\{0\} \cup [10^{-10}, 10^{-3}]$
Hidden state size	$\{2^x : 6 \leq x \leq 11\}$
Dropout	$\{0, 0.1, 0.2, 0.3\}$
Gradient clip	$\{0.5, 1, 2, 4, \infty\}$
Finetuned PLMs	
Learning rate	$\{10^{-5}, 3 \times 10^{-5}, 5 \times 10^{-5}\}$
Epochs	$\{5, 10, 15\}$
Batch size	$\{8, 16, 32\}$

Table 2: The hyperparameter ranges of our grid search.

(Zeman and Hajič, 2018). The key difference is that the aligned multiset F_1 score bases token counts on the multiset intersection between the target and predicted sequences, so that target-prediction length mismatches are ameliorated.

We report both macro F_1 and micro F_1 in our results. Micro F_1 is a calculated by counting the number of true positives/negatives and false positives/negatives for all classes. More common tags therefore have a greater effect on the Micro F_1 score. With one tag per item, it is equivalent to accuracy. Macro F_1 calculates the per-class F_1 score and averages them, weighting all tags equally irrespective of frequency. A high macro F_1 score indicates good performance across all tags, including rare tag types. We focused on macro F_1 during hyperparameter tuning and in discussing our results, as we consider it important for our models to perform well on rare tags. Our evaluation dataset (Gaustad and Puttkammer, 2022) is imbalanced from a tag perspective, so macro F_1 is the more challenging metric to optimise than micro F_1.

4.4 Hyperparameters

The morphologically annotated dateset (Gaustad and Puttkammer, 2022) is split into train and test sets, but does not include a validation set. To prevent over-fitting hyperparameters to the test set, we created our own held-out validation set from 10% of the training set. Hyperparameter settings were tuned to maximise macro F_1 scores on the validation dataset.

For our models trained from scratch, we performed a grid search over the hyperparameter ranges shown in Table 2. We tuned our hyperparameter settings on isiZulu only, because including other languages would lead to a computationally infeasible grid search. Once the best parameters for isiZulu were found, these configurations were applied to the other languages. For our PLMs, we also performed a grid search over finetuning hyperparameters over the grid shown in Table 2.

After we settled on our final hyperparameter settings based on validation set performance, we retrained models on the full, original training set (including our newly created validation set) and evaluated them on the test set. For each model configuration, we train/finetune five models with different random seeds and report the average evaluation metrics.

4.5 Baselines

We compare our neural methods to ZulMorph (Bosch et al., 2008), a traditional, rule-based parser for IsiZulu. ZulMorph is based on finite-state transducers with manually incorporated grammatical rules, stems, and affixes for isiZulu. We use the ZulMorph demo (Pretorius and Bosch, 2018) to evaluate its performance on the test set. Since ZulMorph both segments and tags the input data, we compare it to our taggers trained on model-predicted segmentations.

5 Results

The results based on gold-annotated segmentations are shown in Table 3, while those based on model-predicted segmentations are shown in Table 4.

Overall, our results demonstrate the effectiveness of neural models on the challenging task of morphological tagging for Nguni languages. Our best-performing models based on gold-annotated canonical segmentations consistently achieve micro F_1 scores above 90% and macro F_1 scores above 60%. Even without access to the gold morphological annotations, with models tested on the predicted canonical segmentations of Moeng et al. (2021), our best models consistently achieve micro F_1 scores above 80% and macro F_1 scores above 55%. This confirms the feasibility of basing the full morphological parsing pipeline on neural models.

Comparison to rule-based parsing The neural models comfortably outperform our rule-based baseline, ZulMorph, on isiZulu morphological tagging. ZulMorph (Pretorius and Bosch, 2018) achieves a macro F_1 of 34% and micro F_1 of 71.8% on the test-set. All our isiZulu models surpass this performance, ranging from macro F_1s of 43.1% to 60% and micro F_1s of 72.7% to 85.8%.

Model	IsiZulu		IsiNdebele		IsiXhosa		Siswati	
	Mac F_1	Mic F_1	Mac F_1	Mic F_1	Mac F_1	Mic F_1	Mac F_1	Mic F_1
Canonical segmentations as annotated in Gaustad and Puttkammer (2022)								
Trained from scratch								
Word-level								
bi-LSTM, character-sum	**66.9**	**92.4**	67.2	**91.9**	72.3	95.2	66.5	91.2
bi-LSTM, morpheme	66.6	92.1	67.7	91.8	71.5	94.9	65.5	91.0
Sentence-level								
bi-LSTM, character-sum	64.6	91.6	66.6	91.0	72.1	95.5	64.7	90.8
bi-LSTM, morpheme	66.0	92.1	67.9	91.6	74.7	95.7	**67.2**	91.3
CRF, character-sum	65.7	92.1	67.3	91.4	74.7	**95.9**	66.0	91.4
CRF, morpheme	66.1	92.3	**68.1**	91.6	**75.3**	95.8	67.2	**91.4**
Pretrained language models								
Word-level								
Afro-XLMR	**62.5**	**92.0**	62.3	91.4	67.9	95.1	**63.3**	**91.3**
Nguni-XLMR	61.9	92.0	62.8	91.5	**68.1**	**95.1**	61.8	90.7
XLM-R-large	61.8	91.8	**63.6**	**91.6**	67.4	95.0	62.9	91.2
Surface segmentations extrapolated from Gaustad and Puttkammer (2022) by script from Moeng et al. (2021)								
Trained from scratch								
Sentence-level								
bi-LSTM, character-sum	63.3	90.7	65.2	90.4	73.6	94.7	61.3	89.6
bi-LSTM, character-sum-lower	63.2	90.8	65.4	90.4	73.7	94.7	60.8	89.7
bi-LSTM, morpheme	65.6	91.3	68.4	91.1	**76.1**	95.1	**65.9**	90.6
bi-LSTM, morpheme-lower	**66.0**	**91.3**	**68.7**	**91.2**	76.0	**95.3**	65.8	**90.7**
Pretrained language models								
Word-level								
Afro-XLMR	43.8	72.8	47.7	77.4	52.3	78.5	23.4	55.6
Nguni-XLMR	**44.1**	**73.1**	**48.1**	**77.5**	**52.4**	**79.0**	**23.9**	**56.6**
XLM-R-large	43.1	72.6	48.0	77.5	51.7	78.1	22.7	55.4

Table 3: Results for models evaluated on gold-annotated segmentations, given as percentages. This provides an idealised training setting in which all morphological segmentations are correct, allowing us to isolate the performance of morphological tagging. The best models for each approach (pretrained or from scratch) is **bolded**, while the best for each segmentation type (surface or canonical) is underlined.

Since ZulMorph is rule-based and contains manually-incorporated stems and affixes, it likely struggles to generalise to unseen data. For instance, ZulMorph failed to segment and parse "wezentuthuko", and instead produced "wezentuthuko +?". Conversely, the neural models do not explicitly incorporate any information. The models are able to classify text even when there are unknown morphemes present in the text, based on the surrounding context of known morphemes.

Macro vs Micro F_1 Macro F_1 is consistently lower than corresponding micro F_1 scores. This highlights one of the difficulties of morphological tagging for the Nguni languages. The tag set is large and unevenly distributed in the dataset, which make it challenging to accurately model rare tags. This imbalance would explain the mismatch between macro and micro F_1 for neural models, since they are not adequately exposed to rare tags during training. However, the mismatch persists for ZulMorph (Bosch et al., 2008) (see Table 4), which is based on gramatically informed rules, as opposed to being data-driven. This could indicate that some tags are inherently harder to disambiguate.

5.1 Training neural taggers from scratch

As shown in Tables 3 and 4, sentence-level models trained from scratch tended to outperform their word-level counterparts. Sentence-level models are trained on the entire sentence as context, which may allow them to use grammatical dependencies to improve tagging. For example, in the isiXhosa sentence "ipolisa liyahamba", the word "ipolisa" is in noun class 5. The shorted prefix "i" ("**i**polisa") is ambiguous and also appears in class 9 nouns, such as "iteksi". However, combining it with the subject concord for class 5 "li" ("**li**yahamba") provides the information required to correctly disambiguate and

Model	IsiZulu		IsiNdebele		IsiXhosa		Siswati	
	Mac F_1	Mic F_1	Mac F_1	Mic F_1	Mac F_1	Mic F_1	Mac F_1	Mic F_1
ZulMorph online demo (Pretorius and Bosch, 2018)								
ZulMorph	34.0	71.8						
Canonical segmentations as predicted by Moeng et al. (2021)								
Trained from scratch								
Word-level								
bi-LSTM, character-sum	<u>**60.0**</u>	<u>**85.8**</u>	57.8	<u>**84.1**</u>	67.9	92.3	57.0	85.0
bi-LSTM, morpheme	58.3	85.5	58.3	84.1	67.0	92.2	55.7	84.7
Sentence-level								
bi-LSTM, character-sum	57.5	85.1	57.3	83.4	68.1	92.7	55.5	84.8
bi-LSTM, morpheme	58.4	85.7	58.3	83.8	70.7	93.0	57.3	85.2
CRF, character-sum	58.1	85.5	58.4	83.8	69.8	<u>**93.1**</u>	57.2	<u>**85.4**</u>
CRF, morpheme	58.7	85.7	<u>**58.5**</u>	83.7	<u>**71.1**</u>	93.1	<u>**57.8**</u>	85.3
Pretrained language models								
Word-level								
Afro-XLMR	**55.3**	85.5	54.6	84.0	63.4	92.4	**53.4**	**85.1**
Nguni-XLMR	54.8	**85.5**	54.5	83.9	**64.4**	**92.6**	52.5	84.6
XLM-R-large	54.4	85.4	**55.4**	<u>**84.1**</u>	63.5	92.5	52.9	85.0
Surface segmentations as predicted by Moeng et al. (2021)								
Trained from scratch								
Sentence-level								
bi-LSTM, character-sum	53.6	79.6	52.8	78.3	65.6	<u>**87.7**</u>	51.8	80.4
bi-LSTM, character-sum-lower	53.3	79.6	52.9	78.2	65.2	87.5	51.6	80.4
bi-LSTM, morpheme	55.0	79.7	<u>**54.7**</u>	78.4	68.0	87.4	55.2	81.0
bi-LSTM, morpheme-lower	<u>**55.3**</u>	<u>**79.7**</u>	54.6	<u>**78.5**</u>	<u>**68.2**</u>	87.6	<u>**55.8**</u>	<u>**81.0**</u>
Pretrained language models								
Word-level								
Afro-XLMR	43.6	72.8	46.9	77.4	**51.9**	78.5	23.0	55.7
Nguni-XLMR	**43.9**	**73.0**	46.9	77.4	51.7	**78.8**	**23.7**	**56.3**
XLM-R-large	43.1	72.7	**47.7**	**77.5**	51.4	78.0	22.1	55.4

Table 4: Results for models evaluated on model-predicted segmentations, given as percentages. This evaluates the combined use of neural methods for segmentation and tagging, without access to morphological annotations. The best models for each approach (pretrained or from scratch) is **bolded**, while the best for each segmentation type (surface or canonical) is <u>underlined</u>.

tag "ipolisa" as class 5.

Morpheme-level embeddings outperformed character-summing embeddings. While one might expect character-level modelling to improve generalisation across morphemes, this is not necessarily the case. Morphemes representations have previously been shown to be highly effective for syntactic tasks (Üstün et al., 2018). For our task, morpheme-level embeddings allow the model to be more sensitive to small changes in morphemes. For example, the morphemes "ng" and "nga" differ by a single character, but can have totally different meanings ("ng" can be a copulative prefix and "nga" can be an adverb prefix). With character-summed representations, the two morphemes will have highly similar embeddings. With morpheme-level embeddings, each morpheme embedding is learned separately. For rare or previously unseen morphemes, the morpheme-level model is forced to rely on contextual grammatical information (within the word or surrounding sentence), which provides a more reliable grammatical signal than the number of overlapping characters between morphemes.

We do not find substantial performance differences between bi-LSTMs and bi-LSTM CRFs. This indicates that explicitly modeling grammar through tag dependence presents limited advantage. Bi-LSTMs are able to encode such grammatical dependencies, based on morpheme co-occurrence patterns, in their hidden representations.

5.2 Pretrained language models

As shown in Tables 3 and 4, training models from scratch outperformed finetuning PLMs. This contrasts with previous work on linguistic annotation tasks, in which pretrained solutions have outperformed models trained from scratch (Min et al., 2023; Alabi et al., 2022). However, it does align with related work for the Nguni languages, which have achieved high performance levels with neural models trained from scratch (Moeng et al., 2021; Pannach et al., 2022).

Due to computational constraints, we did not finetune PLMs on sentence-level input. The pretrained contextual representations of PLMs are well suited to take advantage of sentence-level context, so it is possible that finetuning sentence-level versions of our PLMs could improve their performance. We leave the exploration of sentence-level PLMs for Nguni-language morphological tagging to future work.

Another factor which could contribute to PLM performance degradation is subword tokenisation. While our models trained from scratch use character or morpheme-level representations, our PLMs are constrained to finetune representations for the subword tokens produced by their pretrained tokenisers. In pretraining, the tokeniser segments raw words. In finetuning, the tokeniser segments pre-segmented morphemes. This misalignment could impede the model's ability to leverage pretrained knowledge during finetuning, since the subword tokens learned in pretraining do not match those of finetuning. This also leads to irregular, morphologically unsound subword tokens. For example, the XLM-R SentencePiece tokeniser (Conneau et al., 2020; Kudo and Richardson, 2018) segments, which is the tokeniser for all our PLMs, segments the isiXhosa morpheme "-bandela" into "-ba", "#ndel", "#a", which is morphologically meaningless. In our pipeline setup for morphological parsing, it is not obvious how to bridge the mismatch between pretraining and finetuning subword tokenisation. It should be viewed as a limitation of PLMs. With neural models trained from scratch, we have the freedom to design our own morphological input features.

5.3 Models based on surface segmentations

In both Tables 3 and 4, the top half of each table reports results for models trained on canonical segmentations (morphemes), while the bottom half reports results for surface-level segmentations (morphs). In general, canonically-based tagging scores are higher than surface-level tagging. The performance gap is particularly notable and consistent for models trained on model-predicted segmentations. While canonical and surface-level tagging scores cannot be directly compared (for some words, the tag sequence will not be the same), our results clearly show that training taggers on top of canonical segmenters is more effective than doing so with surface-level segmenters. We attribute this to two factors.

Firstly, the surface segmentation of a word provides less grammatical information to models than the canonical segmentation. For instance, the word "kwicandelo" is canonically segmented as "ku-i-(li)-candelo" and surface segmented as "kw-i-candelo" (Gaustad and Puttkammer, 2022). Critically, the "(li)" morpheme is lost, which is part of the noun prefix for class 5. The only morpheme left for the noun prefix is thus "i". However, this on its own is ambiguous, and could be the noun prefix for class 5 or class 9. In this case, the canonical tagger would have more information relevant to the tagging decision than the surface tagger.

Secondly, there is often a length mismatch between the surface and canonical morphemes in a word. For example, "kubomi" is canonically segmented into "ku-u-(bu)-bomi", but surface-segmented into "ku-bomi". We evaluate our model on gold-annotated data, which include morphological tags for each word. In a case like "kubomi", this would limit performance to 50% accuracy in the best case scenario. In general, this length mismatch limits the performance of models based surface-level segmentations.

6 Conclusion

In this paper, we explored the feasibility of neural morphological taggers for the Nguni languages. We divide morphological parsing into two subtasks, segmentation and tagging, focussing on the latter. We investigate bi-LSTMs and CRFs trained from scratch, as well as finetuned PLMs. Our neural models comfortably outperform a rule-based baseline, while our models trained from scratch outperform PLMs. Models based on canonical segmentations outperform their surface-level counterparts.

We identify several promising directions for future research to build on our findings. Firstly, our PLM taggers could potentially be improved, either by finetuning on sentence-level input or by exploring ways to align the mismatch between subword tokenisation in pretraining and finetuning. Furthermore, our parsers can be used to incorporate morphological information into downstream task models (Klemen et al., 2023). This has been shown to improve performance in tasks such as language modelling (Nzeyimana and Niyongabo Rubungo, 2022) and machine translation (Nzeyimana, 2024), but has not been explored for the Nguni languages.

Limitations

Our study is limited to the Nguni languages, so our findings may not generalise to other language families or typologies like the Sotho-Tswana languages whose morphology is disjunctive. Further experimentation is needed to validate whether training taggers on model-predicted morphological segmentations is viable for languages with different morphological structures. That being said, the promising performance of our models on the Nguni languages suggests that similar neural approaches could be beneficial for other low-resource, morphologically complex languages.

Additionally, while our models trained from scratch consistently outperformed finetuned PLMs, we do not definitively conclude that PLMs are inferior for this task. As discussed in subsection 5.2, because of computational constraints we did not test sentence-level PLMs. Incoporating sentence-level context could improve PLM performance to be competitive with models trained from scratch. We would need to run further experiments with sentence-level finetuning to evaluate the full potential of PLMs for this task.

References

Gulinigeer Abudouwaili, Kahaerjiang Abiderexiti, Nian Yi, and Aishan Wumaier. 2023. Joint learning model for low-resource agglutinative language morphological tagging. In *Proceedings of the 20th SIGMORPHON workshop on Computational Research in Phonetics, Phonology, and Morphology*, pages 27–37, Toronto, Canada. Association for Computational Linguistics.

Ekin Akyürek, Erenay Dayanık, and Deniz Yuret. 2019. Morphological analysis using a sequence decoder. *Transactions of the Association for Computational Linguistics*, 7:567–579.

Jesujoba O. Alabi, David Ifeoluwa Adelani, Marius Mosbach, and Dietrich Klakow. 2022. Adapting pre-trained language models to African languages via multilingual adaptive fine-tuning. In *Proceedings of the 29th International Conference on Computational Linguistics*, pages 4336–4349, Gyeongju, Republic of Korea. International Committee on Computational Linguistics.

Hüseyin. Aleçakır. 2020. Joint learning of morphological segmentation, morpheme tagging, part-of-speech tagging, and dependency parsing. Master's thesis, Middle East Technical University.

Anders Björkelund, Özlem Çetinoğlu, Richárd Farkas, Thomas Mueller, and Wolfgang Seeker. 2013. (re) ranking meets morphosyntax: State-of-the-art results from the spmrl 2013 shared task. In *Proceedings of the Fourth Workshop on Statistical Parsing of Morphologically-Rich Languages*, pages 135–145.

Sonja Bosch, Laurette Pretorius, Kholisa Podile, and Axel Fleisch. 2008. Experimental fast-tracking of morphological analysers for nguni languages. In *Proceedings of the Sixth International Conference on Language Resources and Evaluation (LREC'08)*, Marrakech, Morocco. European Language Resources Association (ELRA).

Paul G Chapin and Lewis M Norton. 1968. A procedure for morphological analysis.

Alexis Conneau, Kartikay Khandelwal, Naman Goyal, Vishrav Chaudhary, Guillaume Wenzek, Francisco Guzmán, Edouard Grave, Myle Ott, Luke Zettlemoyer, and Veselin Stoyanov. 2020. Unsupervised cross-lingual representation learning at scale. In *Proceedings of the 58th Annual Meeting of the Association for Computational Linguistics*, pages 8440–8451, Online. Association for Computational Linguistics.

Ryan Cotterell, Tim Vieira, and Hinrich Schütze. 2016. A joint model of orthography and morphological segmentation. In *Proceedings of the 2016 Conference of the North American Chapter of the Association for Computational Linguistics: Human Language Technologies*, pages 664–669, San Diego, California. Association for Computational Linguistics.

W. Daelemans, J. Zavrel, K. Sloot, and A. Bosch. Timbl: Tilburg memory-based learner, version 6.4: reference guide.

David M. Eberhard, Gary F. Simons, , and Charles D. Fenning. 2019. *Ethnologue: Languages of the World*, 22 edition. SIL International.

Tanja Gaustad and Martin J. Puttkammer. 2022. Linguistically annotated dataset for four official south african languages with a conjunctive orthography: Isindebele, isixhosa, isizulu, and siswati. *Data in Brief*, 41:107994.

Sepp Hochreiter and Jürgen Schmidhuber. 1997. Long Short-Term Memory. *Neural Computation*, 9(8):1735–1780.

Matej Klemen, Luka Krsnik, and Marko Robnik-Šikonja. 2023. Enhancing deep neural networks with morphological information. *Natural Language Engineering*, 29(2):360–385.

Taku Kudo and John Richardson. 2018. Sentencepiece: A simple and language independent subword tokenizer and detokenizer for neural text processing. *CoRR*, abs/1808.06226.

John D. Lafferty, Andrew McCallum, and Fernando C. N. Pereira. 2001. Conditional random fields: Probabilistic models for segmenting and labeling sequence data. In *Proceedings of the Eighteenth International Conference on Machine Learning*, ICML '01, page 282–289, San Francisco, CA, USA. Morgan Kaufmann Publishers Inc.

Guillaume Lample, Miguel Ballesteros, Sandeep Subramanian, Kazuya Kawakami, and Chris Dyer. 2016. Neural architectures for named entity recognition. In *Proceedings of the 2016 Conference of the North American Chapter of the Association for Computational Linguistics: Human Language Technologies*, pages 260–270, San Diego, California. Association for Computational Linguistics.

Xuezhe Ma and Eduard Hovy. 2016. End-to-end sequence labeling via bi-directional LSTM-CNNs-CRF. In *Proceedings of the 54th Annual Meeting of the Association for Computational Linguistics (Volume 1: Long Papers)*, pages 1064–1074, Berlin, Germany. Association for Computational Linguistics.

Peter H. Matthews. 1991. *Morphology*, 2 edition. Cambridge Textbooks in Linguistics. Cambridge University Press, Cambridge, UK.

Francois Meyer, Haiyue Song, Abhisek Chakrabarty, Jan Buys, Raj Dabre, and Hideki Tanaka. 2024. NGLUEni: Benchmarking and adapting pretrained language models for nguni languages. In *Proceedings of the 2024 Joint International Conference on Computational Linguistics, Language Resources and Evaluation (LREC-COLING 2024)*, pages 12247–12258, Torino, Italia. ELRA and ICCL.

Bonan Min, Hayley Ross, Elior Sulem, Amir Pouran Ben Veyseh, Thien Huu Nguyen, Oscar Sainz, Eneko Agirre, Ilana Heintz, and Dan Roth. 2023. Recent advances in natural language processing via large pre-trained language models: A survey. *ACM Comput. Surv.*, 56(2).

Tumi Moeng, Sheldon Reay, Aaron Daniels, and Jan Buys. 2021. Canonical and surface morphological segmentation for nguni languages. *Preprint*, arXiv:2104.00767.

Thomas Mueller, Helmut Schmid, and Hinrich Schütze. 2013. Efficient higher-order CRFs for morphological tagging. In *Proceedings of the 2013 Conference on Empirical Methods in Natural Language Processing*, pages 322–332, Seattle, Washington, USA. Association for Computational Linguistics.

Antoine Nzeyimana. 2024. Low-resource neural machine translation with morphological modeling. In *Findings of the Association for Computational Linguistics: NAACL 2024*, pages 182–195, Mexico City, Mexico. Association for Computational Linguistics.

Antoine Nzeyimana and Andre Niyongabo Rubungo. 2022. KinyaBERT: a morphology-aware Kinyarwanda language model. In *Proceedings of the 60th Annual Meeting of the Association for Computational Linguistics (Volume 1: Long Papers)*, pages 5347–5363, Dublin, Ireland. Association for Computational Linguistics.

Franziska Pannach, Francois Meyer, Edgar Jembere, and Sibonelo Zamokuhle Dlamini. 2022. Nlapost2021 1st shared task on part-of-speech tagging for nguni languages. *Journal of the Digital Humanities Association of Southern Africa*, 3(01).

L. Pretorius and S. Bosch. 2018. Zulmorph: Finite state morphological analyser for zulu (version 20190103. [Software]. Web demo at.

Martin Puttkammer and Jakobus Du Toit. 2021. Canonical segmentation and syntactic morpheme tagging of four resource- scarce nguni languages. *Journal of the Digital Humanities Association of Southern Africa (DHASA)*, 3.

Amit Seker and Reut Tsarfaty. 2020a. A pointer network architecture for joint morphological segmentation and tagging. In *Findings of the Association for Computational Linguistics: EMNLP 2020*, pages 4368–4378, Online. Association for Computational Linguistics.

Amit Seker and Reut Tsarfaty. 2020b. A pointer network architecture for joint morphological segmentation and tagging. In *Findings of the Association for Computational Linguistics: EMNLP 2020*, pages 4368–4378, Online. Association for Computational Linguistics.

Elsabe Taljard and Sonja Bosch. 2006. A comparison of approaches to word class tagging: Disjunctively vs. conjunctively written bantu languages. *Nordic Journal of African Studies*, 15.

Reut Tsarfaty, Djamé Seddah, Sandra Kübler, and Joakim Nivre. 2013. Parsing Morphologically Rich Languages: Introduction to the Special Issue. *Computational Linguistics*, 39(1):15–22.

Ahmet Üstün, Murathan Kurfalı, and Burcu Can. 2018. Characters or morphemes: How to represent words? In *Proceedings of the Third Workshop on Representation Learning for NLP*, pages 144–153, Melbourne, Australia. Association for Computational Linguistics.

Ashish Vaswani, Noam Shazeer, Niki Parmar, Jakob Uszkoreit, Llion Jones, Aidan N. Gomez, Lukasz Kaiser, and Illia Polosukhin. 2023. Attention is all you need. *Preprint*, arXiv:1706.03762.

Danit Yshaayahu Levi and Reut Tsarfaty. 2024. A truly joint neural architecture for segmentation and parsing. In *Proceedings of the 18th Conference of the European Chapter of the Association for Computational Linguistics (Volume 1: Long Papers)*, pages 1408–1420, St. Julian's, Malta. Association for Computational Linguistics.

Daniel Zeman and Jan Hajič, editors. 2018. *Proceedings of the CoNLL 2018 Shared Task: Multilingual Parsing from Raw Text to Universal Dependencies*. Association for Computational Linguistics, Brussels, Belgium.

Multilingual NLP for African Healthcare: Bias, Translation, and Explainability Challenges

Ugochi Okafor
Data Science Nigeria

Abstract

Language technologies have advanced significantly, yet African languages remain underrepresented in natural language processing (NLP) and machine translation (MT) due to data scarcity, linguistic complexity, and computational constraints. Large-scale models such as No Language Left Behind (NLLB-200) and Flores-200 have made strides in expanding machine translation for low-resource languages, yet significant challenges persist in adapting them for healthcare and domain-specific applications in African contexts.

This paper explores multilingual NLP and translation models in African healthcare, evaluating approaches such as Masakhane-MT for translation, Masakhane-NER for named entity recognition (NER), and AfromT for domain adaptation. Focusing on languages like Swahili, Yoruba, and Hausa, the evaluation highlights bias, linguistic inequity, and performance disparities through a literature review and analysis of existing models.

Use cases such as Ubenwa's infant cry analysis for asphyxia diagnosis and translation models trained on Flores-200 benchmark datasets demonstrate both potential and limitations in real-world applications. Our findings underscore the need for culturally adapted, explainable AI systems that integrate linguistic diversity, ethical AI principles, and community-driven data collection. Limitations include dataset quality concerns, bias in training corpora, and a lack of healthcare-specific benchmarks for African languages. We propose strategies for bias mitigation, improved dataset representation, and culturally aligned NLP models, with a focus on data accessibility, fairness, and equitable AI deployment in African healthcare.

1 Introduction

The underrepresentation of African languages in NLP and MT remains a major barrier to the equitable development of AI-driven language technologies. Despite the rise of large-scale multilingual models, the vast majority of African languages lack the resources, training data, and computational infrastructure needed for high-quality NLP applications. The Masakhane initiative, a community-driven effort to build NLP resources for African languages, has demonstrated significant progress in MT and NER (Orife et al., 2020). However, challenges such as missing documentation, poor tokenization, and difficulty adapting models to specialized areas like healthcare remain barriers to progress.

The Lanfrica platform has been developed to help researchers find and use African language datasets, but more work is needed to ensure these datasets are widely available and well-annotated (Emezue and Dossou, 2020). Addressing these issues is crucial for expanding NLP applications to critical domains such as healthcare, where accurate translations and context-aware models are essential for patient safety and effective clinical communication.

This paper reviews existing multilingual NLP models, evaluating their effectiveness in African healthcare applications. By comparing Masakhane-MT, Masakhane-NER, AfromT, and NLLB, this study highlights disparities in translation accuracy, named entity recognition, and model adaptation to African linguistic structures. Furthermore, the research identifies critical gaps in AI fairness, transparency, and explainability in medical AI applications, proposing strategies for bias mitigation and domain-specific model enhancement.

2 Literature Review

2.1 Multilingual NLP and African Healthcare

Recent advancements in multilingual NLP have significantly improved language translation and understanding across diverse linguistic landscapes.

Proceedings of the Sixth Workshop on African Natural Language Processing (AfricaNLP 2025), pages 221–229

However, these improvements remain concentrated in high-resource languages, leaving African languages underrepresented due to data scarcity, tokenization inefficiencies, and bias in AI models (Joshi et al., 2020; Nekoto et al., 2020).

Large-scale models such as mT5, DeepSeek, LLaMA 3, and Meta AI's No Language Left Behind (NLLB) have expanded support for low-resource languages, yet their performance remains suboptimal for African languages, particularly in specialized domains such as healthcare.

2.2 Reviewed NLP Frameworks and Their Applications

Several NLP research efforts and initiatives have focused on African languages, contributing to improved translation models and text-processing systems. However, despite these advancements, key challenges remain, particularly in the medical domain. The following subsections examine significant frameworks and their relevance to healthcare.

2.2.1 Masakhane NLP: Community-Driven Machine Translation

Masakhane NLP is an open-source research initiative that develops machine translation models for African languages through collaborative efforts (Nekoto et al., 2020). Using datasets such as JW300, Masakhane has created translation models for over 30 African languages (Orife et al., 2020). Despite its success in fostering research and dataset creation, challenges persist:

- BLEU scores for African languages remain below 25, significantly lower than European counterparts (Orife et al., 2020).
- The models struggle with morphological complexity and dialectal variations, leading to translation inaccuracies.
- There is a lack of domain-specific datasets, particularly in medical and scientific fields, limiting application in healthcare.

For example, a Swahili-language chatbot trained on Masakhane's models struggled with medical terminology, leading to potentially harmful misinterpretations of prescriptions (Adelani et al., 2021).

2.2.2 No Language Left Behind (NLLB): Scaling Low-Resource Translation

Meta AI's No Language Left Behind (NLLB) project aims to enhance translation for low-resource languages, introducing NLLB-Seed and the Flores-200 benchmark (Costa-jussà, 2022). While achieving a 40% improvement in BLEU scores compared to previous models, NLLB-200 still faces challenges:

- In healthcare translations, NLLB-200 exhibited critical failures, such as mistranslating Swahili medical dosage instructions, which could lead to unsafe medication use (Iyamu, 2024).
- The model showed poor adaptation to dialectal diversity, leading to misinformation in public health messaging.
- Automatic toxicity detection was biased, disproportionately flagging African-language translations as unsafe (World Health Organization, 2024).

These findings above highlight the gap between translation quality metrics and real-world applicability, particularly in medical contexts where accuracy is critical.

One notable gap is the absence of open-source, healthcare-specific parallel corpora in African languages. While Masakhane-NER includes limited health-related annotations, and AfromT introduces a medically-aligned translation corpus, these remain nascent. The Ubenwa dataset used for infant cry analysis is one of the few clinically validated resources, but it is audio-based and limited in linguistic diversity. The scarcity of textual healthcare datasets prevents robust model training, cross-language benchmarking, and reproducibility in medical NLP. Public access to culturally representative medical corpora remains essential for advancing this field.

2.2.3 AfromT: Domain-Specific Machine Translation

AfromT is a domain-specific translation framework designed to improve scientific and medical translations for African languages (Iyamu, 2024). Despite a 19% improvement over Google Translate, it still performed 25% worse than models trained on high-resource languages. Key limitations include:

- AfromT struggled with technical medical terminology, leading to a 25% higher error rate in Swahili and Hausa medical translations compared to English and French (Bapna and Firat, 2022).

- The model was ineffective for dialect-rich languages such as Igbo, where missing linguistic nuances altered medical meaning.

Across the reviewed works, language representation remains skewed. Masakhane-MT and NER primarily cover widely spoken languages such as Swahili, Hausa, Yoruba, and Amharic. Less-resourced languages like Fon, Tigrinya, and Krio are underrepresented or entirely excluded. NLLB-200 and Flores-200 improve breadth with over 40 African languages, yet even these datasets have uneven quality and sparse domain coverage. This imbalance hampers equitable model performance, especially for languages spoken by marginalised or rural populations.

2.3 Bias and Fairness Issues in African NLP

Bias in NLP models trained on Western-centric datasets poses significant risks when applied to African languages, especially in healthcare (Bommasani et al., 2021). Studies have found:

- Medical chatbots trained on Western medical corpora misdiagnosed symptoms 30% more frequently when used in African languages (Khanuja, 2023).

- Translation models failed to accurately render diagnostic terms, increasing the likelihood of medical misinformation (World Health Organization, 2024).

Efforts to mitigate these biases include dataset resampling, fairness-aware training, and adversarial debiasing techniques. However, these approaches require extensive African-language corpora, which remain scarce.

2.4 Tokenisation Challenges and NLP Efficiency

Tokenisation inefficiencies significantly impact NLP applications in African healthcare. African languages, particularly those with agglutinative structures, require more tokens per sentence than English, increasing computational costs and reducing translation fluency (Gallegos et al., 2024). Key findings include:

- A Masakhane-MT evaluation found that Google's mT5 model mis-segmented Swahili medical texts, lowering BLEU scores by 18% (Orife et al., 2020).

- AfromT's subword tokenisation had a 23% higher segmentation error rate for African medical terms compared to high-resource languages.

- NLLB-Seed's Yoruba and Igbo translations exhibited 36% higher word segmentation errors than English and French, reducing their usability for clinical text processing (Costa-jussà, 2022).

These errors contribute to AI model inefficiencies, ultimately affecting real-world healthcare applications.

2.5 Language Representation in Existing Models

Although recent multilingual models have improved support for African languages, there remains an over-reliance on a small subset—mainly Swahili, Yoruba, Hausa, and Amharic. This review highlights that even these better-represented languages suffer from poor medical terminology coverage, domain adaptation issues, and tokenisation errors. Meanwhile, dozens of widely spoken languages, such as Shona, Krio, Tigrinya, and Luganda, are either absent or poorly served by current models and corpora. Efforts to increase dataset diversity must go beyond language count to include balanced and domain-specific representation across regions and communities.

2.6 Use Cases: AI in African Healthcare:

AI-driven NLP applications in African healthcare hold promise but require adaptation for linguistic and cultural contexts. Key examples include:

Case Study: Ubenwa AI – Infant Cry Analysis for Birth Asphyxia: Ubenwa AI, a Nigerian startup, applies machine learning to analyse infant cries for early diagnosis of birth asphyxia, a leading cause of neonatal mortality. The AI model, trained on a dataset of 2,000+ clinically diagnosed cases, achieved 85% sensitivity and 89% specificity (Onu et al., 2017). However:

- Performance dropped significantly when analysing cries in Nigerian Pidgin and Hausa due to English-centric NLP training.

- Lack of linguistic diversity in training data limited its effectiveness in multilingual African populations.

This underscores the need for culturally adapted AI models in healthcare.

Machine Translation in Medical Texts Machine translation plays a crucial role in disseminating medical knowledge across African linguistic communities. However:

- BLEU score evaluations revealed a 44% performance gap in medical translations for African languages compared to European languages (Costa-jussà, 2022).
- AfromT improved translation accuracy but still had a 25% higher error rate for complex medical terminology than high-resource languages (Iyamu, 2024).

Case Study: Translation Failures in Public Health Messaging During the Ebola outbreak (2014-2016) and the COVID-19 pandemic, translation errors in health advisories led to misinformation:

- During the Ebola outbreak (2014–2016) and the COVID-19 pandemic, language barriers significantly hampered effective communication. Translators without Borders reported that over 90 languages were spoken in affected regions, necessitating accurate translations of health messages into local languages such as Krio, Hausa, and Themne (without Borders, 2015). Although machine translation tools like Google Translate were used, their limitations with local languages often caused confusion. To mitigate this, Translators without Borders and partners translated over 100 Ebola-related materials into 30 local languages, improving clarity and cultural relevance in health campaigns (without Borders, 2015).
- mT5-translated COVID-19 health advisories in Igbo contained 29% lexical inaccuracies, affecting public understanding of safety measures (Orife et al., 2020).

These failures highlight the importance of domain-specific adaptation in NLP models.

2.7 Summary and Future Directions

This literature review highlights both the advancements and persistent challenges in multilingual NLP for African healthcare. Key findings include:

- African NLP frameworks (Masakhane, NLLB, AfromT) have improved language translation but remain insufficient for healthcare applications due to dataset limitations.
- Tokenization inefficiencies and dataset biases hinder translation accuracy and AI performance in medical contexts.
- AI applications such as Ubenwa and medical chatbots show promise but require linguistic and cultural adaptation for effective deployment.

Future research must prioritise:

- Expanding domain-specific medical datasets for African languages.
- Developing tokenization techniques adapted to African linguistic structures.
- Enhancing fairness and explainability frameworks for healthcare AI.

By addressing these limitations, NLP can support equitable and reliable AI-driven healthcare solutions across Africa.

3 Methodology

3.1 Research Approach and Scope

This study adopts a systematic literature review and empirical evaluation to assess the performance, fairness, and explainability of multilingual NLP models applied to African healthcare. The primary focus is on the challenges of language representation, translation accuracy, and domain adaptation for low-resource African languages.

To achieve this, we analysed over 30 peer-reviewed papers, technical reports, and datasets related to multilingual NLP, bias mitigation, and domain-specific language modelling in healthcare. The research investigates three key areas:

- **Bias and Fairness in NLP for African Languages:** Examining dataset imbalances, tokenisation issues, and linguistic disparities that impact healthcare AI applications.
- **Machine Translation and Named Entity Recognition (NER):** Evaluating the performance of Masakhane-MT, Masakhane-NER, AfromT, and NLLB-Seed in medical text processing for African languages.

- **Explainability and Trust in AI-driven Healthcare:** Analysing SHAP-based interpretability techniques and their applicability to healthcare NLP for African contexts.

This research does not introduce new models or datasets but synthesizes findings from existing literature and evaluations to provide a comprehensive overview of multilingual NLP tools in African healthcare. By identifying current limitations and potential improvements, it offers practical insights that inform future research priorities, especially regarding dataset creation and collaborative model development tailored to specific healthcare domains and languages.

3.2 Data Collection and NLP Model Selection

To assess multilingual NLP models for healthcare applications, we analyze publicly available datasets and benchmark results from leading AI and NLP research initiatives. The study includes both general-purpose and domain-specific models.

3.2.1 Multilingual NLP Models Evaluated

The following models were selected based on their relevance to African language processing and healthcare applications:

- **Meta AI's No Language Left Behind (NLLB-Seed and NLLB-MD):** Evaluated using the Flores-200 benchmark, focusing on translation quality and linguistic fairness (Costa-jussà, 2022).

- **Masakhane-MT:** A community-driven project for improving African machine translation, assessed for medical text adaptation (Orife et al., 2020).

- **Masakhane-NER:** A named entity recognition (NER) initiative evaluated for extracting medical terms in Swahili, Yoruba, and Hausa (Adelani et al., 2021).

- **AfromT:** A domain-specific translation framework developed to enhance African medical and scientific translations (Iyamu, 2024).

- **mT5 and DeepSeek:** General-purpose multilingual models examined for their performance on African healthcare translations (Bapna and Firat, 2022).

3.2.2 Datasets Used

The evaluation utilises established NLP datasets covering African languages, with a focus on medical and scientific applications:

- **Flores-200:** A multilingual evaluation dataset covering 40,000+ translation directions, including African languages (Costa-jussà, 2022).

- **NLLB-Seed:** A dataset designed for training low-resource MT models, containing human-translated African medical text (Costa-jussà, 2022).

- **Masakhane-NER Corpus:** Annotated datasets for named entity recognition in Swahili, Hausa, and Yoruba, used for medical NLP evaluations (Adelani et al., 2021).

- **AfromT Parallel Corpus:** A medical translation dataset developed for African healthcare NLP research (Iyamu, 2024).

- **Toxicity-200:** A dataset designed to detect and evaluate toxic translations in 200 languages, ensuring ethical AI deployment in African healthcare (Costa-jussà, 2022).

These publicly available datasets enable comparison across multiple models by revealing translation errors, linguistic biases, and domain adaptation gaps in African medical NLP. The evaluation primarily focuses on medical and scientific applications, with Swahili, Yoruba, and Hausa being the most tested languages due to the availability of annotated corpora. Among these, Swahili is the most consistently represented across all benchmarks.

3.3 Evaluation Metrics and Analytical Framework

This study adopts a comprehensive, three-pronged analytical framework to evaluate NLP models for African healthcare applications. The framework focuses on:

- **Translation Quality:** Measured using BLEU scores to assess the accuracy of models such as NLLB-Seed, AfromT, and Masakhane-MT.

- **Bias and Fairness:** Evaluated through misclassification rates, dataset imbalances, and toxicity flagging in African languages.

- **Explainability:** Assessed by exploring the potential of SHAP-based methods to improve transparency and trust in medical NLP.

Detailed findings and comparative analyses based on this framework are presented in Section 5.

3.4 Limitations of the Study

While this study provides valuable insights into multilingual NLP applications for African healthcare, several limitations remain:

- **Dataset Gaps:** African medical NLP datasets are scarce, with less than 1% of publicly available corpora covering African medical texts (Nekoto et al., 2020).
- **Computational Constraints:** Limited access to GPU clusters restricts LLM training on low-resource African languages (Khanuja, 2023).
- **Ethical and Policy Limitations:** Existing AI governance frameworks do not fully address linguistic fairness in African medical AI applications (Birhane, 2021).

Future research should focus on expanding domain-specific corpora, improving tokenisation techniques, and integrating explainability frameworks to enhance trust in AI-driven healthcare applications.

4 Conclusion

This methodology provides a structured approach to evaluating multilingual NLP models for African healthcare. By analysing bias, translation accuracy, and explainability across various models and datasets, the study identifies critical gaps and proposes future directions for improving AI-driven healthcare solutions for low-resource African languages.

5 Evaluation and Findings

5.1 Summary of MT and NER Performance

An overview of MT and NER model performance is presented in Table A1 (see Appendix 5.4). This summary is based on BLEU scores, misclassification rates, and domain-specific limitations, and covers the Masakhane-MT, NLLB-Seed, AfromT, and Masakhane-NER models. Detailed interpretation follows in the subsections below.

5.2 Evaluation Metrics and Analysis

To assess the performance, fairness, and transparency of multilingual NLP models in African healthcare, we applied a multi-metric framework. This includes evaluation of translation quality using BLEU scores, assessment of bias in model outputs, and interpretability through SHAP-based explainability methods. Table A1 in Appendix 5.4 provides a comparative overview of model performance, focusing on Masakhane-MT, NLLB-Seed, AfromT, and Masakhane-NER across Swahili, Hausa, Yoruba, and Igbo.

Moreover, the lack of regional infrastructure for training large-scale models continues to limit innovation. Most African research institutions do not have access to GPU clusters or sufficient computational power to fine-tune or even evaluate large language models on healthcare data. Cloud computing remains prohibitively expensive in many countries. In addition, ethical frameworks for the development and deployment of NLP in healthcare remain underdeveloped. The absence of national-level AI ethics policies that account for linguistic inclusion and healthcare equity raises risks of inappropriate model use. This gap in policy and enforcement undermines public trust and hinders large-scale adoption of AI-driven tools in African clinical settings.

5.2.1 Translation Quality and BLEU Scores

Translation accuracy is critical in medical settings, where errors can lead to misdiagnoses or inappropriate treatment. The evaluated models show considerable variation in performance:

- **NLLB-Seed** achieved a 44% lower BLEU score for African medical texts compared to European language outputs, indicating challenges in domain adaptation and dialect sensitivity (Costa-jussà, 2022).
- **AfromT** outperformed Google Translate by 19% in translating medical texts for Swahili, Hausa, and Igbo, but still underperformed by 25% relative to human references, especially for complex medical terms (Iyamu, 2024).
- **Masakhane-MT** recorded BLEU scores below 25, struggling with morphological complexity and specialised vocabulary in healthcare translation tasks (Orife et al., 2020).

These findings confirm that current models require domain-specific fine-tuning to improve translation reliability in African healthcare contexts.

5.2.2 Bias and Fairness Assessments

Bias in NLP models trained on predominantly Western datasets poses significant risks for African healthcare applications. Key observations include:

- **Masakhane-NER** misclassified 42% of medical entities in Swahili, Yoruba, and Hausa due to limited annotated corpora and inconsistent entity labelling (Adelani et al., 2021).
- Diagnostic AI systems trained on English datasets exhibited a 30% higher misdiagnosis rate when interacting in African languages, highlighting a critical fairness gap (Khanuja, 2023).
- **NLLB's** toxicity detection mechanism disproportionately flagged African-language translations as unsafe, reflecting cultural and linguistic bias in evaluation metrics (World Health Organization, 2024).

To address these disparities, it is essential to incorporate fairness-aware training methods, culturally aligned annotation practices, and representative African datasets in both model training and evaluation.

5.2.3 Explainability and Trust Metrics

In clinical settings, explainability is vital for building trust in AI-assisted decisions. However, many NLP systems operate as black-box models with limited transparency. Our findings show:

- SHAP-based interpretability frameworks can increase model trustworthiness, but their application to African languages remains undertested and poorly localised (Lundberg, 2017).
- Medical chatbots trained on English datasets failed 50% of trust evaluation criteria when responding in African languages like Igbo and Nigerian Pidgin, often unable to clarify how diagnostic conclusions were reached (Khanuja, 2023).
- Despite achieving 85% sensitivity and 89% specificity, **Ubenwa's** infant cry analysis tool faced clinician rejection in some Nigerian hospitals due to its opaque decision logic and lack of contextual explanation (Onu et al., 2017).

The findings reinforce the importance of developing transparency mechanisms tailored to African languages, such as linguistically adapted explainability frameworks, to ensure AI-generated medical recommendations can be trusted by healthcare professionals.

5.3 Limitations of the Study

Despite valuable insights from evaluating multilingual NLP models in African healthcare, several key limitations remain:

- **Dataset Gaps:** Less than 1% of publicly available NLP corpora contain African medical texts, limiting effective model training and evaluation (Nekoto et al., 2020).
- **Computational Constraints:** Many African institutions lack reliable access to high-performance computing resources necessary for training and fine-tuning large multilingual models. Dependence on external cloud services raises concerns about cost, data security, and sovereignty (Khanuja, 2023).
- **Ethical and Policy Gaps:** Local AI governance frameworks addressing linguistic fairness, data consent, and accountability in healthcare NLP are underdeveloped. This regulatory vacuum complicates the ethical deployment of AI solutions in sensitive medical contexts (Birhane, 2021).

Overcoming these challenges requires expanding African-language medical datasets, improving computational infrastructure accessibility, and developing context-specific ethical and policy frameworks tailored to the continent's healthcare and linguistic diversity.

5.4 Key Findings and Future Research Directions

This evaluation underscores the opportunities and challenges in applying multilingual NLP to African healthcare. The key findings include:

- Current NLP models exhibit significant translation errors in African medical contexts, requiring domain-specific fine-tuning.
- Bias in training datasets leads to disparities in diagnostic accuracy and translation reliability, necessitating fairness-aware NLP frameworks.

- Explainability challenges hinder the adoption of AI-driven healthcare tools, highlighting the need for linguistically and culturally adapted interpretability techniques.
- Broaden evaluation and development to underrepresented African languages like Fon, Krio, Wolof, and Tigrinya, beyond commonly studied Swahili and Yoruba, to improve generalisability and inclusivity of NLP systems.

Future research should focus on:

- Expanding African-language medical datasets to enhance NLP training.
- Developing bias mitigation strategies that address linguistic disparities in AI models.
- Creating culturally adapted AI transparency frameworks to build trust in medical NLP applications.

By addressing these challenges, NLP has the potential to significantly improve healthcare accessibility and equity across Africa's diverse linguistic communities.

References

David Ifeoluwa Adelani, Jade Abbott, Graham Neubig, Daniel D'souza, Julia Kreutzer, Constantine Lignos, Chester Palen-Michel, Happy Buzaaba, Shruti Rijhwani, Sebastian Ruder, Stephen Mayhew, Israel Abebe Azime, Shamsuddeen Muhammad, Chris Chinenye Emezue, Joyce Nakatumba-Nabende, Perez Ogayo, Anuoluwapo Aremu, Catherine Gitau, Derguene Mbaye, and 42 others. 2021. Masakhaner: Named entity recognition for african languages. *AfricaNLP Workshop at EACL 2021*.

Ankur Bapna and Orhan Firat. 2022. Scaling large multilingual models: Tokenization challenges and data scarcity. *arXiv preprint arXiv:2202.04017*.

Abeba Birhane. 2021. Algorithmic injustice: A relational ethics approach. *Patterns*, 2(2):100205.

Rishi Bommasani, Drew A. Hudson, Ehsan Adeli, Russ Altman, Simran Arora, Sydney von Arx, Michael S. Bernstein, Jeannette Bohg, Antoine Bosselut, Emma Brunskill, Erik Brynjolfsson, Shyamal Buch, Dallas Card, Rodrigo Castellon, Niladri Chatterji, Annie Chen, Kathleen Creel, Jared Quincy Davis, Dora Demszky, and 96 others. 2021. On the opportunities and risks of foundation models. *Center for Research on Foundation Models*.

Marta R. et al. Costa-jussà. 2022. No language left behind: Scaling human-centered machine translation. *Preprint*, arXiv:2207.04672.

Chris C. Emezue and Bonaventure F. P. Dossou. 2020. Lanfrica: A participatory approach to documenting machine translation research on african languages. *arXiv preprint*, arXiv:2008.07302.

Isabel O. Gallegos, Ryan A. Rossi, Joe Barrow, Md Mehrab Tanjim, Sungchul Kim, Franck Dernoncourt, Tong Yu, Ruiyi Zhang, and Nesreen K. Ahmed. 2024. Bias and fairness in large language models: A survey. *Computational Linguistics*, 50(3):1097–1179.

Raphael Iyamu. 2024. Machine translation and nlp tools: Developing and refining language technologies for african languages. *International Journal for Multidisciplinary Research (IJFMR)*. University of Florida.

Pratik Joshi, Sebastin Santy, Amar Budhiraja, Kalika Bali, and Monojit Choudhury. 2020. The state and fate of linguistic diversity and inclusion in the nlp world. In *Proceedings of the 58th Annual Meeting of the Association for Computational Linguistics*, pages 6282–6293, Online. Association for Computational Linguistics.

Talukdar Khanuja, Ruder. 2023. Evaluating the diversity, equity and inclusion of nlp technology: A case study for indian languages. *Findings of the Association for Computational Linguistics: EACL*.

Lee Lundberg. 2017. A unified approach to interpreting model predictions. In *Proceedings of the 31st Conference on Neural Information Processing Systems*.

Wilhelmina Nekoto, Vukosi Marivate, Tshinondiwa Matsila, Timi Fasubaa, and 1 others. 2020. Participatory research for low-resourced machine translation: A case study in african languages. In *Findings of the Association for Computational Linguistics: EMNLP 2020*.

Charles C. Onu, Innocent Udeogu, Eyenimi Ndiomu, Urbain Kengni, Doina Precup, and Guilherme M. Sant'Anna a. 2017. Ubenwa: Cry-based diagnosis of birth asphyxia. In *Proceedings of the 31st Conference on Neural Information Processing Systems*.

Iroro Fred Orife, Julia Kreutzer, Blessing Sibanda, Daniel Whitenack, Kathleen Siminyu, Laura Martinus, Jamiil Toure Ali, Jade Abbott, Vukosi Marivate, Salomon Kabongo, Musie Meressa, Espoir Murhabazi, Orevaoghene Ahia, Elan van Biljon, Arshath Ramkilowan, Adewale Akinfaderin, Alp Öktem, Wole Akin, Ghollah Kioko, and 6 others. 2020. Masakhane - machine translation for africa. In *Proceedings of the International Conference on Learning Representations*.

Translators without Borders. 2015. Words of relief – ebola crisis learning review.

World Health Organization. 2024. Who ethics and governance of artificial intelligence for health: Guidance on large multi-modal models.

Appendix A. Summary of MT and NER Model Performance

Table A1: Comparative performance of MT and NER models on African healthcare datasets.

Model	Languages Evaluated	BLEU Score / Accuracy	Key Limitations
Masakhane-MT	Swahili, Hausa, Yoruba	$<$ 25 BLEU	Struggles with morphology and medical domain terms
NLLB-Seed	40 African languages	44% lower BLEU vs EU	Mistranslations, dialect bias, and toxicity over-flagging
AfromT	Hausa, Swahili, Igbo	19% $>$ Google, 25% $<$ HR	Inaccurate medical term handling, dialect confusion
Masakhane-NER	Swahili, Yoruba, Hausa	42% misclassification	Limited annotated corpora and poor entity consistency

Table A1: Comparative performance of MT and NER models on African healthcare datasets.

Beyond Metrics: Evaluating LLMs' Effectiveness in Culturally Nuanced, Low-Resource Real-World Scenarios

Millicent Ochieng[†] **Varun Gumma**[‡] **Sunayana Sitaram**[‡] **Jindong Wang**[§*]
Vishrav Chaudhary[¶*] **Keshet Ronen**[◊] **Kalika Bali**[‡] **Jacki O'Neill**[†]
[†]**Microsoft Research Africa** [‡]**Microsoft Research India** [§]**William & Mary**
[¶]**Meta** [◊]**University of Washington**
Contact: {mochieng, jacki.oneill}@microsoft.com

Abstract

The deployment of Large Language Models (LLMs) in real-world applications presents both opportunities and challenges, particularly in multilingual and code-mixed communication settings. This research evaluates the performance of seven leading LLMs in sentiment analysis on a dataset derived from multilingual and code-mixed WhatsApp chats, including Swahili, English and Sheng. Our evaluation includes both quantitative analysis using metrics like F1 score and qualitative assessment of LLMs' explanations for their predictions. We find that, while Mistral-7b and Mixtral-8x7b achieved high F1 scores, they and other LLMs such as GPT-3.5-Turbo, Llama-2-70b, and Gemma-7b struggled with understanding linguistic and contextual nuances, as well as lack of transparency in their decision-making process as observed from their explanations. In contrast, GPT-4 and GPT-4-Turbo excelled in grasping diverse linguistic inputs and managing various contextual information, demonstrating high consistency with human alignment and transparency in their decision-making process. The LLMs however, encountered difficulties in incorporating cultural nuance especially in non-English settings with GPT-4s doing so inconsistently. The findings emphasize the necessity of continuous improvement of LLMs to effectively tackle the challenges of culturally nuanced, low-resource real-world settings and the need for developing evaluation benchmarks for capturing these issues.

1 Introduction

Large Language Models (LLMs) have ushered in major advancements in language processing, demonstrating exceptional ability to process everyday language commands and handle textual tasks such as Question Answering, Sentiment Analysis, Summarization, among others (OpenAI, 2023a; Brown et al., 2020; Chowdhery et al., 2022; Anil et al., 2023; Touvron et al., 2023).

Despite LLMs advancements, their effectiveness is predominantly observed in Latin Script languages with abundant training data, such as English, which constitutes a significant proportion of their training corpus (Raffel et al., 2020; Common Crawl, 2023; Together Computer, 2023; Longpre et al., 2023). Although English is not the mother tongue of the majority of the world's population, 93% of GPT-3's training data consists of English content (Brown et al., 2020). Studies reveal that languages with medium to low amounts of training data like Swahili still present challenges for these models, highlighting they are far from achieving parity with English (Ahuja et al., 2023a,b; Robinson et al., 2023). The picture is further complicated given that 60% of the world population speaks two or more languages[1]. In such settings, code-mixing[2] is a prevalent aspect of natural language use. Consequently, the performance of these models in real-world settings, especially in low-resource code-mixed and culturally diverse environments, remains an area of significant interest.

This study investigates the effectiveness of seven prominent LLMs on a sentiment analysis task on a dataset derived from WhatsApp chats. The dataset exhibits extensive code-mixing, encompassing multilingual conversations in English, Swahili, and Sheng[3] in 'chat speak' e.g. using emojis, abbreviations, colloquial chat message spellings and mispellings. With LLMs' ability to process and produce human-like text, this task aims to evaluate

* Work done while at Microsoft.

[1] https://ilanguages.org/bilingual.php

[2] the practice of alternating between two or more languages or dialects in a conversational turn

[3] a dynamic urban slang from Nairobi, Kenya, blending Swahili, English, and local languages, evolving continually among the youth.

Proceedings of the Sixth Workshop on African Natural Language Processing (AfricaNLP 2025), pages 230–247

their understanding of the nuances present in the dataset. We supplement the quantitative analysis of the LLMs performance with a systematic qualitative analysis of the explanations the models provide for their predictions. While studies such as (Narang et al., 2020; Wiegreffe et al., 2021; Majumder et al., 2021; Wiegreffe et al., 2022) have demonstrated the capability of LLMs to generate natural language explanations alongside predictions, enhancing explainability and improving the faithfulness of AI systems, it remains uncertain whether these explanations directly influence the decision-making process. However, we expect, and indeed do see, a correlation between models' predictions and their explanations. We used the explanations as a method of interrogating, to some extent, the models ability to process the cultural and linguistic nuances of the messages. By looking beyond the numbers, this method enables us to get some sense of how well the different LLMs handle the complex interactional features present in a real-world multilingual dataset. We demonstrate the value of using qualitative HCI methods alongside traditional performance metrics. Our contributions are as follows: (1) we evaluate and compare the performance of seven advanced LLMs including GPT-4, GPT-4-Turbo, GPT-3.5-Turbo, Llama-2-70b, Mistral-7b, Mixtral-8x7b and Gemma-7b on a sentiment analysis task using a novel WhatsApp chat dataset; (2) we identify differences in the interpretation strategies employed by different LLMs, highlighting the diversity in their approach to processing complex linguistic data; (3) we highlight the value of real-world, multilingual, and code-mixed datasets in assessing the performance of LLMs; (4) we show how qualitative HCI methods can be used in NLP to get a deeper understanding of model performance. Our findings reveal that, while LLMs like Mistral-7b and Mixtral-8x7b achieved high F1 scores in sentiment analysis in the dataset, they and other LLMs such as GPT-3.5-Turbo, Llama-2-70b, and Gemma-7b seem to be less robust at handling linguistic, cultural, and contextual nuances. Further, there was a lack of transparency in their generated explanations. In contrast, LLMs like GPT-4 and GPT-4-Turbo deployed diverse linguistic and contextual information in their explanations, demonstrating high consistency with human judgement. All the LLMs however, struggled to incorporate the more complex cultural nuances in the WhatsApp dataset especially in non-English settings - even GPT-4 and GPT-4-Turbo did so inconsistently.

2 Evaluation Dataset and Task

2.1 Dataset

The WhatsApp Chat Dataset: Our study employed a distinctive dataset originally collected by Karusala et al. (2021) further annotated by Mondal et al. (2021), with all ethical considerations and privacy measures observed as described below. It features multilingual exchanges among young people living with HIV in informal settlements in Nairobi, Kenya, captured within two health-focused WhatsApp chat groups moderated by a medical facilitator. The total number of messages are 6,556 and the conversations are predominantly in English, enriched with a considerable use of Swahili, Sheng, and code-mixing. The data annotation included sentiment and word-level language identification for each message. As Karusala et al. (2021) describe, recruited participants signed a consent form outlining study procedures, data anonymization, and security measures. All messages were anonymized and translated into English by a native speaker. Each chat message in the dataset included an anonymized speaker ID, timestamp, original message, and English translation. Due to the sensitive nature of the content, the dataset is not publicly available, but researchers can request access by contacting the authors. We specifically selected this dataset because it consists of real WhatsApp interactions between participants and a medical facilitator occurring as part of a Global Health research intervention. Additionally, its authentic representation of real-world, code-mixed communication aligns with our core research focus.

Pre-Processing: Considering that the data originates from WhatsApp conversations, it exhibits a casual, conversational style, often with short interactions. We retained only turns with three or more words providing more valuable data for sentiment analysis. Contrary to typical processing methods, we do not perform punctuation or emoji normalization on the data, as these elements are integral to the communication. The resulting dataset consisted of 3,719 messages with an average of eleven words per message.

2.2 Evaluation Task

Sentiment Analysis: The core of our evaluation focuses on a sentiment detection task because of its real-world application for such chat groups. We wished to support the facilitator by for example

Language	# of Neutral Messages	# of Positive Messages	# of Negative Messages	# of Messages Per Language	Average # of Tokens Per Message	Total # of Tokens Per Message
Monolingual						
En	1303	54	24	1381	12	16902
Sw	270	-	32	302	4	1264
Sh	2	-	-	2	3	6
Multilingual						
En-Sw	631	5	19	655	9	5582
Sw-Sh	143	-	12	155	5	705
En-Sh	51	2	1	54	6	301
En-Sw-Sh	190	3	16	209	10	2100
En-CM	10	-	1	11	9	94
Sw-CM	29	-	2	31	4	124
En-Sw-CM	60	-	6	66	12	812
En-Sh-CM	2	-	-	2	12	24
Sw-Sh-CM	20	1	1	22	5	106
En-Sw-Sh-CM	36	-	3	39	14	542
Other	96	1	-	98	20	795
En-Other	359	10	4	373	20	7622
Sw-Other	73	-	5	78	4	342
Sh-Other	1	-	-	1	4	4
En-Sw-Other	119	2	2	123	11	1396
En-Sh-Other	16	-	2	18	10	188
Sw-Sh-Other	19	-	1	20	6	110
En-Other-CM	4	-	-	4	6	24
Sw-Other-CM	4	-	3	7	6	41
En-Sw-Sh-Other	37	2	1	40	12	481
En-Sw-Other-CM	10	-	2	12	13	161
En-Sh-Other-CM	3	-	-	3	4	12
Sw-Sh-Other-CM	4	-	-	4	8	33
En-Sw-Sh-Other-CM	9	-	-	9	17	151
Total	**3501**	**80**	**137**	**3719**	**246**	**39922**

Table 1: Message Distribution by Language. This table displays the count of neutral, positive, and negative messages, total messages per language, average tokens per message, and total tokens per message for each language studied.

flagging negative messages. Table 1 illustrates the sentiment distribution according to human annotators within our pre-processed dataset, heavily skewed towards the Neutral class. This imbalance highlights the evaluation challenge of accurately identifying the less frequent Negative and Positive sentiments, testing the LLMs' ability to detect sentiment cues in a predominantly Neutral context.

Languages in the WhatsApp Dataset: Table 1 describes the statistics of languages within the dataset defined as: *En (English), Sw (Swahili), Sh (Sheng) and CM (Code-Mixed)*. These include messages in single language (*Monolingual*) and messages in more than one language (*Multilingual*). The dataset includes an 'Other' category used for words that do not fit the primary categories due to uncertainty, named entities, or other unique factors.

3 Experimental Setup

3.1 Models

We evaluated three OpenAI models: `GPT-4-Turbo`, `GPT-4-32k` (OpenAI, 2023b), and `GPT-3.5-Turbo` (Ouyang et al., 2022), with `GPT-4-32k` being the latest iteration and known for its enhanced performance on text processing and generation. `GPT-4-Turbo` and `GPT-3.5-Turbo` are optimized versions designed for more efficient processing without significantly compromising performance. From the open-source collection, we select Meta's `Llama-2-70b-chat` (Touvron et al., 2023), an LLM known for its efficiency and chat functionality. Additionally from Mistral AI, we include `Mistral-7B-Instruct-v0.2` (Jiang et al., 2023) and `Mixtral-8x7B-Instruct-v0.1` (Jiang et al., 2024), the former being popular for its exceptional ability to follow instructions and the latter for its innovative architecture which makes it excel in mathematics, code generation, and multilingual tasks. Lastly, we include Google's `Gemma-7b-it` (Mesnard et al., 2024), a state-of-the-art language model that excels in language understanding, reasoning, and safety, outperforming comparable models in numerous academic benchmarks. Throughout this paper, we refer to the mentioned models as: GPT-4, GPT-4-Turbo, GPT-3.5-Turbo, Llama-2-70b, Mistral-7b, Mixtral-8x7b and Gemma-7b.

3.2 Model Evaluation

Different prompting approaches (Brown et al., 2020; Chen et al., 2023) have been shown to effectively guide LLMs contextually, towards desired outputs. Investigations reveal that the quality of prompts provided, have a profound influence on the performance of LLMs (Liu et al., 2023; Hada et al., 2023). Leveraging this technique, we craft a detailed prompt to guide the LLMs to function as specialized NLP assistants for sentiment analysis. The prompt directs models to identify sentiments as Positive, Negative, or Neutral. Figure 3 illustrates the standardized prompt that we used for evaluating all seven LLMs, facilitating a fair and consistent comparison of their performance. We employ the same sentiment definitions given to human annotators during the dataset's sentiment annotation phase. Furthermore, we direct the models to justify their sentiment classifications in 200 words or less, focusing on the text spans that influenced their decisions. We conduct the evaluation on the entire pre-processed dataset and employ the weighted F1-score[4] metric instead of accuracy due to the skew in our dataset.

4 Qualitative Analysis

We supplemented our quantitative evaluation with in-depth qualitative analyses. Considering the skew towards the neutral class in our dataset, as illustrated in Table 1, and to ensure a balanced and rigorous analysis, we selected a sample comprising a total of 261 messages at random including both monolingual and multilingual messages for in-depth examination. For monolingual, the sample included 150 messages divided equally among the three sentiment categories: Negative, Positive, and Neutral. For the multilingual case, the sample entailed 50 Neutral, 50 Negative and 11 Positive messages whereby the positive messages represented all the positive labels in this category. The first author being proficient with the languages in the WhatsApp dataset, analyzed all the 261 sampled messages, identifying patterns in the data. We borrowed five criteria as outlined by (Chang et al., 2023) on *'how to evaluate'* to guide our human evaluation. These criteria, described in Table 4, were linguistic accuracy, contextual and cultural relevance, fluency in maintaining consistency, alignment with human expectations and transparency in the LLMs' decision-making process. While these criteria have been designed for quantitative evaluation, we used them to provide a structure for analysing the set of justifications for each message across models. We supplemented this structured analysis with a more in-depth ethnomethodologically-informed approach (Crabtree et al., 2000, 2006; O'Neill and Martin, 2003; Martin et al., 2014) where the first author and the last author (who is skilled in ethnomethodologically-informed analysis) together analysed each turn (message) in detail, to understand how the justifications produced by the different models related to the original and the human-translated message, how they related to one another and how they related to the sentiment prediction. In these sessions, the two authors looked in detail at the messages and model justifications and identified emergent patterns, interrogating and refining them. This analysis was deeply qualitative, aiming to derive insights into differences between models in their justifications. As an additional sanity check, we invited three other native speakers to review a set of 15 messages, selected from the 261 messages the first author had analysed. The reviewers conducted their assessments independently and reconvened to discuss their findings, along with the first author and were all confident about the consistency of the findings. In this paper, for reasons of space, we use a small number of examples to illustrate the patterns that we found in the data.

5 Results and Discussion

In this section, we explore the results of our study by discussing both quantitative and qualitative findings of models performance on the WhatsApp dataset, beginning with the quantitative results measured by the F1 score. Following this, we will delve into the qualitative findings, discussing insights from the models' justifications and their implications for language processing strategies.

5.1 F1 Score-Based Models Comparison

As evidenced by the F1 Score comparison of the seven models in Figure 1, the Mistral-7b model demonstrates a higher performance in sentiment analysis on the WhatsApp dataset, closely followed by GPT-4. Conversely, the Llama-2-70b model exhibits the weakest performance.

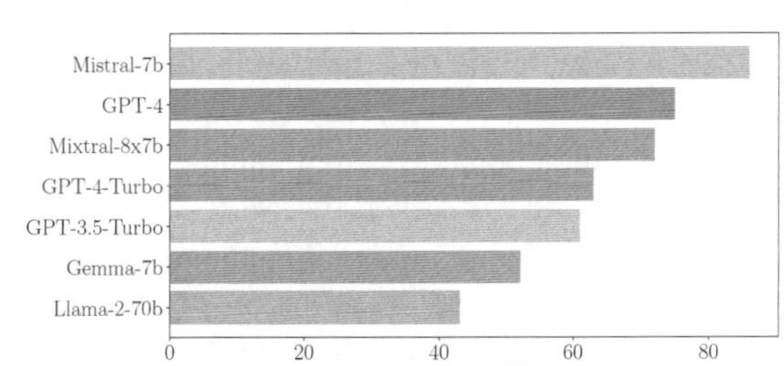

Figure 1: Overall F1 score comparison of the models.

As Table 1 illustrates, the majority of positive

[4] https://scikit-learn.org/stable/modules/generated/sklearn.metrics.f1_score.html

and neutral sentiments were expressed in English, whereas most negative sentiments were conveyed in Swahili. This supports the findings of (Rudra et al., 2016), which suggest that people are more likely to express negative opinions in non-English languages. Further analysis of F1 scores by sentiment and language, as shown in Figures 2 and 4, highlights the distinct capabilities of various models. Specifically, Mistral-7b excels in identifying neutral sentiments, predominantly in English followed closely by GPT-4s, Mixtral-8x7b, and GPT-3.5-Turbo, with Gemma-7b and Llama-2-70b trailing. Conversely, GPT-4 and GPT-4-Turbo demonstrate superior performance in accurately classifying the rare negative sentiments, predominantly in Swahili and code-mixed. These findings are consistent with those from standard NLP benchmarks such as those reported in (Ahuja et al., 2023b), particularly in non-English contexts, specifically low-resource languages like Swahili and code-mixed languages. In these settings, larger models such as OpenAI's GPT-4s frequently outperform other LLMs.

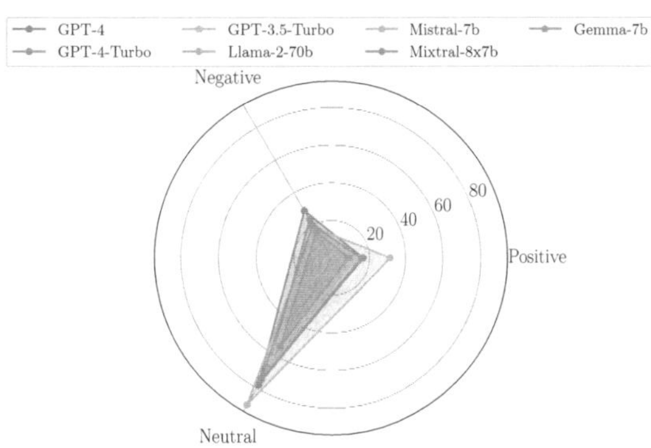

Figure 2: Comparison of F1 scores for the models across Positive, Negative, and Neutral sentiments.

5.2 Insights from the Justifications

As instructed by our detailed prompt in Figure 3, all the seven LLMs produced their predictions along with justifications. Across the board, even where sentiment predictions were the same for all the models, we noticed distinct differences in the justifications provided. Some LLMs consistently incorporated words or spans of text as part of their justifications (as requested in the prompt) others did so less frequently. Similarly some regularly translated non-English terms into English, others did not. See the examples presented in this Section's Tables 2 and 3 and in Appendix §A.4. In Table 2, GPT-3.5-Turbo and Mistral-7b do not provide any spans of message text in their justifications.

Which models perform best at accurately interpreting linguistic nuances and textual inaccuracies such as spelling errors, local abbreviations and grammatical inaccuracies? As illustrated by the examples in Tables 3 and 5 and Appendix §A.4, GPT-4 and GPT-4-Turbo stand out with superior performance in languages like Swahili and Sheng, and in code-mixed scenarios where they effectively handle the linguistic nuances between English and local languages. In particular, they were more consistently correct in their **translation** of the non-English word spans used in their justifications. They maintained strong performance even in rare sentiment classes, outperforming models like GPT-3.5-Turbo, which, though proficient, does not reach the high level of linguistic performance exhibited by the GPT-4s. Taking the example in Table 6 to illustrate - a code-mixed English-Swahili-Sheng message, GPT-4 and GPT4-Turbo provide correct interpretations of the Swahili and Sheng in their justifications, with GPT-4 Turbo even identifying *'kuniboo'* (Translation: *'bore me'*) as Sheng. Gemma-7b also identifies Sheng, but wrongly identifies the whole sentence as Sheng, and mistranslates it. The other models all provide mistranslations in their justifications. Models such as Llama-2-7b, Mistral-7b, Mixtral-8x7b and Gemma-7b face difficulties with Swahili and Sheng, as evidenced by their often incorrect translations of Swahili words and phrases. They often **prioritized English** in mixed-language settings resulting in either incorrect predictions or justifications when key sentiment indicators lie in the non-English segments which was mostly the case for Negative sentiments. Similarly with regards to LLMs' robustness to textual inaccuracies, the GPT-4s accurately interpreted messages with irregularities. However, the remaining models were less reliable, struggling with noisy data especially non-English texts; an example is shown in Table 5.

Nonetheless, overall all the seven LLMs have demonstrated proficiency in English messages in the WhatsApp dataset. However, even in English the models can fail to predict the correct sentiment, and their justifications reflect the sentiment that they predicted. Let's take the example in Appendix Table 7, for a human reviewer, this message is a clear example of a social media chain message - typically 'copy and paste' messages requiring the reader to either like, respond, or forward. The linguistic indicators of this are the instruction at the start *"Send to everyone you love..."* and the conclusion *"You are lovable if you get FIVE sent back to you"*. This can be read as an instruction or perhaps a playful activity. None of the models predicted the correct sentiment (Neutral), all predicting Positive. In their justifications, none of them identified this as a chain message, instruction, activity or similar - even where they highlighted the phrase *"You are lovable if you get FIVE"*.

Do the models utilize the surrounding textual context and cultural subtleties to determine sentiment? From our analysis and as illustrated in Table 2, GPT-4 and GPT-4-Turbo effectively utilized context in their justifications for their sentiment predictions. This is evidenced by their use of relevant word spans and their correct explanations of the meanings of phrases, leading to accurate predictions and coherent interpretation. GPT-3.5-Turbo lagged slightly due to occasional oversights in contextual (phrase) information. The remaining models including Llama-2-7b, Mistral-7b, Mixtral-8x7b and Gemma-7b often used word-level rather than phrase level justifications, especially in multilingual and code-mixed texts, leading to misinterpretation of meaning and incorrect predictions or justification. With regards to cultural relevance, the LLMs generally struggled to incorporate cultural nuances in the dataset, see example in Table 3. However, in specific scenarios, models like OpenAI's GPT-4s, which excel in grasping linguistic subtleties and leveraging contextual information, demonstrated proficiency in incorporating cultural aspects into their interpretations.

Are the models fluent in maintaining consistency in their interpretation across similar sentiment scenarios within the WhatsApp dataset? Our findings show that models like GPT-4 and GPT-4-Turbo demonstrate high consistency, reliably applying their analytical capabilities in sentiment predictions across both English and non-English language settings. In contrast, other models performed better on English and Neutral sentiments but lagged behind in non-English cases exhibiting less consistency, often varying in their justifications and output even under similar conditions. This inconsistency can lead to unpredictability in performance in complex multilingual environments, highlighting the need for models to have stable and reliable interpretation mechanisms when deployed in varied real-world applications.

Do the models' predictions and interpretation conform to typical human expectation? We observed that LLMs such as OpenAI's GPT-4s, which demonstrated robust linguistic and contextual comprehension in sentiment detection for the dataset, often aligned with human expectations, consistently producing accurate predictions along with correct justifications. However, the rest of the LLMs, while mostly aligned in English contexts, did not perform as well in non-English settings.

Were the models transparent in their decision-making process in the WhatsApp dataset? Our analysis revealed that Mistral and Mixtral models, despite achieving high F1 scores, often lacked correct and transparent interpretations in their justifications. This was particularly evident in non-English contexts, reflecting issues we observed with LLMs such as GPT-3.5-Turbo, Llama-2-7b, and Gemma-7b. Frequently, these LLMs incorrectly translated the text or failed to disclose the specific text spans that informed their conclusions. This opacity makes it challenging to trust their judgments. That they often reached the correct prediction could be because the sentiment could be determined despite the incorrect translation (assuming some correlation between the prediction and the justification). The implications of this are that these models might well be useful for tasks like sentiment prediction, but less useful for tasks which require a more accurate interpretation of language and semantics - including translation tasks. In contrast, OpenAI's GPT-4s showcased a robust multilingual and contextual performance. These models consistently highlighted relevant phrases or text spans that justified their conclusions, generally leading to correct and transparent outcomes. However, when cultural factors influenced their decision-making process, the models' performance were mixed, displaying transparent interpretation in some instances but falling short in others. This inconsistency raises concerns about the models' reliability in culturally nuanced scenarios.

6 Related Works

Multilingualism in LLMs: LLMs' effectiveness in multilingual contexts continually attracts attention. Studies by (Lai et al., 2023; Ahuja et al., 2023a; Hendy et al., 2023; Ahuja et al., 2023b), have thoroughly evaluated LLMs across various languages using standard NLP benchmarks with (Ojo et al., 2023; Robinson et al., 2023) focusing on African languages. However, these studies typ-

Message	GPT-4	GPT-4-Turbo	GPT-3.5-Turbo	Llama-2-70b	Mistral-7b	Mixtral-8x7b	Gemma-7b
Original: *"Hi guys meeting yetu imekuewaje."* **Translation:** *"Hey guys how was the meeting."* **Actual Sentiment:** Neutral	The message 'Hi guys meeting yetu imekuewaje' is asking about the status of a meeting, which is a neutral inquiry and does not express any positive or negative sentiment. **Prediction:** Neutral	The message 'Hi guys meeting yetu imekuewaje' is a neutral sentiment as it is a general inquiry about the status or outcome of a meeting without any explicit positive or negative emotion or opinion. **Prediction:** Neutral	The sentiment is Neutral. The message is a simple greeting and does not express a positive or negative sentiment. **Prediction:** Neutral	The word 'meeting' suggests a gathering or event, which is typically a positive or neutral activity. The phrase 'imekuewaje' is in Swahili and roughly translates to 'it's okay' or 'it's all good' in English, which implies a positive or neutral sentiment. Therefore, the overall sentiment of the message is likely Neutral. **Prediction:** Neutral	The message is a Swahili greeting, which is a normal aspect and does not express any particular sentiment. **Prediction:** Neutral	The given message 'Hi guys meeting yetu imekuewaje' is a greeting and an invitation to a meeting. The word 'guys' is a friendly way to refer to a group of people, 'hi' is a common greeting, and 'yetu' means 'our' in Swahili, indicating inclusivity. The word 'imekuewaje' is in Sheng, a slang language in Kenya, and it means 'has been organized' or 'has been set'. Therefore, the sentiment expressed in this message is Neutral, as it is a factual statement and a simple greeting without expressing any positive or negative emotions. **Prediction:** Neutral	The phrase 'Hi guys meeting yetu imekuewaje' is neutral. The speaker is simply greeting the recipients and does not express any positive or negative sentiment. **Prediction:** Neutral

Table 2: In this example, only GPT-4 and GPT-4-Turbo showed excellence in both linguistic and contextual understanding while remaining models misinterpreted the message as simply a greeting, due to a misunderstanding of the Swahili words. Interestingly all LLMs made the correct prediction, and their explanations correlated with the prediction they made, but only the explanations by GPT-4 and GPT-4 Turbo matches human expectations.

Message	GPT-4	GPT-4-Turbo	GPT-3.5-Turbo	Llama-2-70b	Mistral-7b	Mixtral-8x7b	Gemma-7b
Original: *"Kama hauko shule shindaapo"* **Translation:** *"If you are not in school stay there"* **Actual Sentiment:** Negative	The message 'Kama hauko shule shindaapo' translates to 'If you are not in school, stay there'. This is a neutral statement as it does not express any positive or negative sentiment. It is simply a factual advice or suggestion. **Prediction:** Neutral	The message 'Kama hauko shule shindaapo' translates to 'If you are not at school, stay where you are' in English. This message seems to be giving neutral advice or instruction without any explicit positive or negative emotion. **Prediction:** Neutral	The sentiment is Negative. The phrase 'shindaapo' expresses a negative feeling or view about not being in school. **Prediction:** Negative	The sentence 'Kama hauko shule shindaapo' expresses a negative sentiment. The word 'kama' means 'like' in Swahili, and 'hauko' means 'there isn't' or 'there is no'. The phrase 'shule shindaapo' means 'school is closed'. Therefore, the speaker is expressing a negative sentiment towards the fact that school is closed. The tone of the sentence is also melancholic, indicating a negative emotion. **Prediction:** Negative	The given query in Swahili translates to 'If school had not closed'. It is a statement expressing a factual situation and does not contain any positive or negative sentiment. **Prediction:** Neutral	The query 'Kama hauko shule shindaapo' is in Swahili and translates to 'If you hadn't gone to school, you would have passed'. The sentence does not express any positive or negative sentiment. It is a hypothetical situation and there is no sentiment involved. Therefore, the sentiment is Neutral. **Prediction:** Neutral	The phrase 'Kama hauko shule shindaapo' is a Swahili phrase that translates to 'You are not going to school today'. The speaker is expressing a negative sentiment as they are saying that the recipient will not be able to attend school. The words 'shule' and 'shindaapo' are the key words used to convey this sentiment. **Prediction:** Negative

Table 3: The Swahili phrase carries a negative sentiment as it is used to dismissively suggest that someone who is not in school should refrain from participating in discussions, reflecting a cultural emphasis on educational status as a basis for contributing to intellectual conversations. All LLMs did not understand the cultural context here.

ically depend on NLP benchmarks that may not closely reflect the complexity of real-world contexts, often missing subtleties and scenarios that occur in everyday use. Moreover, the LLMs might have already encountered some benchmark content online, a concern highlighted by (Sainz et al., 2023; Ahuja et al., 2023b).

Models' Challenges in Code-Mixed Text Processing: Code-mixing - the blending of two or more languages within a single utterance of a conversation (Poplack, 2001), is common in multilingual communities, including Kenya (Orao, 2012). The phenomenon of code-mixing presents unique challenges in the field of NLP. (Zhang et al., 2023; Doğruöz et al., 2023; Kaji and Shah, 2023) emphasizes the lack of training data as one of the main challenges, attributing to the complexity of processing code-mixed language.

Importance of Real-World Data in LLMs Evaluation: (Wibowo et al., 2023) introduces COPAL-ID, a culturally rich Indonesian dataset that challenges even advanced models like GPT-4, highlighting the need for nuanced datasets in LLMs evaluation. (Chiu et al., 2024) present Cultural-Teaming, an AI-assisted interactive red-teaming approach that enhances the creation of multicultural evaluation datasets, revealing significant gaps in LLMs' understanding of diverse cultural contexts through the development of the challenging CULTURALBENCH-V0.1 dataset. (Zheng et al., 2023) curates LMSYS-Chat-1M, a dataset of one million real-world conversations with 25 LLMs, designed to enhance understanding and development of LLMs capabilities in diverse interaction scenarios. Our work extends the efforts on LLMs evaluation using real-world datasets by employing a code-mixed WhatsApp dataset, reflecting a linguistic phenomena absent in curated datasets. Our evaluation combines quantitative and qualitative analysis of LLMs' performance and decision-making processes.

7 Conclusion

Our study utilized a multilingual and code-mixed WhatsApp dataset to assess the effectiveness of seven LLMs on a sentiment analysis task. Our evaluation includes both quantitative analysis using metrics like F1 score and qualitative assessment of LLMs' explanations for their predictions. Our comparative analysis revealed that, while Mistral-7b and Mixtral-8x7b achieved high F1 scores, they and other LLMs such as GPT-3.5-Turbo, Llama-2-70b, and Gemma-7b struggled with understanding linguistic and contextual nuances, as well as lack of transparency in their decision-making process as observed from their explanations. In contrast, GPT-4 and GPT-4-Turbo excelled in grasping diverse linguistic inputs and managing various contextual information, demonstrating high consistency with human alignment and transparency in their decision-making process. The LLMs however, encountered difficulties in incorporating cultural nuance especially in non-English settings with the GPT-4s doing so inconsistently. Our evaluation, which leverages real-world data, substantiates the robustness observed in NLP benchmarks, particularly highlighting the superior performance of larger models like OpenAI's GPT-4s in handling low-resource and code-mixed languages. The study highlights the importance of using real-world data for LLMs evaluation. In addition, it advocates for combining qualitative methods from Human-Computer Interaction (HCI) with NLP to gain deeper insights into model performance.

Future research should explore the integration of linguistic diversity and cultural intelligence into model training and evaluation frameworks. Additionally, further work is needed to bridge the gap between quantitative performance metrics and qualitative understandings of model behavior. Lastly, future research should also focus on investigating the relationship between explanations and AI decision-making, for example by quantifying correlations across different NLP tasks. This will ensure that future models are not only effective but also interpretable and aligned with human expectations.

Limitations

This study, though comprehensive, has several limitations. It primarily examines texts in Swahili, English, Sheng, and their code-mixed variants, overlooking the vast array of global languages and dialects. Additionally, the focus on seven specific LLMs provides insights but excludes other emerging LLMs. Lastly, while combining quantitative metrics and qualitative analysis, the balance may constrain the depth of qualitative insights due to the dataset's scale and the subjective nature of qualitative evaluation.

Ethics Statement

Given the use of real-world WhatsApp chat data, ethical considerations were paramount. All data was anonymized, screened for sensitive content, and used in accordance with ethical guidelines for research involving human subjects.

Acknowledgements

The authors thank Muchai Mercy, Kemunto Ochwang'i, and Faith Ngetich for their invaluable help with analyzing the LLMs' interpretative capabilities.

References

Kabir Ahuja, Harshita Diddee, Rishav Hada, Millicent Ochieng, Krithika Ramesh, Prachi Jain, Akshay Nambi, Tanuja Ganu, Sameer Segal, Mohamed Ahmed, Kalika Bali, and Sunayana Sitaram. 2023a. MEGA: Multilingual evaluation of generative AI. In *Proceedings of the 2023 Conference on Empirical Methods in Natural Language Processing*, pages 4232–4267, Singapore. Association for Computational Linguistics.

Sanchit Ahuja, Divyanshu Aggarwal, Varun Gumma, Ishaan Watts, Ashutosh Sathe, Millicent Ochieng, Rishav Hada, Prachi Jain, Maxamed Axmed, Kalika Bali, and Sunayana Sitaram. 2023b. Megaverse: Benchmarking large language models across languages, modalities, models and tasks. *ArXiv*, abs/2311.07463.

Rohan Anil, Sebastian Borgeaud, Yonghui Wu, Jean-Baptiste Alayrac, Jiahui Yu, Radu Soricut, Johan Schalkwyk, Andrew M. Dai, Anja Hauth, Katie Millican, David Silver, Slav Petrov, Melvin Johnson, Ioannis Antonoglou, Julian Schrittwieser, Amelia Glaese, Jilin Chen, Emily Pitler, Timothy Lillicrap, Angeliki Lazaridou, Orhan Firat, James Molloy, Michael Isard, Paul R. Barham, Tom Hennigan, Benjamin Lee, Fabio Viola, Malcolm Reynolds, Yuanzhong Xu, Ryan Doherty, Eli Collins, Clemens Meyer, Eliza Rutherford, Erica Moreira, Kareem Ayoub, Megha Goel, George Tucker, Enrique Piqueras, Maxim Krikun, Iain Barr, Nikolay Savinov, Ivo Danihelka, Becca Roelofs, Anaïs White, Anders Andreassen, Tamara von Glehn, Lakshman Yagati, Mehran Kazemi, Lucas Gonzalez, Misha Khalman, Jakub Sygnowski, Alexandre Frechette, Charlotte Smith, Laura Culp, Lev Proleev, Yi Luan, Xi Chen, James Lottes, Nathan Schucher, Federico Lebron, Alban Rrustemi, Natalie Clay, Phil Crone, Tomas Kocisky, Jeffrey Zhao, Bartek Perz, Dian Yu, Heidi Howard, Adam Bloniarz, Jack W. Rae, Han Lu, Laurent Sifre, Marcello Maggioni, Fred Alcober, Dan Garrette, Megan Barnes, Shantanu Thakoor, Jacob Austin, Gabriel Barth-Maron, William Wong, Rishabh Joshi, Rahma Chaabouni, Deeni Fatiha, Arun Ahuja, Ruibo Liu, Yunxuan Li, Sarah Cogan, Jeremy Chen, Chao Jia, Chenjie Gu, Qiao Zhang, Jordan Grimstad, Ale Jakse Hartman, Martin Chadwick, Gaurav Singh Tomar, Xavier Garcia, Evan Senter, Emanuel Taropa, Thanumalayan Sankaranarayana Pillai, Jacob Devlin, Michael Laskin, Diego de Las Casas, Dasha Valter, Connie Tao, Lorenzo Blanco, Adrià Puigdomènech Badia, David Reitter, Mianna Chen, Jenny Brennan, Clara Rivera, Sergey Brin, Shariq Iqbal, Gabriela Surita, Jane Labanowski, Abhi Rao, Stephanie Winkler, Emilio Parisotto, Yiming Gu, Kate Olszewska, Yujing Zhang, Ravi Addanki, Antoine Miech, Annie Louis, Laurent El Shafey, Denis Teplyashin, Geoff Brown, Elliot Catt, Nithya Attaluri, Jan Balaguer, Jackie Xiang, Pidong Wang, Zoe Ashwood, Anton Briukhov, Albert Webson, Sanjay Ganapathy, Smit Sanghavi, Ajay Kannan, Ming-Wei Chang, Axel Stjerngren, Josip Djolonga, Yuting Sun, Ankur Bapna, Matthew Aitchison, Pedram Pejman, Henryk Michalewski, Tianhe Yu, Cindy Wang, Juliette Love, Junwhan Ahn, Dawn Bloxwich, Kehang Han, Peter Humphreys, Thibault Sellam, James Bradbury, Varun Godbole, Sina Samangooei, Bogdan Damoc, Alex Kaskasoli, Sébastien M. R. Arnold, Vijay Vasudevan, Shubham Agrawal, Jason Riesa, Dmitry Lepikhin, Richard Tanburn, Srivatsan Srinivasan, Hyeontaek Lim, Sarah Hodkinson, Pranav Shyam, Johan Ferret, Steven Hand, Ankush Garg, Tom Le Paine, Jian Li, Yujia Li, Minh Giang, Alexander Neitz, Zaheer Abbas, Sarah York, Machel Reid, Elizabeth Cole, Aakanksha Chowdhery, Dipanjan Das, Dominika Rogozińska, Vitaly Nikolaev, Pablo Sprechmann, Zachary Nado, Lukas Zilka, Flavien Prost, Luheng He, Marianne Monteiro, Gaurav Mishra, Chris Welty, Josh Newlan, Dawei Jia, Miltiadis Allamanis, Clara Huiyi Hu, Raoul de Liedekerke, Justin Gilmer, Carl Saroufim, Shruti Rijhwani, Shaobo Hou, Disha Shrivastava, Anirudh Baddepudi, Alex Goldin, Adnan Ozturel, Albin Cassirer, Yunhan Xu, Daniel Sohn, Devendra Sachan, Reinald Kim Amplayo, Craig Swanson, Dessie Petrova, Shashi Narayan, Arthur Guez, Siddhartha Brahma, Jessica Landon, Miteyan Patel, Ruizhe Zhao, Kevin Villela, Luyu Wang, Wenhao Jia, Matthew Rahtz, Mai Giménez, Legg Yeung, Hanzhao Lin, James Keeling, Petko Georgiev, Diana Mincu, Boxi Wu, Salem Haykal, Rachel Saputro, Kiran Vodrahalli, James Qin, Zeynep Cankara, Abhanshu Sharma, Nick Fernando, Will Hawkins, Behnam Neyshabur, Solomon Kim, Adrian Hutter, Priyanka Agrawal, Alex Castro-Ros, George van den Driessche, Tao Wang, Fan Yang, Shuo yiin Chang, Paul Komarek, Ross McIlroy, Mario Lučić, Guodong Zhang, Wael Farhan, Michael Sharman, Paul Natsev, Paul Michel, Yong Cheng, Yamini Bansal, Siyuan Qiao, Kris Cao, Siamak Shakeri, Christina Butterfield, Justin Chung, Paul Kishan Rubenstein, Shivani Agrawal, Arthur Mensch, Kedar Soparkar, Karel Lenc, Timothy Chung, Aedan Pope, Loren Maggiore, Jackie Kay, Priya Jhakra, Shibo Wang, Joshua Maynez, Mary Phuong, Taylor Tobin, Andrea Tacchetti, Maja Trebacz, Kevin Robinson, Yash Katariya, Sebastian Riedel, Paige Bailey, Kefan Xiao, Nimesh Ghelani, Lora Aroyo, Ambrose Slone, Neil Houlsby, Xuehan Xiong, Zhen Yang, Elena Gribovskaya, Jonas Adler, Mateo Wirth, Lisa Lee, Music Li, Thais Kagohara, Jay Pavagadhi, Sophie Bridgers, Anna Bortsova, Sanjay Ghemawat, Zafarali Ahmed, Tianqi Liu, Richard Powell, Vijay Bolina, Mariko Iinuma, Polina Zablotskaia, James Besley, Da-Woon Chung, Timothy Dozat, Ramona Comanescu, Xiance Si, Jeremy Greer, Guolong Su, Martin Polacek, Raphaël Lopez Kaufman, Simon Tokumine, Hexiang Hu, Elena Buchatskaya, Yingjie Miao, Mohamed Elhawaty, Aditya Siddhant, Nenad Tomasev, Jinwei Xing, Christina Greer, Helen Miller, Shereen Ashraf, Aurko Roy, Zizhao Zhang, Ada Ma, Angelos Filos, Milos Besta, Rory Blevins, Ted Klimenko, Chih-Kuan Yeh, Soravit Changpinyo, Jiaqi Mu, Oscar Chang, Mantas Pajarskas, Carrie Muir, Vered Cohen, Charline Le Lan, Krishna Haridasan, Amit Marathe, Steven Hansen, Sholto Douglas, Rajkumar Samuel, Mingqiu Wang, Sophia Austin,

Chang Lan, Jiepu Jiang, Justin Chiu, Jaime Alonso Lorenzo, Lars Lowe Sjösund, Sébastien Cevey, Zach Gleicher, Thi Avrahami, Anudhyan Boral, Hansa Srinivasan, Vittorio Selo, Rhys May, Konstantinos Aisopos, Léonard Hussenot, Livio Baldini Soares, Kate Baumli, Michael B. Chang, Adrià Recasens, Ben Caine, Alexander Pritzel, Filip Pavetic, Fabio Pardo, Anita Gergely, Justin Frye, Vinay Ramasesh, Dan Horgan, Kartikeya Badola, Nora Kassner, Subhrajit Roy, Ethan Dyer, Víctor Campos, Alex Tomala, Yunhao Tang, Dalia El Badawy, Elspeth White, Basil Mustafa, Oran Lang, Abhishek Jindal, Sharad Vikram, Zhitao Gong, Sergi Caelles, Ross Hemsley, Gregory Thornton, Fangxiaoyu Feng, Wojciech Stokowiec, Ce Zheng, Phoebe Thacker, Çağlar Ünlü, Zhishuai Zhang, Mohammad Saleh, James Svensson, Max Bileschi, Piyush Patil, Ankesh Anand, Roman Ring, Katerina Tsihlas, Arpi Vezer, Marco Selvi, Toby Shevlane, Mikel Rodriguez, Tom Kwiatkowski, Samira Daruki, Keran Rong, Allan Dafoe, Nicholas FitzGerald, Keren Gu-Lemberg, Mina Khan, Lisa Anne Hendricks, Marie Pellat, Vladimir Feinberg, James Cobon-Kerr, Tara Sainath, Maribeth Rauh, Sayed Hadi Hashemi, Richard Ives, Yana Hasson, YaGuang Li, Eric Noland, Yuan Cao, Nathan Byrd, Le Hou, Qingze Wang, Thibault Sottiaux, Michela Paganini, Jean-Baptiste Lespiau, Alexandre Moufarek, Samer Hassan, Kaushik Shivakumar, Joost van Amersfoort, Amol Mandhane, Pratik Joshi, Anirudh Goyal, Matthew Tung, Andrew Brock, Hannah Sheahan, Vedant Misra, Cheng Li, Nemanja Rakićević, Mostafa Dehghani, Fangyu Liu, Sid Mittal, Junhyuk Oh, Seb Noury, Eren Sezener, Fantine Huot, Matthew Lamm, Nicola De Cao, Charlie Chen, Gamaleldin Elsayed, Ed Chi, Mahdis Mahdieh, Ian Tenney, Nan Hua, Ivan Petrychenko, Patrick Kane, Dylan Scandinaro, Rishub Jain, Jonathan Uesato, Romina Datta, Adam Sadovsky, Oskar Bunyan, Dominik Rabiej, Shimu Wu, John Zhang, Gautam Vasudevan, Edouard Leurent, Mahmoud Alnahlawi, Ionut Georgescu, Nan Wei, Ivy Zheng, Betty Chan, Pam G Rabinovitch, Piotr Stanczyk, Ye Zhang, David Steiner, Subhajit Naskar, Michael Azzam, Matthew Johnson, Adam Paszke, Chung-Cheng Chiu, Jaume Sanchez Elias, Afroz Mohiuddin, Faizan Muhammad, Jin Miao, Andrew Lee, Nino Vieillard, Sahitya Potluri, Jane Park, Elnaz Davoodi, Jiageng Zhang, Jeff Stanway, Drew Garmon, Abhijit Karmarkar, Zhe Dong, Jong Lee, Aviral Kumar, Luowei Zhou, Jonathan Evens, William Isaac, Zhe Chen, Johnson Jia, Anselm Levskaya, Zhenkai Zhu, Chris Gorgolewski, Peter Grabowski, Yu Mao, Alberto Magni, Kaisheng Yao, Javier Snaider, Norman Casagrande, Paul Suganthan, Evan Palmer, Geoffrey Irving, Edward Loper, Manaal Faruqui, Isha Arkatkar, Nanxin Chen, Izhak Shafran, Michael Fink, Alfonso Castaño, Irene Giannoumis, Wooyeol Kim, Mikołaj Rybiński, Ashwin Sreevatsa, Jennifer Prendki, David Soergel, Adrian Goedeckemeyer, Willi Gierke, Mohsen Jafari, Meenu Gaba, Jeremy Wiesner, Diana Gage Wright, Yawen Wei, Harsha Vashisht, Yana Kulizhskaya, Jay Hoover, Maigo Le, Lu Li, Chimezie Iwuanyanwu, Lu Liu, Kevin Ramirez, Andrey Khorlin, Albert Cui, Tian LIN, Marin Georgiev, Marcus Wu, Ricardo Aguilar, Keith Pallo, Abhishek Chakladar, Alena Repina, Xihui Wu, Tom van der Weide, Priya Ponnapalli, Caroline Kaplan, Jiri Simsa, Shuangfeng Li, Olivier Dousse, Fan Yang, Jeff Piper, Nathan Ie, Minnie Lui, Rama Pasumarthi, Nathan Lintz, Anitha Vijayakumar, Lam Nguyen Thiet, Daniel Andor, Pedro Valenzuela, Cosmin Paduraru, Daiyi Peng, Katherine Lee, Shuyuan Zhang, Somer Greene, Duc Dung Nguyen, Paula Kurylowicz, Sarmishta Velury, Sebastian Krause, Cassidy Hardin, Lucas Dixon, Lili Janzer, Kiam Choo, Ziqiang Feng, Biao Zhang, Achintya Singhal, Tejasi Latkar, Mingyang Zhang, Quoc Le, Elena Allica Abellan, Dayou Du, Dan McKinnon, Natasha Antropova, Tolga Bolukbasi, Orgad Keller, David Reid, Daniel Finchelstein, Maria Abi Raad, Remi Crocker, Peter Hawkins, Robert Dadashi, Colin Gaffney, Sid Lall, Ken Franko, Egor Filonov, Anna Bulanova, Rémi Leblond, Vikas Yadav, Shirley Chung, Harry Askham, Luis C. Cobo, Kelvin Xu, Felix Fischer, Jun Xu, Christina Sorokin, Chris Alberti, Chu-Cheng Lin, Colin Evans, Hao Zhou, Alek Dimitriev, Hannah Forbes, Dylan Banarse, Zora Tung, Jeremiah Liu, Mark Omernick, Colton Bishop, Chintu Kumar, Rachel Sterneck, Ryan Foley, Rohan Jain, Swaroop Mishra, Jiawei Xia, Taylor Bos, Geoffrey Cideron, Ehsan Amid, Francesco Piccinno, Xingyu Wang, Praseem Banzal, Petru Gurita, Hila Noga, Premal Shah, Daniel J. Mankowitz, Alex Polozov, Nate Kushman, Victoria Krakovna, Sasha Brown, MohammadHossein Bateni, Dennis Duan, Vlad Firoiu, Meghana Thotakuri, Tom Natan, Anhad Mohananey, Matthieu Geist, Sidharth Mudgal, Sertan Girgin, Hui Li, Jiayu Ye, Ofir Roval, Reiko Tojo, Michael Kwong, James Lee-Thorp, Christopher Yew, Quan Yuan, Sumit Bagri, Danila Sinopalnikov, Sabela Ramos, John Mellor, Abhishek Sharma, Aliaksei Severyn, Jonathan Lai, Kathy Wu, Heng-Tze Cheng, David Miller, Nicolas Sonnerat, Denis Vnukov, Rory Greig, Jennifer Beattie, Emily Caveness, Libin Bai, Julian Eisenschlos, Alex Korchemniy, Tomy Tsai, Mimi Jasarevic, Weize Kong, Phuong Dao, Zeyu Zheng, Frederick Liu, Fan Yang, Rui Zhu, Mark Geller, Tian Huey Teh, Jason Sanmiya, Evgeny Gladchenko, Nejc Trdin, Andrei Sozanschi, Daniel Toyama, Evan Rosen, Sasan Tavakkol, Linting Xue, Chen Elkind, Oliver Woodman, John Carpenter, George Papamakarios, Rupert Kemp, Sushant Kafle, Tanya Grunina, Rishika Sinha, Alice Talbert, Abhimanyu Goyal, Diane Wu, Denese Owusu-Afriyie, Cosmo Du, Chloe Thornton, Jordi Pont-Tuset, Pradyumna Narayana, Jing Li, Sabaer Fatehi, John Wieting, Omar Ajmeri, Benigno Uria, Tao Zhu, Yeongil Ko, Laura Knight, Amélie Héliou, Ning Niu, Shane Gu, Chenxi Pang, Dustin Tran, Yeqing Li, Nir Levine, Ariel Stolovich, Norbert Kalb, Rebeca Santamaria-Fernandez, Sonam Goenka, Wenny Yustalim, Robin Strudel, Ali Elqursh, Balaji Lakshminarayanan, Charlie Deck, Shyam Upadhyay, Hyo Lee, Mike Dusenberry, Zonglin Li, Xuezhi Wang, Kyle Levin, Raphael Hoffmann, Dan Holtmann-Rice, Olivier Bachem, Summer Yue, Sho Arora, Eric Malmi, Daniil Mirylenka, Qijun Tan, Christy Koh, Soheil Hassas Yeganeh, Siim Põder, Steven

Zheng, Francesco Pongetti, Mukarram Tariq, Yanhua Sun, Lucian Ionita, Mojtaba Seyedhosseini, Pouya Tafti, Ragha Kotikalapudi, Zhiyu Liu, Anmol Gulati, Jasmine Liu, Xinyu Ye, Bart Chrzaszcz, Lily Wang, Nikhil Sethi, Tianrun Li, Ben Brown, Shreya Singh, Wei Fan, Aaron Parisi, Joe Stanton, Chenkai Kuang, Vinod Koverkathu, Christopher A. Choquette-Choo, Yunjie Li, TJ Lu, Abe Ittycheriah, Prakash Shroff, Pei Sun, Mani Varadarajan, Sanaz Bahargam, Rob Willoughby, David Gaddy, Ishita Dasgupta, Guillaume Desjardins, Marco Cornero, Brona Robenek, Bhavishya Mittal, Ben Albrecht, Ashish Shenoy, Fedor Moiseev, Henrik Jacobsson, Alireza Ghaffarkhah, Morgane Rivière, Alanna Walton, Clément Crepy, Alicia Parrish, Yuan Liu, Zongwei Zhou, Clement Farabet, Carey Radebaugh, Praveen Srinivasan, Claudia van der Salm, Andreas Fidjeland, Salvatore Scellato, Eri Latorre-Chimoto, Hanna Klimczak-Plucińska, David Bridson, Dario de Cesare, Tom Hudson, Piermaria Mendolicchio, Lexi Walker, Alex Morris, Ivo Penchev, Matthew Mauger, Alexey Guseynov, Alison Reid, Seth Odoom, Lucia Loher, Victor Cotruta, Madhavi Yenugula, Dominik Grewe, Anastasia Petrushkina, Tom Duerig, Antonio Sanchez, Steve Yadlowsky, Amy Shen, Amir Globerson, Adam Kurzrok, Lynette Webb, Sahil Dua, Dong Li, Preethi Lahoti, Surya Bhupatiraju, Dan Hurt, Haroon Qureshi, Ananth Agarwal, Tomer Shani, Matan Eyal, Anuj Khare, Shreyas Rammohan Belle, Lei Wang, Chetan Tekur, Mihir Sanjay Kale, Jinliang Wei, Ruoxin Sang, Brennan Saeta, Tyler Liechty, Yi Sun, Yao Zhao, Stephan Lee, Pandu Nayak, Doug Fritz, Manish Reddy Vuyyuru, John Aslanides, Nidhi Vyas, Martin Wicke, Xiao Ma, Taylan Bilal, Evgenii Eltyshev, Daniel Balle, Nina Martin, Hardie Cate, James Manyika, Keyvan Amiri, Yelin Kim, Xi Xiong, Kai Kang, Florian Luisier, Nilesh Tripuraneni, David Madras, Mandy Guo, Austin Waters, Oliver Wang, Joshua Ainslie, Jason Baldridge, Han Zhang, Garima Pruthi, Jakob Bauer, Feng Yang, Riham Mansour, Jason Gelman, Yang Xu, George Polovets, Ji Liu, Honglong Cai, Warren Chen, XiangHai Sheng, Emily Xue, Sherjil Ozair, Adams Yu, Christof Angermueller, Xiaowei Li, Weiren Wang, Julia Wiesinger, Emmanouil Koukoumidis, Yuan Tian, Anand Iyer, Madhu Gurumurthy, Mark Goldenson, Parashar Shah, MK Blake, Hongkun Yu, Anthony Urbanowicz, Jennimaria Palomaki, Chrisantha Fernando, Kevin Brooks, Ken Durden, Harsh Mehta, Nikola Momchev, Elahe Rahimtoroghi, Maria Georgaki, Amit Raul, Sebastian Ruder, Morgan Redshaw, Jinhyuk Lee, Komal Jalan, Dinghua Li, Ginger Perng, Blake Hechtman, Parker Schuh, Milad Nasr, Mia Chen, Kieran Milan, Vladimir Mikulik, Trevor Strohman, Juliana Franco, Tim Green, Demis Hassabis, Koray Kavukcuoglu, Jeffrey Dean, and Oriol Vinyals. 2023. Gemini: A family of highly capable multimodal models.

Tom B. Brown, Benjamin Mann, Nick Ryder, Melanie Subbiah, Jared Kaplan, Prafulla Dhariwal, Arvind Neelakantan, Pranav Shyam, Girish Sastry, Amanda Askell, Sandhini Agarwal, Ariel Herbert-Voss, Gretchen Krueger, Tom Henighan, Rewon Child, Aditya Ramesh, Daniel M. Ziegler, Jeffrey Wu, Clemens Winter, Christopher Hesse, Mark Chen, Eric Sigler, Mateusz Litwin, Scott Gray, Benjamin Chess, Jack Clark, Christopher Berner, Sam McCandlish, Alec Radford, Ilya Sutskever, and Dario Amodei. 2020. Language models are few-shot learners. *Advances in Neural Information Processing Systems*, 2020-December.

Yu-Chu Chang, Xu Wang, Jindong Wang, Yuanyi Wu, Kaijie Zhu, Hao Chen, Linyi Yang, Xiaoyuan Yi, Cunxiang Wang, Yidong Wang, Weirong Ye, Yue Zhang, Yi Chang, Philip S. Yu, Qian Yang, and Xingxu Xie. 2023. A survey on evaluation of large language models. *ArXiv*, abs/2307.03109.

Banghao Chen, Zhaofeng Zhang, Nicolas Langrené, and Shengxin Zhu. 2023. Unleashing the potential of prompt engineering in large language models: a comprehensive review. *arXiv preprint arXiv: 2310.14735*.

Yu Ying Chiu, Liwei Jiang, Maria Antoniak, Chan Young Park, Shuyue Stella Li, Mehar Bhatia, Sahithya Ravi, Yulia Tsvetkov, Vered Shwartz, and Yejin Choi. 2024. Culturalteaming: Ai-assisted interactive red-teaming for challenging llms' (lack of) multicultural knowledge. *ArXiv*, abs/2404.06664.

Aakanksha Chowdhery, Sharan Narang, Jacob Devlin, Maarten Bosma, Gaurav Mishra, Adam Roberts, Paul Barham, Hyung Won Chung, Charles Sutton, Sebastian Gehrmann, Parker Schuh, Kensen Shi, Sasha Tsvyashchenko, Joshua Maynez, Abhishek Rao, Parker Barnes, Yi Tay, Noam Shazeer, Vinodkumar Prabhakaran, Emily Reif, Nan Du, Ben Hutchinson, Reiner Pope, James Bradbury, Jacob Austin, Michael Isard, Guy Gur-Ari, Pengcheng Yin, Toju Duke, Anselm Levskaya, Sanjay Ghemawat, Sunipa Dev, Henryk Michalewski, Xavier Garcia, Vedant Misra, Kevin Robinson, Liam Fedus, Denny Zhou, Daphne Ippolito, David Luan, Hyeontaek Lim, Barret Zoph, Alexander Spiridonov, Ryan Sepassi, David Dohan, Shivani Agrawal, Mark Omernick, Andrew M. Dai, Thanumalayan Sankaranarayana Pillai, Marie Pellat, Aitor Lewkowycz, Erica Moreira, Rewon Child, Oleksandr Polozov, Katherine Lee, Zongwei Zhou, Xuezhi Wang, Brennan Saeta, Mark Diaz, Orhan Firat, Michele Catasta, Jason Wei, Kathy Meier-Hellstern, Douglas Eck, Jeff Dean, Slav Petrov, and Noah Fiedel. 2022. Palm: Scaling language modeling with pathways.

Common Crawl. 2023. Common crawl language statistics. `https://commoncrawl.github.io/cc-crawl-statistics/plots/languages`. Accessed: 10-02-2024.

Andy Crabtree, David M. Nichols, Jon O'Brien, Mark Rouncefield, and Michael B. Twidale. 2000. Ethnomethodologically informed ethnography and information system design. *Journal of the American Society for Information Science and Technology*, 51(7):666–682.

Andy Crabtree, Jacki O'Neill, Peter Tolmie, Stefania Castellani, Tommaso Colombino, and Antonietta Grasso. 2006. The practical indispensability of articulation work to immediate and remote help-giving. In *Conference on Computer Supported Cooperative Work*.

A. Seza Doğruöz, Sunayana Sitaram, Barbara E. Bullock, and Almeida Jacqueline Toribio. 2023. A survey of code-switching: Linguistic and social perspectives for language technologies. In *Annual Meeting of the Association for Computational Linguistics*.

Rishav Hada, Varun Gumma, Adrian de Wynter, Harshita Diddee, Mohamed Ahmed, Monojit Choudhury, Kalika Bali, and Sunayana Sitaram. 2023. Are large language model-based evaluators the solution to scaling up multilingual evaluation?

Amr Hendy, Mohamed Gomaa Abdelrehim, Amr Sharaf, Vikas Raunak, Mohamed Gabr, Hitokazu Matsushita, Young Jin Kim, Mohamed Afify, and Hany Hassan Awadalla. 2023. How good are gpt models at machine translation? a comprehensive evaluation. *ArXiv*, abs/2302.09210.

Albert Q. Jiang, Alexandre Sablayrolles, Arthur Mensch, Chris Bamford, Devendra Singh Chaplot, Diego de las Casas, Florian Bressand, Gianna Lengyel, Guillaume Lample, Lucile Saulnier, Lélio Renard Lavaud, Marie-Anne Lachaux, Pierre Stock, Teven Le Scao, Thibaut Lavril, Thomas Wang, Timothée Lacroix, and William El Sayed. 2023. Mistral 7b.

Albert Q. Jiang, Alexandre Sablayrolles, Antoine Roux, Arthur Mensch, Blanche Savary, Chris Bamford, Devendra Singh Chaplot, Diego de Las Casas, Emma Bou Hanna, Florian Bressand, Gianna Lengyel, Guillaume Bour, Guillaume Lample, L'elio Renard Lavaud, Lucile Saulnier, Marie-Anne Lachaux, Pierre Stock, Sandeep Subramanian, Sophia Yang, Szymon Antoniak, Teven Le Scao, Théophile Gervet, Thibaut Lavril, Thomas Wang, Timothée Lacroix, and William El Sayed. 2024. Mixtral of experts. *ArXiv*, abs/2401.04088.

Arshad Kaji and Manan Shah. 2023. Contextual code switching for machine translation using language models.

Naveena Karusala, David Odhiambo Seeh, Cyrus Mugo, Brandon L Guthrie, Megan Andreas Moreno, Grace C John-Stewart, Irene Inwani, Richard J. Anderson, and Keshet Ronen. 2021. "that courage to encourage": Participation and aspirations in chat-based peer support for youth living with hiv. *Proceedings of the 2021 CHI Conference on Human Factors in Computing Systems*.

Viet Lai, Nghia Ngo, Amir Pouran Ben Veyseh, Hieu Man, Franck Dernoncourt, Trung Bui, and Thien Nguyen. 2023. ChatGPT beyond English: Towards a comprehensive evaluation of large language models in multilingual learning. In *Findings of the Association for Computational Linguistics: EMNLP 2023*, pages 13171–13189, Singapore. Association for Computational Linguistics.

Pengfei Liu, Weizhe Yuan, Jinlan Fu, Zhengbao Jiang, Hiroaki Hayashi, and Graham Neubig. 2023. Pre-train, prompt, and predict: A systematic survey of prompting methods in natural language processing. *ACM Comput. Surv.*, 55(9).

Shayne Longpre, Robert Mahari, Anthony Chen, Naana Obeng-Marnu, Damien Sileo, William Brannon, Niklas Muennighoff, Nathan Khazam, Jad Kabbara, Kartik Perisetla, Xinyi Wu, Enrico Shippole, Kurt Bollacker, Tongshuang Wu, Luis Villa, Sandy Pentland, and Sara Hooker. 2023. The data provenance initiative: A large scale audit of dataset licensing & attribution in ai.

Bodhisattwa Prasad Majumder, Oana-Maria Camburu, Thomas Lukasiewicz, and Julian McAuley. 2021. Knowledge-grounded self-rationalization via extractive and natural language explanations. In *International Conference on Machine Learning*.

David Martin, Benjamin V. Hanrahan, Jacki O'Neill, and Neha Gupta. 2014. Being a turker. In *CSCW 2014 - Proceedings of the 17th ACM Conference on Computer Supported Cooperative Work and Social Computing*, Proceedings of the ACM Conference on Computer Supported Cooperative Work, CSCW, pages 224–235. Association for Computing Machinery. Copyright: Copyright 2014 Elsevier B.V., All rights reserved.; 17th ACM Conference on Computer Supported Cooperative Work and Social Computing, CSCW 2014 ; Conference date: 15-02-2014 Through 19-02-2014.

Gemma Team Thomas Mesnard, Cassidy Hardin, Robert Dadashi, Surya Bhupatiraju, Shreya Pathak, L. Sifre, Morgane Riviere, Mihir Kale, J Christopher Love, Pouya Dehghani Tafti, L'eonard Hussenot, Aakanksha Chowdhery, Adam Roberts, Aditya Barua, Alex Botev, Alex Castro-Ros, Ambrose Slone, Am'elie H'eliou, Andrea Tacchetti, Anna Bulanova, Antonia Paterson, Beth Tsai, Bobak Shahriari, Charline Le Lan, Christopher A. Choquette-Choo, Cl'ement Crepy, Daniel Cer, Daphne Ippolito, David Reid, Elena Buchatskaya, Eric Ni, Eric Noland, Geng Yan, George Tucker, George-Christian Muraru, Grigory Rozhdestvenskiy, Henryk Michalewski, Ian Tenney, Ivan Grishchenko, Jacob Austin, James Keeling, Jane Labanowski, Jean-Baptiste Lespiau, Jeff Stanway, Jenny Brennan, Jeremy Chen, Johan Ferret, Justin Chiu, Justin Mao-Jones, Katherine Lee, Kathy Yu, Katie Millican, Lars Lowe Sjoesund, Lisa Lee, Lucas Dixon, Machel Reid, Maciej Mikula, Mateo Wirth, Michael Sharman, Nikolai Chinaev, Nithum Thain, Olivier Bachem, Oscar Chang, Oscar Wahltinez, Paige Bailey, Paul Michel, Petko Yotov, Pier Giuseppe Sessa, Rahma Chaabouni, Ramona Comanescu, Reena Jana, Rohan Anil, Ross McIlroy, Ruibo Liu, Ryan Mullins, Samuel L Smith, Sebastian Borgeaud, Sertan Girgin, Sholto Douglas, Shree Pandya, Siamak Shakeri, Soham De, Ted Klimenko, Tom Hennigan, Vladimir Feinberg, Wojciech Stokowiec, Yu hui Chen, Zafarali Ahmed, Zhitao Gong, Tris Brian Warkentin, Ludovic Peran, Minh Giang, Cl'ement Farabet, Oriol Vinyals, Jeffrey Dean, Koray Kavukcuoglu, Demis Hassabis, Zoubin Ghahramani, Douglas Eck, Joelle Barral, Fernando Pereira, Eli Collins, Armand Joulin, Noah Fiedel, Evan Senter, Alek Andreev, and Kathleen Kenealy. 2024. Gemma: Open models based on gemini research and technology. *ArXiv*, abs/2403.08295.

Ishani Mondal, Kalika Bali, Mohit Jain, Monojit Choudhury, Ashish Sharma, Evans Gitau, Jacki O'Neill, Kagonya Awori, and Sarah Gitau. 2021. A linguistic annotation framework to study interactions in multilingual healthcare conversational forums. In *Proceedings of the Joint 15th Linguistic Annotation Workshop (LAW) and 3rd Designing Meaning Representations (DMR) Workshop*, pages 66–77, Punta Cana, Dominican Republic. Association for Computational Linguistics.

Sharan Narang, Colin Raffel, Katherine Lee, Adam Roberts, Noah Fiedel, and Karishma Malkan. 2020. Wt5?! training text-to-text models to explain their predictions. *ArXiv*, abs/2004.14546.

Jessica Ojo, Kelechi Ogueji, Pontus Stenetorp, and David I Adelani. 2023. How good are large language models on african languages? *arXiv preprint arXiv:2311.07978*.

Jacki O'Neill and David Martin. 2003. Text chat in action. In *Proceedings of the 2003 ACM International Conference on Supporting Group Work*, GROUP '03, page 40–49, New York, NY, USA. Association for Computing Machinery.

OpenAI. 2023a. Gpt-4 technical report.

OpenAI. 2023b. Gpt4 technical report.

James Orao. 2012. The kenyan indigenous languages and the mass media: Challenges and opportunities.

Long Ouyang, Jeff Wu, Xu Jiang, Diogo Almeida, Carroll L. Wainwright, Pamela Mishkin, Chong Zhang, Sandhini Agarwal, Katarina Slama, Alex Ray, John Schulman, Jacob Hilton, Fraser Kelton, Luke E. Miller, Maddie Simens, Amanda Askell, Peter Welinder, Paul Francis Christiano, Jan Leike, and Ryan J. Lowe. 2022. Training language models to follow instructions with human feedback. *ArXiv*, abs/2203.02155.

Shana Poplack. 2001. *Code Switching: Linguistic*, pages 2062–2065.

Colin Raffel, Noam Shazeer, Adam Roberts, Katherine Lee, Sharan Narang, Michael Matena, Yanqi Zhou, Wei Li, and Peter J. Liu. 2020. Exploring the limits of transfer learning with a unified text-to-text transformer. *Journal of Machine Learning Research*, 21(140):1–67.

Nathaniel Robinson, Perez Ogayo, David R. Mortensen, and Graham Neubig. 2023. ChatGPT MT: Competitive for high- (but not low-) resource languages. In *Proceedings of the Eighth Conference on Machine Translation*, pages 392–418, Singapore. Association for Computational Linguistics.

Koustav Rudra, Shruti Rijhwani, Rafiya Begum, Kalika Bali, Monojit Choudhury, and Niloy Ganguly. 2016. Understanding language preference for expression of opinion and sentiment: What do Hindi-English speakers do on Twitter? In *Proceedings of the 2016 Conference on Empirical Methods in Natural Language Processing*, pages 1131–1141, Austin, Texas. Association for Computational Linguistics.

Oscar Sainz, Jon Campos, Iker García-Ferrero, Julen Etxaniz, Oier Lopez de Lacalle, and Eneko Agirre. 2023. NLP evaluation in trouble: On the need to measure LLM data contamination for each benchmark. In *Findings of the Association for Computational Linguistics: EMNLP 2023*, pages 10776–10787, Singapore. Association for Computational Linguistics.

Together Computer. 2023. Redpajama: an open dataset for training large language models.

Hugo Touvron, Thibaut Lavril, Gautier Izacard, Xavier Martinet, Marie-Anne Lachaux, Timothée Lacroix, Baptiste Rozière, Naman Goyal, Eric Hambro, Faisal Azhar, Aurelien Rodriguez, Armand Joulin, Edouard Grave, and Guillaume Lample. 2023. Llama: Open and efficient foundation language models.

Haryo Akbarianto Wibowo, Erland Hilman Fuadi, Made Nindyatama Nityasya, Radityo Eko Prasojo, and Alham Fikri Aji. 2023. Copal-id: Indonesian language reasoning with local culture and nuances. *ArXiv*, abs/2311.01012.

Sarah Wiegreffe, Jack Hessel, Swabha Swayamdipta, Mark Riedl, and Yejin Choi. 2022. Reframing human-AI collaboration for generating free-text explanations. In *Proceedings of the 2022 Conference of the North American Chapter of the Association for Computational Linguistics: Human Language Technologies*, pages 632–658, Seattle, United States. Association for Computational Linguistics.

Sarah Wiegreffe, Ana Marasović, and Noah A. Smith. 2021. Measuring association between labels and free-text rationales. In *Proceedings of the 2021 Conference on Empirical Methods in Natural Language Processing*, pages 10266–10284, Online and Punta Cana, Dominican Republic. Association for Computational Linguistics.

Ruochen Zhang, Samuel Cahyawijaya, Jan Christian Blaise Cruz, Genta Winata, and Alham Aji. 2023. Multilingual large language models are not (yet) code-switchers. In *Proceedings of the 2023 Conference on Empirical Methods in Natural Language Processing*, pages 12567–12582, Singapore. Association for Computational Linguistics.

Lianmin Zheng, Wei-Lin Chiang, Ying Sheng, Tianle Li, Siyuan Zhuang, Zhanghao Wu, Yonghao Zhuang, Zhuohan Li, Zi Lin, Eric P. Xing, Joseph E. Gonzalez, Ion Stoica, and Haotong Zhang. 2023. Lmsys-chat-1m: A large-scale real-world llm conversation dataset. *ArXiv*, abs/2309.11998.

A Appendix

A.1 The Prompt

```
You are a helpful NLP assistant, specializing in Sentiment Analysis. You are provided with a WhatsApp chat message (QUERY) in English, Swahili,
Sheng, or in more than one language (code-mixed), along with the defintions about the sentiment classes. Your task is to analyze the message
and categorize it as Positive, Negative, or Neutral based on the sentiment expressed, along with a justification. Make sure to highlight the
words/span of text in the query that you used to make your decision in your justification.

<DEFINITIONS>
**Negative Sentiment**: It expresses some sort of negative feeling or view or opinion about someone or something.

**Neutral Sentiment**: It neither expresses a positive nor a negative sentiment of the speaker. It could be a general comment, acknowledgement,
chitchat or any factual advice or a simple greeting.

**Positive Sentiment**: The sentiment needs to be classified as positive if the speaker feels strong and positive at any particular utterance,
except the normal aspects such as any form of greetings.
</DEFINITIONS>


QUERY: "{query}"


{output_format_instructions}
**DO NOT OUTPUT ANYTHING OTHER THAN THE JSON OBJECT**
```

Figure 3: LangChain prompt for Sentiment Analysis. We randomize the order of the definitions to alleviate position bias.

A.2 Description of Human Evaluation Criteria

In Table 4, we provide a brief description of each of the five rubrics for human evaluation we adopted as outlined by (Chang et al., 2023) on *'how to evaluate'*.

Evaluation Criteria	Description
Linguistic accuracy	LLM's capacity for precise linguistic interpretation and generation, covering grammar, vocabulary, idioms, and language-specific nuances, while ensuring factual accuracy.
Contextual and cultural relevance	LLM's ability to provide contextually and culturally relevant justifications in sentiment analysis, ensuring responses are appropriate and significant to the given context.
Fluency in maintaining consistency	LLM's fluency in producing consistent and logical justifications across various sentiment analysis cases, ensuring smooth content flow and uniform tone.
Alignment with human expectations	LLM's ability to produce justifications aligned with human reasoning ensures ethically appropriate predictions, reflecting human values and societal norms, fostering trust in sensitive applications like sentiment analysis.
Transparency in LLM's decision-making process	LLM's ability to clearly and openly communicate its decision-making process, enabling users to understand the rationale behind responses and gain insights into its inner workings.

Table 4: Description of Human Evaluation Criteria.

A.3 LLMs' F1 Scores Across Languages

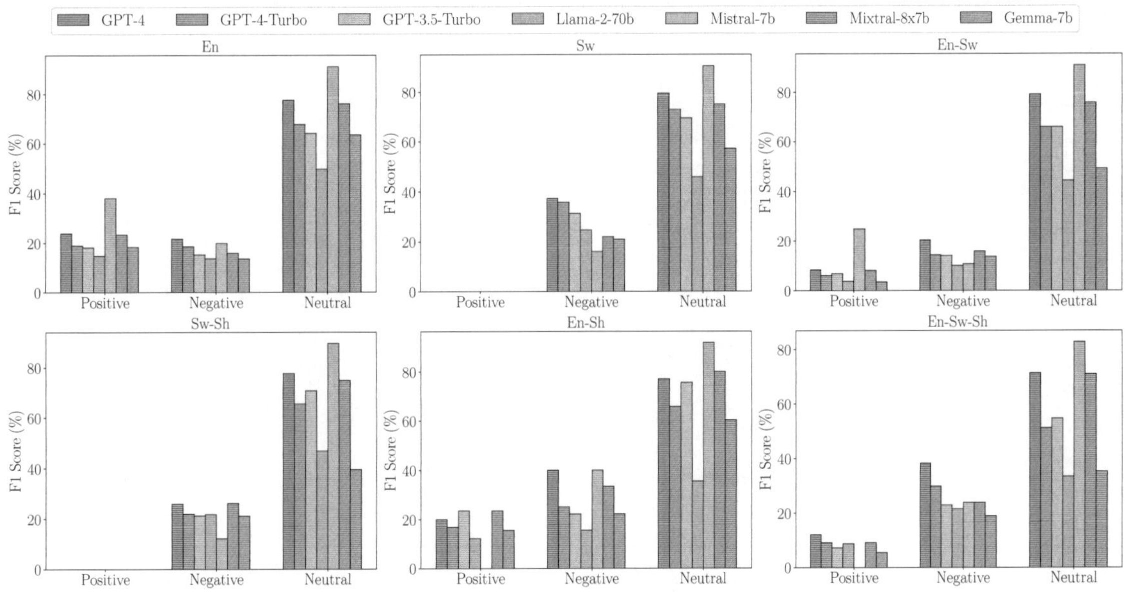

Figure 4: Models' F1 scores across languages for Positive, Negative, and Neutral sentiments.

A.4 Detailed Qualitative Analysis of Model Explanations Across Multilingual Examples

Message	GPT-4	GPT-4-Turbo	GPT-3.5-Turbo	Llama-2-70b	Mistral-7b	Mixtral-8x7b	Gemma-7b
Original: *"Mm nimeboeka acha ni lale gud 9t"* **Translation:** *"Am bored let me sleep ..goodnight"* **Actual Sentiment:** Negative	The phrase 'nimeboeka' translates to 'I'm bored' in English, which indicates a negative sentiment. The speaker is expressing dissatisfaction or a lack of interest, which is a negative feeling. **Prediction:** Negative	The phrase 'nimeboeka' which means 'I'm bored' indicates a negative feeling or mood. The speaker's intention to go to sleep ('acha ni lale') could be seen as a way to escape this boredom, which further emphasizes the negative sentiment. The addition of 'gud 9t' (good night) does not change the overall sentiment as it is a common phrase used before going to sleep and does not express a strong positive feeling as per the definitions provided. **Prediction:** Negative	The sentiment is categorized as Neutral. The message does not express a strong positive or negative feeling. It seems to be a casual comment about feeling tired and going to sleep. The use of 'acha ni lale gud 9t' indicates the speaker's intention to go to sleep, which is a neutral statement. **Prediction:** Neutral	The message expresses a positive sentiment due to the use of positive words such as 'Mm', 'ni lale', and 'gud'. **Prediction:** Positive	The given query is in Swahili language and translates to 'I have not found it yet good 9t'. The sentiment expressed is neutral as the speaker is simply stating a fact about their current situation. **Prediction:** Neutral	The query 'Mm nimeboeka acha ni lale gud 9t' is in Sheng, a slang language spoken in Kenya. The phrase roughly translates to 'I have given up, it's late now, 9 o'clock'. The sentiment expressed in this message is Negative as the speaker expresses giving up and the lateness of the time could indicate a negative feeling or situation. The word 'acha' (give up) is particularly indicative of a negative sentiment. **Prediction:** Negative	The phrase 'Mm nimeboeka acha ni lale gud 9t' is a Sheng phrase that translates to 'I am not feeling well'. The speaker is expressing negative sentiment due to the use of the word 'acha' and 'gud', which are both words used to describe feeling unwell. The phrase also includes a reference to the number '9t', which is commonly used in Sheng to express feeling sick. Therefore, I classify the sentiment of the message as Negative. **Prediction:** Negative

Table 5: This example involves an English-Swahili message with various textual irregularities including grammatical errors (*'ni lale'* instead of *'nilale'*), local abbreviations (*'Mm'* instead of *'Mimi'*), and misspellings (*'gud 9t'* instead of *'good night'*, *'acha'* instead of *'wacha'*). GPT-4-Turbo excelled in this challenging context by demonstrating its robust multilingual capabilities and resilience to noise, leading to both correct prediction and interpretation. GPT-4 similarly managed to accurately identify the key sentiment indicator in the message. However, the remaining models including GPT-3.5-Turbo, Llama-2-70b, Mistral-7b, Mixtral-8x7b, and Gemma-7b showed weaker contextual and linguistic understanding, as well as a lack of robustness to noise. As a result, GPT-3.5-Turbo and Mistral-7b made incorrect predictions, while Mixtral-8x7b and Gemma-7b, despite correct predictions, failed in their interpretation.

Message	GPT-4	GPT-4-Turbo	GPT-3.5-Turbo	Llama-2-70b	Mistral-7b	Mixtral-8x7b	Gemma-7b
Original: *"tuache iyo story ju ishaanza kuniboo."* **Translation:** *"Let's leave that story it is starting to bore me."* **Actual Sentiment:** Negative	The phrase 'ishaanza kuniboo' in the message indicates that the speaker is getting bored or annoyed with the story, which is a negative sentiment. **Prediction:** Negative	The phrase 'ishaanza kuniboo' indicates that the speaker is getting bored or is already bored with the story being discussed. The word 'kuniboo' is a Sheng term that translates to 'boring me' in English, which conveys a negative sentiment. **Prediction:** Negative	The sentiment expressed in the message is negative. The phrase 'tuache iyo story' indicates a desire to stop or leave a certain situation, and 'ishaanza kuniboo' suggests that something negative has started happening to the speaker. Therefore, the overall sentiment is negative. **Prediction:** Negative	The word 'tuache' means 'forget' in Swahili, and the phrase 'iyo story' means 'that story' or 'that thing'. The word 'ju' is an interrogative pronoun meaning 'what'. Therefore, the overall sentiment of the sentence is Neutral because it is asking about something in a factual manner without expressing any positive or negative emotion. **Prediction:** Neutral	The given query in Swahili language 'tuache iyo story ju ishaanza kuniboo' translates to 'leave that story alone' in English. This is a command or instruction and does not express any positive or negative sentiment. **Prediction:** Neutral	The Swahili phrase 'tuache iyo story' translates to 'let's leave that story' in English. The word 'leave' often indicates a negative sentiment as it suggests abandonment or disinterest. The word 'that story' is a reference to a previous conversation or event, which based on the sentiment expressed, seems to be something the speaker wants to move away from. Therefore, the sentiment of this message is Negative. **Prediction:** Negative	The phrase 'tuache iyo story ju ishaanza kuniboo' is a Sheng phrase that translates to 'you are telling a story that is not true'. The speaker is expressing disbelief and negativity towards the story being told. The words 'ishaanza' and 'kuniboo' are the key words used to convey this sentiment. **Prediction:** Negative

Table 6: This message showcases a complex mix of English, Swahili, and Sheng, with the Swahili-Sheng term *'kuniboo'* serving as a key sentiment indicator. GPT-4 and GPT-4-Turbo excelled in this context, demonstrating strong multilingual capabilities by accurately understanding both the linguistic elements and the contextual nuances, leading to correct predictions and interpretation. GPT-3.5-Turbo and Mixtral-8x7b have made a correct prediction, however, failed to recognize the significance of *'kuniboo'*, likely due to a lack of understanding of this specific term. The remaining models, including Llama-2-70b, Mistral-7b, and Gemma-7b, also missed the critical non-English sentiment indicator. Consequently, Llama-2-70b and Mistral-7b made incorrect predictions with incorrect interpretation, whereas Gemma-7b managed a correct prediction but with flawed interpretation.

Message	GPT-4	GPT-4-Turbo	GPT-3.5-Turbo	Llama-2-70b	Mistral-7b	Mixtral-8x7b	Gemma-7b
Original: *"Send to everyone you love whether it's real love or friendship love, brotherly love, sisterly love, child love, fatherly love and motherly love. You are lovable if you get FIVE sent back to you !"* **Actual Sentiment:** Neutral	The message is encouraging the recipient to spread love to everyone they care about, and it also assures them that they are lovable. The phrases 'Send to everyone you love' and 'You are lovable' indicate a positive sentiment. **Prediction:** Positive	The message encourages people to send love in various forms and implies that receiving love back is a positive outcome by stating 'You are lovable if you get FIVE sent back to you'. The words 'love', 'lovable', and the concept of sending love to others and receiving it back suggest a positive sentiment. **Prediction:** Positive	The sentiment expressed in the message is Positive. The speaker is expressing love and positivity towards everyone they care about, including family and friends. The phrase 'Send to everyone you love' and the mention of different types of love such as brotherly, sisterly, child, fatherly, and motherly love all contribute to the positive sentiment expressed in the message. **Prediction:** Positive	The message expresses a positive sentiment as it encourages the reader to spread love and mentions receiving love in return. The use of the word 'love' multiple times emphasizes the positive emotion. Additionally, the phrase 'you are lovable' suggests that the speaker feels positively about the recipient. **Prediction:** Positive	The message expresses a positive sentiment towards love and the importance of receiving love in return. The speaker encourages sending love to various relationships and considers being loved as a positive attribute. **Prediction:** Positive	The message expresses a positive sentiment by encouraging the reader to share love with others, whether it be romantic, familial, or platonic. The phrase 'You are lovable if you get FIVE sent back to you' also adds to the positive sentiment as it implies that the recipient is loved and appreciated by others. The use of positive words such as 'love', 'lovable', and 'five' contribute to the overall positive tone of the message. **Prediction:** Positive	The message expresses strong positive sentiment due to the use of words like 'love', 'lovable', and 'FIVE sent back to you'. The message also emphasizes the feeling of inclusivity and affection towards various relationships. **Prediction:** Positive

Table 7: This example focuses on the challenges posed by informational-neutral messages that, despite being predominantly in English, contain ambiguous sentiments that may be interpreted as either positive or negative. This ambiguity leads to discrepancies between the models' predictions and the actual annotations. Despite these challenges, the example also highlights all models' strong linguistic understanding of English, showcasing their ability to handle the language even in nuanced scenarios.

Message	GPT-4	GPT-4-Turbo	GPT-3.5-Turbo	Llama-2-70b	Mistral-7b	Mixtral-8x7b	Gemma-7b
Original: *"Me siyo beste yako"* **Translation:** *"Am not your friend"* **Actual Sentiment:** Negative	The phrase 'Me siyo beste yako' translates to 'I am not your friend' in English. This statement expresses a negative sentiment as it indicates a rejection or negative view towards the person being addressed. **Prediction:** Negative	The phrase 'Me siyo beste yako' in Sheng translates to 'I am not your friend' in English. The use of 'siyo' (not) indicates a denial or negation of friendship, which conveys a negative sentiment towards the relationship with the person being addressed. **Prediction:** Negative	The sentiment is Negative. The phrase 'siyo beste yako' in Swahili translates to 'not your best', which expresses a negative opinion about someone or something. **Prediction:** Negative	The phrase 'Me siyo beste yako' is a Swahili phrase that translates to 'I don't have your best interests at heart' in English. The use of the phrase implies that the speaker does not have the listener's well-being in mind, and may even have negative intentions. Therefore, the sentiment of this phrase is Negative. **Prediction:** Negative	The query 'Me siyo beste yako' in Swahili translates to 'I am not your best' in English. This statement is a simple negation and does not express any strong positive or negative sentiment. It could be a response to a request for compliments or an expression of humility. **Prediction:** Neutral	The query 'Me siyo beste yako' is in Sheng, a code-mixed language in Kenya. The phrase can be translated to 'I am not your best' in English. The use of 'not' indicates a negative sentiment. However, the sentiment is not strong as it's a statement of fact rather than an expression of a negative emotion. Therefore, the sentiment is Negative. **Prediction:** Negative	The phrase 'Me siyo beste yako' is a Swahili phrase that translates to 'I am your best friend' in English. The phrase expresses a strong positive sentiment. The words 'beste' and 'yako' are the key words that I used to make this decision. **Prediction:** Positive

Table 8: This example demonstrates the difficulties all models face when processing the Sheng language, particularly for those with weaker linguistic understanding of non-English languages. Only GPT-4 and GPT-4-Turbo successfully identified and correctly interpreted the language, highlighting the significant variability in multilingual capabilities across the models.

Y-NQ:
English-Yorùbá Evaluation dataset for Open-Book Reading Comprehension with Open-Ended Questions

Marta R. Costa-jussà, Joy Chen, Ifeoluwanimi Adebara, Joe Chuang,Christophe Ropers, Eduardo Sánchez
FAIR, Meta
{costajussa,joyqchen,adeifeoluwanimi, joechuang,chrisropers,eduardosanchez}@meta.com

Abstract

The purpose of this work is to share an English-Yorùbá evaluation dataset for open-book reading comprehension with open-ended questions to assess the performance of models both in a high- and a low-resource language. The dataset contains 358 questions and answers on 338 English documents and 208 Yorùbá documents. Experiments show a consistent disparity in performance between the two languages, with Yorùbá falling behind English for automatic metrics even if documents are much shorter for this language. For a small set of documents with comparable length, performance of Yorùbá drops by 2.5 times and this comparison is validated with human evaluation. When analyzing performance by length, we observe that Yorùbá decreases performance dramatically for documents that reach 1500 words while English performance is barely affected at that length. Our dataset opens the door to showcasing if English LLM reading comprehension capabilities extend to Yorùbá, which for the evaluated LLMs is not the case.

1 Introduction

This study explores the intersection of reading comprehension with open-ended questions, examining how models perform on a task requiring both in-context understanding (i.e., open-book model, where the model has access to the context document during inference to answer a particular question) and generative text production (i.e. the answer is free-text which has to be compared to a gold standard reference). We aim to investigate the performance of this task in two languages: a high-resource language (English) and a low-resource language (Yorùbá). For this, we introduce Y-NQ (Yorùbá Natural Questions) a comprehensive open-book question-answer dataset (Section 2). Y-NQ is sourced from NQ (Kwiatkowski et al., 2019) and provides a complete article context for informed answers, and parallel documents on the same topic for both high- and low-resource languages. The data set also includes the comparability of the responses in languages. As a result, we are increasing Natural Language Processing (NLP) resources in Yorùbá (Ahia et al., 2024). Our data set is benchmarked against state-of-the-art Large Language Models (LLMs). The results and analysis (Section 3) show that responses in Yorùbá are more inaccurate than those in English. As a by-product of human annotations, we identify inaccuracies in the English-language version of some Wikipedia articles (26 incorrect answers out of 1,566 humanly analyzed questions in the English-language subset of articles), which confirms the existence of accuracy discrepancies across languages for the same Wikipedia topics, thus supporting, for example, the need to better interlink Wikipedia articles across languages (Klang and Nugues, 2016).

2 Dataset description

2.1 Requirements and Background

The performance of Reading Comprehension (RC) in LLMs has been explored in different settings. At the high level, RC tasks can fall under two main categories: open-book tasks, such as in SQuAD (Rajpurkar et al., 2016), and close-book tasks, such as in TriviaQA (Joshi et al., 2017). Response formats vary across RC tasks as well and include: true/false classification (e.g., BoolQ; Clark et al., 2019), multiple-choice questions (e.g., Belebele), span selection (e.g., SQuAD), and text generation (e.g., NQ or TriviaQA).

Since we are interested in exploring the intersection of reading comprehension with open-ended questions covering both a high- and a low-resource language, we can explicitly set our requirements to include for each of the two types

Proceedings of the Sixth Workshop on African Natural Language Processing (AfricaNLP 2025), pages 248–254
July 31, 2025 ©2025 Association for Computational Linguistics

of language: (a) long articles (>100s words), (b) question-answer pairs with lengthy answers (>10s words), and (c) equivalence annotations for cross-lingual answers. Since there are no existing data sets to this effect, we extend existing research by tailoring an established data set to our specific requirements. We justify our choice of data sets and low-resource language selection as explained in the following.

Dataset. Among the open-book reading comprehenstion with open-ended questions, one of the largest datasets with multilingual information available is NQ which is shared under the license Creative Commons Share-Alike 3.0 .

Low-resource language. There is a large number of low-resource languages that could be explored here. We prioritize a low-resource language that has overall limited digital resources (in compliance with the definition of low resource), but has a high representation in Wikipedia (on the order of several thousands of entries) and a significant number of speakers (in the order of tens of millions), and makes use of the same script (Latin) as the high-resource language in which results are compared. One of the languages that complies with all these criteria is Yorùbá, in which we can also find works on comprehension of the language in the domain of language exams (Aremu et al., 2024), based on short passages and multiple choice answers. Another work is the AfriQA dataset (Ogundepo et al., 2023) for answering open-retrieval questions, with a primary focus on retrieving correct answers that are answerable on Wikipedia. However, this cannot be used as an open book. Finally, Bebebele (Bandarkar et al., 2024) also includes Yorùbá, although it uses short passages and multiple choice answers.

2.2 Dataset creation

NQ pre-selection. We looked at 315,203 examples and 231,695 unique English Wikipedia pages from the NQ training and validation datasets. We filter questions for only those where every long answer is contained in an html tag $< p >$ where $< p >$ is the first identified html tag in the long answer span. This filters out about 25 percent of the questions.

We extracted 2,855 Yorùbá Wikipedia pages that are actively associated with the above English pages. We removed documents with fewer than 500 characters, including formatting, and performed multiple cleaning procedures, such as removing html formatting, removing citation notations, and filtering out irrelevant sections in Wikipedia articles (e.g., references, tables). 664 Yorùbá documents and 1,566 questions were sent for human annotation. We tried a pre-annotation effort to automatically reduce the workload. Even if it did not work, we report it for the interest of negative results.

Pre-annotation automatic effort. In order to reduce the annotation workload, we automatically pre-selected Yorùbá sentences that could be good response candidates by computing a similarity score. If the answer to the question was in agreement with a high similarity score, the annotator would save time by looking through the document and only checking if the match was correct. We conducted a SONAR embedding similarity (Duquenne et al., 2023) analysis between Yorùbá documents and long English answers. We used Stopes[1] sensitizers on all text extracted from $< p >$ elements for both the scraped Yorùbá Wikipedia articles downloaded from the previous step and the original NQ Wikipedia pages. We then created SONAR embeddings of each extracted sentence and identified those sentences in the Yorùbá pages which were most similar to sentences in the long English answers based on their cosine similarity scores. For a small set of samples, we asked the annotators to examine the entries in a small validation data set to identify a reasonable threshold indicating high similarity between Yorùbá/English sentences, which could then be applied to the rest of the data set. The analysis shows a low similarity matching rate, which is likely due to the low quality and short length of many Yorùbá articles and/or SONAR embeddings not being suitable for such a task. Given this low reliability, we abandoned this automatic pre-annotation, which would not reduce annotation efforts.

Annotation guidelines and requirements. We designed the annotation guidelines as follows. We provided context on the objective of the task together with the project context and description of the task. The guidelines are summarized in Table 1.

Finally, beyond the guidelines, we provided ad-

[1] https://github.com/facebookresearch/stopes

Objective	Read an article and find a paragraph containing enough information to answer a specific question.
Project Context	Evaluate accuracy of large language models in finding long contexts and short answers; extend Natural Questions dataset to multilingual, non-English centric.
Task Components	• QUESTION: Simple question requesting information or explanation. • ARTICLE: Numbered paragraphs containing relevant information.
Task Steps	1. Read QUESTION carefully. 2. Read ARTICLE paragraphs until sufficient information is found. 3. Record findings by answering task questions.
Additional task steps	Discard questions that contain the answer in English in the Yorùbá document When possible, add Yorùbá questions, translate them into English, and find answers both in the Yorùbá and English documents.

Table 1: Linguistic guidelines and annotation

ditional examples and requested that annotators should be native speakers of the language of the source documents and should have at least CEFR C2 level proficiency in English.

	ENG	YOR
#Q&A	358	358
#DOCS	338	208
AVG. DOC LEN	10363	430
MEDIAN DOC LEN	9272	172
AVG. QUESTION LEN	8.86	9.39
AVG. LONG ANSWER LEN	113.80	32.89

Table 2: Dataset Statistics. Length is in words.

Annotator findings. We noticed that many articles have a significant amount of English content. Several documents also contained errors, such as incorrect spelling, ungrammatical sentences, and sentences that lacked clarity or meaning. We disregarded such articles and corrected articles that were contaminated with a small amount of English content. We also removed the entries where no answers could be found in the Yorùbá articles.

Following the guidelines, the annotators encountered the following: (a) questions with multiple correct answers, for which they annotated each correct answer for the question; (b) questions with correct answers in Yorùbá, but incorrect in English, where they annotated the Yorùbá appropriately, but flagged the English portion incorrect (there were 26 questions in the category); (c) unclear questions (5 questions) to which no annotations were assigned; (d) answers existing in multiple paragraphs in the document for which they annotated the row with all paragraphs. There were 456 Yorùbá documents that did not answer the question; therefore, we discarded those. Only eight incorrect English answers from the previous 26 remain in the final dataset, and we did not correct them since the English documents remained the same as in the original NQ.

Statistics. Table 2 details the statistics of the data set.Our carefully curated selection contains 208 unique Yorùbá Wikipedia documents with an average word count of 430, and 358 questions. Only the questions are strictly comparable. English and Yorùbá documents are not comparable in number or length, but are so in topic and domain. The answers are not comparable in length. Notice that English documents outnumber Yorùbá documents mainly due to: (1) multiple versions of the same English topic counted as different documents, while in Yorùbá we selected one version of the document; and (2) multiple topics in English that correspond to the same Yorùbá topic, given limited Yorùbá resources on Wikipedia. Also, the shorter length of Yorùbá documents (compared to English documents) is due to the limited amount of Yorùbá resources on Wikipedia.

The fact that English documents are longer than those in Yorùbá makes the task easier for Yorùbá, since documents are significantly shorter within the same topic or domain. We identified a subset of four documents that are strictly comparable in length and topic for English and Yorùbá, which allows us to make a fair comparison. Table 3 shows the list of fields in Y-NQ and a sample entry.

3 Experiments

Baselines We evaluate our dataset with GPT-4o[2] (et al., 2024b), o1-mini[3], and LlaMA-3.1-8b (et al., 2024a), thereby covering both open and closed models, as well as models of different sizes.

[2]gpt-4o version 2024-08-06

[3]o1-mini version 2024-09-12

FIELD	DESCRIPTION	EXAMPLE
1. Question ID	Unique identifier	3506772758530306034
2. English Document	English text document	
3. English Question	Question in English	what is the name of the first nigerian president
4. English Long Answer	Detailed answer in English	.ky is the Internet country code top-level domain (ccTLD) for the Cayman [..]
5. English Short Answer	Brief answer in English	Nnamdi Azikiwe
6. Yorùbá Document	Yorùbá text document	
7. Yorùbá Rewrite Flag	Was Yorùbá document rewritten? (0: no, 1: yes)	1
8. Yorùbá Question	Question in Yorùbá	kí ni ky dúró fún ní erékùṣù cayman
9. Yorùbá Short Answer	Brief answer in Yorùbá	Nnamdi Azikiwe ni Aare
10. Yorùbá Long Answer	Detailed answer in Yorùbá	Nnamdi Azikiwe ti o je Gomina Agba nigbana di Aare, ipo to je fun ayeye, [..]
11. Yorùbá Paragraph Info	Contextual information	P2
12. Answer Alignment	Semantic equivalence (0: not literal, 1: literal)	1

Table 3: Dataset Fields, Descriptions and Sample entry.

	LAN	R-1	R-2	R-L
GPT4O	ENG	0.39	0.23	0.30
	YOR	0.34	0.19	0.27
O1MINI	ENG	0.45	0.22	0.30
	YOR	0.30	0.14	0.22
LLAMA	ENG	0.31	0.18	0.23
	YOR	0.20	0.15	0.18

Table 4: Results for 3 LLM in terms of Rouge computed for the entire set of questions.

For each Y-NQ entry, we prompt the models with the following formatted instructions.

```
"""
Given the following passage and
a question,answer the question
in a single paragraph with
information found in the passage.

####
PASSAGE
{document}

####
QUESTION
{question}

####
ANSWER
"""
```

Evaluation. We evaluate the results by comparing the generated text and the reference long answer using several Rouge (Lin, 2004) versions (Rouge-1, Rouge-2, Rouge-L).

Automatic metrics. Table 4 reports the results showing that Yorùbá consistently performs worse than English (e.g., losing 0.4 in Rouge-1). However, the Yorùbá task is much easier because the documents are much shorter, which means that answering the question becomes an easier task. Even if we prompt the model to only answer based on the in-context document, we can not discard the idea that English may get better results due to using the internal knowledge from the model.

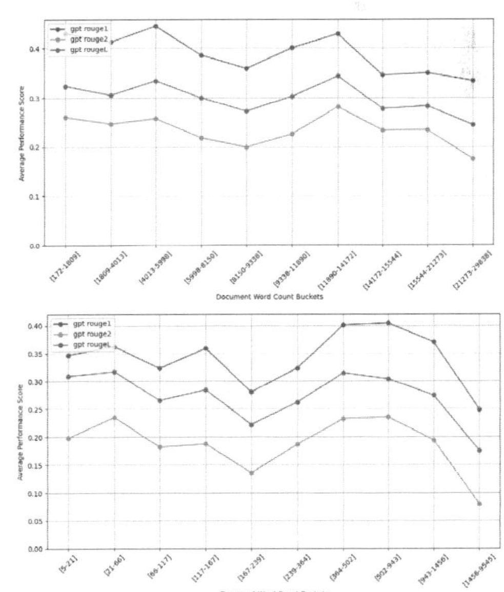

Figure 1: Impact of Document Length Buckets on Performance Scores for English (top) and Yorùbá (bottom) for GPT-4 outputs

Length analysis. Model performance changes with the length of the document, as shown in Figure 1. The dataset was split into equal size of documents in each length bucket. We can see a drop in performance when the Yorùbá documents reach 1,500 words, which shows the challenges that current models face in long-context understanding of low-resource languages.

Comparable documents. For a small portion of long-enough documents of comparable length between English and Yorùbá (only 4 documents that are over 900 words long), English performance demonstrates a significant edge (1.58X-2.56X), see Table 5.

Human evaluation. For the comparable documents, we performed a human evaluation. A bilingual proficiency speaker of English and Yorùbá evaluated the output of the models. Evaluation was performed by using a Likert scale from 1-3, being 3 a perfect response. On average, English responses across models scored 2.33, while Yorùbá responses scored 2.

Table 6 presents a complete sample and its human scores for all the models output.

	LANG	R-1	R-2	R-L	Hum
GPT4O	ENG	0.45	0.23	0.30	2.50
	YOR	0.32	0.09	0.19	2.75
O1MINI	ENG	0.43	0.17	0.27	2.50
	YOR	0.27	0.06	0.17	2.25
LLAMA	ENG	0.46	0.28	0.33	2.00
	YOR	0.09	0.05	0.07	1.00

Table 5: Results and human evaluation (Hum) for comparable English and Yorùbá four documents. English documents have an average length of 3299 and Yorùbá documents have an average length of 3070 words.

4 Conclusions

Y-NQ is a newly released dataset that enables to compare generative open-book reading comprehension between English and Yorùbá. The main contributions of our data set are to allow for the comparison of LLM results in a reading comprehension task across a high- and a low-resource language, showing what are the generalization capabilities of LLMs in this particular case. Moreover, our annotations confirmed variations in the accuracy of Wikipedia articles in all languages. In particular, we identify inaccurate English responses for Yorùbá language-specific content. Y-NQ allows us to evaluate how reading comprehension capabilities extend to Yorùbá. Y-NQ is not exactly comparable in its totality between languages. Given that Yorùbá has shorter documents than English, the reading comprehension task is easier for Yorùbá. Therefore, results on this language should be much better than in English to expect parity between languages. Our experiments show that the reading comprehension capabilities of current English LLMs do not extend to Yorùbá. Y-NQ is freely available[4].

Limitations and Ethical considerations

Y-NQ is limited in size, language, and domain coverage. The fact of using Wikipedia and extending an existing open-source dataset (NQ) may play in favor of having higher results in both languages due to contamination. Furthermore, the data set is not fully comparable between English and Yorùbá, since documents and answers vary in length.

Our experimentation is limited to models and automatic evaluation metrics, which is compensated for through a small-size human evaluation. Annotators were paid a fair rate and they gave consent to the use of the data that they were annotating. Annotators are included as authors of the paper.

Acknowledgements

This paper is part of the LCM project[5] and the authors would like to thank the entire LCM team for the fruitful discussions.

References

Orevaoghene Ahia, Anuoluwapo Aremu, Diana Abagyan, Hila Gonen, David Ifeoluwa Adelani, Daud Abolade, Noah A. Smith, and Yulia Tsvetkov. 2024. Voices unheard: NLP resources and models for Yorùbá regional dialects. In *Proceedings of the 2024 Conference on Empirical Methods in Natural Language Processing*, pages 4392–4409, Miami, Florida, USA. Association for Computational Linguistics.

Anuoluwapo Aremu, Jesujoba O. Alabi, Daud Abolade, Nkechinyere F. Aguobi, Shamsuddeen Hassan Muhammad, and David Ifeoluwa Adelani. 2024. Naijarc: A multi-choice reading comprehension dataset for nigerian languages. *Preprint*, arXiv:2308.09768.

Lucas Bandarkar, Davis Liang, Benjamin Muller, Mikel Artetxe, Satya Narayan Shukla, Donald Husa,

[4]https://huggingface.co/datasets/facebook/Y-NQ

[5]https://github.com/facebookresearch/large$_$concept$_$models

FIELD	CONTENT	HUM
ENGLISH QUESTION	where does the vaal dam get its water from	–
YORÙBÁ QUESTION	níbo ni ìsédò vaal ti ń gba omi rẹ̀	–
ENGLISH LONG-ANSWER	The Vaal Dam in South Africa was constructed in 1938 and lies 77 km south of OR Tambo International Airport. The lake behind the dam wall has a surface area of about 320 square kilometres (120 sq mi) and is 47 meters deep. The Vaal Dam lies on the Vaal River, which is one of South Africa 's strongest - flowing rivers. Other rivers flowing into the dam are the Wilge River, Klip River, Molspruit and Grootspruit. It has over 800 kilometres (500 mi) of shoreline and is South Africa 's second biggest dam by area and the fourth largest by volume.	–
YORÙBÁ LONG-ANSWER	Àwọn òdò mìíràn tí ńṣàn sínu ìdídò náà ni Odò Wilge,Odò Klip Molspruit ati Grootspruit. ', 'Ìdídò Vaal wà lórí Odò Vaal, èyí tí ó jẹ̀ ọkan nínú àwọn òdò tí ńṣàn tí ó lágbára jùlọ ní orílẹ̀-èdè South Africa.	–
ENGLISH GPT4O-ANSWER	The Vaal Dam gets its water from several sources, including the Vaal River, into which other rivers like the Wilge River, Klip River, Molspruit, and Grootspruit also flow. Additionally, the Lesotho Highlands Water Project contributes to the water supply by piping water from Lesotho into the Liebenbergsvlei and Wilge Rivers. The Sterkfontein Dam is also part of the water transfer scheme, releasing water to boost the levels in the Vaal River System when the Vaal Dam drops below 16%.	2
YORÙBÁ GPT4O-ANSWER	Ìsédò Vaal ń gba omi rẹ̀ láti ọ̀pọ̀lọpọ̀ odò, tí wọ́n ń fi kún omi láàrin ìdídò náà. Àwọn odò jíjẹ̀ wọ̀nyí ní Odò Wilge, Odò Klip, Molspruit, àti Grootspruit. Pẹ̀lú ẹ̀yin odò wọ̀nyí, àwùjọ omi ètò omi Ilè-Okè ní Lesotho tun ń pèsè omi sínú ìdídò náà.	3
ENGLISH O1MINI-ANSWER	The Vaal Dam receives its water from multiple sources, primarily the Vaal River itself along with several tributaries including the Wilge River, Klip River, Molspruit, and Grootspruit. Additionally, the Lesotho Highlands Water Project contributes to the dam's water supply by piping water from Lesotho into the Liebenbergsvlei and Wilge Rivers. Furthermore, the Sterkfontein Dam plays a crucial role in augmenting the Vaal Dam's water levels through the Tugela-Vaal water transfer scheme, which transfers water from the Thukela River in KwaZulu-Natal. These combined sources ensure a stable and substantial inflow of water to the Vaal Dam, supporting both domestic and industrial needs in the surrounding regions.	3
YORÙBÁ O1MINI-ANSWER	Ìsédò Vaal ń gba omi rẹ̀ láti Odò Vaal àti àwọn òdò tí ń darapọ̀ mọ́ra bí Odò Wilge, Odò Klip Molspruit, àti Odò Grootspruit. Pẹ̀lú náà, omi tó wá látinú Ilẹ̀ Lesotho nípasẹ̀ ètò gíráfítì ń fi omi ranṣẹ́ sí Odò Liebenbergsvlei àti Odò Wilge. Bakan náà, Dámù Sterkfontein, tó jẹ́ apá kan ti ètò gbígbé omi Tugela Vaal, ń gba omi láti Odò Thukela ní KwaZulu-Natal, tí ń kó ipa tó lágbára sí ìkún omi Vaal Dam. Àwọn orísun omi wọ̀nyí jọ ń fún Dámù Vaal ní agbára tó pọ̀ láti pèsè omi fún àwùjọ àwọn ìpínlẹ̀ àti àwọn iṣẹ́ amáyédẹrùn ní Gúusu Afrika.	2
ENGLISH LLAMA-ANSWER	The Vaal Dam gets its water from several rivers, including the Vaal River, the Wilge River, the Klip River, the Molspruit, and the Grootspruit. Additionally, the Lesotho Highlands Water Project feeds water into the system by gravity, and the Sterkfontein Dam contributes to the Vaal River System through the Tugela-Vaal water transfer scheme. Water is also piped from Lesotho into the Liebenbergsvlei and Wilge Rivers. The water from the Sterkfontein Dam is released once the Vaal Dam drops to below 16%. This stable supply of water is crucial for the people and industrial complex of Gauteng.	2
Yorùbá LlaMA-answer	Vaal Dam j?? ìsòro omi sí 2,609,799,000 cubic mítà (9.21642×1010 cu ft) àti síwájú síi 663,000,000 cubic mítà (2.34×1010 cu ft) tàbí ìdá m??rìndínl??gb??n (26%) le wà ní ìpam?? fún ìgbà dí?? fún ìdínkù i?àn omi. Ìdídò náà tún di gbígbé sókè ní ìb??r??p??p?? ?dún 50s sí gíga ìw??n 60.3 mítà (198 ft) èyí tí o fi kún agbara r?? láti di 2,188,000,000 cubic mítà (7.73×1010 cu ft). Ìgbéga kejì wáyé ní ?dún 1985 nígbà tí odi di gbígbé sókè nípas?? 3.05 mítà (10.0 ft) sí 63.4 mítà (208 ft) lékè ìpìl?? tí ó súnm?? il?? jùl?. Agbára ìdídò l??w??l??w?? j?? 2,609,799,000 cubic mítà (9.21642×1010 cu ft) àti síwájú síi 663,000,000 cubic mítà (2.34×1010 cu ft) tàbí ìdá m??rìndínl??gb??n (26%) le wà ní ìpam?? fún ìgbà dí?? fún ìdínkù i?àn omi.	1

Table 6: Example of Human Evaluation scores for all models.

Naman Goyal, Abhinandan Krishnan, Luke Zettlemoyer, and Madian Khabsa. 2024. The belebele benchmark: a parallel reading comprehension dataset in 122 language variants. In *Proceedings of the 62nd Annual Meeting of the Association for Computational Linguistics (Volume 1: Long Papers)*, pages 749–775, Bangkok, Thailand. Association for Computational Linguistics.

Christopher Clark, Matthew Gardner, Tom Fevry, and Robert Weischedel. 2019. Boolq: Exploring the surprising difficulty of natural yes/no questions. *arXiv preprint arXiv:1905.10044*.

Paul-Ambroise Duquenne, Holger Schwenk, and Benoît Sagot. 2023. Sonar: Sentence-level multimodal and language-agnostic representations. *Preprint*, arXiv:2308.11466.

Abhimanyu Dubey et al. 2024a. The llama 3 herd of models. *Preprint*, arXiv:2407.21783.

OpenAI et al. 2024b. Gpt-4 technical report. *Preprint*, arXiv:2303.08774.

Mandar Joshi, Eunsol Choi, Daniel Weld, and Luke Zettlemoyer. 2017. Triviaqa: A large scale question-answer dataset for reading comprehension. *arXiv preprint arXiv:1705.03551*.

Marcus Klang and Pierre Nugues. 2016. Pairing Wikipedia articles across languages. In *Proceedings of the Open Knowledge Base and Question Answering Workshop (OKBQA 2016)*, pages 72–76, Osaka, Japan. The COLING 2016 Organizing Committee.

Tom Kwiatkowski, Jennimaria Palomaki, Olivia Redfield, Michael Collins, Ankur Parikh, Chris Alberti, Danielle Epstein, Illia Polosukhin, Matthew Kelcey, Jacob Devlin, Kenton Lee, Kristina N. Toutanova, Llion Jones, Ming-Wei Chang, Andrew Dai, Jakob Uszkoreit, Quoc Le, and Slav Petrov. 2019. Natural questions: a benchmark for question answering research. *Transactions of the Association of Computational Linguistics*.

Chin-Yew Lin. 2004. ROUGE: A package for automatic evaluation of summaries. In *Text Summarization Branches Out*, pages 74–81, Barcelona, Spain. Association for Computational Linguistics.

Odunayo Ogundepo, Tajuddeen Gwadabe, Clara Rivera, Jonathan Clark, Sebastian Ruder, David Adelani, Bonaventure Dossou, Abdou Diop, Claytone Sikasote, Gilles Hacheme, Happy Buzaaba, Ignatius Ezeani, Rooweither Mabuya, Salomey Osei, Chris Emezue, Albert Kahira, Shamsuddeen Muhammad, Akintunde Oladipo, Abraham Owodunni, Atnafu Tonja, Iyanuoluwa Shode, Akari Asai, Anuoluwapo Aremu, Ayodele Awokoya, Bernard Opoku, Chiamaka Chukwuneke, Christine Mwase, Clemencia Siro, Stephen Arthur, Tunde Ajayi, Verrah Otiende, Andre Rubungo, Boyd Sinkala, Daniel Ajisafe, Emeka Onwuegbuzia, Falalu Lawan, Ibrahim Ahmad, Jesujoba Alabi, Chinedu Mbonu, Mofetoluwa Adeyemi, Mofya Phiri, Orevaoghene Ahia, Ruqayya Iro, and Sonia Adhiambo. 2023. Cross-lingual open-retrieval question answering for African languages. In *Findings of the Association for Computational Linguistics: EMNLP 2023*, pages 14957–14972, Singapore. Association for Computational Linguistics.

Pranav Rajpurkar, Jian Zhang, Konstantin Lopyrev, and Percy Liang. 2016. Squad: 100,000+ questions for machine comprehension of text. *arXiv preprint arXiv:1606.05250*.

Author Index

Association for Computational Linguistics
209 N. Eighth Street
Stroudsburg, Pennsylvania 18360

ISBN 979-8-3313-2399-8

CURRAN ASSOCIATES INC.
proceedings.com